THE NEW AMERICAN COMMENTARY

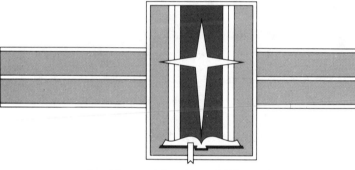

An Exegetical and Theological
Exposition of Holy Scripture

THE NEW AMERICAN COMMENTARY

Volume
5

JOSHUA

David M. Howard, Jr.

BROADMAN
& HOLMAN
PUBLISHERS

Nashville, Tennessee

© 1998 • Broadman & Holman Publishers
All rights reserved
ISBN 0–8054–0105–9
Dewey Decimal Classification: 222.20
Subject Heading: BIBLE. O.T. JOSHUA
Library of Congress Catalog Number: 98–40576
Printed in the United States of America
08 07 06 05 04   8 7 6 5 4

Library of Congress Cataloging-in-Publication Data

Howard, David M., Jr.
    Joshua / David M. Howard, Jr.
      p.   cm. — (The new American commentary ; v. 5)
    Includes bibliographical references and indexes.
    ISBN 0–8054–0105–9 (hardcover)
    1. Bible. O.T. Joshua—Commentaries.   I. Title.   II. Series.
BS1295.3.H68   1998
222'.2077—dc21

To

Christina

Author Preface

The book of Joshua forms the logical end point for much that is found in the Pentateuch. It shows Israel in possession of the land that God had promised for centuries to Abraham and his descendants. It tells of the fulfillment of many of the promises given earlier, and it shows a God who was faithful to his promises. This God was at once warm and demanding: he repeatedly took the initiative to bless his people, to keep his promises, and to give them the land, and yet, an integral part of this involved his demands that Israel forsake all other allegiances and completely destroy the land's inhabitants. God's awesome holiness forms the backdrop to such destruction, but his never-ending love and abundant provision for his people is also revealed in the book. The book ends on a peaceful, satisfying note, showing how God had been faithful to his promises and how the people had been obedient. Such a picture is drawn broadly (since there are also hints in the book about the people's failings), but it is one that nevertheless was true at the end of Joshua's life, and one not often found in other Old Testament historical books.

The book contains many familiar stories: of Rahab and the Israelite spies, of the "battle" of Jericho, of the sun and moon's "stopping" in the sky, of fierce battles up and down the land of Canaan. Yet, often Christians only know the plot lines of such stories, but not the underlying theological truths nor what they reveal about God. Careful study of the book will reveal many valuable theological insights even from these familiar stories. The book also contains much that is unfamiliar to most Christians, primarily in the extensive land distribution lists of chaps. 13–21, but here, too, the book contains many rich treasures waiting to be mined.

This commentary has been written as an exposition of the text of Joshua in the context of the Christian church. As such, it attempts to lay out clearly the meaning of the words, sentences, paragraphs, and larger units in the book. The primary focus is upon the *text* of the book, and the greatest effort has gone into expounding the meaning of the text. Readers will find the results of this effort in the main body of the commentary. They should thus be able to follow the flow of the book's argument as they work their way through this portion of the commentary. Many readers will find their needs met by reading only the body, while ignoring the footnotes, excursuses, and the introduction, and this is certainly acceptable.

However, because most readers also come to commentaries with questions that do not immediately address the meaning of the text itself—questions concerning the reliability of the text in presenting historical data, the historical and archaeological background of many texts, ethical questions arising from aspects of the text, etc.—the commentary also deals with these. Such questions are dealt with in the introduction to the commentary, in the footnotes, and in several excursuses found throughout the work. The effort has been made to place the exposition of the text in the main body of the commentary and to address these other questions elsewhere, although complete consistency has not been achieved. (A further statement about what a commentary is and how it can best be used is found in my article "Evaluating Commentaries on Joshua," *The Southern Baptist Journal of Theology* 2.3 [Fall 1998]: 4–10. Readers are advised that three theme issues on the book of Joshua have appeared in 1998: *Review and Expositor* 95.2 [Spring]; *The Southern Baptist Journal of Theology* 2.3 [Fall]; and *Southwestern Journal of Theology* 40.3 [Fall], which can contribute further to their understanding of the book.)

I am indebted to many people who contributed in various ways to the final product. I thank E. Ray Clendenen, General Editor of the New American Commentary, for the invitation to contribute to this series and for his competent and gracious shepherding of the manuscript through to completion. A competent scholar of the book of Joshua himself, he made numerous suggestions that have greatly improved the work.

I also thank Dr. Charles S. Kelley, Jr., President of New Orleans Baptist Theological Seminary, for very graciously offering me a short sabbatical leave during the first term I was here at the Seminary, during which time I was able to make significant progress on the project. I thank the Seminary, as well, for providing generous help in the form of graduate assistant and secretarial support.

I also thank the following persons who read or discussed with me portions of the manuscript and provided helpful feedback: John J. Bimson, Trent C. Butler, Octave Bourgeois, R. Dennis Cole, Richard W. Johnson, Francis X. Kimmitt, William F. Warren, and Bryant G. Wood. Several ethicists read and commented on my treatment of Rahab's lie in chap. 2, and I thank them for their labors: David Clark, Bruce Fields, Walter C. Kaiser, Jr., Erwin W. Lutzer, Steve W. Lemke, John Warwick Montgomery, and Joe E. Trull. The following graciously made available to me unpublished materials of theirs that were very helpful: David W. Baker, Phyllis A. Bird, Trent C. Butler, David A. Dorsey, Ronald A. G. du Preez, Richard S. Hess, H. Van Parunak, John H. Walton, Bryant G. Wood, and K. Lawson Younger, Jr. Students in classes at Trinity Evangelical Divinity School and New Orleans Baptist Theological Seminary also have contributed to my understanding of the book of Joshua by their comments and questions. I alone bear the responsibility for any and all faults remaining, however.

Thanks also are due to Moody Press for granting permission to use materials from chap. 2 of my *An Introduction to the Old Testament Historical Books* (Chicago: Moody, 1993).

My two graduate assistants, Joseph A. Vadnais and William L. McDonald, deserve special thanks and commendation: they laboriously proofread the entire manuscript, checked the Scripture references, tracked down bibliographical materials, provided helpful feedback, and generally saved me from many errors and infelicities along the way. Both of them graciously volunteered their services during times when they were not being compensated, as well. My secretary, Carl Kelley, also provided valuable help at different stages of the project.

My family has shouldered a heavy burden in tolerating their dad's and husband's preoccupation with this project, especially in the last five months, when the project deadline imposed its cruel will upon us all. I thank my wife, Jan, for her encouragement, affirmation, and patience through it all, and our daughters, Christina and Melody, for putting up with Dad's obsession with Joshua.

This book is dedicated to Christina on the occasion of a significant milestone in her life: her thirteenth birthday. She has been a source of incredible joy to Jan and me, and it is her mother's and my prayer that she will hold fast to the faith that has been entrusted to her, which is now blossoming in her life, and that she will display the faith of Rahab, who committed her life to the true God in no uncertain terms (Josh 2:9–11).

It is in him that we live and move and have our being, and it is for the service of his Church, and to his glory, that this commentary is offered.

New Orleans, Louisiana
October 5, 1998

Editors' Preface

God's Word does not change. God's world, however, changes in every generation. These changes, in addition to new findings by scholars and a new variety of challenges to the gospel message, call for the church in each generation to interpret and apply God's Word for God's people. Thus, THE NEW AMERICAN COMMENTARY is introduced to bridge the twentieth and twenty-first centuries. This new series has been designed primarily to enable pastors, teachers, and students to read the Bible with clarity and proclaim it with power.

In one sense THE NEW AMERICAN COMMENTARY is not new, for it represents the continuation of a heritage rich in biblical and theological exposition. The title of this forty-volume set points to the continuity of this series with an important commentary project published at the end of the nineteenth century called AN AMERICAN COMMENTARY, edited by Alvah Hovey. The older series included, among other significant contributions, the outstanding volume on Matthew by John A. Broadus, from whom the publisher of the new series, Broadman Press, partly derives its name. The former series was authored and edited by scholars committed to the infallibility of Scripture, making it a solid foundation for the present project. In line with this heritage, all NAC authors affirm the divine inspiration, inerrancy, complete truthfulness, and full authority of the Bible. The perspective of the NAC is unapologetically confessional and rooted in the evangelical tradition.

Since a commentary is a fundamental tool for the expositor or teacher who seeks to interpret and apply Scripture in the church or classroom, the NAC focuses on communicating the theological structure and content of each biblical book. The writers seek to illuminate both the historical meaning and contemporary significance of Holy Scripture.

In its attempt to make a unique contribution to the Christian community, the NAC focuses on two concerns. First, the commentary emphasizes how each section of a book fits together so that the reader becomes aware of the theological unity of each book and of Scripture as a whole. The writers, however, remain aware of the Bible's inherently rich variety. Second, the NAC is produced with the conviction that the Bible primarily belongs to the church. We believe that scholarship and the academy provide an indispensable foundation for biblical understanding and the service of Christ, but the editors and authors of this series have attempted to communicate the findings of their research in a manner that will build up the whole body of Christ. Thus, the commentary concentrates on theological exegesis while providing practical, applicable exposition.

THE NEW AMERICAN COMMENTARY's theological focus enables the reader to see the parts as well as the whole of Scripture. The biblical books vary in content, context, literary type, and style. In addition to this rich variety, the editors and authors recognize that the doctrinal emphasis and use of the biblical books differs in various places, contexts, and cultures among God's people. These factors, as well as other concerns, have led the editors to give freedom to the writers to wrestle with the issues raised by the scholarly community surrounding each book and to determine the appropriate shape and length of the introductory materials. Moreover, each writer has developed the structure of the commentary in a way best suited for expounding the basic structure and the meaning of the biblical books for our day. Generally, discussions relating to contemporary scholarship and technical points of grammar and syntax appear in the footnotes and not in the text of the commentary. This format allows pastors and interested laypersons, scholars and teachers, and serious college and seminary students to profit from the commentary at various levels. This approach has been employed because we believe that all Christians have the privilege and responsibility to read and seek to understand the Bible for themselves.

Consistent with the desire to produce a readable, up-to-date commentary, the editors selected the *New International Version* as the standard translation for the commentary series. The selection was made primarily because of the NIV's faithfulness to the original languages and its beautiful and readable style. The authors, however, have been given the liberty to differ at places from the NIV as they develop their own translations from the Greek and Hebrew texts.

The NAC reflects the vision and leadership of those who provide oversight for Broadman Press, who in 1987 called for a new commentary series that would evidence a commitment to the inerrancy of Scripture and a faithfulness to the classic Christian tradition. While the commentary adopts an "American" name, it should be noted some writers represent countries outside the United States, giving the commentary an international perspective. The diverse group of writers includes scholars, teachers, and administrators from almost twenty different colleges and seminaries, as well as pastors, missionaries, and a layperson.

The editors and writers hope that THE NEW AMERICAN COMMEN-

TARY will be helpful and instructive for pastors and teachers, scholars and students, for men and women in the churches who study and teach God's Word in various settings. We trust that for editors, authors, and readers alike, the commentary will be used to build up the church, encourage obedience, and bring renewal to God's people. Above all, we pray that the NAC will bring glory and honor to our Lord who has graciously redeemed us and faithfully revealed himself to us in his Holy Word.

SOLI DEO GLORIA
The Editors

Abbreviations

Bible Books

Gen	Isa	Luke
Exod	Jer	John
Lev	Lam	Acts
Num	Ezek	Rom
Deut	Dan	1, 2 Cor
Josh	Hos	Gal
Judg	Joel	Eph
Ruth	Amos	Phil
1, 2 Sam	Obad	Col
1, 2 Kgs	Jonah	1, 2 Thess
1, 2 Chr	Mic	1, 2 Tim
Ezra	Nah	Titus
Neh	Hab	Phlm
Esth	Zeph	Heb
Job	Hag	Jas
Ps (pl. Pss)	Zech	1, 2 Pet
Prov	Mal	1, 2, 3 John
Eccl	Matt	Jude
Song	Mark	Rev

Apocrypha

Add Esth	*The Additions to the Book of Esther*
Bar	*Baruch*
Bel	*Bel and the Dragon*
1,2 Esdr	*1, 2 Esdras*
4 Ezra	*4 Ezra*
Jdt	*Judith*
Ep Jer	*Epistle of Jeremiah*
1,2,3,4 Mac	*1, 2, 3, 4 Maccabees*
Pr Azar	*Prayer of Azariah and the Song of the Three Jews*
Pr Man	*Prayer of Manasseh*
Sir	*Sirach, Ecclesiasticus*
Sus	*Susanna*
Tob	*Tobit*
Wis	*The Wisdom of Solomon*

Commonly Used Sources

AASOR	Annual of the American Schools of Oriental Research
AB	Anchor Bible
ABR	*Australian Biblical Review*
ABD	*Anchor Bible Dictionary,* ed. D. N Freedman
ABW	*Archaeology and the Biblical World*
AC	An American Commentary, ed. A. Hovey
AcOr	*Acta orientalia*
AEL	M. Lichtheim, *Ancient Egyptian Literature*
AJBI	*Annual of the Japanese Biblical Institute*
AJSL	*American Journal of Semitic Languages and Literature*
Akk.	Akkadian
AnBib	Analecta Biblica
ANET	*Ancient Near Eastern Texts,* ed. J. B. Pritchard
ANEP	*Ancient Near Eastern Pictures,* ed. J. B. Pritchard
Ant.	*Antiquities*
AOAT	Alter Orient und Altes Testament
AOS	American Oriental Society
AOTS	*Archaeology and Old Testament Study,* ed. D. W. Thomas
ArOr	Archiv orientální
AS	Assyriological Studies
ATD	Das Alte Testament Deutsch
ATR	*Anglican Theological Review*
AusBR	*Australian Biblical Review*
AUSS	*Andrews University Seminary Studies*
AV	Authorized Version
BA	*Biblical Archaeologist*
BAGD	W. Bauer, W. F. Arndt, F. W. Gingrich, and F. W. Danker, *Greek-English Lexicon of the New Testament*
BALS	Bible and Literature Series
BARev	*Biblical Archaeology Review*
BASOR	*Bulletin of the American Schools of Oriental Research*
BBR	*Bulletin for Biblical Research*
BDB	F. Brown, S. R. Driver, and C. A. Briggs, *Hebrew and English Lexicon of the Old Testament*
BETL	Bibliotheca ephemeridum theologicarum lovaniensium
BFT	Biblical Foundations in Theology
BHS	*Biblia hebraica stuttgartensia*
Bib	*Biblica*
BibOr	Biblica et orientalia
BibRev	*Bible Review*
BJRL	*Bulletin of the Johns Rylands University Library*
BJS	Brown Judaic Studies
BKAT	Biblischer Kommentar: Altes Testament
BN	*Biblische Notizen*
BO	*Bibliotheca orientalis*

EvQ	*Evangelical Quarterly*
ExpTim	*Expository Times*
FB	Forschung zur Bibel
FOTL	Forms of Old Testament Literature
Gk.	Greek
GBH	P. Joüon, *A Grammar of Biblical Hebrew,* 2 vols., trans. and rev. T. Muraoka
GKC	Gesenius's Hebrew Grammar, ed. E. Kautzsch, trans. A. E. Cowley
GTJ	*Grace Theological Journal*
HALOT	*Hebrew and Aramaic Lexicon of the Old Testament,* ed. L. Koehler et al.
HAR	*Hebrew Annual Review*
HAT	Handbuch zum Alten Testament
HBD	*Harper's Bible Dictionary,* ed. P. Achtemeier
HBT	*Horizons in Biblical Theology*
HDR	Harvard Dissertations in Religion
Her	Hermeneia
HKAT	Handkommentar zum Alten Testament
HS	*Hebrew Studies*
HSM	Harvard Semitic Monographs
HT	Helps for Translators
HTR	*Harvard Theological Review*
HUCA	*Hebrew Union College Annual*
IB	*Interpreter's Bible*
IBC	International Bible Commentary, ed. F. F. Bruce et al.
IBD	*Illustrated Bible Dictionary,* ed. J. D. Douglas and N. Hillyer
IBHS	B. K. Waltke and M. O'Connor, *Introduction to Biblical Hebrew Syntax*
IBS	*Irish Biblical Studies*
ICC	International Critical Commentary
IDB	*Interpreter's Dictionary of the Bible,* ed. G. A. Buttrick et al.
IDBSup	Supplementary volume to *IDB*
IEJ	*Israel Exploration Journal*
IES	Israel Exploration Society
IJT	*Indian Journal of Theology*
Int	*Interpretation*
INT	Interpretation: A Bible Commentary for Teaching and Preaching
IOS	*Israel Oriental Society*
ISBE	*International Standard Bible Encyclopedia,* rev. ed., G. W. Bromiley
ITC	International Theological Commentary
ITQ	*Irish Theological Quarterly*
JAAR	*Journal of the American Academy of Religion*
JAARSup	*Journal of the American Academy of Religion,* Supplement

JANES	*Journal of Ancient Near Eastern Society*
JAOS	*Journal of the American Oriental Society*
JBL	*Journal of Biblical Literature*
JBR	*Journal of Bible and Religion*
JCS	*Journal of Cuneiform Studies*
JEA	*Journal of Egyptian Archaeology*
JETS	*Journal of the Evangelical Theological Society*
JJS	*Journal of Jewish Studies*
JNES	*Journal of Near Eastern Studies*
JNSL	*Journal of Northwest Semitic Languages*
JPOS	*Journal of Palestine Oriental Society*
JPST	Jewish Publication Society Torah
JRT	*Journal of Religious Thought*
JSJ	*Journal for the Study of Judaism in the Persian, Hellenistic, and Roman Period*
JSOR	*Journal of the Society for Oriental Research*
JSOT	*Journal for the Study of the Old Testament*
JSOTSup	JSOT—Supplement Series
JSS	*Journal of Semitic Studies*
JTS	*Journal of Theological Studies*
JTSNS	*Journal of Theological Studies, New Series*
JTT	*Journal of Translation and Textlinguistics*
KAT	Kommentar zum Alten Testament
KB	L. Koehler and W. Baumgartner, *Lexicon in Veteris Testamenti libros*
KB³	L. Koehler and W. Baumgartner, *The Hebrew and Aramaic Lexicon of the Old Testament,* trans. M. E. J. Richardson
KD	*Kerygma und Dogma*
LBBC	Layman's Bible Book Commentary
LBI	Library of Biblical Interpretation
LCC	Library of Christian Classics
LLAVT	E. Vogt, *Lexicon Linguae Aramaicae Veteris Testamenti*
LSJ	Liddell-Scott-Jones, *Greek-English Lexicon*
LTQ	*Lexington Theological Quarterly*
LW	*Luther's Works: Lecture's on Genesis,* ed. J. Pelikan and D. Poellot, trans. G. Schick
LXX	Septuagint
MT	Masoretic Text
NAB	New American Bible
NASB	New American Standard Bible
NAC	New American Commentary, ed. R. Clendenen
NB	*Nebuchadrezzar and Babylon,* D. J. Wiseman
NBD	*New Bible Dictionary,* ed. J. D. Douglas
NCBC	New Century Bible Commentary
NEAEHL	*The New Encyclopedia of Archaeological Excavations in the Holy Land,* ed. E. Stern

NEB	New English Bible
NIB	The New Interpreter's Bible
NICNT	New International Commentary on the New Testament
NICOT	New International Commentary on the Old Testament
NIDOTTE	*The New International Dictionary of Old Testament Theology and Exegesis,* ed. W. A. VanGemeren
NJB	New Jerusalem Bible
NJPS	New Jewish Publication Society Version
NKZ	*Neue kirchliche Zeitschrift*
NLT	New Living Translation
NovT	*Novum Testamentum*
NRSV	New Revised Standard Version
NRT	*La nouvelle revue the'ologique*
NTS	*New Testament Studies*
NTT	Norsk Teologisk Tidsskrift
OBO	Orbis biblicus et orientalis
Or	*Orientalia*
OTL	Old Testament Library
OTP	*The Old Testament Pseudepigrapha,* ed. J. H. Charlesworth
OTS	*Oudtestamentische Studiën*
OTWSA	*Ou-Testamentiese Werkgemeenskap in Suid-Afrika*
PCB	*Peake's Commentary on the Bible,* ed. M. Black and H. H. Rowley
PEQ	*Palestine Exploration Quarterly*
POTT	*Peoples of Old Testament Times,* ed. D. J. Wiseman
POTW	Peoples of the Old Testament World, ed. A. E. Hoerth, G. L. Mattingly, and E. M. Yamauchi
PTMS	Pittsburgh Theological Monograph Series
PTR	*Princeton Theological Review*
RA	*Revue d'assyriologie et d'archéologie orientale*
RB	*Revue biblique*
REB	Revised English Bible
ResQ	*Restoration Quarterly*
RevExp	*Review and Expositor*
RSR	Recherches de science religieuse
RTR	*Reformed Theological Review*
SANE	Sources from the Ancient Near East
SBLDS	Society of Biblical Literature Dissertation Series
SBLMS	Society of Biblical Literature Monograph Series
SBLSP	Society of Biblical Literature Seminar Papers
SBT	Studies in Biblical Theology
SJT	*Scottish Journal of Theology*
SJOT	*Scandinavian Journal of the Old Testament*
SJLA	Studies in Judaism in Late Antiquity
SLJA	*Saint Luke's Journal of Theology*

SOTI	*A Survey of Old Testament Introduction,* G. L. Archer
SP	Samaritan Pentateuch
SR	Studies in Religion/Sciences religieuses
ST	*Studia theologica*
STJD	Studies on the Texts of the Desert of Judah
Syr.	Syriac
TD	*Theology Digest*
TDNT	*Theological Dictionary of the New Testament,* ed. G. Kittel and G. Friedrich
TDOT	*Theological Dictionary of the Old Testament,* ed. G. J. Botterweck and H. Ringgren
Tg(s).	Targum(s)
TJNS	Trinity Journal—New Series
TLOT	*Theological Lexicon of the Old Testament,* ed. E. Jenni and C. Westermann
TLZ	*Theologische Literaturzeitung*
TNTC	Tyndale New Testament Commentaries
TOTC	Tyndale Old Testament Commentaries
TrinJ	*Trinity Journal*
TS	*Theological Studies*
TToday	*Theology Today*
TWAT	*Theologisches Wörterbuch zum Alten Testament,* ed. G. J. Botterweck and H. Ringgren
TWOT	*Theological Wordbook of the Old Testament*
TynBul	*Tyndale Bulletin*
UF	*Ugarit-Forschungen*
Ug.	Ugaritic
UT	C. H. Gordon, *Ugaritic Textbook*
Vg	Vulgate
VT	*Vetus Testamentum*
VTSup	Vetus Testamentum, Supplements
WBC	Word Biblical Commentaries
WEC	Wycliffe Exegetical Commentary
WHJP	*World History of the Jewish People,* ed. B. Mazer
WTJ	*Westminster Theological Journal*
WMANT	Wissenschaftliche Monographien zum Alten und Neuen Testament
ZAW	*Zeitschrift für die alttestamentliche Wissenschaft*
ZDMG	*Zeitschrift der deutschen morgenländischen Gesellschaft*
ZDPV	*Zeitschrift des deutschen Palästina-Vereins*
ZPEB	*Zondervan Pictorial Encyclopedia of the Bible*
ZTK	*Zeitschrift für katholische Theologie*

Contents

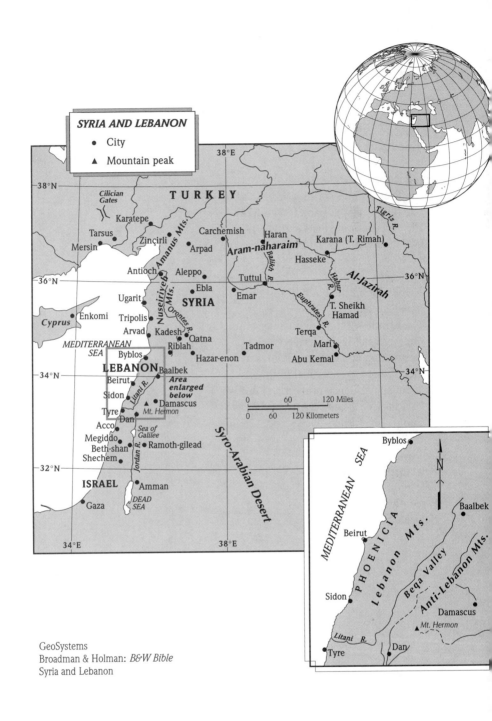

SYRIA AND LEBANON
- • City
- ▲ Mountain peak

TURKEY

Cilician Gates
Karatepe
Tarsus
Zinçirli
Mersin
Antioch
Carchemish
Haran
Arpad
Aram-naharaim
Karana (T. Rimah)
Hasseke
Aleppo
Tuttul
Al-Jazirah
Ebla
Ugarit
SYRIA
Emar
Cyprus
Enkomi
Tripolis
T. Sheikh Hamad
Arvad
Kadesh
Qatna
Terqa
Mari
MEDITERRANEAN SEA
Riblah
Tadmor
Byblos
Hazar-enon
Abu Kemal
LEBANON
Baalbek
Beirut
Area enlarged below
Sidon
Damascus
Tyre
Dan
Mt. Hermon
Acco
Sea of Galilee
Megiddo
Beth-shan
Ramoth-gilead
Shechem
ISRAEL
Amman
Gaza
DEAD SEA

Amanus Mts.
Nuseiriyeh Mts.
Orontes R.
Litani R.
Jordan R.
Syro-Arabian Desert
Tigris R.
Balikh R.
Habur R.
Euphrates R.

0   60   120 Miles
0   60   120 Kilometers

Byblos
MEDITERRANEAN SEA
Baalbek
Beirut
PHOENICIA
Lebanon Mts.
Beqa Valley
Anti-Lebanon Mts.
Sidon
Damascus
Mt. Hermon
Litani R.
Tyre
Dan
N

GeoSystems
Broadman & Holman: B&W Bible
Syria and Lebanon

Joshua

—————————————— INTRODUCTION ——————————————

Most people who know anything about the Book of Joshua think first (if not entirely) of its battles, typified by the old spiritual "Joshua Fit the Battle of Jericho." As with most stereotypes, there is some truth to this picture, but there are distortions as well. Certainly the book contains accounts of great victories and great miracles by God on his people's behalf: it affirms repeatedly that God fought for Israel (10:14; 21:44; etc.). The Israelites entered the land of Canaan and with considerable ease took a series of cities with dramatic victories (chaps. 6–12). Who does not thrill to read of the miraculous collapse of the walls of Jericho? Who does not puzzle and marvel at the sun and moon "stopping" in the sky? Who is not awed by the unstoppable march through southern and northern Canaan?

And yet, the Book of Joshua is far more than its battles. Indeed, its battles were not "battles" at all in the typical sense of the word: they were not massive military-style confrontations between well-trained forces, with the Israelites prevailing via a combination of superior force and tactics. Rather, the Israelites won with the Lord's help, often through direct divine intervention (most dramatically, at Jericho and Gibeon), and always with his help and guidance. It was God who gave the victories and the Israelites who reaped the benefits. Also, the Israelites were not like most conquering armies, in that for the most part they left intact the cities that they conquered. They killed the inhabitants and then were able to settle in cities and houses they had not built, as a gift from God (Deut 6:10–11; Josh 24:13).

Beyond its "battles," the Book of Joshua is far more interested in the land of Canaan, whose possession was the goal of the conflicts. This land had been promised for centuries to Abraham and his descendants, and the book tells of the joyful fulfillment of God's long-standing promises. The book begins with the detailed and careful preparations that were necessary before Israel embarked on its campaign to take this land (chaps. 1–5). These preparations had a primarily spiritual nature, emphasizing that before Israel could inherit the land, they must stand in right relationship with their God, who was graciously giving them the land.

Even in the taking of the land (chaps. 6–12), spiritual concerns were paramount. Jericho was not taken directly, but only after a series of religiously significant marches around the city. Sin in the camp caused Israel's only defeat in the land. When the Israelites took the bulk of the land, it was God who went before them.

Along with the section telling of the actual conflicts (chaps. 6–12), the heart of the book comes when the long-promised land was actually distributed among the tribes (chaps. 13–21). In these chapters—which most Christians do not read at all, or else in the most cursory fashion—the contours of God's promises are fleshed out in the extensive details about each tribes' lands. In the detailed listings of the cities inherited by each tribe and in the drawing of each tribe's boundary lines, the message that God was true to his promises and that he was equitably treating each of the tribes cannot be missed.

The book ends with Joshua's reflections about what God had done for his people and his exhortations about life ahead in the land (chaps. 22–24). The book ends on a satisfying note, with the people settled in their lands and everything seemingly in order.

In all of this, God emerges as the primary mover in the book. He was the cause of Israel's successes and the giver of their lands. He was the God who attracted the dramatic conversion of Rahab, a Canaanite prostitute. He was the God whose actions on his people's behalf demanded their continued remembrance of what he had done. His holiness demanded the horrific extermination of the current occupants of the land because their sins had so defiled the land. He was the one who kept all of his promises to his people.

Thus, to read the Book of Joshua and only to see its battles is seriously to misunderstand the book. It is a richly textured book, one that shows God in all his glory, graciously helping those who were his people and who had responded to him, and yet, true to his nature, not tolerating those who would stubbornly reject him. It represents a satisfying conclusion to the story-line of the Pentateuch, which consistently looks ahead to God's gift of the land. It also represents the beginning of Israel's life in the land. The outlook for Israel was only positive. And yet the book also contains hints of the apostasy that was soon to set in, as revealed in the Book of Judges and subsequent books. Thus it is a very realistic book, one that glorifies God and shows his mercies on his people, but one that warns of the dangers of rebellion and disobedience against him as well.

1. Joshua: Title and Man[1]

The Book of Joshua received its title from its major character, who was Moses' successor and Israel's leader. Some have supposed that the title has indicated authorship (see below), but this does not necessarily follow. Joshua's name means "Yahweh saves" or "Yahweh delivers."[2] His name is rendered in the Old Greek traditions (LXX) as *Iēsous*, which is the same form

---

[1] Portions of this chapter are taken from chap. 2 of *An Introduction to the Old Testament Historical Books*, by David M. Howard, Jr. Copyright 1993, Moody Bible Institute of Chicago. Moody Press. Used by permission.

[2] His name was יְהוֹשֻׁעַ. Twice his name is spelled as יְהוֹשׁוּעַ (Deut 3:21; Judg 2:7), with same meaning. In Neh 8:17 his name is given in a shortened form as "Yeshua" (יֵשׁוּעַ).

as Jesus' name in the New Testament. His original name was "Hoshea," which means "salvation" or "deliverance" (Num 13:8; Deut 32:44). Numbers 13:16 explains that Moses himself gave Hoshea his new name, "Joshua."

A significant amount of information about Joshua is presented in the Pentateuch. He first appears as the military commander who defeated the Amalekites in the wilderness, at Rephidim, and as a close aide and confidant of Moses (Exod 17:8–13). He had been Moses' aide since his youth (Exod 33:11; Num 11:28), and he accompanied Moses up to Mount Sinai (Exod 24:13). He was one of the twelve spies sent into the land of Canaan, and he and Caleb were the only ones who brought back a positive report (Numbers 13–14). As a result, only they were allowed to enter the promised land (Num 14:30,38; 26:65).

Joshua was designated as Moses' successor by the Lord, and Moses brought him before the Lord to commission him (Num 27:15–23). He was a man in whom God's Spirit resided (Num 27:18).[3] The commissioning service was a solemn affair, with the entire congregation in attendance and Eleazar the high priest presiding. During the ceremony, Moses passed his authority to Joshua through the laying on of his hands. Along with Eleazar the priest, Joshua was to distribute the lands to the tribes (Num 32:28; 34:17), a role they carried out when they reached the land (Josh 14:1; 19:51).

When Moses reached the end of his life, he reminded the people that Joshua was his successor as their leader, designated as such by God himself (Deut 31:1–8). He charged him to "be strong and courageous" (v. 7), just as the Lord would do later (Josh 1:6,9). When Moses was about to die, Joshua went with him to the tent of meeting to meet God (Deut 31:14), and God encouraged him to be strong and courageous, assuring Joshua that he would be with him and that Joshua would bring the Israelites into the land (Deut 31:23). These words were a brief foreshadowing of the longer charge that he gave to Joshua later, in Josh 1:2–9. After Moses died, the Israelites listened to Joshua; a spirit of wisdom was upon him because Moses had laid hands on him (Deut 34:9).

As he is presented in the book bearing his name, Joshua is a worthy successor to Moses, Israel's great leader and lawgiver. He had proven his worth earlier by being one of two spies (out of twelve) who counseled entering the land of Canaan despite seemingly prohibitive odds (Numbers 13–14). Now—despite clear differences between the two men both in terms of personality and office—he was called by God to function as Moses' successor (1:1–9). The book is clear that God was with him and that he enjoyed the same stature

---

[3] The text of Num 27:18 states only that "the spirit" was in him. The NIV's text note states that it may have been "the Spirit," i.e., God's Spirit. Alternatively, "the spirit" here may refer to "the spirit of wisdom," which is mentioned in Deut 34:9.

that Moses did (1:9,16–18; 3:7; 4:14; 6:27; 10:14; 11:15,23). The entire nation vowed to obey him at the beginning of his ministry (1:16–18),[4] and they obeyed his challenge at the end of his life as well in vowing with him to follow the Lord (24:16–18).

Joshua appears throughout the book speaking and acting with authority, and he is as eloquent as Moses in his farewell speeches (Joshua 22–24). He is referred to at the beginning of the book merely as "Moses' aide" (1:1), but he appears in the end as the "servant of the Lord" (24:29), just as Moses was (1:1). This indicates that he was indeed a worthy successor to Moses (cf. also Deut 34:9). Joshua died at the ripe old age of 110, and he was buried in the land of his own inheritance (Josh 19:49–50; 24:29–31). During his lifetime, the people served the Lord, which speaks well of his leadership (24:31). He is mentioned in the New Testament twice: in Acts 7:45 and Heb 4:8.

2. Authorship and Date of Composition

(1) Authorship

The book is anonymous. The Talmud and some rabbis (Rashi, David Kimchi) attributed it to Joshua, but some saw parts of the book as written by later hands (e.g., the account of Joshua's death or other fragments). Avravanel attributed it to Samuel, due especially to the phrase "to this day" (4:9; 5:9; 7:26; etc.).[5] Modern critical scholars generally attribute the book to the Deuteronomistic writer(s), ca. seventh and sixth centuries B.C. (see below). Joshua undoubtedly wrote portions of the book: 24:26 states that "Joshua recorded these things in the Book of the Law of God," referring to the covenant that the people had made at Shechem. But there are no further indications here or elsewhere in the Bible concerning the book's authorship.

(2) Date of Composition

There are no formal indicators in the book or elsewhere about the date of its writing. However, the formula "until this day"[6] can be instructive in indicating a general date for the book, or at least parts of it. B. S. Childs has noted that the use of the formula in Josh 15:63 and 16:10 points to a period not later than the tenth century B.C.[7] This is because 15:63 mentions people from the tribe of Judah living in Jerusalem alongside Jebusites, whom they could not drive out. Since David captured Jerusalem from the Jebusites ca. 1003 B.C.

---

[4] For a defense of this statement, see the commentary on 1:12 and 1:16.

[5] M. H. Woudstra, *The Book of Joshua*, NICOT (Grand Rapids: Eerdmans, 1981), 5.

[6] See 4:9; 5:9; 6:25; 7:26[2x]; 8:28,29; 9:27; 13:13; 14:14; 15:63; 16:10.

[7] B. S. Childs, "A Study of the Formula, 'Until This Day,'" 292.

(2 Sam 5:6–10), presumably the Jebusites did not live there in any significant numbers much later than that time. Furthermore, 16:10 mentions Canaanite inhabitants of Gezer among the Ephraimites. Since an Egyptian pharaoh—probably Siamun (ca. 978–959 B.C.)[8]—destroyed the Canaanites at Gezer and gave the town to Solomon as a dowry (1 Kgs 3:1; 9:16), the reference to Canaanites in Gezer would have come from a period prior to that. Other references to "until this day" would seem to make more sense if a relatively long period of time had elapsed between the events and the time of writing.

The reference in 6:25, however, about Rahab still being alive "to this day" would seem to indicate a date much earlier. Furthermore, the boundary descriptions in chaps. 18–19 seem to have come from survey descriptions written at the very time (see 18:4,6,8,9), and Joshua was responsible for writing about the covenant renewal ceremony in chap. 24. The reference to Rahab, however, is not conclusive because it may be her descendants in view just as the reference to David in Hos 3:5 refers to his descendants, not to him.

We conclude that portions of the book were written in Joshua's day and that it was substantially complete by the time of David at the latest.[9]

3. Purpose

In general, Joshua was written to provide an interpretive history of one slice of Israel's life as a people. More specifically, it interprets the period in which Israel entered and settled in the land promised to Abraham and his descendants. Again and again it shows God to be in control of the events of history, not only in dramatic miracles but also in the consistent way he is given credit for *all* of Israel's victories. God's activity in all of this was in order that he might give to Israel the land he had promised to Abraham and his descendants.

Thus, the major purpose of the Book of Joshua is to describe God's giving of the promised land of Canaan to his people Israel. That it was a gift from God is repeatedly emphasized in the book, as well as its being a fulfillment of the promise to Israel's ancestors. The taking and distributing of the land are emphasized in the two central portions of the book (chaps. 6–12 and 13–21). Concern with the land is part of the warp and woof of every chapter. The book forms the fitting resolution of issues left unresolved at the end of the Pen-

---

[8] K. A. Kitchen, *The Bible in Its World* (Downers Grove: InterVarsity, 1977), 100–101, 105–6.

[9] Mainstream critical scholarship usually assigns the composition of Joshua to the time of Josiah or later. For a Josianic date, see N. Na'aman, "The 'Conquest' of Canaan in the Book of Joshua and in History," in I. Finkelstein and N. Na'aman, eds., *From Nomadism to Monarchy: Archaeological and Historical Aspects of Early Israel* (Jerusalem: Israel Exploration Society, 1994), 218–81; R. D. Nelson, "Josiah in the Book of Joshua," *JBL* 100 (1981): 531–40. For later dates see n. 50 below.

tateuch; indeed, Israel's inheriting and settling in the land are the focal points toward which the Pentateuch moves in a purposeful and consistent way.

4. Historical and Cultural Context for the Book of Joshua

(1) Date of the Events

There are no firm synchronisms in the Book of Joshua with known dates that would enable a precise dating of its events. The problem of the date of these events is bound up with that of the date of the exodus from Egypt, which is one of the knottiest and most-discussed issues in Old Testament chronology.[10] The biblical evidence is not entirely clear, and the archaeological evidence has been interpreted variously. In general, the biblical evidence has tended to support an early date for the exodus, while the archaeological evidence has been interpreted to support a late date.

Early Dating of the Exodus. On the face of it, the problem is simple enough, since two biblical data are unambiguous and point to an early date. First, in 1 Kgs 6:1, we read that Solomon began building the Temple in the 480th year after the exodus, which was the fourth year of Solomon's reign. This year was 966 B.C., using Thiele's chronology.[11] Thus, the exodus would have occurred in 1446 B.C. Second, in Judg 11:26 Jephthah the judge, in speaking with his Ammonite adversaries, mentioned that for the three hundred years since Israel had first settled in Transjordan, the Ammonites had not disputed Israel's claims to that territory. Jephthah came relatively late in the period of the judges, perhaps ca. 1100 B.C.; thus this number would indicate a settlement in Transjordan ca. 1400 B.C.[12]

---

[10] Entrée into the discussion may be obtained via the following: W. F. Albright, "Archaeology and the Date of the Hebrew Conquest of Palestine," *BASOR* 58 (1935): 10–18; id., "The Israelite Conquest of Canaan in the Light of Archaeology," *BASOR* 74 (1939): 11–23; H. H. Rowley, *From Joseph to Joshua: Biblical Traditions in the Light of Archaeology* (London: Oxford University, 1950); Kitchen, *Ancient Orient and Old Testament*, 57–75; J. M. Miller, "The Israelite Occupation of Canaan," in *Israelite and Judaean History*, ed. J. H. Hayes and J. M. Miller (Philadelphia: Westminster, 1977), 213–84; C. F. Aling, *Egypt and Bible History* (Grand Rapids: Baker, 1981), 77–96; J. J. Bimson, *Redating the Exodus and Conquest*, 2d ed. JSOTSup (Sheffield: Almond Press, 1981); J. J. Bimson and D. Livingston, "Saving the Biblical Chronology," *BARev* 13.5 (1987): 40–53, 66–68; W. H. Shea, "Exodus, Date of the," *ISBE* 2.230–38; E. H. Merrill, *Kingdom of Priests: A History of Old Testament Israel* (Grand Rapids: Baker, 1987), 66–67; H. M. Wolf, *An Introduction to the Old Testament Pentateuch* (Chicago: Moody, 1990), 141–48.

[11] E. R. Thiele, *The Mysterious Numbers of the Hebrew Kings*, 3d ed. (Grand Rapids: Zondervan, 1983), 79–81 and *passim*. The alternative would be ca. 956 B.C., found in D. N. Freedman and E. F. Campbell, Jr., "Chronology of Israel and the Ancient Near East," *The Bible and the Ancient Near East* (Winona Lake: Eisenbrauns, 1979), but Thiele's appears to have stood the test of new evidence. In either case, 480 years prior to this time places the exodus in the fifteenth century B.C.

[12] An early date for the exodus is defended by Bimson, Aling, Shea, Merrill, and Wolf among those in n. 10.

However, other biblical data are not so clear, and the archaeological evidence has been interpreted to point in other directions.

Late Dating of the Exodus. The prime impetus for a late dating of the exodus has come from archaeology. A fairly consistent and widespread layer of destructions has been discovered in Palestine dating to the middle and late thirteenth centuries B.C., and 1200 B.C. is used as the date of convenience for the end of the Late Bronze Age and the beginning of the Early Iron Age. These destructions have been attributed to the entering Israelites, and the exodus is placed forty years previous to that.[13]

According to this view a *terminus a quo* for the exodus would be ca. 1279 B.C., the beginning of the reign of the pharaoh Ramses II (ca. 1279–1213 B.C.).[14] This is because Exod 1:11 mentions the Israelites building two store-cities for the Egyptians, Pithom and Rameses. The latter city logically would have been named for this long-lived pharaoh known for his building projects.[15]

A *terminus ad quem* for Israel's presence in the land is usually seen to have been ca. 1207 B.C. since a stele of the Egyptian pharaoh Mer-ne-Ptah (ca. 1213–1203 B.C.) from his fifth year mentions Israel as a people whom he encountered and subdued in a campaign into Canaan.[16]

In this understanding, the above biblical data are seen to have been later glosses, mistakes, or round or symbolic numbers. The number "480" in 1 Kgs 6:1, for example, is interpreted as a symbolic number, representing twelve generations of forty years. If the actual lifespan at that time was closer to twenty-five years, then the time span mentioned in 1 Kgs 6:1 would be closer to three hundred years, placing the exodus early in the thirteenth (rather than in the fifteenth) century B.C.

Other biblical data seem to be incompatible with the number 480 (and with Jephthah's number of 300). Adding up the total of dates in Joshua, Judges, and

---

[13] See the works of Albright, Rowley, Kitchen, and Miller in n. 10 for a defense of this late-date view. Kitchen, e.g., dates the exodus to 1290/1260 B.C. (*Ancient Orient and Old Testament*, 61).

[14] The *terminus a quo* is the time before which the exodus could not have occurred, according to this scheme. The Egyptian dates used here are the "low" dates laid out by Kitchen in "The Basics of Egyptian Chronology in Relation to the Bronze Age," 37–55. There is near unanimity now among Egyptologists concerning a low dating scheme, particularly after the accession of Ramses II (1279 B.C.). Previously, the date of Ramses was given as 1290–1224 B.C. (e.g., J. Bright, *A History of Israel*, 468), and the year 1290 is widely mentioned in earlier literature as the *terminus a quo*.

[15] Ramses I, the founder of the Nineteenth Egyptian Dynasty (the first Ramesside dynasty), reigned less than two years, ca. 1295–1294 B.C. and is not reckoned by scholars to have commissioned any such projects.

[16] The *termius ad quem* is the time after which the exodus could not have occurred, according to this scheme. For the Merneptah Stele, see *ANET*, 376–78; *DOTT*, 137–41. The fact that Israel is the only name in Merneptah's list designated as belonging to a people, rather than to a land, is taken by some to suggest that Israel was not yet completely settled, but rather was a relatively recent entrant into the land.

Samuel, for example, gives more than 470 years.[17] Added to forty wilderness years, forty years for David, and the first years of Solomon, this yields a minimum total of 553 years (plus three unknown amounts) for the 480-year period referred to in 1 Kings 6:1.[18] Thus, these numbers, and especially those in the Book of Judges, are seen to be round or symbolic as well. Also, the chronologies in the Book of Judges may have been overlapping rather than consecutive, and thus the period easily could be telescoped into a shorter time span.[19]

Evaluation. There are good arguments for both dating schemes as well as weaknesses in both. In general, mainstream critical scholarship has tended to favor late dating schemes, while evangelical scholars have tended to favor the early one.[20]

The view in this commentary favors an early date for the exodus. This is partly because the late dating schemes have tended to arise out of interpretations of the archaeological data: since archaeology tended to show large-scale destructions at a late date, the biblical data then were adjusted to accommodate it. However, there are several flaws with such attempted correlations. First, the Bible itself does not support the models constructed on the basis of these destructions. This is because the Bible specifically states that only three cities were destroyed by fire—Jericho, Ai, and Hazor. For the rest, only the destruction of people is mentioned. This accords well with the biblical data emphasizing that the Israelites would inherit "a land with large, flourishing cities you did not build, houses filled with all kinds of good things you did not provide, wells you did not dig, and vineyards and olive groves you did not plant" (Deut 6:10–11; cf. Josh 24:13: "So I gave you a land on which you did not toil and cities you did not build; and you live in them and eat from vineyards and olive groves that you did not plant"). Most of the cities the Israelites took were *not* destroyed, and thus we should not expect to see in the widespread destructions ca. 1200 B.C. any evidence of the Israelite "conquest."[21] Indeed, the account of the destruction of Hazor goes so far as to point out that Joshua did not burn the other cities on their tells (Josh 11:13).

Second, the destructions in Canaan that once were thought to have been

---

[17] See Kitchen, "Chronology of the Old Testament," *NBD,* 3d ed., 192.

[18] Kitchen, *Ancient Orient and Old Testament,* 72–73; Rowley, *From Joseph to Joshua,* 87–88.

[19] Kitchen, *Ancient Orient and Old Testament,* 73–75.

[20] Some evangelicals have favored the late date as well, however. See, e.g., Kitchen, *Ancient Orient and Old Testament,* R. K. Harrison (*Introduction to the Old Testament,* [Grand Rapids: Eerdmans, 1969], 174–77 and *passim*), and R. S. Hess (*Joshua: An Introduction and Commentary,* TOTC [Downers Grove: InterVarsity, 1996], 139–43).

[21] This point is made by B. K. Waltke, "Palestinian Artifactual Evidence Supporting the Early Date for the Exodus," *BSac* 129 (1972): 33–47; Merrill, "Palestinian Archaeology and the Date of the Conquest: Do Tells Tell Tales?" *GTJ* 3 (1982): 107–21; J. K. Hoffmeier, *Israel in Egypt: The Evidence for the Authenticity of the Exodus Tradition* (New York: Oxford University, 1997), 34–35, 43–44.

due to the Israelite invasion actually are now known to have been part of a far-ranging pattern of upheaval that covered much of the eastern Mediterranean area, not just Canaan.[22] Evidence for this can be seen, for example, in the migrations of the Land and Sea Peoples.[23] Thus, there is no special compulsion for seeing Israel involved in any exceptional way in these upheavals.

Third, the evidence from Merneptah's stele shows that Israel was settled for some time in Canaan, not recently established. As Bimson states: "Israel was well established in the region by Merenptah's day, and not a people newly arrived or only just emerging as a distinct people. In other words, Israel's origins must lie earlier than the final decades of the thirteenth century BCE."[24] In addition, it would appear that the many Iron I small settlements in the hill country that have been discovered and associated with the Israelites should be dated to the twelfth century, not the thirteenth.[25] If so, this dissociates even further these settlements from Israel's emergence in the land. Thus Bimson concludes, "The archaeology of the Iron I settlements can only provide information about Israel's *sedentarization* [not its emergence in the land]" (p. 24; italics Bimson). That is, the transition from the Late Bronze Age to the Iron Age was indeed a turbulent one, which is reflected in the archaeological record in numerous ways. However, this does not signify anything about Israel's *entry* into the land. Rather, if we hold to the early date of the exodus, then the upheavals ca. 1200 B.C. happened during the period of the judges, and the Bible says nothing about them at all. The chaos around 1200 B.C. certainly finds its counterpart in the spiritual chaos depicted in the Book of Judges, but the Bible is not concerned to tell us about these external events.[26]

---

[22] For bibliography, see Howard, "Philistines," *Peoples of the Old Testament World* [Grand Rapids: Baker, 1994), 233–34, n. 9); see also V. R. d'A. Desborough, "The End of Mycenaean Civilization and the Dark Age," *CAH,* 2.2:658–77; G. E. Mendenhall, "Ancient Israel's Hyphenated History," in *Palestine in Transition,* ed. D. N. Freedman and D. F. Graf (Sheffield: Almond/ASOR, 1983), 91–103.

[23] See Mendenhall, "The 'Sea Peoples' in Palestine," *Palestine in Transition,* 142–73; R. D. Barnett, "The Sea Peoples," *CAH,* 2.2:359–78; N. K. Sandars, *The Sea Peoples* (London: Thames & Hudson, 1978), 105–15, 198–201.

[24] Bimson, "Merenptah's Israel and Recent Theories of Israelites Origins," *JSOT* 49 (1991): 3–29; the quote is from p. 23.

[25] Bimson, "Merenptah's Israel," 9–13, relying on work by B. G. Wood ("Palestinian Pottery of the Late Bronze Age: An Investigation of the Terminal LB IIB Phase" (Ph.D. diss., University of Toronto, 1985).

[26] Such silence about important external events is not limited to the Book of Judges. In a later period, a significant battle between Shalmaneser, king of Assyria, and a coalition of western kings (including Ahab of Israel), which took place at Qarqar on the Orontes River (853 B.C.), is not mentioned at all in the Bible. We know of it only from Shalmaneser's own inscriptions (see *ANET,* 278–79). Also Omri, a king who is mentioned several times in extrabiblical inscriptions as a significant and powerful king, is allotted a mere eight verses in Scripture (1 Kgs 16:21–28), and no mention at all is made of his military might or his international significance.

Several lines of evidence argue in favor of an early dating. First, as we have noted, the two most direct pieces of evidence in the Bible concerning date—"480 years" in 1 Kgs 6:1 and "300 years" in Judg 11:26—both point to an early exodus. In connection with this, we should note that nowhere in the Bible is a large number (such as "480 years") used to symbolize a certain number of generations, which would argue against the late-date interpretation of this number.[27]

Second, with a conquest of Canaan dated to ca. 1200 B.C., this leaves merely 150 years before the rise of King Saul, which was ca. 1050 B.C. Granted that there may have been some flexibility and overlap in the Judges accounts and chronologies, it nevertheless appears to be too short a period to accommodate everything in that book. This is particularly so when one considers a scheme such as Mendenhall's, who places the "Yahwistic revolution" that he postulates (see below) as having occurred no earlier than 1150 B.C.[28] This leaves no more than a century for the events in Judges, which would seem to be an impossibly short time frame for these all to have occurred. In an early-date scheme, the numbers in Judges still need to be considered to have overlapped somewhat, but not nearly so drastically as under a late-date scheme.

Third, the archaeological and historical data from the fifteenth century B.C. do fit the biblical data well, even though most scholars have concentrated their attention on the thirteenth century.[29]

We should note that scholars favoring an early date for the exodus differ among themselves about the exact date. Most accept 1446 B.C.,[30] but Bimson places it earlier, ca. 1470 B.C. Thus, he accepts the number in 1 Kgs 6:1 as approximately accurate, although not exactly so.[31] These differences, however, do not materially undermine the arguments for the early date.[32]

---

[27] On this point, see Hoffmeier, *Israel in Egypt*, 125.

[28] Mendenhall, "Ancient Israel's Hyphenated History," 100. Several other scholars also, on various grounds, argue for placing the conquest in the twelfth century B.C., rather than the thirteenth (see J. Bright, *A History of Israel*, 3d ed. (Philadelphia: Westminster, 1981), 133 and n. 68; G. Rendsburg, "The Date of the Exodus and the Conquest/Settlement: The Case for the 1100s," 510–27; Howard, "Philistines," 239, n. 31).

[29] See especially the treatments by Bimson and Shea in n 10, but also the others and works cited therein. See also the excursus on "The Archaeology of Jericho and Ai" at the end of chap. 6.

[30] E.g., Shea (ca. 1450 B.C.), Aling, and Merrill (see n. 10).

[31] Bimson, *Redating the Exodus and Conquest*, 74–79. However, Bimson has recently reevaluated his dating scheme, based upon new data.

[32] H. Goedicke has proposed an even earlier date, 1477 B.C., based on completely independent evidence—i.e., postulating that a tidal wave caused by the volcanic eruption from that year that destroyed the Minoan civilization was the cause of the Egyptian army's drowning in the Red Sea (H. Shanks, "The Exodus and the Crossing of the Red Sea, According to Hans Goedicke," *BARev* 7.5 [1981]: 42–50). This proposal has not met with any general acceptance, however.

(2) Nature of the Events

Four major models now exist to explain the nature of Israel's entrance into Canaan. The first two see the Israelites entering into the land of Canaan from the outside, while the latter two see "Israel" emerging as a national entity from within Canaan. The first model sees Israel's entry into the land in terms of a traditional "conquest": a large-scale, hostile Israelite invasion, resulting in major destructions of Canaanite cities and towns. The second sees it in terms of a peaceful, sedentary infiltration into the land, with the Israelites settling down among the Canaanites. The third sees it in terms of an internal upheaval, a "peasant revolt," perhaps precipitated by the entrance of a small group of outsiders (who formed the core of "Israel"). A fourth approach has emerged in the last decade, seeing Israel as an outgrowth of an evolutionary (not a revolutionary) process of change in Canaan. Its proponents differ widely among themselves, and it is too early to speak definitively of only one, separate "model."[33]

The Conquest Model.   On their face, the biblical accounts speak plainly enough of a forced entry into the land of Canaan by the Israelites. They spied out the land, then entered it, conquered a gateway city in central Canaan (Jericho), and then proceeded to defeat several other cities in this area. Following this, they embarked on a southern campaign and a northern campaign, thereby taking effective control of the land.[34]

This is the traditional viewpoint (although it often has assumed far greater material destructions than the Bible actually indicates), and it was not seriously questioned until the twentieth century. The archaeological evidence of destructions ca. 1200 B.C. mentioned above has been interpreted as confirming that these destructions did take place, and many scholarly treatments have merged this evidence with the biblical accounts in attempting to reconstruct the events of Joshua's day.[35]

---

[33] The literature on all of these is vast. For the first three models, see the overviews by N. K. Gottwald, *The Tribes of Yahweh* Maryknoll, N.Y.: Orbis, 1979), 189–233; G. W. Ramsey, *The Quest for the Historical Israel* (Atlanta: John Knox, 1981), 65–98; M. Chaney, "Ancient Palestinian Peasant Movements and the Formation of Premonarchic Israel," in *Palestine in Transition,* ed. D. N. Freedman and D. F. Graf (Sheffield: Almond/ASOR, 1983), 39–90; B. S. J. Isserlin, "The Israelite Conquest of Canaan: A Comparative Review of the Arguments Applicable," *PEQ* 115 (1983): 85–94. More recently, convenient overviews of all four models have been made by several evangelical scholars: Bimson, "The Israelite Conquest of Canaan: An Examination of Recent Theories," *Themelios* 15.1 (1989): 4–15; Hess, "Early Israel in Canaan: A Survey of Recent Evidence and Interpretations," *PEQ* 125 (1993): 125–42; Merrill, "The Late Bronze/Early Iron Age Transition and the Emergence of Israel," *Bsac* 152 (1995), 145–62; K. L. Younger, Jr., "Early Israel in Recent Biblical Scholarship," in B. T. Arnold and D. W. Baker, eds., *The Face of Old Testament Studies* (Grand Rapids: Baker, forthcoming).

[34] A survey such as L. Wood's *Survey of Israel's History* (rev. ed. [Grand Rapids: Zondervan, 1986], 137–53), essentially summarizes the biblical account in this way.

[35] E.g., Albright, "Archaeology and the Date of the Hebrew Conquest of Palestine," 10–18; Bright, in his first edition (1959): *A History of Israel*, 110–27; G. E. Wright, *Biblical Archaeology*, 69–85; P. W. Lapp, "The Conquest of Palestine in the Light of Archaeology," 283–300.

The Settlement Model. In this century an alternative model has been proposed, whereby the Israelites are seen to have been a loosely connected group of pastoral nomads from independent tribes who gradually infiltrated Canaan from the desert and settled there in a largely peaceful enterprise. Any conflicts with Canaanites were certainly not military in nature but rather natural ones between settled farmers and incoming nomads.[36] Once in the land, for various reasons these tribes banded together into a loose federation that eventually came to be called "Israel."

This model was based on a traditio-historical approach, which exhibited a thoroughgoing skepticism concerning the accuracy of both the biblical and archaeological records. It was never accepted by those with confidence in either or both of these records, and it has been severely criticized from both directions.[37] A recent, important defense of Alt's position has been mounted by I. Finkelstein based upon archaeological research, but it too has problems.[38]

The Revolt Model. In 1962 a third alternative was proposed[39] that gained significant acceptance in the field until recently, with varying modifications.[40] This model proposes that the turmoil in Canaan visible in both the biblical and archaeological records was not due to any significant external force entering the land but rather to an internal peasants' revolt that toppled existing Canaanite power structures, located primarily in the large urban centers. This may well have been precipitated by the entry into the land of a small band of worshipers of Yahweh, perhaps an escaped band of slaves from Egypt (thus is the exodus accounted for!) who provided the religious (or political-ideological) glue that melded together the diverse groups in the revolt, forming a Yahwistic tribal confederation. These groups were not descended from a common ancestor, as the Bible pictures it, but rather came together around this common ideology.

This model is based on various sociological approaches. While it incorporates the archaeological evidence into its considerations, it dismisses much of

---

[36] This was first proposed by A. Alt, "The Settlement of the Israelites in Palestine," in *Essays on Old Testament History and Religion,* trans. R. A. Wilson (Garden City: Doubleday, 1968), 173–221, and then accepted by many scholars, such as M. Noth, *The History of Israel,* trans. P. R. Ackroyd (New York: Harper & Row, 1960), 53–109; M. Weippert, *The Settlement of the Israelite Tribes in Palestine* (London: SCM, 1971); id., "The Israelite 'Conquest' and the Evidence from Transjordan," in *Symposia,* ed. F. M. Cross (Cambridge, Mass.: ASOR, 1979), 15–34; V. Fritz, "Conquest or Settlement?" *BA* 50 (1987): 84–100.

[37] E.g., Chaney, "Ancient Palestinian Peasant Movements"; Merrill, *Kingdom of Priests,* 122–26.

[38] Finkelstein, *The Archaeology of the Israelite Settlement* (Jerusalem: Israel Exploration Society, 1988). See the reviews by R. S. Moorey, in the *Journal of Jewish Studies,* 238–40; D. L. Esse, *BARev* 14.5 (1988): 6–12.

[39] Mendenhall, "The Hebrew Conquest of Palestine," 100–120.

[40] Note especially Gottwald, *The Tribes of Yahweh.* See also Mendenhall's *Tenth Generation*; the essays in the special theme issue of *JSOT* 7 (1978); and Chaney, "Ancient Palestinian Peasant Movements."

the biblical record that does not fit the theory.[41] It self-consciously uses modern sociological and anthropological models, and fits the biblical data into them.[42] Criticisms of this model have come from many directions as well.[43]

The Evolutionary Model. The fourth model is in actuality a set of models, all of them assuming that what emerged as "Israel" came from people living within Canaan but that this occurred peacefully, not via a revolutionary process. Thus, for several scholars the emergence of Israel was more of an evolutionary process, as peoples native to Canaan resettled in new sites and took on an identity that eventually came to be known as "Israelite." There are many variations among such models, but all take into account the singular phenomenon that a plethora of many small village sites emerged for the first time in the hill country of Palestine immediately following 1200 B.C. These are taken by many scholars to have been Israelite sites, since the Book of Joshua indicates that the Israelites had the most success in taking territories in the hill country. The previous history and identity of the peoples occupying these sites is debated, but the phenomenon of these sites is foundational to these models.[44]

---

[41] Several have attempted to integrate the traditional conquest model and this revolt model. See Bright, *A History of Israel,* 133–143; R. G. Boling, *Joshua,* 128–32 and passim.

[42] This especially is Gottwald's approach. Note that Mendenhall strenuously objects to being classified with Gottwald ("Ancient Israel's Hyphenated History," 91–103), but their two approaches are similar enough to be grouped in the same discussion, despite their differences.

[43] See, e.g., the debate in several essays in *JSOT* 7 (1978): 2–52, and *JSOT* 8 (1978): 46–49; B. J. Beitzel, "Review of Norman Gottwald, in *The Tribes of Yahweh*," *TJ* 1 (1980): 237–43; N. P. Lemche, *Early Israel: Anthropological and Historical Studies on Israelite Society before the Monarchy,* VTSup 37 (Leiden: Brill, 1985); B. Halpern, "Sociological Comparativism and the Theological Imagination: The Case of the Conquest," in M. Fishbane et al., eds., *"Shaʿarei Talmon": Studies in the Bible, Qumran, and the Ancient Near East Presented to Shemaryahu Talmon* (Winona Lake: Eisenbrauns, 1992), 53–67; Younger, "The 'Collapse Model' and the Origins of the Israelites and Arameans"; paper read at the annual meeting of the American Schools of Oriental Research, November 17, 1997, San Francisco.

[44] For different expressions of this approach, see W. G. Dever, "The Late Bronze-Early Iron I Horizon in Syria-Palestine: Egyptians, Canaanites, 'Sea Peoples,' and 'Proto-Israelites,'" in *The Crisis Years: The Twelfth Century B.C. from beyond the Danube to the Tigris* (Dubuque: Kendall/Hunt, 1992), 99–110; id. "Israel, History of (Archaeology and the 'Conquest')," *ABD* 3:545–58; R. B. Coote and K. W. Whitelam, *The Emergence of Early Israel in Historical Perspective* (Sheffield: Almond, 1987); Lemche, *Early Israel*; id., *Ancient Israel: A New History of Israelite Society,* The Biblical Seminar 5 (Sheffield: JSOT, 1988); T. L. Thompson, *Early History of the Israelite People from the Written and Archaeological Sources,* Studies in the History of the Ancient Near East 4 (Leiden: Brill, 1992); G. W. Ahlström, *The History of Ancient Palestine from the Palaeolithic Period to Alexander's Conquest,* JSOTSup 146 (Sheffield: Academic Press, 1993). Finkelstein's first book (*Archaeology of the Israelite Settlement*) reaffirmed the Alt-Noth settlement model, but his more recent work reflects change toward the direction of the evolutionary model. See Finkelstein, "The Emergence of Early Israel: Anthropology, Environment and Archaeology," *JAOS* 110 (1990): 677–86; id., "The Emergence of Israel in Canaan: Consensus, Mainstream, and Dispute," *SJOT* 2 (1991): 47–59; id., "The Emergence of Israel: A Phase in the Cyclical History of Canaan in the Third and Second Millennia BCE," in *From Nomadism to Monarchy: Archaeological and Historical Aspects of Early Israel* (Jerusalem: IES, 1994), 150–78. For overviews of these "evolutionary" models, see Hess, "Early Israel in Canaan," 131–32; Younger, "Early Israel in Recent Biblical Scholarship."

Evaluation. Each of the models outlined above has contributed to our understanding of the biblical materials in some measure. The conquest model takes seriously the biblical accounts, but it has tended to overemphasize violent destruction of cities, which is not indicated in the biblical record for the most part. The revolt model has highlighted the fact that Israel was not an undifferentiated ethnic identity but rather consisted of diverse strands, including at least some marginal, lower-class groups (see such passages as Exod 12:38 and Num 11:4, which mention a "mixed multitude" and the "rabble" that were part of Israel's company). Here and there throughout the biblical texts are traces of what could be seen as evidence that "Israel" was an outcast, lower-class entity. It certainly cannot be denied, even using the conquest model, that the Israelites would have been poorer and less well-equipped than the Canaanites, in the cosmopolitan Canaanite societies of the Middle or Late Bronze Ages.[45] The settlement and evolutionary models can account for some of the biblical evidence, such as Rahab's family and the Gibeonites (and perhaps others like them), who were already part of Canaan and whose transformation into "Israelites" was nothing very dramatic externally.

However, the settlement, revolt, and evolutionary models (and their offshoots) are at root profoundly skeptical of the biblical records as they now stand, and they are for the most part alien models imposed on the biblical data. They do not adequately account for important biblical data, and thus they ultimately fall short. We must conclude that even given the schematic approach and selectivity of narration of the data that we find in the Book of Joshua, a modified version of the conquest model is the one that best understands and represents the biblical material.

This model must be modified, however, because the stereotypical model of an all-consuming Israelite army descending upon Canaan and destroying everything in its wake cannot be accepted. The biblical data will not allow for this. For example, nowhere in Joshua does Israel win a battle on the basis of superior force in an all-out, frontal offensive attack. Rather, it used various means (ambush, diversionary tactics), along with God's direct help at times, to defeat its enemies.[46] Also, as we noted above, Israel actually physically destroyed very few cities in its conquest of Canaan. Furthermore, the evidence in Judges 1 suggests that Israel's victories over Canaanite peoples were also somewhat incomplete.

We conclude, then, that the biblical picture of an "Israel" descended from

---

[45] The biblical text even suggests this, in Num 13:27–29, where the Israelite spies were awed by the wealth they encountered there. See also J. A. Thompson, *The Bible and Archaeology*, 3d ed. (Grand Rapids: Eerdmans, 1982), 89–92, 96–98, on the disparity between Canaanite and Israelite cultures and standards of living.

[46] See Y. Yadin, *The Art of Warfare in Biblical Lands*, 1, 1–31, 76–114, 182–245; A. Malamat, "Israelite Conduct of War in the Conquest of Canaan," 35–55.

Abraham entering Canaan from without and engaging and defeating various Canaanite forces, but without causing extensive material destruction, is the most reasonable and defensible model, and that is the one assumed here.[47]

(3) Challenges to the Historicity of the Events

As the preceding discussions indicate, the period of Israel's entry into the land of Canaan is the subject of much discussion and lively debate. Not only are the dates and the nature of the events much debated, but also the reliability of the texts that discuss them. That is, for many scholars the Book of Joshua gives an accurate picture of Israel's entry into the land when it is correctly understood. This is the position taken by most believing Christians through the centuries. However, for many scholars, especially in recent years, the Book of Joshua—indeed, the Bible as a whole—is almost worthless as a source of historical information, and the very idea that there was an entity called "Israel" during or at the end of the Late Bronze Age and in the Early Iron Age is challenged. The debate concerning whether any events took place as the Bible depicts them pits what are sometimes called "maximalists" against "minimalists." "Maximalists" differ among themselves concerning the Bible's reliability—evangelicals would affirm it in its entirety, properly interpreted, whereas others would affirm its general usefulness as a historical source, although by no means every detail—but they use it and other written materials alongside archaeological evidence in reconstructing the history of this period. Most "minimalists," on the other hand, insist that archaeological evidence alone should be used in such reconstructions because written texts—most especially the Bible—are late, tendentious, and ideologically biased.

The minimalist approach has its roots in a reaction to the "biblical archaeology" approach espoused by G. E. Wright, W. F. Albright, and others. For Wright, Albright, and many others the Bible was generally considered to be accurate historically, and archaeology usually confirmed its reliability. The so-called biblical archaeology movement thus provided a positive alternative to the negative conclusions about the Bible's reliability that had been in place since the middle of the nineteenth century. J. Wellhausen had claimed that "the text tells us something only from the time when it was written down,"[48] that is, that the text of Joshua and the other historical books, which he claimed were written many hundreds of years after the events, could only give us information about the times in which they were written, not the earlier periods that they discussed.

---

[47] See also the following surveys by evangelical scholars: Merrill, *Kingdom of Priests,* 93–128; Bimson, "The origins of Israel in Canaan" 4–15; Waltke, "The Date of the Conquest," 181–200.

[48] Quoted in Dever, "'Will the Real Israel Please Stand Up?' Archaeology and Israelite Historiography: Part I," *BASOR* 297 (1995): 64.

Beginning in the 1970s, a neo-Wellhausenian reaction to the biblical archaeology movement set in,[49] and in the last ten to fifteen years a thorough-going skepticism has set in among a group of influential scholars. Many of these would date the Old Testament's historical books—including the Book of Joshua—very late, to the period of the exile or later.[50] More to the point, almost all of the minimalist scholars would dispense with the Old Testament entirely as a source for historical reconstruction. Thus, for example, Lemche states: "I propose that we decline to be led by the Biblical account and instead regard it, like other legendary materials, as essentially ahistorical, that is, as a source which only exceptionally can be verified by other information."[51] Similarly, Coote and Whitelam employ an approach "which assigns priority to interpreting archaeological data within a broad interdisciplinary frame-work."[52] T. Thompson puts it even more starkly: "It is ... the independence of Syro-Palestinian archaeology that now makes it possible for the first time to begin to write a history of Israel's origins. Rather than in the bible (sic), it is in the field of Syro-Palestinian archaeology, and the adjunct fields of ancient Near Eastern studies, that we find our primary sources for Israel's earliest history."[53]

A profound skepticism toward the reliability of the biblical accounts is embedded in the work of minimalist scholars. Thus, J. Strange asserts: "It goes without saying that the book [of Joshua] as such does not relate any actual conquest and division of the promised land to Joshua. Everybody (sic) agrees on that."[54] Similarly, Coote claims: "The writers of the Hebrew Scriptures knew little or nothing about the origin of Israel, although the Scriptures can provide much information relevant to the investigation of early Israel. The period under discussion, therefore, does not include the periods of the patriarchs, exodus, conquest, or judges, as devised by the writers of the Scriptures. These periods never existed."[55] J. Van Seters believes that "there

---

[49] Most especially represented by T. L. Thompson, *The Historicity of the Patriarchal Narratives: The Quest for the Historical Abraham*, BZAW 133 (Berlin: de Gruyter, 1974), and J. Van Seters, *Abraham in History and Tradition* (New Haven: Yale University, 1975).

[50] P. R. Davies, e.g., dates almost all of the OT to the Persian period (fifth–third centuries B.C.) ("In Search of 'Ancient Israel,'" JSOTSup 148 [Sheffield: Sheffield Academic Press, 1992], 76). J. Strange dates the Book of Joshua even later, to the second century B.C. ("The Book of Joshua: A Hasmonean Manifesto?" in *History and Traditions of Early Israel: Studies Presented to E. Nielsen, May 8th, 1993,* ed. A. Lemaire and B. Otzen, VTSup 50 [Leiden: Brill, 1993], 136–41), as does G. Garbini *(History and Ideology in Ancient Israel* [New York: Crossroad, 1988], 132).

[51] Lemche, *Early Israel,* 415.

[52] Coote and Whitelam, *Emergence of Early Israel,* 8.

[53] T. L. Thompson, *The Origin Tradition of Ancient Israel,* JSOTSup 55 (Sheffield: JSOT, 1987), 27.

[54] Strange, "The Book of Joshua: A Hasmonean Manifesto?" 141.

[55] Coote, *Early Israel: A New Horizon* (Minneapolis: Fortress, 1990), 2–3.

is no justification for trying to associate archaeological ruins of the end of the Late Bronze Age with a conquest narrative written 600–700 years later. [The Deuteronomistic Historian] did not have any records from Israel's earliest period, nor did he follow old oral traditions. The invasion of the land of Canaan by Israel under Joshua was an invention of [the Deuteronomistic Historian]. The conquest narrative is a good example of ancient historiography but it cannot pass for historical by any modern criteria of historical evaluation."[56]

Because of such skepticism, many of these scholars now attempt to reconstruct the history of the Late Bronze Age and Early Iron Age in Palestine primarily or entirely without reference to the Bible. These include Coote and Whitelam,[57] T. L. Thompson,[58] Ahlström,[59] and Lemche,[60] among others.[61] For most of these scholars, "Israel" is merely a modern scholarly construct and the product of the imaginations of late biblical writers. A nation of "Israel" actually living in Palestine at the end of the second millennium B.C. was not to be found, at least not in any form close to that described in the Bible. The outer limits of skepticism are reached in the work of Davies, for whom a "historical Israel" as depicted in the Bible simply never existed,[62] or Whitelam, for whom "ancient Israel" is solely an invention of ideologically driven biblical writers who have been followed in the modern day by biblical scholars, historians, and archaeologists with their own ideological (i.e., political) agendas in favor of the modern-day state of Israel (as over against the

---

[56] J. Van Seters, "Joshua's Campaign of Canaan and Near Eastern Historiography," *Scandinavian Journal of the Old Testament* 1 (1990): 1–12 (quote is from p. 12).

[57] Coote and Whitelam, *Emergence of Early Israel*; Coote, *Early Israel;* Whitelam, *The Invention of Israel: The Silencing of Palestinian History* (London: Routledge, 1996).

[58] T. L. Thompson, *Early History of the Israelite People from the Written and Archaeological Sources*, Studies in the History of the Ancient Near East 4 (Leiden: Brill, 1992).

[59] Ahlström, *History of Ancient Palestine*. He dismisses the historical value of the biblical records, stating that "the historiography of certain periods for which there are no other sources available than those of the biblical writers will rest on shaky ground because of the subjective presentation and religious *Tendenz* of the material" (p. 32).

[60] Lemche, *Early Israel;* id. *Ancient Israel;* id. *The Canaanites and Their Land: The Tradition of the Canaanites*, JSOTSup 110 (Sheffield: Sheffield Academic Press, 1991).

[61] Two recent works with essays by some of these scholars, as well as others, are V. Fritz and P. R. Davies, eds., *The Origins of the Israelite States,* JSOTSup 228 (Sheffield: Sheffield Academic Press, 1996); L. L. Grabbe, ed., *Can a "History of Israel" Be Written?* (Sheffield: Sheffield Academic Press, 1997).

[62] For Davies there are three "Israels": (1) "biblical Israel," which existed (and exists) *only* as a literary construct in the pages of the Bible; (2) the "historical Israel," which refers to "the inhabitants of the northern Palestinian highlands during part of the Iron Age" and "whose resemblance to biblical Israel is superficial and not substantive"; and (3) "ancient Israel," which is a modern scholarly construct built from the first two "Israels" (*In Search of "Ancient Israel,"* 11, 18).

modern Palestinian cause).[63]

It should be obvious that in these constructions the Bible in general and the Book of Joshua in particular have suffered greatly in terms of their reliability, that is, of their status as sources of information for the period claimed in the Book of Joshua, whether it be the fifteenth or the thirteenth century B.C. Such minimalist constructions are profoundly skeptical of the biblical record, which is approached with what is often called "a hermeneutic of suspicion," that is, they are assumed to be in error until they can be proven to be correct by some independent means of verification.

This skeptical approach, although currently very much in vogue in some wings of biblical scholarship, has not gone unchallenged by critical scholars or evangelicals. Most of these represent something closer to a "maximalist" approach to the Bible and the Book of Joshua, where the book is treated as entirely, or in good measure, reliable as a source of historical information.

Thus, for example, Miller has pointed out the inconsistency of many of the minimalists' efforts to reconstruct a history of Israel, in that they rely on the Bible in much of what they do, notwithstanding their stated aims to the contrary. With reference to Coote and Whitelam, for example, he states that "either they assume information that can only have come from the Hebrew Bible, or they appeal to scholarly consensus, which itself rests on the Bible. In short, their study does not bypass the Hebrew Bible, it only bypasses any critical evaluation of it."[64]

A more serious flaw is the methodological assumption that written texts are of necessity corrupted by ideology or theology and therefore are worthless for any true historical investigation. Thus, not only do these scholars reject the Bible as a valid source, but they resist reading extrabiblical texts that intersect with the Bible in any way that would reinforce the biblical picture. That is, they go out of their way to read certain extrabiblical materials, which most scholars understand to refer to people or events found in the Bible, in ways that deny such connections. Thus, to cite but two examples, the reference to "the house of David" found in an inscription discovered in 1993 at Tel Dan (which was the first extrabiblical mention of David discovered in the ancient

---

[63] For Whitelam, to search for an ancient Israel in Canaan (Palestine) is to commit a methodological sin, and it is at the expense of the search for other, equally valid histories, particularly Palestinian history. See Whitelam, *The Invention of Israel*. Two critiques of Whitelam's work are H. Shanks, "Keith Whitelam Claims Bible Scholars Suppress Palestinian History in Favor of Israelites," *BARev* 22.2 (1996): 54, 56, 69; I. W. Provan, "The End of (Israel's) History? K. W. Whitelam's *The Invention of Ancient Israel*: A Review Article," *JSS* 42 (1997): 283–300.

[64] Miller, "Is it Possible to Write a History of Israel without Relying on the Hebrew Bible?" in *The Fabric of History: Text, Artifact and Israel's Past*, ed. D. V. Edelman, JSOTSup 127 (Sheffield: Sheffield Academic Press, 1991), 93–102.

Near East)[65] has been vigorously disputed by Davies,[66] even though his objections fly in the face of the grammar and epigraphy of the inscription.[67] Another example is Whitelam's dismissal of the Merneptah inscription's reference to Israel as ideologically tainted and thus worthless for historical inquiry. He argues that the inscription itself is ideological and, further, that modern-day attempts to equate the "Israel" of the inscription and the "Israel" of the Bible are themselves ideologically driven.[68] It appears that both Davies' and Whitelam's objections stem primarily from their own ideological commitments to the unreliability not only of the Scriptures but also of any text that would lend any support to the biblical picture.

Indeed, one common thread among such skeptical scholars is a bias in favor of the supposedly "untainted" or "objective" data of archaeology. However, this stance ignores the fact that archaeological remains are mute and can give only limited information without written texts. For example, excavations at Tell Mardikh, a large site in northwestern Syria, began in 1964 with no knowledge about the identity of the ancient site. In 1968 a statue was found identifying the site as ancient Ebla—a name known for more than one hundred years from Mesopotamian documents. From 1964 to 1968, much was learned about the site, primarily about buildings, pottery types, and artifacts; even the physical size of the site gave clues as to its importance. With the identification of the site in 1968, knowledge was advanced further. However, knowledge about the site was revolutionized in 1974 when the first of what turned out to be thousands of tablets were discovered. The earlier discoveries had given insights into social, administrative, political, economic, and religious life; and they fit the site into the context of known history in other areas. But with the texts the earlier picture was fleshed out, and vast amounts of new information became available about life in the third millennium B.C.[69]

Mute archaeological records must be interpreted. As soon as individuals begin the process of interpretation, the archaeological remains take on a voice, but only that voice supplied by the interpretation. It is certainly true that in studying the written records of history "value-neutrality is impossible. The unconscious assumptions of the historians' own age are inescapable. The historian himself is part of the historical process, powerfully influenced by his

---

[65] See A. Biran and J. Naveh, "An Aramaic Stele Fragment from Tel Dan," *IEJ* 43 (1993): 81–98; Shanks, "'David' Found at Dan," *BARev* 20.2 (1994): 26–39.

[66] Davies, "'House of David' Built on Sand: The Sin of the Biblical Maximizers," *BARev* 20.4 (1994): 54–55.

[67] Rainey, "The 'House of David' and the House of the Deconstructionists: Davies Is an Amateur Who 'Can Safely Be Ignored,'" *BARev* 20.6 (1994): 47; D. N. Freedman and J. C. Geoghegan, "'House of David' Is There!" *BARev* 21.2 (1995): 78–79.

[68] Whitelam, *The Invention of Ancient Israel*, 206–10.

[69] Introductions to the excavations at Tell Mardikh (Ebla) may be found in W. S. LaSor, "Tell Mardikh," *ISBE* 4:750–58; R. D. Biggs, "Ebla Texts," *ABD* 2:263–70.

time and place."[70] However, the same is the case with the study of mute archaeological remains: they must be interpreted, and modern-day interpretations can sometimes cloud the issues rather than clarify them.

Another assumption of many "minimalist" scholars is that the Bible, as a theological document (or, for many, an ideological one) and one written (they claim) many centuries after events depicted is less reliable than other written records from the ancient Near East. For example, Lemche states that ordinarily, such external sources [Assyrian, Babylonian royal inscriptions] are regarded as providing more reliable information than the Old Testament does, since they are contemporaneous with the events they depict."[71] Yet W. F. Hallo notes: "The Biblical record must be ... scrutinized like other historiographical traditions of the ancient Near East, neither exempted from the standards demanded of those other traditions, nor subjected to severer ones than they are."[72] Using such standards, he concludes: "One can hardly deny the reality of a conquest from abroad, implying a previous period of wanderings, a dramatic escape from the prior place of residence and an oppression there that prompted the escape."[73]

The larger challenges to a reading of the Bible (and the Book of Joshua) presented by minimalist approaches cannot be adequately responded to here. However, not only are such approaches profoundly antibiblical in most respects but they also founder methodologically in the ways in which they use and interpret the evidence, both biblical and extrabiblical. Numerous rejoinders to such minimalist approaches have pointed out their many shortcomings.[74] An especially important recent example is the challenge in the recent

---

[70] D. Bebbington, *Patterns in History: A Christian View* (Downers Grove: InterVarsity, 1979), 6.

[71] Lemche, *Ancient Israel*, 70.

[72] W. H. Hallo, "The Limits of Skepticism," *JAOS* 110 (1990): 187–99; quote is from p. 193. This was the 1989 Presidential Address of the American Oriental Society.

[73] Ibid., 194.

[74] Also see responses of nonevangelicals such as Dever ("Will the Real Israel Please Stand Up?" *BASOR* 297 [1995], 61–80; id. *BASOR* 298 [1995]: 37–58; id., "The Identity of Early Israel," *JSOT* 72 [1996]: 3–24; id., "Revisionist Israel Revisited," *CR:BS* 4 [1996]: 35–50; id., "Philology, Theology, and Archaeology: What Kind of History Do We Want, and What Is Possible?" in *The Archaeology of Israel,* ed. N. A. Silberman and D. Small [Sheffield: Academic Press, 1997], 290–310); A. F. Rainey ("Uncritical Criticism," *JAOS* 115 [1995]: 101–4); A. Hurwitz ("The Historical Quest for 'Ancient Israel' and the Linguistic Evidence of the Hebrew Bible," *VT* 47 [1997]: 301–15; as well as evangelicals such as V. P. Long (*The Art of Biblical History* [Grand Rapids: Zondervan, 1994]); I. W. Provan ("Ideologies, Literary and Critical: Reflections on Recent History Writing on the History of Israel," *JBL* 114 [1995]: 585–606; id., "The End of [Israel's] History?" 283–300); J. K. Hoffmeier ("The Evangelical Contribution to Understanding the [Early] History of Ancient Israel in Recent Scholarship," *BBR* 7 [1997]: 77–90; id., *Israel in Egypt,* esp. chaps. 1–2); R. S. Hess ("Fallacies in the Study of Early Israel: An Onomastic Perspective," *TynBul* 45 [1994]: 339–54; id., "Non-Israelite Personal Names in the Book of Joshua," *CBQ* 58 [1996]: 205–14; id., "West Semitic Texts and the Book of Joshua," *BBR* 7 [1997]: 63–76; id., "Getting Personal: What Names in the Bible Teach Us," *BibRev* 13.6 [1997]: 30–37); and Younger (*Ancient Conquest Accounts: A Study in Ancient Near Eastern and Biblical History Writing,* JSOTSup 98 (Sheffield: Academic Press, 1990), esp. chap. 1; id., "Early Israel in Recent Biblical Scholarship").

46

edited *Faith, Tradition, and History.*[75] This contains critiques of minimalist approaches, but, equally significant, numerous positive contributions to the study of Israel's history in all periods, including that of the Book of Joshua.

The more immediate challenges to reading and understanding the history presented in the Book of Joshua center around the available archaeological evidence and its interpretation, the viability of the different models used to speak of Israel's entry or emergence in the land of Canaan, and the date assigned to it. Entrée into these issues may be had via the discussions above on "Date of the Events" and "Nature of the Events," as well as in the commentary proper (see especially the excursus on "The Archaeology of Jericho and Ai" at the end of chap. 6).

(4) Historical Setting of the Conquest

If the Israelites entered Canaan about 1400 B.C., it was during the Late Bronze Age (ca. 1550–1200 B.C.).[76] The Middle Bronze Age II period (ca. 1750–1550 B.C.) probably was the peak of civilization throughout the entire ancient Near East.[77] The greatest myths and epics originated in this period,[78] pottery was at its technical peak, and the great law code of Hammurabi had just been codified.[79] Economically, this was a time of great prosperity for Canaan, which was on the trade routes between Africa and Asia.

On the international scene, there were three great power centers during the Middle Bronze Age: in Mesopotamia (under the Babylonians), in Asia Minor (under the Hittites), and in Egypt (under the Egyptians). These groups constantly struggled with each other for supremacy, and the small states and

---

[75] A. R. Millard, J. K. Hoffmeier, D. W. Baker, eds., *Faith, Tradition, and History: Old Testament Historiography in Its Near Eastern Context* (Winona Lake: Eisenbrauns, 1994). E. A. Yamauchi's lead essay, "The Current State of Old Testament Historiography" (pp. 1–36) represents another able critique of minimalist scholarship.

[76] Under Bimson's scheme, the Middle Bronze Age came to an end more than a century later than is commonly accepted, ca. 1430–1400 B.C. (see his convenient chart on p. 222), and the conquest would have been roughly during this time. However, Bimson himself has reevaluated this scheme, although he has not published any extensive reworking of this to date. See p. 176, n. 33.

[77] The most thorough summary of the period may be found in the essays of the *Cambridge Ancient History,* Vol. II, pt. 1: *The Middle East and the Aegean Region c. 1800–1380 B.C.* A convenient short summary of the period immediately preceding and following Israel's entry into the land may be found in Merrill, *Kingdom of Priests,* 94–108.

[78] Convenient translations of the great Ugaritic myths about Baal and the other gods may be found in *ANET,* 129–55; J. B. Pritchard, ed., *The Ancient Near East: An Anthology of Texts and Pictures* (Princeton, N.J.: Princeton University, 1958), 92–132; *DOTT,* 118–33; G. R. Driver, *Canaanite Myths and Legends*; C. H. Gordon, "Poetic Legends and Myths From Ugarit," 5–133, and M. D. Coogan, *Stories from Ancient Canaan.*

[79] Ca. 1792–1750 B.C., using the "middle chronology" proposed by several scholars (see Harrison, *Introduction to the Old Testament,* 159–66). See the translation of this law code in *ANET,* 163–80; *DOTT,* 27–37.

regions between them were under their economic and military domination. Canaan in this period was relatively unstable, undoubtedly under the influence of the Hyksos groups that can be seen in Egypt at this time. Most were Semites who came into Egypt from the north and who dominated its institutions until they were expelled ca. 1550 B.C.[80]

The Egyptian expulsion of the Hyksos usually is seen as marking the transition to the Late Bronze Age. Other than this political change, the differences between the Middle and Late Bronze Ages are relatively minor compared, perhaps, to those between the Bronze and Iron Ages. The Late Bronze Age (ca. 1550–1200 B.C.) continued as a period of prosperity, although it declined as the period progressed. In Canaan, the system of relatively small, independent city-states under loose foreign domination gave way to one of large empires (Egyptian, Hittite, etc.) that maintained tighter control over these city-states. The land that Israel occupied was dominated in the coastal areas and low-lying hills by Egypt and by its vassals in the hill country. The interdependence throughout the region is illustrated by the fact that at Ugarit, in the far north, at least five different writing systems and eight different languages found among the texts have been discovered there.[81]

At the time of Israel's entry into Canaan, the two kingdoms to the north—the Hittite Empire, under Suppiluliumas, and the smaller Mitannian Empire, under Tushratta—were engaged in struggles for control.[82] The Hittites prevailed but did not push their territorial claims southward into Egyptian territory; rather, a fragile but peaceful balance of power prevailed. Egypt, under Amenophis III (ca. 1390–1352 B.C.) and his son, the reformer king Amenophis IV (Akhenaten, ca. 1352–1336 B.C.), was not much interested in military affairs.[83] Thus, a relative power vacuum existed in southern Canaan[84] that Israel was able to exploit.

Ugarit.   The ancient city of Ugarit, on the northeast Mediterranean coast, was just entering its golden age when Israel entered Canaan, far to the south. It was a city-state that had existed for centuries but whose existence climaxed in the period from 1400–1200 B.C. It sat astride significant trade routes, and its commercial influence was widespread. Its special significance for biblical studies lies in the texts (about 1400) that have been unearthed at its site (modern Ras Shamra) since its discovery in 1929. These tablets date to the Late

---

[80] See W. W. Hallo and W. K. Simpson, *The Ancient Near East: A History* (New York: Harcourt Brace Jovanovich, 1971), 250–60; W. C. Hayes, "Egypt: From the Death of Ammenemes III to Seqenenre II," *CAH* 2.1:54–73.

[81] P. C. Craigie, *Ugarit and the Old Testament* (Grand Rapids: Eerdmans, 1983), 22.

[82] A. Goetze, "The Struggle for the Domination of Syria (1400–1300 B.C.)," 1–20.

[83] W. C. Hayes, "Egypt: Internal Affairs From Thutmosis I to the Death of Amenophis III," *CAH* 2.1:338–46; C. Aldred, "Egypt: The Amarna Period and the End of the Eighteenth Dynasty," *CAH* 2.2:49–63.

[84] K. M. Kenyon, "Palestine in the Time of the Eighteenth Dynasty," *CAH* 2.1:526–56.

Bronze Age, and they give a vivid picture of life in the land that Israel entered under Joshua and lived in during the period of the judges. We can see a flourishing internationalism, and we are given thorough insights into Canaanite religion and culture. The long mythological texts about the Canaanite gods have shed light on the challenge that faced Israel in keeping its worship pure (see below); they also have shed much light on our understanding of the Hebrew language and its poetry.[85] The city's and its texts' direct relevance to the Book of Joshua are relatively minor however.

The Amarna Letters.   Israel entered Canaan just before a period of considerable social and political unrest there, which is attested in a series of more than 350 documents (mostly letters) uncovered at Tell el-Amarna, in middle Egypt, beginning in 1887 and a few discovered in Palestine.[86] These letters are now dated to the middle of the fourteenth century B.C. They are primarily correspondence from the petty kinglets in Canaan appealing (in a rather shrill manner) to their Egyptian overlords—Amenophis III and IV—for assistance against rivals and threats from the general populace, and they portray fairly chaotic conditions throughout Canaan. Their data would correlate well with the chaotic conditions portrayed in the Bible during the period of the judges.

The Hapiru.   In the Amarna letters, groups of persons called "Hapiru" are mentioned regularly as a source of trouble for the kinglets.[87] Because of the similarities between this word and the biblical word "Hebrew" (*ʿibrî*) and because of the close correspondence in dates between the biblical chronology and the Amarna letters, the Hapiru were initially assumed to be the invading Hebrews of the biblical accounts.

However, it has been shown that the Hapiru in Canaan were not an external, invading ethnic force but rather a disparate band of internal groups linked by political and social realities, and not ethnic ties. They were a marginal group, consisting of disenfranchised persons who became disaffected with the power systems in Canaan; "outlaw" is an English word that approximates their status. They withdrew from everyday life in Canaan and eventually turned against the power structures, causing the turmoil seen in the Amarna letters. People and towns could *become* Hapiru; the term was used pejoratively in almost all its references. Furthermore, references to these groups have been found in far-ranging areas, outside of Canaan, and from late in the

---

[85] Entrée into the vast literature on Ugarit may be had via A. Curtis, *Ugarit (Ras Shamra)*; M. S. Drower, "Ugarit," 130–60; Craigie, *Ugarit and the Old Testament;* M. Liverani, *ISBE,* 4, s.v. "Ugarit, Ugaritic." Translations of the texts are mentioned in n. 77.

[86] See Campbell, "The Amarna Letters and the Amarna Period," 54–75; Drower, "The Amarna Age," 483–93; Albright, "The Amarna Letters From Palestine," 98–116; R. F. Youngblood, *ISBE,* 1, s.v. "Amarna Tablets"; Nadab Na'aman, *ABD,* 1, s.v. "Amarna Letters."

[87] These people are also known as *ʿapiru* and *Habiru.*

third millennium B.C., not just the Amarna period.[88]

Study of the Hapiru has been a major element in the formulation of the "revolt" model of the "conquest" discussed earlier. The assumption has been that the biblical Hebrews (and thus the biblical Israelites) and Amarna Hapiru were the same people, and the biblical picture thus has been radically revised to fit the Amarna data. The "invasion" by an external, ethnically related force is seen instead as an internal revolt by marginalized groups who eventually created a fictional ancestry (i.e., that which is found in the Bible) to link them together.

However, this equation has been challenged on two grounds. First, there is serious question about whether the two terms (ʿapiru and ʿibrî) truly are related to each other etymologically.[89] It would appear that this equation was made originally at least partly because the date of the Amarna Hapiru fit the prevailing date of the Israelite conquest, and it has survived among those who question this early dating. However, those making the equation do not focus as much attention on the Hapiru outside Canaan in other periods as they do on the Amarna Hapiru.

A second challenge is independent of the etymological argument, and it is that one cannot equate the biblical terms "Hebrew" and "Israelite" in too facile a manner. It should be noted, for example, that in the Bible the term "Hebrew" is mainly found on the lips of foreigners.[90] Thus, it is entirely conceivable that non-Israelites used the term in describing the Israelites but that the Israelites did not normally call themselves that.[91] Certainly an equation between the terms "Hebrew" and "Hapiru" could have been made in some people's minds (i.e., as a popular etymology), even if linguistically there was no actual etymological connection.

We should note, further, that acceptance of the equation of Hapiru=Hebrew and a redefinition of the biblical Hebrews as marginal "outlaws" — seeing them as related only socially, legally, or religiously — discounts the clear and

---

[88] See M. Greenberg, *The Hab/piru*; id., "Hab/piru and Hebrews," *WHJP* 2:188–200; Mendenhall, "The Hebrew Conquest of Palestine"; id., *The Tenth Generation*, 122–41; H. Cazelles, "The Hebrews," in *Peoples of Old Testament Times*, ed. D. J. Wiseman (Oxford: Oxford University Press, 1973), 1–28; Gottwald, *The Tribes of Yahweh*, 401–9 and *passim*; Beitzel, *ISBE*, 2, s.v. "Habiru"; Rainey, "Who Is a Canaanite? A Review of the Textual Evidence," *BASOR* 304 (1996): 1–15.

[89] Greenberg, *The Hab/piru*, 90–96; Weippert, *The Settlement of the Israelite Tribes in Palestine*, 63–102; Beitzel, *ISBE*, 2, s.v. "Habiru" and "Hebrew (People)."

[90] E.g., in Gen 39:14,17; Exod 2:6; 1 Sam 4:6,9. See, briefly, Cazelles, "The Hebrews," 1–3.

[91] This may have been due to its pejorative associations in the popular mind, but it certainly need not have been; it could have been because the terms were indeed understood differently (see Beitzel, *ISBE*, 2, s.v. "Hebrew [People]").

unanimous biblical picture of them as also, if not primarily, related ethnically to each other.[92]

It does not seem appropriate, then, to equate the Amarna Hapiru with the biblical Israelites in too firm a way. It certainly is conceivable that some among the Israelite tribes became "Hapiru" after encountering them in Canaan[93] or that they were perceived as such by the Canaanites,[94] but to see the Israelites simply as identical with the Hapiru stretches the evidence too far.

The significance of the above indicates that Israel entered a Canaan that was beginning to be destabilized due to the Hapiru problem. This destabilization led to a gradual decline in Late Bronze Age culture and institutions until they collapsed around 1200 B.C.

5. The Place of Joshua in the Canon

(1) Joshua and the Pentateuch

The Book of Joshua forms the logical conclusion of much that is found in the Pentateuch. In particular, it has much in common with the book of Deuteronomy. They each chronicle events at a pivotal time in Israel's history, they each focus on a great leader's words and actions, and they are logically connected with each other. The one anticipates the other and picks up where the other left off. To understand the Book of Joshua, then, one must know something about Deuteronomy.

The Book of Deuteronomy claims to be the words Moses spoke at the end of his life to the generation of Israel that was poised to enter the promised land. As such, it is the last of the "Books of Moses." Several times Moses' speaking to the people is mentioned: Deut 1:1,5; 4:44–45; 5:1; 27:1; 29:2[Hb. 1]; 31:1,30; 33:1. He is also depicted as writing: 31:9,22,24.[95]

The book looks back to the Sinai and wilderness experiences, and it uses these as the basis for exhortation about the future. It looks ahead to life in the promised land and speaks of centralization of worship (chap. 12) and many other concerns. It is in a real sense a "second law" (which is what its title means) since much of it is devoted to recapitulating and expanding upon the law that had been given earlier (chaps. 12–26).

MAINSTREAM CRITICAL VIEWS OF DEUTERONOMY. Critical scholar-

---

[92] See Beitzel, "Hapiru," *ISBE* 2:589–90, and "Hebrew (People)" for these and other objections to equating the Amarna Hapiru and the biblical Hebrews.

[93] See, e.g., Bimson, *Redating the Exodus and the Conquest*, 224–30, esp. 228–29.

[94] Merrill, *Kingdom of Priests*, 100–8.

[95] Other Pentateuchal references to Moses' writing include Exod 17:14; 24:4; 34:27–28; Num 33:2.

ship in the last two centuries has taken a very different view of the book's provenience and purpose. To generalize, it is seen as a product of the seventh century B.C., dating from—or just prior to—the time of Josiah (2 Kings 22–23). It was the "book of the Law" that was "discovered" in the temple during the repairs of the temple commissioned by Josiah, and it formed the basis for the further reforms he instituted. It is usually seen as a "pious fraud," ascribed to Moses by its seventh-century author(s) in order to give it the maximum authority. It supposedly was written, then, to stimulate religious reform in the wake of the apostasy of the time of Manasseh and Amon (2 Kings 21).[96]

This view of Deuteronomy is part and parcel of what has come to be known as the "documentary hypothesis" of the sources of the books of Genesis–Deuteronomy. In brief, four major, independent literary sources for the present Pentateuch are postulated, sources that came together over time, woven as strands into the present narrative. Most of Deuteronomy is seen as a discrete unit, coming from the time of Josiah.

DEUTERONOMY, JOSHUA, AND THE "HEXATEUCH." Because of the obvious continuities in thought, subject matter, and style between Joshua and Deuteronomy, Joshua has been seen as the logical conclusion of the Pentateuch, and the idea of a "Hexateuch" (i.e., a literary unit composed of six books: Genesis–Joshua) has been given credence.[97] At root was the thought that the Pentateuch was incomplete, that it "remains a torso,"[98] without the Pentateuchal land promises being fulfilled in Joshua.

Fundamental to this idea is the assumption that the documentary strands found in the Pentateuch can also be found in the Book of Joshua. Accordingly, many scholars favoring this hypothesis have focused on identifying these strands in Joshua.[99]

An obvious strength of this idea is that it is based on an undisputed fact: the Pentateuch does end somewhat inconclusively. D. J. A. Clines speaks of the "partial fulfillment—which implies also the partial nonfulfillment—of the promise to or blessing of the patriarchs."[100] It is obvious to the reader at the end of Deuteronomy that there is more to come.

On the other hand, there are several problems with the hypothesis of a

---

[96] See the reviews of work on Deuteronomy in O. Eissfeldt, *The Old Testament: An Introduction*, 171–76, 219–33; Harrison, *Introduction to the Old Testament*, 637–53; Childs, *Introduction to the Old Testament as Scripture*, 204–10; M. Weinfeld, *ABD*, 2, s.v. "Deuteronomy, Book of."

[97] See the classical formulations of this in S. R. Driver, *Introduction to the Literature of the Old Testament*, rev. ed. (New York: Scribners, 1913), 1–159; G. von Rad, "The Form-Critical Problem of the Hexateuch," 1–78.

[98] Childs, *Introduction to the Old Testament as Scripture*, 231.

[99] E.g., W. H. Bennett, *The Book of Joshua: A New English Translation,* Polychrome Bible (New York: Dodd, Mead, 1899); Eissfeldt, *The Old Testament: An Introduction*, 241–48, 250–57; G. Fohrer, *Introduction to the Old Testament*, 192–205.

[100] D. J. A. Clines, *The Theme of the Pentateuch*, JSOTSup 29.

"Hexateuch." First, despite the fact that Deuteronomy does not end with the patriarchal promises fulfilled, it does end at a very logical place, namely, at the death of Moses, the major character of the last four books of the Pentateuch. Taken on its own terms, it represents Moses' last words, given to a people poised to enter the land. Life in the land begins in the next book and continues in the land through the rest of Israel's history.

A second problem with the "Hexateuch" hypothesis lies in its severing of the many obvious ties that Joshua (and Deuteronomy) has with the material following it (see below). The Book of Judges is a strange place for another large, independent work to have begun.[101]

A third problem concerns the documentary hypothesis itself. On the one level, there is little agreement about the various "sources" themselves, both within the Pentateuch itself or within Joshua. On a more fundamental level, there is not even agreement about the existence of *any* such "sources," ones that are intertwined strands of material. Conservative Christian scholars have questioned this hypothesis from the beginning,[102] and they were joined over the years by others.[103] Currently, the entire hypothesis is being radically reworked among mainstream critical scholars and even widely rejected or ignored.[104]

(2) Joshua and the "Deuteronomistic History"[105]

An alternative hypothesis that has implications for the Book of Joshua (and the books following it) was given its classical formulation in 1943 by M. Noth.[106] Noth saw a literary unity beginning with Deuteronomy and

---

[101] See also D. N. Freedman, *IDB*, 2, s.v. "Hexateuch"; Childs, *Introduction to the Old Testament as Scripture*, 231.

[102] See, e.g., W. H. Green, *The Unity of the Book of Genesis* (New York: Scribners, 1895); id., *The Higher Criticism of the Pentateuch*; O. T. Allis, *The Five Books of Moses* (Nutley, N.J.: Presbyterian & Reformed, 1949); Harrison, *Introduction to the Old Testament*, 495–541; G. F. Archer, Jr., *A Survey of Old Testament Introduction* (Chicago: Moody, 1974); E. E. Carpenter, *ISBE*, 3, s.v. "Pentateuch"; Wolf, *Introduction to the Old Testament Pentateuch*, 62–71; D. Garrett, *Rethinking Genesis: The Source and Authorship of the First Book of the Pentateuch* (Grand Rapids: Baker, 1991), 13–33.

[103] See C. H. Gordon, "Higher Critics and Forbidden Fruit," 131–34; U. Cassuto, *The Documentary Hypothesis and the Composition of the Pentateuch,* trans. I. Abrahams (Jerusalem: Magnes, 1961); M. H. Segal, *The Pentateuch—Its Composition and Authorship—and Other Biblical Studies* (Jerusalem: Magnes, 1967).

[104] See, e.g., R. Alter, *The Art of Biblical Narrative*; I. M. Kikawada and A. Quinn, *Before Abraham Was: The Unity of Genesis 1–11*; Y. T. Radday and H. Shore, *Genesis: An Authorship Study*; Rendsburg, [Two Book Reviews] *JAOS* 107 (1987): 554–57.

[105] For fuller discussion of the "Deuteronomistic History," see Howard, *Introduction to the Old Testament Historical Books,* 179–82.

[106] M. Noth, *The Deuteronomistic History,* JSOTSup 15, 2d ed. (Sheffield: JSOT, 1991).

stretching through 2 Kings that he called the "Deuteronomistic History." He contended that this was the work of a single theologian, the "Deuteronomist," who wrote after the fall of Jerusalem to offer a historical-theological explanation for the events of 722 and 587 B.C. (the falls of Samaria and Jerusalem). Noth saw this work as attempting to demonstrate that these events were the direct consequence of Israel's unrepentant following after other gods and their failure to obey God. As such, it had essentially a negative purpose.[107]

Basic themes in the "Deuteronomistic History" are (1) the graciousness of Yahweh's covenant, (2) the evils of idolatry and a decentralized cult, (3) and the inevitability of reward and punishment according to obedience or disobedience.[108] A primary emphasis here is in the keeping of the Mosaic covenant (although the Abrahamic and Davidic covenants do figure as well).[109]

There are some obvious strengths to this approach. First, there *is* a strong "Deuteronomistic" influence found throughout Joshua–2 Kings, one that is not nearly so visible in Genesis–Numbers.[110] Second, the theory of consecutive, discrete blocks of literary materials joined together at various "seams" (as Noth envisioned in the case of the Deuteronomistic History) is easier to countenance than is the "documentary" theory of various intertwined strands coming together. Third, on the whole, there is more of a unity, both in content and in outlook, to Deuteronomy–Kings than there is to Genesis–Joshua.

However, there are some deficiencies as well. First, this approach does not take seriously the biblical witnesses to Deuteronomy's provenience at a far earlier period in Israel's history than the time of Josiah or the exile.[111] Second, the removal of Deuteronomy from Genesis–Numbers leaves that corpus as a torso; the resulting "Tetrateuch" is most unsatisfactory as a literary unit. Third, Noth's essentially negative understanding of the Deuteronomist's pur-

---

[107] Recent reviews of work on the Deuteronomistic History may be found in G. Gerbrandt, *Kingship According to the Deuteronomistic History*, SBLDS 87 (Atlanta: Scholars Press, 1986), 1–18; S. L. McKenzie, *The Trouble with Kings: The Composition of the Book of Kings in the Deuteronomistic History* (Leiden: Brill, 1991), 1–19; id., *ABD*, 2, s.v. "Deuteronomistic History."

[108] The first and third points here conflict somewhat; both patterns can be seen, however. See R. Polzin, *Moses and the Deuteronomist* (New York: Seabury, 1980), 144–45 and *passim* on this.

[109] See Howard, "The Case for Kingship in Deuteronomy and the Former Prophets," 113–14, on the merging of these divergent covenants in the "Deuteronomistic History."

[110] Thus, there can be some value in speaking of a "Deuteronomistic" philosophy of history (i.e., one in which there is a strong—and almost always immediate—correlation between obedience and reward, disobedience and punishment) or a "Deuteronomistic" history (i.e., a corpus of books that reflects the same viewpoints found in Deuteronomy). The term thus can be used adjectivally, with no conclusions concerning authorship or date of Deuteronomy implicit in its use.

[111] See G. Wenham, "The Date of Deuteronomy," Part One, *Themelios* 10.3 (1985): 15–20; "The Date of Deuteronomy," Part Two, *Themelios* 11.1 (1985): 15–18.

pose has not been generally accepted: "It is hard to imagine a negative cause as sufficient reason to compose and preserve the tradition."[112]

(3) Joshua and the Present Canon

The present order of books from Genesis to Esther in the Protestant canon, and from Genesis to 2 Kings in the Hebrew canon, is basically chronological with reference to the events in them. In the former order, the first five books generally are known as the "books of Moses," the "Pentateuch," or the "Law." In the Jewish traditions, the five Mosaic books form the "Torah," and the narrative books from Joshua to 2 Kings are part of a larger corpus entitled the "Prophets." Within this division are the "Former Prophets" (Joshua to 2 Kings) and the "Latter Prophets" (Isaiah, Jeremiah, Ezekiel, and the "Twelve"). References to the "Prophets" as a canonical division are found very early, in the Prologue to the book of Ecclesiasticus (Sirach) (ca. 180 B.C.), Josephus,[113] and the New Testament.[114] The Bible itself refers to the "former prophets" (Zech 1:4; 7:7), but these would seem to be references to the classical prophets in the tradition of Elijah, Amos, or Jeremiah, and not to a canonical corpus. The earliest extant reference to the "Former Prophets" as a canonical division comes from the Middle Ages.[115]

In many ways both Deuteronomy and Joshua act as fulcrums between the material preceding and following. The first part of Deuteronomy (1–11) is Moses' personalized review of the past, along with his exhortations and warnings about the future. The core of the book (12–26) is a restatement—with many additions—of the law given earlier; the changes and additions reflect a concern for life in the land, which Israel is about to begin. Childs has noted the importance in this connection of von Rad's idea of "actualization" in Deuteronomy, whereby each generation appropriates and enters into the covenant for itself.[116] The best examples of this are in Deut 5:2–3 and especially 29:14–5 (Hb. 13–14), but it occurs throughout the book. That is, the book is more than merely a historical review for one generation; it applies the Sinai experiences and Law to all succeeding generations as well (cf., e.g., Deut 4:25–31; 6:7,20–25).

Similarly, Joshua builds upon the Pentateuch, most notably with respect to the fulfillment of the land promises but also with respect to the continued

---

[112] Childs, Introduction to the Old Testament as Scripture, 237. See further the discussion in chap. 6 below.

[113] Josephus, Against Apion 1.7–8.

[114] Matt 5:17; 7:12; 11:13; 22:40; Luke 16:16,29,31; 24:27; 24:44; John 1:45; Acts 13:15; 24:14; 26:22; 28:23; Rom 3:21. Each of these cases refers to two of the three canonical divisions: "the Law and the Prophets" or to "Moses and the Prophets"; Luke 24:44 refers to all three divisions: "the Law of Moses, the Prophets, and the Psalms."

[115] Childs, Introduction to the Old Testament as Scripture, 230.

[116] Ibid., 214–15, 222.

story line involving people such as Joshua himself, who earlier had been introduced. At the end of the book, Joshua and the people renew the covenant. This has a backward-looking component as well as a forward-looking one. Also, the book as a whole looks ahead to settled life in the land.

Despite all of this, the testimony throughout both Protestant and Hebrew canons is unanimous and unambiguous in seeing a major canonical break between Deuteronomy and Joshua.[117] Both of the above theories—of a "Hexateuch" and a "Deuteronomistic History"—have cogently made valid observations about the flow of thought across Deuteronomy and Joshua. However, they are modern critical constructs, and they both cut across the present canonical division, thus ignoring some important features in the biblical text.

One such feature is Joshua's position at the head of the Prophets, which must be taken seriously. The prophetic tradition was one which carried God's words to the people. While the "Former Prophets" are "historical" books in the main, they are "prophetic" in that they are God's words, and they "bear testimony to the working out of the prophetic word in the life of the nation."[118] It is interesting to note the wholesale incorporation of historical material in the books of the prophets, which softens the distinction between the two types of books (cf., e.g., Isaiah 36–39 // 2 Kings 18–20; Jer 40:7–9 // 2 Kgs 25:23–26; Jer 52:1–27, 31–34 // 2 Kgs 24:18–25:21,27–30).[119]

A second feature is Joshua's position at the head of the books whose history is played out in the promised land. In Joshua the capture of the land is recounted, and in 2 Kings the loss of the land is related. All the history in between takes place in this land that God gave to Israel. The Book of Joshua, then, plays an important role in introducing us to this land.

Third, we may notice that Joshua the man is very different from Moses. Joshua is Moses's successor (Joshua 1) as leader of the nation, and yet he does not occupy the same office as Moses. He is not called a prophet, as Moses is (Deut 34:10). Moses is the "servant of the LORD," whereas Joshua is merely "Moses' aide" (Josh 1:1). Joshua is not the recipient of the Law as Moses was, but rather only its guardian; Moses was the great law-giver, whose role is not duplicated in Israel's history.

Fourth, we may also notice that Joshua is the first in the line of leadership that received its full expression in the kings of Israel and Judah. Joshua was not a king, yet several facts about him show that elements of his leadership foreshadowed the leadership the kings were to exercise. For example, the

---

[117] In the Syriac version, Job is placed between Deuteronomy and Joshua, on the theory that Job was written by Moses, and in some early Christian traditions mention is made of a "Heptateuch" and even an "Octateuch" (Harrison, *Introduction to the Old Testament*, 665). However, these did not survive as mainstream traditions, and they never were part of the Jewish traditions.

[118] Childs, *Introduction to the Old Testament as Scripture*, 236.

[119] Ibid.

emphasis in Josh 1:1–9 on his keeping the law, the fact that he was responsible for Israel's entering and keeping the land, and the very fact that there is a narrative devoted to his entering his office[120] all place him in this line of leadership, since all of these are characteristic of the kings.[121]

Finally, despite its own status as God's prophetic Word, the Book of Joshua also recognizes the existence of an earlier, authoritative, written word of God: the Book of the Law (e.g., Josh 1:8; 8:31,32,34). The words of God Moses wrote down and deposited in the ark (Deut 31:24) have an authoritative function as written Scripture in Joshua. This idea certainly is not as visible with respect to what Joshua himself said. The Pentateuch as a whole forms an authoritative basis for the Book of Joshua; indeed, it does so throughout the rest of the Old Testament.[122]

6. Theology of the Book of Joshua

At least seven major themes can be seen in the Book of Joshua: (1) the land, (2) God's promises, (3) the covenant, (4) obedience, (5) purity of worship (holiness), (6) godly leadership, and (7) rest. These combine to form a rich theology that consistently points to God as the major character in the book. He was the giver of the land in fulfillment of his promises, the one to whom allegiance and obedience were owed, who was a holy and jealous God, who appointed Joshua as Moses' designated successor, and who fought for his people and gave them rest. The book, then, for all its battles and land distributions, points to God above all else.

(1) The Land

The major theme in the book is the possession of the promised land.[123] The land had been promised to Abraham (Gen 12:7; 13:14–15,17; 15:18–21; 17:8; 22:17) and also to Isaac (Gen 26:3–4), to Jacob (Gen 28:4,13; 35:12), and to succeeding generations (see Gen 15:13–21; 48:4; 50:24).

The land is a central goal toward which the action and thought in the Pentateuch moves. Moses was called to bring God's people to "a good and broad land, a land flowing with milk and honey" (Exod 3:8,17; cf. also 6:4,8). The Book of Exodus shows the beginning of the move toward that land, and the

---

[120] In contrast to the absence of such in the accounts of the prekingship charismatic judges.

[121] See Gerbrandt, *Kingship According to the Deuteronomistic History*, 116–23.

[122] See Childs, *Introduction to the Old Testament as Scripture*, 223–24, 233, for more on this point.

[123] We have dealt at length with important components of the land motif in the book in several excursuses below, and the information there will not be repeated here. See (1) "The Giving of the Land in Joshua" (at 1:3); (2) "Israel's Inheritance of the Land" (at 13:7); and (3) "Patterns in the Land Distribution Lists" (at the end of chap. 13).

Book of Numbers shows the continuation of the journey. Indeed, it has been noted[124] that twelve "journeying" texts in these two books form their framework[125] in the same way that the "generations" formulas form the framework of Genesis.[126] Beyond this, several chapters in Numbers are concerned with tribal and individual land inheritances: Num 27:1–11; 32; 34–36.

The land is related to God's gift to Israel over and over again in the Pentateuch, especially in Deuteronomy.[127] In Joshua the concept occurs more than fifty times.[128] As a gift of God, the land never belonged absolutely to Israel: it belonged to God (Lev 25:23; Deut 9:4–5). The dividing of the land by lot further indicates that it was at God's disposal (Num 26:55–56; Josh 14:2; 18:1–10), as does the demand for the land's firstfruits to be given to God (Deut 14:22–29; 26:9–15).[129]

The fact that a major portion of the Book of Joshua is devoted to detailing the specific inheritances of individuals and the tribes (chaps. 13–21) is important in this regard. Although these chapters do not make for easy (or interesting) reading, their importance lies in their showing that the land promises were now indeed being fulfilled in tangible ways. It is as if the author of the book were saying, "If you don't believe it, here is the 'map,' and here are the details; you can check them out for yourself."[130]

(2) God's Promises

An integral part of the book's major theme, the possession of the promised land, is the idea that Yahweh was a promise-keeping God. The land that is the book's focus was not just any land, but it was the land that had long been promised to Abraham and his descendants (see the references above). The Book of Joshua shows God being faithful to his promises in every respect, including promises that were not directly about the land.

The book begins with God's repeating his promises about giving Israel the land (1:2–4; cf. Deut 7:24; 11:25). God also promised Joshua that he would

---

[124] F. M. Cross, *Canaanite Myth and Hebrew Epic* (Cambridge: Harvard University, 1973), 308–17.

[125] Exod 12:37a; 13:20; 14:1–2; 15:22a; 16:1; 17:1a; 19:2; Num 10:12; 20:1a; 20:22; 21:10–11; 22:1. Note also the "journeying" chapter at the end of Numbers: chap. 33.

[126] Gen 2:4; 5:1; 6:9; 10:1; 11:10; 11:27; 25:12; 25:19; 36:1; 36:9; 37:2.

[127] See, e.g., Exod 6:4, 8; Deut 1:6–8; 4:38,40; 5:31; 7:13; 8:1–10; 9:4–6; 11:8–12,17; 26:1,9; 32:49,52; 34:4.

[128] See the excursus on "The Giving of the Land in Joshua" at 1:3 for a full discussion of this.

[129] See also P. D. Miller, Jr., "The Gift of God: The Deuteronomic Theology of the Land," *Interpretations* 23 (1969): 451–65; von Rad, "The Promised Land and Yahweh's Land in the Hexateuch," 79–93; B. L. Bandstra, *ISBE*, 3, s.v. "Land."

[130] For a fuller introduction to this aspect of chaps. 13–21, see the excursus on "Patterns in the Land Distribution Lists" at the end of chap. 13.

be with him (1:5,9; cf. Deut 31:8,23), and that no one would be able to withstand him (1:5). God had promised rest to his people (Exod 33:14; Deut 12:10; 25:19), and he repeated this promise to them before they entered the land (Josh 1:13,15). This promise was fulfilled as the events of the book unfolded: the land had rest from war, and Israel had rest from its enemies (Josh 11:23; 14:15; 21:44; 23:1). God promised the Israelites that they would inherit a land whose cities they did not build, houses filled with good things they did not provide, wells they did not dig, and vineyards and olive groves they did not plant (Deut 6:11), and this was explicitly fulfilled in the Book of Joshua (24:13).

God's promises to the entire nation about the land are the most prominent in the book. Yet other promises also are mentioned. For example, God promised Joshua that he would exalt him in Israel's eyes (3:7), and according to 4:14 this came about precisely as God had promised. Also, God promised the daughters of Zelophehad that they would receive a portion in the land, even though their father had no sons (Num 27:7–11), and this promise was explicitly kept (Josh 17:3–6). Furthermore, God promised his people to drive out the Canaanites from before them (Deut 9:3–5; Josh 3:10; 13:6; 23:5), and he did this (23:9) or enabled the people to do this (13:12; 14:12; 15:14; 17:18).

The most dramatic illustration of the importance of God's keeping his promises comes in the summary of his activities at the end of the land distributions in 21:43–45: "So the LORD gave Israel all the land he had sworn to give their forefathers, and they took possession of it and settled there. The LORD gave them rest on every side, just as he had sworn to their forefathers. Not one of their enemies withstood them; the LORD handed all their enemies over to them. Not one of all the Lord's good promises to the house of Israel failed; every one was fulfilled." Here we have an all-encompassing affirmation of Yahweh as the promise-keeping God.[131]

(3) The Covenant

Another prominent theme in Joshua is the covenant. The focus is on God's *fulfilling* the covenant (see comments on "God's Promises" above), as well as on Israel's *keeping* of the covenant. Like Deuteronomy, the book stresses obedience to the law (the covenant) and the cause-and-effect relationship of obedience and blessing, disobedience and punishment. Obedience to the law and the covenant is urged upon Joshua (1:7–8), upon the Transjordan tribes (22:5), and upon the people (23:6,16; 24:15). These references emphasize the law, that is, the Mosaic Covenant, but the book also emphasizes the Abrahamic Covenant when it speaks of the promises about the land.

---

[131] On passages that stand in tension with these affirmations, see the commentary on 10:40–43 and 21:43–45.

Two covenant renewal ceremonies are recorded in the book. The first took place on Mount Ebal, when Joshua built an altar to the Lord and offered sacrifices (Josh 8:30–35). There "Joshua copied on stones the law of Moses, which he had written" (8:32). Then he read the entire law to the people (8:34–35). In doing so, Joshua was fulfilling the requirements that a king was supposed to keep (Deut 17:18–19).

The covenant renewal ceremony at Shechem in chap. 24 also is very significant. According to vv. 25–27, Joshua wrote the words of their covenant renewal in "the Book of the Law of God" and erected a large stone as a witness and a memorial for them. The people also committed themselves to keeping the law (24:16–18,21–22,24,27).

The importance of the covenant in Joshua is even clearer in the book's emphasis on the ark of the covenant. It occupies an especially important place in the account of the crossing of the Jordan in chap. 3 as well as in chap. 8, where it was part of the covenant renewal ceremony. The ark was a symbol of God's presence, and the covenant was a sign of his relationship with his people. In chap. 3 the priests were responsible for carrying the ark, in accordance with the Mosaic legislation.[132] Since the ark was the symbol of God's presence, a healthy distance was to be maintained between it and the people (Josh 3:4). The ark is referred to in various ways in this chapter, the most common phrase being "the ark of the covenant."[133] In chap. 8 the ark was at the center of the ceremony when Israel recommitted themselves to the covenant (8:33), again highlighting the close relationship between the ark and the covenant.

(4) Obedience

Closely related to the idea of the covenant is Israel's adherence to it. Over and over again in the book, we read of the importance of obedience to the law. God charged Joshua to obey all the words of the law (1:7). Joshua charged the Transjordan tribes to obey God's commandments, to keep the law (22:5), and he charged the entire nation to do the same thing (23:6). In the context of the covenant renewal ceremony, the people committed themselves to serving and obeying the Lord (24:24).

The law of Moses is mentioned eight times in the Book of Joshua, and in each case the context concerns obedience to this law. Either Joshua or the people were being urged to obey it (1:7–8; 22:5; 23:6), or they were committing themselves to do so (24:24), or they were copying and reading it (8:32,34), or they were actually obeying it (8:31).

The point is made in Joshua (echoing a motif found more prominently in

---

[132] Deut 10:8; cf. 31:9. The ark was to be carried with poles and not touched: Exod 25:12–13; 37:3–5; Num 4:4–15.

[133] On this point see further the commentary on 3:3.

Deuteronomy) that possession and retention of the land were tied to Israel's obedience to the law. In Joshua, for example, the complete possession of the land and extermination of its inhabitants is seen as a result of Joshua's obedience to God's command (10:40; 11:20, 23; 23:9–13). Furthermore, Israel's continued possession of the land was tied to its obedience (23:9–13,15–16).[134]

Not only is obedience to God's law important, however, but also, more immediately, obedience to his specific commands. In several places we see God commanding something and Joshua and the people carefully obeying, down to the smallest detail. Examples of this include 3:8,15; 4:2–3,10,12; 5:2–3; 8:8,27; 8:30–35; and 11:6,9.

An obvious example of Israel *disobeying* God's commands and suffering the consequences is in the case of Achan in chap. 7 (cf. 6:18; 7:1). Other examples include the texts where Israel failed to drive out the inhabitants of various territories (13:13; 15:63; 16:10; 17:11–12; 19:47).

In addition to obedience to God, obedience to Joshua's commands is also important in the book. Israel committed itself to obey Joshua and to punish those who did not (1:17–18). They obeyed Joshua's instructions in the matter of memorializing the crossing (4:8,10). In this case, Joshua's instructions had come from Moses and God himself (4:10). Thus, obedience to Joshua was also obedience to the Lord. Joshua was revered all the days of his life, a process that had begun on the occasion of the crossing and the memorializing of that crossing (4:14). Joshua's instructions at Jericho about Rahab were obeyed to the letter (6:22–23). The nation obeyed Joshua when he told them to bring out the five kings who had opposed Israel at Gibeon (10:22–24). And the Transjordan tribes fully obeyed Joshua in what he and Moses had commanded them (22:2–3).

(5) Purity of Worship (Holiness)

The idea of Israel's separate identity in Canaan—especially religiously—pervades the Book of Joshua. That is the essence of holiness in the Old Testament: the Hebrew word *qādôš* ("holy") has at its core the idea of separateness—away from the everyday and the mundane, from evil, and set apart for the sacred, the good.

The word "holy" occurs only three times in the book (5:15; 24:19,26), but the idea is much more important than these three references would indicate. The fact that the Israelites were to maintain a distance of one thousand yards between themselves and the ark of the covenant showed them that theirs was a holy God; they could not get too close to him (3:4; cf. Exod 19:12–13,23–24).

---

[134] In Deuteronomy see Deut 4:1,25–27,40; 6:17–18; 8:1; 11:8; 30:15–20; 32:46–47.

In Josh 24:19 Joshua confronted the people with the uncomfortable fact that they could not serve the Lord and reminded them that he was a holy and jealous God. His holiness set him apart from them.

Wherever God was to be found, that was a holy place. He was most closely identified with the ark (see esp. chap. 3), but also with the tent of meeting (18:1). When the people presented themselves "before God" at Shechem (24:1), this was undoubtedly before the ark (see commentary on 24:1 on this point). When Joshua met the commander of the Lord's army, he was standing on holy ground, just as Moses had been (5:15; cf. Exod 3:5).

An important passage in Joshua that speaks of holiness is chap. 5. Here we find recorded several ceremonies, all of which show the importance of ritual purity. First, there is a circumcision ceremony (5:2–9) in which those who had not been circumcised in the wilderness were now circumcised. Second, the Passover was kept (5:10–12), after which the manna stopped appearing and the Israelites ate from the fruit of the land. Third, Joshua met the commander of the Lord's army (5:13–15). In this little episode the key to the encounter lies in Joshua's falling face down to the ground and in the commander's indications that Joshua was standing on holy ground and that he should remove his sandals (vv. 14–15).

Thus, all three episodes concern holiness in one way or another. That such spiritual preparations preceded the actual "conquest" of the land illustrates the biblical priorities, that is, proper relationship with God was the key to success (see 1:7–8; cf. Matt 6:33). Thus, the real "action" of the book is delayed by several important—even essential—preliminaries: memorializing God's miraculous help (chap. 4) and sanctifying the people (chap. 5). The tasks ahead of battle were far too important to enter lightly—to enter unprepared in any way, including spiritually.

Another passage that speaks of purity of worship is found in Joshua 22. Here, when the Transjordan tribes built an altar of commemoration, the other tribes were greatly concerned that this was a rival and illegitimate altar of sacrifice, which would compromise the purity of the one true altar of the Lord.

Holiness is rooted in God's very nature. Leviticus 19, a crucial chapter in a book on holiness, shows that the commands to be holy are rooted in God's own character since he himself is holy (19:2): "Be holy, because I, the LORD your God, am holy." This command was behind Israel's self-understanding in the land of Canaan. An important insight into holiness is given us in Numbers 16 as well. This chapter concerns the rebellion of various individuals against the authority God had given Moses and Aaron. In v. 38[Hb. 17:3], the censers of the sons of Korah are seen as holy because they had been offered to the Lord (see vv. 17–18).

Thus, *dedication to the Lord* is an important part of the concept of holiness. Such dedication had the effect of separating the individual who was dedicated from the ordinary or the profane (i.e., the common). This is the thrust of the rituals in Joshua 5. Circumcision marked the dedication of the individual to the Lord, to the covenant he had established with Abraham and his descendants. The Passover observance also marked the individuals' dedication to him and commemorated the separating out of the Israelites from the Egyptians years earlier.

It is here that we enter another of the book's important motifs: the destruction of the Canaanites. This destruction was accomplished so that the Israelites might take possession of the land and that they might punish the great wickedness of the Canaanites. However, it was also for the purpose of cleansing the land, of dedicating its inhabitants—even its cities and its booty—to the Lord. These were to be devoted to the Lord for destruction, emphasizing his absolute holiness and his intolerance of evil. When the land and its inhabitants were thus "dedicated" to him, they became "holy" and thus fit to be his people's inheritance.[135]

(6) Godly Leadership[136]

The beginning of the Book of Joshua places the reader at a significant transitional point. Israel's great leader, Moses, who was "the servant of the LORD," had just died; and Joshua, who was merely "Moses' aide," was his designated replacement (1:1; cf. Num 27:15–23; Deut 31:1–8; 34:9). Moses was a prophet par excellence: no one like him had arisen since in Israel (Deut 34:10–12). He was the great lawgiver and one whom the Lord knew face to face, who had performed mighty deeds in the sight of all Israel.

Moses' stature as the Lord's servant is reiterated in Joshua. He is called "the servant of the LORD" fourteen times in the book (out of a total of eighteen times in the entire Old Testament). The book carefully avoids this title for Joshua until the time of his death, when it is clear that he had indeed fulfilled his obligations as Israel's leader and Moses' successor (24:29).

Joshua stepped into Moses' shoes and did well the job that was expected of him. God promised him his own presence, just as he had been with Moses (1:5; 3:7), and he exalted Joshua in the people's eyes (3:7; 4:14). Over and over again in the book, what Joshua said carried the authoritative weight of what God said, just as Moses' words had. People listened to him and obeyed (see, e.g., 1:12–18; 4:1–8,15–18; 6:2–11; etc.). In this respect, this theme is tied in closely with that of obedience, which we have discussed above.

The key to Joshua's success lay not in administrative or military genius—although he appears to have had abilities in both areas—but in his devotion

---

[135] For further development of the motif of the destruction of the Canaanites, see the excursus "Destruction and Devoted Things in Joshua" at the end of chap. 6.

[136] See also the section above on "Joshua: Title and Man."

to God. God instructed him that he was to be rooted in the law, and therein would lie his success (1:7–8). In this regard, Joshua was to be a leader in the model of the godly kings, for whom the key to success was also a rootedness in the law, not a dependence on their own wealth or military might (Deut 17:14–20). Joshua wrote the words of the law at the covenant renewal ceremony on Mount Ebal (8:32), just as would be required of a king (Deut 17:18–19).

The results of Joshua's godly leadership were impressive: the land was pacified, the people settled in their allotted territories, and Joshua was buried in his own land at a ripe old age (24:29–31). Things had gone well, and not one of the Lord's good promises had failed (21:43–45).

Yet the book contains several hints that all was not well. Several foreign peoples remained entrenched within Israel's borders (13:13; 15:63; 16:10; 17:11–12; 19:47), and this fact would come back to haunt Israel during the period of the judges. Furthermore, even though the nation served the Lord during Joshua's days (24:31), the Book of Judges recounts that a new generation arose who did not know the Lord nor what he had done for Israel (Judg 2:10). This is a tragic fact, although curious, since so much emphasis had been placed on remembering what God had done (esp. chap. 4) and on obeying (see chaps. 23–24). Had there been a godly leader in place like Joshua, the situation certainly would not have deteriorated to the degree that it did. The Book of Judges affirms the value of godly leadership when it states "In those days Israel had no king; everyone did as he saw fit" (Judg 17:6; 21:25). If Israel had had a king in place, leading as a godly king should (Deut 17:18–20), then things would have been different.[137]

Joshua did not designate a successor, as Moses had done, and Butler has suggested that this fault can be laid at his feet.[138] However, this is not clear because nowhere is Joshua condemned for not having done this. Nevertheless, what can be asserted with clarity is that despite the positive picture of Joshua's leadership in the book, its effects were short-lived. In this regard, the lessons of godly leadership laid out in Deut 17:14–20 are confirmed: Israel needed godly leaders who depended on God, or it would fall into apostasy. Almost no judge provided such leadership in the way that Moses and Joshua had done.

---

[137] See Howard, "The Case for Kingship in Deuteronomy and the Former Prophets," *WTJ* 52 (1990), 101–15.

[138] T. C. Butler, *Understanding the Basic Themes of Joshua* (Dallas: Word, 1991), 27; id., "The Theology of Joshua," *RevExp* 95 (1998): 214. For Butler the Book of Joshua is a "biography of a leader," and the theme of Joshua's leadership is paramount (*Basic Themes of Joshua*, 6–16, 23–34). However, as important as the leadership theme may be, to elevate it to a status as the primary theme of the book, and to classify the book as a biography, seems to stretch the evidence overmuch.

(7) Rest

The idea of the possession of the land as the accomplishment of God's "rest" is important as we consider the Book of Joshua.[139] The "rest" is a gift, part of the inheritance. The inheritance is of two parts: (1) the land and (2) "rest" from conflict with enemies.[140] This was promised from the beginning. To the Transjordan tribes, Joshua said: "Remember the command that Moses the servant of the LORD gave you: The LORD your God is giving you rest and has granted you this land" (Josh 1:13). This refers back to promises given in Num 32:20–22 and repeated in Deut 3:18–20. The idea of rest for the entire nation from their enemies is found in such passages as Deut 12:10 and 25:19, and it is echoed in the summarizing passages in Josh 21:44 and 23:1. In two places we are told that the land itself had rest from war.[141] This anticipates the same idea repeated several times in Judges: "And the land had rest XX years."[142]

Typologically, the New Testament equates the Old Testament concept of rest with entering into Christ's "rest." Hebrews 3 and 4 develops this in greatest detail and speaks of God resting on the seventh day of creation. Hebrews 4 quotes several times from Psalm 95, mentioning the rebellious wilderness generation, whose disobedience prevented them from entering the Lord's rest (building upon Heb 3:7–11, which quotes all of Ps 95:7d–11). The offer of rest to that generation was rejected, but in the "today" of Ps 95:7d and Heb 3:7,15; 4:7, the offer is repeated. Hebrews 4:8 mentions Joshua, under whom the rebellious generation was *not* allowed to enter the land; it was rather a new generation to whom the offer of rest was made. This was an offer which was to be appropriated in each generation.

7. The Text of Joshua

The Book of Joshua was written in Hebrew more than three millennia ago,[143] and it was copied painstakingly over the centuries. In the process, however, human errors in copying inevitably crept in. Furthermore, over time the book was translated into various ancient languages and eventually into modern languages. The most complete Hebrew manuscript of the Old Testament available as the basis for translation is the so-called Leningrad Codex, dating from A.D. 1008, more than one thousand years after the completion of

---

[139] von Rad, "There Remains Still a Rest for the People of God," 79–93.

[140] The passages in Joshua about Israel or the land having rest are the following: 1:13,15; 11:23; 14:15; 21:44; 22:4; 23:1.

[141] Josh 11:23; 14:15; cf. Deut 12:9–10; 25:19; 2 Sam 7:1,11; 1 Kgs 8:56.

[142] Judg 3:11; 3:30; 5:31; 8:28.

[143] See above for a more nuanced discussion of the dating of the book.

the last Old Testament book. [144] This serves as the basis of the critical edition of the Hebrew Bible used as the foundation of every modern Bible translation: the *Biblia Hebraica Stuttgartensia.* [145]

A discussion of "The Text of Joshua" is focused on the degree to which this manuscript—and others in its tradition, collectively known as the "Masoretic Text" (hereafter "MT"), along with the manuscripts of other traditions into which the Hebrew text was translated—reflects the original text of Joshua as it left the pen of its author, since the original text no longer exists. The two major traditions used by scholars for the Book of Joshua are (1) the MT, represented primarily by the Leningrad Codex and later manuscripts, and (2) the Old Greek traditions, often collectively known as the "Septuagint" (LXX), which date to ca. 250–100 B.C., although the earliest complete manuscripts do not date before the fourth century A.D.

An important third tradition used by scholars has only recently become available, represented by several fragments of scrolls written in Hebrew, discovered near the Dead Sea; they are known as the "Dead Sea Scrolls" or the "Qumran Scrolls" (after the name of the site near which they were discovered). These by no means represent anywhere near a complete manuscript of the Hebrew text however.

The Masoretic Hebrew text of Joshua is for the most part intelligible and represents a version that probably reflects the original Hebrew in most respects. The Old Greek represents a text that is shorter than the Hebrew text by no more than four to five percent, [146] and many scholars today believe that it translates a Hebrew text that was somewhat different from the Hebrew text represented in the MT, that is, that these two traditions go back to two different originals, which must have diverged from each other in the copying process sometime in the next few centuries after the actual original of the book was produced. [147] The evidence from Qumran tends to support the MT

---

[144] For introductions to the Leningrad Codex and the other manuscripts, both Hebrew and in other languages, that form the basis for determining as closely as possible the original text of the Bible, see the convenient handbooks by E. R. Brotzman, *Old Testament Textual Criticism* (Grand Rapids: Baker, 1994), 37–96; E. Würthwein, *The Text of the Old Testament,* 2d ed. (Grand Rapids: Eerdmans, 1995), 10–104. In more depth, see E. Tov, *The Textual Criticism of the Hebrew Bible* (Minneapolis: Fortress, 1992), 21–154. The so-called Aleppo Codex is a complete Masoretic manuscript ca. 100 years older than the Leningrad Codex, but it has not been published in a full critical edition as yet. See the discussions of this manuscript in the works just cited.

[145] Stuttgart: Deutsche Bibelstiftung, 1977, ed. K. Elliger et al. (hereafter "BHS").

[146] A. Rofé, "The Editing of the Book of Joshua in the Light of 4QJosha," in G. J. Brooke and F. G. Martinez, eds., *New Qumran Texts and Studies,* STDJ 15 (Leiden: Brill, 1994), 326.

[147] See L. Greenspoon, "The Qumran Fragments of Joshua: Which Puzzle Are They Part of and Where Do They Fit?" in *Septuagint, Scrolls and Cognate Writings,* ed. G. J. Brooke and B. Lindars, SBLSCSS 33 (Atlanta: Scholars Press, 1992), 175–77 and bibliography there (the full article is on 159–94). On some of the difficulties of attempting to reconstruct an "original" text, see B. K. Waltke, "Aims of OT Textual Criticism," *WTJ* 51 (1989): 93–108.

against the Old Greek, which supports the MT's case for being closer to the true original (see below).

Study of the Old Greek traditions must begin with the magisterial and painstaking work of M. Margolis, who produced a critical edition of the Greek text and all of its variants from different manuscripts.[148] Further important studies are those of L. Greenspoon,[149] A. G. Auld,[150] and others.[151] The Qumran Hebrew fragments have only begun to be published in the 1990's. Fragments of two manuscripts have been published by E. Ulrich and E. Tov, designated as 4QJosha and 4QJoshb.[152] Additional studies are now forthcoming.[153]

The Qumran materials reflect the MT Hebrew text in almost every place where they can be compared, including places where the MT and the Old Greek diverge, which lends support to the priority of the MT tradition as we have it. Greenspoon states that "there are no qualitatively important readings definitively shared by the LXX and 4QJoshua. ... It is, therefore, tempting simply to locate the Qumran material in the same tradition as the MT. This would explain their many shared secondary expansions and also, in my opinion, independent additions on the part of the Qumran scribe."[154]

The most important divergence from the MT among the Qumran materials is the presence in one fragment of Josh 8:34–35 immediately after 5:1, not in its expected position at the end of chap. 8. The passage in question (8:30–35) is an important one in several respects, and the curiosity of its placement is heightened when we note that in the Old Greek traditions it occurs in yet a

---

[148] M L. Margolis, ed., *The Book of Joshua in Greek*, 4 vols. (Paris: Paul Geuthner, 1931–1938); id., *The Book of Joshua in Greek*, Part V: *Joshua 19:39–24:33* (Philadelphia: Annenberg Research Institute, 1992). The final volume, with an introduction to the entire work, will be published by Greenspoon.

[149] Greenspoon, *Textual Studies in the Book of Joshua*, Harvard Semitic Monographs 28 (Chico: Scholars Press, 1983).

[150] A. G. Auld, "Studies in Joshua: Text and Literary Relations" (Ph.D. diss., University of Edinburgh, 1976).

[151] E.g., L. Mazor, "The Septuagint Translation of the Book of Joshua," *Bulletin of the International Organization for the Septuagint and Cognate Studies* 27 (1994): 29–38 (this is an abstract of her Ph.D. dissertation at the Hebrew University, and it provides a helpful summary of the relationship of the Old Greek to the MT). For further bibliography, see Butler, *Joshua*, xvii.

[152] Publication of 4QJoshuaa is to be found in E. Ulrich, "4QJoshuaa and Joshua's First Altar in the Promised Land" in *New Qumran Texts and Studies,* 89–104; and id., "4QJosha," in Ulrich et al., eds., Qumran Cave 4 (IX: Deuteronomy, Joshua, Judges, Kings, DJD 14 (Oxford: Clarendon, 1995), 143–52. Publication of 4QJoshuab is to be found in Tov, "4QJoshb," in *Intertestamental Essays in Honour of Josef Tadeusz Milik,* ed. Z. J. Kapera (Krakow: Enigma, 1992), 1:205–12; and id., "4QJoshb," in Ulrich et al., eds., *Qumran Cave 4 IX,* 153–60.

[153] Two important studies are Rofé, "The Editing of the Book of Joshua in the Light of 4QJosha" and Greenspoon, "The Qumran Fragments of Joshua."

[154] Greenspoon, "The Qumran Fragments of Joshua," 164–65.

third position, after 9:2![155] Probably the most significant divergence between the MT and the Old Greek traditions comes at the end of the book (24:28–33), where the MT is much shorter and the Old Greek gives significant and interesting information not found in the Hebrew text.

In this commentary the MT as found in the *BHS* forms the basis of the discussion, for reasons of convenience (it is the text behind all major English versions, including the NIV), as well as of prudence (textual critics of Joshua still have not produced a definitive eclectic text of the book, and they have not established definitively the priority of any other manuscript tradition over that of the MT). Important textual variants will be discussed as warranted, but in keeping with the nature of the New American Commentary series, these are not extensive.[156]

---

[155] See the discussion of the placement of this passage at the introduction to 5:2–15 and at 8:30–35.

[156] The best verse-by-verse discussions of textual matters may be found in the commentaries by R. G. Boling, T. C. Butler, and R. D. Nelson, and especially in the official publications of the Committee for the Textual Analysis of the Hebrew Old Testament (D. Barthélemy et al., eds. *Preliminary and Interim Report on the Hebrew Old Testament Text Project*. Vol. 2: *Historical Books* (New York: UBS, 1979), 1–67; id., *Critique textuelle de l'Ancien Testament*, Orbis Biblicus et Orientalis 50/1. Vol. 1: *Josué, Juges, Ruth, Samuel, Rois, Chroniques, Esdras, Néhémiah, Esther* (Fribourg: Éditions Universitaire, 1982), 1–72).

OUTLINE OF THE BOOK

I. PREPARATIONS FOR INHERITING THE LAND (1:1–5:15)
  1. Instructions for Inheriting the Land (1:1–18)
    (1) God's Charge to Joshua (1:1–9)
    (2) Joshua's Instructions for Breaking Camp (1:10–11)
    (3) Joshua's Charge to the Transjordan Tribes (1:12–15)
    (4) All Israel's Response (1:16–18)
  2. A Foreigner's Welcome (2:1–24)
    (1) Rahab's Faith in Action (2:1–8)
    (2) Rahab's Faith in Words (2:9–14)
    (3) Sealing the Agreement (2:15–24)
  3. Crossing the Jordan (3:1–5:1)
    (1) Instructions for Crossing: Stage One (3:1–6)
    (2) Instructions for Crossing: Stage Two (3:7–13)
    (3) The Miracle of the Crossing (3:14–17)
    (4) Memorializing the Crossing: Stage One (4:1–10)
    (5) The Crossing Completed: Stage One (4:11–14)
    (6) The Crossing Completed: Stage Two (4:15–18)
    (7) Memorializing the Crossing: Stage Two (4:19–5:1)
  4. Ritual Preparations (5:2–15)
    (1) Circumcision (5:2–9)
    (2) Passover (5:10–12)
    (3) A Call to Holiness (5:13–15)
Joshua 1–5: Theological Reflections

I. PREPARATIONS FOR INHERITING THE LAND (1:1–5:15)

Israel was about to undertake a great enterprise as they entered the land of Canaan. This land had been promised for centuries, and the Pentateuch points repeatedly to it. Now the time had come for the nation to enter the land and take possession of their inheritance. But before they could do this, they needed to undertake several steps of preparation.

The first preparation was of their leader, Joshua. God encouraged him by promising to remain with him, and he charged Joshua to keep the law diligently (1:1–9). If Joshua did this, he would have success. The nation then affirmed Joshua as leader (1:16–18). The nation's unity was an issue as well, and before the people embarked on their campaigns, a unity in this task needed to be assured (1:12–18).

The story of Rahab in chap. 2 shows that the Canaanites were ripe for the taking, since they had heard of Israel and its God and were terrified of them. But Rahab stands as a shining example of a true believer, a Canaanite convert, and she was spared.

The Jordan River was a natural barrier that needed to be crossed. However, the story of the crossing in chap. 3 emphasizes two things: (1) God's presence with his people, symbolized by the ark, and (2) God's wondrous miracle in stopping up the waters of the river. This was such a marvel that all of chap. 4 is devoted to reflecting upon it, to memorializing it.

Final preparations before embarking on the first stage of the "battles" in Canaan included ceremonial preparations in chap. 5 that reminded Israel of their commitments to God (circumcision) and of his faithfulness to them (Passover). The Lord's own army commander met with Joshua in an episode reminiscent of Moses' encounter with God at the burning bush. Only after such ceremonial and spiritual preparations would the nation be ready to engage the Canaanites in battle.

1. Instructions for Inheriting the Land (1:1–18)

This chapter begins the story of God's giving the land of Canaan to the Israelites, and what a beginning it is! We find here God's charge to Joshua (vv. 1–9), in which he promised Joshua that he would be with him in the same way he had been with Moses the prophet, whom God had met face to face (Deut 34:10–12). This is a very impressive promise! The issue of whether Joshua was up to the job also begins to be addressed here. Indeed he would be, because of God's presence with him, if he was careful to keep his priorities correctly lined up: the key to success for Joshua was that he was to be immersed in God's word (vv. 7–8). Here are Joshua's initial instructions about entering the land, which set the stage for action later (vv. 10–11; cf. chap. 3). We also read about special instructions for the tribes who planned to settle west of the Jordan River (vv. 12–15); these concern their commitment to their fellow Israelites and raise the issue of the unity of the nation, which is a concern throughout the book. Finally, these tribes, along with the rest of the nation, affirm Joshua's place of leadership and encourage him in this (vv. 16–18).

(1) God's Charge to Joshua (1:1–9)

¹After the death of Moses the servant of the LORD, the LORD said to Joshua son of Nun, Moses' aide: ²"Moses my servant is dead. Now then, you and all these people, get ready to cross the Jordan River into the land I am about to give to them—to the Israelites. ³I will give you every place where you set your foot, as I promised Moses. ⁴Your territory will extend from the desert to Lebanon, and

from the great river, the Euphrates—all the Hittite country—to the Great Sea on the west. [5]No one will be able to stand up against you all the days of your life. As I was with Moses, so I will be with you; I will never leave you nor forsake you.

[6]"Be strong and courageous, because you will lead these people to inherit the land I swore to their forefathers to give them. [7]Be strong and very courageous. Be careful to obey all the law my servant Moses gave you; do not turn from it to the right or to the left, that you may be successful wherever you go. [8]Do not let this Book of the Law depart from your mouth; meditate on it day and night, so that you may be careful to do everything written in it. Then you will be prosperous and successful. [9]Have I not commanded you? Be strong and courageous. Do not be terrified; do not be discouraged, for the LORD your God will be with you wherever you go."

1:1 The Book of Joshua begins as though it were a continuation of something written previously, which, of course, it is. A wooden translation of the first portion of the verse would read "And it happened, after the death of Moses the servant of the LORD, that the LORD said to Joshua ..." The phrase "the death of Moses" ties this material in with an earlier event (which is recounted in the preceding chapter in the Bible: Deut 34:1–8).[1]

Several other books in the Old Testament narrative corpus also begin with a reference to a leading person's death by using the wording found here: "and it happened, after the death of ____." These include the books of Judges (Joshua's death), 2 Samuel (Saul's death), and 2 Kings (Ahab's death).[2]

Moses' death was an important event in the life of the new nation of Israel. He is the towering figure who casts his shadow not only across the entire corpus of Exodus–Deuteronomy, but also across the Book of Joshua and later Scriptures. Deuteronomy ends by affirming,

> Since then, no prophet has risen in Israel like Moses, whom the LORD knew face to face, who did all those miraculous signs and wonders the LORD sent him to do in Egypt—to Pharaoh and to all his officials and to his whole land. For no one has ever shown the mighty power or performed the awesome deeds that Moses did in the sight of all Israel (Deut 34:10–12).

This sounds like an evaluative passage added many years after Moses had died. It would not be a very impressive comment if it were penned, for example, only a decade or less after his death. The longer the interval between Moses'

---

[1] The Hb. syntax reinforces this, as the form opening the verse is וַיְהִי. The "*wāw*-consecutive" construction here clearly presupposes preceding material, even though in this case, that which precedes comes from a different book and author, probably written many years earlier. This form commonly signals a new episode in narrative texts (see, e.g., GKC § 111f.; *GBH* §118c), and even books may begin with it (see, e.g., Judg 1:1; 2 Sam 1:1); however, in almost all cases, this form also connects the new material with what precedes. Other books in the OT's narrative corpus that begin with the *waw*-consecutive construction are Leviticus, Numbers, Joshua, Ruth, 1 Samuel, 2 Kings, and Esther. For more on the function of וַיְהִי in a text, see the comments below, at 4:11.

[2] In the case of 2 Kgs 1:1, the wording is slightly different: "And Moab rebelled against Israel after the death of Ahab" (author translation).

death and the writing of this evaluation, the more impressive Moses' stature becomes.[3] Yet Moses' death should not cripple the nation. The Lord was faithful in all ages, and he would be in this instance as well. Joshua was designated as Moses' successor, and the people were to carry on under him. As one scholar notes, "Yahweh's fidelity does not hinge on the achievement of men, however gifted they may be, nor does it evaporate in the face of funerals or rivers."[4]

As we noted in the Introduction, Moses was the great lawgiver and leader par excellence. He is here called the "servant of the LORD." This title for Moses is found far more often in the Book of Joshua than in the rest of the Old Testament combined (fourteen of eighteen times.[5] This is a special title used in the Old Testament only of Moses (fourteen times), Joshua (Josh 24:29; Judg 2:8), David (Pss 18:1; 36:1), and, pejoratively, of the nation of Israel (Isa 42:19).[6]

This labeling of Moses as the Lord's servant is important in the Book of Joshua, since Joshua, for whom the book is named, is only called the "servant of the LORD" once, at the end of the book (24:29). The Book of Joshua is concerned with showing how God's earlier promises were now in process of being fulfilled and with how God's commands were being carried out. Many of these promises and commands were spoken by Moses, who is depicted in this book as the Lord's special servant.

God is referred to in this verse as "the LORD." This rendering, found in most English versions (as well as the Septuagint, which renders it *kurios,* "lord"), obscures the fact that here is God's personal name, which most scholars today agree was pronounced "Yahweh."[7] This is the most holy, personal

---

[3] The fact remains that we do not know when or by whom these verses were penned. Even evangelicals, almost all of whom maintain a Mosaic authorship for the Pentateuch, allow that portions or all of Deuteronomy 34 were written by someone other than Moses. See, e.g., E. H. Merrill, *Deuteronomy,* NAC (Nashville: Broadman & Holman, 1994), 455; G. L. Archer, Jr., *A Survey of Old Testament Introduction,* 3d ed. (Chicago: Moody, 1994), 89, n. 1, 276.

[4] D. R. Davis, *No Falling Words: Expositions of the Book of Joshua* (Grand Rapids: Baker, 1988), 18.

[5] The references in Joshua are 1:1,13,15; 8:31,33; 11:12; 12:6[2x]; 13:8; 14:7; 18:7; 22:2,4–5. The references elsewhere are Deut 34:5; 2 Kgs 18:12; 2 Chr 1:3; 24:6.

[6] Several other characters are called "my [i.e., God's] servant"—e.g., Abraham (Gen 26:24), Caleb (Num 14:24), David (twenty-three times), Job (Job 1:8; 2:3; 42:7,8[2x]), Isaiah (Isa 20:3), Nebuchadnezzar (Jer 25:9; 27:6; 43:10), Zerubbabel (Hag 2:23), and others—or "his servant"—e.g., Solomon (1 Kgs 8:59), Elijah (2 Kgs 9:36; 10:10), Jonah (2 Kgs 14:25)—but the exact phrase "servant of the LORD" is not used.

[7] The exact meaning, etymology, and pronunciation of this name remain somewhat uncertain. "Yahweh" is rendered in older Bible versions and hymnody as "Jehovah"; most modern versions render it as "the LORD" (with smaller capital letters, to distinguish it from another name used of God in the OT—"Adonay" [אֲדֹנָי]—which is more properly a title meaning "Lord, Master"). On "Yahweh" (יהוה), see R. L. Harris, "The Pronunciation of the Tetragram," in J. H. Skilton, ed., *The Law and the Prophets* (Nutley, N.J.: Presbyterian & Reformed, 1974), 215–24; and B. J. Beitzel, "Exodus 3:14 and the Divine Name: A Case of Biblical Paronomasia," *TrinJ* 1 (1980): 5–20, for two treatments arguing for alternatives to the prevailing scholarly consensus that יהוה comes from היה, particularly the view that it is a *hiphil* of היה.

name of God, revealing much of his character,[8] and it is praised repeatedly throughout the Psalms.[9] It is the name whose meaning was revealed to Moses at the burning bush (Exod 3:11–15; cf. 6:2–3), and it tells us about God's eternal existence and his enduring faithfulness to his people.[10] "Yahweh" was God's personal name just as "Baal" and "Marduk" were the personal names of the high gods of the Canaanites and the Babylonians, respectively.

In addition to Moses and Yahweh, Joshua the son of Nun, the main protagonist of the Book of Joshua, also is introduced in v. 1. He is named about 205 times in the Old Testament, 148 times in this book.[11] After this, his name appears most often in Exodus, Numbers, Deuteronomy, and Judges. Joshua is mentioned twice in the New Testament, first, in Stephen's speech, where Joshua's leadership in bringing the tabernacle into the land of Canaan is mentioned (Acts 7:45) and second, in the Book of Hebrews, in the great passage on rest (Heb 3–4): Joshua's rest is depicted here as incomplete, not fulfilled until one enters Christ's rest (4:8).

Joshua's name usually is given in the Hebrew Bible as "Yehoshua," which means "Yahweh saves/delivers."[12] His name is rendered in the Greek traditions (LXX) as *Iēsous,* which is the same form as Jesus' name in the New Testament. His original name was "Hoshea," which means "salvation" or "deliverance" (Num 13:8 and Deut 32:44). Numbers 13:16 explains that Moses himself gave Hoshea his new name "Joshua." Joshua stands out from the other characters listed in the Numbers 13 passage (vv. 3–16, which list the twelve spies Moses sent into the land of Canaan), by virtue of this explanatory gloss about his name: "Moses gave Hoshea son of Nun the name Joshua." Joshua is the first person in the Bible to be explicitly given a name that incorporates God's holy, personal name, "Yahweh."[13]

---

[8] On God's name as revelatory of his character, see R. J. Wyatt, "God, Names of," *ISBE* 2:504–5; E. Jacob, *Theology of the Old Testament* (New York: Harper & Row, 1958), 43–55; g. von Rad, *Old Testament Theology* (New York: Harper & Row, 1962), 1:179–90; W. Eichrodt, *Theology of the Old Testament* (Philadelphia: Westminster, 1961), 1:178–205.

[9] See, e.g., Pss 8:1,9; 9:2; 18:49; 29:2; 30:4; 34:3; 54:6; 68:4; 72:19; 86:12; 89:12,16; 92:1; 96:2,8; 97:12; 99:3; 100:4; 103:1; 106:47; 113:1–3.

[10] See U. Cassuto, *A Commentary on the Book of Exodus* (Jerusalem: Magnes, 1967), 35–40; W. Kaiser, "Exodus," EBC 2:318–24, 340–42, on the meaning of the revelation of this name. For treatments of God's personal name in general, see J. B. Payne [and R. L. Harris], "יהוה, הָיָה," *TWOT*, 210–12; V. P. Hamilton, "הָיָה," *TWOT*, 214; and D. N. Freedman and M. O'Connor, "יהוה YHWH," *TDOT* 5:500–521.

[11] Several other characters named "Joshua" appear in the OT (and the Apocrypha), but none is as prominent as Joshua son of Nun. On the other Joshuas, see D. F. Roberts and J. E. Hartley, "Jeshua," *ISBE* 2:1033; S. E. Porter and W. S. Green, "Joshua," *ABD* 3:1000–1002.

[12] Twice his name is spelled as יְהוֹשׁוּעַ (Deut 3:21; Judg 2:7), with the same meaning. In Neh 8:17 his name is given in a shortened form as "Yeshua" (יֵשׁוּעַ).

[13] "Jochebed," Moses' mother's name, is also based on the name "Yahweh" (Exod 6:20; Num 26:59), but the meaning of her name is not elaborated upon by the biblical writers, as is Joshua's.

While the Book of Joshua does not make a point of saying anything about the meaning of his name, surely his name change by Moses is significant since (1) it is singled out for mention in Numbers 13, and (2) it went from a generic name meaning "deliverance" to one containing a glorious affirmation of trust in God: "Yahweh delivers" (or perhaps "may Yahweh deliver"). That God himself was Israel's deliverer is an important point made repeatedly in the Book of Joshua, and Joshua's new name is a not-so-subtle reminder of this.[14]

Joshua's father's name was "Nun."[15] Nothing is known of his father except for his lineage: 1 Chr 7:20–29 gives a list of descendants of Ephraim and some of their holdings; Joshua and Nun are mentioned in v. 27.[16]

Finally, v. 1 tells us that Joshua was "Moses' aide." This too is a significant fact. First, Joshua is distinguished from Moses in that he is not called "the servant of the LORD," as Moses is. A question throughout the book is whether Joshua would be worthy of filling Moses' shoes. On one level, the answer was "no"; no one would succeed Moses as Israel's lawgiver, and no prophet would arise like him (Deut 34:10). The Book of Joshua carefully refrains from calling Joshua by this honorific title until the very last chapter; when Joshua dies, he is finally accorded the title of "servant of the LORD" (24:29) as we already have noted. In contrast, Moses is called by this title seventeen times in the book. Yet, on another level, the fact that Joshua finally does receive this title shows that he did indeed fulfill the instructions that God gave him, in a similar way to Moses.[17]

Joshua is called "Moses' aide" only four times in Scripture: Exod 24:13; 33:11; Num 11:28; Josh 1:1. The word for "aide" here *(měšārēt)* means "one who serves." Usually this Hebrew word refers to service in a worship context, but it can also mean (as here) service to an individual.[18] An interesting and important theological truth can be seen by comparing the two sets of relation-

---

[14] The new name avoids the potential confusion of Joshua's original name, Hoshea (meaning "deliverance"), which might have suggested to people that Joshua himself was primarily responsible for Israel's deliverance (rather than Yahweh).

[15] Joshua is called "son of Nun" thirty times in the Bible, including ten times in Joshua and eleven times in Numbers. Elsewhere in the Pentateuch, Joshua is identified this way only once in Exodus (33:11) and four times in Deuteronomy (1:38; 31:23; 32:44; 34:9). Later in the OT, we find the phrase once each in Judges (2:8), 1 Kings (16:34), 1 Chronicles (7:27), and Nehemiah (8:17). The use of the surname "son of Nun" in Kings, Chronicles, and Nehemiah is primarily to distinguish Joshua from other men with the same name in these books. In the other cases, no clear pattern of use presents itself, except that the surname adds a measure of formality to the mention of Joshua. In Numbers, Joshua is mentioned by name eleven times, ten of these with his surname attached.

[16] For speculations about the meaning of Nun's name, see J. A. Soggin, *Joshua*, OTL (Philadelphia: Westminster, 1972), 1, n. 1; R. G. Boling, *Joshua*, AB 6 (Garden City: Doubleday, 1982), 120.

[17] He is called this again only once, in Judg 2:8.

[18] See also 1 Kgs 19:21, where Elijah appears as Elisha's "aide" (NIV has "attendant" there).

ships in this verse: (1) Yahweh and Moses (Yahweh's "servant") and (2) Moses and Joshua (Moses' "aide"). The relative sociological distance between a "servant" and his master was far greater than that between an "aide" and the one he served. Here then is a subtle yet powerful reminder that God's sovereignty is infinite and that he was infinitely greater than even the towering figure of Moses. The gulf between Moses and God was infinitely greater than that between Joshua and Moses.[19]

1:2–5 The initial portion of God's charge to Joshua is concerned with (1) the land that God had promised to Israel, (2) God's encouragement of Joshua in his new role as Moses' successor, and (3) God's promise to be Israel's strong protector. In vv. 2–4, God addressed not merely Joshua, but all of the Israelites (the grammatical forms for "you" and "your" are plural); in v. 5, Joshua himself is addressed. Portions of these verses are very similar to Deut 11:24–25a, where Moses promised the Israelites the land and God's protection.[20] Compare the following:

Joshua	Deuteronomy
I will give you every place where you set your foot, as I promised Moses. (1:3)	Every place where you set your foot will be yours. (11:24a)
Your territory will extend from the desert to Lebanon, and from the great river, the Euphrates—all the Hittite country—to the Great Sea on the west. (1:4)	Your territory will extend from the desert to Lebanon, and from the Euphrates River to the western sea. (11:24b)
No one will be able to stand up against you all the days of your life. (1:5a)	No man will be able to stand against you. (11:25a)

Such careful repetitions assure us that God was indeed committed to keeping his promises. The very same words he had uttered earlier through his servant Moses indicate that there was no reneging on the promises and no "revising" of them. Both of these passages hark back to earlier promises of God, beginning with the promises to Abraham (Gen 12:7; 15:18–20). The

---

[19] On the way Joshua is presented in the Book of Joshua and the Pentateuch see further G. C. Chirichigno, "The Use of the Epithet in the Characterization of Joshua," *TrinJ* 8 (1987): 69–79.

[20] Considerable scholarly speculation has been devoted to the minor differences between the two passages. Soggin states that "it is impossible to tell how this textual corruption came about" (*Joshua*, 26). T. C. Butler devotes detailed attention to the differences, suggesting that at least one difference ("this" in the phrase "this Lebanon") may have been a late gloss (*Joshua*, WBC 7 [Waco: Word, 1983], 3–4); for more on "this Lebanon," see comments on 1:4. Neither of these explanations (textual corruption or late gloss) is *required*, however; the variations may simply reflect the (slightly) different wording used on the two occasions.

wording in Deut 11:24–25 and Josh 1:3–5 also is anticipated closely in Exodus 23.[21]

The most direct route from Egypt to the land of Canaan would *not* involve crossing the Jordan River. However, the Israelites had earlier forfeited their right to enter the land directly when they embraced the spies' discouraging report about the impossibility of taking the land (Num 13–14). God sentenced the people to wander in the wilderness for forty years, during which time the generation that came out of Egypt would die off (Num 14:26–35). The Israelites attempted an entrance directly into the land from the south, but they were rebuffed by the Canaanites there (Num 14:40–45). Consequently, they wandered for another thirty-eight years and arrived at the entrance to the land of Canaan at a different spot, this time east of the Jordan River, on the plains of Moab (Num 22:1; 33:48–50; 36:13; Deut 1:1–5). This is where the Book of Joshua begins.

1:2 God stated in v. 2 that he was "about to give" the land to the Israelites (so NIV; cf. RSV, NASB: "I am giving"). According to v. 3, "every place upon which the sole of your foot will tread, to you I have given it" (literal translation). In both verses the pronouns are plural, embracing not just Joshua, but all Israel. Also in these verses, the two forms of the verb "give" are different in Hebrew,[22] and their use here reflects two significant truths about God's giving of the land to his people. In one sense God was still in process of giving Israel the land. After all, Israel had not yet even crossed the Jordan River, and only the land east of the Jordan actually had been taken by Israel. Most of the land remained to be taken. But in another sense God had *already given* Israel the land. It is as though Israel already possessed legal title to the land (ever since Abraham's day), but they were awaiting God's timing for the actual possession. In Gen 15:16 God promised Abraham that it would be several generations before his descendants would actually possess the land, since "the sin of the Amorites [i.e., Canaanites] has not yet reached its full measure."

1:3 Verse 3 ends by stating that this gift of the land was in fulfillment of God's promise to Moses. God's promises, and their fulfillment, receive special attention in Deuteronomy and the Former Prophets (i.e., Joshua–2 Kings). Whereas in the Latter Prophets (i.e., Isaiah, Jeremiah, Ezekiel, and the

---

[21] Note Exod 23:23,27,31: "My angel will go ahead of you and bring you into the land of the Amorites, Hittites, Perizzites, Canaanites, Hivites and Jebusites, and I will wipe them out. ... I will send my terror ahead of you and throw into confusion every nation you encounter. I will make all your enemies turn their backs and run. ... I will establish your borders from the Red Sea to the Sea of the Philistines, and from the desert to the River. I will hand over to you the people who live in the land and you will drive them out before you."

[22] In v. 2, it is נֹתֵן, a *qal* participle, whereas in v. 3, it is נְתַתִּיו, a *qal* "perfect" (plus suffix). The participle's normal translation is "I am giving" or "I am about to give," whereas the "perfect's" normal translation is "I have given" or "I gave."

twelve Minor Prophets), the fulfillment of most prophecies is not indicated, the opposite is usually the case in the Former Prophets: the words of the true prophets are usually shown to come to pass. In 1, 2 Kings, for example, G. von Rad has identified eleven cases where a prophecy is given and its fulfillment is explicitly detailed, to which several more can be added.[23] In each case, these are explicitly stated to be in fulfillment of "the word of the LORD" or of a prophet speaking for the Lord.

EXCURSUS: THE GIVING OF THE LAND IN JOSHUA

Introduction. The giving of the promised land to Israel is an important motif in the Book of Joshua, and it is viewed from several different perspectives. Each of these contributes something important to our overall understanding of the motif. For example, the land was Israel's "inheritance" or "possession," promised to Israel many years earlier. It was God's gift to Israel. Yet, another perspective shows that it was "taken" by Israel. Furthermore, while it was *God*'s gift to Israel, several different people engaged in giving the land and/or its inhabitants into the possession of different recipients. In addition, the land already belonged to Israel from one perspective, but it was not yet theirs from another.

One of the most important ways that the gift of the land can be understood is by understanding the verb "give" and its use in Joshua. After a brief, general look at this verb, we will consider it from two primary perspectives: (1) Who gives the land? and (2) When is the land given? We will then summarize our findings in more detail.

The Verb "to Give" *(ntn).* The verb "to give" (the Hb. root is *ntn*) is one of the most common in the Old Testament, occurring more than two thousand times. It is one of the fifteen most common words in the Old Testament (excluding particles). Its semantic range is very broad: in Joshua alone, the NIV translates it "give," "grant," "deliver," "put," "let," "hand over," "assign," "do," "subject," "designate," "allot," and "make." Elsewhere, its meanings range even further, including "place," "lay," "allow," "surrender," "submit," and "raise (one's voice)."[24]

The Giver(s) of the Land. The verb *ntn* occurs eighty-nine times in Joshua.[25] In sixty-nine instances, it refers to the giving of the land of Canaan in

---

[23] G. von Rad, "The Deuteronomistic Theology of History in the Books of Kings," *Studies in Deuteronomy*, SBT 9 (London: SCM, 1953), 78–81. The passages are 2 Sam 7:13 // 1 Kgs 8:20; 1 Kgs 11:29ff. // 1 Kgs 12:15; 1 Kgs 13:2 // 2 Kgs 23:16–18; 1 Kgs 14:6ff. // 1 Kgs 15:29; 1 Kgs 16:1ff. // 1 Kgs 16:12; Josh 6:26 // 1 Kgs 16:34; 1 Kgs 22:17 // 1 Kgs 22:35ff.; 1 Kgs 21:21ff. // 1 Kgs 21:27–29 [cf. 2 Kgs 9:7]; 2 Kgs 1:6 // 2 Kgs 1:17; 2 Kgs 21:10ff. // 2 Kgs 24:2 [cf. also 2 Kgs 23:26]; 2 Kgs 22:15ff. // 2 Kgs 23:30. Von Rad does not mention the following cases: 1 Kgs 13:3 // 1 Kgs 13:5; 1 Kgs 21:23 (and 2 Kgs 9:10) // 2 Kgs 9:30–37. Note that one of the sets of passages concerns the rebuilding of Jericho: Josh 6:26 // 1 Kgs 16:34.

[24] *HALOT*, 733–35.

[25] The various nouns built upon the root נתן are all relatively rare, and they all refer to specific gifts people give to one another and the Lord, never to the land as a gift from God. None of them occurs in the Book of Joshua in any case.

some way: the land as a whole, or cities within the land, or a tribe's or a person's inheritance, or a plot of ground.

God as Giver of the Land.   God is the one who gives the land; even when humans are the agents of the verb's action, they act on God's behalf. For example, God is said to give the land in twenty-four of the sixty-nine times *ntn* is used in this way.[26] In an additional eight cases, God gives *people* of the land into Israel's hands.[27]

Moses and Joshua as Givers of the Land.   God's human agents, Moses and Joshua, also gave or parceled out the land on his behalf. Moses is the agent giving (or not giving) the land seventeen times. In the following cases, we read that he gave the Israelites (or various tribes therein) their allotted land: 1:14,15; 9:24; 12:6; 13:8,15,24,29; 14:3a; 17:4; 18:7; 22:4,7. Concerning the Levites, Moses did *not* give them an inheritance, since their inheritance was offerings by fire, or God himself: 13:14,33; 14:3b. Joshua also appears nine times as the agent giving the land: 11:23; 12:7; 14:12,13; 15:13; 17:4,14; 21:2;[28] 22:7.

Israel as Giver of the Land.   The nation of Israel itself gave the land in fourteen cases: 19:49,50; 20:2,4,8; 21:2,3,8,9,11,12,13,21; 24:33.[29] The first time it did so, this action came at the end of the land distribution process for the tribes west of the Jordan, which is described in chaps. 14–19. Here, the Israelites gave Joshua *his* inheritance (19:49–50). It was not for Joshua to give himself his own land; the entire nation acted as God's agent to do this.

This fact brackets the section under consideration (chaps. 14–19), since at the beginning of the section (in 14:5) we read that not just Joshua (and Eleazar the priest) but also representatives of the entire nation were involved in the land distribution: "So the Israelites divided the land,[30] just as the LORD had commanded Moses." After the reference to the Israelites' giving Joshua his land (in 19:49–50), the Israelites were heavily involved in designating and giving the cities of refuge (chap. 20) and the Levitical cities (chap. 21).

It would appear that the nation as a whole was especially involved in giving special individuals their lands. Not only was this true for Joshua (19:49–50), but it was also true for the Levites (21:2–3,8–9,11), Caleb (21:12), Aaron's descendants (21:13), and Phinehas, Eleazar's son (24:33).[31]

Caleb as Giver of Land to His Daughter.   The above references account for sixty-six of the sixty-nine references in Joshua to land giving using *ntn*. The final three uses of *ntn* in this sense are more limited. Three times in 15:19, we read of

---

[26] Josh 1:2,3,6,11,13,15a; 2:9,14,24; 5:6; 6:2,16; 8:1,7,18; 10:30,32; 18:3; 21:43[2x]; 23:13, 15,16; 24:13.

[27] Josh 10:8,12,19; 11:6,8; 21:44; 24:8,11.

[28] In this case, he is included with Eleazar the priest and the heads of the families in Israel as codistributor (see 21:1).

[29] Also, in 14:4, we read that they did *not* give the Levites land.

[30] The verb here is not נתן, but חלק, "to apportion, distribute."

[31] The verb here is passive *(niphal)*, the only such occurrence of נתן in the entire book; the agents are the people of Israel (see both vv. 32 and 33).

Caleb's giving part of his inheritance to his daughter: land in the Negev and a water supply (upper and lower springs).

Time Reference and Verb Forms in the Giving of the Land. When we consider when and in what manner (temporally) the land is given, we glean even more instructive information. The verb forms used to speak of the giving of the land show this.

The Perfect. The Hebrew "perfect" forms most often convey the idea that the land had already been given, that the complete act of giving is in view.[32] Israel was not *about* to be given the land, but it already *had* been given it.

In Joshua, the perfect of *ntn* occurs forty-two times, twenty-four of which show that God's giving of the land or its inhabitants was an already-accomplished fact.[33] Most often it refers to God's gift of the land as a whole.[34] Other times it refers to something more specific, such as the cities of Jericho or Ai (6:2,16; 8:1), or Joshua's or Caleb's or Joseph's individual inheritances (15:13; 17:14; 19:50). Occasionally it refers to God's giving the land's inhabitants into Israel's hands (8:1; 10:8,19).

Of the twenty-four occurrences of the perfect as already-accomplished, complete actions, in fully one-half of the cases (twelve), the perfect is used to describe the giving as already accomplished in its entirety when, in the actual historical reality, this was *not* the case.[35] This makes the important theological point that God was in control of the granting of the land and that the title to the land was already Israel's, even if they had not yet taken all of it.

In the Pentateuch, the perfect of *ntn* is used similarly. There the perfect is used twenty-eight times referring to God's giving of the land of Canaan as an already-accomplished fact. These include two references in Genesis,[36] eight in Num-

---

[32] On the perfective aspect of verbs, especially the idea of "complete" actions (i.e., not just "completed" actions, but actions in their entireties—which includes, but is not limited to, actions that are terminated), see the important work of B. Comrie, *Aspect: An Introduction to the Study of Verbal Aspect and Related Problems* (Cambridge: University Press, 1976). For the perfect in biblical Hebrew (i.e., suffixed verb forms), see *IBHS* §§ 29.6a–d (relying on Comrie) and chap. 30.

[33] The giving of the land appears in Josh 1:3,14–15; 2:24; 6:2,16; 8:1 (land and inhabitants); 10:8 and 10:19 (inhabitants); 13:8[2x]; 14:3; 15:13; 17:14; 18:3,7; 19:50; 22:4,7[2x]; 23:13,15–16; 24:33. In four additional cases, the Levites' lack of a portion (13:14,33; 14:3–4) is mentioned with נָתַן (perfect).

[34] The land as a large entity—whether as an all-inclusive, comprehensive whole or as the entirety of the Transjordan tribe's inheritance—is in view as God's gift to Israel in thirteen passages: Josh 1:3,14–15; 2:24; 13:8[2x]; 14:3; 18:3,7; 22:4,7[2x]; 23:13,15–16.

[35] The clearest such references are eight in number: Josh 1:3; 2:24; 6:2,16; 8:1; 10:8,19; 18:3. In four additional cases (17:14; 23:13,15,16), where the land distribution would appear already to have been accomplished, it can be argued that the giving was not actually fully completed, since internal evidence in Joshua, as well as Judges 1, shows that much land remained in Canaanite hands.

[36] Gen 15:18; 35:12.

bers,[37] and eighteen in Deuteronomy.[38] In three additional cases in Deuteronomy, God speaks of giving *other* lands to other peoples: the descendants of Esau and Lot.[39] This shows that *all* lands—not just Canaan—belong to God (cf. Ps 24:1: "The earth is the LORD's, and everything in it, the world, and all who live in it").

Of these twenty-eight occurrences, only six refer to land that historically had already been possessed.[40] Thus, fully twenty-two references to God's giving of the land of Canaan in the Pentateuch present this as a *fait accompli*, even before the fact.

The Imperfect.   Two verb forms speak of the land as yet to be given, or in process of being given: the imperfect and the participle. The imperfect—which is usually future-oriented[41]—of *ntn* is used only four times in Joshua, only once to refer to giving the land: 8:18 (referring to God's giving Ai into Israel's hands).

In the Pentateuch, the imperfect is found thirty-five times referring to God's intent to give land. Twenty-one times it refers to the land of Canaan.[42] Ten times it refers to cities of refuge.[43] Three times it refers to God's giving other lands to other peoples.[44] Twice it refers to God's giving people into Israel's hands: Exod 23:31; Num 21:1. In all these cases, the imperfect is used consistently, to denote God's (future) intent to give lands to people.

The Participle.   The participle is the second verb form used to speak of the in-process or yet-to-come nature of the gift of the land. The participle by itself does not indicate a time frame. However, it often denotes present (ongoing) or future time,[45] and in this sense the participle of *ntn* is found several times in the Pentateuch and Joshua. It can thus be translated (with, e.g., a first-person reference) as "I give," "I am giving," "I will give," or "I am about to give."

In Joshua, the participle of *ntn* occurs only four times, but three of these refer to God's giving the land to Israel: 1:2,11,15. In each case, the reference is to the anticipated gift of the land (God is giving it, or he is about to give it).[46]

In the Pentateuch, the participle of *ntn* is used overwhelmingly to speak of God's imminent giving of the land. Of fifty-six occurrences of the participle, forty-five refer to the gift of the land. Of these, six references are in Exodus–

---

[37] Num 20:12,24; 21:34; 26:62; 27:12; 32:7,9; 33:53.

[38] Deut 1:8,21; 2:12,24,36; 3:2,12,13,15,16,18,19,20; 8:10; 9:23; 12:1; 26:15; 28:52.

[39] Deut 2:5,9,19.

[40] Deut 2:24,36; 3:12,13,15,16.

[41] See *IBHS* chap. 31 for a more precise characterization of the imperfect (i.e., prefixed verb form).

[42] Gen 12:7; 13:15,17; 24:7; 23:9[2x]; 26:3; 28:13; 35:12[2x]; Exod 12:25; 32:13; 33:1; Lev 20:24; Num 10:29; 26:54; 27:7; 32:5; Deut 1:36,39; 34:4. Two of these references are to Abraham's significant land purchase of the cave of Machpelah, where he buried his wife Sarah (23:9[2x]).

[43] Num 35:2,4,6[2x],7,8[2x],13,14[2x].

[44] Deut 2:5,9,19 (descendants of Esau and Lot).

[45] The participle used as a predicate roughly approximates the imperfect (*GBH* §§121a–h; *IBHS* §§ 37.6e–f). It can refer to present time (primarily a durative aspect) or to future time, usually expressing "certainty, often with immanency—the so-called *futurum instans* participle" (*IBHS* § 37.6f).

[46] In the fourth case (11:6), God is about to give the Canaanite coalition into Israel's hands.

Numbers,[47] while thirty-nine are found in Deuteronomy.[48] Most of these references are some variation on the formulaic "the land the LORD your God is giving you"; the three references in Joshua are of this type.

Other Verb Forms. Of the remaining verb forms (imperative, infinitive absolute, and infinitive construct),[49] the infinitive construct of *ntn* is the most common and most significant in Joshua and the Pentateuch. It is most often translated "to give," in an expression such as "the land which I swore to give." It occurs nine times in Joshua, seven times referring to the land or individuals' inheritance), and twice referring to people. In the Pentateuch it occurs fifty-six times, twenty-two times referring to the land, twice referring to people.

The instances of the imperative and infinitive absolute referring to the giving of the land in Joshua and the Pentateuch are rare and never refer to the land as a whole, only to specific plots of land or inheritances.

Summary. This survey of *ntn* ("to give") in Joshua reveals several things. First, the land of Canaan was God's gift to his people Israel. He alone was the giver. When Moses, Joshua, or the nation as a whole were the agents of the giving, it was nevertheless at God's behest, and it was the land that God had promised to his people that they were giving. Second, God gave the land's *peoples* into Israel's hands as well. They were not taking this land on their own, nor through any strength or merits of their own.[50] Third, God was doing this in Joshua's day in fulfillment of the many promises he had made to do so: to the patriarchs, to Moses, to earlier generations of Israelites.

Fourth, the giving of the land is viewed from two distinct perspectives. In one (*ntn* in the perfect), the land already belongs to Israel; God has already given it to them (i.e., given them the rights or title to it). In the other (*ntn* in the imperfect and participle), the giving was yet to be accomplished; it was either imminent or in process. In both perspectives, God was the giver and the guarantor of the process.

1:4 The extent of the land that God was giving Israel is detailed in v. 4, a "map" of sorts. The description is general, giving the southern and northern boundaries first: "the desert" in the south and "Lebanon" in the north. "The desert" is a generic term that may refer in the Old Testament to any barren

---

[47] Exod 20:12; Lev 14:34; 23:10; 25:2; Num 13:2; 15:2.

[48] Deut 1:20,25; 2:29; 3:20; 4:1,21,40; 5:16,31; 9:6; 11:17,31; 12:9; 13:12; 15:4,7; 16:5,18,20; 17:2,14; 18:9; 19:1,2,10,14; 20:16; 21:1,23; 24:4; 25:15,19; 26:1,2; 27:2,3; 28:8; 32:49,52.

[49] The *qal* passive participle occurs eight times in Joshua or the Pentateuch, but it is never used to refer to the land.

[50] This is explicitly stated in Deut 7:1–2: "(1) When the LORD your God brings you into the land you are entering to possess and drives out before you many nations—the Hittites, Girgashites, Amorites, Canaanites, Perizzites, Hivites and Jebusites, seven nations larger and stronger than you—(2) and when the LORD your God has delivered them over to you and you have defeated them, then you must destroy them totally." See also Deut 6:10–11: Canaan was "a land with large, flourishing cities you did not build, houses filled with all kinds of good things you did not provide, wells you did not dig, and vineyards and olive groves you did not plant."

area; the reference here to a southern desert is deduced from the context.[51]

"Lebanon" is roughly what is present-day Lebanon, north of Israel, including two mountain ranges. This name occurs seventy-one times in the Old Testament, but here in 1:4 is the only time it is called "this Lebanon."[52] A similar phrase, "this Jordan," occurs in 1:2 (see NASB, RSV), as well as five other times in the Old Testament.[53] In all of these cases, the Jordan River was visible at hand when the phrase "this Jordan" was uttered. However, Lebanon is not visible near at hand to someone east of the Jordan. The statement "this Lebanon," then, may have been an ironic one, intended to emphasize the inclusion of this (not-visible) land.[54]

After the general north-south boundaries are delimited, the east-west ones are given. The Euphrates River is often designated as "the great river" when it is mentioned in the Bible (as here).[55] In reality, the Euphrates represents the northeastern border; the Jordan River or the Arabian desert is the true eastern border. However, in biblical geography, the Euphrates represented a convenient eastern border. The "Great Sea on the west" is the Mediterranean Sea.

The land between the eastern and western extremities is called here "all the Hittite country." The term "Hittite" is used to mean different peoples in the Bible. Here, it is essentially a synonym for "Canaanites," perhaps designating all of the hill country west of the Jordan,[56] although there was a great Hittite

---

[51] The exact identity of the desert here is unclear. C. J. Goslinga suggests that it is the desert of Zin (*Joshua, Judges, Ruth,* BSC [Grand Rapids: Zondervan, 1986], 37; cf. Num 33:36; 34:3; etc.); Boling states that it could be the Negev desert in southern Judah or southern Transjordan or both (*Joshua,* 122). M. H. Woudstra states that it "is probably the region which borders the cultivated land of Palestine to the south and east," although he states (curiously) that it also could refer to the Syrian [i.e., northeastern!] desert (*The Book of Joshua,* NICOT [Grand Rapids: Eerdmans, 1981], 60 and n. 29). The fact that the desert is Israel's southern border, however, should be clear. The territorial description here is very general. In an early "map" passage (Gen 15:18), God tells Abram that his land would extend from "the river of Egypt [in the southwest] to the great river, the Euphrates [in the northeast]." Thus, in Josh 1:4, "the desert" certainly stands for the southern border.

[52] See NASB, RSV, NRSV; the NIV ignores the demonstrative adjective "this."

[53] A total of six times in the OT: in Gen 32:10 [Heb 11]; Deut 3:27; 31:2; Josh 1:2,11; 4:22.

[54] Boling suggests that the utterance of "this" was accompanied by a sweeping gesture of the hand (*Joshua,* 122). Goslinga suggests that Joshua was standing in an elevated place (as was Moses in Deut 34); he states that "Mount Hermon [in Lebanon] is visible from Mount Nebo, at whose base the Israelites were encamped" (*Joshua, Judges, Ruth,* 36). Butler suggests that "this" is a late gloss (*Joshua,* 4).

[55] The Tigris River is called the "great river" once: Dan 10:4.

[56] So Boling, *Joshua,* 122–23. For other options, see R S. Hess, *Joshua: An Introduction and Commentary,* TOTC (Downers Grove: InterVarsity, 1996), 70 and n. 2 (pp. 70–71); Woudstra, *Joshua,* 60. See also the commentary on 3:10, following.

kingdom to the north in roughly the period of Joshua (and preceding).[57]

As we have noted, this is a general description of Israel's borders. The intent here is not to give the specific boundaries of the land, or of various tribes' inheritance within the land, that we find in many other passages (see especially Josh 14–19). Rather, it is a general summary painted with broad brush strokes. The details will come later.

1:5 This verse is the spiritual climax and highlight of the first part of God's charge to Joshua. It is a heart-warming promise to Joshua himself[58] that (1) his and the Israelites' efforts would succeed and (2) God would never leave him. It is doubly encouraging when we see that God promised to be with Joshua *in the same way* that he was with Moses. The words in the first part of the verse are identical to those in God's promise to Moses in Deut 7:24b: "No one will be able to stand up against you; you will destroy them." The promise is repeated almost verbatim in Deut 11:25a: "No man will be able to stand against you."

God's impressive promise to Joshua in the second half of the verse that he would be with him just as he was with Moses begins to answer the question whether Joshua would be able to fill Moses' shoes as a leader (see comments on v. 1). On the one hand, as we have noted, no one could ever do this. Yet, God's presence would accompany Joshua just as it had Moses. The words "I will be with you" recall identical promises made to Isaac (Gen 26:3), Jacob (31:3), Moses (Exod 3:12), and Joshua himself (Deut 31:8,23).[59] The promise to Moses in Exod 3:12 is especially significant, since it is tied in with the revelation of God's very name, "Yahweh" (Exod 3:14–15). This God whose name was Yahweh promised Moses that he would be with him; indeed, his name was inextricably tied in with this idea of his keeping covenant to be with his people.[60]

The promises to Joshua in Deuteronomy likewise are most significant. In 31:8, Moses assured Joshua that God would be with him, and in 31:23, God

---

[57] Late remnants of this kingdom may be referred to in the list of Solomon's trading partners in 1 Kgs 10:29. For introductions to the Hittites, see O. R. Gurney, *The Hittites,* rev. ed. (Baltimore: Penguin, 1954); H. A. Hoffner, "The Hittites and Hurrians," in D. J. Wiseman, ed., *Peoples of Old Testament Times* (Oxford: Clarendon, 1973), 197–228; id., "Hittites," in A. Hoerth et al., eds., *Peoples of the Old Testament World* (Grand Rapids: Baker, 1994), 127–55. See also these works and Woudstra (*Joshua,* 60–61, nn. 33–34) on the relationship between the biblical Hittites and those found in the ancient Near East.

[58] The grammatical references here are singular.

[59] These promises hark back to a promise made to Abraham, when God said to him about his descendants: "I will be their God" (Gen 17:8).

[60] See the wordplay between "I will be with you" in Exod 3:12 (אֶהְיֶה עִמָּךְ) and God's reply to Moses when Moses asked him his name (Exod 3:14): "I will be what I will be" (see NIV marginal note) (אֶהְיֶה אֲשֶׁר אֶהְיֶה). See Cassuto, *Book of Exodus,* 30–40; Kaiser, "Exodus," 2:319–22.

himself stated the same thing. The verbatim repetitions of God's promise here are yet another way in which the Book of Joshua shows how God was being faithful to his words spoken in earlier times. He was faithful to whatever generation of Abraham's descendants he was dealing with. Jesus told his disciples that "surely I am with you always, to the very end of the age" (Matt 28:19–20), showing that God's presence was not just promised to particular generations, but to every generation of faithful believers.

In the last clause of the verse, God expands on this promise to Joshua of his presence: he would never leave nor forsake him. This too echoes earlier promises, most notably in Deut 11:25a[61] and Deut 31:6,8.

The second part of God's charge to Joshua consists of his instructions and encouragement. Three things stand out prominently here. First, as in the first section, much of the language derives from God's earlier instructions and encouragement. Second, the threefold command to "be strong and courageous" (vv. 6,7,9) is important, and it also helps to give structure to the section. Third, the emphasis on Joshua's keeping of the law in order to succeed in his responsibilities (vv. 7–8) is significant.

The command to "be strong and courageous" brackets this paragraph, introducing it and bringing it to a close (vv. 6,9). The middle occurrence of this command is highlighted by the addition of the modifier "very" (*mĕʾōd*, "be strong and *very* courageous"). This introduces the heart of the paragraph, God's instructions about Joshua's keeping the law (vv. 7–8).

1:6 The verb "to be strong" *(ḥzq)* is common in Hebrew (occurring almost three hundred times), but the verb "to be courageous" *(ʾmṣ)* occurs only forty-one times. Both words are actually similar in meaning.[62] The context in Joshua 1 shifts back and forth between "courage" and "resoluteness" for the latter verb. "Courage" is perhaps more appropriate in vv. 6 and 9, which are coupled with statements about conflict ("no one will be able to stand up against you" [v. 5]; "do not be terrified; do not be discouraged" [v. 9]). However, God's commands to Joshua in vv. 7–8 about keeping the law call for "resoluteness" rather than "courage." In about one-third of its uses, the latter verb *(ʾmṣ)* is used as a command (fourteen times). Whenever this is the case, it is invariably coupled with *ḥzq*.[63]

God was echoing identical exhortations that he and Moses gave to Joshua earlier (Deut 31:6,7,23). With these words Moses had exhorted the people (Deut 31:6), the people would exhort Joshua (Josh 1:18), and Joshua would later encourage the people (10:25). Each statement is accompanied by an

---

[61] Where the "you" is plural vs. the singular "you" here.

[62] The primary meaning for both verbs is given in BDB and *HALOT* as "be strong, firm, stout" (s. v.). NJPSV renders the clause as "be strong and resolute," which captures well the meaning here.

[63] The references are Deut 31:6,7,23; Josh 1:6,7,9,18; 10:25; 1 Chr 22:13; 28:20; 2 Chr 32:7 *(qal* stem); Deut 3:28; Isa 35:3; Nah 2:1 [Hb. 2] *(piel* stem).

assurance that God would be with Joshua or the Israelites, or that he would fight for them. This motif of God's presence is an important one throughout the Old Testament.[64]

The need for Joshua to be strong and resolute was acute because he was the instrument for the people to inherit the land. The Hebrew grammatical construction here highlights Joshua himself: if he, of all people, was weak and irresolute, then the cause was in deep trouble.[65]

Not only did God promise Moses that he would give the land to the Israelites (v. 3), but this had been promised to earlier generations too, and God specifically acknowledged this here (on these promises, see on v. 3).

1:7–8 The heart of God's instructions to Joshua is introduced by a variant of the command in vv. 6 and 9, adding the word "very," which highlights the instructions here about keeping the law.[66] In a paragraph of this length, the amount of space devoted to keeping the law might seem to be disproportionate (about half: forty-five of ninety-two words); however, keeping the law would be the key to Joshua's success. It is striking that God's instructions here to Joshua are not about military matters, given that Joshua and the Israelites faced many battles ahead. However, the keys to his success were spiritual, directly related to the degree of his obedience to God. The keys to Joshua's success were the same as those for a king: being rooted in God's word rather than depending upon military might (Deut 17:14–20, esp. vv. 16,18–19).[67]

The command in v. 7 to be strong and very resolute is to ensure Joshua's scrupulous obedience to the law of Moses. The NIV's wording ("Be careful to obey") translates the verbs *šmr* and *ʿśh*. The first, *šmr*, means "to keep, observe," and the second, *ʿśh*, means "to do, obey." They are used as a word pair forty times in the Old Testament, almost always with reference to keeping and obeying God's words or commands.[68] In such cases, *šmr* is often trans-

---

[64] See H. D. Preuss, "אֵת *ʾēth*; עִם *ʿim*," *TDOT* 1:449–63.

[65] The rendering "you are the one who will cause [this people] to inherit" captures the nuance of the construction here: אַתָּה תַּנְחִיל. The language in Deut 31:7,23 similarly highlights Joshua by fronting of אַתָּה before the verb (בוא in these cases).

[66] Boling confirms this judgment in commenting upon the use of רַק, "Only" (not in NIV here) and מְאֹד, "very": "This is not a radical editorial disjunction in the address, but an emphatic imperative at the center of it" (*Joshua*, 124).

[67] See G. Gerbrandt, *Kingship according to the Deuteronomistic History*, SBLDS 87 (Atlanta: Scholars Press, 1986), and D. M. Howard, Jr., "The Case for Kingship in Deuteronomy and the Former Prophets," *WTJ* 52 (1990): 101–15, for more on this downplaying of the king's military role in Israel. Joshua fit the model for kings, even though he was not a king himself (Gerbrandt, *Kingship according to the Deuteronomistic History*, 116–23).

[68] Thirty-nine of forty times it is used this way. The one exception is in Deut 23:24. These forty occurrences represent cases where the two roots are adjacent to each other. In many more cases, these two roots occur in close proximity, separated by one or more words and used in essentially the same way, as an exhortation to keep the law.

lated "be careful" and ʿśh "do, obey" (as NIV does here).[69]

The importance of obedience to the law as the key to Joshua's success cannot be overestimated. This is emphasized over and over in these two verses. (1) Joshua was to "be careful to do" this law (v. 7a). (2) It was "all" the law that was to be obeyed (v. 7a). (3) Joshua was not to deviate from it even slightly, neither to the right nor to the left (v. 7b).[70] (4) The Book of the Law was not to depart from Joshua's mouth, since he was to meditate upon it by day and by night (v. 8a). The idea of meditating here is not the one commonly familiar in the late twentieth century, namely, of emptying the mind and concentrating on nothing or on self or on visualizations of various types; much of this type of meditation is indebted to Eastern mystic religions. Rather, the Old Testament concept of meditation involves two things: First, a focus upon God himself (Ps 63:6[Hb.7]), his works (Pss 77:12[Hb. 13]; 143:5), or his law (Josh 1:8; Ps 1:2), and second, an activity that was done aloud.[71] This is why God told Joshua that this lawbook should not leave his *mouth* (as opposed to, e.g., his heart or his mind).[72] (5) Joshua was to "be careful to obey" everything[73] *written* in the lawbook. This represents something permanent, since it was written down.[74]

The result (ʾāz, "then") of Joshua's keeping the law was that his way would prosper and be successful. Joshua's obedience to God's will (vv. 7–8) and God's presence with him (v. 9) guaranteed this. Many Christians make

---

[69] The construction שׁמר לעשׂה, where עשׂה occurs as an infinitive construct, is the most frequent, occurring twenty-seven of the forty times these two lexemes occur together (including three times in Josh: 1:7,8; 23:6). The construction לשׁמר לעשׂה, where both lexemes occur as infinitive constructs "to observe to do" or "to be careful to obey," occurs another eight times (including twice in Joshua: 1:7; 23:6).

[70] This idea of not deviating from God's commands either to the right or to the left is found again in Deut 2:27; 5:32; 17:20; 28:14; Josh 23:6. In addition, Prov 4:27 and Isa 30:21 speak of not deviating from the proper path in life, and 2 Kgs 22:2 // 2 Chr 34:2 speaks of Josiah's not deviating from the way of David his father.

[71] The Hb. word rendered "meditate" here (הגה) is translated elsewhere in NIV as "plot" (Ps 2:1), "growls" (Isa 31:4), or "lament" (Isa 16:7). The common thread here is an activity that is done aloud. With reference to meditating upon the law, the idea is that one reads or recites the law aloud to oneself. In the ancient world, almost all reading was done aloud. Augustine remarked in a well-known passage in his *Confessions* (6.3) that he noticed St. Ambrose reading without moving his lips, a spectacle odd enough for him to comment upon. Silent reading was rare, although not unknown in the ancient world (see F. D. Gilliard, "More Silent Reading in Antiquity: *Non Omne Verbum Sonobat*," *JBL* 112 [1993]: 689–96).

[72] C. F. Keil makes the valuable observation that the word here, "meditate" (הגה), "does not mean theoretical speculation about the law, such as the Pharisees indulged in, but a practical study of the law, for the purpose of observing it in thought and action, or carrying it out with the heart, the mouth, and the hand" (*The Book of Joshua* [Grand Rapids: Eerdmans, 1975 reprint], 30).

[73] The wording is the same here as in v. 7a (see points (1) and (2) above).

[74] Examples where people are instructed to write something down so it can be preserved for posterity include Exod 17:14; Deut 31:19; Neh 9:38; Dan 12:4.

much of passages such as this in the Old Testament that speak of prosperity and success. Other passages often cited include the following:

"Whatever [the righteous] does prospers" (Ps 1:3).
"The lions may grow weak and hungry, but those who seek the LORD lack no good thing" (Ps 34:10).
"I was young and now I am old, yet I have never seen the righteous forsaken or their children begging bread" (Ps 37:25).
"The wealth of the rich is their fortified city, but poverty is the ruin of the poor" (Prov 10:15).
"Commit your works to the LORD, and your plans will succeed" (Prov 16:3).
"If they obey and serve him, they will spend the rest of their days in prosperity and their years in contentment" (Job 36:11).

Many Christians read these and other passages as guarantees that all Christians will (or should!) succeed in every venture they undertake and that they will prosper financially if they are truly following God. Christians who do not succeed, or who are not financially well off, are condemned as living in some persistent sin or lacking in proper faith.

Much could be said in response, but here we will make only three points.[75] First, the message of the Book of Job points in precisely the opposite direction as that argued by these Christians. That is, Job was stripped of his financial wealth for reasons that had nothing to do with any lack of faith or obedience. Job's wealth was restored again at the end of the book, but he came to a position of peace with God and acceptance of God's will in his life *before* his wealth was restored (Job 42:5–6). This was because he had now had a firsthand encounter with God, whereas previously his knowledge of God had been primarily secondhand.

Second, the Book of Proverbs, which contains many statements about wealth and prosperity (see the passages quoted above, and such passages as Prov 3:1–10), nevertheless is clear about a balanced view of wealth. Kaiser notes that "Proverbs does emphasize the moral restraints that God has placed on gaining wealth. It is not to be achieved through deceit (21:6), or by using false balances (20:10), or by shifting boundary markers (22:28), or through oppression (23:10–11)."[76] Such verses as Prov 23:4–5 and 30:7–9 show us

---

[75] The issue of Christians and prosperity in general is too broad a topic to enter into here. The discussion here focuses primarily on the terms for prosperity and success used in Josh 1:7–8 (צלח and שׂכל) and the implications arising out of their usage in the OT (and their misuse by many Christians). For treatments of the broader topic from an OT perspective, see W. C. Kaiser, Jr., "The Old Testament Case for Material Blessings and the Contemporary Believer," in D. Moo, ed., *The Gospel and Contemporary Perspectives* (Grand Rapids: Kregel, 1997), 27–41, 185–86 [reprinted from *TrinJ* 9 (1988): 151–70]; H. G. M. Williamson, "The Old Testament and the Material World," *EvQ* 57 (1985): 5–22.

[76] Kaiser, "The Old Testament Case for Material Blessings," 36.

that wealth is *not* the ultimate good to be sought or even guaranteed by God:

> "Do not wear yourself out to get rich; have the wisdom to show restraint. Cast but a glance at riches, and they are gone, for they will surely sprout wings and fly off to the sky like an eagle" (Prov 23:4–5).
>
> "Two things I ask of you, O LORD; do not refuse me before I die: Keep false-hood and lies far from me; give me neither poverty nor riches, but give me only my daily bread. Otherwise, I may have too much and disown you and say, 'Who is the LORD?' Or I may become poor and steal, and so dishonor the name of my God (Prov 3:7–9).[77]

Third, the two words we find here in our passage in Joshua (1:7–8) speak-ing of prosperity and success are almost never used in the Old Testament to speak of financial success. Rather, they speak of succeeding in life's proper endeavors. This happens when people's lives are focused entirely on God and obedience to him. The focus of people's endeavors is *not* to be prosperity and success but rather holiness and obedience. A believer's consuming obsession should be holiness, for God himself is holy (Lev 11:45; 19:2, etc.), to love God with one's entire being (Deut 6:5), to keep his word with the same fervor (Deut 6:6; 2 Kgs 23:25; Ezra 7:10; etc.), and to "fear God and keep his com-mandments" (Eccl 12:13). When this happens, then God does bless (usually!), although not always in exactly the ways we might like him to. In this, the Old Testament has the same message that Jesus spoke when he said, "Seek first his kingdom and his righteousness, and all these things [food, drink, clothing] will be given to you as well" (Matt 6:33). Our priority is to seek God.

The Hebrew roots in question here are *ṣlḥ* ("prosper") and *śkl* ("be success-ful"). The first term occurs sixty-nine times in the Old Testament, and the major-ity of the time (fifty-nine times) it means "to prosper [or, better, "to succeed"] in one's endeavors," almost always because of God's gracious and ever-present hand.[78] For example, Abraham's servant was given success by God in his mis-sion to find a wife for Isaac (Gen 24:12,40,42,56). Joseph succeeded in Potiphar's household because God was with him (Gen 39:2,3,23). The Messiah himself, when he was bruised, nevertheless would cause God's will to "prosper"

---

[77] For more on this issue in Proverbs, see the helpful treatments by B. K. Waltke, "Does Prov-erbs Promise Too Much?" *CBRF Journal* 128 (1992): 17–22, and R. C. Van Leeuwen, "Wealth and Poverty: System and Contradiction in Proverbs," *HS* 33 (1992): 25–36. More broadly focused treat-ments on how to read Proverbs and the issue of "guarantees" therein include W. Zimmerli, "The Place and Limit of Wisdom in the Framework of Old Testament Theology," *SJT* 17 (1964): 146–58; G. von Rad, *Wisdom in Israel* (Nashville: Abingdon, 1972), 97–100; and D. P. Bricker, "The Doctrine of the 'Two Ways' in Proverbs," *JETS* 38 (1995): 501–17.

[78] The root (or possibly a second, identical one) is used ten times to mean "penetrate, advance, rush," and it is the term used, e.g, in Judges and 1 Samuel speaking of God's Spirit coming with power upon Samson, Saul, or David (see, e.g., Judg 14:19; 15:14; 1 Sam 10:6,10; 11:6; 16:13). On the issue of one or two roots of צלח, see BDB, 852; *HALOT,* 1025–27.

in his hand (Isa 53:10). Jeremiah spoke several times of the wicked not succeeding in their evil intents (Jer 2:37; 5:28; 13:10; 22:30[2x]; 32:5). Daniel and his friends succeeded in their efforts in exile in Babylon, with God's help (Dan 3:30; 6:28[Hb. 29]). The people's efforts in Ezra and Nehemiah also succeeded because of God's good hand upon them (Ezra 5:8; 6:14; Neh 1:11; 2:20). Solomon succeeded as king and as builder (1 Chr 22:11,13; 29:23; 2 Chr 7:11).

A very revealing passage comes in 1 Chr 22:13, when David was giving his son Solomon instructions about building the temple. The key to Solomon's success was the same as for Joshua: "Then you will have success if you are careful to observe the decrees and laws that the LORD gave Moses for Israel. Be strong and courageous. Do not be afraid or discouraged." The vocabulary in this passage echoes that of Joshua 1 in remarkable ways. In both cases, God's chosen leader was to focus on knowing and obeying God's laws. That was the key to their success as leaders.

The second term in Josh 1:8 (*śkl*, "to be successful") occurs a total of seventy-eight times in the Old Testament (as a verb or a noun), most commonly with the meaning of "have insight, understanding, be wise." In ten or eleven cases—including twice here in Josh 1:7–8—it means "to have success."[79] And, in these cases, almost without exception, success is to be achieved because individuals seek the Lord earnestly or carefully obey his commandments. Success is specifically equated with obeying God's law or the covenant in Deut 29:9 [Hb. 8]; Josh 1:7–8; 1 Kgs 2:3; and 2 Kgs 18:7. In 1 Kgs 2:3, for example, David instructed Solomon to "observe what the LORD requires: Walk in his ways and keep his decrees and commands, his laws and requirements, as written in the Law of Moses, so that you may prosper in all you do and wherever you go." Hezekiah was a good king who trusted in the Lord, clung to him, and "kept the commands the LORD had given to Moses" (2 Kgs 18:5–6). As a result of this, he enjoyed God's presence with him, and "he was successful in whatever he did" (18:7). David succeeded because God was with him (1 Sam 18:5,14–15). He was "a man after God's own heart" who, the text of 1 Sam 13:14 implies, "kept the LORD's command," and God's Spirit was upon him (1 Sam 16:13). Jeremiah speaks of false religious leaders who do *not* seek the Lord, and, as a result, they are *not* successful (Jer 10:21).

The context here in Joshua is very clear about what is to be the key to Joshua's success (1:7–8): he is "to be careful to obey all the law"; he is not to turn from it to the right or the left; he is to have it constantly on his lips and to meditate on it at all times; and he is carefully to do everything written in it. His focus is to be upon God's word and will; then, as he leads Israel in taking the land of Canaan, success will come to him.

---

[79] The references are Deut 29:9 [Hb. 8]; Josh 1:7–8; 1 Sam 18:5,14–5; 1 Kgs 2:3; 2 Kgs 18:7; Prov 17:8; Jer 10:21; also possibly Isa 52:13 (cf. NIV note).

Nothing at all is said here about financial success. In fact, of the fifty-nine times that *śkl* refers to success, and the ten to eleven times that *śkl* does, only *once* are finances even remotely in view. This is in Ezek 16:13, which states about the city of Jerusalem, "So you were adorned with gold and silver; your clothes were of fine linen and costly fabric and embroidered cloth. Your food was fine flour, honey and olive oil. You became very beautiful and rose to be a queen." In this passage, the NIV's "rose to be" translates *śkl*, and it refers to Jerusalem and God's blessing upon her. It can scarcely be used to justify personal financial reward for individuals as the meaning of *śkl*.

Thus, in the Old Testament "prosperity" is not financial in its primary orientation, if at all. Rather, it refers to succeeding in proper endeavors. Also, it comes only when it is not the focus of one's efforts in any case. It comes when one's focus is on God and one's relationship with him. The success is granted by God, not attained by human achievement.

Here in Josh 1:8 is the only place in the entire Old Testament that these two words are found together. Their use in this fashion underscores the importance of Joshua's mission in leading Israel in taking possession of the land of Canaan, particularly the importance of his obedience and faithfulness to God. The same, it can safely be said, would be the case today: the keys to success in life lie in being intensely focused upon God and in consistent faithfulness to him and his revealed word.

1:9 God's charge to Joshua ends by reiterating words of encouragement and commitment (see esp. vv. 5–6). Joshua was not to fear or be discouraged precisely because the Almighty God promised him his presence (see on v. 5).

(2) Joshua's Instructions for Breaking Camp (1:10–11)

10So Joshua ordered the officers of the people: 11"Go through the camp and tell the people, 'Get your supplies ready. Three days from now you will cross the Jordan here to go in and take possession of the land the LORD your God is giving you for your own.'"

1:10 The "officers" here are more administrative officials than military officers. Previously, God had appointed them to help Moses in his administrative duties. They were respected leaders in Israel, who had the Spirit of the Lord on them (Num 11:16–17; Deut 1:15–16), and who had some judicial and/or religious (Levitical) duties (Deut 1:15–16; 16:18; 2 Chr 19:11; 34:13).

A key word in chap. 1 is "order, command" *(ṣwh)*, which occurs in 1:7,9,10,11,13,16,18. The word is especially important in the Pentateuch and in Joshua,[80] referring most often to God's commands for his people. How-

---

[80] The word occurs 496 times in the Hb. Bible, of which about 60 percent are found in these six books: twenty-seven times in Genesis, fifty-four times in Exodus, thirty-five times in Leviticus, forty-eight times in Numbers, eighty-eight times in Deuteronomy, and forty-three times in Joshua.

ever, as we noted earlier with reference to "give," God also delegated his authority to various representatives. Here, God commanded Joshua (1:7,9), who in turn commanded the officials (1:10). The officials were to pass on Joshua's commands to the people (1:11), and the people pledged to respond in obedience to Joshua's commands (1:16,18). This adds to the picture of Joshua's leadership painted in this book.

1:11 In keeping with the nonmilitary instructions that God gave to Joshua in vv. 6–9, Joshua's instructions to the people here likewise concern not military strategy or equipment, but for breaking camp, for readying food supplies for their journey.[81] The possession of the land was, in effect, an already-accomplished fact; the Israelites merely needed to load up with supplies, since God would be giving the land into their hands (see the end of v. 11).

Joshua told the officials that sometime within the next three days they would be crossing the Jordan River in order to take possession of the land. It is possible that Joshua meant they would merely be setting out from their present encampment within three days, not actually crossing within three days.[82] Or, it may indicate that his estimate of when they would be able to set out simply was erroneous, since, as it turned out, the crossing did not take place until the seventh day, due to delays encountered, as there are two three-day periods mentioned in chap. 3. The first three-day period was spent preparing provisions (1:11), at the same time the spies went into Jericho and then hid in the hills (see 2:22; 3:2). Then, it was another three days before Israel actually crossed the Jordan (see 3:2).[83]

The purpose of the Jordan crossing was that Israel might go in and actually take possession of the land that the Lord their God was giving them as part of their inheritance. Just as God's *giving* of the land is important in Joshua, so also are the related concepts of Israel's *inheriting* and *taking possession* of the land. Israel inherited the land that God gave and then had to take possession of it. These latter two concepts are expressed by two related Hebrew words: *nḥl*, "to inherit" (used in v. 6), and *yrš*, "to take possession" (used twice here in v. 11, which are obscured somewhat by the NIV's rendering as "take possession" and "for your own," respectively). These are very important words, integral to the theology of the Book of Joshua and are dealt with at length in

---

[81] The word here (צֵידָה) and its cognates mean "food for a journey" (or simply "hunted game"). Despite Boling's objection (*Joshua,* 125–26) that military provisions are to be included here, the evidence does not point in this direction (*HALOT,* 1020–21); see also Soggin (*Joshua,* 32–33), who notes that the text here presents the conquest as a peaceful process, with little to worry about, since God had already given the people the land.

[82] See Keil, *Joshua,* 31–32; Goslinga, *Joshua, Judges, Ruth,* 40.

[83] For a fuller explanation of this, see my "Three Days in Joshua 1–3: Resolving a Chronological Conundrum," *JETS* 41 (1998), and the commentary below at 2:22–24 and 3:2.

an excursus entitled "Israel's Inheritance of the Land of Joshua," after 13:7.

(3) Joshua's Charge to the Transjordan Tribes (1:12–15)

¹²But to the Reubenites, the Gadites and the half-tribe of Manasseh, Joshua said, ¹³"Remember the command that Moses the servant of the LORD gave you: 'The LORD your God is giving you rest and has granted you this land.' ¹⁴Your wives, your children and your livestock may stay in the land that Moses gave you east of the Jordan, but all your fighting men, fully armed, must cross over ahead of your brothers. You are to help your brothers ¹⁵until the LORD gives them rest, as he has done for you, and until they too have taken possession of the land that the LORD your God is giving them. After that, you may go back and occupy your own land, which Moses the servant of the LORD gave you east of the Jordan toward the sunrise."

Joshua's charge to the two-and-one-half tribes who were to settle east of the Jordan (in Transjordan) springs from their earlier transaction with Moses, when these tribes were granted the right to settle there (see Num 32:1–42; Deut 2:26–3:17). Verses 13–15 here quote Deut 3:18–20 virtually word for word. A change in v. 14, from Deuteronomy's "cities" to Joshua's "land," highlights the Book of Joshua's special interest in the land as a whole. These Transjordan tribes were required to keep covenant solidarity with their brethren settling west of the Jordan (Cisjordan) by helping them in the conquest. They agreed to do this (vv. 16–18), just as they had earlier pledged (Num 32:25–27). Joshua 22 indicates that they followed through on their commitments, and Joshua blessed them for their faithfulness in this matter (Josh 22:1–8).

1:12 The grammatical construction introducing Joshua's words to the Transjordan tribes in vv. 13–15 sets off these words from the three other speeches in chap. 1.[84] Usually commentators assume that vv. 12–18 are a unit consisting of Joshua's instructions to the Transjordan tribes and their response. They assume that the disjunction in v. 12 shows that these verses are an "aside" and that the main narrative action does not resume until 2:1.[85] The close correspondence between Joshua's words in vv. 13–15 and the people's response in vv. 16–18 naturally reinforces this assumption.

However, this is only an assumption, made possible by the fact that the verb in v. 16—*wayyaʿănû*, "Then they answered"—does not specify who pre-

---

[84] I.e., the narrative framework of the chapter (vv. 1,11,12,16a), which surrounds the speeches, consistently uses the normal narrative verbal construction *(wayyiqtol)*, except in v. 12, where the *waw* + *yiqtol* verb sequence is interrupted by a disjunctive *wāw* followed by three prepositional phrases.

[85] See, e.g., Butler, *Joshua*, 18–23; Boling, *Joshua*, 126–28; Soggin, *Joshua*, 212; J. Gray, *Joshua, Judges, Ruth*, NCBC, 3d ed. (Grand Rapids: Eerdmans, 1986), 60–61; Goslinga, *Joshua, Judges, Ruth*, 39–42.

cisely did the answering. In reality, it is more probable that the disjunction in v. 12 functions to tie Joshua's two speeches together into one unit, so to speak, and that the response recorded in vv. 16–18 represents not just the Transjordan tribes of vv. 12–15 but also the representatives of the entire nation addressed in vv. 10–11.[86] Thus, what transpired here was that Joshua first gave his instructions to the officials of the people (vv. 10–11), then gave another set of instructions to the Transjordan tribes (vv. 12–15), and finally the nation as a whole (or its representatives) responded by affirming his leadership (vv. 16–18).[87]

1:13 "Moses' command" is the one recorded in Num 32:20–22 and reiterated in Deut 3:18–20 and here. The promise of "rest" is found in all of these passages, and it is God's gift, part of Israel's inheritance. In Exod 33:14 God had stated: "My Presence will go with you, and I will give you rest." Not only would Israel inherit the land, however, but they would have rest from their enemies while they were in that land (see, e.g., Deut 12:10; 25:19). In addition, the land itself would have rest from war (Josh 11:23; 14:15; cf. similar passages in 2 Sam 7:1,11; 1 Kgs 8:56).[88]

1:14 Contrary to the usual deemphasis on military matters in the book, we find in this verse a cluster of military vocabulary. "Fully armed" translates a Hebrew term *(ḥămušîm)* whose exact meaning is disputed. The Hebrew word is related to the words for "five" *(ḥāmēš)* and "fifty" *(ḥămiššîm)*, and many scholars suggest it means something like "lined up in battle array, in groups of fifty," but it must be admitted that this is only a guess.[89] The term is used in a similar way in Exod 13:18; Josh 4:12; Judg 7:11; and elsewhere. The "fighting men" *(gibbōrê haḥayil)* are the "mighty men of valor" or "valiant warriors" of other versions (e.g., KJV, NKJV; and NASB, respectively). These men were the military elite. Joshua chose thirty thousand of them for the ambush at Ai (Josh 8:3) and took them into battle at Gilgal (10:7). Groups of four hundred mighty men (1 Sam 22:2) and later six hundred (27:2) accompanied David when he was fleeing from Saul; later, we read of an elite group of thirty or more who were his special warriors (2 Sam 23:8–39).

---

[86] The disjunction represents a clause of the type that F. I. Andersen (*The Sentence in Biblical Hebrew* [The Hague: Mouton, 1974], 65–66) called a "paragraph-level circumstantial clause," which performs the function of coordination, representing two events as happening simultaneously or roughly at the same time. The two events in this case are Joshua's two sets of instructions, in vv. 10–11 and 12–15.

[87] I have defended this understanding of the verbal sequence and the events here at length in "All Israel's Response to Joshua: A Note on the Narrative Framework of Joshua 1," in A. Beck et al., ed., *Fortunate the Eyes That See: Essays in Honor of David Noel Freedman in Celebration of His Seventieth Birthday* (Grand Rapids: Eerdmans, 1995), 81–91.

[88] The passages on rest in Joshua are 1:13,15; 11:23; 14:15; 21:44; 23:1. For more on this important concept, see "Introduction" and Butler, *Joshua*, 21–22.

[89] E.g., *HALOT*, 331; Boling, *Joshua*, 127; Gray, *Joshua, Judges, Ruth*, 61–62.

1:15 The importance of the unity of the nation comes out clearly in Joshua's words here. They echo motifs already introduced: rest (v. 13), possession of the land (v. 11), the land as a gift from God (vv. 2–3), the men's responsibilities (v. 14; cf. Num 32:17,22; Deut 3:19–20), and even Moses' role (v. 13). These provide a fitting wrap-up to this short set of instructions.

(4) All Israel's Response (1:16–18)

¹⁶Then they answered Joshua, "Whatever you have commanded us we will do, and wherever you send us we will go. ¹⁷Just as we fully obeyed Moses, so we will obey you. Only may the LORD your God be with you as he was with Moses. ¹⁸Whoever rebels against your word and does not obey your words, whatever you may command them, will be put to death. Only be strong and courageous!"

1:16 As already indicated, the grammar of the narrative framework of the chapter (vv. 1,10,12,16a) points to this response coming from representatives of all twelve tribes of Israel. That is, the officials of the people (v. 10) and the Transjordan tribes (v. 12) joined together in affirming their loyalty to Joshua and his instructions to them after he had spoken to each of them (see above on 1:12).

The people's affirmation of Joshua was warm and enthusiastic, and it echoed elements of God's charge to Joshua in vv. 1–9. They blessed him with the statement about the Lord his God being with him, just as he had been with Moses (v. 17; this is similar to God's promise to Joshua of his presence in v. 5). Also in these verses is the fourth and final occurrence of the exhortation to be strong and courageous (v. 18c; see also vv. 6, 7, 9), which forms a fitting conclusion to this chapter, one that is full of exhortations and encouragements.

On the face of it, the people's pledges of obedience and loyalty to Joshua certainly must have been encouraging to this new leader who was not yet worthy of being called the "servant of the LORD" (see note on v. 1). And there is no indication in the text that the people were anything but sincere in their words.

However, the Israelites had been a very disobedient people over the years, despite earlier promises to obey. For example, when Moses brought them the laws that God had given him and read from the Book of the Covenant, they had solemnly sworn obedience, saying, "Everything the LORD has said we will do" and "We will do everything the LORD has said; we will obey" (Exod 24:3,7). Yet, within a very short time, Aaron was leading the people in building a golden calf (Exod 32); and the Israelites' subsequent history is replete with examples of complaining, rebellion, and outright disobedience. So, we must wonder about the people's words here. If their promise was to obey Joshua in the same way they had obeyed Moses, the prospects were not as bright as they might first appear, since, of course, they did *not* "fully obey" Moses.[90] Quite to the contrary! And Israel did not fully follow through on

---

[90] I am indebted to my student Timothy Simpson for stimulating my thinking in this direction.

their obligations in Joshua's day either. For example, it is abundantly clear that the Israelites were to annihilate the Canaanites when they entered the land. God had so informed Moses that Israel was to carry out this complete destruction in Canaan (Deut 7:2; 20:16–17; Josh 11:15,20), and Moses had so instructed Joshua (11:12,15; cf. 10:40). God spoke to Joshua directly about this, as well (6:17, with reference to Jericho).

And yet, Israel did not follow through on these instructions in many instances. The most notorious incident of disobedience was Achan's taking of the spoils of Jericho when the explicit instructions were to the contrary (6:17–19; cf. 7:1). Furthermore, on several occasions the people as a whole did not follow through on their obligations to drive out the land's inhabitants (see 11:22b; 13:1; 15:63; 16:10; 17:12–13). Thus, a tension is introduced here between the people's words and their actions, one that simmers below the surface throughout the entire book (see Introduction).[91]

1:17 The aforementioned tension is evidenced by use of the adverb *raq,* meaning "only," which occurs in the middle of this verse (NIV does not translate it). Before an imperfect verb form (as here), it "expresses something which either contradicts or varies from that which precedes it."[92] The question is, What is there in vv. 16–17a that contrasts with what follows in v. 17b? In light of the discussion immediately above, the answer should be obvious: Joshua would not be able to rely on the people's obedience—despite their promises! Rather, his success would come from the Lord's presence, not from the people's obedience (or lack of it). The people's words may have been well-intentioned, but their use of this word—and what follows—makes it very clear where Joshua needed to look for help: not to their obedience to him, but to God.[93]

---

[91] L. D. Hawk points out some tensions in this chapter, but he does not make the observation about the irony of the people's promise to obey Joshua just as they had Moses. Most of Hawk's observations about the tensions here strain credulity (*Every Promise Fulfilled: Contesting Plots in Joshua* [Louisville: Westminster/John Knox, 1991], 58–59).

[92] *HALOT,* 1286. BDB similarly states concerning the construction we find here, "prefixed to *sentences,* [רַק is used] to add a limitation on [something] previously expressed (or implied)" (BDB, 956).

[93] Whether or not they intended this (i.e., to undermine their own promise of obedience and loyalty) is unclear, but the effect is certainly to show from where Joshua would receive his true help. Hawk reads רַק differently: as a challenge by the eastern tribes to Joshua that he himself needed to obey God—he states that "the eastern tribes … [declare] that they will be obedient insofar as Yahweh is with Joshua"—and he translates, "However *[raq]* Yahweh must be with you as he was with Moses" (Hawk, *Every Promise Fulfilled,* 59). Hawk believes that the use of רַק in vv. 7 and 18 is to be understood in the same way as in v. 17 (functioning as a contrast) and that the Transjordan tribes were giving Joshua only qualified obedience, contingent upon the Lord's being with him (as if they suspected that God might *not* be with him). However, Hawk ignores the difference in grammatical constructions: in vv. 7 and 18, רַק introduces an imperative and should be translated as "only" or "just" (not "however"; it does not introduce a contrast in these cases, but rather a restriction, an emphasis, or a focusing), whereas in v. 17, it introduces an imperfect verb form, which does introduce a contrast (see previous note).

The NIV's rendering here ("Only may the LORD your God be with you") gives the impression that this is the people's wish or blessing for Joshua. However, the verb form behind NIV's "may" is indicative in mood, not jussive, and the clause should therefore be translated, "Only the LORD your God will be with you" (i.e., substituting "will" for "may"). It is a statement of fact, not wish. The verse affirms that, in the end, the Lord will indeed be with Joshua.

1:18 The words in this verse echo the sentiments already expressed several places in the chapter. The statement "Whoever rebels against your word" is literally "Whoever rebels against your mouth."[94] This expression is found previously in Scripture only three times, all referring to the earlier generation of Israelites' rebellions against God's commands (Deut 1:26,43; 9:23). Here, the next generation commits itself, in word at least, to obeying Joshua's commands and to imposing severe sanctions (death) to anyone who would disobey. The final "Be strong and courageous" is the fourth time this exhortation has appeared in the chapter, the first three coming from God himself (vv. 6,7,9).

2. A Foreigner's Welcome (2:1–24)

(1) Rahab's Faith in Action (2:1–8)

¹**Then Joshua son of Nun secretly sent two spies from Shittim. "Go, look over the land," he said, "especially Jericho." So they went and entered the house of a prostitute named Rahab and stayed there.**

²**The king of Jericho was told, "Look! Some of the Israelites have come here tonight to spy out the land."** ³**So the king of Jericho sent this message to Rahab: "Bring out the men who came to you and entered your house, because they have come to spy out the whole land."**

⁴**But the woman had taken the two men and hidden them. She said, "Yes, the men came to me, but I did not know where they had come from.** ⁵**At dusk, when it was time to close the city gate, the men left. I don't know which way they went. Go after them quickly. You may catch up with them."** ⁶**(But she had taken them up to the roof and hidden them under the stalks of flax she had laid out on the roof.)** ⁷**So the men set out in pursuit of the spies on the road that leads to the fords of the Jordan, and as soon as the pursuers had gone out, the gate was shut.**

⁸**Before the spies lay down for the night, she went up on the roof**

---

[94] Hawk misunderstands the *hiphil* of מרה, rendering it as "cause your mouth to rebel" (*Every Promise Fulfilled*, 59). However, the *hiphil* of this verb does not have a causative sense: it means to "shew disobedience, rebelliousness" (BDB, 598), "to behave rebelliously" (*HALOT*, 633).

Chapter 2 consists of a relatively self-contained episode that tells of the Israelite spies' initial contact with Rahab, a Canaanite woman who was a prostitute and the first Canaanite convert to a belief in Israel's God.[95] It shifts the focus from Joshua and Israel to Rahab and the Canaanites, and its events unfold during the three-day period spoken of in 1:11 and 2:22. The chapter is an important bridge linking chaps. 1 and 6: chap. 1 speaks of the Israelites' taking the land of Canaan as something still in the future, and chap. 6 shows the first stage of this taking place when the Israelites actually take Jericho. Chapter 2, where most of the action takes place in Jericho, naturally anticipates chap. 6, where Jericho is actually taken. It also forms a contrast with chap. 7, where Israel's unfaithfulness is exemplified by Achan's sin; conversely, here, Rahab, a Canaanite, is shown to be faithful.

2:1 The author's use of Joshua's full name here signals a new episode. The norm in the book is to call him merely "Joshua" (138 times). Only ten times is "Joshua son of Nun" used, and in fully half of these occasions (including here), the full name is a narrative structuring device.[96] In this section of the book, new episodes consistently are marked grammatically in some way,[97] and this phrase serves that function here.

Joshua dispatched his spies "secretly" *(ḥrš).*[98] Despite his intent that this be secret, the very next verse states that their presence was known immediately to the king of Jericho. As agents of stealth, they were singularly ineffectual![99]

---

[95] Most critical scholars see this chapter as coming from a different hand than chaps. 1 and 3, but they differ concerning whether the chapter is unified internally or is composed of different sources. See the reviews of such positions in Soggin, *Joshua*, 37–38; Woudstra, *Joshua*, 69, n. 2; and especially Butler, *Joshua*, 27–32.

[96] The ten references are in 1:1; 2:1,23; 6:6; 14:1; 17:4; 19:49,51; 21:1; 24:29. Of these ten references, four times the phrase is in conjunction with "Eleazar the priest" in the context of land distribution (14:1; 17:4; 19:51; 21:1) and one other time in connection with the priests (6:6). The remaining five times, it performs a structural function, identifying Joshua in episode-initial or episode-closing statements (1:1; 2:1,23; 19:49; 24:29).

[97] E.g., in 3:1, with a special verb: שׁכם "to get up early [in the morning]"; in 1:1 and 4:1, with a וַיְהִי-plus-time-margin construction; in 5:2, with an initial time marker: "at that time"; in 6:1, with a nominal clause.

[98] The adverb *ḥereš* is found only here in BH; scholarly consensus links it with a verb meaning "to be deaf; to keep silent" (*HALOT*, 357–58; A. E. Hill, "חָרֵשׁ," *NIDOTTE* 2:298).

[99] R. Polzin (*Moses and the Deuteronomist* [Bloomington: Indiana University Press, 1980], 86) sees the sending out of the spies in a negative light, as a sign of timidity and lack of faith: "Joshua timidly sends out spies to reconnoiter the country, and we are immediately alerted that Joshua may not be as strong and resolute as God and the people had encouraged him to be." Hawk's assessment of this is similar (*Every Promise Fulfilled*, 61). However, Calvin long ago anticipated this objection and countered it well: "Are we to approve of [Joshua's] prudence [in sending out spies]? or are we to condemn him for excessive anxiety …? … although it is perfectly obvious that [Joshua] would never have thought of moving the camp unless God had ordered it, it is also probable that in sending the spies he consulted God as to his pleasure in the matter, or that God himself, knowing how much need there was of this additional confirmation, had spontaneously suggested it to the mind of his servant" (J. Calvin, *Commentary on Joshua* [Grand Rapids: Eerdmans, n.d.], 43).

The place from which Joshua sent the spies was Shittim, near the Jordan River.[100] Two earlier episodes are echoed here. (1) This place was where the Israelites had rejected their God earlier and prostituted themselves by consorting with Moabite women and gods at Balaam's instigation (Num 25:1–3; 31:16). (2) Joshua's dispatch of two spies also recalls Moses' sending out of 12 spies into Canaan from the wilderness, a group that included Joshua himself (Num 13–14). That incident ended with a negative report from ten of the spies and the people's rebellion, with the result that they were condemned to wander in the wilderness for forty years until the entire rebellious generation died off (except for Joshua and Caleb).

Given the negative experiences of these earlier episodes, we might wonder whether trouble lay in store for this new spying expedition.[101] However, God himself had ordered the earlier spying expedition (Num 13:1), and here Joshua acted as a leader on God's behalf, in Moses' mold, by ordering the same thing. Also, despite the sexual improprieties that took place earlier at Shittim, and the possibility that vocabulary of the end of Josh 2:1 could connote sexual liaisons (the words "entered" and "stayed there" in v. 1—literally, "came" and "lay there"—are often used elsewhere of sexual intercourse; see, e.g., Gen 6:4; 16:2; 30:3; 34:7; 39:7,10,12),[102] the text here carefully avoids the suggestion that the spies and Rahab had any sexual relations.[103] The verb bw° ("entered") is used commonly for entering a building (e.g., Judg 9:5; 2 Sam 12:20; 2 Kgs 19:1), and when it *is* used to indicate a sexual liaison no direct object (such as "the house") is used; the pattern is for a preposition to follow, e.g., "and Samson went in [entered] *to* her" (Judg 16:1; cf. Gen 6:4; 16:2; 30:3; etc.). Also, when the verb *škb* ("lay there") is used to indicate a sexual liaison, it occurs with a following preposition such as $^{\circ}im$ or $^{\circ}et$ "with,"[104] which is not the case here.

Rahab's house was likely a way station, inn, tavern, or a combination of these. It would have been a logical place for spies to frequent, as a public gath-

---

[100] On Shittim's location, see the commentary on 3:1.

[101] Indeed, Hawk makes much of these data, arguing that the episode is "dark and disturbing" and that Rahab, as a prostitute, "is a synthesis of all that is most threatening to Israel" (*Every Promise Fulfilled*, 60–61). He sees the chapter almost entirely in a negative light, as an example of Israel's disobedience, by consorting with this pagan Canaanite prostitute. However, he ignores the strong message of grace evident here in the promise of protection for Rahab, and he reads into the vocabulary of v. 1 a sexual message that is not truly there, despite his and other scholars' assertions to the contrary (see below). Against this, G. Mitchell judges that the stories of Rahab and the Gibeonites present "a relatively positive image of foreigners" (*Together in the Land: A Reading of the Book of Joshua*, JSOTSup 134 [Sheffield: Sheffield Academic Press, 1993], 187; see also pp. 161–65), although Mitchell accepts uncritically the suggestions about the supposed sexual overtones in the passage.

[102] For more references of such usage, see Hawk, *Every Promise Fulfilled*, 62.

[103] This point is made well by Hess, *Joshua*, 83.

[104] Ibid. See also BDB, 1012.

ering place and a potential source of information, but it is not necessary to suggest that the spies themselves had (or intended to have) a sexual encounter with Rahab.[105] In addition to these points, we can also note that in the early chapters of Joshua, maintaining ritual purity and doing things exactly as God had commended were very important, and, if the spies had acted inappropriately, we should expect some indication of this (as we see when Achan sinned; note 7:1).

The NIV correctly translates Joshua's instructions as "Go, look over the land ... especially Jericho," despite the surface impression given by the Hebrew, which reads (literally), "the land *and* Jericho." Joshua's intent was for them to concentrate their energies and attentions on Jericho, and not the entire land of Canaan, if only because he specified that city and that city only.[106] We can also deduce this from his instructions in 1:11: he certainly would not have told the Israelite leaders that they would be beginning their crossing within three days if his intent was for the spies to reconnoiter the *entire land* of Canaan. We should recall that the earlier spying expedition, of which he was a part, took a full forty days to complete (Num 13:25).

The action in vv. 2–8 moves along quickly and is described in rather choppy Hebrew.[107] It is a straightforward account, however, of events setting the stage for the dramatic conversations of vv. 9–14 and 16–21.

2:2–3 The king of Jericho is prominent in these verses, although he is not named.[108] He was informed by unspecified agents[109] of the Israelite spies' presence in the city (v. 2), and so he sent a message to Rahab demanding that she deliver up the spies because of their intent to spy out the entire land (v. 3).

---

[105] See Hess, *Joshua*, 83–84 and M. Weinfeld, *The Promise of the Land: The Inheritance of the Land of Canaan by the Israelites* (Berkeley: University of California Press, 1993), 142–44, on the existence and function of such inns in Canaan and the ANE. This evidence renders even more plausible the grammatical evidence just noted against a sexual encounter having taken place. The suggestion that this was an inn and not a brothel is common and goes as far back as Josephus (*Ant.* 5.1.2).

[106] This understanding of the *wāw* phrase here, explained by P. Wilton as a *wāw explicativum* and translated by him as "*that is,* Jericho" ("More Cases of the *Waw Explicativum*," *VT* 44 [1994]: 126]), is echoed in many commentators and translations. Among commentators, see, e.g., Gray, *Joshua, Judges, Ruth,* 63; Woudstra, *Joshua,* 69; Soggin, *Joshua,* 36. Among translations, see, e.g., NASB, NIV, NRSV ("especially Jericho") and NJPSV ("the region of Jericho").

[107] The normal narrative verb form—*wāw*-consecutive-plus-prefixing verb—describing normally progressing action is found in only three places in the narrative of these verses: in vv. 2 (וַיֵּאָמֵר), 3 (וַיִּשְׁלַח), and 4 (וַתֹּאמֶר). This is partly because the section is broken up by reported speech in several places (portions of vv. 2–5,9), but also because there are several disjunctive syntactical patterns, as well (vv. 6–8, as well as the "pluperfect" וְהִיא הֶעֱלָתַם in v. 4a [see on v. 4]). As to a possible reason for this choppiness, see the comments on v. 8.

[108] In actuality, he would have been more like a "kinglet," i.e., not a great sovereign over a large empire, like the Egyptian pharaohs or the Assyrian or Babylonian kings. During most of its history, local rule in Canaan was by petty kings whose sovereignty was limited to small kingdoms dominated by one city; they were, in effect, city-states. See the references in the Book of Joshua to kings of such cities as Ai (8:1), Jerusalem (10:1), Hebron, Jarmuth, Lachish, Eglon (10:3), Makkedah (10:28), Gezer (10:33), and Hazor (11:1).

[109] The verb is passive and impersonal here, literally "and it was told to the king of Jericho."

It is interesting that the men and the king assumed the spies were there to spy out the entire land, even though Joshua's interest was more specifically limited to Jericho (see comments on 2:1). These men may have been unaware of this, or, if they knew of it, their exaggerated comments about the entire land may betray some of the hysterical fear and paranoia that gripped the inhabitants of the city that Rahab told the spies about in vv. 9–11. Also interesting is that the spies' presence is noted immediately and that the king of Jericho sent immediately to the very house where they were staying. The king's agents did not tell him her name, yet he directed them at once to Rahab's house. This confirms the author's interest in this section in just telling the bare facts; he omits much that he could have included, because his interest is focused more on the conversations to come in vv. 9–14 and 16–21 (esp. vv. 9–14).

2:4–6 Apparently Rahab knew of the spies' mission and was sympathetic to it,[110] because she had hidden the spies prior to the king's agents' arrival.[111] According to vv. 4–6 she misled the king's agents by lying about what she knew of the spies.[112] Verse 6 is a parenthetical aside,[113] telling us in more detail what we had already known generally from v. 4: the specifics of her hiding the spies under the stalks of flax that she had laid out on the roof.[114]

---

[110] Another example of events unreported in this section, due to the author's specific interests here.

[111] The NIV has two "pluperfect" verbs here (one that expresses a past action that was completed before another past action): "the woman *had taken* the men and *hidden* them" (the NASB and NJPSV also understand the verb in this way). Strictly speaking, these verbs are in the normal narrative sequential verb forms (*waw* consecutive plus prefixing ["imperfect"] verb forms), and so one would expect a translation such as the NRSV's: "But the woman took the two men and hid them." However, it is difficult to countenance a situation in which Rahab, being demanded to produce the spies, would have been able to sequester the men in that very moment. More plausible is imagining her having done this some time previously. This is an example of what has been called "dischronologized narrative" (another example occurs in vv. 15–16). See W. J. Martin, "'Dischronologized' Narrative in the Old Testament," *VTSup* 17 (Leiden: Brill, 1969), 179–86; *IBHS* § 33.2.3a. For a more complete discussion and fuller documentation of this phenomenon, see my "Three Days in Joshua 1–3," *JETS* 41 (1998).

[112] See the following excursus (after v. 14) for ethical issues arising from this lie.

[113] N. Winther-Nielsen calls it an "explanatory background satellite" (*A Functional Discourse Grammar of Joshua: A Computer-assisted Rhetorical Structural Analysis*, Coniectanea Biblica, Old Testament Series 40 [Stockholm: Almqvist & Wiksell, 1995], 126).

[114] Boling makes the intriguing observation that "this would probably have been regarded as quite providential, since it is most likely that flax was not being cultivated in that early period. ... It was, rather, more likely wild flax, the relative scarcity of which would heighten the sense of escape 'by the skin of your teeth'" (*Joshua*, 146). Many scholars believe that flax is mentioned in the Gezer calendar, an extrabiblical calendar listing the seasons of crop harvesting dating to the tenth century B.C., and that this demonstrates that flax *was* cultivated in Canaan during Rahab's time, several centuries earlier (e.g., Soggin, *Joshua*, 41; J. K. Hoffmeier, "פֶּשֶׁת," *NIDOTTE* 3:711). However, Boling's observation carries more weight, since it is based on the careful study by S. Talmon: "The Gezer Calendar and the Seasonal Cycle of Ancient Canaan," *JAOS* 83 (1963): 177–87. Talmon shows in convincing detail that, while flax was cultivated in Egypt and elsewhere, there was a curious lack of such in Canaan during most of the OT period. Thus, the "flax" mentioned here would most likely have been some wild flax that Rahab had laid out for drying.

2:7–8 In response to Rahab's incorrect information, the king's agents set out in hot pursuit of the spies, heading in a logical direction (toward the Jordan), where the spies would likely be returning to report to Joshua across the Jordan. A comical note is sounded, not only in these agents being sent off by Rahab on a futile chase, but also in the statement that the city gate was shut behind them as soon as they left! Since Rahab reported that the spies had just escaped before the gates were to close (v. 5a), the pursuers must have thought that they were hot on their trail.[115] This note also reinforces the picture of Jericho as a heavily guarded city and it explains why Rahab let the spies out of the city through her window (v. 15) rather than escorting them out of the gate.

Verse 8 shows that the men were not yet asleep, even though they had been lying under the stalks of flax, and it shows that the statement in v. 1 about "staying" in Jericho is an anticipatory one describing a sleepless stay (and, when it was all said and done, a rather short one, as well!).

The syntax of vv. 7–8 (indeed, vv. 6–8) is rather herky-jerky. That is, the narrative does not flow easily, but diverges first here, then there, in fits and starts, with several back references and asides.[116] It is very plausible that the text's author is making an intentional point by this, deliberately stumbling over himself in a literary sense, in order to reach what in his mind is the heart of his story, namely Rahab's great confession of faith in vv. 9–11. He can hardly wait to tell his story and his style becomes more breathless as this great confession nears.[117]

(2) Rahab's Faith in Words (2:9–14)

9and said to them, "I know that the LORD has given this land to you and that a great fear of you has fallen on us, so that all who live in this country are melting in fear because of you. 10We have heard how the LORD dried up the water of the Red Sea for you when you came out of Egypt, and what you did to Sihon and Og, the two kings of the Amorites east of the Jordan, whom you completely destroyed. 11When we heard of it, our hearts melted and everyone's courage failed because of you, for the LORD your God is God in heaven above and on the earth below.

---

[115] Boling renders הָרֹדְפִים (NIV: "the pursuers") as "the posse" throughout this chapter (*Joshua*, 138–39). This delightful word choice helps to capture the incompetent and futile group mind-set of this misguided band of king's agents. Butler also notes the following comical irony: "The royal messengers are transformed into 'pursuers' though the game they pursue lies behind them at the starting gate" (*Joshua*, 32).

[116] See Winther-Nielsen (*Discourse Grammar of Joshua*, 125–28) for the most detailed consideration of the narrative flow and logic here.

[117] This phenomenon of the literary style or texture changing to reflect something important in the story has been noted by many observers. See, e.g., R. Alter's observations on David's mourning for Bathsheba's dead son (*The Art of Biblical Narrative* [New York: Basic, 1981], 128–29 or S. Bar-Efrat's analysis of the story of Amnon's rape of Tamar (*Narrative Art in the Bible*, JSOTSup 70 [Sheffield: Almond, 1989], 239–82, esp. 260–61 and 264–66).

¹²Now then, please swear to me by the LORD that you will show kindness to my family, because I have shown kindness to you. Give me a sure sign ¹³that you will spare the lives of my father and mother, my brothers and sisters, and all who belong to them, and that you will save us from death."

¹⁴"Our lives for your lives!" the men assured her. "If you don't tell what we are doing, we will treat you kindly and faithfully when the LORD gives us the land."

The New Testament rightly commends Rahab for her faith, emphasizing what she did for the Israelite spies: "By faith the prostitute Rahab, because she welcomed the spies, was not killed with those who were disobedient" (Heb 11:31), and "Was not even Rahab the prostitute considered righteous for what she did when she gave lodging to the spies and sent them off in a different direction?" (Jas 2:25). In Josh 2:4–8, we see her faith outwardly at work in precisely this way. However, her faith was not merely external: 2:9–11 shows her speaking words that reveal a fundamental change in her belief orientation as she embraced Israel's God as her own.[118]

2:9–11   These verses furnish information about Israel's reputation, the Canaanites' fear, and Rahab's faith.[119] Clearly, Israel's reputation had preceded them: Rahab knew that Israel's God had given her people's land to Israel (v. 9), and the entire land was melting in fear because of Israel (vv. 9,11).[120] God already had dramatically delivered the Israelites in several ways in its brief history as a nation, and Rahab mentioned two of these great events in v. 10: God's drying up of the Red Sea (Exodus 14) and the victories over two kings east of the Jordan, Sihon and Og (Num 21:21–35). Also, not only the people of Jericho had heard of the Israelites' God, but "all who live in this country" (v. 9; literally,

---

[118] Verses 9–11 represent the heart of the passage, both in content and in structure. On the passage's structure, see Davis (*No Falling Words,* 25–26), who sees a concentric structure highlighting Rahab's confession of faith:

Commission by Joshua (v. 1a)

    Arrival/Concern: Protection of the spies (vv. 2–7)

        Confession of Faith (vv. 8–14)

    Escape/Concern: Protection of Rahab and family (vv. 15–21)

Return to Joshua (vv. 22–24)

[119] Many scholars believe that vv. 9–11 were inserted by the "Deuteronomist" hundreds of years later and that Rahab never actually spoke these words. Butler presents a clear articulation of this view: "The one thing that does appear to be clear is that the Deuteronomist has introduced his own theological conception into the mouth of Rahab in vv. 9–11. The tradition of the fear of the nations, the drying up of the waters…, the two kings of the Amorites, and the divine title (12b) all bear Deuteronomic stamp. … Here then is pre-Deuteronomic literature given a Deuteronomic stamp" (Butler, *Joshua,* 31). The text itself, of course, clearly states that Rahab did speak these words.

[120] Indeed, the song that the Israelites sang on the occasion of their deliverance from the Egyptians predicted precisely this sort of terror: "The people of Canaan will melt away, terror and dread will fall upon them" (Exod 15:15b–16a).

"all the inhabitants of the land"). This fact was confirmed later, when the Gibeonites mentioned the very same episodes to Joshua (9:9–10).

Rahab's statement in v. 11b bears some reflection, for it is a most remarkable statement in the mouth of a foreigner. Not only did she affirm that this— her own land—was to be given to the Israelites and that Israel's God had done some impressive things for his people (vv. 9–11a), but she went further than that and affirmed that "the LORD your God is God in heaven above and on the earth below" (v. 11b). This statement is remarkable for at least three reasons.

First, on its own merits, Rahab affirmed that Israel's God had dominion over the realms of the heavens and the earth—an extremely broad scope that surely encompassed the domains of many of the gods that her people worshiped. We know from many biblical passages that the Canaanites worshiped many gods (see Exod 23:24,32–33; 34:15; Deut 11:16,28; 12:2–3,30–31; etc.). This is also clear from extrabiblical materials, ranging from Canaanite religious texts about their gods to temples and religious artifacts that have been recovered from archaeological digs.[121] Here was Rahab, a Canaanite prostitute who presumably knew her culture's religious traditions, affirming that Israel's God ruled over the very heavens and earth that her own religious traditions asserted belonged to Baal, Asherah, and others.

Second, Rahab stated that Israel's God, Yahweh, was indeed (the only) God: "the LORD your God is God." "Yahweh" was the true God's personal name, just as "Baal" or "Asherah," "Marduk," or "Ishtar" were the personal names of Canaanite and Babylonian gods, respectively. Thus, when Rahab stated that "Yahweh your God is God," she was stating that Baal, Asherah, and the rest were not true gods. This affirmation echoes similar language found several times in the Pentateuch, where God's exclusive claims to sovereignty (e.g., Deut 4:35; 10:17) or revelations about his character (e.g., Deut 7:9; 10:17) are found.

Third, Rahab's words become even more significant when we realize that the last part of her affirmation—the phrase "in the heavens above and the earth below"—is found only three times prior to this, all in contexts that affirm God's exclusive claims to sovereignty.

> You shall not make for yourself an idol in the form of anything in heaven above or on the earth beneath or in the waters below (Exod 20:4).
> Acknowledge and take to heart this day that the Lord is God in heaven above and on the earth below. There is no other (Deut 4:39).
> You shall not make for yourself an idol in the form of anything in heaven above or on the earth beneath or in the waters below (Deut 5:8).

Two of these references (the first and third) prohibit making or worshiping

---

[121] On "Canaanite Religion and Culture," see my *Introduction to the Old Testament Historical Books* (Chicago: Moody, 1993), 106–7, and the bibliography in n. 24 there. See further J. Day, "Canaanite Religion," *ABD* 1:831–37, and bibliography there.

idols. They are from the Ten Commandments and establish God's exclusive claim to worship. The other reference states flatly: "There is no other [god]."

Thus, when we read these words coming from Rahab's mouth, we cannot escape the implications: she was doing far more than merely trying to save her skin or that of her family. She was acknowledging that this God she had heard about was the one and only true God, the only one—out of dozens that she as a good Canaanite knew about—who was worthy of worship and allegiance.

This constitutes her statement of faith in words. This is surely what gave impetus to her actions in vv. 4–8. Now we know why she did what she did: she may have been afraid, as were all the other Canaanites, but she also had come to believe in her heart that there was only one true God. This God's actions on behalf of his people had convinced her, and she had changed her life and belief system because of it.

How did Rahab know all of this? How did she know enough to make such a strong declaration of faith, using the very words of the Israelites' revealed Scripture? The answer is that we do not know. Although many scholars would assert that she never said these words at all, it is not difficult to imagine Israel's reputation preceding it in the way Rahab described. More difficult is her intimate knowledge of specific language from the Pentateuch. However, given that her initial knowledge of Israel's God developed into a faith displayed in deed (vv. 4–8) and word (vv. 9–11), we can perhaps imagine that she had taken further steps to learn about this God, that she was at least passingly familiar with the exclusive claims that this God made, and that she used language affirming this in a simple, yet profound statement.[122]

One further observation can be made about Rahab before leaving these verses. She is a prime example of a foreigner who responded in faith to Israel's God. In the New Testament, Rahab is included with four other women in Jesus' genealogy in Matthew 1: Tamar, Ruth, Bathsheba, and Mary. All but Mary were foreigners who became part of Israel. This reflects the inclusiveness intended in the Abrahamic covenant, whereby God stated that he would bring blessing to the nations—to those who were not descendants of Abra-

---

[122] The possibility that her words recorded here are not the sum total of the exact words she spoke must also be considered, with some caution. As Woudstra states, "We believe the substance of these words to be truly that of Rahab. However, her conversation with the spies may well have been longer than actually reported. If so, a summary by the Israelite writer had to be supplied. In such an outline, various thoughts of the Pentateuchal books may have influenced the report, but not to such an extent as to cast doubt upon the basic veracity of the words and on the sentiments expressed" (*Joshua*, 73). This issue of the verbatim citation of words spoken is addressed well by P. D. Feinberg with respect to the words of Jesus in the Gospels: "*Inerrancy does not demand that the* Logia Jesu *(the sayings of Jesus) contain the* ipsissima verba *(the exact words) of Jesus, only the* ipsissima vox *(the exact voice).* ... When a New Testament writer cites the sayings of Jesus, it need not be that Jesus spoke those exact words. ... It is thus impossible for us to know which of the sayings are direct quotes, which are indirect discourse, and which are even freer renderings" ("The Meaning of Inerrancy," in N. L. Geisler, ed., *Inerrancy* [Grand Rapids: Zondervan, 1979], 301 [emphasis Feinberg]).

ham, like Rahab—through Abraham and his descendants (see Gen 12:2–3). If the example of Nineveh is any indication (Jonah 3–4), then we can presume that Jericho could have been spared destruction if it had demonstrated faith in God, casting itself upon God's mercy in the same way as did the inhabitants of Nineveh, or as did Rahab. The inhabitants of Jericho presumably had the same opportunity to embrace Israel's God that Rahab did, but only she seized the opportunity, and consequently only she and her family were spared destruction.

2:12–13   Because of her "kindness" *(ḥesed)*[123] to the spies, Rahab asked the spies to take an oath of protection for her and her household. Oath-taking was a serious practice, as illustrated by the Israelites' ill-advised oath with the Gibeonites that they could not take back (9:15–21).

Some scholars have noted that Israel's interactions with Rahab were a violation of God's commands not to enter into any relations at all with the Canaanites, and certainly not to make any promises to them or treaties with them. In Deut 7:1–5 and 20:16–18, for example, God gave explicit instructions about not entering into any treaties with the peoples of the land of Canaan, but he ordered them to annihilate its inhabitants completely. R. Polzin thus judges that the spies' co-mingling with Rahab—specifically the promise they made to her in vv. 14,17,20—is "in direct disobedience to the Mosaic rules for holy war in Deuteronomy."[124] Hawk is harsher by far.[125] For him, almost every aspect of the story of Rahab is "dark and disturbing. The entire incident relates a situation expressly forbidden to Israel and articulates an opposition to the introductory affirmations of obedience [in chap. 1]."[126] Rahab represents everything that threatens Israel: she is a (dominating and aggressive) woman, a prostitute, and a Canaanite. Her request for amnesty in vv. 12–13 is simply another example of her domination and aggressiveness because of its bold and insistent language,[127] and the spies' agreement to her "demands" ensures disaster, from Hawk's perspective: "the two Israelite spies have ... been mastered and ensnared by their Canaanite counterpart."[128]

---

[123] This word is theologically rich and is translated in many different ways, according to context: "kindness," "mercy," "steadfast love," "loyalty," "faithfulness," etc. There is a strong relational aspect to the word's use, in describing human-human relationships (as here) and, more frequently, the divine-human relationship. See H.-J. Zobel, "חֶסֶד," *TDOT* 5:44–64; D. A. Baer and R. P. Gordon, "חסד," *NIDOTTE* 2:211–18.

[124] Polzin, *Moses and the Deuteronomist*, 86.

[125] Hawk, *Every Promise Fulfilled*, 59–71.

[126] Ibid., 60.

[127] The language is indeed insistent, but it can be explained by the urgency of the situation and Rahab's genuine concern for her family, impelled by her newly expressed faith in a new God, not by reference to her "dominance" and "mastery" over the passive Israelite spies.

[128] Hawk, *Every Promise Fulfilled*, 68.

Both scholars have rightly noted that Israel was expressly forbidden by God to enter into covenantal agreements with Canaanites. The story of Israel's treaty with the Gibeonites in chap. 9 vividly highlights the pitfalls of this, and the Book of Judges is replete with examples of the consequences of Israel's failures to drive out all the Canaan and disentangle themselves with them.

However, the story of Rahab is of a far different nature. The crucial difference is Rahab's confession of faith in Israel's God. By this, she made herself an Israelite, so to speak. She chose to cast her lot with Israel's God, not the Canaanites' gods. Prior to this confession of faith, the spies showed no intentions of entering into any treaties or agreements with her or any other Canaanite. However, her confession of faith made all the difference. She was, in effect, no longer a Canaanite. Thus, the spies were not guilty of the gross disobedience that these scholars accuse them of. Her presence in the book of Joshua is a positive feature, displaying the outworkings of the Abrahamic covenant, God's inclusive interest in all who would confess him as sovereign Lord, and his providential care for his own people.

2:14 The spies solemnized this agreement with Rahab by putting their own lives on the line if Rahab and her family were harmed. However, they added a condition: Rahab was not to betray them. Then, and only then, would they be able to guarantee that she would be treated well. They responded to Rahab with reassuring words ("we will treat you kindly and faithfully"), echoing words she had used in her request to them. Their pledge of their lives was in effect the "sure sign" that Rahab had asked for.[129]

EXCURSUS: ON RAHAB'S LIE

A troublesome aspect of the Rahab story for many people is that she apparently uttered a bold-faced lie by telling the king of Jericho's messengers that the Israelite spies had fled when in fact they were hiding in her own house (Josh 2:4), and she was never censured for it. In fact, she and her family were spared by the Israelites (Josh 6:25) and the New Testament twice commends her in very glowing terms (Heb 11:31; Jas 2:25). How could she have been accorded such a positive treatment in the face of this lie that she told?

Generations of Christian ethicists have considered Rahab's case carefully in constructing broader systems of ethics. In her case, two absolute principles of moral behavior seem to have come into conflict: (1) the principle that it is wrong to tell a lie and (2) the principle that one must protect human life. In Rahab's case, it appears that, in order to save the spies' life, she had no alternative but to lie. Or, conversely, had she told the truth and revealed the spies' position, their lives

---

[129] The two words here in v. 14 are וֶאֱמֶת חֶסֶד. The first (חֶסֶד: NIV "kindly") echoes precisely Rahab's request in v. 12 ("show kindness"), while the second (אֱמֶת: NIV "faithfully") is also found in Rahab's words in v. 12, in the phrase "a *sure* (אֱמֶת) sign."

would most likely have been forfeited and Israel's inheritance of the land may have been jeopardized.

Generally, orthodox Christian ethicists argue one of three positions concerning situations in which Biblical principles of behavior seem to conflict with each other.[130] The first position involves what many call "conflicting absolutes" or "the lesser of two evils." Christians holding this position argue that in a fallen world, sometimes two or more absolute principles of moral behavior will conflict absolutely, and that there is no recourse in the situation but to sin.[131] In such a case, the Christian's obligation is to commit the lesser of the two sins, and then to repent of it. So, for Rahab, the lesser sin was to lie, thus sparing the spies' life, but she was wrong to lie. She also would have been wrong if she told the truth, resulting in the spies' exposure and death. Thus, she faced a situation in which it was impossible to avoid sinning. This is not God's ideal, and it may seem unfair, but it is the best humans can expect in a fallen, sinful world. This position is sometimes called "realism" by its proponents, since it attempts to deal with situations in the real (fallen) world: it admits that people might sometimes be compelled to sin, and it encourages them to cast themselves on God's mercy to forgive that sin (see 1 John 1:9).[132] Martin Luther's impatience with what he saw as an undue fastidiousness toward sin is often quoted in this regard: "If you are a preacher of grace, then preach a true grace and not a fictitious grace. ... Be a sinner and sin boldly, but believe and rejoice in Christ more boldly, for he is victorious over sin, death, and the world."[133]

The second position is often labeled "hierarchicalism" or "graded absolutism." Here, many Christians argue that there is an ordered hierarchy of absolutes, such that some values have priority over others. In cases of conflict, where it is impossible[134] to obey both commands, one should act according to the greater good (or the higher norm), and is thus "exempt" from the lower norm. Thus, in some strictly defined situations, certain actions usually labeled as sins are not in fact sins, that is, their usual nature as sins is set aside, redefined. In Rahab's case,

---

[130] Surveys of the wider range of positions may be found in many works, including N. L. Geisler, *Ethics: Alternatives and Issues* (Grand Rapids: Zondervan, 1971), 28–136; id., *Christian Ethics: Options and Issues* (Grand Rapids: Baker, 1989), 17–132; J. E. Trull, *Walking in the Way: An Introduction to Christian Ethics* (Nashville: Broadman & Holman, 1997), 103–31, 307–13.

[131] J. W. Montgomery concludes that "our sin in Adam has created an ethical mess from which we sometimes cannot extricate ourselves" (personal communication, February 9, 1998).

[132] This position is held especially (although not exclusively) among Lutherans. See the representative treatments by E. J. Carnell, *Christian Commitment* (New York: Macmillan, 1957), 223–30; H. Thielecke, *Theological Ethics: Foundations* (Philadelphia: Fortress, 1966), vol. 1 (on lying per se, see pp. 520–66); Montgomery, *Human Rights and Human Dignity* (Grand Rapids: Zondervan, 1986), 178–79 and nn. 346–48, 376 (pp. 300, 302); id., in J. Fletcher and J. W. Montgomery, *Situation Ethics* (Minneapolis: Bethany Fellowship, 1972), passim.

[133] M. Luther, "Letter to Philip Melanchthon, August 1, 1521," in *Luther's Works*, vol. 48 (Philadelphia: Fortress, 1963), 281–82, quoted in R. Higginson, *Dilemmas: A Christian Approach to Moral Decision Making* (Louisville: Westminster/John Knox, 1988), 131.

[134] Hierarchicalists would say that it *is* impossible to obey both, while nonconflicting absolutists (see next paragraph) would say that it only *appears* impossible.

the greater good was to save the spies' life rather than to tell the truth, and thus she did not sin in telling the lie, because she was exempted from it by the higher norm of saving lives. Biblical support for this is adduced from cases where it appears that God sanctioned breaking of some laws in favor of following others, such as (1) the Hebrew midwives' lying to the pharaoh in order to save the Israelite boys (Exod 1:15–21); (2) Jesus' injunction that people should hate their fathers, mothers, wives, children, brothers, and sisters and follow him instead (Luke 14:26); or (3) Jesus' statement that there were some matters of the law—such as tithing of certain spices—that were less important than others—such as justice, mercy, and faithfulness (Matt 23:23–24).[135]

The third position speaks of "nonconflicting absolutes," whereby, in any given situation, seemingly opposed absolute norms do not conflict in reality. In this view, God does not set aside or exempt certain absolutes in certain situations, but he holds to them absolutely. In situations where these may seem to conflict, there will always be some "third way" that avoids sin. Biblical support for this comes from Paul's strong rejection of the "ends-justifies-the-means" argument of those who would say, "Let us do evil that good may result" (Rom 3:7–8), as well as his assurance that, when Christians are tempted to sin, "God is faithful; he will not let you be tempted beyond what you can bear. But when you are tempted, he will also provide a way out so that you can stand up under it" (1 Cor 10:13). In Rahab's case, then, she should not have lied, but she should have trusted God to provide for her a way to protect the spies that did not necessitate sinning.[136]

Each of these positions takes the Bible seriously and attempts to do justice to Biblical principles, yet each has aspects that appear to be unsatisfactory, as well, at least on the surface. Concerning the first position, it is difficult to conceive of God's holding people responsible for sinning when their only choice is to do just that. Furthermore, if Jesus was in all ways tempted as we are, and yet remained sinless (Heb 4:15), then certainly he would not have committed a lesser sin in order to avoid a greater one.[137]

---

[135] This position is widely held among evangelical Christians and is defended in Geisler, *Ethics*, 114–36; id., *Christian Ethics*, 113–32; M. J. Erickson, *Relativism in Contemporary Christian Ethics* (Grand Rapids: Baker, 1974), 129–53; J. J. Davis, *Evangelical Ethics: Issues Facing the Church Today* (Phillipsburg, N.J.: Presbyterian & Reformed, 1985), 12–16; P. Barnes, "Was Rahab's Lie a Sin?" *RTR* 54 (1995): 1–9; among many others.

[136] This position is also widely held among evangelical Christians. See the representative treatments by J. Murray, *Principles of Conduct: Aspects of Biblical Ethics* (Grand Rapids: Eerdmans, 1957), esp. pp. 123–48; E. W. Lutzer, *The Morality Gap: An Evangelical Response to Situation Ethics* (Chicago: Moody, 1972), 75–113; W. C. Kaiser, Jr., *Toward Old Testament Ethics* (Grand Rapids: Zondervan, 1983), esp. pp. 222–34 and 271–74; id., *Hard Sayings of the Old Testament* (Downers Grove: InterVarsity, 1988), 95–97; R. V. Rakestraw, "Ethical Choices: A Case for Non-Conflicting Absolutism," *CTR* 2 (1988): 239–67. Two early Church writers who took this position with respect to the issues of truth-telling and lying were Augustine and Thomas Aquinas; see Augustine, *On Lying* and *To Consentius: Against Lying*, in P. Schaff, ed., *A Select Library of the Nicene and Post-Nicene Fathers of the Christian Church* (Grand Rapids: Eerdmans, 1980 reprint), 3:455–500; Thomas Aquinas, *The Summa Theologica* (London: Burns Oates and Washbourne, 1922), 12:76–98.

[137] See Geisler, *Christian Ethics*, 106–10, on this point.

For this reason, many Christians adopt the second position, in which God "exempts" people from certain sins in certain situations. This is attractive because it does indeed appear that some biblical values are more important than others or that some sins are lesser than others (Matt 23:23). However, whether sins are greater or lesser, they are still sins. As Lutzer points out, "Nowhere is there any indication in the Scriptures that sin has not been committed when a moral law was violated because someone was acting with a higher norm in view."[138] Furthermore, nowhere does the Bible lay out an ordered hierarchy of values or exemptions, and so human judgments necessarily play a part in establishing these, introducing an element of human subjectivity at a critical point in making ethical decisions. Although this position is different in many important ways from the relativistic, situation ethics of J. Fletcher, for whom the only guiding ethical norm is the law of love,[139] they also are similar in several ways.[140]

The third position is often criticized as naïve, since in Rahab's case, it appears she had no choice: lie or the spies would die. For us—operating with the cool light of hindsight and in the non-threatening comfort of our homes, offices, classrooms, or churches—to condemn Rahab for lying in the heat of a very real, stressful, and life-threatening situation is to condemn her unjustly. Many claim that it is a naïve legalism that would require her to find another way out in such a situation.

Despite some apparent problems, the position here is that "nonconflicting absolutism" would best seem to fit the scriptural data, entailing the fewest difficulties. The ends do not justify the means (Rom 3:7–8), as some hierarchicalists seem to argue.[141] To act otherwise shows a lack of faith in God's ability to protect or provide, even in desperate situations. To act otherwise also fails to recognize that some moral norms are indeed absolutes, for which the Bible gives no exceptions (e.g., the prohibition against lying), while others are provided with exceptions (e.g., the command not to kill has the exception in cases of capital punishment, e.g., in Exod 21:12–17 or Gen 9:6). The crucial difference from hierarchicalism is that the exceptions stem from God himself, not human judgments or extrapolations.[142]

---

[138] Lutzer, *The Morality Gap*, 101.

[139] J. Fletcher, *Situation Ethics* (Philadelphia: Westminster, 1966).

[140] Orthodox Christian ethicists who hold to this position differ strongly with Fletcher concerning most key points, and rightly so. However, their positions do approximate each other's in several important ways. The most extended critique of hierarchicalism is R. A. G. du Preez, "A Critical Study of Norman Geisler's Ethical Hierarchicalism" (Th.D. diss., University of South Africa, 1997). Du Preez concludes that hierarchicalism "turns out to be a relativistic ethical scheme that operates in a utilitarian way" and that "in its actual application it ends up with only one contentless 'absolute,' which is really no absolute at all" (pp. 298–99). In this system, "there is no real difference between an 'intention' [Geisler's term] and an 'end' [Fletcher's term]" (p. 299). (I thank Dr. du Preez for making available to me the major portions of his dissertation.)

[141] Otherwise, for an extreme example, one might argue that Judas was justified in betraying Jesus since Jesus' death was part of God's plan for humanity and great good came out of it. But Jesus demolished that argument: "The Son of Man will go just as it is written about him. But woe to that man who betrays the Son of Man! It would be better for him if he had not been born" (Matt 26:24).

[142] See Lutzer, *The Morality Gap*, 106–7.

In Rahab's case, then, she should not have told the lie, since the Bible is very clear about lying. It roots truth-telling in God's very nature, because he is truth (e.g., John 14:6; 1 John 5:20) and he cannot lie (Titus 1:2; Heb 6:18). Truth comes from God (Ps 43:3), and his word is truth (John 17:17). As we are to be holy because God is holy, so we are to be truthful because he is truthful.[143] Lying is uniformly condemned in both Old and New Testaments (e.g., Lev 19:11; Prov 12:22; Eph 4:25).

The best examples used by hierarchicalists to argue that lying is sometimes justified are the cases of Rahab and the Hebrew midwives in Egypt. In the latter instance, the midwives did not obey the pharaoh, who had ordered them to kill Hebrew male infants, and they lied to him about it (Exod 1:17–19).[144] Many Christians point out that the text commends the midwives, by stating that God was kind to them and gave them families of their own (Exod 1:20–21). However, a careful reading of the text shows that the author's central concern was the midwives' reverence for God (their "fear" of him: 1:17,21), and the only causative construction here is in connection with this reverence: "And because *(kî)* the midwives feared God, he gave them families of their own" (1:21).[145] God was kind to them (v. 20) and gave to them abundantly (v. 21) because they feared him rather than the pharaoh (vv. 17,21), not because they lied.

In Rahab's case, since the New Testament commends her so highly, many Christians argue that this justifies lying in some instances. Hebrews 11:31 states that "By faith the prostitute Rahab, because she welcomed the spies, was not killed with those who were disobedient." James 2:25 says that "Was not even Rahab the prostitute considered righteous for what she did when she gave lodging to the spies and sent them off in a different direction?" However, here again, a careful reading shows that nowhere is Rahab's lie per se commended.[146] Her faith is rightfully commended, and her actions in helping the spies are, as well. The James passage seems especially explicit. It mentions two actions: (1) giving lodging to the spies and (2) sending them out by a safer route. It does not mention Rahab's lying, or even her "protection" of the men accomplished by the lie. James very well might have omitted mentioning the deception deliberately, to avoid the appearance of condoning it, since the passage is fairly explicit otherwise.

---

[143] Murray, *Principles of Conduct*, 127.

[144] Some have argued that they merely told a partial truth, since, when they claimed that Hebrew women gave birth before the midwives arrived, this may have been true in some cases. However, it is unlikely that this was true in every case.

[145] The NIV is misleading in v. 20, when it renders the *wāw*-consecutive at the beginning of the verse as "So" rather than simply "and," implying that God was kind to the midwives *because of* the lie they had told in v. 19. There is no grammatically causal relationship between vv. 19 and 20. See NASB and NJPSV, which correctly render the *wāw* here as "and."

[146] If being sinless were a requirement of an individual's having been listed as a hero of the faith in Hebrews 11, the chapter would have been extraordinarily short. We know of the sins of several other individuals in that chapter, as well (e.g., Noah, Abraham, Jacob, Moses, Samson, Jephthah, David).

Many have objected that such analyses of the two episodes are wrongheaded and overly legalistic, since the midwives' and Rahab's lies were part and parcel of the deliverance that they were able to effect. However, this ignores the points noted earlier about truth's being rooted in God's very own nature, and Paul's arguments that the ends do not justify the means (Rom 3:7–8) and that God promises deliverance from the necessity of sinning (1 Cor 10:13). Also, if Christ was in all ways tempted as we are and yet remained sinless (Heb 4:15), as we noted above, then surely he faced difficult situations and emerged sinless. There is no record that he broke (or "transcended") lower norms in favor of higher ones— how much less so that he ever committed the lesser of two sins!—except perhaps in matters involving the ceremonial laws (such as supposed sabbath breaking, e.g., in Mark 2:23–27). Here again, however, the exceptions come from God himself, not human judgments or extrapolations.[147]

How could Rahab have avoiding lying and still protected the spies? We do not know exactly; we may only speculate. Kaiser, for example, suggests that "Rahab should have hidden the spies well and then refused to answer the question whether she was hiding them. She could, for instance, have volunteered, 'Come in and have a look around,' while simultaneously praying that God would have made the searchers especially obtuse."[148] Even in the tragic, hypothetical case in which, had Rahab not lied, and the spies had been found out, we can note that even protection of human life is not the highest good. If that were the case, there would never had been any Christian martyrs or there would never be any need to lay down one's life for someone else. To lie and deny the faith would be justified as reasonable under the circumstances, and yet the Bible and Christian history are replete with examples where people chose death over betraying God or others.[149]

One further factor must be considered here. Christian ethicists of almost all varieties agree that sometimes people have forfeited their right to know the truth, and that it is legitimate at times to conceal the truth, even if it is not permissible to lie outright.[150] Many argue that warfare constitutes a special case in which lying is permissible, in which opposing combatants do not have a right to know the full truth.[151] Thus, Rahab, since the Canaanites ostensibly were at war with Israel, did not sin by lying to the Canaanites. The gap between hierarchicalists and non-conflicting absolutists in such a case appears to narrow considerably, since the latter acknowledge—by appealing to the special conditions of warfare

---

[147] See Lutzer, *The Morality Gap*, 111–12, on the issue of Christ's temptation.

[148] Kaiser, *Hard Questions*, 97.

[149] Lutzer, *The Morality Gap*, 109–10.

[150] Even ethicists arguing for non-conflicting absolutes acknowledge this. See, e.g., Murray, *Principles of Conduct*, 139–40,146–47; Kaiser, *Toward Old Testament Ethics*, 225–27. Concerning what constitutes a lie, Augustine's definition is foundational: a lie is "a false signification with will of deceiving" (Augustine, *Against Lying*, 494). Or, as he states elsewhere, "that man lies, who has one thing in his mind and utters another in words, or by signs of whatever kind" (id., *On Lying*, 458). See further Kaiser, *Toward Old Testament Ethics*, 222–28 and bibliography therein.

[151] E.g., Erickson, *Relativism in Contemporary Christian Ethics*, 151; L. B. Smedes, *Mere Morality* (Grand Rapids: Eerdmans, 1983), 232–33; R. McQuilkin, *An Introduction to Biblical Ethics* (Wheaton: Tyndale House, 1989), 433–34.

and certain people's right to know the truth or not—what the former hold on a different basis, namely, that higher norms come into play here.[152]

However, even if one grants the assumption that warfare requires different norms—an assumption not clearly taught in the Scriptures in any case—it is not clear that warfare for the Israelites in Joshua's day required the same suspension of norms. God himself was to be Israel's warrior, and even Rahab the Canaanite knew this. She acknowledged the facts that had the entire land of Canaan melting with terror: that Israel's God had given it the land, and that he had gone before it in parting the waters of the Red Sea and in defeating Sihon and Og (Josh 2:9–11). Over and over again in Joshua (and Judges: see especially the story of Gideon), God acted as Israel's warrior. Israel needed scarcely to fight, as God routed its enemies. This is something that Rahab would have known, given her intimate knowledge of Israel, its God, and its history to that point (see below, on vv. 9–11), and thus her lie betrayed a lack of trust in this God, to whom we see her committing her life (commendably so!). Her sin was not only the lie per se, but also a lack of trust in God. The elders of Israel who asked Samuel for a king "to lead us and to go out before us and fight our battles" (1 Sam 8:20) also sinned in this way. They (and she) did not trust God to provide for and protect them. They attempted to solve the problem by looking to a military-style king, and she did so by lying.

Thus, in evaluating Rahab, we must render a mixed verdict, one that condemns her lie and momentary lack of trust in God, but one that commends her faith, both in deed and in word. As Calvin stated, "those who hold what is called a dutiful lie to be altogether excusable, do not sufficiently consider how precious truth is in the sight of God. Therefore, although our purpose be to assist our brethren, to consult for their safety and relieve them, it never can be lawful to lie, because that cannot be right which is contrary to the nature of God. And God is truth. And still the act of Rahab is not devoid of the praise of virtue, although it is not spotlessly pure. For it often happens that while the saints study to hold the right path, they deviate into circuitous courses."[153] It was to Rahab's credit, however—and to God's— that her clear and enduring faith in Israel's God prevailed in the end over her momentary lapse into a lie. God judged her ultimately by her enduring faith, not by her lie (Heb 11:31; Jas 2:25).

(3) Sealing the Agreement (2:15–24)

[15]So she let them down by a rope through the window, for the house she lived in was part of the city wall. [16]Now she had said to them, "Go to the hills so the pursuers will not find you. Hide yourselves there three days until they return, and then go on your way."

---

[152] Geisler makes this point particularly forcefully (*Christian Ethics*, 91–92), as does C. Curran, who notes that the critical question is the definition of lying, and that situationalists and nonconflicting absolutists "can agree on the question of truth telling in particular situations" (C. Curran, "Dialogue with Joseph Fletcher," *The Homiletical and Pastoral Review* 67 [1967]: 829, quoted in Erickson, *Relativism in Contemporary Christian Ethics*, 151, n. 15).

[153] Calvin, *Commentaries on the Book of Joshua*, 47.

[17]The men said to her, "This oath you made us swear will not be binding on us [18]unless, when we enter the land, you have tied this scarlet cord in the window through which you let us down, and unless you have brought your father and mother, your brothers and all your family into your house. [19]If anyone goes outside your house into the street, his blood will be on his own head; we will not be responsible. As for anyone who is in the house with you, his blood will be on our head if a hand is laid on him. [20]But if you tell what we are doing, we will be released from the oath you made us swear."

[21]"Agreed," she replied. "Let it be as you say." So she sent them away and they departed. And she tied the scarlet cord in the window.

[22]When they left, they went into the hills and stayed there three days, until the pursuers had searched all along the road and returned without finding them. [23]Then the two men started back. They went down out of the hills, forded the river and came to Joshua son of Nun and told him everything that had happened to them. [24]They said to Joshua, "The LORD has surely given the whole land into our hands; all the people are melting in fear because of us."

After securing the men's pledge of protection, Rahab helped them to escape by letting the spies down through the window of her house using a rope. We read in this section more details of the oath of protection, including Rahab's responsibilities of putting a scarlet cord in her window and bringing her entire family into her house. The spies then hid in the hills for three days until their pursuers gave up looking for them and went home. Then the men returned to Joshua and told him that the inhabitants of the land were terrified of them, and that the Lord was indeed giving them the land.

2:15   The exact nature of Rahab's house is unclear. Some Bible versions place her house "on" the wall (e.g., KJV, NASB), but the Hebrew preposition here is b-, which is the normal word for "in." Two different words for "wall" are used here as well; the phrase here might be rendered as "in the double walls.[154] This would call to mind the defensive fortifications found in many cities in biblical times, called "casemate" walls, in which a double wall was erected, with cross-walls built to create chambers that were then filled with rubble for strengthening, or else made into storage areas or living quarters.[155] Rahab's family may have lived in one of these residences, although her window must have been rather high, since she let the spies down using a rope. Perhaps the house was indeed atop the wall, but built "into" the wall in such a way that it was considered an integral part of it. The NRSV renders v. 15b as "her house was on the outer side of the city wall and she resided within the wall itself," while the NJPSV's translation is essentially the same.

---

[154] Although literally, it is "in the wall of the wall." The two Hb. words in question are קִיר and חוֹמָה.

[155] See Boling, *Joshua*, 148, and Hess, *Joshua*, 87, n. 2 for further explanation and bibliography.

The NIV's "the house she lived in was part of the wall" would allow for any of the above possibilities.

2:16 On the face of it, after she let the spies down by the rope, Rahab initiated a rather extensive conversation with them while they were at the foot of the wall (vv. 16-21). This appears rather strange, however, given the state of alert that the city was in and the spies' need for secrecy. Thus, the NIV renders the Hebrew verb form here as a "pluperfect" or "past perfect": "Now [Rahab] *had said* to them."[156] In this understanding, the conversation took place not with the spies at the foot of the wall (or, worse yet, dangling precariously from a rope!) but rather in Rahab's home, before she actually let them down. The conversation perhaps is placed here because of the reference to the window introduced in v. 15 and the subsequent references to it in vv. 18 and 21.

Rahab continued to demonstrate her concern for the spies' safety by her instructions to hide in the hills for three days until the pursuers had given up looking for them. She shrewdly sent them in the opposite direction from where the pursuers had gone: they had headed east, toward the Jordan River and its fords (see v. 7 and comment there), whereas the hills near Jericho were to the west of it, as it lay in the Jordan valley.[157]

2:17–21[158] The conversation about Rahab's rescue, the first part of which is found in vv. 12–14, now continues. In the first part, Rahab extracted a promise of mercy for her and her family because of her kindness to the spies. The spies agreed to spare her, contingent upon her not betraying them. Here in vv. 17–20, they reiterated the conditions and added to them. In v. 18, the NIV, NJPSV, and NASB all translate *hinnēh* here (which is normally translated as "Look!" or "Behold!") as "unless," understanding the conditions that Rahab must fulfill to be (1) the hanging of the scarlet thread from her window and (2) the gathering of her family into her house.[159] Alternatively, one could argue that the primary condition has already been stated in v. 14 (and reiterated in v. 20, i.e., Rahab must not betray the spies), and that it is understood implicitly at the end of v. 17.[160] Then, the two further conditions are introduced in v. 18. In either case, all three conditions mentioned in vv. 14 and 18 were necessary for Rahab to be spared.

In vv. 18–20, the conditions are gone over in explicit detail, and the condi-

---

[156] This is a prime example of "dischronologized narrative," discussed above in note on 2:4–6.

[157] See C. G. Rasmussen, *NIV Atlas of the Bible* (Grand Rapids: Zondervan, 1989), 94. Goslinga (*Joshua, Judges, Ruth,* 48) mentions the "Qarantal Hills west of Jericho, an area with numerous caves and grottos," and Keil (*Joshua,* 38–39) discusses these hills in more depth.

[158] Several grammatical forms in these verses are anomalous, but they do not materially affect the syntax or the understanding of the text here. See Woudstra, *Joshua,* 75, n. 35; Hess, *Joshua,* 94, n. 1.

[159] The NRSV's understanding is similar, rendering *hinnēh* as "if."

[160] So Woudstra, *Joshua,* 74 and n. 30.

tions of guilt or innocence are carefully spelled out. The last words the men spoke (v. 20a) repeat the major condition, with which they had begun their part of the conversation (v. 14a): Rahab must not tell what they were up to. In v. 21, Rahab agreed to all the conditions, and she sent them away, tying the scarlet cord in her window.

An intriguing part of this narrative is the scarlet cord that the spies instructed Rahab to hand out her window. This is a different cord than the rope Rahab used to let them down with (v. 15), since the Hebrew words are different (*hebel*, "rope" in v. 15, and *tiqwat hûṭ haššānî hazzeh* in v. 18, lit., "this cord of scarlet thread").[161] Furthermore, if the conversation in vv. 16-21 took place before Rahab let the spies down out of the window (as seems likely), then the spies' reference to "*this* cord" suggests that the cord was something immediately at hand, perhaps something they had brought with them or something lying in Rahab's house.[162] Its function is clear: it would be a sign to the Israelites that this was the house where Rahab and her family were, and that they should be spared.

The thread's color has attracted attention by students of the Bible, many of whom have argued that its color—the color of blood—is significant, since only through shed blood can redemption come to anyone, whether it be the blood of sacrificial animals in the Old Testament or the blood of Christ in the New Testament (of which the animals' blood was merely an anticipation). This interpretation is very ancient, going back to the church fathers.[163]

This is a typological approach to understanding Scripture, and it is one that the Scriptures themselves employ and endorse. For example, Paul argues that Adam was a "type" of Christ in Rom 5:12–21; in v. 14, he states explicitly that Adam "was a pattern ['type'][164] of the one to come." Peter argues that the waters from which Noah was saved were a "type" of the water baptism that saves Christians "by the resurrection of Jesus Christ" (1 Pet 3:20–21). It certainly is legitimate to look for true types in Scripture, given proper cautions.[165]

---

[161] In v. 20, the reference is simply to "the scarlet cord": *tiqwat haššānî*.

[162] Bird suggests that the scarlet cord was something already associated with Rahab's house, perhaps as an "advertisement" of her services as a prostitute, since the sudden appearance of a new, very visible decoration outside her house might have attracted unwanted attention to it ("The Harlot as Heroine: Narrative Art and Social Presupposition and Three Old Testament Texts," *Semeia* 46 [1989]: 119–39; the suggestion is on p. 130, n. 34).

[163] Goslinga, *Joshua, Judges, Ruth*, 49; Woudstra, *Joshua*, 75. Woudstra states that "Rahab herself was considered a symbol of the Church, since she by her faith and kindness secured the safety of her family" (ibid.).

[164] The Greek word is *tupos*, from which we derive "type" and "typology" in English.

[165] See L. Goppelt, "τύπος," *TDNT* 8:246–59; A. Berkeley Mickelsen, *Interpreting the Bible* (Grand Rapids: Eerdmans, 1963), 236–64; D. J. Moo, "The Problem of *Sensus Plenior*," in D. A. Carson and J. D. Woodbridge, eds., *Hermeneutics, Authority, and Canon* (Grand Rapids: Zondervan, 1986), 195–98.

However, it is questionable as to whether the typology pointed out here—
that the scarlet thread represents shed blood or the blood of Christ and that
Rahab represents the Church—is truly warranted. Probably the best reason for
questioning this particular typological association is that the word for "scarlet" here *(šānî)* is used exclusively in connection with thread or fabrics, primarily referring to the tabernacle curtains and priestly robes (see throughout
Exodus 28 and 35–39), not to blood.[166] The only time that the color of blood
is specified in the Old Testament is in 2 Kgs 3:22, which states that "the water
looked red—like blood." The color word here is the normal word for "red":
ʾādōm (not *šānî*).[167] Another reason for questioning the typological interpretation here is that nowhere does the New Testament even hint at such an association between Rahab's scarlet thread and the blood of Christ.

Having said this, two associations between this passage and others can be
made with more certainty. The first is with the word "scarlet [cord]," which is
found in Gen 38:28,30 *(šānî)* referring to the scarlet cord that Tamar, Judah's
daughter-in-law, wrapped around the wrist of one of her twin boys as he was
being born. This son was named Zerah, and he is remembered in Jesus' genealogy (Matt 1:3). We noted above (in commentary on 2:9–11) that Rahab and
Tamar are linked together in being two of the four foreign women in this same
genealogy. Now we see a further link between the two women in the scarlet
cord. In God's providence, these two women—both of them foreigners, societal outcasts, prostitutes,[168] and in possession of a scarlet cord—came to be
part of the lineage of Jesus Christ himself. It is part of the Bible's pattern that
shows God working in unexpected ways, through unexpected people, often
the poor, the disadvantaged, the outcast.

A second association is with the Passover, as described in Exodus 12.
There, the Israelites were to be protected by painting of blood on the door-
posts and lintels of their homes as a sign for the Lord as he went through the
land to destroy the Egyptians (Exod 12:13,22–23). Likewise, Rahab's scarlet

---

[166] It occurs a total of forty-two times in the OT, in all cases but one referring to literal scarlet
thread or yarn or cloth (it occurs twenty-six times in Exodus). The one exception is in Isa 1:18,
where God says to his people, "Though your sins are like scarlet, they shall be as white as snow;
though they are red as crimson, they shall be like wool." Here, however, the usage is consistent: the
comparison is not with scarlet-colored blood, but (in keeping with the normal usage of the word)
with scarlet-colored cloth or thread.

[167] There actually are several words cognate to each other in the semantic field for "red,"
including אָדֹם, אֲדַמְדָּם, אַדְמוֹנִי, and מְאָדָּם. On these, see the standard treatment by A. Brenner, *Colour Terms in the Old Testament*, JSOTSup 21 (Sheffield: JSOT, 1982), 58–80. On other
terms related to these that denote some sort of reddish color, see Brenner, *Colour Terms*, 106–
15,127–32. Brenner does not treat Josh 2:18,21 in any significant detail, except to note what we
have already pointed out, that "scarlet" *(šānî)* is a textile-related term *(Colour Terms, 143)*.

[168] Tamar was not actually a prostitute, but she dressed up like one to entrap Judah into doing
his familial duties by her, since her husband, Judah's son, had died.

cord was to be a sign for the Israelites as they entered Jericho to destroy it. Furthermore, in both cases, those being protected were not, under any circumstances, to venture outside their houses (Exod 12:22; Josh 2:19). God spared those faithful to him in both cases, obedient Israelites in the one case and obedient non-Israelites in the other.

2:22–24 The chapter wraps up quickly, telling of the spies' hiding in the hills for three days, their pursuit being called off, their return to Joshua across the Jordan, and their confident report to him. During these three days, we can presume that the people were making ready for their journey according to Joshua's instructions in 1:11, where he stated that "Three days from now you will cross the Jordan."

The three days in view here were not three complete twenty-four-hour units. The normal system of time reckoning in the Old Testament was inclusive. As E. R. Thiele states, "reckoning was according to the inclusive system, whereby the first and last units or fractions of units of a group were included as full units in the total of the group."[169] Thus, one scholar notes that "three days" need only signify parts of three days, as in "part of today, tomorrow, and part of the next day."[170] Furthermore, the counting of days was on a morning-to-morning basis here.[171] That is, each day began with the light of the morning and ended with the last hours of darkness of the next morning. The first day, then, was when Joshua sent out two spies into Jericho (2:1) and they arrived at Rahab's house. They hid there and then escaped sometime that night into the hills. The end of the hours of darkness constitutes the first of the three days of hiding mentioned in 2:22. On the second day, the spies continued hiding in the hills (2:22). On the third day, they continued hiding, and then returned sometime during this day to report to Joshua (2:22–23). Joshua is called the "son of Nun" here, as he is in v. 1, indicating the close of the episode that opened in 2:1 (see above, on 2:1, and note there).

The spies' report in v. 24 is simple, confident, and direct, in contrast to the detailed and pessimistic majority report from the twelve spies sent out earlier (see Num 13:27–29,31–33). These two spies' words are taken essentially word for word from Rahab's statement to them in v. 9, and the way is paved for the action that begins at Jericho in chap. 6. The chapter thus ends with a positive word for Israel and the go-ahead for it finally to enter the land of Canaan.

---

[169] E. R. Thiele, *The Mysterious Numbers of the Hebrew Kings*, 3d ed. (Grand Rapids: Zondervan, 1983), 52; see also n. 12.

[170] J. A. Wilcoxen, "Narrative Structure and Cult Legend: A Study of Joshua 1–6," in J. C. Rylaarsdam, ed., *Transitions in Biblical Scholarship* (Chicago: University of Chicago Press, 1968), 62 and n. 31.

[171] Wilcoxen, "Narrative Structure and Cult Legend," 62, n. 30.

3. Crossing the Jordan (3:1–5:1)

Chapters 3–4 belong together, since they both discuss the crossing of the Jordan River. The emphasis in these two chapters is not so much on the crossing per se—this could have been mentioned in a few short verses—as it is on Israel's proper observance and remembrance of this great, defining event. The crossing itself was an event on a par with the crossing of the Red Sea. Both involved God's miraculous intervention in parting (the Red Sea) or stopping up (the Jordan River) waters that were barriers to Israel. These are the only two events in the entire Bible where this type of divine intervention on behalf of the nation takes place.[172]

Because of the miraculous and "amazing things" (3:5) that God was about to do for Israel, the author of the book slows down here and lets us savor this wonderful event, from a slow, deliberate buildup (3:1–13) to a deliberate and repetitive climax (3:14–17), followed by a satisfying and drawn-out reflection on its significance (4:1–5:1). Thus, two major episodes make up these chapters: (1) the miraculous crossing of the Jordan River and (2) the setting up of memorial stones to commemorate the event. The story of the crossing is told in a fairly straightforward fashion in chap. 3, with a few exceptions that will be noted below. In chap. 4, however, the story becomes much more repetitive, as the author reflects on the glorious event that has transpired. In the process, the chronology becomes difficult to follow in several places. However, the author's primary concern is not chronology but theological reflection.[173]

---

[172] Cp. 2 Kgs 2:8, where the Jordan was parted before Elijah and Elisha. The Bible, however, does not reflect on the wonders of the miracle in the way that it does about the other two.

[173] The following commentary attempts to do justice to both. These chapters (esp. chap. 4) are exceedingly difficult to outline, due to the shifting nature of the perspectives adopted by the author. Accordingly, many scholars believe that these chapters represent a classic conflation of hypothetical literary sources. Nelson speaks of "[t]he convolutions of chapters 3 and 4" (*Joshua*, 55), and he states that beyond a few simple observations about "deuteronomistic redaction and the conspicuous gloss of [chap. 3] v. 4a, further attempts to reconstruct the literary history of chapters 3–4 are probably doomed to failure" (p. 57). For representative surveys of the manifold attempts to sort out the issues here, most of them postulating extremely complicated histories of redactional layers, see Nelson, *Joshua*, 55–60, 65–68; Butler, *Joshua*, 41–44; Soggin, *Joshua*, 50–54. One study that surveys in depth the critical literature and then offers its own, rather convoluted solution is B. Peckham, "The Composition of Joshua 3–4," *CBQ* 46 (1984): 413–31. Three studies emphasizing the literary and thematic coherence in chaps. 3–4 are P. P. Saydon, "The Crossing of the Jordan: Josue 3; 4," *CBQ* 12 (1950): 194–207; Polzin, *Moses and the Deuteronomist*, 91–113; and Winther-Nielsen, *Functional Discourse Grammar of Joshua*, 169–90. The discussion following finds much common ground with these last three treatments.

(1) Instructions for Crossing: Stage One (3:1–6)

¹Early in the morning Joshua and all the Israelites set out from Shittim and went to the Jordan, where they camped before crossing over. ²After three days the officers went throughout the camp, ³giving orders to the people: "When you see the ark of the covenant of the LORD your God, and the priests, who are Levites, carrying it, you are to move out from your positions and follow it. ⁴Then you will know which way to go, since you have never been this way before. But keep a distance of about a thousand yards between you and the ark; do not go near it."

⁵Joshua told the people, "Consecrate yourselves, for tomorrow the LORD will do amazing things among you."

⁶Joshua said to the priests, "Take up the ark of the covenant and pass on ahead of the people." So they took it up and went ahead of them.

Finally, after centuries of waiting, the Israelites were now about to cross into the land promised to Abraham their ancestor. Before the actual crossing, final instructions were in order, and the author spends considerable time reviewing these (vv. 1–13). A literary break occurs at v. 7, and so we may for convenience speak of the instructions in two stages. In this first stage, the focus is on the ark of the covenant and the people's relation to it: they were not to get too close. They also were to make proper preparations for witnessing the great wonders that God had in store for them (v. 5).

3:1   Joshua and "all Israel" set out early in the morning from Shittim,[174] where they had been encamped since their triumph over Sihon and Og in the wilderness (see Num 25:1).

3:2   The people encamped at Shittim for three days. Under the system of inclusive time reckoning found in the Hebrew Bible, this period would include the end of the day on which they arrived at the Jordan (v. 1), a second day during which we are not told what transpired, and a third day, when they actually crossed the Jordan (vv. 14–17). At the end of this period, the officers[175] went through the camp with instructions for the people (vv. 2b–3a). At first glance, this appears to be the officer's carrying out of Joshua's orders to them in 1:11, and, for this reason, many scholars see the three days in 1:11 and 3:2 to be one and the same time period. However, the language in the two verses is clearly different. In the first place, the *time* of the officers' passing through the camp is different in the two contexts. In 1:11, Joshua expected that the actual crossing would take place three days hence, so the officers were to pass through the camp *before* that ("within three days"), whereas in

---

[174] The name "Shittim" means "the Acacia trees." It always takes the definite article (-הַ) in the six times it occurs in the OT (Num 25:1; 33:49; Josh 2:1; 3:1; Mic 6:5; Joel 4:18). Its exact location is unknown, but it was no more than ten miles east of the Jordan, depending on its site identification. For the three major options proposed for its location, see W. S. LaSor, "Shittim," *ISBE* 4:490; J. C. Slayton, "Shittim," *ABD* 5:122–23.

[175] See comment on 1:10 for more on these officers (or officials).

3:2, the officers passed through the camp at the *end* of a three-day period.[176] Second, the actual instructions given are different on the two occasions. In 1:11, the instructions were limited to preparations of provisions for the short trip ahead of them, whereas in 3:2, the instructions concerned what the people were to do when they saw the ark of the covenant going before them. This period, then, was actually the fifth through the seventh days after the action of the book began in chap. 1. As to what took place on the sixth day (the second day of the three mentioned in 3:2), we do not know exactly, but it may have involved ritual preparations for the crossing, since Joshua instructed the people that they should sanctify themselves in preparation for what God was going to do (v. 5). On the seventh day of the book's action, God performed the miracle of the crossing.

3:3 The ark of the covenant is mentioned here for the first time in the Book of Joshua, and it is an important focal point in this chapter.[177] The ark was the most holy physical possession of Israel since it symbolized God's very presence (Exod 25:22; Num 7:89; 10:35–36; 1 Sam 4:4), and it contained three symbols of Israel's relationship with God: (1) the tablets of the Ten Commandments, (2) Aaron the high priest's rod, and (3) a jar of manna (Exod 25:16,21; 40:20; Heb 9:4). The priests were responsible for carrying it here (v. 3), in accordance with the Mosaic legislation, which accorded that responsibility to the tribe of Levi (Deut 10:8; cf. 31:9). The ark was to be carried with poles and was not to be touched (Exod 25:12–13; 37:3–5; Num 4:4–15). As the symbol of God's presence, a healthy distance was to be maintained between it and the people (Josh 3:4).

The ark is referred to in various ways in this chapter, the most common phrase being "the ark of the covenant." However, several references to it elevate it to even more prominent status when the Hebrew is read carefully. The following are literal renditions of the Hebrew: In v. 11, the reading is "the ark of the covenant, the Lord of all the earth"; in v. 14, it is "the ark, the covenant"; and in v. 17, we find "the ark, the covenant of the LORD."[178] These references suggest such a close relationship between the ark and the covenant it represents that it is almost as if the ark *is* the covenant. God, whose very presence is associated with the ark, is closely associated with the covenant as

---

[176] The respective phrases here are בְּעוֹד שְׁלֹשֶׁת יָמִים "within three days" (1:11), and מִקְצֵה שְׁלֹשֶׁת יָמִים, "at the end of three days" (3:2).

[177] It is mentioned ten times in this chapter (vv. 3,6[2x],8,11,13,14,15[2x],17) and an additional seven times in chap. 4 (vv. 5,7,9,10,11,16,18).

[178] In each case, a definite article is found that breaks up a construct chain. Thus, assuming the text is correct as it stands and assuming a consistent application of the normal canons of Hebrew grammar regarding construct chains (e.g., GKC § 127a–i; *IBHS* § 9.7a), the NIV's and other versions' renderings of these, which ignore the definite article's presence, are incorrect. They obscure the richness and diversity by which the ark is described.

well, and these ways of referring to the ark highlight this.

The "priests, who are Levites," were to carry the ark. Since all legitimate priests were Levites (Num 3:10),[179] the expression here is redundant.[180] It may be a special reminder that these priests were indeed legitimate, and thus everything was in order.[181] Also, the fact that the *priests* were to carry the ark highlights the importance of this special occasion, since it appears to have been more usual for Levites who were not priests to carry the ark.[182] The priesthood was restricted to Levites (in general) and Aaron's family (specifically) in the Mosaic legislation (Num 25:7–13, esp. vv. 12–13; Deut 18:5). Although all legitimate priests were Levites, not all Levites were priests; their duties were different.[183]

3:4 The NIV reverses the sentence order in this verse. The verse begins with an emphatic particle *(ʾak)* that introduces the warning about keeping a one-thousand-yard distance[184] from the ark, and the first sentence might be translated, *"Be very sure* that a distance of a thousand yards remains between you and it." This emphasizes the sacredness of the ark and the awesomeness of God's glory. Even though the ark symbolized God's presence among his people, his presence among them was not to be taken lightly or abused (as it was on a later occasion, when the ark was taken into battle in order to "guarantee" a victory over the Philistines [see 1 Sam 4:3–11]). When the Israelites prepared for receiving the Ten Commandments at Mount Sinai, they were to keep their distance from that mountain where God was as well (Exod

---

[179] The priests mentioned in Exod 19:22,24 may have been non-Levitical priests, since the restriction of the priesthood to the tribe of Levi did not come until later.

[180] The term is found several times in Deuteronomy; see 17:9,18; 18:1; 24:8; 27:9.

[181] See also J. A. Thompson, *The Book of Jeremiah,* NICOT (Grand Rapids: Eerdmans, 1980), 602–3, where he agrees, seeing this expression as perhaps "another way of referring to 'legitimate priests.'"

[182] The task was normally assigned to the Kohathite branch of the Levites (Num 4:15), but other passages are more general in just mentioning the Levites (e.g., Deut 10:8; 31:25; 1 Chr 15:4–15, esp. v. 15). However, the Levites were not to touch the holy things in preparation, just carry them. The priests were to prepare the holy things for carrying by the Levites: Num 4:5–6,15.

[183] The exact nature of the priesthood in all periods in the OT—and its exact relationship to the Levites—is the subject of a vast amount of scholarly discussion. Critical assumptions about the lateness of the priesthood have been a linchpin in the documentary hypothesis, and they formed an important part of J. Wellhausen's theory of an evolutionary development of Israel's religion. See the judicious reviews of the subject by G. J. Wenham, *Numbers: An Introduction and Commentary,* TOTC (Downers Grove: InterVarsity, 1981), 74–77; W. O. McCready, "Priests and Levites," *ISBE* 3:965–70; D. A. Hubbard, "Priests and Levites," *NBD,* 956–60; and E. H. Merrill, *Deuteronomy,* 262 (on 17:9) and 267 (on 18:1).

[184] The Hb. says "2,000 cubits." The cubit was the length between a man's fingertips and his elbow, about eighteen inches. Two thousand cubits was the radius of the pastureland around the Levitical towns (Num 35:5), and it became the accepted distance for a Sabbath day's journey, based on Exod 16:29 and Num 35:5 (Woudstra, *Joshua,* 81, n. 11; cf. Boling, *Joshua,* 163). The short distance from the Mount of Olives to Jerusalem is called "a Sabbath day's walk" in Acts 1:12.

19:12,23–24). These two aspects of God's nature—his close, comforting presence and his awesome, fearsome glory—are kept in a healthy balance in the Bible, but the latter is in danger of being forgotten in some wings of the church today.

The distance was for the purpose of the people's knowing the way they should walk in, since they had never traveled that way before. The meaning of this statement surely was meant literally and physically: these Israelites had certainly not crossed a river in the way in which they would soon be doing, and they had not been in Canaan before.

However, it is very possible that a spiritual meaning is intended here as well. That is because figurative references to walking in God's way(s) are common in the Old Testament. In the Pentateuch alone, there are some eighteen references to this.[185] In these cases, what is meant is not a literal road or path, but right living. In two cases (Exod 18:20 and Deut 8:2), *knowing* or *remembering* the right way to go is stressed. Surely this was an appropriate charge for the Israelites as they entered the unknown land of Canaan with a mandate to do something they had never done before: take the land and exterminate its inhabitants. The Israelites, as they kept a proper, reverent distance from the ark of the covenant, would be shown in which way they should walk, both physically and spiritually.

We find another wordplay here, this time with the verb "know." In v. 4, the Israelites would "know" the right way to go as a result of their keeping their distance form the ark. In v. 7, they would also "know" that God was with Joshua, as a result of God's exalting him on that day, and in v. 10, they would "know" that God was with them, as a result of his driving out the various Canaanite peoples before them.

3:5 After the officials had completed their instructions, Joshua gave them an additional task: to consecrate themselves. The Hebrew root here *(qdš)* is in the same semantic field as such English words as "consecrate," "sanctify," "holy," and "sacred." Although the term is not used very many times in Joshua,[186] holiness is an important concept in the Old Testament, and the Israelites had had extensive instruction in God's holiness and their own need for holiness in the years prior to this, especially in the Book of Leviticus. The core idea is that of "separation" from things that are unclean or common, that is, anything that would contaminate one's relationship with a perfect God. Here, the people (and not just the priests) were to consecrate themselves.

---

[185] In the singular (as is the case here), we find nine such references: Gen 18:19; Exod 18:20; 32:8; Deut 5:33; 8:2; 9:12,16; 11:28; 31:29, while in the plural, we also find nine: Exod 33:13; Deut 8:6; 10:12; 11:22; 19:9; 26:17; 28:9; 30:16; 32:4.

[186] Some form of קדשׁ is found only six times in the book (3:5; 5:15; 6:19; 7:13[2x]; 20:7), but in each case but one (20:7) it has a significant theological meaning. In 20:7 it refers to the "setting apart" of a city of refuge.

Their proper preparation would have included extensive and rigorous ritual preparation, including thorough washings and abstinence from sexual relations and certain foods. God had instructed the Israelites in a similar way at Mount Sinai (Exod 19:5–10; see also Num 11:18).[187]

The Hebrew word behind NIV's "amazing things" *(niplāʾôt)* is the closest word in the Old Testament for what we today call "miracles." These wonders were such impressive acts that they astonished people and called forth their praise of God (see Pss 9:1; 96:3). They included God's miraculous works among the Egyptians (i.e., the plagues: Exod 3:20; Mic 7:15) and at the Red Sea and in the wilderness (Ps 78:12–16). They were so abnormal as to be unexplainable to people experiencing them except as mighty acts of God. Here in Joshua 3, the "wonders" were the stopping up of the waters of the Jordan (see vv. 14–17).[188]

(2) Instructions for Crossing: Stage Two (3:7–13)

[7]And the LORD said to Joshua, "Today I will begin to exalt you in the eyes of all Israel, so they may know that I am with you as I was with Moses. [8]Tell the priests who carry the ark of the covenant: 'When you reach the edge of the Jordan's waters, go and stand in the river.'"

[9]Joshua said to the Israelites, "Come here and listen to the words of the LORD your God. [10]This is how you will know that the living God is among you and that he will certainly drive out before you the Canaanites, Hittites, Hivites, Perizzites, Girgashites, Amorites and Jebusites. [11]See, the ark of the covenant of the Lord of all the earth will go into the Jordan ahead of you. [12]Now then, choose twelve men from the tribes of Israel, one from each tribe. [13]And as soon as the priests who carry the ark of the LORD—the Lord of all the earth—set foot in the Jordan, its waters flowing downstream will be cut off and stand up in a heap."

The instructions before the people crossed the Jordan continued, this time with God speaking to Joshua (vv. 7–8) and then Joshua speaking again to the people (vv. 9–13). The long build-up to the miraculous stopping of the waters continues.

3:7 God speaks in vv. 7–8 to Joshua for the first time since his charge in 1:1–9. The words here are in fulfillment of those in chap. 1, especially about God's being with Joshua just as he had been with Moses, confirming his place as Israel's new leader (see also 1:5,17; 4:14). God's presence with him was important in encouraging him and validating him as Israel's leader (see on 1:5). The initial confirmation of Joshua's leadership would be the great miracle that God would do on Israel's behalf. Interestingly, Joshua was not directly involved in the miracle at all (except in giving the people and the

---

[187] See Boling, *Joshua*, 163.
[188] For more on this term, see P. A. Kruger, "פלא," *NIDOTTE* 3:615–17.

leaders their instructions), but he would nonetheless be made great[189] in Israel's eyes because of this. Butler well notes that it was God's initiative and God's work: "Joshua's claim to power does not rest on anything he has accomplished. It rests on what God has accomplished at the Jordan and on the obedience of Joshua to the words and example of Moses."[190]

The purpose of God's exalting Joshua was not for Joshua's own sake. Rather, it was for the larger purpose that Israel would know that God was with him. This is the thrust of the word translated here as "so that,"[191] and it also is reinforced by the special verb form of the verb "know." This verb has a suffixed consonant known as a *paragogic nun,* whose function involves "contrastivity."[192] Here the author is emphasizing that the people would indeed know something they would *not* otherwise know: that God was with Joshua in a special way. How would they know this? Through the great miracle that God would perform, which is looked at from so many different angles throughout chaps. 3 and 4.

3:8   The second part of God's instructions to Joshua is more prosaic than the first: the priests carrying the ark were actually to enter the water and stand there. This anticipates what would happen when they did this: the waters would actually stop flowing.

3:9–10   With v. 9, the text begins an inexorable movement toward the chapter's climax in vv. 14–17. Joshua assembled the people to hear God's words, and he stated that there would be a specific way that they would know that God was in their midst and that he would drive out the nations. This way

---

[189] The verb here is the *piel* of גדל, "to be great," which carries a causative sense: "make great, magnify, exalt." Waltke and O'Connor point out (relying on work by E. Jenni) that this "causative" (they use the term "factitive") nature of the *piel* is very specific: it focuses on the bringing about of *a state of being,* rather than on the *process* of causation. A verb such as גדל, which is intransitive in the *qal* ("to be great"), becomes transitive in the *piel* (i.e., it takes an object). The object of causation—in this case, Joshua—"is inherently passive in part" (*IBHS* § 24.1i). The focus here, then, is *on God's bringing about of this state of exaltation* to Joshua, which is a "real" one, i.e., it is "an objective event, an event that can be seen or felt apart from the participants" (*IBHS* § 24.2e). (Waltke and O'Connor discuss this specific example at § 24.2g: "Israel is to experience physically YHWH's making Joshua great.")

[190] Butler, *Joshua,* 46. Butler's well-founded observation is confirmed by the grammatical observations just made in the previous note.

[191] The word is אֲשֶׁר, a relative pronoun usually translated as "who, which." However, in many contexts (as here), it is used as a conjunction meaning "so that." (See BDB, 83 [§ 8b]: "It is resolvable into *so that*"; and *HALOT,* 99 [§ B.d]: "giving the consequence "so that.")

[192] The verb is יֵדְעוּן, occurring in a subordinate clause introduced by אֲשֶׁר. In this type of construction, the paragogic *nun* indicates a concern "with an aim which will certainly be attained (provided the action in the principal clause takes place)," according to J. Hoftijzer, in *The Function and Use of the Imperfect Forms with Nun Paragogicum in Classical Hebrew* (Assen: Van Gorcum, 1985), 44. In this passage, the action in the principal clause is God's exalting of Joshua, and the construction indicates a surety that the people will indeed know that God is with Joshua.

is not stated until v. 13, when the "wonderful things" previewed in v. 5 are revealed to be the stopping of the Jordan's flow.

Verse 10 is introduced by a short prepositional phrase: "By this you will know ...."[193] "This" refers to the miraculous sign of the water stoppage in v. 13, which is emphasized by the repeated verbs and the vivid imagery there. God's actions here were for a larger purpose than just Israel's crossing the Jordan. It was to demonstrate to Israel that the "living God" was among them.

The reference here to the "living God" is most likely intended to contrast Israel's living, powerful God with the "dead," false gods of the seven peoples who are named in the verse. In Hos 1:10[Hb. 2:1], the same term is used, and the context there is also part of a contrast. There, God had instructed Hosea to name his third child "Not my people" as an ironic reminder to Israel that they had gone astray and were like the pagans around them, not worthy of being called God's people (Hos 1:9). However, a promise of restoration follows (1:10–11[Hb. 2:1–2]), and to those who would taunt Israel with the name "Not my people," God responds forcefully that the Israelites were in reality "the sons of the living God." Other uses of the term in the Old Testament also denote a contrast, usually between Israel's God and hostile pagan gods or forces.[194] Here, then, the term "the living God" is used as a polemic against God's enemies, who were also Israel's enemies. It was a forceful reminder to Israel that their God was *not* like the gods of the nations around them, nations whom they were going to displace (v. 10b), but rather he was a powerful and living God, able to effect the type of miracle in view here. And this living God was "among you," literally, "in your midst," affirming the promise of God's presence that he had made to Joshua (see 1:5,9).

The wordplay of "knowing" (vv. 4,7) is continued in v. 10. The events that were soon to follow were not just for the purpose of getting the Israelites across the Jordan River. They were to attest to the fact "that the living God is among you"! These wonderful acts were testimonies to God's glorious presence among his people, working on their behalf. This exact wording—"This is how you will know ..."—is found only one other time in the Old Testament, in Num 16:28, where God was authenticating Moses' position as his chosen leader (cp. similarly Exod 7:17). Here, he is doing the same for Joshua.

---

[193] The verb "know" occurs again with a *paragogic nun* (see on v. 7), referring again to the miracle.

[194] The term here, אֵל חַי, "living God," occurs only four times in the OT: in Josh 3:10; Pss 42:2[Hb. 3]; 84:2[Hb. 3]; and Hos 1:10[Hb. 2:1]. The term "my living God" (or "the God of my life" [NIV]) is found in Ps 42:8[Hb. 9]. In the three Psalms passages, death or estrangement from God lurk in the background, and the "living God" is a source of life for the psalmists. Variations of אֵל חַי are אֱלֹהִים חַי (2 Kgs 19:4,16 // Isa 37:4,17), אֱלֹהִים חַיִּים (Deut 5:23; 1 Sam 17:26,36; Jer 10:10; 23:36), and אֱלָהָא חַיָּא (Dan 6:20,26 [Aram 6:21,27]). In the case of each of these variant forms, the "living God" is contrasted with hostile pagan gods or forces.

Seven peoples are listed in v. 10. Twenty-three times in the Old Testament we find such lists, including five times in Joshua (3:10; 9:1; 11:3; 12:8; 24:11). The number and order of the names vary in each list, but seven is used often, probably as a number symbolic of completeness. Twelve peoples occur in all, but a core of seven—the seven mentioned here—comprises the "standard" list.[195]

In Joshua, these seven nations are listed at 3:10 and 24:11, while six nations are listed in the other three references. The primary way in which the lists are used in the Old Testament is in connection with Israel's possession of the land of Canaan.[196] These were the peoples whom they were to displace. And the fact that they are commonly listed as separate nations—as opposed to being described simply as "the people who live in the land" (Exod 23:31), or inclusively as "the Canaanites"—shows a contrast between the ethnic divisions among them, as opposed to the national unity that was so important for Israel.[197] Furthermore, the lists of peoples functioned to help the Israelites define themselves: they were not these wicked, divided nations, but rather one people, God's people.[198]

The term "Canaanites"[199] sometimes is an all-inclusive term denoting any people living in Canaan, regardless of their ethnic identity (e.g., Gen 12:6; 36:2–3; Exod 13:11; Ezek 16:3). Often, however, the Canaanites are distinguished from others who lived in Canaan, as they are here (e.g., Josh 7:9; Judg 1:27–29). In this case, they probably are the peoples living near the sea and near the Jordan River (see 5:1, which mentions Canaanites along the coast, and Num 13:29, which mentions them by the sea and near the Jordan).[200]

The Hittites appear in the Bible primarily in the hill country of Judah (e.g., Hebron: Genesis 23; Beersheba: Gen 26:34; Bethel: Judg 1:22–26; Jerusalem:

---

[195] The most detailed study of the lists is E. C. Hostetter, *Nations Mightier and More Numerous: The Biblical View of Palestine's Pre-Israelite Peoples*, BIBAL Dissertation Series 3 (N. Richland Hills, Tex.: BIBAL Press, 1995). See also T. Ishida, "The Structure and Historical Implications of the Lists of Pre-Israelite Nations," *Bib* 60 (1979): 461–90, and Mitchell, *Together in the Land*, 122–33.

[196] Hostetter, *Nations Mightier and More Numerous*, 141–42.

[197] See Hostetter (ibid., 143) on this point. See the commentary on 1:13–15 and chap. 22 on the importance of Israel's unity in the Book of Joshua.

[198] Hostetter, *Nations Mightier and More Numerous*, 143–45.

[199] All the names in this verse are singular (i.e., "the Canaanite," "the Hittite," etc.), but they refer to the groups represented.

[200] On these people's geographical distribution and the dual use of their name (i.e., all-inclusive and more limited), see Hostetter, *Nations Mightier and More Numerous*, 57–62. Extrabiblically, much is known of the Canaanites (and the Phoenicians, who carried the Canaanite traditions into the first millennium B.C.). See A. R. Millard, "The Canaanites," in D. J. Wiseman, ed., *Peoples of Old Testament Times* (Oxford: Clarendon, 1973), 29–52; J. Day, "Canaan, Religion of," *ABD* 1:831–37; K. N. Schoville, "Canaanites and Amorites," *POTW*, 157–82.

Ezek 16:3,45).[201] Here in Joshua, the reference to them appears to be the same (Josh 11:3 specifically states that they lived in the hill country). As we noted in the comment on 1:4, there was a great Hittite kingdom of the middle and late second millennium B.C. to the north of Israel's lands in northern Syria, and vestiges of this kingdom appear to be in view in the reference to Solomon's trading partners in 1 Kgs 10:29.[202]

The next three peoples in the list are relatively obscure.[203] The Hivites were located in the mountainous region to the north, in what is today Lebanon (Josh 11:3; Judg 3:3). The Perizzites appear to have lived in the forested areas of central Palestine, in the highlands of Samaria (Gen 13:7; Josh 17:15). The Girgashites appear in the Bible only in the lists of peoples. Based on where the other peoples lived, Hostetter suggests that the only area left for the Girgashites was toward the north of Palestine. All three of these peoples are unknown outside the Bible.

Like the term "Canaanite," the term "Amorite" is sometimes used as an all-inclusive term, referring to anyone living in Canaan (see Gen 15:16; 36:2–3; Josh 24:15; Judg 1:34–35; Ezek 16:3). Elsewhere it is a more limited term, referring to areas in the central hill country of Canaan (Num 13:29; Deut 1:7) or to kingdoms east of the Jordan River (Num 21:26; Deut 4:46; Josh 13:10, 21). Here, it probably refers to the people east of the Jordan. Outside the Bible, "Amorites" are known from early texts in Mesopotamia, and there they are "westerners," that is, people coming from the west (from Syria, Lebanon, and Palestine). Later, an "Amorite" kingdom is known, with its capital at Sidon.[204]

The Jebusites were the pre-Israelite inhabitants of Jerusalem (see Josh 15:8; 18:28). They are the only ones in the list named for a city ("Jebus" was the name of Jerusalem when David captured it [1 Chr 11:4–9]). Outside the Bible, the Jebusites are known from archaeological remains in Jerusalem, but not from literary sources.[205]

The "standard" list of seven peoples includes several very obscure peoples alongside several more prominent ones, yet the list was selective, since addi-

---

[201] See Boling, *Joshua*, 122–23.

[202] For the Hittites' geographical distribution, see Hostetter, *Nations Mightier and More Numerous*, 66–72. For more general introductions to the Hittites, see the works mentioned at 1:4.

[203] On the Hivites, see Hostetter, *Nations Mightier and More Numerous*, 72–76, and D. W. Baker, "Hivites," *ABD* 3:234–35. On the Perizzites, see Hostetter, *Nations Mightier and More Numerous*, 80–83, and S. A. Reed, "Perizzite," *ABD* 5:231. On the Girgashites, see Hostetter, *Nations Mightier and More Numerous*, 62–66, and D. W. Baker, "Girgashite," *ABD* 2:1028.

[204] On the Amorites, see Hostetter, *Nations Mightier and More Numerous*, 51–57; M. Liverani, "The Amorites," in *Peoples of Old Testament Times*, 100–133; G. E. Mendenhall, "Amorites," *ABD* 1:199–202; Schoville, "Canaanites and Amorites," *POTW*, 157–82.

[205] On the Jebusites, see Hostetter, *Nations Mightier and More Numerous*, 76–80; R. K. Harrison, "Jebus; Jebusite," *ISBE* 2:973–74; S. A. Reed, "Jebus," *ABD* 3:652–53.

tional peoples are mentioned in some texts. Why were these particular seven chosen? This probably was due in part, if not entirely, to the complete geographical picture obtained, since these peoples occupied the lands that the Israelites took.[206]

3:11–13 Joshua now focused the Israelites' attention on the ark by using an attention-getting word *hinnēh* ("See!" "Look!" "Behold!"). The ark was to be their guide, and its position at the water's edge would signal the beginning of the miracle. The Hebrew in v. 11 has, literally, "the ark of the covenant, the Lord of all the earth," which all versions correct to read "the ark of the covenant *of* the Lord of all the earth." However, if the Hebrew is correct as it stands, then the ark is identified all that much more closely with God himself, that is, the ark (or the covenant) is equated with the Lord himself.

Joshua's words in v. 12 about choosing twelve men look ahead, anticipating the actions Israel was to take after the crossing.[207] God spoke these words to Joshua almost verbatim in 4:2, adding that these men were to take up twelve stones for a memorial (4:3–7). This demonstrates again the slow building up of the story we have already noted: it shows a skilled author at work, who will repeat himself at different points or suspend his story and then resume it, in the interests of weaving an ordered, intricate story. We see this in the portrayal of the priests in this chapter: they are introduced in 3:3, but their role is made clearer in 3:8, and then clearer still in 3:13. We also see it in the repetition of the crossing motif at several points: 3:1,14,16,17; 4:1,10,11.[208]

Finally, in v. 13, the substance of the "amazing things" spoken of in v. 5 is revealed: when the priests carrying the ark stepped into the Jordan, the waters would stop flowing! The entire chapter thus far has been building to this revelation. In reality, probably most Israelites—and most readers—would have guessed long before this what was going to happen. However, the author's presentation of the information draws out the suspense on a literary level and highlights the magnificence of the miracle.

Here the Lord is identified as sovereign over all the earth, although the word for "earth" (*ʾereṣ*) can also mean "land"; if this is the intended meaning, it is nevertheless appropriate, since the Lord was not only sovereign over all

---

[206] See Hostetter, *Nations Mightier and More Numerous*, 83, 142–43, on this point and his map on p. 151.

[207] That it is a slight interruption in the immediate concerns of the story is indicated by the disjunctive particle *wěʿattâ* ("So, now") that begins the verse. These words thus may not have been spoken in actuality until later, but they are introduced here to anticipate the second part of the story, the memorializing of the crossing.

[208] Hess (*Joshua*, 103) makes the point well: "Like a film in which the camera switches back and forth between the various scenes of action, the narrative moves back and forth between these three groups [the priests, the twelve men, and the people]." See also Woudstra, *Joshua*, 86. Critical commentators see v. 12's placement as yet another indication of tangled literary sources in this part of Joshua (e.g., Soggin, *Joshua*, 59–60; Nelson, *Joshua*, 55).

the earth, but also the entire land of Canaan, which he was in process of giving to Israel.

The stoppage of the waters is viewed in two ways here, anticipating the further elaboration in vv. 16–17 and in several places in chap. 4: they would be "cut off," and they would "stand up in a heap."

(3) The Miracle of the Crossing (3:14–17)

[14]So when the people broke camp to cross the Jordan, the priests carrying the ark of the covenant went ahead of them. [15]Now the Jordan is at flood stage all during harvest. Yet as soon as the priests who carried the ark reached the Jordan and their feet touched the water's edge, [16]the water from upstream stopped flowing. It piled up in a heap a great distance away, at a town called Adam in the vicinity of Zarethan, while the water flowing down to the Sea of the Arabah (the Salt Sea) was completely cut off. So the people crossed over opposite Jericho. [17]The priests who carried the ark of the covenant of the LORD stood firm on dry ground in the middle of the Jordan, while all Israel passed by until the whole nation had completed the crossing on dry ground.

These verses are the climax of the chapter—indeed, of all of chaps. 3–4. Here, the narrative slows to a crawl, so that the reader can savor the wonder of the miracle and view it from as many different perspectives as possible. The author, by writing in this way, affirms God's greatness and power and intervention on his people's behalf. The point is not so much that the people were able to cross over the Jordan, but the *manner* in which they were able to cross: by a glorious and mighty miracle of God. The immediate purpose of the miracle was obviously to get Israel across the Jordan. However, the larger purpose was—as it is with all miracles—to testify to God's greatness and faithfulness, both to Israel (v. 10) and to all the peoples of the earth (4:24a), and to stimulate proper worship of him (4:24b).

That we are to be awed by the wonder of the miracle is clear as we read these two chapters, and especially when we reach the climax itself. This is accomplished in several ways: by the many verbs describing the water stoppage in vv. 13 and 16, by the verbs of standing or resting in the Jordan (vv. 8,13,15,17), by the references to high water or dry ground (vv. 15,17), and by the very syntactical constructions in vv. 14–16. This emphasis is confirmed in chap. 4, where many of the same motifs are repeated: see especially 4:7,18, 22–23.

3:14–16 Here finally we read the account of the miracle that has been anticipated from the beginning of the chapter. It is truly a remarkable one: the Jordan River, at flood stage, was completely stopped up when the priests carrying the ark stepped into it, and the people were able to cross over on dry land!

In Hebrew, these verses constitute one long, drawn-out statement about the stopping up of the waters, followed by a short, terse statement about the people's crossing over. The drawn-out nature of vv. 14–15 especially highlights the suspense and wonder until the powerful statements in v. 16 about the miracle itself. Unfortunately the NIV has obscured this by breaking the passage into four sentences and changing some of the clause order.

A more literal translation of vv. 14–16 would read as follows:[209]

> *And it happened*—when the people set out from their tents to cross the Jordan, with the priests carrying the ark of the covenant before them, and when those carrying the ark came as far as the Jordan, and [when] the feet of the priests carrying the ark were dipped into the edge of the waters (now the Jordan overflows all its banks all the days of the harvest)— *that the waters coming down from above stood! They rose up [in] one heap,* a very far distance away, at Adam, the city that is opposite Zarethan,[210] *and the [waters] coming down upon the Sea of the Arabah, the Salt Sea,*[211] *were completely cut off.* And the people crossed opposite Jericho."

Two things should be observed here about the syntax, because it is highly unusual and appears to many scholars to be overcomplicated and thus a signal that different literary sources lie behind these verses.[212] (1) The statements in vv. 14–15 are all in subordinate clauses of some type, which means that the author, having begun his main thought with *and it happened,* leaves us suspended as to what actually happened until v. 16. The same is true for the statement at the end of v. 16, telling of the actual crossing: it is in a subordinate clause, and it is included as a statement of what happened, but clearly the focus is on the miracle, not the crossing. (2) When v. 16 *is* finally reached, the language changes, and in quick succession two verbs appear describing the water's stoppage: *they stood* and *they rose up.* A few words later, two more verbs occur, describing this from a different perspective: *they were completely*

---

[209] The words in brackets are not in the Hebrew, but they are necessary in making the transition from one language to another. The words in italics constitute the main "story line" of these verses, whereas those not italicized constitute the subordinate clauses containing background material of various types.

[210] The cities were some fifteen to twenty miles upriver from where the Israelites crossed. On their locations, see M. J. Fretz, "Adam (Place)," *ABD* 1:64; H. O. Thompson, "Zarethan," *ABD* 6:1041–43.

[211] The reference here is to the Dead Sea. The "Arabah" is part of the great Rift Valley that runs north and south in eastern Africa. In the Bible, it includes the Jordan Valley, the Dead Sea, and the depression running southward from the Dead Sea to the Gulf of Aqaba. See R. K. Harrison, "Arabah," *ISBE* 1:218–20; Boling, *Joshua*, 170.

[212] R. Nelson, e.g., sees "the complex, overfull sentence in vv. 14–16" as "undoubtedly the result of a complicated history of composition and redaction" (*Joshua*, 55). Other scholars are more sensitive to the dramatic unfolding of the narrative. See, e.g., Polzin, *Moses and the Deuteronomist*, 91–110 (on all of 3:1–5:1); Winther-Nielsen, *Functional Discourse Grammar of Joshua*, 176–79 (on 3:14–17).

cut off.[213] In the short space of one verse, then, we find four different verbs reflecting on what happened to the waters. The language "piles up" in a manner that reminds us of the waters themselves piling up!

Thus the passage's climax tells us, in a very impressive way, that the waters of the Jordan River, which was at flood stage, were stopped up so that God's people could cross over and begin their mission in the promised land.

3:17 Here we have a wrap-up, highlighting things already stated and adding a bit more that makes the miracle even more impressive. Just as the waters had *stood* (v. 16), now the priests *stood firm*[214] in the midst of the Jordan. After the reference to *the people* at the end of v. 16, they are referred to again twice in v. 17, in different ways: *all Israel* and *the whole nation*. Just as the waters were *completely* cut off (v. 16), so now the entire nation *completed* its crossing. This last point effectively wraps up this portion of the episode.

Something new is introduced as well: the twofold reference to *dry ground*. This gives us a still different perspective on the miracle: the waters were so completely stopped up that the priests stood and the people crossed on dry ground! No shallow fords were to be found, since the waters were at flood stage at this time of year, so a true miracle was needed. The end of v. 15 (see the translation above) refers to the early summer harvest, when the river was still swollen from spring melting and spring rains. The crossing was actually done on the tenth day of the first month (4:19), which corresponds to March-April. Thus, the fact that Israel not only crossed the Jordan during the flood stage but did so *on dry ground* (and not muddy, mucky ground) makes the miracle even more impressive.

These events naturally call to mind the Red Sea crossing in Exodus 14–15. There too God miraculously separated the waters that allowed the Israelites to cross on dry ground.[215] There too the waters stood in a "heap" (Exod 15:8).[216] There too the miracle was for the immediate purpose of crossing a great watery barrier, but it was for the larger purpose of glorifying God and confirming his chosen leader (Moses) in the eyes of the people (Exod 14:31), just as the later miracle glorified God (3:10; 4:24) and confirmed his chosen leader, Joshua (3:7; 4:14).

---

[213] The Hebrew here literally reads, "They completed, they were cut off."

[214] "Firm" translates הָכֵן, the *hiphil* infinitive absolute of כוּן, "to be firm"; it is used adverbially here. See GKC §§ 113h–x and *IBHS* § 35.3.2 on the adverbial function of the infinitive absolute.

[215] The word in Josh 3:17 [2x] and 4:18 is חָרָבָה, "dry land," which is also found in Exod 14:21. The more common word is יַבָּשָׁה "dry ground" (found in Exod 14:16,22,29; 15:19; Josh 4:22), whose meaning is essentially the same.

[216] The word is *nēd*, which the NIV translates in Exodus as "wall" and in Joshua as "heap."

(4) Memorializing the Crossing: Stage One (4:1–10)

[1]When the whole nation had finished crossing the Jordan, the LORD said to Joshua, [2]"Choose twelve men from among the people, one from each tribe, [3]and tell them to take up twelve stones from the middle of the Jordan from right where the priests stood and to carry them over with you and put them down at the place where you stay tonight."

[4]So Joshua called together the twelve men he had appointed from the Israelites, one from each tribe, [5]and said to them, "Go over before the ark of the LORD your God into the middle of the Jordan. Each of you is to take up a stone on his shoulder, according to the number of the tribes of the Israelites, [6]to serve as a sign among you. In the future, when your children ask you, 'What do these stones mean?' [7]tell them that the flow of the Jordan was cut off before the ark of the covenant of the LORD. When it crossed the Jordan, the waters of the Jordan were cut off. These stones are to be a memorial to the people of Israel forever."

[8]So the Israelites did as Joshua commanded them. They took twelve stones from the middle of the Jordan, according to the number of the tribes of the Israelites, as the LORD had told Joshua; and they carried them over with them to their camp, where they put them down. [9]Joshua set up the twelve stones that had been in the middle of the Jordan at the spot where the priests who carried the ark of the covenant had stood. And they are there to this day.

[10]Now the priests who carried the ark remained standing in the middle of the Jordan until everything the LORD had commanded Joshua was done by the people, just as Moses had directed Joshua. The people hurried over,

Chapter 4 celebrates the great miracle of the crossing by going over much of the same ground as chap. 3, adding to it, and looking at the event from still different perspectives than seen heretofore. It also solemnly gives instructions for the memorializing of this event by the building of an altar, which was to stand as a perpetual reminder to Israel and the nations of God's great hand.

The chapter may be divided into two major sections: vv. 1–14 and vv. 15–24 (with 5:1 forming the proper conclusion to the second section).[217] At the end of each section, the author offers his own evaluative comment about the effect of the events thus far:

That day the LORD exalted Joshua in the sight of all Israel; and they revered him all the days of his life, just as they had revered Moses (4:14).

Now when all the Amorite kings west of the Jordan and all the Canaanite kings along the coast heard how the LORD had dried up the Jordan before the Israelites until we had crossed over, their hearts melted and they no longer had the courage to face the Israelites (5:1).

---

[217] Almost all commentators agree in seeing a significant break after v. 14. The contour of the analysis here is particularly indebted to Polzin, *Moses and the Deuteronomist*, 91–113, esp. 99–104.

The first of these evaluative comments shows the effect of the events *in Israel*: Joshua was exalted by God in the Israelites' eyes, just as Moses had been. The second of these shows the effects of the events *outside Israel:* the kings of the land were terrified because of Israel. Furthermore, as Polzin points out, the events in 4:1–14 *"are narrated from a vantage point outside of the promised land, whereas [those in 4:15–5:1] are narrated from a vantage point inside of the promised land."*[218]

Several smaller divisions are found within these two major sections. They mirror each other, as the following shows:

Memorializing the Crossing: Stage One (4:1–10)
The Crossing Completed: Stage One (4:11–14)
The Crossing Completed: Stage Two (4:15–18)
Memorializing the Crossing: Stage Two (4:19–5:1)

The first of these divisions details the setting up of memorial stones to commemorate the crossing of the Jordan (4:1–10).

4:1–3 Verse 1 resumes the action in chap. 3 by repeating the last seven words of 3:17 almost verbatim.[219] This repetition helps to tie the materials in the two chapters together. A look backward is taken (by the repetition), but a move forward is signaled by the new construction here: *"And it happened, when all the nation had completed crossing the Jordan, that the LORD spoke to Joshua, saying …"*

Verse 2 is God's command to Joshua to pick out twelve men, one from each tribe, a command that Joshua himself already had uttered in 3:12. Either 3:12 or 4:2 is out of place chronologically. Whichever one is displaced, however, the words in 3:12 have the effect of tying the story in chap. 3 with what follows in chap. 4 by anticipating God's command. Most likely, God's command came first in real time, and Joshua's words followed.[220] The recording of both sets of words shows us that God's command was indeed carried out. This pattern of anticipation/confirmation or command/fulfillment is common in these two chapters. See, for example, God's words in 3:7 promising Joshua that he would exalt him in Israel's eyes, and the report in 4:14 that this came about precisely as God had promised, or Joshua's words in 3:13 about what would happen to the waters of the Jordan when the priests entered them, and the report in 3:16–17 showing that this was exactly what happened.[221]

---

[218] Polzin, *Moses and the Deuteronomist*, 101 (emphasis Polzin).

[219] The NIV obscures this by its dynamic equivalent translation. The words in question are כַּאֲשֶׁר־תַּמּוּ כָל־הַגּוֹי לַעֲבוֹר אֶת־הַיַּרְדֵּן, "when all the nation had completed crossing the Jordan" (cp. the end of 3:17: "until all the nation had completed crossing the Jordan").

[220] In real time, Joshua's command fits best between 4:2 and 4:4–7, i.e., between God's command to choose twelve men to carry the stones and Joshua's commands to the men he chose.

[221] Polzin details this phenomenon at some length (*Moses and the Deuteronomist*, 104–7).

God's command in 4:2–3 is more detailed than Joshua's words in 3:12. In 4:3, the actual duties of these men are revealed: the men were to take twelve stones from the middle of the Jordan, from the spot where the priests were standing firmly,[222] and carry them to their lodging place for the night. Surprisingly, the word the NIV renders as "put them down" is literally "cause them to rest." The word choice—"rest" rather than the more common "set" or "place"—may be intentional, tying even the memorial stones into the theme of "rest" in the book.[223]

4:4–7 In these verses, the pattern of repetition and addition continues. Here are Joshua's commands to the twelve men, in fulfillment of God's command to him, and the first explanation of the meaning of the stones.

In v. 4, the references to the twelve men, one from each tribe, is another back reference, to the words in 3:12 and 4:2. However, "choose" in those verses is replaced by "appointed" here. The verb "appointed" is from the same root *(kwn)* as that translated "firm" and "firmly" in 3:17 and 4:3. Just as the priests had stood "firmly" in the midst of the Jordan, now Joshua was causing the twelve men to be (firmly) established.

Joshua's commands in vv. 5–7 began by instructing the men each to pass before the ark into the midst of the Jordan and to take a stone from there, and he explained that the number *twelve* corresponded to the number of tribes of Israel (v. 5). This is an obvious point, but it is a reminder of the nation's essential unity: it was a twelve-tribe nation, not nine and one-half tribes.[224] These men too were to "go over" *(ʿbr)* before the ark, just as the people "passed by" *(ʿbr:* 3:17) and "crossed" *(ʿbr:* 4:1). God's abiding presence with his people, symbolized by the ark, is an overarching motif in these two chapters (see on 3:3).

The men were to take the stones for the specific purpose revealed in vv. 6–7. The stones' purpose was to be a testimony and a memorial to Israel's descendants that God had worked a great miracle in stopping up the waters of the Jordan. They were not to be an altar for sacrifice, but a pile of stones for a "remembrance."[225] This is reminiscent of the twelve "stone pillars" (NIV) erected by Moses at the foot of Mount Sinai, in the context of a covenant-making ceremony (Exod 24:4; the Hb. word is *maṣṣēbâ*). The memorial was to

---

[222] The NIV omits הָכִין, "firmly," which is an obvious echo of הָכֵן, "firm" in 3:17, another link between the chapters.

[223] On "rest," see the Introduction. The Hb. root here is נוח, "rest," but the roots שׂים, "put, set, place," or שׁית, "put, set, lay," are more common and would be expected here.

[224] See the commentary on 1:13–15 for more on the motif of unity.

[225] The Hb. word here is זִכָּרוֹן, "memorial, remembrance." It is related to זָכַר, "remember." Similarly in English, the words "memory," "remember," etc. are etymologically related to each other. Two "memorial stones" were to be part of the ephod the high priest wore (Exod 28:9–12; 39:7), but there the symbolism lay in the names of the twelve tribes that were inscribed on the stones. They were to be constant reminders to God, so to speak. The idea is somewhat different from the stones Israel was to erect here.

be a highly personalized one: literally, the Hebrew at the end of v. 6 reads, "What are these stones *to you?*" The Israelites' children would be asking them what these stones symbolized for them personally, and they were to have an answer ready that told of the miracle that God had performed and the ark's role in it. (Similar examples of the parents teaching their children about God's grace, protection, and provision in responding to their children's questions about the meaning of certain symbols or rituals may be found in Exod 12:26–27; 13:14–16; Deut 6:20–25.) The syntax of v. 7 is again somewhat repetitive and choppy, to focus attention on these two things: the miracle and God's presence. Verse 7 ends by stating that these stones were to be a *perpetual* reminder to Israel. God would not always perform such dramatic miracles, but, by means of these stones, Israel could remember when he did work in this way.

4:8–10 This section completes the story of the twelve memorial stones by reviewing what had transpired up until this point. Verse 8a affirms that everything was done in accordance with God's commands. In vv. 2–3, God had given instructions about the memorial stones, and in vv. 4–7, Joshua had repeated and amplified them. Whatever Joshua said was in effect a command from God; conversely, what God said, Joshua repeated. What is important is obedience: Joshua's obedience to God and the people's obedience to God and his spokesman Joshua (see on 4:2).

In the remainder of v. 8, the author tells us how the people obeyed Joshua, and he reviews what Joshua and the Lord had commanded in vv. 3 and 5. The wording here shows that the twelve chosen men acted on Israel's behalf, in that "the people" (not the twelve men) are said to have obeyed Joshua. The wording of Joshua's report concerning the people's obedience comes almost entirely from vv. 3 and 5, although rearranged somewhat.[226] The close identification of God's words and Joshua's words is reinforced, first of all, when we read that the people obeyed *Joshua*. In fact, the words here echo what the Lord had commanded Joshua, not what Joshua had commanded the people. We can safely infer from this that Joshua had faithfully repeated everything that God had commanded him. Second, when v. 8 states that the people were acting "as the LORD had told Joshua," the identification of God's words and Joshua's words is also reinforced, since the statement about the number of the tribes is found earlier in Joshua's instructions, not God's (v. 5). Even though Joshua is never called a "prophet," he acts here and throughout most of the book just as a true biblical prophet would act: as a spokesman for God.[227]

---

[226] Most of the report repeats information from v. 3, but the statement "according to the number of the tribes of the Israelites" comes from v. 5.

[227] For good introductions to the phenomenon of biblical prophecy, see C. H. Bullock, *An Introduction to the Old Testament Prophetic Books* (Chicago: Moody, 1986), 11–40; G. V. Smith, "Prophet; Prophecy," *ISBE* 3:986–1004; idem, *The Prophets as Preachers: An Introduction to the Biblical Prophets* (Nashville: Broadman & Holman, 1994), 5–46.

Verse 9 seems at first glance to introduce a second set of twelve stones into the story, which have not been mentioned yet (and are not mentioned again). The first set would be those that the twelve men took up from the middle of the river and set up on the bank (vv. 3,5,8), and the second set would be those that Joshua set *in* the riverbed (v. 9). The first set, then, would be the true memorial stones, and the second set would mark the very spot where the priests had stood, perhaps coming visible during the dry season. The textual traditions represented by the Septuagint (Greek) and the Vulgate (Latin) support this by referring to "twelve *other* stones" here.[228]

However, more likely, only one set of stones existed. Most of v. 9 is best read as a parenthetical aside, telling us that Joshua had initially set up twelve stones *in the riverbed itself*, where the priests had stood.[229] This is new information (that Joshua himself set up the stones initially), since the earlier commands in vv. 3 and 5 mention only the twelve chosen men. When we read about the twelve men taking up twelve stones from the riverbed to set up on the banks of the river, it becomes clear that they were taking up the twelve stones that Joshua had set down previously. Their purpose initially was to mark the importance of the spot where the priests stood with the ark.[230] However, when the crossing was complete, these stones were set up on the riverbank as a perpetual memorial. That is the significance of the statement at the end of v. 9 ("And they are there to this day"). "There" refers to the stones on the riverbank (not in the riverbed), echoing (literally) "they laid them to rest *there*" at the end of v. 8.[231]

---

[228] Several commentators understand there to have been two sets of twelve stones. See Woudstra, *Joshua*, 92; Butler, *Joshua*, 49; Polzin, *Moses and the Deuteronomist*, 95, 114. Saydon omits v. 9 as a late interpolation ("The Crossing of the Jordan," 203). Curiously, Saydon—who provides a holistic reading of the text and affirms that "the whole narrative, in spite of some blunt edges, is a well knit account, logically constructed, and utterly free of contradictions and inconsistencies" ("The Crossing of the Jordan," 207)—feels compelled to delete part of the text in order to be able to affirm its freedom from inconsistencies.

[229] The word for "set up" here *(hēkîm)* continues the wordplay on "firm" noted at v. 4.

[230] Whether they were standing in a pile next to the priests or laid out at (or under) their feet is not exactly clear. Boling speaks of a "stone platform" (*Joshua*, 174) and Nelson of a "processional causeway" (*Joshua*, 69). Unless they were smooth, cut stones, however, it is more plausible to consider them as standing in a pile at the priests' feet, not laid out as a platform or causeway.

[231] The syntax of the verse is as follows: all of the verse until the last clause is a lengthy (parenthetical) circumstantial clause introduced by the disjunctive direct object (וּשְׁתֵּים עֶשְׂרֵה אֲבָנִים, "And twelve stones"). The final clause (after the *athnach*) resumes the narrative of v. 8: "And they [i.e., the twelve stones that the twelve men took to the riverbank] have been there [i.e., on the riverbank] until this day." The copula introducing this clause (וַיִּהְיוּ "and they have been") is unnecessary grammatically, since we would translate the clause in the same way if it were missing: "And (they have been) there until this day." The clause would then begin with וְשָׁם or שָׁם or וְהֵמָּה. The copula's presence indicates a special grammatical feature, in this case, a resumption of the narrative suspended at the end of v. 8. See also Winther-Nielsen, *Discourse Grammar of Joshua*, 179–82, who reads the verse similarly (although he does not seem to believe that Joshua set up the stones in the riverbed, despite the clear evidence of "under the place where the feet of the priests were standing"—הַכֹּהֲנִים תַּחַת מַצַּב רַגְלֵי). Keil's understanding is closest to that here (*Joshua*, 48–49).

Verse 10 summarizes the action up to this point and adds a few bits of new information. The beginning of the verse affirms again (see 3:17a) that the priests were standing in the midst of the Jordan. In chap. 3, they stood there until the entire nation had "completed" (the verb is *tmm*) its crossing; in chap. 4, they stood there until everything[232] God (and Moses) had commanded was "completed" (or "fulfilled"; the verb is again *tmm*). The emphasis in this verse is again on obedience and the fulfillment of the spoken word. God's recorded commands to Joshua include those in his charge in 1:2–9 and, more immediately, in 3:7; 4:2–3. In addition, we have noted that God's commands were behind Joshua's words in several cases (see 3:3–6; 4:4–7). Moses' commands to Joshua concerning the entering and taking of the land were more general. On at least one occasion, Moses encouraged Joshua with words similar to those in God's charge to Joshua: in Deut 31:3,7–8, Moses reminded the people that Joshua was to cross the Jordan ahead of them, and he exhorted Joshua to be strong and courageous. More specific commands are found in Num 32:28–30, where Joshua and Eliezer the priest were commanded to make sure the Transjordan tribes crossed over, well armed, with everyone else; significantly, in Josh 4:12–13, the Transjordan tribes are specifically singled out as crossing over well armed.

The verse ends tersely: the people crossed over the Jordan quickly.[233] The message is clear: when God's people obeyed what they knew they were supposed to do, things went well for them. The first example of disobedience in the book comes in chap. 7, and the results are disastrous. God's desire was ultimately to glorify himself and have his people revere him (4:24).

(5) The Crossing Completed: Stage One (4:11–14)

[11]**and as soon as all of them had crossed, the ark of the LORD and the priests came to the other side while the people watched. **[12]**The men of Reuben, Gad and the half-tribe of Manasseh crossed over, armed, in front of the Israelites, as Moses had directed them. **[13]**About forty thousand armed for battle crossed over before the LORD to the plains of Jericho for war.**

[14]**That day the LORD exalted Joshua in the sight of all Israel; and they revered him all the days of his life, just as they had revered Moses.**

4:11 Attention is now focused on the crossing of the Jordan again, instead of the memorial stones, but the action moves forward only slowly.

---

[232] Or every "word" was fulfilled. The term used here is *dābār*, which can mean "word" or "thing."

[233] The NIV's "hurried" can be misleading. The operation was completed quickly and easily because of the obedience of all those involved. It was a quick, effortless action. "Hurried" might lead one to infer that they made haste because of fear or some other motivation, but that is not in view here at all. (See Woudstra, *Joshua*, 93 on this.)

Verse 11 begins almost identically to v. 1: "*And it happened*, when all the people had completed crossing the Jordan ...,"[234] which itself closely echoes
3:17. The construction here signals a new episode (contrary to NIV's rendering);[235] the new element consists in looking at the crossing from yet another
perspective, this time from the perspective of fulfilled commands or promises.
In v. 11b, after the people had crossed over, the priests and the ark did too.
Now, finally, after several assertions about the people's crossing over, the text
for the first time tells of the priests' crossing. The end of the entire glorious
episode is in sight.

4:12–13   These verses single out the Transjordan tribes for special attention, noting that they were acting in fulfillment of Moses' commands that they
should cross over with their brethren (see Num 32:20–22; Deut 3:18–20). The
language clearly echoes the instructions Joshua gave these tribes in 1:13–14.
New information here includes the number of fighting men who gathered
(forty thousand)[236] and the fact that they gathered near Jericho ready for battle. The significance of these verses is twofold: (1) they show another example
of obedience to a command, and (2) they provide another look at the issue of
Israel's unity (see also 1:15 and chap. 22).

In v. 13 is the first reference to Jericho in the story of the crossing. It foreshadows the dramatic events to follow in chap. 6. Jericho lay six miles west of
the Jordan River, ten miles north-northwest of the northern end of the Dead
Sea, in the deep Jordan River Valley. Its location was near a large fresh-water
spring, 825 feet below sea level.[237]

4:14   Verse 14 not only summarizes this immediate paragraph, but the
entire first section of the chapter. It represents the fulfillment of God's promise to Joshua in 3:7 that he would exalt him. Joshua's words were consistently
obeyed; and, most especially, when he told the people what was going to happen to the waters of the Jordan (3:13), it happened precisely the way he predicted (3:14–16). As a result, the people "revered" *(yrᵓ)* him all the days of his

---

[234] The only two differences are that v. 11 has "people" instead of "nation," and the verb in v.
11 is singular instead of plural.

[235] The construction is an episode-initial one: וַיְהִי plus a prepositional phrase indicating a time
frame followed by a *wayyiqṭol* verb form. Such is the analysis of, e.g., GKC § 111f; *GBH* § 118c.
A. Niccacci provides a further perspective on the specific construction here. He maintains that וַיְהִי
is a "macro-syntactic sign" of narrative, serving to introduce a new element into a narrative. When
it precedes a temporal clause (as here), it does so in order to connect the material in the temporal
clause in a close and integral way with what immediately follows. (See A. Niccacci, *The Syntax of
the Verb in Classical Hebrew Prose*, JSOTSup 86 [Sheffield: JSOT, 1990], §§28, 30, 127.) This
same type of construction occurs several times earlier in Joshua, e.g, in 1:1; 3:14–16; 4:1.

[236] On the issue of large numbers in Joshua and elsewhere, see the note at 7:2–5.

[237] An impressive mound where the ancient city lay rises today close to eighty feet at its highest
point. For more on Jericho and its excavations, see R. A. Coughenour, "Jericho," *ISBE* 2:992–96;
K. Kenyon et al., "Jericho," *NEAEHL* 2:674–97. See also below, p. 175f.

life, just as they had Moses. The word "revered" is literally "feared" (see its
use in the NIV of v. 24). When used of God, it denotes a holy fear, reverence,
awe, or worship. When used of humans, the idea is similar. It can denote terror on the one extreme (e.g., Exod 14:10 [the Israelites feared *(yr')* the Egyp-
tians]; Deut 2:4 [the inhabitants of Seir feared *(yr')* the Israelites]; etc.) and
respect or honor on the other extreme (e.g., Lev 19:3 ["respect *(yr')* your
mother and father"]; 1 Kgs 3:28 [the Israelites held Solomon "in awe" *(yr')*
because of his wise decision]; etc.).[238]

Joshua is now, in effect, the "new Moses." After the great crossing of the
Red Sea, "the people feared the LORD and put their trust in him and in Moses
his servant" (Exod 14:31b). Here, now, Joshua found himself in a remarkably
similar position after a remarkably similar miracle. He was growing into
Moses' job as Israel's leader.[239]

Thus ends the first section of chap. 4, with a reflection on events within
Israel, from a vantage point outside the promised land. From this point on, the
focus shifts to events outside of Israel, from a vantage point inside Canaan.
Polzin notes that "up to this point both priests and people are described as
crossing over *('ābar)* the river. ... [After this, the narrative] *never* refers to the
crossing of the river, but to the *coming out* or *up* from the Jordan *('ālāh
mittōk* or *mîn hayyardēn)*."[240]

(6) The Crossing Completed: Stage Two (4:15–18)

**15Then the LORD said to Joshua, 16"Command the priests carrying the ark of
the Testimony to come up out of the Jordan."**

17So Joshua commanded the priests, "Come up out of the Jordan."

**18And the priests came up out of the river carrying the ark of the covenant of
the LORD. No sooner had they set their feet on the dry ground than the waters of
the Jordan returned to their place and ran at flood stage as before.**

The chapter ends with two paragraphs detailing the completion of the
crossing and revisiting the story of the memorial stones. Consistent with the
pattern throughout the chapter, both look backward at what has already been
stated, yet both advance the story line as well.

---

[238] See H. F. Fuhs, "יָרֵא *yārē'*," *TDOT* 6:290–315; M. V. Van Pelt and W. C. Kaiser, Jr., "ירא,"
NIDOTTE 2:527–33.

[239] See the commentary on 1:1 on Joshua's subordinate role to Moses and the issue of leadership in the book. See also D. J. McCarthy, "The Theology of Leadership in Joshua 1–9," *Bib* 52
(1971): 165–75; T. C. Butler, *Understanding the Basic Themes of Joshua* (Dallas: Word, 1991),
23–34; and J. A. Vadnais, "The Characterization of Joshua: From Minister of Moses to Servant of
the Lord," (Ph.D. diss., New Orleans Baptist Theological Seminary, in progress).

[240] Polzin, *Moses and the Deuteronomist,* 101 (emphasis Polzin). The Hb. *'ālāh mittōk* and
mîn hayyardēn means "to come up from the midst" and "[to come up] from the Jordan." In 4:11–
24, Polzin's statement is true when the reported speech of vv. 22–23 is excluded.

4:15–18 Here the commands to the priests to come up out of the Jordan are recorded. Strictly chronologically, they belong before v. 11, which tells us that the priests and the ark crossed over to the other side. Here, though, as we have noted, the perspective is from within the land: they did not "cross over" here (as in v. 11), but rather they "came up" from the Jordan.

The ark of the "Testimony" is mentioned here for the first time.[241] The word "testimony" is always used to refer to God's testimony or covenant. It often describes the tabernacle ("the tabernacle of the Testimony": Exod 38:21; Num 1:50,53) and the ark ("the ark of the Testimony": Exod 25:22; 26:33,34; etc.). It sometimes stands alone referring to the ark ("the Testimony": Exod 27:21; 30:36; Lev 16:13). It also sometimes refers to the two tablets of stone that were *in* the ark (Exod 25:21; 40:20). The "Testimony" is even equated with the covenant itself (cp. Exod 31:18: "the two tablets of the Testimony" and Deut 9:11: "the tablets of the covenant"). The written words of the law constitute the Testimony, and the use of this term here is appropriate in the context of command or promise and fulfillment that we have seen in chaps. 3–4. God's word was to form the basis of everything Joshua and Israel did (cf. 1:7–8).

The final stage in the miracle of the crossing was the priests' leaving the Jordan riverbed and the waters returning to their place (v. 18). This verse is a mirror image of 3:15: its language echoes the earlier passage almost word for word as it describes the priests' feet touching dry ground as they came out (instead of the river water as they entered it) and the waters overflowing its banks. Just as in 3:15 the syntax leading up to the stopping up of the waters is drawn out, so here too the wording slowly builds up to the denouement where the waters returned to their place. The miraculous nature of the crossing event, so prominent throughout chaps. 3–4, is once again highlighted in the statement that the waters returned to their flood stage the moment the priests' feet touched the dry ground.

(7) Memorializing the Crossing: Stage Two (4:19–5:1)

¹⁹On the tenth day of the first month the people went up from the Jordan and camped at Gilgal on the eastern border of Jericho. ²⁰And Joshua set up at Gilgal the twelve stones they had taken out of the Jordan. ²¹He said to the Israelites, "In the future when your descendants ask their fathers, 'What do these stones mean?' ²²tell them, 'Israel crossed the Jordan on dry ground.' ²³For the LORD your God dried up the Jordan before you until you had crossed over. The LORD your God did to the Jordan just what he had done to the Red Sea when he dried it up before

---

[241] On other designations for the ark in these chapters, see the commentary on 3:3. On the term here (עֵדוּת), see C. Schultz, "ʿēdût," *TWOT* (Chicago: Moody, 1980), 649–50; P. Enns, "עֵדוּת," *NIDOTTE* 3:328–29.

us until we had crossed over. [24]He did this so that all the peoples of the earth
might know that the hand of the LORD is powerful and so that you might always
fear the LORD your God."

[1]Now when all the Amorite kings west of the Jordan and all the Canaanite
kings along the coast heard how the LORD had dried up the Jordan before the
Israelites until we had crossed over, their hearts melted and they no longer had
the courage to face the Israelites.

With its interpretive comments on the significance of the crossing, this section brings the story of the crossing to an end. It consists primarily of Joshua's
final words to Israel about the crossing. In these words to the Israelites, he
picks up on the ideas stated in vv. 5–7 about the meaning of the memorial
stones, and he concludes with an evaluation of the purpose of the entire affair
(v. 24). In 5:1, a short, independent paragraph concludes the section, telling
about the terror that the Israelites' reputation had spread among the kings
west of the Jordan. This evaluative paragraph brings the second major section
of chap. 4 (4:15–5:1) to a close, with a perspective on the events from within
Canaan and outside of Israel. This contrasts with 4:14, the evaluative comment at the end of the first major section, which focuses on events from outside of Canaan and within Israel, as we have already noted.

4:19 The crossing of the Jordan River happened on the tenth day of the
first month (i.e., the month of Nisan [also known as Abib], which corresponds
with March-April). This was an important day, since it coincided with the day
that the Passover lamb was to be selected (Exod 12:3). It foreshadowed the
keeping of the Passover in 5:10 on the fourteenth day of the month in accordance with the Passover calendar (when the lamb actually was killed) (Exod
12:6,18). And the fact that this happened at Passover helps to connect the
crossing of the Jordan even more closely with the events of the exodus and the
crossing of the Red Sea, which is made explicit in v. 23.

The Israelites encamped at Gilgal, just east of Jericho in the Jordan Valley.[242] Gilgal was the first of three religious bases the Israelites occupied in
Joshua's day. The second was Shiloh (18:1), and the third was Shechem (24:1;
cf. 8:30). This is the first reference in the Book of Joshua to this important
religious site. Here, the Israelites celebrated several religious rituals, including circumcision and Passover (Joshua 5), and it was the place where a sanctuary and an altar were built for God (9:23,27). It remained as an important
place of sacrifice for many centuries later (see 1 Sam 10:8). It was one of the
cities where Samuel judged (1 Sam 7:16) and where Saul was made king
(1 Sam 11:14–15). However, worship there eventually became apostate, and

---

[242] The exact phrase used here is "at the east edge of Jericho" (בִּקְצֵה מִזְרַח יְרִיחוֹ). This is
the only geographical clue in the OT as to its location; its exact site is unknown. See Boling,
Joshua, 192, and W. R. Kotter, "Gilgal," *ABD* 2:1025, on the geographical possibilities.

two eighth-century prophets condemned it (Hos 9:15; 12:11; Amos 4:4; 5:5).

4:20 Joshua now erected the stones that the twelve men had brought up out of the Jordan River (v. 8) as a memorial in a permanent site, at Gilgal. He had earlier set them up in the middle of the Jordan, at the spot where the priests were standing (v. 9).[243]

4:21–23 The twelve stones were to be a memorial for Israel, to pass along to their children, as Joshua had stated earlier (vv. 6–7). The wording here is slightly different from that of vv. 6–7. Here, the crossing itself is mentioned, and not just the miracle of the stoppage of the waters. However, the miracle is still clearly in view: the "dry land" is mentioned in v. 22,[244] and a new fact is introduced: the Lord "dried up" the Jordan until the Israelites crossed over (v. 23).

The similarities of this crossing of the Jordan and the crossing of the Red Sea have been noted (see comments on 3:17). Lest we miss the point, the text makes this connection explicit in 4:23. God did here exactly what he had done earlier: he "dried up" the waters. The wonder of the miracle is enhanced even further by this comparison with the defining moment at the Red Sea.

4:24 The miracle was performed for a greater purpose than merely getting the Israelites across the Jordan River. Here, two purposes are given:[245] (1) it was to be a "sign" to all peoples that God himself was mighty, that is, a testimony to his greatness, and (2) an inducement to the Israelites to fear God all their days, that is, accord to him (and him alone) the worship and allegiance due him. The miracle was so amazing that it should call forth such a response from God's people.

The statement about the miracle being a testimony to all the peoples recalls the words of Rahab, who acknowledged that the inhabitants of Jericho had indeed heard about how great Israel's God was, when he defeated Sihon and Og in the wilderness (2:10–11). It also recalls the purpose of the tenth plague in Egypt, which was much more than merely to convince the pharaoh to release the Israelites. Exodus 12:12 states that the tenth plague (if not also all the others) was God's challenge to the Egyptian gods: "I will bring judgment on all the gods of Egypt." All of these cases show that God performed miracles to attest to himself, along with the more immediate purposes of accomplishing certain ends for the people involved.

5:1 This verse is a final summary of the effect of the miracle on the nations. The first purpose for the miracle in chap. 3, as it is expressed in

---

[243] The verb in both vv. 9 and 20 is the same: *hēkîm*, "set up, established (firmly)."

[244] The word here is יַבָּשָׁה (see n. on 3:17).

[245] That it was performed for these purposes is made clear by the word לְמַעַן, "so that, for the purpose of," which is found twice in the verse, introducing the two major clauses. The statements in v. 24 are thus subordinate grammatically to those in vv. 22–23, showing that the actions there were for the purposes described here.

4:24, was now accomplished: the nations did indeed realize that God's hand was powerful, and they were terrified because of it. This reinforces the message of the "giving" of the land in chap. 1 and Rahab's confession in 2:9–11. As Butler states, "Before Israel has fought a single battle, the entire land is hers for the taking."[246] It also is the fulfillment of the prophetic words in the Song of the Sea (Exodus 15), where the Israelites celebrated God's great deliverance from the Egyptians at the Red Sea. Part of that song looks ahead to Israel's entering the land and the nations cowering in terror before them (Exod 15:14–16).

This verse echoes closely some of the language of 4:23. Compare the following portions:[247]

> 4:23: *the LORD* your God *dried up the waters of the Jordan from before* you *until* you *crossed over*
> 5:1: *the LORD dried up the waters of the Jordan from before* the sons of Israel *until* we/they[248] *crossed over.*

Here again we have the author confirming that the words of God or his servant —in this case, Joshua—came true.

This verse also confirms the truth of Rahab's words in 2:10–11. Compare the following portions:

> 2:10–11: *How the LORD* your God *dried up the waters of the* Red Sea *from before you* ... *and* our *heart melted and no spirit* rose *in* any man *again on* your *account*
> 5:1: *How the LORD dried up the waters of the* Jordan *from before* the sons of Israel ... *and* their *heart melted and no spirit* was *in* them *again on account* of the sons of Israel.

Such reactions of fear or opposition were common as Israel entered the land (see 9:1–4; 10:1–2; 11:1–5). What is noteworthy here is that this reaction came before any military encounter had taken place. The wonder of the miracle God performed is thus highlighted in even sharper detail. Once more the author equates the miracles at the Red Sea and the Jordan River (see also 3:17; 4:14).

Those standing in awe and terror of Israel here are all the kings of the Canaanites and the Amorites, two of the seven peoples mentioned in 3:10. Here, they appear to stand for all seven groups.

---

[246] Butler, *Joshua*, 51.

[247] Here and in the next selection, the words in italics are those identical in both texts.

[248] The NIV has "we" here, following the consonantal text of the Masoretic text and echoing the same wording in v. 23. However, more logical is "until they crossed over," which is the reading suggested by the Masoretes and found in many ancient manuscripts and versions. NASB, NJPSV, and NRSV all have "they."

In addition to looking back one last time, 5:1 looks ahead.[249] Since all of the inhabitants of Canaan were terrified of Israel, the possession of the land promised to be an easy task. In addition, the Canaanites' fear conveniently immobilized them just at the time the Israelites performed a mass circumcision ceremony (5:2–9), after which they would have been vulnerable to a military attack (cp. Gen 34:25).

Such is the end of the story of Israel's crossing the Jordan. It was accomplished by a mighty miracle of God, which is reflected upon in depth in chaps. 3 and 4, and it caused Israel's enemies in Canaan to be paralyzed with fear. The stage was now set for Israel to move into the land and to take it. Before they did, however, further preparations were required. These are presented in chap. 5.

4. Ritual Preparations (5:2–15)

Joshua 5 records the first actions of Joshua and the Israelites in Canaan after they had crossed the Jordan and memorialized it with the stones. Three episodes make up the chapter in the Hebrew Bible, and they continue in the spirit of chap. 4, since they are all concerned with ritual preparations or holiness in one way or another, not with military preparedness or with "getting on with the action." That such spiritual preparations preceded the actual "conquest" of the land illustrates the priorities we have noted: God was going to give Israel the land, and Israel's task was to be sure it obeyed and was adequately prepared spiritually. Thus, the real "action" of the book is delayed by several important—even essential—preliminaries: the admonitions to Joshua about keeping the law and to the Transjordan tribes about keeping unity within the nation (chap. 1), memorializing God's miraculous help (chap. 4), and sanctifying the people (chap. 5). The tasks ahead of battle were far too important to enter lightly—to enter unprepared in any way, including spiritually. Interestingly enough, the ritual ceremonies in this chapter are highlighted and emphasized in that they are bracketed by two seven-day periods: the first involved crossing of the Jordan (see the commentary on 3:2), and the second involved marching around Jericho (6:15). Each of these seven-day periods was climaxed by a mighty work of God: the stopping of the Jordan's waters in the first instance and the destruction of Jericho in the second.

---

[249] Most commentators' outlines include 5:1 with what follows instead of with what precedes. It begins with an episode-initial construction (וַיְהִי plus prepositional phrase with a temporal reference plus *wayyiqtol* verb form), and so this is certainly defensible. However, it may be serving as an independent wrap-up of the entire two chapters preceding and thus stands alone grammatically. Contentwise, it looks back more than it looks ahead, although in reality it functions as a hinge, looking back and ahead.

At this juncture in the text, one of the most important divergences from the Masoretic manuscript traditions upon which our Bible translations are based is found in the Qumran scrolls.[250] In one short fragment, portions of Josh 8:34–35 and an editorial transition not found in any other extant Bible manuscript immediately precede Josh 5:2.[251] The portion is very fragmentary, but it is almost certain that all of 8:30–35 preceded 5:2. This shows a radically different order and arrangement from the majority Masoretic text of the Hebrew Bible upon which almost all Bible translations are based today.[252]

The account in 8:30–35 tells of a covenant renewal ceremony during which Joshua built an altar of uncut stones on Mount Ebal, sacrifices were offered (burnt offerings and fellowship offerings), the law was copied onto stones, and the people stood on Mounts Gerizim and Ebal for the reading of the law. All of this was in accordance with the law of Moses, specifically Deut 27:2–8,12–13. Joshua 8:30–35 states—five different times, no less!—that these things were done in strict observance of Moses' commands. In Deuteronomy 27, the same elements are found: instructions to build an altar of uncut stones (vv. 5–6), to copy the law onto stones (vv. 3,8), to offer burnt offerings and fellowship offerings (vv. 6–7), to do it on Mount Ebal when Israel crossed the Jordan (v. 4), divided into two groups, one on Mount Gerizim and one on Mount Ebal (vv. 12–13).

In its present placement in the MT, the passage in 8:30–35 records the Isra-

---

[250] These are the so-called Dead Sea Scrolls, discovered in the 1940s and 1950s. These are the oldest Hb. documents available today, dating to the second and first centuries B.C. and the first century A.D. For general introductions to the Dead Sea Scrolls, see L. Schiffman, *Reclaiming the Dead Sea Scrolls: The History of Judaism, the Background of Christianity, the Lost Library of Qumran* (Philadelphia: Jewish Publication Society, 1994); J. C. Vanderkam, *The Dead Sea Scrolls Today* (Grand Rapids: Eerdmans, 1994). In Joshua, portions of two scrolls have been found, both in Cave 4, labeled 4QJosh[a] and 4QJosh[b]. They have only recently been published: (1) 4QJosh[a] by E. Ulrich, in two publications: "4QJoshua[a] and Joshua's First Altar in the Promised Land," in G. J. Brooke and F. G. Martinez, eds., *New Qumran Texts and Studies*, STDJ 15 (Leiden: Brill 1994), 89–104; id., "4QJosh[a]," in E. Ulrich et al., eds., *Qumran Cave 4 (IX: Deuteronomy, Joshua, Judges, Kings*, DJD 14 (Oxford: Clarendon, 1995), 143–52; and (2) 4QJosh[b] by E. Tov, "4QJosh[b]," in Z. J. Kapera, ed., *Intertestamental Essays in Honour of Josef Tadeusz Milik* (Krakow: Enigma, 1992), 1:205–12; id., "4QJosh[b]," in *Qumran Cave 4 (IX)*, Ulrich et al., eds., 153–60.

[251] The addition is found in 4QJosh[a], and it is about one and one-half lines long, of which about half is missing. What can be read is as follows: "After which [i.e., the covenant renewal ceremony just described], the[ir feet?] were drawn out ... the book of the law after this, those carrying the ark went up ..." (author's translation, restoring עלו ["went up"] with A. Rofé ["The Editing of the Book of Joshua in the Light of 4QJosh[a]," in *New Qumran Texts and Studies*, ed. Brooke and Martinez, 78]).

[252] This fragment—along with other fragments most likely belonging to the same scroll—have been published by Ulrich (see earlier note). They are also discussed by Rofé ("The Editing of the Book of Joshua in the Light of 4QJosh[a]," 73–80. L. Greenspoon discusses most of the Joshua fragments from Cave 4, but not this one ("The Qumran Fragments of Joshua: Which Puzzle Are They Part of and Where Do They Fit?" in *Septuagint, Scrolls and Cognate Writings*, ed. G. J. Brooke and B. Lindars, SBLSCSS 33 [Atlanta: Scholars Press, 1992], 159–94).

elites' fulfillment of these instructions, but the timing was significantly delayed, since it did not take place until after the taking of Jericho and the initial defeat and eventual victory at Ai. The instructions clearly stated (three times: Deut 27:2,3,4) that this was to be done upon crossing the Jordan; the clear implication is that this was to be done immediately.

Thus, the evidence from Qumran that Joshua and the Israelites fulfilled these instructions immediately after the crossing is very important. This evidence is buttressed by Josephus's account (the first-century Jewish historian), who mentions the building of an altar immediately after the crossing.[253] If the original manuscripts of Joshua did have this covenant renewal ceremony between 5:1 and 5:2, then this shows the Israelites attempting to obey Moses' commands as closely as possible. This fits in very well with the following two episodes in chap. 5: the ceremonies of circumcision and Passover. Both of these (or all three) show the continuing attention in the book's early chapters to the command-fulfillment pattern we have observed and to the Israelites' ritual proper preparation before they began their military encounters.[254]

(1) Circumcision (5:2–9)

[2]At that time the LORD said to Joshua, "Make flint knives and circumcise the Israelites again." [3]So Joshua made flint knives and circumcised the Israelites at Gibeath Haaraloth.

---

[253] Josephus, *Ant.* 5.1.4. He also mentions what apparently is a second ceremony after the conquest of the land (after chap. 12: *Ant.* 5.1.18–20), which is not recorded elsewhere, so his evidence cannot be considered determinative. However, the combination of the Qumran evidence and Josephus's evidence for the ceremony taking place before 5:2 is difficult to ignore.

[254] It is impossible to be certain here. The Old Greek traditions represented in the LXX place the covenant renewal ceremony close to where it is in the MT, but displaced until after 9:2, when a coalition of Canaanite kings had assembled to oppose Israel. This placement of the ceremony is the least plausible, since it is difficult to imagine such an event taking place in the face of such a threat. Whether the ceremony took place immediately after the crossing (after 5:1) or after the victory at Ai (after 8:29), the Israelites would have had to travel some distance to get to Mount Ebal: it was about twenty-five miles from Gilgal to Shechem (the town at the base of Mount Ebal) and about twenty miles from Ai to Shechem; so in either case, the Israelites would have had to make a special journey to get there. (See Rofé, "The Editing of the Book of Joshua in the Light of 4QJosh[a]," 77, and Rasmussen, *NIV Atlas of the Bible*, 94 [map] on the distances here.) The presence in the Qumran manuscript of an editorial transition between the account of the covenant renewal and 5:2 might signal that this manuscript was not a text of Scripture per se, but a commentary or a liturgical work of some type that included excerpts of Scripture along with other materials. This type of work was common at Qumran (see Ulrich et al., "Introduction," *Qumran Cave 4* (IX, 1). Hess judges that the Joshua manuscript in question was probably this type of work (*Joshua*, 20), and Nelson considers that it too neatly fits into a fulfillment pattern to have been original (*Joshua*, 73). On the other hand, Ulrich concludes that the Qumran text does reflect the original ("4QJosh[a]," 145–46), and Rofé seems to agree, even adducing some rabbinical evidence that points in the same direction as does the Qumran and Josephus evidence ("The Editing of the Book of Joshua in the Light of 4QJosh[a]," 77–79).

⁴Now this is why he did so: All those who came out of Egypt—all the men of military age—died in the desert on the way after leaving Egypt. ⁵All the people that came out had been circumcised, but all the people born in the desert during the journey from Egypt had not. ⁶The Israelites had moved about in the desert forty years until all the men who were of military age when they left Egypt had died, since they had not obeyed the LORD. For the LORD had sworn to them that they would not see the land that he had solemnly promised their fathers to give us, a land flowing with milk and honey. ⁷So he raised up their sons in their place, and these were the ones Joshua circumcised. They were still uncircumcised because they had not been circumcised on the way. ⁸And after the whole nation had been circumcised, they remained where they were in camp until they were healed.

⁹Then the LORD said to Joshua, "Today I have rolled away the reproach of Egypt from you." So the place has been called Gilgal to this day.

The first episode in chap. 5 is the ceremony of circumcision. Circumcision was an original sign of the covenant with Abraham (Gen 17:11), and it was to be done for every male in every generation. However, it was not done during the wilderness wanderings (v. 5). This is ironic, since Moses, Israel's leader at the time, had had an experience earlier in which the Lord had tried to kill him because he had not circumcised his own son (Exod 4:24–26), yet he had apparently not been too concerned to encourage circumcision in the wilderness, because an entire generation had now crossed the Jordan who were not circumcised. This episode marks the beginning of Israel's true identification with the land of Canaan, and it contrasts the present generation of Israelites very starkly with the preceding generation, which rebelled against Moses and the Lord.[255]

5:2 This verse begins with "At that time," a phrase found again in Joshua at 6:26; 11:10,21. Each time it introduces a statement or a specific act by Joshua, except here, where God speaks, although Joshua then obeyed (v. 3).[256] This fact reinforces the close link between God and Joshua that we have noted earlier (e.g., see on 3:7; 4:1–3,8–10).

---

[255] In 5:2–9, the Old Greek differs significantly from the Hb. text, so much so that it must be judged to have come from a different Hb. exemplar, now lost. It is considerably shorter, omitting two significant portions: (1) the reference in v. 2 to "again … a second time" (NIV simply has "again" here) and (2) most of v. 4, which gives the reason for the second circumcision. It also states that some were uncircumcised when the Israelites left Egypt (v. 5), whereas the Hb. of v. 5 states that all who left Egypt *were* circumcised. For details of the differences here, see Butler, *Joshua*, 54–55, and Nelson, *Joshua*, 72–74. However, we should note that the MT is perfectly coherent on its own merits.

[256] Hess, *Joshua*, 118.

Joshua was to make flint knives[257] with which to circumcise the Israelites. Only in two episodes in the historical narratives of the Old Testament is the word "flint" found: here and in Exod 4:25, in the story of Moses' wife's circumcision of their son. God's instructions here to the Israelites to make flint knives for circumcision undoubtedly were intentionally designed to recall that earlier incident. Possibly, they were special knives, used for ceremonial purposes only (since they are only mentioned in Scripture in connection with circumcision). Their importance is reinforced by the Old Greek text of 24:30, which states that these knives were buried with Joshua (see the commentary on 24:30).

Circumcision in Israel involved cutting off the male foreskin in accordance with the instructions given to Abraham, as a sign of the covenant God had made with him and his descendants (Gen 17:10–14). Israel was not the only nation that practiced the rite: Jeremiah mentions Egypt, Edom, Ammon, Moab, and others as nations who practiced it but who were "uncircumcised" in their hearts (Jer 9:25–26).[258] In contrast to the practice in these nations, however, circumcision had special covenantal significance in Israel.[259]

The circumcision was done "again ... a second time." This phrase reflects the information given in vv. 4–5: when the Israelites had left Egypt, that generation of males had been circumcised, but they had died in the wilderness, and the practice had been neglected in the wilderness. Thus, it was necessary to do again, especially before the important celebration of the Passover. The original instructions for the Passover had emphasized the importance of circumcising all participants before the ceremony (Exod 12:44,48), and Israel here was acting in accordance with those commands.

5:3 Joshua obeyed God's command explicitly—the wording is identical in the command (v. 2) and the report of the execution of the command, except for the necessary changes in verb forms—and circumcised the Israelites at a

---

[257] The term is lit. "swords [=knives] of stones." Flint is a rock found in abundance in biblical lands, and its use is documented in almost all periods of occupations; many flint knives have been found in excavations. Flint was gradually replaced by harder metals (copper, bronze, iron), but it continued to be used long after these metals were introduced. A. R. Millard suggests that, in circumcision rites, this was probably due to a concern for cleanliness: sharp stone flakes could easily be struck from the rocks and then discarded. See Millard, "Back to the Iron Bed: Og's or Procrustes'?" *Congress Volume (Paris 1992)*, VTSup 61 (Leiden: Brill, 1995), 195–97. On flint in general, see R. K. Harrison, "Flint; Flinty (Rock)," *ISBE* 2:315.

[258] See J. M. Sasson, "Circumcision in the Ancient Near East," *JBL* 85 (1966): 473–76, on the practice outside of Israel. A well-known Egyptian text tells of one man's experience of circumcision (see J. A. Wilson, trans., "Circumcision in Egypt," in *ANET*, 326), and a scene from an Egyptian tomb shows young boys being circumcised by "mortuary priests" with flint knives (see *ANEP*, 206 [fig. #629]).

[259] See R. deVaux, *Ancient Israel* (New York: McGraw Hill, 1961), 46–48; E. Isaac, "Circumcision as Covenant Rite," *Anthropos* 59 (1964): 444–56, esp. 450–54; and M. Fox, "Sign of the Covenant: Circumcision in the Light of the Priestly ʿôt Etiologies," *RB* 81 (1974): 537–96.

place called "Gibeath-Haaraloth."[260] As the NIV text note indicates, this name means "hill of foreskins." This is the first of two names given to the site; the second is "Gilgal" (v. 9), which already has been introduced into the text at 4:19.

Both names' meanings have significance to the story. Gibeath-Haaraloth's is obvious ("Hill of Foreskins").[261] Gilgal's is a play on the word *gālal*, which means "to roll." In v. 9, the spot is called "Gilgal" because God had "rolled away" the reproach of Egypt. The first name is found only here in the Old Testament, while the second is found forty times, including three times before this story (Deut 11:30; Josh 4:19,20).[262]

5:4–7 The text gives a detailed explanation as to just why this circumcision was done and why it was necessary. Of the adult males who came out of Egypt, all had been circumcised in Egypt. However, those born after the exodus from Egypt had not been circumcised (v. 5). This is why there was a need for a "second" circumcision (see v. 2).[263] The reason for this appears to have been the older generation's rebelliousness, typified by their refusal to enter the land and their complaining to Moses (Numbers 14). As a result, God sentenced them to die in the wilderness during a wandering of forty years (Num 14:28–35).[264] This applied to all those who were twenty years old or older (Num 14:29). This text in Joshua confirms the fulfillment of that divine sentence: the older rebellious generation had indeed died off, and a new one replaced it.

The disobedience spoken of in v. 6 cannot be correlated with a specific act of disobedience to a specific command of God or Moses, but it clearly refers

---

[260] We presume Joshua was assisted in this task by others, given that there were thousands of Israelite males to circumcise. A similar individualizing of a large task can be seen in 23:4, where Joshua tells the nations that *he* had conquered the Canaanite nations; the book makes clear in chaps. 6–12 that God did the lion's share of the fighting and that the people helped as well.

[261] Whether the reference is to a "hill" of severed foreskins piled up or to an actual hill near the spot where the circumcision took place is unclear. Since its location and the location of Gilgal are unknown (see note at 4:19 for Gilgal), no certainty is possible.

[262] See the commentary on 4:19 for more on Gilgal. The references in 4:19–20 and Deut 11:30 refer to the site by its common name, derived from the incident here in Joshua 5. The reference in Deuteronomy likely was added by someone after Moses, who inserted the site's common name in later years.

[263] It is not because a first circumcision was done in the Egyptian manner (i.e., a slitting—not a cutting off—of the foreskin) and now these same males needed to be circumcised in the "Israelite" manner (contrary to Sasson's assertions, "Circumcision in the Ancient Near East," 473–74). Those circumcised in Egypt were now all dead, except perhaps for those who had been underage when they left Egypt (v. 4). The second circumcision was performed on all those born in the desert.

[264] The Old Greek traditions have "forty-two" years here, since, strictly speaking, the Israelites rebelled in their second year after leaving Egypt (see Num 10:11–12), and forty more years of wandering would yield a total of forty-two. But, passages such as Deut 1:3 and Acts 7:36 support the Hebrew reading of "forty" here; indeed, Deut 2:14 states that thirty-eight years passed after the rebellion. Thus, the forty-year sentence on the rebellious Israel must be seen as a round number that included the first two years before their rebellion at Kadesh Barnea in Numbers 14.

to the events in Numbers 14, where the twelve spies had been sent into the
land at God's command and the people had rebelled. The clear implication
there is that, given a favorable report from the spies about the wondrous land
that awaited them, the people should enter and take it. After all, God was giving them the land, and he ordered the spying expedition, presumably to
encourage Israel about the land he was giving them (Num 13:2). Yet, they
refused to enter the land, due to the spies' majority report, which was negative. In Josh 5:7, the younger generation of Israelites had been uncircumcised,
and this was at best an act of negligence by the Israelites and at worst a defiant
act of disobedience, since circumcision had been required of Israel since the
time of Abraham (Gen 17:11).[265] It was this younger generation that stood in
need of circumcision, and that Joshua did circumcise (v. 7).

The unity of Israel in matters both good and bad is visible in this passage.
There are two groups in view: the earlier, circumcised group and the present,
uncircumcised group. The word "all" *(kōl)* is found six times in vv. 4–8,
referring to the totality of one or the other of these groups (vv.
4[2x],5[2x],6,8). In vv. 4–5a, and 6, the references are to the circumcised but
rebellious group that had *all* died out. The two references in vv. 5b and 8 are
to the uncircumcised ones, *all* of whom Joshua circumcised.[266] A play on the
word "finished off, completed" *(tmm)* is found in vv. 6,8: in v. 6, the entire
rebellious nation was "finished off" *(tmm),* and in v. 8, the entire new generation's circumcision was "completed" *(tmm).* The wordplay helps to draw the
sharp contrast between each group.[267]

Verse 6b contains a trenchant insight into the nature of the Abrahamic covenant. God had promised Abraham this land (Gen 12:7; 15:7,16,18–21; etc.),
and it was to belong to his descendants in perpetuity (Gen 17:8). Yet, because
of the wilderness generation's rebelliousness, God had sworn to them that
they would *not* see this land (see Num 14:20–23). While the elements of this
covenant would not be broken by God and they remained in effect throughout
all generations, each generation of Israelites—indeed, each individual Israelite—had to make its own decision whether to obey the covenant. That is the
point of circumcision as the sign of the covenant (Gen 17:9–14): an individual's failure to circumcise was tantamount to breaking the covenant, and whoever did not do this was cut off from the rest of Israel (17:14). However, the
covenant as a whole remained in effect for the nation; it was the rebellious
individual or group who was cut off.[268] If the entire nation sinned, God would

---

[265] Keil argues that the suspension of circumcision was at God's behest, despite the absence of
any such indications in the text itself (*Joshua*, 55–57).

[266] See Hess, *Joshua*, 120.

[267] See Nelson, *Joshua*, 77.

[268] See W. C. Kaiser, Jr., *Toward an Old Testament Theology* (Grand Rapids: Zondervan, 1978),
92–94, for an introduction to this issue.

take the land completely away from them (Deut 4:25–27; 8:19–20; 30:17–18; etc.), but even when it did happen at the time of the exile, God brought Israel back to the land (Jer 29:10; Ezra 1–2; etc.). God's promises to Abraham's descendants would be fulfilled to the nation as a whole, but not every last individual would automatically participate; faith and obedience were required. Joshua 5:7 shows this by stating that God raised up another generation to replace the one he had consigned to perish in the wilderness.

The land that God was giving to Israel was a bountiful one: it was "a land flowing with milk and honey" (v. 6b). This colorful phrase occurs only here in the Book of Joshua. It evokes images of a fertile land ready to supply all the Israelites' needs. It is first found in God's promises to Moses about the land, in Exod 3:8, and it is used fifteen times in the Pentateuch to describe this "good and large land" (Exod 3:8).

Two final, miscellaneous notes can be made here. (1) the NIV's "men of military age" in v. 4 is literally "the males, all the men of war." Numbers 14:29 shows that these were the men twenty years old and older. (2) In v. 6, the NIV's "the land that he had solemnly promised their fathers to give *us*" is a good reminder that the promises to Abraham were for every generation of Israelites and that Joshua could truthfully say that the earlier promises were for "us."[269]

5:8–9 The syntax at the beginning of v. 8 indicates a final paragraph in this section. It contains two summarizing statements: (1) the author's report concluding the story of the circumcision and (2) God's words interpreting the significance of the event.

The men were not able to move easily after their circumcision, so they remained at Gilgal until they were healed (v. 8). The chronological indicators in 4:19 and 5:10 show that the Passover began four days after they arrived at Gilgal. The healing was not likely completed within three to four days, but the men apparently had enough vigor to observe the activities of the Passover; we do not know exactly how long after this the events associated with Jericho began.

God interpreted the event for Joshua by telling him that the "reproach of Egypt" had been rolled away. We have already noted the similarity of the name "Gilgal" to the Hebrew for "roll": *gilgāl* and *gālal*. The "reproach of Egypt" has been understood variously by commentators, but the most straightforward understanding is that this was the reproach heaped upon Israel by Egypt (i.e., Egypt's scorn), in the same way as the "reproach of Moab" (Zeph 2:8) was the derision heaped upon Judah by Moab because of God's punishment of his own people or the "reproach" of the daughters of Aram/

---

[269] There is some manuscript evidence that reads "to them" here, but it is not nearly as compelling as the evidence for "they" (instead of "we") in v. 1 (see above on v. 1).

Edom[270] and others (Ezek 16:57) was the scorn directed at Judah because of God's punishment on it.[271] Egypt's "reproach" would have been occasioned by the Egyptians' observing that Israel was wandering aimlessly in the wilderness for forty years, concluding that Israel's God had abandoned it and heaping scorn on Israel because of this. This is precisely what Moses predicted Egypt would do in the event that God punished his people because of their sins (Exod 32:12; Num 14:13–16; Deut 9:28).[272] Thus, now that Israel was being so careful to obey God in every way possible, culminating with the first observance of circumcision in a generation, God effectively put Israel's "reproach" stage behind it, rolling it away. Israel was now making a new start, one in which neither Egypt nor any other nation could deride it for its God's having seemingly abandoned it.

(2) Passover (5:10–12)

¹⁰On the evening of the fourteenth day of the month, while camped at Gilgal on the plains of Jericho, the Israelites celebrated the Passover. ¹¹The day after the Passover, that very day, they ate some of the produce of the land: unleavened bread and roasted grain. ¹²The manna stopped the day after they ate this food from the land; there was no longer any manna for the Israelites, but that year they ate of the produce of Canaan.

The celebration of the Passover marked a significant turning point in Israel's life, since immediately following this, they began to live off of the land they were about to possess. The miraculous provision of manna in the wilderness stopped now. This momentous event, closing off an epoch in Israel's history, is emphasized by several repetitions in the verses here. The event also is presented in such a way as to recall the first Passover, recounted in Exodus 12. This text, then, is a transitional one, looking back to two important parts of Israel's history—the first Passover and the provision of manna— and also looking forward to life in the land, when Israel would live off of its produce.

5:10 Verse 10 harks back to 4:19: both include a date, a reference to Israel "encamping" *(ḥnh)*, and a geographical reference to the vicinity of Jer-

---

[270] Most MT manuscripts, the LXX, and the Vg have "Aram" here; some Hb. manuscripts and the Syr. have "Edom."

[271] Uncircumcision is described as a "reproach" (NIV: "disgrace") in Gen 34:14, i.e., as an evil, shameful thing. However, this cannot be the meaning of the phrase "the reproach of Egypt" (i.e., that the Israelites' uncircumcision was the reproach), since the Egyptians themselves were uncircumcised (Jer 9:25–26), and they were in no position to offer such a reproach. The wording in Josh 5:9 suggests that the reproach was something directed *at* Israel, which the Lord rolled away, rather than something that Israel had done (or not done).

[272] See Keil, *Joshua*, 59; Goslinga, *Joshua, Judges, Ruth*, 64; Woudstra, *Joshua*, 102, for this solution.

icho. Israel came up out of the Jordan on the tenth day of the first month (4:19), and now they celebrated the Passover on the fourteenth day (5:10). This was "on the evening" of the fourteenth day, which shows once again that the Israelites were scrupulous in following instructions. In this case, Exod 12:6 instructed them to kill the Passover lamb at precisely this time: on the fourteenth day of the month, "at twilight."[273] The Passover lamb is not mentioned here, but the focus in this passage is not so much on the food of the Passover meal as it is on (1) the fact that the festival was observed, symbolizing more of Israel's preparations (v. 10), and (2) the food provided in the new land, symbolizing a new transition (vv. 11–12).[274]

We should note, however, that the Passover is important as a proper preparation before taking the land (along with circumcision)[275] and as a reminder of another important transition. While the Israelites did celebrate the Passover in the wilderness (see Num 9:1–5), the reference to it here is almost certainly intended to recall the first Passover in Egypt, not any wilderness observances.[276] This is because (1) preparations on the tenth day of the month are mentioned both in Exod 12:3 and in Josh 4:19—and not in any of the accounts of the Passover celebration in the wilderness or in the legislation concerning the Passover (see Exod 23:15; 34:18; Lev 23:5; Num 9:1–5; 28:16–25; 33:3; Deut 16:1–8)— and (2) Canaan is described as "a land flowing with milk and honey" in connection with both occasions (Exod 13:5; Josh 5:6). The Passover celebration in Joshua would now mark Israel's entrance into Canaan just as it had earlier marked Israel's exodus from Egypt.

5:11–12 The emphasis in vv. 11–12 is on the end of the manna and the food Israel ate in their new land. The details of the Passover celebration are not given. The reference to unleavened bread in v. 11 naturally recalls the seven-day Feast of Unleavened Bread, which began on the fifteenth day of the month (Lev 23:6–8), the day after the Passover. However, it is not clear that Israel paused here for the full seven days of that feast. The references to the unleavened bread and the roasted grain in Josh 5:11 emphasize the transition to the new land, with a new diet (see above, on v. 10), and not so much the possible observance of the feast.[277]

---

[273] The root is the same in both verses (עֶרֶב, "evening"). Exod 12:3 states that on the tenth day of the month, the Israelite families were to select their lambs for slaughter on the fourteenth day. Josh 4:19 does not mention this event, but, if the Israelites were strictly observing this ceremony, then they would have chosen the lambs on the day they came up out of the Jordan.

[274] On the second emphasis, see Butler, *Joshua*, 60; C. Brekelmans, "Joshua v 10–12: Another Approach," *OTS* 25 (1989): 89–95; Hess, *Joshua*, 124–25.

[275] And, possibly, with the covenant renewal ceremony (see discussion above of the placement of 8:30–35).

[276] See Hess, *Joshua*, 123 on this point.

[277] It is also possible that the seven days of the feast coincided with the seven days of marching around Jericho.

Three times the text of vv. 11–12 states that the Israelites "ate" (*ʾkl)* of the produce of Canaan. The first two times, the word for "produce" is *ʿābûr,* a word found only here in the Old Testament, while the third time it is *tĕbûʾat;* both words mean essentially the same thing: the harvest-yield of the land.[278] When the text becomes more specific, it lists unleavened bread and roasted grain (v. 11b). The element common to both of these is that they were "foods of disordered circumstances and time pressures, involving uncomplicated preparation."[279] For example, unleavened bread was prepared by Lot for his night visitors (Gen 19:3) and by the Israelites when they left Egypt in a hurry (Exod 12:34). Roasted grain was part of the rations David's father gave him to take to his brothers (1 Sam 17:17) and part of what Abigail prepared in a hurry to take to David (1 Sam 25:18). The Israelites would have plenty of time in years to come to enjoy the full range of Canaan's produce, but on this occasion, the emphasis was on quick consumption.

The occasion was a momentous one for Israel, in that it ended forty years of wilderness living, a daily symbol of which was manna. Exodus 16:35 anticipates the event mentioned here: "The Israelites ate manna forty years, until they came to a land that was settled; they ate manna until they reached the border of Canaan." The Israelites had tired of this diet, however (see Num 11:4–6), and the stopping of the manna marked an important transition in several ways. The importance of this occasion is signaled by the repetitions in vv. 11–12, not only of the idea of the Israelites' eating of the land's produce but also in the twofold reference to the manna's ending in v. 12. The second reference to this reads, literally, "and there was not again for the sons of Israel manna." The syntactical construction echoes those in 2:11 ("and there arose not again any spirit [i.e., courage] in any man") and 5:1 ("and there was not in them again any spirit").[280] God's people's entrance into the land of Canaan put an end not only to the wilderness manna but also to their enemies' courage. Israel's consumption of the land's food was also a symbol of its taking possession of the land: God had promised it a bounteous land, with "houses filled with all kinds of good things you did not provide, wells you did not dig, and vineyards and olive groves you did not plant" (Deut 6:11), and now Israel was enjoying the firstfruits of that promise.

The text carefully dates the events here. On the fourteenth day of the month, the Israelites celebrated the Passover (v. 10). The next day, they ate the land's produce (v. 11). The day after that, the manna stopped (v. 12). The text ends by mentioning that this happened "in that year." Since no specific year has been mentioned prior to this, the reference can only be seen as a

---

[278] This fits the statement in 3:15 that it was harvesttime when Israel crossed the Jordan.

[279] Nelson, *Joshua,* 79.

[280] Nelson, *Joshua,* 78, makes this trenchant observation.

concluding device to signal the end of the *forty* years in the wilderness (see
v. 6 and Exod 16:35, noted above). What a joyous occasion this was, for the
Israelites finally to be able to partake of the promised land's goodness and to
see a tangible sign that their wilderness exile was over!

(3) A Call to Holiness (5:13–15)

¹³**Now when Joshua was near Jericho, he looked up and saw a man standing in
front of him with a drawn sword in his hand. Joshua went up to him and asked,
"Are you for us or for our enemies?"**
    ¹⁴**"Neither," he replied, "but as commander of the army of the LORD I have
now come." Then Joshua fell facedown to the ground in reverence, and asked him,
"What message does my Lord have for his servant?"**
    ¹⁵**The commander of the LORD's army replied, "Take off your sandals, for the
place where you are standing is holy." And Joshua did so.**

The concluding episode in chap. 5 is somewhat different from the earlier
ones, but it is linked with them in that it concerns holiness (the word "holy"
is used for the first time in the chapter in v. 15), just as the earlier episodes
concern the people's proper ritual preparation and relationship with God. All
of the chapter's episodes reflect the same outlook noted in connection with
1:7–8, that spiritual concerns—not military preparations—were to be of first
importance to the Israelites in their tasks ahead. This principle, of course, is
one that still stands today: God wants our undivided loyalties and our holiness. Indeed, Lev 19:2 ("Be holy because I, the LORD your God, am holy")
is quoted by the apostle Peter (1 Pet 1:16) as still valid for Christians.

This brief episode forms the introduction to the conquest narratives that
follow, since it tells of the commander of the Lord's army meeting with the
commander of Israel's army. There is no clear resolution to this episode, but
the obvious implication here is that the Lord will fight for Joshua and Israel as
long as they maintain the proper priorities, and this is played out in the following chapters.

5:13 By subject matter and syntax, a new episode begins here. The stage
is set with Joshua near Jericho.[281] He was surprised by seeing a man standing
before him "with a drawn sword in his hand." This was a threatening sight,

---

[281] The preposition here is -בְּ, commonly translated "in." This has occasioned some unnecessary exegetical gymnastics, such as Keil's statement that Joshua was "inside [Jericho] in thought,
meditating upon the conquest of it" (*Joshua*, 62). But the preposition also frequently means "at"
(*HALOT* 104), and "at Jericho" fits the scenario easily: Joshua was somewhere near it, not within
its walls (cf. 6:1, which says that Jericho was tightly shut up because of the Israelites).

and Joshua's question about the man's loyalties should not surprise us.[282] The exact language here—"with a drawn sword in his hand"—is found again only twice in the Old Testament, referring to the angel of the Lord: (1) in Num 22:23,31, where the angel of the Lord stood before Balaam, barring his way, and (2) in 1 Chr 21:16, where the angel of the Lord stood before David, threatening Israel because of David's sin.[283] Joshua apparently did not initially recognize the man as a divine messenger. A literal translation of his acts of perception is "and he lifted up his eyes and looked, and, behold, a man was standing opposite him." The word "behold" here indicates a change in perspective, from the narrator's all-knowing perspective to Joshua's more limited perspective, and it captures some of his surprise at seeing this threatening sight. We might paraphrase here by saying, "He looked, and what do you know! A man was standing opposite him."[284] Joshua's question of this man reflects a natural human concern with the immediate: he was concerned with the battles ahead and whether or not he could count on this man.

5:14 The stranger did not answer Joshua's question directly. With his no he was stating that his interest was not the same as Joshua's, which was to know if this man was for him or against him.[285] Instead, he asserted something far more important: he was the commander of the army of the Lord. The more general term "commander of the army" refers most commonly in the Old Testament (thirty-five times) to a human, military commander such as Phicol, the Philistine commander (Gen 21:22,32; 26:26), Sisera, the Canaanite commander (Judg 4:2,7; 1 Sam 12:9), Abner, Saul's commander (1 Sam 14:50; 17:55; etc.), Shobach, the Syrian commander (2 Sam 10:16,18); Joab, David's commander (1 Kgs 1:19,25; 2:5), Omri, the Israelite commander (1 Kgs 16:16), or Naaman, the Syrian commander (2 Kgs 5:1). In each of

---

[282] Hawk reads far too much into the threatening aspect of the encounter, stating that the commander's "menacing appearance, his evasive answer to Joshua's initial question, and the episode's abrupt ending all lend an uncanny and ominous tone to the encounter" (*Every Promise Fulfilled*, 23). He ignores the fact that, despite God's representative's unwillingness to answer Joshua directly, God himself gives detailed assurances and instructions to Joshua just a few verses later, in 6:2–5. The point in 5:13–15 is to emphasize proper priorities for Joshua: faith in God's power and authority (see below, on v. 15).

[283] The clause is בְּיָדוֹ שְׁלוּפָה וְחַרְבּוֹ, "and his sword was drawn in his hand."

[284] On the function of *hinnēh*, "behold," to mark a change in viewpoint to a character's more limited perspective, see Andersen, *Sentence*, 94–95; A. Berlin, *Poetics and Interpretation of Biblical Narrative* (Sheffield: Almond, 1983), 62–63; S. Bar-Efrat, *Narrative Art in the Bible*, JSOTSup 70 (Sheffield: Almond, 1989), 35–36.

[285] We should read לֹא "no" ("And he said, 'No. For I am the commander…'") at the beginning of the verse, with the MT and most text traditions, rather than לוֹ, "to him" ("And he said to him, 'For I am the commander …'"), which is found in some Hb. manuscripts and the Gk. and Syr. text traditions. The NIV's "neither" implies that the man was telling Joshua that he was not on anyone's side, yet surely he was indeed on Israel's side. The point here is that Joshua was asking the wrong question.

these cases, the commander was the supreme military authority, but he was subordinate to someone else, the king. In almost every case, the commander's name is found only along with the king's name, not by itself. Thus, the designation here—"the commander of the army of the LORD"—indicates an authority figure, yet one whose superior is the king, who in this case is God himself.[286]

The identity of the "army" *(ṣābāʾ)* of the Lord has been the subject of much discussion. Was it the army of Israel, acting on God's behalf as it fought, or was it a celestial army, fighting for Israel? A first possibility is that this man whom Joshua encountered might have been saying that *he* was the commander of the Israelite army that Joshua had heretofore commanded, that is, that Israel's army was in view here. The exact phrase "the army of the LORD" is found only in this passage (vv. 14–15), but it is found once more, in the plural, in Exod 12:41: "all the armies of the LORD,"[287] referring to the ranks of Israelites as they left Egypt. In keeping with this latter usage, we find Israel's armies designated as God's armies in several places. For example, in Exod 7:4, God said to Moses, "I will bring out my divisions *[ṣābāʾ]*, my people the Israelites," and in 1 Sam 17:45, David responded to Goliath's taunts by saying he came against him "in the name of the LORD Almighty *[ṣābāʾ]*, the God of the armies of Israel." These examples would suggest that Israel's army may have been in view here.

However, an equally common usage of *ṣābāʾ* ("army") refers to the realm of the heavenlies, referring to God's armies. A common designation of God is "the LORD of hosts," which occurs more than 250 times in the Old Testament (NIV renders this as "the LORD Almighty" in most instances). The stars (or, more generally, all the heavenly bodies) are in view in many of these uses of *ṣābāʾ*. Note, for example, Gen 2:1, where the heavens and the earth and "all their vast array" *(ṣābāʾ)* were completed, or Isa 40:26, where God told his people to contemplate the "starry host" *(ṣābāʾ)* that he created and named. Alternatively, the angels of heaven sometimes are in view, as in 1 Kgs 22:19, where Micaiah saw "the LORD sitting on his throne with all the host *[ṣābāʾ]* of heaven standing around him," or Ps 103:19–21, where God's "heavenly hosts" *(ṣābāʾ)* are equated with his mighty angels. Thus, it is also possible that the man whom Joshua encountered was saying that he was the commander of the heavenly army that would fight for Israel.

In this passage, the likelihood is that it was Yahweh's heavenly army,

---

[286] In one case, Dan 8:11, the term שַׂר־הַצָּבָא, "the commander of the army" (NIV has "the Prince of the host" here) refers to a divine being similar to the figure mentioned in Joshua 5. Most commentators rightly see the figure in Dan 8:11 as God himself. See, e.g., J. E. Goldingay, *Daniel*, WBC 30 (Dallas: Word, 1989), 210–11; S. R. Miller, *Daniel*, NAC (Nashville: Broadman & Holman, 1991), 226–27.

[287] The NIV has "all the LORD's divisions" in Exod 12:41.

poised to fight on Israel's behalf. There is no indication that the man Joshua met was taking personal command of Israel's army, displacing Joshua, and the language of v. 15 (concerning holy ground) strongly suggests that this is a divine being representing God and his hosts. Even the syntax of v. 14 highlights the commander: a literal translation of his response is "No. For I, I am the commander of the army of the LORD." The focus on himself points to a divine being with a divine mission.[288]

Joshua recognized this man's authority, and he prostrated himself on the ground and "worshiped" him.[289] Whether this was an act of true worship of God or a more general gesture of respect for a superior (since both can be signified by the verb used here) has been debated. However, Joshua called him "my lord," using the generic term *ădōnî*[290] rather than "my Lord," using God's name *ădōnāy*, which suggests that he may still have been unclear as to whether or not he was speaking with God himself.[291] In either case, however, he clearly knew that he was in the presence of an extraordinary superior being because he did bow down, and he did not pursue his question about the man's loyalties any further. Rather, he humbly asked, "What message does my [lord] have for his servant?" In this response, Joshua displayed three attitudes: (1) a humble, expectant, obedient attitude, indicated by the question itself; (2) a recognition of the man's superior (and God-sent) position, indicated by the term "my lord"; and (3) a recognition of his own inferior position and a readiness to serve, indicated by his use of the term "his servant" to refer to himself.

5:15 Even though the man refused to answer Joshua's question, it is clear that he would be "for" Israel, not "against" it. Why, then, did he not speak more forthrightly with Joshua and tell him that he was indeed for Israel? It appears to have been to teach Joshua a lesson about priorities. God had already promised Joshua that he would be with him just as he was with Moses (1:5), so Joshua needed not worry. The lessons Joshua needed here were to be able to recognize when he was in God's presence and when to trust in him. The man's instructions to Joshua about removing his sandals because he was standing on holy ground obviously recalled God's words to Moses at the

---

[288] On the "hosts" or "armies" *(ṣābā³)* of the Lord, see C. J. H. Wright, "God, Names of," *ISBE* 2:507; T. Longman III, "צבא," *NIDOTTE* 3:733–35; T. Fretheim, "Yahweh," *NIDOTTE* 4:1297–98.

[289] The NIV has "in reverence" for the verb *ḥwh* (חוה), which is usually translated "bow down, worship." See *HALOT*, 295–96, and BDB, 1005 (BDB identifies the verb's root as *šḥh* [שחה], reflecting an older scholarly consensus as to this word's root). The language here is somewhat repetitive, emphasizing Joshua's prostration. Literally, it reads "and Joshua fell down upon his face to the ground and bowed down (or 'worshiped')."

[290] Which is used to refer to human superiors. See, e.g., Num 36:2; Judg 4:18; 1 Sam 22:12.

[291] The NIV renders אֲדֹנִי here as "my Lord," judging that this was a manifestation of God himself and thus capitalizing "Lord." However, this goes against the morphological evidence and reads as if the word were אֲדֹנָי.

burning bush (Exod 3:5).[292] In yet another way, Joshua was now being affirmed as Moses' successor and God's presence was being promised to him.

The identity of the commander of the Lord's army would appear to be similar to that of the "angel of the LORD," which appeared numerous times to people in the Old Testament.[293] Like the Lord's angel, who brought messages from God, the commander brought a word from God to Joshua; and, to his credit, Joshua responded appropriately, prostrating himself and taking off his shoes. The commander's appearance and words form a fitting prelude to God's more specific words of instruction in 6:2–5. Thus, the distinction between Yahweh and his commander is not a sharp one.[294]

This ends the first section of the Book of Joshua. Some scholars maintain that this episode is incomplete and that some of it has been lost or else that the commander's instructions are found in 6:2–5.[295] However, 5:13–15 easily stands alone as God's final encouragement—through his emissary—to Joshua. The enigmatic nature of his reply to Joshua and the seemingly incomplete reply only heighten the mystery and focus our attention on the divine nature of this emissary and on the holiness of the occasion. Just as the earlier episodes of the chapter focus on proper preparation in the spiritual realm before doing battle at Jericho, this episode does as well. Joshua was reminded here of the important lesson that God—the holy God, to whom Joshua owed all allegiance—would fight for him. In this case, the more important lesson was about God's holiness, not about the coming conflicts.

Excursus: The Identity of the Angel of the Lord[296]

Because of the close association of the angel of the Lord and the Lord himself in many passages of Scripture, many students have wondered about the precise identity of this angel. Essentially, there are three options.[297] (1) It is simply an angel with a special commission. (2) It may be a momentary descent of God himself into visibility. (3) It may be the Logos himself (i.e., Christ) "a kind of temporary preincarnation of the second person of the trinity."[298] Because of the close

---

[292] The wording is identical in the two passages, except for one additional word in Exodus and insignificant spelling differences.

[293] The term "angel of the LORD" (מַלְאַךְ יהוה) occurs fifty-nine times, and "angel(s) of God" (מַלְאַךְ אֱלֹהִים) occurs twelve times. The Hb. term *malʾāk* can be translated either as "angel" or "messenger"; God's angels were his messengers to humans in special cases.

[294] See the following excursus, "The Identity of the Angel of the Lord."

[295] Nelson (*Joshua*, 81–82) is confident that the commander's original concluding words are missing. Goslinga (*Joshua*, 67) sees 6:2 as the continuation of 5:15, as does Hess (*Joshua*, 128–29).

[296] Two critical scholars who deal with the issue are W. Eichrodt, *Theology of the Old Testament*, 2:23–29; G. von Rad, *Old Testament Theology*, 1:285–89. Several evangelical treatments are represented in the following notes.

[297] J. M Wilson, *ISBE*, 1. s.v. "Angel," 125.

[298] Ibid.

relationship—even alternation—of the angel of the Lord and the Lord himself, it would seem that the first option is not adequate. The angel represents God himself in very real ways.

Exodus 23:20–23 is a key text in this regard, since it shows how this angel carries the Lord's character and authority. Exodus 23:21 shows that the angel has the authority to forgive sins and that the Lord's name is "in him"; vv. 21–22 both specify the angel's authority to speak for God. On the other hand, in Exod 32:34–33:17 we see more of a distinction between the Lord and his angel: the Lord pledges to send his angel before Israel, despite their sin (32:24; 33:2), but he himself will not go with them (33:3). This seems to distinguish this "angel" from God himself. When the passage speaks in 33:14 of God's presence with Israel, it does not refer to his "angel" but rather his "face" (*pānay:* lit. "my face") that goes with them.

Some evangelical interpreters take these manifestations of the angel of the Lord to be pre-New Testament revelations of Christ.[299] In support, the descriptions of an angelic-type being[300] in Dan 10:6 and Ezek 1:26–28 are compared with John's descriptions of Jesus (Rev 1:14,16). Also it is noted that the angel of the Lord is not mentioned in the New Testament when Jesus is on earth. Furthermore, the fact that Jesus was "sent" to do his Father's work (John 8:18) is compared to the angel's also being sent by God. Thus, G. B. Funderburk concludes that "only the Logos, or some other manifest personification of God, would be able to [speak with authority as if he were God himself]."[301]

However, we should note that the New Testament, which certainly is not loath to identify Jesus Christ with Old Testament figures (as King and Messiah, as Priest, as the "Word" of God Incarnate) *never* makes such an identification. Obviously, Jesus was the self-expression of God in the New Testament, but nothing in the Scriptures requires our understanding God's self-expressions prior to Jesus' birth to have been this self-same Person. T. McComiskey's conclusion is a judicious one: "It is best to see the angel as a self-manifestation of Yahweh in a form that would communicate his immanence and direct concern to those to whom he ministered."[302] The exact nature or personality of this divine self-revelation are not known precisely because the Scriptures are silent on the question. This self-revelation of God certainly anticipated Christ in a typological way, even if it was not Christ himself. This may be analogous to the way in which "wisdom"—as it is described and personified in Job 28 and Proverbs 8—displays remarkable affinities with the Incarnate Word.[303]

---

[299] E. g., J. B. Payne, *The Theology of the Older Testament* (Grand Rapids: Zondervan, 1962), 167°70; G. B. Funderburk, *ZPEB,* s.v. "Angel," 1:162–63; W. C. Kaiser, Jr., *Hard Sayings of the Old Testament* (Downers Grove: InterVarsity, 1966), 98–100.

[300] Although the term "angel" is not used in these passages.

[301] Funderburk, *ZPEB,* s.v. "Angel," 1:162–63.

[302] T. E. McComiskey, *EDOT,* s.v. "Angel," 1:48. See also M. Erickson, *Christian Theology* (Grand Rapids: Baker, 1986), 443, who has a similar conclusion.

[303] See H. Gese, "Wisdom, Son of Man', and the Origins of Christology: The Consistent Development of Biblical Theology," *HBT* 3:23–57.

JOSHUA 1–5: THEOLOGICAL REFLECTIONS

At the end of the first main section of the Book of Joshua, the Israelites stand well-prepared for their first major encounter with the Canaanites whose land they were to inherit. They were well prepared because (1) God was very much with them, (2) because he had given them a leader who was already in process of becoming a worthy successor to Moses, (3) because the entire nation was taking care to obey God's commands to the letter (from Joshua and the priests on down to the people), and (4) because they were careful to sanctify themselves properly before engaging the Canaanites.

Several important notes are sounded in these chapters that set the stage for later developments. First and foremost, the God whom Israel was to follow identified himself clearly to Israel. In general terms, he did so by his charge to Joshua in 1:1–9. More specifically, he did so by his promises to be with Joshua in 1:5,9. In the process, it was clear that this God was the same one who had been with earlier generations and that he would be with Joshua and Israel in the same way. Furthermore, the important symbolism of the ark of the covenant in chap. 3 demonstrated to Israel that this God was very much in their midst. The different ways in which the ark is spoken of in this chapter reinforce the close identity of the physical box with the transcendent—but also very much immanent—God.

God also demonstrated the awesomeness of his presence with Israel via the great miracle of stopping up of the waters of the Jordan River (chap. 3), a miracle on the order of the parting of the Red Sea in an earlier generation and one whose magnitude was seldom if ever seen again in Old Testament times. The awesomeness of this miracle is confirmed by the extended reflection on it in chap. 4. In this reflection, the Israelites were taught not only what God did, but also how they should respond to such mighty deeds: by keeping alive the memory of these deeds and teaching their children of their significance. The Israelites learned that this was for the dual purpose of announcing Yahweh's power to the nations at large and of stimulating Israel to revere him properly (4:24; 5:1).

God's presence with his people was further revealed through Joshua's encounter with the commander of the Lord's army (5:13–15). The holiness of the ground where Joshua stood revealed to him and to Israel that God was present and that he would be with them just as he had been with Moses (Exodus 3) and that the task upon which they were about to embark was essentially spiritual in nature.

The importance of the people's proper ritual preparation for the taking of the land of Canaan flowed out of God's own holy nature. Joshua found himself standing on holy ground because God was there and God was holy. The entire land and its people were to be "dedicated" to God, and some of its cities and all of its people were to be destroyed in order to rid the land of the uncleanness that had built up there for centuries (Gen 15:16; Deut 7:2; 20:16–

18). For Israel to enter such a land, then, it needed to be properly prepared and in right relationship with God, just as the priests were to enter into their duties properly prepared, cleansed, and in right relationship with God. Indeed, Israel itself was to be a "kingdom of priests and a holy nation" (Exod 19:6), and the preparations for entering the land reinforce this. These preparations included, most obviously, the circumcision and the keeping of the Passover (5:2–12).[304]

The instructions to the Transjordan tribes about their responsibilities to the other tribes and the importance of unity within the nation (1:12–18) also were part of Israel's preparation for the taking of the land. This was not to be an every-man-for-himself rush to secure his own land at the expense of others, but very much a corporate exercise in which God's people functioned together in unity and as a unity received God's blessings.

God's charge to Joshua, with its emphasis on meditating on and keeping the law as the keys to his success, also demonstrates the importance of proper preparation. Joshua and Israel were to do something analogous to what Christ later told his disciples: "But seek first his kingdom and his righteousness, and all these things will be given to you as well" (Matt 6:33). They would have success to the degree they focused on seeking God and obeying him, not to the degree they employed superior military forces or strategies.

Proper preparations also are represented by the erecting of memorial stones and the extended reflections in chap. 4 about the significance of God's miracle. The taking of land was not so important that Israel did not have time to stop and reflect upon God's greatness and graciousness in performing such wonders on his people's behalf.

Proper leadership for the nation is an important topic addressed in the early chapters of the book. Moses, the servant of the Lord, like whom a prophet had not arisen since in Israel (Deut 34:10–12), was dead, and someone was needed to take his place. Joshua was his designated successor (Num 27:15–23; Deut 31:14,23; 34:9; Josh 1:2–9). Just like the later kings, leaders whose success was to be measured in terms of their adherence to God's word (Deut 17:18–20) and *not* by their military prowess (Deut 17:16), so too Joshua's success was to be measured by the degree to which he adhered to God's word (Josh 1:7–8). God himself was going to fight for Israel, and Joshua's and the people's role was to be properly prepared, rooted in God's word, and to take the land according to his instructions.

Joshua's leadership was visible by the manner in which he gave commands to the Israelites throughout the first five chapters, and especially by the manner in which he spoke for God. He functioned in a manner analogous to a prophet, in that he passed on to the people the words that God had spoken to him. Unlike the prophets, however, the people obeyed him in everything he commanded (at

---

[304] And possibly the renewal of the covenant, as well (see the introductory comments before 5:2).

least until Achan's sin in chap. 7). And God himself exalted Joshua before all Israel, just as he had Moses, as a sign of his presence with him (3:7; 4:14).

The importance of God's word is clear in the early chapters of the Book of Joshua. In a formal sense, this is indicated by the references to the Torah found in 1:7–8. Elsewhere this is indicated by the references to God's spoken words and commands, which were faithfully passed on by Joshua and executed by him and the people. Furthermore, the emphasis on things being in Joshua's day just as they were in Moses' day highlights the faithfulness of God's words and promises to his people.

A related idea to God's faithfulness is that of continuity with the past. Many of the commands or promises about the land and the people that are found in the Pentateuch are reiterated, often word-for-word, in Joshua 1–5. In addition, Moses, although dead, casts a long and important shadow across the entire Book of Joshua. In these chapters alone he is mentioned fifteen times.

The book's central message—that of Israel's possession of the promised land in fulfillment of God's promises—is found in every one of its aspects in the early chapters of the book. The land was God's gift to his people; he was its legal owner and could give it to whom he willed. He was in process of giving it to the Israelites now (1:2), and yet he had already given it to them (1:3). The already-accomplished nature of the act emphasizes the connections with earlier times and that God had already given Israel legal title to the land (Gen 12:7; 15:18–20; Deut 1:8,21; etc.). Despite the fact that the Israelites were receiving the land as God's gift, however, they still had to enter into the land and take possession of it as their inheritance. The battles ahead are deemphasized—after all, the Lord would be giving Israel its victories—but Israel's taking possession and inheriting the land is foreshadowed in the early chapters.

In these chapters, Israel actually entered the land (chap. 3), the importance of which can hardly be overstated. This event had been prophesied centuries earlier (Gen 15:13–16), and it is the event toward which the entire Pentateuch moves. Its importance is signaled by the extraordinary way in which the story is told in chap. 3 and reflected upon in chap. 4. And when Israel did enter the land, an important break with the previous forty years occurred: perhaps the most visible symbol of God's providential care in the wilderness—the manna—stopped being provided, since the land itself would now provide for God's people (5:11–12).

Finally, the significance of Rahab and the blessing on this foreigner are highlighted in chap. 2, showing one outworking of the promise of the Abrahamic covenant that God would bless those who blessed Abraham and that through him all families of the earth would be blessed (Gen 12:2–3). Rahab, through her remarkable faith—demonstrated in both deed and word—secured the promise of a blessing for her family, which was fulfilled when Jericho was taken (chap. 6). Later Scripture shows that Rahab was an ancestor of Israel's greatest king—David—and ultimately of Jesus Christ (Matt 1:5).

II. INHERITING THE LAND (6:1–12:24)
    1. The Destruction of Jericho (6:1–27)
        (1) Instructions for Taking Jericho (6:1–7)
        (2) The "Battle" of Jericho (6:8–21)
        (3) Aftermath of the "Battle" of Jericho (6:22–27)
    2. Covenant Disobedience (7:1–26)
        (1) The Sin (7:1)
        (2) The Defeat (7:2–5)
        (3) Joshua's Lament (7:6–9)
        (4) The Lord's Instructions (7:10–15)
        (5) Discovery and Consequence (7:16–26)
    3. The Destruction of Ai (8:1–29)
        (1) Instructions for Taking Ai (8:1–2)
        (2) Preparations for the Battle of Ai (8:3–13)
        (3) The Battle of Ai (8:14–23)
        (4) Aftermath of the Battle of Ai (8:24–29)
    4. Covenant Affirmations (8:30–35)
    5. The Gibeonite Treaty Established (9:1–27)
        (1) Introduction (9:1–2)
        (2) The Gibeonites' Deceit (9:3–15)
        (3) The Gibeonites' Lot (9:16–27)
    6. The Gibeonite Treaty Tested; Southern Campaign Begun (10:1–27)
        (1) Southern Coalition Gathered against Gibeon (10:1–5)
        (2) The Battle of Gibeon: Stage One (10:6–11)
        (3) The Battle of Gibeon: Stage Two (10:12–15)
        (4) Southern Coalition Kings Defeated (10:16–27)
    7. Southern Campaign Completed (10:28–43)
        (1) Seven Cities Destroyed (10:28–39)
        (2) Summary of the Campaign (10:40–43)
    8. Northern Campaign Begun (11:1–15)
        (1) Northern Coalition Gathered against Israel (11:1–5)
        (2) The Battle of Merom (11:6–9)
        (3) Northern Coalition Defeated (11:10–15)
    9. Northern Campaign Completed (11:16–23)
        (1) Summary of the Campaigns (11:16–17)
        (2) Conclusion (11:18–23)
   10. List of Conquered Kings and Land (12:1–24)
        (1) The Kings and Land of Transjordan (12:1–6)
        (2) The Kings and Land of Cisjordan (12:7–24)
Joshua 6–12: Theological Reflections

──────── II. INHERITING THE LAND (6:1–12:24) ────────

After the important preliminaries laid out in chaps. 1–5, the book now enters the core phase of the Israelites' taking of the land of Canaan. The section begins with a slow, detailed account of the first military-style encounter with the Canaanites—at Jericho—(chap. 6), an equally slow account of Israel's first defeat, at Ai (chap. 7), and another detailed account of Israel's victory over Ai (chap. 8). Concerns for keeping proper covenantal relations are then addressed (chaps. 8–9), leading up to the schematic descriptions of Israel's stunning victories in the south and the north of the land (chaps. 10–11). The section concludes with a detailed listing of the kings and lands defeated (chap. 12).

This section of seven chapters contains the only military-style actions in the book. Thus, we must remember that such activity forms only one part of the book's message. From the ritual preparations leading up to this activity to the careful distribution of the land after this activity, we realize that the book's primary message is not a militaristic one per se. The military-style encounters are a means to two ends: (1) God's giving Israel its inheritance, the land that had long been promised it, and (2) his punishing the local inhabitants of the land for their wickedness. Throughout all parts of the book, Israel's God was fulfilling his promises to his people, caring for them, directing them, and, when needed, fighting on their behalf.

An important backdrop to all the episodes in this section is Deut 20:16–18, the passage that instructs the Israelites on how to treat the cities of the peoples it was to displace in the land of Canaan. The passage states that "in the cities of the nations the LORD your God is giving you as an inheritance, do not leave alive anything that breathes. Completely destroy them—the Hittites, Amorites, Canaanites, Perizzites, Hivites and Jebusites—as the LORD your God has commanded you. Otherwise, they will teach you to follow all the detestable things they do in worshiping their gods, and you will sin against the LORD your God." Joshua reiterated that the Israelites were to destroy the inhabitants of Jericho completely and were not to take any of its booty (Josh 6:17–19), sparing only Rahab and her family on the basis of her hiding of the spies (v. 17) and her confession of faith (see commentary on 2:9–11). When one Israelite—Achan—violated the commands by taking booty, Israel suffered a defeat at Ai, and he and his family suffered the fate intended for the Canaanites (chap. 7). After the stain of Achan's sin was removed by his elimination, God relaxed the stricture against taking any booty and explicitly stated that the Israelites *could* take booty from Ai (8:2), which they did (8:27).[1] The episode involving the Gibeonites in chap. 9 also refers back to Deuteronomy 20, since the Israelites were allowed to make peace with peoples who were not from nearby, that is, in the Canaanite territories devoted to destruction (Deut 20:10–15). The initial battle in Joshua 10 (vv. 1–27) was one that tested the Israelites' commitment to their treaty with the Gibeonites (see 9:15), and the battles in the remainder of chaps. 10 and 11 were fought using the model of total destruction described in Deut 20:16–18.

1. The Destruction of Jericho (6:1–27)

The story of Israel's first victory in the land is told in exquisite detail. Just as the crossing of the Jordan was treated as an important event to be solemnly undertaken, with proper ritual preparation and commemoration, so also the taking of Jericho was to be done properly and in order. God gave precise instructions for the taking of the city, which involved careful ceremonial circling of the city rather than classic military tactics (vv. 2–5). Joshua, as God's faithful representative, instructed the people accordingly (vv. 6–7). The dramatic buildup and climax of the action is told in vv. 8–21, and, in the aftermath, several loose threads are tied up. The story is repetitive, and the Old Greek version is shorter than the MT version, leading many scholars to postulate very complex histories of the supposed growth and development of the account, by the accretion of either many literary strands or many separate traditions. As with chaps. 3–4, however, such postulates are not required by the text, and here too one can make sense of the Hebrew text on its own merits.[2]

The detail with which the account is told emphasizes the importance of this city and its destruction.[3] It was the first city captured by the Israelites, and, as such, its capture represented the entire takeover of the land.[4] The

---

[1] See R. Polzin, *Moses and the Deuteronomist: A Literary Study of the Deuteronomistic History*, Part One: *Deuteronomy, Joshua, Judges* (Bloomington: Indiana University, 1981), 113–15.

[2] For source-critical and tradition-historical readings, see especially T. C. Butler, *Joshua*, WBC 7 (Waco: Word, 1983), 66–70, and R. D. Nelson, *Joshua: A Commentary*, OTL (Louisville: Westminster John Knox, 1997), 83–90. N. Winther-Nielsen (*A Functional Discourse Grammar of Joshua: A Computer-assisted Rhetorical Structural Analysis*, Coniectanea Biblica, Old Testament Series 40 [Stockholm: Almqvist & Wiksell, 1995]), reviews many such diachronic treatments (pp. 191–92), but offers his own synchronic reading (pp. 193–210). Two other literary readings are R. C. Culley, "Stories of the Conquest: Joshua 2, 6, 7 and 8," *HAR* 8 (1984): 25–44 (for Joshua 6, see pp. 35–37); R. Robinson, "The Coherence of the Jericho Narrative: Literary Reading of Joshua 6," *Konsequente Traditionsgeschichte*, OBO 126 (Fribourg: Universitätsverlag Freibourg, 1993), 311–35. Culley's comment about the unfolding of the text shows the chapter's narrative similarities to chaps. 3–4: "The narrative proceeds from announcement to occurrence by means of small movements in the action which are very much like action sequences: an instruction is given, and then it is reported that the instruction has been obeyed" (Culley, "Stories of the Conquest," 36). Cp. the comments on 3:12; 4:1,11; etc.

[3] On the archaeology of this city, see the excursus "The Archaeology of Jericho and Ai" at the end of this chapter.

Israelites' taking of other cities and their kings is compared several times to what happened to Jericho (8:1–2; 10:28,30). And at the end of Joshua's life, when he summarized the taking of the land, Jericho was the only city he mentioned by name, even though he mentioned seven nations and several kings who fought against Israel (24:8–13).

(1) Instructions for Taking Jericho (6:1–7)

[1]Now Jericho was tightly shut up because of the Israelites. No one went out and no one came in.
[2]Then the LORD said to Joshua, "See, I have delivered Jericho into your hands, along with its king and its fighting men. [3]March around the city once with all the armed men. Do this for six days. [4]Have seven priests carry trumpets of rams' horns in front of the ark. On the seventh day, march around the city seven times, with the priests blowing the trumpets. [5]When you hear them sound a long blast on the trumpets, have all the people give a loud shout; then the wall of the city will collapse and the people will go up, every man straight in."
[6]So Joshua son of Nun called the priests and said to them, "Take up the ark of the covenant of the LORD and have seven priests carry trumpets in front of it." [7]And he ordered the people, "Advance! March around the city, with the armed guard going ahead of the ark of the LORD."

6:1 This verse sets the stage for the episode at Jericho and is grammatically and syntactically not part of the narrative story line.[5] The problem is stated: Jericho was "tightly shut up." This would appear to have been a dual problem: it was a problem for the inhabitants of Jericho, since it was "because of the Israelites" that this happened, but it also was a problem for the Israelites, since their task of taking the city was made all that much harder because of this. The difficulty of the task magnified the great accomplishment of the taking of the city when it did take place. In this sense, v. 1 functions in the same way that 3:15 does, which precedes the other great miracle in the book ("Now the Jordan overflows all its banks all the days of the harvest"): both

---

[4] J. R. Vannoy makes this point in his summary of the work of H. J. Koorevaar (Vannoy, "Joshua, Theology of," *NIDOTTE* 4:812, summarizing Koorevaar, *De opbouw van het boek Jozua* [Heverlee: Centrum voor bijbelse vorming Belgie, 1990]).

[5] It consists of a circumstantial clause and contains no finite verb forms (only participles). Many commentators see this verse as an intrusion or an aside and see the literary unit here as legitimately beginning in 5:13. In this way, Joshua's unanswered question is seen to be answered by the Lord's words in 6:2–5. See C. F. Keil, *COT: The Book of Joshua* (Grand Rapids: Eerdmans, 1975 reprint), 61–64; C. J. Goslinga, *Joshua, Judges, Ruth*, BSC (Grand Rapids: Zondervan, 1986), 66–68; R. S. Hess, *Joshua: An Introduction and Commentary*, TOTC (Downers Grove: InterVarsity, 1996), 126–32; Winther-Nielsen, *Discourse Grammar of Joshua*, 193–94. These scholars make a plausible argument. However, 5:13–15 has important ties with the earlier parts of the chapter, and the instructions in 6:2–5 do not appear to be those of the commander of the Lord's army (see the introductory comments on 5:13–15 and further, on 5:15).

show a great potential obstacle that is then overcome effortlessly by a mighty act of God.

6:2–5 God's instructions to Joshua about the taking of Jericho contain no reference to military strategy but rather indicate that it is essentially to be a ritual ceremony. God's words consist of an encouraging assurance to Joshua (v. 2), instructions for Israel's part in the episode (vv. 3–5a), and a statement about the amazing results (v. 5b).

The ritual nature of the episode is suggested by the absence of any military strategy, by the blowing of the trumpets, by the prominence of the priests and the ark of the covenant, by the solemn processionals, and by the prevalence of the number "seven," which occurs four times in v. 4 alone and fourteen times in the chapter. "Seven" is the number of totality, completion, and perfection in the Scriptures;[6] and its predominance in this chapter emphasizes the completeness of Yahweh's victory on Israel's behalf. This spiritual exercise is a natural outgrowth of the rituals of holiness in chap. 5, since Jericho was dedicated to destruction for Yahweh, that is, it was "set apart" to him, as were all things holy (see v. 17).

The outcome of the entire affair is announced to Joshua at the outset: God had already given Jericho, its king, and its warriors into Joshua's hand (v. 2).[7] Thus, the extensive marching, blowing of trumpets, and shouting that the Israelites were to engage in is shown to be essentially ceremonial because God was giving the victory. This is reinforced by the comment at the end of v. 5, where God stated clearly that the wall would collapse through no effort on the people's part beyond the ceremonial actions just mentioned.

Seven priests blowing seven trumpets[8] were to march in front of the ark around Jericho for seven days, once each day and seven times on the seventh day (vv. 3–4). The wall would "fall down under itself," that is, "collapse" (NIV), and the people would enter the city seemingly effortlessly (v. 5).

6:6–7 As he did several times earlier in connection with the crossing of

---

[6] See B. C. Birch, "Number," *ISBE* 3:559; P. P. Jenson, "שֶׁבַע," *NIDOTTE* 4:34–37. The number's significance as seen in the Scriptures is found in almost all ancient Near Eastern cultures as well.

[7] The form of the verb is perfect, indicating a complete action here (see comments on 1:3, note 31, and the excursus there on "The Giving of the Land in Joshua").

[8] Three different terms for horns or trumpets are used in this chapter, in several combinations. They were all animal horns, not metallic trumpets, and were more noisemakers than music makers. The *qeren* was made from an animal's horn; in v. 5 is the only time it is used in the OT as an instrument (appearing in combination with *yôbēl*); otherwise it refers to the horn as part of the actual animal. The *šôpār* is the most commonly mentioned instrument, and it was a ram's horn used primarily for signaling, especially in wartime. It is found in Joshua fourteen times, all in chap. 6: vv. 4[2x],5,6,8[2x],9[2x],13[3x],16,20[2x]. The *yôbēl* (v. 5) was also a ram's horn, and it was used as a signal when the Israelites were allowed to approach Mount Sinai (Exod 19:13). On these horns, see D. A. Foxvog and A. D. Kilmer, "Music," *ISBE* 3:439; Butler, *Joshua*, 70.

the Jordan (chaps. 3–4), Joshua passed along to the people what we are told God had commanded him. Beyond this is the instruction in v. 7 about the "armed guard" that was to walk in front of the ark, along with the priests. Joshua also expanded upon the way in which the ark was referred to: "the ark *of the covenant*" (v. 6) and "the ark *of the LORD*" (vv. 6–7), focusing the people's attention on it and its significance.[9] Joshua's command to "Advance!" (NIV) is literally "Cross over" (*ʿbr*), which is the key verb in Joshua 3–4. This helps further to connect the two sets of events.

(2) The "Battle" of Jericho (6:8–21)

[8]When Joshua had spoken to the people, the seven priests carrying the seven trumpets before the LORD went forward, blowing their trumpets, and the ark of the LORD's covenant followed them. [9]The armed guard marched ahead of the priests who blew the trumpets, and the rear guard followed the ark. All this time the trumpets were sounding. [10]But Joshua had commanded the people, "Do not give a war cry, do not raise your voices, do not say a word until the day I tell you to shout. Then shout!" [11]So he had the ark of the LORD carried around the city, circling it once. Then the people returned to camp and spent the night there.

[12]Joshua got up early the next morning and the priests took up the ark of the LORD. [13]The seven priests carrying the seven trumpets went forward, marching before the ark of the LORD and blowing the trumpets. The armed men went ahead of them and the rear guard followed the ark of the LORD, while the trumpets kept sounding. [14]So on the second day they marched around the city once and returned to the camp. They did this for six days.

[15]On the seventh day, they got up at daybreak and marched around the city seven times in the same manner, except that on that day they circled the city seven times. [16]The seventh time around, when the priests sounded the trumpet blast, Joshua commanded the people, "Shout! For the LORD has given you the city! [17]The city and all that is in it are to be devoted to the LORD. Only Rahab the prostitute and all who are with her in her house shall be spared, because she hid the spies we sent. [18]But keep away from the devoted things, so that you will not bring about your own destruction by taking any of them. Otherwise you will make the camp of Israel liable to destruction and bring trouble on it. [19]All the silver and gold and the articles of bronze and iron are sacred to the LORD and must go into his treasury."

[20]When the trumpets sounded, the people shouted, and at the sound of the trumpet, when the people gave a loud shout, the wall collapsed; so every man charged straight in, and they took the city. [21]They devoted the city to the LORD and destroyed with the sword every living thing in it—men and women, young and old, cattle, sheep and donkeys.

The deliberate buildup to the climactic destruction of Jericho slowly unfolds in this section. The actions of the first two days are described in detail

---

[9] See the comment on the terminology for the ark at 3:3.

(vv. 8–14), and then those of the seventh day are narrated (vv. 15–21). The narrative pacing is slow, the action advancing by small steps, with much repetition, just as we have seen in chaps. 3–4. In both passages, the events spoken of were great works of God, to be reflected upon in great detail. There is no true battle, no clash of opposing armies. Rather, it was a one-sided affair in which God gave the city into the Israelites' hands, and they were able to destroy the city's inhabitants, apparently without any losses of their own.

6:8–11   Verses 8–9 report on the execution on the first day of God's and Joshua's commands in vv. 2–7. Little new substantive information is found here except that, in addition to the armed guard and the trumpet-blowing priests preceding the ark, there was also a "rear guard"[10] following the ark (v. 9). All this time the horns were sounding (vv. 9,13).[11] The close identification of the ark with God himself noted in chap. 3 is also here in the explanation that the priests were "before the LORD" (v. 8); in v. 4, the phrase is "before the ark," and in v. 6 it is "before the ark of the LORD."[12]

The noise appears to have been solely from the horns, since v. 10 states that Joshua had previously[13] instructed the people that they were not to make any sounds until the day on which he would instruct them to shout. The reference to "until the day" *(ʿad yôm)* indicates that from the beginning, Joshua expected that this "campaign" would be several days in duration, not just one day. The silence is enjoined in three ways: (1) they were not to raise a shout *(rwʿ)*, (2) they were not to make their voices heard *(šmʿ)*, and (3) they were not to utter a word *(dbr)*. A wordplay apparently is at work in the use of *rwʿ*, "to raise a shout."[14] It is commonly used in the Old Testament to designate a war cry or shout of alarm (e.g., Judg 7:21; 1 Sam 17:52; Isa 42:13; 2 Chr 13:15[2x]). However, it is also commonly found as part of the vocabulary of praise in the Psalms and similar contexts and can be translated there as "to raise a glad cry" (e.g., Ezra 3:11,13; Pss 95:1–2; 98:4,6; 100:1). Both meanings of the term would be appropriate in the context of the circling of Jericho: by raising such a shout, the people would at the same time have been sound-

---

[10] The term here is מְאַסֵּף, used only four times to indicate a rear guard: twice here (vv. 9,13); once in Num 10:25, comprised of the tribes of Dan, Asher, and Naphtali when Israel set out from Sinai; and once figuratively of God, in Isa 52:12.

[11] Nelson believes the text indicates that the rear guard was blowing horns, along with the priests, and that this is one of the many indications of a confusion and conflation of sources in the chapter (*Joshua*, 88). However, the verbs indicating horn blowing more properly indicate that the priests were the sole ones blowing the horns in vv. 8–9,13 (see NIV, NASB, NRSV, NJPSV, and NLT, which all indicate this).

[12] Robinson makes this observation about the language of chap. 6 ("The Coherence of the Jericho Narrative," 324).

[13] The syntax indicates what is deducible from common sense: Joshua gave these instructions prior to their setting out, not as they were walking along.

[14] Butler makes this trenchant suggestion (*Joshua*, 70).

ing a war cry, which would frighten the inhabitants of Jericho, and also praising God for the victory he was giving them.

Verse 11 prosaically tells of the circling of the city one time on the first day
and the return to spend the night at the encampment.

6:12–14   The activity on the second day was exactly the same as on the
first, and it is reported as such (v. 13 echoes vv. 8–9 very closely, and v. 14
echoes v. 11).[15] The narrator, now that the pattern is established, states that
the same happened on the first six days (v. 14c), and the stage is set for the
climactic seventh day. Verse 12 begins with the statement that "Joshua got up
early in the morning," which is exactly the same wording as we find in 3:1,
another passage where an important march was to be taken. Both were undertaken with the priests carrying the ark and Joshua exercising leadership over
the entire process.

6:15–16   The climactic episode is initiated by the episode-beginning
wayĕhî, "and it happened,"[16] and the same verb, "to get up early (when the
dawn broke)," found in v. 12. The actions were the same as previously (see
NIV's "in the same manner"), but they were executed seven times on this day
(hence the early start, undoubtedly). The second half of v. 15 shows that it
was only *(raq)* on this day (and no other) that this happened.[17] The marching
action on the seventh day is described much more quickly than for days one
and two, since the story's climax quickly approaches.

In strict accord with God's instructions (vv. 4–5), Joshua commanded the
people to shout when the priests gave one long, sustained blast on their horns
(v. 16). Once again, the already-accomplished fact that the Lord had given
Israel the land is reported (now, it is "the city," v. 16). The report of the execution of his command is delayed until v. 20, however, by his instructions
regarding the Israelites' treatment of Rahab and their handling of the things
that had been devoted to destruction.

6:17–19   The bulk of Joshua's instructions in vv. 17–19 had to do with
how the Israelites were to deal with the city of Jericho, its inhabitants, and its
booty once these fell into their hands. First, he made it clear that these all
were to be completely destroyed. The NRSV's rendering in v. 17a captures
the nuances: "And the city and all that is within it shall be devoted to the

---

[15] We learn in v. 13 that the priests walked directly ahead of the ark, and the armed guard
marched ahead of the priests, information that is not found in the earlier references to these two
groups in vv. 4,6,7.

[16] This construction is also found at the very climax of the episode, in v. 20, marking off the
actual climax itself from the rest of the episode.

[17] The NIV's "except" is confusing and misleading here. Better is the NJPSV: "That was the
only day that they marched around the city seven times" (see also NASB, NRSV, NLT). The particle רק here is used in its restrictive sense, meaning "only, exclusively, alone" (see *HALOT*, 1286,
§ 2a).

LORD for destruction." Things "devoted to the LORD" were off limits to the Israelites because they were to be completely destroyed, as an offering of sorts to the Lord.

Rahab was specifically exempted from this destruction in the book's first reference to her since chap. 2 (v. 17b). This exemption stands in tension with Yahweh's instructions for dealing with the peoples in Canaan in Deut 7:1–5 and 20:16–18. Deuteronomy 20:16–18 states, "However, in the cities of the nations the LORD your God is giving you as an inheritance, do not leave alive anything that breathes. Completely destroy them—the Hittites, Amorites, Canaanites, Perizzites, Hivites and Jebusites—as the LORD your God has commanded you. Otherwise, they will teach you to follow all the detestable things they do in worshiping their gods, and you will sin against the LORD your God." However, as we have seen earlier, the crucial difference between Rahab and the other Canaanites was her demonstration of faith, both in deeds and words.[18]

These verses contain the first significant discussion in the Book of Joshua of the related concepts of "devoted things," "devoting a city to the LORD," and the complete destruction of the Canaanites.[19] We have already noted the instructions in v. 17 to devote the entire city of Jericho to destruction. Behind this idea is the Hebrew verb *ḥāram* and noun *ḥērem*. The verb can be rendered "to devote to the LORD" or "to devote to destruction" or "to completely destroy," and the noun can be rendered as "devoted things" or "destruction." The NIV text note makes clear the connection between the idea of devotion and destruction: "The Hebrew term refers to the irrevocable giving over of things or persons to the LORD, often by totally destroying them."

Verse 18 gives further details: "But keep away from *the devoted things [ḥērem]*, so that you will not *bring about your own destruction [ḥāram]* by taking any of *[the devoted things (ḥērem)]*. Otherwise you will make the camp of Israel liable to *destruction [ḥērem]* and bring trouble on it."[20] Certain items were to be set apart for destruction, and if they were not, Israel itself would be subject to the same fate; Israel itself would become "a devoted thing." Verse 19 continues to develop this idea. The treasures of Jericho were to be set apart for the Lord, since they were sacred, that is, holy. As such, they were to go into his treasury. The term here for "treasury" (*ʾôṣar*) is the same one used for those in Solomon's temple, built many years later (1 Kgs 7:51).

---

[18] On Rahab's faith, see especially the comments on 2:9–11; and on her exemption from destruction, see on 2:12–13.

[19] The idea is first encountered in Rahab's reference to the Israelites' complete destruction of Sihon and Og (Josh 2:10). For a fuller discussion of the issue, see the excursus on "Destruction and Devoted Things in Joshua" at the end of this chapter.

[20] God's warning that disobedience would "bring trouble" (*ʿkr*) on the camp anticipates the problem that developed in Achan's case, where the same term is used (see commentary on 7:25).

However, since no temple stood in Joshua's day, the exact nature and location of this treasury is unknown. The "treasury of the LORD's house" is mentioned in v. 24; it may have been associated with the "house of God" at Gilgal mentioned in 9:23. The sacred tent at Shiloh in Samuel's day was also called "the house of the LORD" (1 Sam 1:7). There is no need to suppose that this referred, anachronistically, to the later temple. In Ps 27:4,6, the words "house of the LORD" and "his tabernacle" are used interchangeably, and the references here in Joshua may have been to the tabernacle as the Lord's house, not the temple.

6:20–21 The actual "battle" of Jericho is described very briefly in v. 20, and the story line suspended after v. 16 is now resumed, with the report of the execution of Joshua's command that the people should shout. The story reaches its climax here, and the terse telling of the climactic moments has a dramatic effect. Initially, the text is choppy and wordy, as we can see in a wooden translation: "And the people shouted, and they blew on the ram's horns. And it happened, when the people heard the sound of the ram's horn, that the people shouted a great shout, and the wall fell down under itself and the people went up to the city, each man opposite himself, and they captured the city." Those blowing on the horns were the priests (v. 16), not the people, and the sequence of action would have been that the priests blew on the horns (vv. 16a,20a), and then the people shouted, as Joshua commanded (vv. 16b,20a).

The middle of v. 20 contains an episode-initial marker (*wayĕhî*, "and it happened"), followed by a temporal clause setting the time frame ("when the people heard the sound of the ram's horn"), which repeats and adds to information found in the first part of the verse. This introduces a more sequential telling of the events, leading to the terse description of the walls' collapse and the city's capture.[21] Verse 21 expands on the description at the end of v. 20: the Israelites' taking of the city entailed their devoting everything in it to destruction. The totality of the destruction is reinforced by the two word pairs in v. 21—"men and women," "young and old"—and by the listing of the animals, which can be translated as "and even including cattle, sheep, and donkeys."

In contrast to the detailed telling and retelling of the great miracle at the Jordan River (3:14–17 and throughout chap. 4), the great miracle of the walls collapsing is told here in one terse statement at the end of v. 20. However, this fits the general outlook of the book, that military matters belonged to God and that he would effortlessly fight Israel's battles. Protracted attention to battle details would undermine this sense of the effortless taking of the land of Canaan. What *is* emphasized in this account are the ritual preparations for the

---

[21] A detailed accounting of the syntax here is found in N. Winther-Nielsen, *Discourse Grammar of Joshua*, 200–202. On וַיְהִי and the construction here, see the note at 4:11.

battle (vv. 2–19) and the follow-up to the taking of the city, in which faithfulness to earlier commands and agreements is highlighted (vv. 22–26). The Book of Hebrews adds to this perspective: it was "by faith the walls of Jericho fell, after the people had marched around them for seven days" (Heb 11:30).

(3) Aftermath of the "Battle" of Jericho (6:22–27)

²²Joshua said to the two men who had spied out the land, "Go into the prostitute's house and bring her out and all who belong to her, in accordance with your oath to her." ²³So the young men who had done the spying went in and brought out Rahab, her father and mother and brothers and all who belonged to her. They brought out her entire family and put them in a place outside the camp of Israel.
²⁴Then they burned the whole city and everything in it, but they put the silver and gold and the articles of bronze and iron into the treasury of the LORD's house. ²⁵But Joshua spared Rahab the prostitute, with her family and all who belonged to her, because she hid the men Joshua had sent as spies to Jericho—and she lives among the Israelites to this day.
²⁶At that time Joshua pronounced this solemn oath: "Cursed before the LORD is the man who undertakes to rebuild this city, Jericho:

"At the cost of his firstborn son
    will he lay its foundations;
at the cost of his youngest
    will he set up its gates."
²⁷So the LORD was with Joshua, and his fame spread throughout the land.

After spending considerable space building up to the destruction of Jericho (vv. 1–19) and quickly recounting the destruction proper (vv. 20–21), the author of Joshua concludes the story of the "battle" of Jericho by emphasizing four things: (1) the fulfillment of the spies' oath to Rahab (vv. 22–23,25), (2) the total destruction (v. 24), (3) the curse placed upon Jericho (v. 26), and (4) an evaluative statement about Joshua's place as Israel's leader (v. 27).

6:22–25 Just as earlier the book is concerned to show that Joshua and the people had faithfully obeyed the commands of Yahweh and Moses,²² the same is true in this section. In v. 22 are found Joshua's instructions for the two spies—the spies who had earlier made the oath with Rahab to spare her and her family on the basis of her faith, which had been demonstrated in her actions and her words (see commentary on chap. 2, esp. on 2:14). The instructions were that they should bring Rahab and her family out of the city alive, in accordance with their oath to her, and they did precisely that (v. 23). It is perhaps especially fitting that the two spies who had first met Rahab were given the assignment to go into the city and bring her and her family out.

The entire city was put to the torch, except for the articles that had been men-

---

²² See comments on 4:2–3,10,12.

tioned in v. 19, the valuables that were saved for the Lord's sanctuary: the articles of silver, gold, bronze, and iron (v. 24). Rahab and her family and extended household were spared because of what she did for the spies, and, the author tells us, she still lived there until the day that he wrote those words (v. 25). At first glance, this last statement would suggest that the Book of Joshua was written within a few years after the events described in the book, and that very well may have been the case. However, the reference to "Rahab" living among the Israelites "to this day" could have referred to her *descendants,* in the same way that the reference to "David" in Hos 3:5 indicates David's descendants rather than David himself. Thus, this verse cannot be used conclusively to date the writing of the Book of Joshua. However, the point of the verse is not to date the writing of the book, but rather to indicate something of the lasting effects of the agreement the two spies had made with Rahab: it was a binding agreement, one that Israel honored, because of Rahab's faith.

6:26 Joshua pronounced a curse against anyone who would rebuild the city of Jericho. This echoed Moses' instructions in Deut 13:12–16 [Hb. 13–17] that the Israelites should completely destroy any city in which wicked men arose to lead people astray by worshiping other gods. Many years later, this curse found a fulfillment when Hiel, a man from Bethel, "rebuilt Jericho. He laid its foundations at the cost of his firstborn son Abiram, and he set up its gates at the cost of his youngest son Segub, in accordance with the word of the LORD spoken by Joshua son of Nun" (1 Kgs 16:34). The key words of the curse are found in both texts, showing the strict faithfulness of the Lord to his own words or those legitimately spoken on his behalf. The city was used as a place of habitation on occasion (see Josh 18:21; Judg 3:13; 2 Sam 10:5), but Hiel's actions represented the first time that someone had actually attempted to rebuild the city in a systematic way, restoring its foundations and its gates, in violation of the curse.[23]

6:27 The statement here about the Lord's being with Joshua and his fame spreading throughout the land echoes two earlier statements, where God promised Joshua his presence, just as he had been with Moses (3:7) and where God began to exalt Joshua in the eyes of the people (4:14). This statement builds naturally upon those, reiterating that God was with Joshua, but adding that his fame now spread throughout all the land.[24]

---

[23] On this point, see M. H. Woudstra, *The Book of Joshua,* NICOT (Grand Rapids: Eerdmans, 1981), 116.

[24] Hess's point about the emphasis here on Joshua rather than Yahweh indicating a focus on Joshua as military leader (*Joshua,* 136) ignores the fact that Yahweh was Israel's commander (see also 5:13–15), and that the exaltation of Joshua began earlier, in contexts that clearly were not military. Winther-Nielsen's comment that 6:27 should be read as opening the story told in chap. 7 is somewhat mystifying (*Discourse Grammar of Joshua,* 214), since he justifies this by comparing the syntactical construction here with the very different episode-initial constructions of 9:1; 10:1; 11:1. The וַיְהִי functions very differently here from the way it does in 9:1; 10:1; 11:1.

EXCURSUS: THE ARCHAEOLOGY OF JERICHO AND AI

The Bible records that three cities—Jericho, Ai, and Hazor—were burned with fire and destroyed, whereas for the others, only destruction of people is specified. It should be possible, then (given proper site identifications and proper recovery and analysis of evidence), to verify these destructions archaeologically. In the case of Hazor, this can be done with some degree of confidence (see note on 11:1). However, in the cases of Jericho and Ai, this is much more difficult. Indeed, the archaeological evidence—or rather, the lack of it—has been a major difficulty for those who would attempt to root the biblical account of Joshua in historical realities, and it has been an important piece of evidence for others who argue that the biblical account is not rooted in such realities. Therefore, we devote some attention to each of these sites in turn.

Jericho

Archaeologically, Jericho is known very well; it is one of the oldest cities in the world, having been occupied since the eighth millennium B.C.[25] However, it does not appear to have been occupied during the latter part of the Late Bronze Age (ca. 1400–1200 B.C.), and this has raised problems for understanding the biblical accounts.

Jericho's early excavator, John Garstang, had found a large wall that was destroyed, and he had dated it to ca. 1400 B.C., attributing its fall to the Israelite takeover.[26] However, it is now known that this wall dates almost 1000 years earlier, in the Early Bronze Age. Garstang also had dated the end of his "City IV" to 1400 B.C., but Jericho's later excavator, Kathleen Kenyon, raised this date to 1550 B.C. Furthermore, she dated its period of nonoccupation from 1550 until ca. 1100 B.C., except for a brief period immediately following 1400 B.C.[27] This has caused difficulties for anyone attempting to correlate the Bible and the archaeological data.

Whether one proposes a fifteenth-century date for the events in Joshua or one in the thirteenth century, the problem of erosion in precisely the period in question, the Late Bronze Age, is a serious one, and so all-encompassing, definitive conclusions are impossible. For example, Kitchen (a proponent of the thirteenth-century date) states that "it seems highly likely that the washed-out remains of the last Late Bronze Age city are now lost under the modern road and cultivated land along the E side of the town mound, as the main slope of the mound is from W down to E."[28]

---

[25] See J. R. Bartlett, *Cities of the Ancient World: Jericho* (Grand Rapids: Eerdmans, 1982); T. A. Holland and E. Netzer, "Jericho," *ABD* 3:723–40; K. M. Kenyon, "Jericho," *NEAEHL* 2:674–81; Holland, "Jericho," *The Oxford Encyclopedia of Archaeology in the Near East* (New York: Oxford University Press, 1997), 3:220–24.

[26] See his popular presentation of the city's excavations, done with his son: J. Garstang and J. B. E. Garstang, *The Story of Jericho*, 2d ed. (London: Marshall, Morgan, & Scott, 1948). He did not live to produce a final excavation report.

[27] See Kenyon, "Jericho," *NEAEHL* 2:678–80.

[28] K. A. Kitchen, "Jericho," *NBD,* 555.

However, in what is potentially a very significant advance, B. Wood has reaffirmed Garstang's dating of the fall of City IV, which occurred ca. 1400 B.C., based on examination of the pottery and other evidence from Jericho made available by Kenyon's final reports on the site, published posthumously in the 1980s.[29] This calls into question Kenyon's dating of its fall—she placed it ca. 1550 B.C.[30]—and accords very well with the biblical record. Wood presents strong evidence that Kenyon's methodology in dating the Late Bronze Age pottery at Jericho was flawed, using as it did imported pottery types from tombs for its typology rather than the more common local, domestic wares found much more widely throughout the Jericho mound.[31] He presents several lines of evidence that Garstang's dating of the demise of City IV and its walls[32] was indeed correct, ca. 1400 B.C.[33] If he is correct—and his evidence is very persuasive—then the archaeological evidence from Jericho fits the biblical picture very well.

Ai

The problems with Ai are of a different sort from Jericho because there are legitimate questions as to whether the ancient site of Ai has been correctly identified. If it has, then the problems are similar to Jericho's, but, if it has not, then we cannot say anything definitive about the question of Ai and the archaeological record.

In this century, the site of Ai has been identified by most scholars with et-Tell, a mound two miles east of Beitin (usually assumed to be biblical Bethel).[34] The

---

[29] B. G. Wood, "Did the Israelites Conquer Jericho? A New Look at the Archaeological Evidence," *BARev* 16.2 (1990): 44–58. The final scholarly report on the excavations (vols. 3–5) was published posthumously in the 1980s (see particulars in *NEAEHL* 2:681; *ABD* 3:740). Wood's conclusions are challenged by P. Bienkowski ("Jericho Was Destroyed in the Middle Bronze Age, Not the Late Bronze Age," *BARev* 16.5 [1990]: 45–46, 69), but he presents a well-reasoned rebuttal ("Dating Jericho's Destruction: Bienkowski Is Wrong on All Counts," *BARev* 16.5 [1990]: 45, 47–49, 68–69).

[30] Kenyon, "Jericho," *NEAEHL* 2:680.

[31] Bienkowski's independent and thorough review of the evidence (*Jericho in the Late Bronze Age* [Warminster: Aris & Phillips, 1986]) would appear to suffer from the same methodological problem that Kenyon's does, since it relies on her dating schemes.

[32] This is a different set of walls from the Early Bronze Age walls mentioned above.

[33] J. J. Bimson (*Redating the Exodus and Conquest*, 2d ed., JSOTSup 5 [Sheffield: Almond, 1981], 106–36) gives a good review of the evidence and comes to similar conclusions, but following somewhat different lines of evidence. Among other things, he redates the end of the Middle Bronze Age from ca. 1550 B.C. to much later, ca. 1430 B.C., a redating that has won almost no scholarly approval. However, Bimson's redating depends heavily on analyses of the evidence from Jericho available only through the 1970s; he has now reconsidered his views, based on the new data available through the final publications of Kenyon's excavations, including Wood's work. However, the lack of any burning at Hazor ca. 1400 B.C. still poses a problem for the larger question of the dating of the conquest (Bimson, personal communication, July 1998). See also J. J. Bimson and D. Livingston, "Redating the Exodus," *BARev* 13.5 (1987), 40–53, 66–68, especially the note on p. 52.

[34] See J. A. Callaway, "Ai (et–Tell): Problem Site for Biblical Archaeologists," in L. G. Perdue, L. E. Toombs, G. L. Johnson, eds., *Archaeological and Biblical Interpretation* (Atlanta: John Knox, 1987), 87–99; id., "Ai," *NEAEHL* 1:39–45. On the problems of equating Beitin with Bethel, see the works in n. 39.

site's Arabic name means "mound (on which is a ruin)," and the biblical site's Hebrew name (which has the definite article "the" *(hā-)* attached to it), *hā‘ay*, is assumed to mean "the Ruin," based on (1) the statement in Josh 8:28 that it was "a permanent heap of ruins, a desolate place to this day," and (2) the supposed similarity with the Arabic meaning.

The problem with this site identification is that et-Tell was unoccupied from ca. 2400–1200 B.C. The settlement on the mound after 1200 B.C. was a small one, only on one corner of the mound, and it only lasted 150 years. These facts have caused problems for those concerned with the reliability of the biblical record, whether they have held to a date for the entrance into Canaan in the fifteenth or the thirteenth centuries B.C.

If indeed et-Tell is ancient Ai, then either the biblical record is hopelessly mistaken or any remains from the time of Joshua have eroded away. The former is the position taken by most critical scholars,[35] while the latter is held by many scholars who would reconcile the Bible and the archaeological record.[36]

Another possibility is that the identification of Ai with et-Tell is mistaken. The identification of the two on linguistic grounds is not sustainable, for several reasons.[37] For one thing, the site in question is only one of six called "et-Tell" in Transjordan alone, some of whose ancient names are known with certainty; this renders the equation of "Ai = et-Tell" suspect. Also, "Ai" was the *name* of a place, not a generic *label,* meaning "the ruin." The fact that several other places were named "Ai" (or a name related to "Ai" linguistically), without the article, makes it clear that "Ai" was a name: one in Transjordan (Jer 49:3), one on the border of Moab (Iyim: Num 33:45), one in southern Judah (Iim: Josh 15:29).

Furthermore, Ai was inhabited during much of the biblical period (not an abandoned ruin): in the time of Abraham (Gen 12:8; 13:3), Joshua (Joshua 7–8), and the monarchy (1 Chr 7:28; Ezra 2:28 // Neh 7:32), all periods when et-Tell was not inhabited. By contrast, the only time et-Tell was inhabited (1200–1050 B.C.) was during the time when the Bible indicates Ai lay as a ruin (Josh 8:28).

Because of these and other difficulties, several scholars have pointed to other mounds in the immediate vicinity as more plausible possibilities for Ai. Some argue that Ai was at Khirbet Nisya,[38] while others suggest that it was at Khirbet el-Maqatir.[39] These alternate site proposals have been vigorously disputed,[40] but it would nevertheless seem that a good case can be made that et-Tell is not Ai and that an alternate site proposal must be sought. However, a definitive answer as to which of several mounds in the vicinity is ancient Ai is not yet forthcoming, and

---

[35] E.g., Callaway (see previous note); Z. Zevit, "The Problem of Ai," *BARev* 11.2 (1985): 58–69.

[36] E.g., K. A. Kitchen, *The Bible in Its World* (Downers Grove: InterVarsity, 1977), 89–90; R. K. Harrison, "Ai," *ISBE* 1:83.

[37] On these points, see J. Simons, *The Geographical and Topographical Texts of the Old Testament* (Leiden: Brill, 1959), § 465, and J. M. Grintz, "'Ai Which Is Beside Beth-Aven': A Reexamination of the Identity of 'Ai," *Bib* 42 (1961): 201–16, esp. 207–11. Z. Zevit also disputes the linguistic equation of the names "Ai" and "et–Tell" as both meaning "ruin," although he nevertheless believes that et–Tell is the site of ancient Ai and that the biblical record is mistaken (Zevit, "The Problem of Ai," 58–69, esp. 62–63).

the true site of Ai would seem to remain as yet unidentified, subject to further excavation and exploration.

EXCURSUS: DESTRUCTION AND DEVOTED THINGS IN JOSHUA[41]

In Joshua 6 (vv. 17–21), we encounter the first significant discussion in the Book of Joshua of the related concepts of "devoted things," "devoting a city to the LORD," and the complete destruction of the Canaanites. In v. 17, Joshua instructed the people that Jericho and everything in it was "to be devoted to the LORD," then in v. 18 he elaborated: "But keep away from *the devoted things*, so that you will not bring about your own *destruction* by taking any of *[the devoted things]*. Otherwise you will make the camp of Israel liable to *destruction* and bring trouble on it." The common element behind the italicized words is the Hebrew root *ḥrm:* it occurs in the Old Testament both as a verb (fifty-one times) and as a noun (twenty-nine times). The verb can be rendered "to devote to the LORD" or "to devote to destruction" or "to completely destroy," and the noun can be rendered as "devoted things" or "destruction." The NIV text note makes clear the connection between the idea of devotion and destruction: "The Hebrew term refers to the irrevocable giving over of things or persons to the LORD, often by totally destroying them."

The importance of this concept in Joshua is apparent from the number of times the root occurs, more than in any other Old Testament book. Of the forty-

---

[38] D. Livingstone, "Further Considerations on the Location of Bethel at el–Bireh," *PEQ* 126 (1994): 154–59, esp. 159. Ten seasons of excavations had been completed by 1994, but the results are somewhat equivocal. The author claims to have found remains that match the biblical account, published in his doctoral dissertation ("Khirbet Nisya, 1979–1986: A Report on Six Seasons of Excavation" [Ph.D. diss., Andrews University, 1979]), but one of his own doctoral examiners questions his success at making his case (B. K. Waltke, "The Date of the Conquest," *WTJ* 52 [1990]: 193).

[39] G. A. Byers, "Khirbet el–Maqatir 1996–97: Preliminary Report," *Near East Archaeological Society Newsletter* (1997), 1–2. A third season of excavation was carried out in June 1998 (B. G. Wood, personal communication). Wood presents his case against Ai being at Khirbet Nisya in "Notes on the Locations of Ai and Beth Aven" (unpublished notes, 1998).

[40] The issue also includes questions about the location of Bethel, since it was near Ai (see Josh 7:2). The equation of Ai with et–Tell and Bethel with Beitin is questioned by Livingstone, "Location of Biblical Bethel Reconsidered," *WTJ* 33 (1971): 20–44, with a vigorous rebuttal by A. F. Rainey, "Bethel Is Still *Beitîn*," *WTJ* 33 (1971): 175–88, and a surrebuttal by Livingstone, "Traditional Site of Bethel Questioned," *WTJ* 34 (1971): 39–50. The debate has continued in Rainey, "Rainey on Bethel and Ai," *BARev* 14.5 (1988): 67–68; Livingstone, "The Location of Bethel at el–Bireh." See also Bimson, *Redating the Exodus and Conquest*, 201–11, who reviews the debate and cautiously adds several arguments to Livingstone's.

[41] Introductions to the concept may be found in the following works: N. Lohfink, "חָרַם *ḥāram*; חֵרֶם *ḥērem*," *TDOT* 5:180–99; C. Brekelmans, "חֵרֶם *ḥērem* **ban**," *TLOT*, 474–77; J. A. Naudé, "חרם," *NIDOTTE* 2:276–77. See also P. D. Stern, *The Biblical Ḥerem: A Window on Israel's Religious Experience,* BJS 211 (Atlanta: Scholars Press, 1991); J. P. U. Lilley, "Understanding the *Ḥerem*," *TynBul* 44 (1993): 169–77. On the broader issue of holy war, see n. 52. On the ethical issues arising from the *ḥērem*, see the discussion below and the works in n. 57.

eight times the verb occurs in the Old Testament, fourteen times are in Joshua.[42] Of the twenty-nine occurrences of the noun, thirteen are in Joshua.[43]

Lohfink provides the following definitions for *ḥrm*. The verbal form (*hiphil*, the "causative" stem") means to "consecrate something or someone as a permanent and definitive offering for the sanctuary; in war, consecrate a city and its inhabitants to destruction; carry out this destruction; totally annihilate a population in war; kill." The noun form means "the object or person consecrated in the sense of the *hiphil* or condemned in the sense of the *hophal* (passive of the *hiphil*) or contaminated by entering into their deadly sphere; the act of consecration or of extermination and killing."[44] A common rendering of *ḥrm* as "ban" or "to place under the ban" is inappropriate, because it does not carry the ideas of secular outlawry or ecclesiastical excommunication that these definitions carry.[45] Lilley stresses that the essence of *ḥrm* "is an irrevocable renunciation of any interest in the object 'devoted'" and that it denotes "uncompromising consecration without possibility of recall or redemption."[46]

The concept of *ḥrm* is often found in sacred contexts, in which it has a strong connection with the idea of holiness. As such, these things were forbidden to common use, but rather were to be an "offering" to the Lord. Leviticus 27:28–29 illustrates this well: "But nothing that a man owns and devotes [*ḥrm*, twice][47] to the Lord—whether man or animal or family land—may be sold or redeemed; everything so devoted [*ḥrm*] is most holy to the LORD. No person devoted to destruction [*ḥrm*, twice][48] may be ransomed; he must be put to death." If something is dedicated or devoted to the Lord, it is "most holy." We find this idea in Joshua as well. In 6:18–19, the devoted things are holy (sacred): "But keep away from the devoted things [*ḥrm*], so that you will not bring about your own destruction [*ḥrm*] by taking any of them [*ḥrm*]. Otherwise you will make the camp of Israel liable to destruction [*ḥrm*] and bring trouble on it. All the silver and gold and the articles of bronze and iron are sacred to the Lord and must go into his treasury." In 7:13, the people were to consecrate themselves (i.e., make themselves holy) and remove the devoted things from them: "Go, *consecrate* the people. Tell them, '*Consecrate* yourselves in preparation for tomorrow; for this is what the LORD, the God of Israel, says: That which is devoted [*ḥrm*] is among you, O Israel. You cannot stand against your enemies until you remove it.'

More commonly, the idea of *ḥrm* is found in contexts of war. Numbers 21:2–3 illustrates this well: "Then Israel made this vow to the Lord: 'If you will deliver these people into our hands, we will totally destroy [*ḥrm*] their cities.' The LORD

---

[42] Josh 2:10; 6:18,21; 8:26; 10:1,28,35,37–38,40; 11:11–12,20–21.

[43] Josh 6:17,18[3x]; 7:1[2x],11,12[2x],13[2x],15; 22:20.

[44] Lohfink, *TDOT* 5:188.

[45] Ibid.

[46] Lilley, "Understanding the *Ḥerem*," 176,177.

[47] The NIV obscures the two references to *ḥrm* here. A literal rendering would be "every devoted thing [*ḥrm*] which a man devotes [*ḥrm*] to the LORD."

[48] Here again, *ḥrm* occurs twice: "every devoted thing [*ḥrm*] which is devoted [*ḥrm*] to the LORD that is human."

listened to Israel's plea and gave the Canaanites over to them. They completely destroyed *[ḥrm]* them and their towns; so the place was named Hormah" (*ḥormāh*, i.e., something completely destroyed). In Joshua, this is represented too. In most of the cities mentioned in the campaigns in chaps. 10 and 11, the Israelites completely destroyed their inhabitants (10:28,35,37,39–40; 11:11,12,20–21). And, in the case of cities such as Hazor, the destruction was of everything, including the city itself: "Everyone in it they put to the sword. They totally destroyed them *[ḥrm]*, not sparing anything that breathed, and he burned up Hazor itself. Joshua took all these royal cities and their kings and put them to the sword. He totally destroyed them *[ḥrm]*, as Moses the servant of the LORD had commanded" (11:11–12).

We should not make too hard and fast a distinction, however, between the sacred and the war contexts. The context of the destruction of Jericho, for example, makes it clear that the destruction was not a secular activity, but a deeply sacred one: most of chap. 6 is devoted to the sacred ceremonial rituals of marching around the city, and only briefly is the actual conflict told. Thus, things would be offered to God by being utterly destroyed. This could happen with respect to material wealth,[49] people,[50] or even entire cities.[51]

Scholars have spoken of the idea of "holy war" to describe a large complex of motifs in the Old Testament, in which the Lord fights for his people and gives them the victory. Essential in this is that the people be properly prepared and consecrated to receive this gift of victory from the Lord's hands. The idea of "holy war" is much broader than the idea of *ḥrm* under discussion here, but the *ḥrm* is an important part of the "holy war."[52]

This practice, while referred to extensively in the Old Testament, is not commonly seen in surrounding cultures. This is somewhat remarkable, given the bellicose nature of so many of these cultures and also given their developed religious systems. There is only one clear occurrence of this meaning of the root *ḥrm* in cognate Semitic literature.[53] Second Kings 19:11 mentions the Assyrian kings "utterly destroying" *(ḥrm)* lands they conquered, but it is not in the context of reli-

---

[49] E.g., Josh 6:18–19; 7:1,11.

[50] E.g., Josh 10:28, 35,39–41; 11:11,20.

[51] E.g., Josh 6:21; 8:26; 10:1,37; 11:12,21.

[52] The foundational study is G. von Rad, *Holy War in Ancient Israel* (Grand Rapids: Eerdmans, 1991); see the introduction by B. C. Ollenburger (pp. 1–33) for a helpful essay placing von Rad's work into context in OT scholarship since the work first appeared in German (1952). See also P. D. Miller, Jr., *The Divine Warrior in Early Israel* (Cambridge: Harvard University, 1973); M. Lind, *Yahweh Is a Warrior: The Theology of Warfare in Ancient Israel* (Scottsdale: Herald, 1980); S.-M. Kang, *Divine War in the Old Testament and in the Ancient Near East*, BZAW 177 (Berlin: de Gruyter, 1989); T. Longman, III and D. G. Reid, *God Is a Warrior* (Grand Rapids: Zondervan, 1995). A good bibliography may be found in R. M. Good, "The Just War in Ancient Israel," *JBL* (1985): 385–86, n. 1.

[53] This is in the Moabite Stone, where Mesha, king of Moab, states that he had devoted Nebo and its inhabitants for destruction to Ashtar-Chemosh (see *ANET*, 320). Brekelmans claims that the root *ḥrm*, with the meaning "to consecrate," occurs in almost all Semitic languages (*TLOT*, 474), but cf. Lohfink, *TDOT* 5:189–93.

gious destruction. Some parallels between biblical "holy war" and ancient Near East warfare do exist,[54] but the specific idea of *ḥrm* and parallels to it are rare.[55]

The special emphasis at the time of Joshua was that Israel was to keep itself holy, undefiled, and the land itself was to be undefiled. In the particular circumstances of the Israelites entering the long-promised land as a newly constituted nation, it was vitally important that they do so uncontaminated by pagan worship. Already they had yielded to temptation in connection with the Baal of Peor in the wilderness (Num 25; 31:1–4). In Deuteronomy, the Lord had made his desires clear: "You shall utterly destroy them … *precisely so that* they might not teach you to do according to all their abominations which they have done on behalf of their gods" (20:17–18; author translation).

When Israel did not obey the command utterly to destroy things, this did indeed contaminate its religion. This is most visible in the story of Achan's and Israel's "breaking faith" concerning things devoted to the Lord (Joshua 7). When Israel was defeated at Ai as a result of this, Joshua and the elders of the people went into mourning (7:7–9).

God's response to Israel's faithlessness was couched in terms of holiness (7:10–15). Israel (not just Achan) had sinned, and he would not tolerate it. This passage shows that God is not open to the charge of a double standard with reference to his treatment of Israel and the Canaanites. Earlier, he had ordered Israel to exterminate the Canaanites because of their sin (see below), but now he also held all Israel responsible for the sin of one man. The overriding concern in *all* such episodes was his demand for holiness and obedience and the concern for purity of worship. Thus, Josh 7:11 underlines the seriousness of the offense attributed to the nation: Israel had (1) "sinned," (2) "violated" the Lord's covenant, (3) "taken some of the devoted things," (4) "stolen," (5) "lied," and (6) put the things among their own possessions. The quick, staccato accumulation of these verbs in v. 11 accentuates the severity of the action, since it was essentially one act, but it is described in these various ways. Verse 12 shows that the people of Israel themselves now were, literally, "a thing for destruction" (as Jericho had been) as a result of this. God would no longer be with Israel, until the sin was removed from the camp. Verse 13 again emphasizes the importance of holiness in God's eyes: the people were to sanctify themselves, since they had been defiled by the presence of the devoted things.

Achan was found out, and he and his family were stoned and burned (7:16–26). Because he had violated God's command concerning the booty from Jericho, Achan found himself in the position of the inhabitants of Jericho: he himself was devoted to destruction. He in effect had become a Canaanite by his actions.

Another illustration of the effects of not completely destroying pagan influences comes in the Book of Judges. Despite the indications in Joshua 10–11 that Israel completely carried out the requirements of the complete annihilation, Judges 1 indicates that the various tribes did not fully obey.[56] Judges 2—and

---

[54] See J. J. Niehaus, "Joshua and Ancient Near Eastern Warfare," *JETS* 31 (1988): 37–50.

[55] See Lohfink, *TDOT* 5:189–93.

[56] See esp. Judg 1:19,21,28–34. See comments on 10:40–43 for a discussion of the different perspectives in Joshua 10–11 and Judges 1.

indeed the rest of the book of Judges—shows the effects this had on Israel's life: the people turned to the Baals, the gods of the Canaanites living among them, and forsook the Lord. Israel's worship did not remain pure.

One question that arises for many people is, How can a holy, just, loving God have commanded such harsh actions?[57] Many people today are repelled by what they see as a bloodthirstiness displayed by the Israelites and the God who had demanded the annihilations of the *ḥērem*.[58] R. Goetz is representative when he states that "the book of Joshua is embarrassment enough, with its ferocity and its religious advocacy of mass murder." He speaks of Calvin's "cold-blooded acceptance of the Deuteronomic theology of the *ḥērem*."[59] He goes on to speak of "the guilt of the living God" because of activities that, were they not committed or commanded by God, we would condemn as unspeakable and unjustifiable atrocities.[60]

Indeed, the biblical record is stark and unblinking when it speaks of these things, which are indeed horrible and should cause all of us as human beings to cringe when considering them. However, the human perspective is not always the divine perspective. God had informed Moses that Israel was to carry out this complete destruction in Canaan (Deut 7:2; 20:16–17; Josh 11:15,20), and Moses had so instructed Joshua (11:12,15; cf. 10:40). God spoke to Joshua directly about this as well (6:17, with reference to Jericho). Thus, the question arises concerning God's basic justice.

The Bible does not address the question in this way, but we can discern the outlines of an answer along two main trajectories. The first is that Israel's worship was to be maintained absolutely pure, without any taint of the false worship found in its surroundings. This point has been reviewed earlier. The second trajectory focuses on the Canaanites' sin. We can speak of their sin in general and also in terms of their rebellion against the God of Israel.

Concerning sin, we should first note that, from God's perspective, *all* peoples have sinned and fallen short of his standards (Rom 3:23) and thus are deserving of the severest punishment (Rom 6:23). Thus, on this level, the Canaanites only received what all peoples—then and now—deserve, and any peoples who have been spared are so spared only by God's grace. Sin is a harsh reality, but its absolute affront to the holy God is clearly taught in the Scriptures and too often ignored in the modern day.

While it is completely true that the Canaanites only received what all people deserve, and thus it could legitimately stand as the complete answer to the question, this answer is somewhat incomplete, since it is clear that God did not choose

---

[57] Other treatments of the ethical issues raised by the *ḥērem* may be found in W. B. Green, "The Ethics of the Old Testament," *PTR* 28 (1929): 313–66 (reprinted in W. C. Kaiser, Jr., ed., *Classical Evangelical Essays in Old Testament Interpretation* [Grand Rapids: Baker, 1972], 206–35; see esp. pp. 213–16); and Kaiser, *Toward Old Testament Ethics* (Grand Rapids: Zondervan, 1983), 67–72, 266–69.

[58] See esp. 6:21; 8:22; 10:26,28,30,32–33,35,37,39–40; 11:8,10–14.

[59] R. Goetz, "Joshua, Calvin, and Genocide," *TToday* 32 (1975): 263–74; quotes from p. 264.

[60] Goetz, "Joshua, Calvin, and Genocide," 273.

to annihilate other peoples in biblical times (or since) who also were sinful. What was distinctive about the Canaanite situation that triggered the unprecedented injunctions to destroy everyone and everything?

A preview of the Canaanites' sin was presented to Abraham, where he was told that the fulfillment of the promise to him would be delayed, in part because "the sin of the Amorites is not yet complete" (Gen 15:16). That is, the return of Abraham's descendants finally to inherit the land would have as part of its mission the punishing of the Canaanites for their sin.[61] For many years, the Canaanites' sins apparently would not justify the annihilation that would come when the Israelites took the land. However, that time *would* arrive, and it did arrive in the time of Joshua.

The sins of the Canaanites appear in several places. In Lev 18:24–30, Israel is solemnly warned to abstain from the many abominations that the Canaanites had practiced (see also v. 3). The larger context makes it clear that the entire list of sins in 18:6–23 were sins that the Canaanites practiced. These included engaging in incest, adultery, child sacrifice, homosexual activity, and bestiality. Furthermore, in Deut 9:4–5, "the wickedness of the nations [in the land of Canaan]" is given as a major reason why the Lord would drive them out before Israel. So again the Israelites' displacement of the Canaanites was in part a punishment for their wickedness. We can add that the promise to Abraham included the provision that God would curse anyone who cursed Israel (Gen 12:3), and the Canaanites sought to destroy Israel on at least three occasions (Josh 9:1–2; 10:1–5; 11:1–5).[62]

By the standards of most cultures, the sins of Lev 18:6–23 are particularly heinous. The evidence outside the Bible confirms the biblical picture of a particularly debased culture in Canaan. Archaeological excavation has shown that the practice of child sacrifice was particularly the province of the Canaanites and their descendants who migrated westward to Carthage.[63] Furthermore, texts and artifacts of the cults of the Baals, spoken of frequently in the Bible, have been discovered in the soil of Syria, Lebanon, and Israel. Among the common cultic practices was ritual prostitution.[64]

---

[61] The term "Amorite" in Gen 15:16 is synonymous with "Canaanite" here. See the commentary on 3:10.

[62] We should be very clear that Israel was not inheriting Canaan because of any merit of their own. Deut 9:5 states that "it is not because of your righteousness or your integrity that you are going in to take possession of their land; but on account of the wickedness of these nations."

[63] See L. E. Stager and S. R. Wolff, "Child Sacrifice at Carthage: Religious Rite and Population Control?" *BARev* 10.1 (1984): 30–51.

[64] Good introductions to the religion of the Canaanites may be found in D. Harden, *The Phoenicians*, 2d ed. (New York: Frederick A. Praeger, 1963), 82–114; W. F. Albright, *Yahweh and the Gods of Canaan* (Garden City: Doubleday/Anchor, 1968), 110–52; S. Moscati, *The World of the Phoenicians* (London: Weidenfeld & Nicholson, 1968), 30–41, 136–44; H. Ringgren, *Religions of the Ancient Near East* (Philadelphia: Westminster, 1973), 27–54. More recent introductions are J. Day, "Canaan, Religion of," *ABD* 1:831–37; P. C. Schmitz, "Phoenician Religion," *ABD* 5:357–63.

Another perspective on the sins of the Canaanites is provided in the Book of Joshua.[65] Beyond being a punishment for their sins in general—which were especially heinous, judged against those of nations around them—the destruction of the Canaanites was also due to their hardened hearts and their rebellion against God and his people. According to Josh 11:19–20, "Except for the Hivites living in Gibeon, not one city made a treaty of peace with the Israelites, who took them all in battle. For it was the LORD himself who hardened their hearts to wage war against Israel, so that he might destroy them totally, exterminating them without mercy, as the LORD had commanded Moses." This passage shows that the destruction of the Canaanites in chaps. 10–11 was orchestrated by God himself: he hardened their hearts so that he could completely destroy them. They had followed a pattern of opposing God by attacking the Israelites (see 9:1; 10:1–5; 11:1–5). Thus, the text is stark and harsh: the idea and activity of hardening originated from God himself, and it was for the purpose of destroying the Canaanites through battle, with no mercy.

The reference to God's hardening the Canaanites' hearts obviously recalls the same idea in the events of the exodus, where God hardened the pharaoh's heart (Exod 9:12; 10:1,27; 11:10; etc.) and sent the plagues. A careful reading of the Exodus passages, however, shows that God's actions in Egypt were tied to the pharaoh's defiance. His hardening of the pharaoh's heart must be seen in the context of the pharaoh's own stubbornness and resistance to God. Ultimately, he was not doing to the pharaoh anything that his heart was not already predisposed to do.

The Canaanites' resistance to the Lord can be seen in a similar light. They heard about Israel's victories (2:9–11; 5:1; 9:1,3; 10:1; 11:1), and most of them resisted Israel and its God; as a result, they were shown no mercy and were annihilated. God's hardening of their hearts (11:20) must be seen in the same way as the hardening of the pharaoh's heart: in the context of their own stubbornness and resistance of Israel's God. Had they been willing to react as Rahab (or even the Gibeonites) had done, undoubtedly the results would have been different.

Thus, the Canaanites' sins can be seen from two perspectives. First, they are condemned as particularly heinous and deserving of destructive punishment (Gen 15:16; Lev 18:6–30; Deut 9:4–5). Second, they consist in rebelling against Israel's God, in resisting him (Josh 11:19–20). For both reasons—as well as to keep Israel's faith uncontaminated—God commanded these terrible annihilations.

We should note that the instructions to Israel to annihilate the Canaanites were specific in time, intent, and geography. That is, Israel was not given a blanket permission to do the same to any peoples they encountered, at any time or in any place. It was limited to the crucial time when Israel was just establishing itself as a theocracy under God, to protect Israel's worship, as well as to punish these specific peoples. Thus, harsh as it is to our sensibilities, we should remember that it was for very clearly stated reasons, and it was very carefully circumscribed.[66]

---

[65] See the commentary on 11:19–20 for a fuller discussion of this perspective.

[66] God commanded Saul to annihilate the Amalekites (an order he did not carry out; 1 Sam 15) and Ahab to do the same to Ben–hadad (1 Kgs 20:42), but these again were circumscribed and limited orders. (See W. C. Kaiser, Jr., *Hard Sayings of the Old Testament* [Downers Grove: InterVarsity, 1988[, 106–9, on the Amalekite situation.)

Christians should remember this in attempting to apply the principles of the *ḥērem* to the modern day. While God abhors evil of every kind and Christians are to oppose it vigorously, the extremes of the *ḥērem* are not enjoined upon Christians to practice today. Even in what some people see as "barbaric" Old Testament times, the *ḥērem* was limited. God worked against evil during most of the Old Testament period, as he does today, in less drastic ways.

2. Covenant Disobedience (7:1–26)

The account in this chapter is organically bound up with that in the following chapter (8:1–29), so much so that many scholars subsume both chapters under one heading. The sin that Achan committed, its consequences for the nation, and the process of discovery and punishment of the sin are all related here. The defeat at the hands of the men of Ai here is followed by victory over these same men in chap. 8. The victory was made possible because of the cleansing of the nation that had been defiled by Achan's sin.

Several parallels exist between the accounts in Joshua 2 and 7. In Joshua 2, Rahab, a believing Canaanite, acted faithfully and, as a result, was promised deliverance from destruction. In effect, she became an Israelite. In Joshua 7, Achan, a disbelieving Israelite, acted faithlessly and, as a result, was not delivered but destroyed. In effect, he became a Canaanite. Achan thus stands as a foil to Rahab, and the two characters embody striking contrasts.[67]

(1) The Sin (7:1)

¹But the Israelites acted unfaithfully in regard to the devoted things; Achan son of Carmi, the son of Zimri, the son of Zerah, of the tribe of Judah, took some of them. So the LORD's anger burned against Israel.

7:1 This verse is a transition between the story of the conquest of Jericho and that of the defeat at Ai. It anticipates for the reader the information that emerges in more detail throughout the chapter, especially in vv. 20–21, where Achan admits the wrong that he had committed.

The positive state of affairs for the Israelites that existed after their taking of Jericho and that is indicated by the favorable comments of 6:27 was quickly shattered by sin. The specific sin was that Achan, who was from the favored tribe of Judah,[68] took some of the things in Jericho that had been

---

[67] For more details on lexical and thematic links between the two chapters, see Nelson, *Joshua*, 102–3; D. Dorsey, *Structure and Meaning in the Old Testament* (Grand Rapids: Baker, forthcoming), ad loc. See also L. L. Rowlett, *Joshua and the Rhetoric of Violence: A New Historicist Analysis*, JSOTSup 226 (Sheffield: Academic Press, 1996), 176–79, although her work as a whole represents an ideological reading of Joshua that has many problems.

[68] A rather detailed genealogy is given for Achan here, which is found again in 1 Chr 2:6–7, where Achan's name is "Achor" (see note at v. 26). This family listing foreshadows the step-by-step identification of Achan in vv. 16–17.

devoted to destruction. By doing so, he was violating the prohibition against taking these things that Joshua had uttered in 6:17–19. Apparently Achan acted alone, but the verse twice mentions the "Israelites"[69] as the guilty party (i.e., the one man's sin infected the nation as a whole).

More generally, the sin was that Israel "acted unfaithfully" with regard to the things devoted to destruction. The term in question here *(mᶜl)* is used to describe a wife's adultery (see Num 5:12–13): it was a betrayal of a trust that existed between two parties. In almost every use of this term in the Bible, the trust broken is that between God and humans.[70] So, in taking the devoted things, Achan was acting in a way that broke the fundamental covenantal relationship between God and Israel, and vv. 11 and 15 make that explicit: Israel had broken God's covenant. The damage was not repaired until the cause of the betrayal of trust had been removed from the nation (v. 26); then God's anger abated. And, in its present position, the covenant renewal ceremony of 8:30–35[71] shows that shortly thereafter the damaged covenant was renewed and repaired.

The sin was more than simple theft (a violation of the Eighth Commandment, Exod 20:15), since the term *mᶜl,* "to act unfaithfully," is used (and not *gnb,* "to steal").[72] The same term *(mᶜl)* is used seven times in Joshua 22, where the tribes west of the Jordan accused the two and one-half Transjordan tribes of acting unfaithfully by building an altar they thought was a source of idolatry and false worship.[73] These tribes accused the Transjordan tribes of acting in exactly the same way that Achan had (see 22:20), even though the specific actions of Achan and these tribes were different. The point of continuity in both episodes is the betrayal of God's trust and the pursuing of some other object of affection. In this sense, Achan's sin was a violation of the First Commandment, which prohibited having any other gods before the Lord (Exod 20:3).[74]

(2) The Defeat (7:2–5)

²Now Joshua sent men from Jericho to Ai, which is near Beth Aven to the east of Bethel, and told them, "Go up and spy out the region." So the men went up and spied out Ai.
³When they returned to Joshua, they said, "Not all the people will have to go up against Ai. Send two or three thousand men to take it and do not weary all the

---

[69] The NIV has "Israel" in the second instance, but in both cases the phrase is, literally, "the sons of Israel."

[70] See the excellent discussion by R. Knierim: "מעל‎ *mᶜl* "to be unfaithful," *TLOT* 2:680–82. In more depth, see J. Milgrom, *Leviticus 1–16,* AB 3A (New York: Doubleday, 1991), 345–56, who translates מעל‎ as "sacrilege." Hess's attempt to find a verbal linkage with a scattered sequence of letters in 6:24 that yield *m-ᶜ-l* is somewhat forced (Hess, *Joshua,* 143–44).

[71] See the discussions at 5:2 and 8:30 on differing placements of this account.

[72] Although גנב‎ is used in v. 11 (see below).

[73] Josh 22:16[2x],20[2x],22,31[2x].

[74] This trenchant observation was first made by Lohfink (*TDOT* 5:185) and is expanded upon by Robinson, "The Coherence of the Jericho Narrative," 333.

people, for only a few men are there." ⁴So about three thousand men went up; but they were routed by the men of Ai, ⁵who killed about thirty-six of them. They chased the Israelites from the city gate as far as the stone quarries and struck them down on the slopes. At this the hearts of the people melted and became like water.

7:2–5 After the spectacular success of the operations at Jericho, the Israelites turned their attention next to Ai.[75] As he had in the case of Jericho, Joshua sent out spies again (v. 2). The spies' report was optimistic (v. 3), as had been the earlier spies' report, but with a difference. The earlier spies were confident that the Lord had given Jericho into Israel's hands, and they had stated that all the people were "melting" *(mwg)* in fear (2:24), which is what Rahab had told them (2:9,11); in this case, however, God was not part of the equation at all. As a result of their spying expedition, the spies at Ai recommended two to three thousand men to engage in the operation. This was a small number compared to the much larger numbers available. For example, Josh 4:13 mentions forty thousand armed men just from the two and one-half Transjordan tribes alone, and Num 26:51 gives 601,730 as the total number of Israelite men twenty years old and older able to serve in its army shortly before the nation entered Canaan.[76]

---

[75] Ai is always referred to with the definite article—הָעַי—and it is mentioned thirty-eight to forty times in the OT. The meaning of its name is commonly taken to be "The Ruin." However, this equation of the Hb. הָעַי with the Arabic "tell" (which refers to a mound on which there is a ruin) is not sustainable. Its location is given with some precision in v. 2: it was near Beth-Aven and east of Bethel. On the archaeological and geographical evidence for Ai, as well as the meaning of its name, see the excursus on "The Archaeology of Jericho and Ai" at the end of chap. 6. On Bethel, see the commentary at 8:17.

[76] The accuracy of the large totals for the nation of Israel in the Books of Exodus, Numbers, Joshua, and elsewhere is a vexing question that cannot be addressed adequately here. Many different proposals have been advanced, but none is without its problems. Among conservative and evangelical scholars, Keil interprets the numbers literally *(COT: The Pentateuch,* 2:46–47, and esp. 3:4–14). J. W. Wenham argues that the Hebrew term *ʾelep* (usually translated "thousand") sometimes means "family leader" and sometimes "thousand" and that, in the large numbers, these two meanings were sometimes confused in the writing or copying of the OT ("The Large Numbers of the Old Testament," *TynBul* 18 [1967]: 19–53). G. J. Wenham states that "there is no obvious solution to the problems posed," but he appears to favor interpreting the numbers symbolically, linked with multiples of various astronomical periods *(Numbers: An Introduction and Commentary,* TOTC 4 [Downers Grove: InterVarsity, 1981], 60–66). R. B. Allen interprets the large numbers symbolically, arguing that they have been deliberately overstated by a factor of ten in order to bring greater glory to God ("Numbers," EBC 2 (Grand Rapids: Zondervan, 1990), 680–91). D. M. Fouts makes a similar argument but is freer than Allen in his advocacy of hyperbole ("The Use of Large Numbers in the Old Testament with Particular Emphasis on the Use of *ʾelep*" [Th.D. diss., Dallas Theological Seminary, 1992]); id., "A Defense of the Hyperbolic Interpretation of Large Numbers in the Old Testament," *JETS* 40 [1997]: 377–87). For a survey of population estimates of Canaan in ancient times, see Fouts, *Use of Large Numbers,* 53–67, and an overview of most proposals, pp. 154–70. A recent proposal, related somewhat to J. W. Wenham's, is C. J. Humphreys, "The Number of People in the Exodus from Egypt: Decoding Mathematically the Very Large Numbers in Numbers I and XXVI," *VT* 48 (1998): 196–213. The proposals of J. W. Wenham and Humphreys, or, alternatively, that of Allen, appear to have the most validity, but absolute certainty is not possible.

The spies' estimate was obviously inadequate, based on the results of the battle and also based on the number of people of Ai who fell in the destruction of the city: twelve thousand men and women (8:25).[77]

The actual account of the Israelites' defeat at Ai is briefly told in vv. 4–5. The reversal of fortunes is told with a focus on the Israelites: "And about three thousand men from the people went up there, but they fled before the men of Ai!"[78] Thirty six Israelites were killed—a very small number compared to the numbers of Israel's fighting forces, but it was thirty-six more than are recorded for the Jericho campaign—and the men of Ai gave chase for some distance. The attention here to the extended chase provides a backdrop for the Israelites' victory in the next chapter, where they laid an ambush and drew the men of Ai out of the city and this time were able to kill them all (8:9–23).[79]

As a result of the defeat, the Israelites feared greatly: their hearts "melted" *(mwg)*, and they became like water. The wordplay involving "melting" here—recalling Rahab's and the spies' statements in 2:9,11,24—is obvious: because of Achan's sin, Israel had now become like the Canaanites, alone, without any true god to protect them, and melting away with fear.

(3) Joshua's Lament (7:6–9)

⁶Then Joshua tore his clothes and fell facedown to the ground before the ark of the LORD, remaining there till evening. The elders of Israel did the same, and sprinkled dust on their heads. ⁷And Joshua said, "Ah, Sovereign LORD, why did you ever bring this people across the Jordan to deliver us into the hands of the Amorites to destroy us? If only we had been content to stay on the other side of the Jordan! ⁸O Lord, what can I say, now that Israel has been routed by its enemies? ⁹The Canaanites and the other people of the country will hear about this and they will surround us and wipe out our name from the earth. What then will you do for your own great name?"

7:6   Joshua's reaction to the turn of events was dramatic. He mourned in

---

[77] However, the reason for the Israelites' defeat was that they had sinned, not that they took an inadequately sized army; so, even if they had taken a larger force, the text's implication is that they would have been defeated.

[78] Author's translation. The NIV's "were routed" obscures the focus on the overconfident Israelites in the verse.

[79] The location of the "stone quarries"—the word is rendered in the NIV text note and some versions as a place name, "Shebarim"; see, e.g., NASB, NKJV, NRSV, NJPSV—is unknown.

the Lord's presence (before the ark), and the elders joined him (v. 6).[80] He then cried out to God, lamenting the present state of affairs (vv. 7–9).

7:7 Joshua's words were bitter ones, ones that echoed various complaints by the Israelites in the wilderness (see Exod 16:3; 17:3; Num 11:4–6; 14:2–3; 20:3–5). Like the Israelites who questioned why God had brought them into the wilderness only to let them die (in their view), Joshua now questioned why God had brought them across the Jordan only to let them die at the hands of the Canaanites (v. 7a).[81] For both the Israelites and Joshua, the certainty of the past was preferable to the difficulties of the present and the uncertainty of the future. Joshua's desire to have remained east of the Jordan (v. 7b) shows his selective memory, since God had shown himself to be very much on Israel's side in the case of Jericho. Conversely, the wilderness sojourn had not been without its many problems, and, indeed, when they were in the wilderness, the Israelites had longed to be back in slavery in Egypt rather than in the wilderness (Num 11:4–6). Joshua probably was thinking that east of the Jordan they had had two significant victories over the land's inhabitants, Sihon, king of the Amorites, and Og, king of Bashan (Num 21:21–35) and that now that Transjordan had been pacified, it would be a comfort to live there. He appears to have forgotten God's promises that no one would be able to withstand Israel and that he would be with his people (1:5–9). He concluded that God intended to destroy Israel, and he did not consider the possibility that there might be sin in the camp.

The name used of God in v. 7— "Sovereign LORD" in the NIV and the NLT—is *ʾădōnāy yhwh*, which is rendered in many versions as "the Lord GOD" (e.g., NASB, NKJV, NJPSV, NRSV). God is called most commonly by one of three names in the Old Testament: (1) *ʾĕlōhîm*, translated as "God"; (2) *yhwh*, "Yahweh," rendered as "the LORD" (or, in ASV, "Jehovah"); and (3) *ʾădōnāy*, translated as "the Lord." As we noted at 1:1, "Yahweh" was God's personal name, and it was the subject of the Third Commandment: "You shall not misuse the name of the LORD [Yahweh] your God" (Exod 20:7). The reason that most modern versions render "Yahweh" as "the LORD" is that the Jews, fearful of violating the Third Commandment even by mispronouncing the holy Name of God, began substituting *ʾădōnāy*, "Lord," in oral

---

[80] The actions of mourning here are much more dramatic than most mourning customs in the modern Western world. However, they were common in Israel and the ancient Near East. Other mourning customs indicated in the OT include weeping (Ps 6:6; Jer 9:1), beating the chest (Isa 32:12), lifting up of the hands (Ps 141:2; Ezra 9:5), lying or sitting in silence (Judg 20:26; 2 Sam 12:16), bowing the head (Lam 2:10), fasting (2 Sam 3:35), wearing of sackcloth (Gen 37:34), sprinkling of ashes, dust, or dirt (as here; 2 Sam 15:32). There was even a class of professional women mourners who could be called to mourn on specific occasions (Jer 9:17, 20; Amos 5:16–17). Israelites were strictly prohibited from practicing some pagan mourning rites, however, such as cutting the flesh or shaving the beard (Lev 19:28; Deut 14:1; Jer 16:6).

[81] See note on 3:10 on the term "Amorites." Here it is used generically to refer to Canaanites.

reading—although not in writing—when they came to the name "Yahweh." In time, this convention was taken into written translations into other languages. In most English versions, the convention has continued, but these versions (including the NIV) make distinctions by rendering the names differently. The Hebrew in the present passage in oral reading would have created a redundant-sounding *ʾădōnāy ʾădōnāy.* In these special cases, the Jews substituted *ʾelōhîm* for "Yahweh" in their oral reading, yielding the phrase *ʾădōnāy ʾelōhîm.*[82] This term is used almost three hundred times of God in the Old Testament, and it expresses a special attitude of worship and respect for him, acknowledging the covenant-keeping, personal God of Israel *(yhwh)* as the Lord *(ʾădōnāy)* who is sovereign over all.

7:8 The import of the rout that Israel suffered is seen in the words Joshua chose here to describe it. Instead of stating that Israel had "fled" *(nws),* for example (a more common and expected expression), he declared that Israel had (lit.) "turned the back of its neck before its enemies." The word translated "turned" here *(hpk)* more usually is translated "overturned" and is a word indicating great turmoil. This is the only place in the Old Testament where this dramatic expression—"turned the back of its neck"—is used, and it vividly captures the shame and turmoil involved for Israel (see also v. 12, where the language is slightly different).

7:9 Joshua's concern took two tracks: he was concerned immediately for his own survival and the survival of the nation. However, he also was concerned for the Lord's reputation, which is indicated by his reference to the Lord's "great name." He was conscious of Israel's status as Yahweh's chosen people, and he knew that Yahweh's reputation among the nations would be linked by them to the fortunes of his people. That the nations did look at Israel and judge it and its God by its fortunes is indicated by God's reference to the "reproach of Egypt" in 5:9 and by Moses' words in Num 14:13–16.[83]

The meaning of God's name, the way in which it revealed aspects of his character, the importance of people's bowing at the sound of his name and praising it, and its connection with God's reputation—these are all components of a great "name" theology in the Old Testament. Humans first began calling on the name of the Lord in Gen 4:26, and the problem with the building of the tower of Babel was that its builders wanted to exalt their own name in the process, not God's (Gen 11:4). God revealed the meaning of his name to Moses at the burning bush (Exod 3:14–15). The psalmists often urged that

---

[82] Perhaps the best place for a reader to notice the interplay between these names of God is in Amos 6:8, in which the three names for God are found four times in quick succession: *ʾădōnāy yhwh … yhwh ʾelōhîm ṣebāʾôt.* The NIV reads "The Sovereign LORD has sworn by himself—the LORD God Almighty declares," while a more literal version, the NASB, reads "The Lord GOD has sworn by Himself, the LORD God of hosts has declared."

[83] See the comments at 5:9 for more on this.

Israel praise the name of the Lord (e.g., Pss 113:1–3; 135:1–3; 148:5,13). Just as in English today, a reference in Hebrew to people's names referred to their reputation and their character (we speak of maintaining—or restoring—our good name, meaning our good reputation).[84]

(4) The Lord's Instructions (7:10–15)

[10]The LORD said to Joshua, "Stand up! What are you doing down on your face? [11]Israel has sinned; they have violated my covenant, which I commanded them to keep. They have taken some of the devoted things; they have stolen, they have lied, they have put them with their own possessions. [12]That is why the Israelites cannot stand against their enemies; they turn their backs and run because they have been made liable to destruction. I will not be with you anymore unless you destroy whatever among you is devoted to destruction.

[13]"Go, consecrate the people. Tell them, 'Consecrate yourselves in preparation for tomorrow; for this is what the LORD, the God of Israel, says: That which is devoted is among you, O Israel. You cannot stand against your enemies until you remove it.

[14]"'In the morning, present yourselves tribe by tribe. The tribe that the LORD takes shall come forward clan by clan; the clan that the LORD takes shall come forward family by family; and the family that the LORD takes shall come forward man by man. [15]He who is caught with the devoted things shall be destroyed by fire, along with all that belongs to him. He has violated the covenant of the LORD and has done a disgraceful thing in Israel!'"

The Lord's response to Joshua's and the elders' mourning was directed to Joshua alone, and it was a rebuke couched in holiness terms. *Israel* (not just Achan; see v. 1) had sinned, and God would not tolerate it. This passage shows that God was not open to the charge of a double standard with reference to his treatment of Israel and the Canaanites. He had ordered Israel to exterminate the Canaanites because of their sin, but here he allowed all Israel to be affected by the sin of one man. The overriding concern in all such episodes was his demand for holiness and obedience and the concern for purity of worship.[85]

7:11 Despite the indication in 7:1 that only Achan had violated the instructions concerning the things banned, this verse extends the responsibil-

---

[84] For more on the theology of God's name, see J. B. Payne, *The Theology of the Older Testament* (Grand Rapids: Zondervan, 1962), 144–51; E. Jacob, *Theology of the Old Testament* (New York: Harper & Row, 1958), 43–64; W. Eichrodt, *Theology of the Old Testament* (Philadelphia: Westminster, 1961), 1:178–205; G. von Rad, *Old Testament Theology* (New York: Harper & Row, 1962), 1:179–87; W. C. Kaiser, Jr., *Toward an Old Testament Theology* (Grand Rapids: Zondervan, 1978), 106–7.

[85] My student William McDonald points out that the Lord's words occur at the structural midpoint of the chapter (private communication).

ity to the entire nation, in an example of what has been called "corporate solidarity."[86] This concept embraces at least the following ideas: (1) the entire group is treated as a unity; (2) sometimes the entire group is represented by a single individual; and (3) sometimes the individual and the group are merged.[87] The third of these ideas is embodied here; the individual and the group are closely identified: the verse affirms that "Israel has sinned," and yet later Achan confesses, "I have sinned" (v. 20).

This verse indicates the seriousness of the sin and God's outrage at it, because of the slow, climactic buildup of the language and the differing terms for sin, which become more specific with every word. First, the general word "sin" *(ḥāṭāʾ)* is used. Next, the more specific term "violated" is used (*ʿābar*, lit., "crossed over [the line], transgressed"). Next, the specific sin is mentioned in two different ways: the Israelites had taken *(lāqaḥ)* some of the devoted things and they had stolen *(gānab)*. They had also lied *(kiḥāš)*, and they had put *(śām)* the devoted things among their own things. Six verbs are thus used to describe Achan's (=Israel's) actions, four of which indicate sin in their own right and the other two do so in this context. The successive clauses are all linked by the word *gam,* usually translated "also."[88] Here, the linking of the verbs and clauses in this way indicate a progressive buildup of specificity and, in the process, they describe the totality of what Achan did.

Israel had violated God's covenant. The word "covenant" refers to many different dealings of God with his people at different times, but here the specific reference appears to be to the portion of the covenant he had made with his people through Moses that referred to the annihilation of the Canaanites (Deut 20:10–20).

7:12 The reason for Israel's defeat is now revealed: Israel itself—just as Jericho before it—was made liable to destruction because of *its* sin, and it had suffered a humiliating defeat because of this. What's more, God would no

---

[86] The idea of "corporate personality" was introduced by H. W. Robinson, *Corporate Personality in Israel* (Philadelphia: Fortress, 1964). Robinson's formulation has been criticized by many, and the term "corporate solidarity" is often used, which avoids many of the pitfalls of Robinson's model. See, e.g., J. R. Porter, "The Legal Aspects of Corporate Personality in the Old Testament," *VT* 15 (1965): 361–68; J. W. Rogerson, "The Hebrew Conception of Corporate Personality," *JTS* 21 (1980): 1–16; id., "Corporate Personality," *ABD* 1:1156–57; W. C. Kaiser, Jr., *Toward Old Testament Ethics* (Grand Rapids: Zondervan, 1983), 67–70.

[87] Kaiser, *Toward Old Testament Ethics*, 69.

[88] On the functions of גַּם, see *HALOT*, 195–96; *IBHS* §§ 39.3.4; T. Muraoka, *Emphatic Words and Structures in Biblical Hebrew* (Leiden: Brill; Jerusalem: Magnes, 1985), 143–46; C. J. Labuschagne, "The Emphasizing Particle *GAM* and Its Connotations," *Studia Biblica et Semitica: Theodoro Christiano Vriezen Festschrift*, ed. W. C. van Unnik and A. S. van der Woude (Wageningen: Veenman & Zonen, 1966), 193–203. Muraoka makes a good case for גַּם being almost exclusively an additive word, not an emphatic one (as opposed to Labuschagne, who argues for the priority of emphasis).

longer be with Israel, until they (the "you" is now plural) removed the sin from the camp. God's threatened withdrawal of his presence was a serious thing, since he had specifically promised to be with his people earlier in the book (1:5,9). God's presence was withdrawn on two occasions in later times, with dire consequences: 1 Sam 4:19–22; 16:14. This threat to withdraw emphasizes once again God's absolute standards and demands of holiness.

7:13–15 The sin needed to be dealt with, and vv. 13–15 detail God's instructions for this. In v. 13, the instruction is again to Joshua: he was to sanctify the people in preparation for what God would do on the morrow. The language here echoes that of 3:5 in an ironic way, where Joshua ordered the people, "Consecrate yourselves, for tomorrow the LORD will do amazing things among you." Here, the people also were to consecrate *(qdš)* themselves, but, in contrast with the "amazing things" *(niplāʾôt)* that would be "among" *(bĕqereb)* the Israelites, now the "devoted things" *(ḥērem)* were "among" *(bĕqereb)* them. The need for purification was due to very different things in the two cases.

Verse 14, by its orderly instructions and by the verb used here, indicates that the Lord was in control of the entire process of identifying the culprit through the basic social units of society: tribe, clan, and family.[89] Three times the verb "catches" or "captures" is used in v. 14 *(lqd)*, again at the beginning of v. 15 and once each in vv. 16–18. The NIV translates it "takes" (as do most versions),[90] but the idea indicated by "catches" is much more expressive, as well as accurate.

The punishment was severe and total: Achan and everything that belonged to him were to be burned with fire (v. 15), a sentence that was carried out after stoning (v. 25). Caleb's sin involved violating the Lord's covenant and doing a "disgraceful thing" *(nĕbālâ)*. The latter concept denotes "disorderly and unruly action in breaking a custom" or "behaving treacherously toward God."[91]

(5) Discovery and Consequence (7:16–26)

[16]Early the next morning Joshua had Israel come forward by tribes, and Judah was taken. [17]The clans of Judah came forward, and he took the Zerahites. He had the clan of the Zerahites come forward by families, and Zimri was taken. [18]Joshua had his family come forward man by man, and Achan son of Carmi, the son of Zimri, the son of Zerah, of the tribe of Judah, was taken.

[19]Then Joshua said to Achan, "My son, give glory to the LORD, the God of

---

[89] On these social units, see R. G. Boling, *Joshua*, AB 6 (Garden City: Doubleday, 1982), 226; Woudstra, *Joshua*, 127; in more depth, see N. P. Lemche, *Early Israel: Anthropological and Historical Studies on the Israelite Society before the Monarchy* (Leiden: Brill, 1985), 245–90.

[90] But see NJPSV marginal note, which has "catches."

[91] C.-W. Pan, "נבל," *NIDOTTE* 3:11.

Israel, and give him the praise. Tell me what you have done; do not hide it from me."

²⁰Achan replied, "It is true! I have sinned against the LORD, the God of Israel. This is what I have done: ²¹When I saw in the plunder a beautiful robe from Babylonia, two hundred shekels of silver and a wedge of gold weighing fifty shekels, I coveted them and took them. They are hidden in the ground inside my tent, with the silver underneath."

²²So Joshua sent messengers, and they ran to the tent, and there it was, hidden in his tent, with the silver underneath. ²³They took the things from the tent, brought them to Joshua and all the Israelites and spread them out before the LORD.

²⁴Then Joshua, together with all Israel, took Achan son of Zerah, the silver, the robe, the gold wedge, his sons and daughters, his cattle, donkeys and sheep, his tent and all that he had, to the Valley of Achor. ²⁵Joshua said, "Why have you brought this trouble on us? The LORD will bring trouble on you today."

Then all Israel stoned him, and after they had stoned the rest, they burned them. ²⁶Over Achan they heaped up a large pile of rocks, which remains to this day. Then the LORD turned from his fierce anger. Therefore that place has been called the Valley of Achor ever since.

Achan was found out for the sin he had committed, and he and his family were stoned and burned. Because he had violated God's command concerning the booty from Jericho, Achan found himself in the position of the inhabitants of Jericho: he himself was devoted to destruction. He in effect had become a Canaanite by his actions. This account masterfully builds, slowly and deliberately, to its climactic dénouement in v. 26.

7:16–18   Chapter 3 is again echoed (see on 7:13) here, since the first three words in Hebrew are identical to those in 3:1: "And Joshua arose early in the morning."[92] The first time, it was for a noble cause: to prepare the Israelites for entering the land. This time, it was for a far more grim cause: to identify and punish the one who had violated the covenant.

In vv. 16–18, Achan is methodically and inexorably identified by the process God specified in v. 14. The specific means by which he was identified is not indicated (by lot? by Urim and Thummim?), but the expressive vocabulary of v. 14 continues here: Achan was "caught" by the process.

7:19   Joshua addressed Achan as "my son," an indication of his assuming a leadership—even paternal—role in the incident. He issued four commands to Achan: "ascribe glory to the LORD," "give him praise," "tell me what you did," and "do not hide it from me." The first two clearly parallel each other, as do the second two. However, it would appear that the two sets of verbs also parallel each other. That is, the four actions commanded by Joshua are part and parcel of one event. By confessing (and not hiding) his sin, he was indeed

---

[92] The NIV's dynamic equivalent renderings in 3:1 and 7:16 obscure the parallels.

glorifying and praising God. Joshua was not instructing Achan to indulge in a disengaged act of glorifying and praising God and *then* to confess his sin; rather, by his very confession, he was glorifying God. The same wording is found in John 9:24, where the Pharisees spoke these words—"Give glory to God"—in urging a blind man whom Jesus had healed to tell the truth (and, in their minds, by doing so, he would have needed to confess his sin of lying when he claimed that Jesus had healed him).

7:20–21 Achan immediately confessed that he was guilty (v. 20) and gave the details of what he had done (v. 21). He had taken plunder that was very valuable. The "beautiful robe from Babylonia" was literally "one beautiful garment of Shinar" (see the NIV text note). The land of Shinar is mentioned in Gen 11:2 as the place where men built the Tower of Babel (i.e., the "Tower of Babylon").[93] The two hundred shekels of silver weighed more than eighty ounces, and the fifty-shekel "wedge"[94] of gold weighed about twenty ounces.[95]

Achan's actions, besides violating (1) the Eighth Commandment (about stealing: Exod 20:15), (2) God's instructions in Deut 20:10–20 (see on v. 11), (3) the injunction against lying (Lev 19:11), and (4) the First Commandment (about not having any other gods before the Lord: Exod 20:3; see on v. 1), also directly violated the Ninth Commandment (about coveting: Exod 20:17). A telling parallel to this passage if Gen 3:6, where the same verbs are used of Eve: both she and Achan "saw" *(rʾh)* and "desired" (or "coveted") *(ḥmd)* and "took" *(lqḥ)* what was forbidden to them.

Achan attempted to hide his sin from the God from whom nothing could be hidden (see Ps 139:7–12). A subtle wordplay connects vv. 19 and 21: Joshua instructed Achan not to hide *(kḥd)* anything from him when he confessed (v. 19), but Achan had hidden *(ṭmn)* the things he stole (v. 21).[96]

7:22–26 This section brings the Achan incident to a brisk conclusion, in a continuous narrative stream. In v. 22, the veracity of Achan's words in his confession (v. 21) is confirmed, since the wording concerning where the booty would be and how it was arranged (with the silver below) is identical in both verses. Achan now was indeed telling the truth and "glorifying" God (see v. 19). In v. 23, the items of booty were "spread out" before the Lord. The word used

---

[93] "Shinar" is a term used for Babylonia eight times in the OT. D. M. Stec has recently questioned the accuracy of the account here, due to the lack of references elsewhere to garments associated with Shinar ("The Mantle Hidden By Achan," *VT* 41 [1991]: 356–59). However, A. R. Millard has shown that the textile industry was an integral part of Babylonian trade since earliest times ("Back to the Iron Bed: Og's or Procrustes'?" *Congress Volume [Paris 1992]*, VTSup 61 [Leiden: Brill, 1995], 197–99).

[94] It probably was a gold bar. The Hb. literally calls it a "tongue of gold."

[95] The shekel was the basic unit of weight for coins, and it weighed slightly more than 0.4 ounces. See E. M. Cook, "Weights and Measures," *ISBE* 4:1053–54.

[96] The words are different, but they are part of the larger semantic field for words of hiding. For a listing of this semantic field, see *NIDOTTE* 5:102.

here *(yṣr)* is significant, since it is translated most commonly as "poured out," referring to the use of oil in anointing and other religious contexts. The stolen items were "poured out" before the Lord, returning to him what belonged to him.

Achan was brought out to be stoned, not only with each of the items he had stolen, but also with all his possessions and his entire household, including his children (v. 24). This was an extremely severe punishment (see the excursus on "Destruction and Devoted Things in Joshua" at the end of chap. 6), but it illustrates again God's absolute demands of holiness. Achan's sin had infected the entire nation of Israel (7:1), and ridding Israel of the stain of this sin required the annihilation of everything with which he had had intimate contact. Ironically—and tragically—for Achan, God allowed the Israelites to take booty in the next victory, at the second battle of Ai (8:2). He could have had anything he wanted if he had only waited on God. Like Adam and Eve, he lost sight of the character of our generous God and thought that satisfaction required taking. Achan's greed was his downfall. Also ironically, it was Joshua and "all Israel" who did this to Achan. Previously, all of Israel had been indicted because of Achan's sin (v. 1), but now the nation was acting to purge itself of the contamination, and it could again move ahead confidently in the task of taking the land of Canaan. Achan's self-centered actions resulted in terrible consequences not only for himself but also for his family. This illustrates the principle that sin does have its consequences.

Joshua's question in v. 25—"Why have you brought this trouble on us?"— is turned on its head by his next statement, an assertion that the Lord would now bring trouble on Achan. Joshua used the same word for "bringing trouble" here *(ʿkr)* that he had earlier used in warning the people against taking the devoted items, since doing so would "bring trouble" *(ʿkr)* on the entire camp (6:18). The story of Achan proves the veracity of Joshua's earlier words. Sin always would have its consequences. The root here *(ʿkr)* forms the basis for the name of the site in later times ("Achor," vv. 24,26).

The punishment for Achan and his household was stoning and burning (v. 25b). The exact sequence of events is not entirely clear. The text reads, literally, "And all Israel 'stoned' him [with] a stone, and they burned them with fire, and they 'stoned' them with stones." The two verbs for stoning here are different, and the burning with fire seems to be misplaced (i.e., it would most likely have happened after—not before—the stoning of everyone: see NIV). The overall impression forged by the repetitions is one of completeness. It is possible that one of the words for stoning refers more properly to the heaping up of a pile of stones over Achan's corpse, a point made explicitly in v. 26.[97]

---

[97] According to *HALOT*, the first term for stoning (רגם) means "to cover over with stones," whereas the second (סקל) means "to kill by hurling stones" (*HALOT*, 768; cf. p. 1187). If so, the pile of stones would have been only over Achan, as v. 26 states. BDB does not distinguish between the two terms. Keil suggests that the second term (סקל) denotes the piling up of stones, in which case the pile would have been covering both Achan and his family (*Book of Joshua*, 83).

A great pile of stones was heaped over Achan, one that remained "to this day," that is, until the time of the writing about this event (v. 26a). This was also done to the king of Ai when Israel had finally defeated him (8:29), as well as to Absalom after he was dead (2 Sam 18:17); in each case, the wording is almost identical to that here.[98] In Josh 8:29, the wording is exactly the same, making the point clearly that God would not favor his own people when they blatantly disobeyed, any more than he would favor wicked Canaanites. Because of his sin, Achan was expelled from Israel and treated as a Canaanite. In this way, the Lord's anger was abated.

The connection between this pile of stones and the earlier set of twelve memorial stones that Joshua erected on the banks of the Jordan River is hard to ignore. The reason for each one was different, but both piles of stones remained in their place "until this day" (4:9; 7:26; see also 10:27). The first set was specifically to be a reminder to Israel of God's presence with them (see 4:7). The pile of stones over Achan is not infused with the same meaning, but the very fact that it remained "until this day" shows us that it was a reminder to Israel of the story of Achan and the consequences of sin.

The name of the place—"Valley of Achor"—means "Valley of Trouble" (see NIV text note), undoubtedly given to it because of the events that transpired here. Achan's name in several places in the Greek translation of Joshua is "Achor," which no doubt represents a fusing of the two names.[99] It too had retained its name "to this day."[100]

3. The Destruction of Ai (8:1–29)

The account of the destruction of Ai follows immediately upon the story in chap. 7 of Achan's sin, the resulting defeat at Ai, and the punishment of that sin (see the introductory comments to chap. 7). In the larger perspective of the book, there should never have been any question concerning the Israelites' ability to take Ai, since Yahweh would be its warrior and guarantor of the land (cf. 1:2–9). However, in the immediate context of Achan's sin, the defeat at Ai brought great distress: it caused Joshua and the people to fear and to raise questions of God (7:5–9).

---

[98] See Hess, *Joshua*, 155–56, on stone mounds or cairns in antiquity.

[99] The names of Achan and his forebears found in 7:1 are found again in 1 Chr 2:6–7. Achan's name there is "Achor," while his grandfather Zabdi's name there is Zimri. Minor changes in spelling are common between early and late texts such as these: even David's name is spelled slightly differently in 1, 2 Chronicles from the way it is in 1, 2 Samuel. Also see the note on Achan at 7:1. For more on the names here, see Hess, "Achan and Achor: Names and Wordplay in Joshua 7," *HAR* 14 (1994): 89–98.

[100] The wording is the same in the two parts of the verse.

The trauma was alleviated by Israel's rooting out the evil in its midst, the abatement of Yahweh's anger, and the great victory achieved after the events of chap. 7. God was no longer angry with Israel, since atonement had been made for its sin, and the task now was to get on with the conquest. Thus, he gave the city of Ai into the Israelites' hands: they captured it via an elaborate ambush. In chap. 8, that victory is described in some detail, more so than for any other battle in the book. It is the first true military victory recounted (since the taking of Jericho can hardly be called a "battle") and involved a military strategy for which the Lord gave instructions.[101]

The chronology and geography in this chapter are difficult.[102] The chapter seems to describe two ambush forces, sent out on two different days (vv. 3–9 and 10–13). However, this is not according to the Lord's instructions in v. 2, and it presents the particular difficulty of the first (improbably large) ambush force of thirty thousand men (v. 3) being forced to spend two nights and a day in hiding near Ai—a city with only twelve thousand inhabitants of its own, less than half of the numbers in ambush force—without being detected by its inhabitants.

More probably, there was just one ambush force and only one night involved. Verses 3–9 describe the main aspects of the preparations. Verse 10 describes the commencement of the battle the next morning. Then, vv. 11–13 contain a flashback, expanding upon the narrative of vv. 3–9. This is indicated by the syntax of vv. 11 and 14. Verse 11 begins with a disjunctive, circumstantial clause construction[103] and thus introduces the retrospective account of vv. 11–13.[104] The signal that this account is concluded—and that the main narrative is resuming—comes at the beginning of v. 14, which begins with the paragraph marker *wayĕhî* ("and it happened"), followed by a stage-setting time reference in a subordinate clause ("when the king of Ai

---

[101] Many scholars have noted the similarities between this account and that of the Israelite ambush of Gibeah in Judges 20. In both cases, Israel suffered an initial defeat, and then God provided assurances of success. Also, both cases involved an ambush, the only two times in the Bible where such a tactic was employed. There are several striking parallels in story line and even vocabulary; see Butler, *Joshua*, 80–81, Hess, *Joshua*, 161–62, and Nelson, *Joshua*, 111–12, for these and for further bibliography.

[102] For reviews of the problems from various critical perspectives, postulating various (conflicting) sources or traditions, see J. A. Soggin, *Joshua*, OTL (Philadelphia: Westminster, 1972), 96–104; Boling, *Joshua*, 236; Nelson, *Joshua*, 110–11 (Nelson presents a more holistic reading on pp. 112–13). For reviews more sympathetic to the integrity of the text, see Keil, *Book of Joshua*, 84–87; Woudstra, *Joshua*, 136–40; Goslinga, *Joshua, Judges, Ruth*, 186–87.

[103] וְכָל־הָעָם הַמִּלְחָמָה אֲשֶׁר אִתּוֹ עָלוּ: "And all the people of war who were with him had gone up."

[104] Boling, *Joshua*, 12, and NIV correctly render the verb in v. 12 as past perfect ("had taken"), but they do not account for the disjunction at the beginning of v. 11, which suggests that the verbs in v. 11 should also be rendered as past perfects.

saw") and a normal resumptive verb form.[105] This solution is not without its problems—the main one being the number "thirty thousand" in v. 3 (on which, see below)—but it fits best the syntax of the passage.

Thus, the sequence of events would be as follows. Joshua commissioned a group of men to lie in ambush west of Ai, as the Lord had instructed (vv. 3b–4,12–13). He sent them out (v. 9a), then he went with the main fighting force to be stationed north of the city (vv. 3a,11) and spent the night with this group (vv. 9b,13b).[106] He and the people went up to Ai the next morning (v. 10), which was seen by the king of Ai (v. 14), who mustered his people to meet Israel in battle. The Israelites put their ruse into effect, pretending to flee, drawing out of the city its entire population (vv. 15–17).[107]

At the same time, the ambush force was arising (v. 19), and when Joshua stretched out his javelin toward Ai, they entered the city and set it ablaze (vv. 18–19). When the Aiites saw this, they realized that they were surrounded before and behind, and they succumbed to a slaughter that left none alive except their king (vv. 20–26). The Israelites took the cattle and booty as spoil (v. 27)—which had been authorized this time by God (v. 2)—and burned the city, exposing the body of its king in an act of humiliation before burying it under a great pile of stones (vv. 28–29).

(1) Instructions for Taking Ai (8:1–2)

[1]Then the LORD said to Joshua, "Do not be afraid; do not be discouraged. Take the whole army with you, and go up and attack Ai. For I have delivered into your hands the king of Ai, his people, his city and his land. [2]You shall do to Ai and its king as you did to Jericho and its king, except that you may carry off their plunder and livestock for yourselves. Set an ambush behind the city."

---

[105] The Hb. and a literal translation are as follows: וַיְהִי כִּרְאוֹת מֶלֶךְ־הָעַי וַיְמַהֲרוּ וַיַּשְׁכִּימוּ וַיֵּצְאוּ אַנְשֵׁי־הָעִיר לִקְרַאת־יִשְׂרָאֵל: "And it happened, when the king of Ai saw [these things], that the men of Ai hurried and got up early and went out to meet Israel." The resumptive verb form is the *wayyiqtol* form וַיְמַהֲרוּ, to be translated in this context as "that [the men of Ai] hurried." Most Eng. versions ignore the presence of the episode-initial וַיְהִי. This pattern is also found at the beginning of v. 24.

[106] Verse 9 states that "Joshua spent that night with the people," whereas v. 13 states that "that night Joshua went into the valley." This would involve Joshua spending the night with the people, *across* the valley from Ai, but late in the night getting up and *going into* the valley in preparation for the day's events. Or, if the alternative reading in the Syriac version is followed—"Joshua spent that night with the people," which involves changes in only two consonants of the Hb. text—then both vv. 9b and 13b state exactly the same thing.

[107] Verse 17 mentions Bethel, as well. Either the men of Bethel also came out and were routed (in which case this is the only reference to the defeat of that significant city, curiously enough), or else the word *bêt-ʾēl* simply means "house of [the] god" here (i.e., the sanctuary at Ai); then the scenario is that the Aiites left their city, even its sanctuary, unguarded (see Boling, *Joshua*, 240, on the latter suggestion).

8:1 Yahweh's words of encouragement to Joshua in 8:1 reinforce the statement of 7:26, that he was no longer angry with Israel. Atonement had been made for the nation's sin, and the task at hand was to get on with the conquest. The encouragement consisted of two parts. The first—"Do not be afraid"—is found more than seventy times in the Old Testament, most commonly (but not exclusively) in battle contexts: see, for example, Exod 14:13; Deut 1:21; 3:2; 7:18; 20:1; 31:8; it is repeated in Josh 10:8,25; 11:6. The second—"do not be discouraged"—is similar, and it echoes God's encouragement to Joshua in 1:9.[108] God's encouragement here is a fitting introduction to a battle narrative and represents a welcome promise from God, particularly in light of the previous problems. We should note that there were no words of promise, assurance, or guidance from God when Israel attacked Ai the first time, a significant contrast. He was not with them because of their sin. God's assurance that he had already given the king of Ai and all his people and their lands into Joshua's hand echoes the same past-time perspective we noted at 1:3.

8:2 The Israelites were now to do to Ai just as they had done to Jericho, but now they could take and keep the spoils of war for themselves rather than devote them to the Lord (cf. 6:18–19,21,24). This contrast with the previous instructions is indicated by the contrastive use of *raq*, "only" (see also v. 27).[109]

(2) Preparations for the Battle of Ai (8:3–13)

³So Joshua and the whole army moved out to attack Ai. He chose thirty thousand of his best fighting men and sent them out at night ⁴with these orders: "Listen carefully. You are to set an ambush behind the city. Don't go very far from it. All of you be on the alert. ⁵I and all those with me will advance on the city, and when the men come out against us, as they did before, we will flee from them. ⁶They will pursue us until we have lured them away from the city, for they will say, 'They are running away from us as they did before.' So when we flee from them, ⁷you are to rise up from ambush and take the city. The LORD your God will give it into your hand. ⁸When you have taken the city, set it on fire. Do what the LORD has commanded. See to it; you have my orders."

⁹Then Joshua sent them off, and they went to the place of ambush and lay in wait between Bethel and Ai, to the west of Ai—but Joshua spent that night with the people.

---

[108] The expression "do not be discouraged" (with the negative particle אַל) is used sixteen times in the OT, usually (twelve times) in the exact combination found here ("do not fear and do not be discouraged"): Deut 1:21; Josh 8:1; 10:25; 1 Chr 22:13; 28:20; 2 Chr 20:15,17; 32:7. In the following passages, the two expressions are separated by a few words: Isa 51:7; Jer 30:10; 46:27; Ezek 2:6. The expression occurs another four times with the negative particle לֹא: Deut 31:8; Isa 31:4; 51:6; Job 39:22, once in the combination found here: Deut 31:8.

[109] See *HALOT*, 1287 on the use of רַק here, and above, on 1:17 and 6:15, for more on the functions of רַק.

10Early the next morning Joshua mustered his men, and he and the leaders of Israel marched before them to Ai. **11**The entire force that was with him marched up and approached the city and arrived in front of it. They set up camp north of Ai, with the valley between them and the city. **12**Joshua had taken about five thousand men and set them in ambush between Bethel and Ai, to the west of the city. **13**They had the soldiers take up their positions—all those in the camp to the north of the city and the ambush to the west of it. That night Joshua went into the valley.

Joshua's detailed instructions for attacking Ai are given here (vv. 4–8), along with other information leading up to the battle (vv. 3,9–13). The chronology of the events is not completely clear, but vv. 11–13 appear to be a flashback, covering the same ground as vv. 3 and 10 (see the introduction to chap. 8).

8:3 Initially, Joshua and the "whole army" set out to begin the attack on Ai. The language here and in v. 10 is slightly different: here, the activity was begun—the language reads, literally, "And Joshua and all the people arose *to go up* (to) Ai," that is, the *intent* was "to go up"—whereas in v. 10, the next morning, they actually did go up.

The NIV's "whole army" translates an expression that literally reads "all the people *[ʿam]* of war." The usual term is "men *[ʾanšê]* of war" (21 times in the OT; see, e.g., Num 31:28,49; Deut 2:14,16; Josh 5:4,6; 6:3; 10:24). This phrase "all the people of war" is found in the Old Testament only in the Book of Joshua (8:1,3,11; 10:7; 11:7). These uses seem to emphasize the unity of the entire nation in doing battle (cf. the concern for unity in 1:12–15), even though it was most likely only men who actually engaged in the battles.

The number of men here sent out for the ambush—thirty thousand—seems inordinately large.[110] For a group of this size to hide itself west of a city of only twelve thousand inhabitants (v. 25) would have been very difficult, if not impossible. In addition, v. 12 states that five thousand men were sent out for an ambush force. This was not likely another ambush force, but rather the same one, since we understand vv. 11–13 as a flashback (see above). Thus, if vv. 3 and 12 refer to the same ambush force, then one of the numbers is obviously incorrect, most likely the number here. That is, an early copyist's error[111] would have erroneously changed "five thousand" to

---

[110] On the issue of interpreting the large numbers of the OT in general, see the note at 7:3.

[111] Such an error would have to have been very early, since there is no manuscript evidence for any error here. See also Keil, *Book of Joshua,* 86, and n. 1; Woudstra, *Joshua,* 137–38. It is a drastic measure to postulate an emendation with no manuscript support, but it seems to be the best solution to a difficult problem.

"thirty thousand" in v. 3.[112]

8:4–8   Joshua's instructions to the ambush force were straightforward. The ambush force was to hide "behind" the city (i.e., to its west; cf. v. 9), not very far away from it and on the alert, and Joshua and those with him would advance in plain sight (vv. 4–5). Joshua and the main force would be stationed north of the city (vv. 12–13). The initial action would be reminiscent of the first battle: the men of Ai would come out and the Israelites would flee (v. 5), just as they had done earlier (7:4). However, this time the Israelites' action was an intentional lure into a trap (v. 6). When the Aiites took the bait and left the city in pursuit of the Israelites, the men lying in ambush were to arise and take the city, setting it on fire (vv. 7–8).

In vv. 7–8, religious concerns are visible again. This time, Ai fell to the Israelites because God was involved, in contrast to the first time, when he was not (see on v. 1). It was at God's command that Israel would take Ai (v. 8) and with his help (v. 7). The unfolding of the story in the rest of the chapter shows that the Israelites strictly obeyed God's commands this time.

8:9–10   The ambush force obeyed Joshua and hid west of Ai, between Ai and Bethel (Ai was east of Bethel: Gen 12:8; Josh 7:2). In the meantime, Joshua spent the night with the people (v. 9).[113]

Verse 10 introduces a new phase of the action by focusing on the new start on the new day. Joshua mustered the people, and he and the elders went up to Ai before the people. This last statement in the verse is reminiscent of the religious aspects of the crossing of the Jordan, where the priests carrying the ark

---

[112] Hess (*Joshua*, 162) states that the number in v. 12 (five thousand, or, in his estimation, five military units) represented the ambush force sent out, while the number in v. 3 (thirty thousand, or thirty military units) represented the entire force. Thus, when Joshua dispatched five thousand men for the ambush, twenty-five thousand men remained with him. This is possible, but it does not deal adequately with the language of vv. 3b–4, which states clearly that the entire number of thirty thousand (five thousand?) men were being *sent out* by Joshua, whereas the main force of people—a separate group, not part of the same group—remained with him (vv. 3a,10,11). L. R. Bush suggests another alternative: "Perhaps the thirty thousand is the total number involved in the operation (including the entire support system for this strategy). The five thousand would be a supplementary detail telling how many of the thirty thousand actually engaged in the physical attack on the city. In other words, twenty-five thousand provided logistical support for the operation with five thousand literally advancing on the city to take it as a front line force. This is another possible reading that does not require emendation of the text" (personal communication, September 1998).

[113] We have noted in the introduction to chap. 8 that certain textual issues arise when comparing vv. 9 and 13, since both refer to Joshua's activity at night. The Old Greek traditions (LXX) do not record the information in v. 9b, so there is no repetition concerning Joshua's activities at night, and the statement in v. 13 is straightforward enough. Other manuscript traditions have both statements, however. As noted above, the simplest solution is found in the Syr., where the reading in both verses is the same. However, even the *lectio difficilior* ("the more difficult reading") of the MT can be understood, if we imagine Joshua spending most of the night with the people (v. 9) and then setting out before daybreak into the valley (v. 13).

were to go before the people (3:3–4,6,11,14), and also of the taking of Jericho, where a similar procession preceded the people (6:7–8). Even in this account, where the military aspect is far more prominent than in any other battle in the book, there are still reminders such as this that, ultimately, religious concerns were paramount (see also vv. 7–8).

The new phase of the action is obvious by virtue of the subject matter here and in later verses. It also is evident in the precise wording at the beginning of the verse—"And Joshua arose early in the morning"—which is identical to that in 3:1, where Joshua embarked on a new endeavor, leading the people as they left Shittim for the Jordan River.

8:11–13 As we noted in the introduction to this chapter, these verses represent a flashback, adding more details to the events introduced already in vv. 3–10. While v. 3 states that Joshua began his preparations to go up to Ai and v. 10 states that he actually went up to Ai the next morning, v. 11 looks back to the day before and tells about the Israelite forces' movements after v. 3 and before v. 10. They had gone up and approached the city, arriving opposite it, and encamped north of the city, across the valley from it.

Verse 12 reiterates the information in v. 9, telling what Joshua had done with the ambush force of five thousand men.[114] Verse 13 mentions "the people" setting up the camp, with the main force north of the city and the ambush force to the west. This continues the special emphasis on everyone—and not just the military forces—that we noted at v. 3.[115] The term for "valley" in this verse *(ʿēmeq)* is different from the one in v. 11 *(gay[ʾ])*. There is little difference between the two terms, but *ʿēmeq* seems to refer to a broader, wider geographical feature.[116] The reason for the use of two different terms here may be to echo the term for "valley" in 7:24,26 ("Valley of Achor": *ʿēmeq ʿākôr),* which was a term of approbation. Here, the use of the same term may have been a subtle reminder that the city of Ai was itself worthy of approbation.

Concerning Joshua's night activity, as the text stands here, it would appear that Joshua spent the night with the people, across the valley from Ai (vv. 9,11), but late in the night he got up and went into the valley in preparation for the day's events (v. 13). Alternatively (following readings in the Old Greek or Syriac versions), vv. 9 and 13 state that Joshua merely went into the valley (in the morning) but did not spend the night there.[117]

(3) The Battle of Ai (8:14–23)

14When the king of Ai saw this, he and all the men of the city hurried out early in the morning to meet Israel in battle at a certain place overlooking the Arabah.

---

[114] See on v. 3 for a discussion of the discrepancy in numbers between vv. 3 and 12.

[115] The NIV's "they" is actually "the people" (הָעָם).

[116] See C. Rasmussen, "עֵמֶק," *NIDOTTE* 3:440.

[117] See earlier footnote.

But he did not know that an ambush had been set against him behind the city. [15]Joshua and all Israel let themselves be driven back before them, and they fled toward the desert. [16]All the men of Ai were called to pursue them, and they pursued Joshua and were lured away from the city. [17]Not a man remained in Ai or Bethel who did not go after Israel. They left the city open and went in pursuit of Israel.

[18]Then the LORD said to Joshua, "Hold out toward Ai the javelin that is in your hand, for into your hand I will deliver the city." So Joshua held out his javelin toward Ai. [19]As soon as he did this, the men in the ambush rose quickly from their position and rushed forward. They entered the city and captured it and quickly set it on fire.

[20]The men of Ai looked back and saw the smoke of the city rising against the sky, but they had no chance to escape in any direction, for the Israelites who had been fleeing toward the desert had turned back against their pursuers. [21]For when Joshua and all Israel saw that the ambush had taken the city and that smoke was going up from the city, they turned around and attacked the men of Ai. [22]The men of the ambush also came out of the city against them, so that they were caught in the middle, with Israelites on both sides. Israel cut them down, leaving them neither survivors nor fugitives. [23]But they took the king of Ai alive and brought him to Joshua.

The main narrative that was suspended in v. 10 resumes now, indicated by a new syntactical pattern.[118] When the king of Ai saw that Joshua and his people had come out against him and his city (vv. 10,14), he mustered his people to meet Israel in battle (v. 14). The Israelites put their ruse into effect, pretending to flee, drawing out of the city its entire population (vv. 15–17). At the same time, the Israelite ambush force was arising (v. 19), and when Joshua stretched out his spear toward Ai, they entered the city and set it ablaze (vv. 18–19). When the Aiites saw this, they realized that they were surrounded before and behind, and they succumbed to a slaughter that left none alive except their king (vv. 20–23).

8:14–15 Two geographical terms are found in these verses. The Arabah (v. 14) is the great Rift Valley in which Jericho, the Jordan River, and the Dead Sea are found, indicating that the view from the battle looked down into this depression, toward the east.[119] The NIV's "the desert" in v. 15 is more properly "the way of the wilderness," and this may have been the name of a particular road or escape route. However, no such route is known today for this area; in addition, the exact site of Ai is disputed.[120] More probably, the phrase is more general, indicating merely that the men of Ai fled in disarray into the wilderness. The same phrase is found again in a similar context,

---

[118] See the introduction to this chapter.

[119] On the Arabah, see R. K. Harrison, "Arabah," *ISBE* 1:218–20; Rasmussen, *NIV Atlas of the Bible*, 19–22, 51.

[120] See the excursus "The Archaeology of Jericho and Ai" at the end of chap. 6.

where a coalition of Israelites set an ambush for the Benjaminites at Gibeah; and when they turned on the Benjaminites, they fled by "the way of the wilderness" (Judg 20:42; NIV has "in the direction of the desert" here). The phrase occurs again only in Exod 13:18, referring to the route the Israelites took out of Egypt through the desert.

8:16–17 At first glance, the activity here (v. 16) is identical to that in chap. 7: the men of Ai were pursuing the Israelites (the verb "pursue" *[rdp]* is the same here and in 7:5). However, in the first instance, the Aiites' success was real; in this instance, of course, it was merely an illusion, since the Israelites had planned an ambush.

The Aiites were completely fooled by the Israelites' ruse: not one man was left in either Ai or Bethel who did not come out of their cities to pursue the Israelites (v. 17). They left their city wide open in their pursuit *(rdp)* of Israel.

The reference to Bethel in v. 17 in connection with the encounter with Ai is a little surprising. Bethel was an important city in its own right in biblical times. It had a fine pedigree that went back to patriarchal times, when Abraham offered a sacrifice to God there (Gen 12:8; 13:3) and Jacob had a dream from God there (Gen 28:10–22). It had been a Canaanite city in the centuries preceding the Israelites' arrival in the land. Bethel was near Ai, to the west (Gen 12:8; Josh 7:2), although its exact location is uncertain.[121] Here, the inhabitants of Bethel came out of their city to help the men of Ai. Since the Israelite ambush was stationed between Bethel and Ai (8:9,12), the inhabitants of Bethel may have felt threatened by the Israelites as well. Or Ai may have been a small outpost for the larger city of Bethel (see 7:3, which shows the spies' estimate of Ai as a small, insignificant city), and an attack on Ai was understood to be an attack on Bethel as well. The reference to Bethel here is somewhat puzzling, however, since it is not mentioned again in the chapter. No record of its defeat is found, although its king is listed as among those conquered by Joshua in 12:16. It may be that, in the defeat of Ai, readers of the Book of Joshua understood that Bethel also was defeated, and no further reference was needed.

8:18–19 Joshua was to hold out the weapon in his hand as a signal for the ambush force to begin their attack on Ai. God's provision was evident here, as we can see in a play on the words "your hand": Joshua was to stretch out the weapon "in your hand" *(bĕyadkā)* because God was going to give the city "into your hand" *(bĕyadkā)*. The weapon itself was not going to win the victory; God was going to give it.

As soon has Joshua did this, the ambush force accomplished their task, setting the city on fire. Just as was Jericho's fate (6:24), so also Ai was torched. After this, only one other city is mentioned as having been burned

---

[121] See the excursus "The Archaeology of Jericho and Ai."

with fire (Hazor: 11:11).

The nature of the signal is not clear. It is difficult to imagine, if Joshua and the people were fleeing away from Ai and if the men hiding in ambush were on the other side of the city, that they were able to see clearly Joshua's outstretched arm; we may imagine perhaps that this signal was relayed in some way to those lying in wait. The term for Joshua's weapon here *(kîdôn)*—rendered by NIV, NASB, and RSV as "javelin"—is not the usual word for "spear" *(ḥănît)*; it may actually have been a short sword of some type.[122] In addition to its use as a signal, it was a symbol of God's presence and sovereignty (see on v. 26). It remained a sign for the duration of the battle because Joshua kept it outstretched until the entire population of Ai had been killed (vv. 25–26).

8:20–23 The battle's climax came quickly. The ambush worked to perfection, and the men of Ai were caught between the ambush force, which now came out of the city and attacked the Aiites, and the main force, which turned back and also attacked the Aiites. The destruction was complete: there were neither survivors nor fugitives remaining (v. 22).

The language in v. 22 vividly captures the Aiites' predicament. It begins by highlighting the men of the ambush, who now came out of the city to attack the Aiites, just as v. 21 had highlighted Joshua and all those with him.[123] The focus here, then, is on the two forces that surrounded the Aiites. However, the reason for this focus is to emphasize the predicament that the Aiites found themselves in: they were (lit.) "in the midst of Israel—these over here and these over there,"[124] that is, they were completely surrounded by the two Israelite forces.

---

[122] The term *kîdôn* is the same one used of Goliath's bronze "javelin" (1 Sam 17:6,45). It has been identified as a scimitar, a heavy, curved sword, which was a weapon common in the second millennium B.C. but replaced by the straight sword after that. At Qumran, the term is used of a short sword. For details, see, briefly, *HALOT,* 472, and, in more depth, Boling, *Joshua,* 240–41, and G. Molin, "What Is a *Kidon?" JSS* 1 (1956): 334–37. The word only occurs eight times in the OT, only here (vv. 18,26) and in the story of Goliath in historical contexts. The NRSV has "sword" here. The wording of the command in v. 19 is a bit curious, as the Hb. states, lit., "Stretch out with [-ב] the sword/javelin that is in [-ב] your hand." Usually in contexts such as this, the verb נטה ("to stretch out") is followed by the direct object "hand" (e.g., Exod 14:21,26–27; Isa 5:25). Here, the instrument is also indicated, but, since it is introduced by the preposition "with," the underlying syntax would appear to be as follows: "Stretch out [your hand] *with* the sword/javelin that is your hand." A similar construction is found in Exod 8:5,17[Hb. 8:1,13]: "Stretch out your hand with your staff … and Aaron stretched out his hand with his staff."

[123] Both verses accomplish this highlighting syntactically by fronting the subject in the sentence: "And *Joshua and all Israel* saw …" (v. 21); "And *these* [the ambush force] went out from the city to meet them [the men of Ai]" (v. 22). The focus, then, in the two verses is on the two forces surrounding the Aiites.

[124] "These" (אֵלֶּה) refers in both cases to the Israelite forces, not the Aiites. Cf. the use of the same word to refer to the men of the ambush at the beginning of v. 22.

The Israelites took the king of Ai alive. God had commanded them to treat the king of Ai exactly as they had the king of Jericho (8:2). Chapter 6 does not specify what they did to the king of Jericho, but we can infer from 8:29 that they killed him and exposed his body in a humiliating way (see also on 8:27).

(4) Aftermath of the Battle of Ai (8:24–29)

24When Israel had finished killing all the men of Ai in the fields and in the desert where they had chased them, and when every one of them had been put to the sword, all the Israelites returned to Ai and killed those who were in it. 25Twelve thousand men and women fell that day—all the people of Ai. 26For Joshua did not draw back the hand that held out his javelin until he had destroyed all who lived in Ai. 27But Israel did carry off for themselves the livestock and plunder of this city, as the LORD had instructed Joshua.

28So Joshua burned Ai and made it a permanent heap of ruins, a desolate place to this day. 29He hung the king of Ai on a tree and left him there until evening. At sunset, Joshua ordered them to take his body from the tree and throw it down at the entrance of the city gate. And they raised a large pile of rocks over it, which remains to this day.

A new phase of the narrative is signaled by the syntactical pattern here, the same as in v. 14. After the Israelites had killed all the men who had come out of the city, they then returned to Ai and killed its inhabitants (vv. 24–26), taking only their livestock and possessions as booty (v. 27). This taking of booty had been explicitly authorized this time by God (v. 2), in contrast to the explicit prohibition against such at Jericho (6:17–19). The Israelites finished burning the city, exposing the body of its king in an act of humiliation before burying it under a great pile of stones (vv. 28–29).

8:24–25 The destruction was complete: it included both those who had chased the Israelites and those who remained in the city, a total of twelve thousand men and women. Those remaining in the city must have been only women and children, since vv. 16–17 state that every man left the city in pursuit of the Israelites.[125] This is the only battle in the book for which a numerical total is given for the dead, consistent with the detailed description of all parts of the battle.

8:26 Joshua maintained his arm outstretched, with his sword in his hand, until the defeat of Ai was complete. This shows that the outstretched sword was more than a signal to start the battle (see on v. 18): it was also a symbol of God's presence and help in the battle. This confirms God's promise of his

---

[125] The gruesome nature of the destruction of the Canaanites comes close to the surface of the text here, in the slaughter of those remaining in an undefended city, and it can hardly help but make us shudder. Yet the Book of Joshua does not shrink from including even such details because of the overarching larger picture of the Canaanites' sin and pollution of the land. See the excursus on "Destruction and Devoted Things in Joshua" at the end of chap. 6.

presence, indicated in v. 1.

The episode closely echoes that in Exod 17:8–16, where the Israelites battled the Amalekites and Moses stretched out his hand with "the rod of God" in it (v. 9). Moses' outstretched hand also was a symbol of God's presence because the battle went in Israel's favor when Moses' hands were up, and it went against Israel when he tired and dropped his hands. Undoubtedly this episode in Joshua was included in the book to show yet another way in which Joshua was the worthy successor to Moses (see the commentary on 1:1,5; 24:29). Joshua had been the military leader carrying the battle to the Amalekites when Moses stretched out his hand (Exod 17:9–10), and now Joshua was in Moses' position, while others carried the battle to the Aiites.

A subtle reminder that Joshua was Israel's leader comes in the indicator that "he" destroyed all who lived in Ai. He certainly did not do this single-handedly (see the plural verbs of destruction in vv. 22,24), and he may not have personally killed anyone if he was standing with an outstretched sword throughout the battle. However, he was Israel's leader, and the statement here that "he had destroyed all who lived in Ai" reminds us of the uniqueness and importance of his position.

8:27 This time, the Israelites were careful to obey the word of the Lord. He had specified earlier that the Israelites could take of the city's possessions and livestock, but nothing else (v. 2), and this verse indicates that they carried out his instructions to the letter.

8:28 This verse states that Joshua burned the city, which is probably to be understood in the same way as the statement in v. 26 that he destroyed everyone in Ai (see on v. 26). The men in the Israelite ambush force had already set the city on fire (v. 19). The verb in v. 19 properly means "to kindle, set on fire" (*yṣt*), whereas the verb here (*śrp*) is more general, meaning simply "to burn," so v. 28 looks at the accomplished fact (the city was burned up) while v. 19 focuses on the initial lighting of the fire.

The NIV's "heap of ruins" translates Hebrew *tēl*. Ancient cities usually were built on high points of land near water supplies; and, when a city was destroyed, the new city was built on the same site, atop the packed and settled debris from the former city. Thus, over time, high mounds arose, topped by the current city. Ai was not rebuilt, and it remained a heap of ruins. This word is found only at Deut 13:16[Hb. 17]; Josh 8:28; 11:13; Jer 30:18; 49:2; and it survives in such place names in the Bible as Tel Abib (Ezek 3:15) or Tel Melah and Tel Harsha (Ezra 2:59). The Arabic word is "tell," and it survives today in the names of many sites in Israel.

The ruin was "permanent" and "a desolate place" visible "to this day," that is, at the time of the writing of the book. The totality of the destruction of Ai is again emphasized here.[126]

8:29 Joshua executed the king of Ai and hung his body on a tree, just as he would do later to the five kings of the Amorite coalition (10:26). This practice of exposure is known in both Assyria and Egypt as a wartime practice;[127] it is found in the Bible here and in connection with criminal penalties as well (Deut 21:22). The king's body was taken down at sundown, in accordance with the injunction in Deuteronomy that a body could not remain exposed overnight (Deut 21:22–23). Here again, Joshua was observing the law as closely as possible (cf. v. 27).

The Israelites' encounter with Ai had begun at the city gate (7:5); at its conclusion, the king's body was dumped at that very spot, and a pile of stones was erected over it. Just as the city, now a heap of ruins, was a sign "until this day" (v. 28), so also its king's body, under a heap of stones, was a sign "until this day."

The king's fate here was exactly the same as Achan's fate in 7:26 (where the words are exactly the same: "They erected over him a large pile of stones, [which is there] until this day").[128] This makes the point clearly that God would not favor his own people when they blatantly disobeyed any more than he would favor wicked Canaanites; Achan was expelled from Israel and treated as a Canaanite.

With this verse ends the first phase of Israel's taking the land. The victory at Jericho and the defeat and subsequent victory at Ai were significant events in Israel's taking the land, since they were all "firsts." Most later victories (see chaps. 10–11), while certainly just as dramatic, receive very little individual attention in the telling compared to that devoted to Jericho and Ai. The lessons about God's standards of holiness and obedience were dramatic: at Jericho, the city fell to Israel in a ritual event, but one man, Achan, violated God's commands. Thus, Israel as a nation suffered a defeat, and Achan and his family paid with their lives, all for one contaminating act of disobedience. In the end, however, Ai also paid dearly for its resistance to Israel's God: not only was it completely annihilated, but its ruin and the heap of stones over its dead king stood as mute reminders of this for decades, if not for centuries ("to this day": vv. 28–29). The symmetry between Achan and the people of Ai is underscored at many points, not the least of which is that both he and their king were buried under great piles of stones (7:26; 8:29).

4. Covenant Affirmations (8:30–35)

30Then Joshua built on Mount Ebal an altar to the LORD, the God of Israel,

---

[126] Many commentators mention a wordplay here between the city's name, "Ai," which is taken to mean "ruin," and the statement here in this verse. This equation, however, is not sustainable. See the excursus at the end of chap. 6 on "The Archaeology of Jericho and Ai" on this point.

[127] See K. L. Younger, Jr., *Ancient Conquest Accounts: A Study in Ancient Near Eastern and Biblical History Writing*, JSOTSup 98 (Sheffield: Academic Press, 1990), 222–23 and n. 88.

[128] The NIV's dynamic equivalent translation does not render the two statements identically.

[31]as Moses the servant of the LORD had commanded the Israelites. He built it according to what is written in the Book of the Law of Moses—an altar of uncut stones, on which no iron tool had been used. On it they offered to the LORD burnt offerings and sacrificed fellowship offerings. [32]There, in the presence of the Israelites, Joshua copied on stones the law of Moses, which he had written. [33]All Israel, aliens and citizens alike, with their elders, officials and judges, were standing on both sides of the ark of the covenant of the LORD, facing those who carried it—the priests, who were Levites. Half of the people stood in front of Mount Gerizim and half of them in front of Mount Ebal, as Moses the servant of the LORD had formerly commanded when he gave instructions to bless the people of Israel.

[34]Afterward, Joshua read all the words of the law—the blessings and the curses—just as it is written in the Book of the Law. [35]There was not a word of all that Moses had commanded that Joshua did not read to the whole assembly of Israel, including the women and children, and the aliens who lived among them.

Before taking Jericho and Ai, Israel had paused at Gilgal to memorialize its crossing (chap. 4) and to observe various rituals of purification (chap. 5). Now, after these victories (as well as a defeat) and before further encounters with the Canaanites, Israel again paused, to confess and to celebrate with sacrifices and covenant renewal at a different place, Mount Ebal. After the sin of Achan and the defeat at Ai, the nation again needed a ceremonial reminder of its relationship with God. First, the cause of the sin and the defeat was removed (7:25–26), and then victory was secured (8:1–29). But, before proceeding further, sacrifices and a renewal of the nation's covenant obligations were in order.

Israel had violated the Lord's covenant (7:11,15), and it was now more fitting than ever that the nation reaffirm that covenant. So, the Israelites interrupted their campaign to take the land and traveled some distance from where they were in order to renew the covenant at Mounts Ebal and Gerizim (vv. 30,33). From the standpoint of military strategy and Israel's location near Ai, the journey northward through Canaanite territory to Mounts Ebal and Gerizim does not make good sense. This region was about twenty miles from the region of Ai and Bethel,[129] and a major city—Shechem—was situated between the two mountains.[130] Yet, the imperatives for Israel of getting back on track with its God, of obedience to the law of Moses, necessitated such an interruption.

The location chosen was significant. In the first place, Mount Ebal was the place where Moses had commanded the Israelites that they should build an altar when they entered the land (Deut 27:4–5). In the second place, Mounts Ebal and Gerizim were the location where the twelve tribes were to stand— six tribes on each mountain—for the pronouncing of blessings and curses in connection with renewing of the covenant (Deut 11:26–32; 27:12–13). In addition, the city of Shechem was located between the two mountains, Ebal to the north and Gerizim to the south. The city is not mentioned by name until the boundary lists in chap. 17, but it was the site of the important covenant-

---

[129] Boling, *Joshua*, 247; Rasmussen, *NIV Atlas of the Bible*, 94.

renewal ceremony with which the book ends (24:1).[131] Shechem had an ancient tradition of religious significance and covenant making in Israel that went back to Abraham. For example, Abraham built an altar to the Lord after the Lord had appeared to him there (Gen 12:6–7). Jacob bought land there, he too erected an altar there (Gen 33:18–20), and the city eventually became the family's home (Gen 35:4; 37:12–14).

As we noted in the introduction to chap. 5 (after 5:1), the episode found here (vv. 30–35) is located in three different places in manuscript traditions, such that it sometimes is called a "floating pericope."[132] In the MT, it is found here, just following the victory at Ai. At Qumran, it is found just before the observances of circumcision and Passover, between 5:1 and 5:2. In the Old Greek, it is found just after the notice of a Canaanite coalition that came against the Israelites, after 9:2. We can see, then, that this account is not too firmly anchored in its present position. Syntactically, the episode is set off from its surroundings as well. It begins with a disjunctive adverb, ʾāz, "then" (8:30), and it is followed by an episode-initial construction in 9:1,[133] so it is

---

[130] Many scholars disbelieve this account in its entirety, in part because a journey of this magnitude through presumably hostile territory strains credulity. However, the Shechemites may have been friendly with the Israelites, perhaps due to the earlier ties between the city and Israel that we have noted. The Book of Joshua does not record any taking of the city, which may have been settled peacefully, or it may have made an alliance of some type with Israel. The account here twice mentions aliens among the Israelites (vv. 33,35), some of whom may have been Shechemites. (See Hess, *Joshua*, 173, on this point.) B. G. Wood also sees the Shechemites as friendly to Israel ("The Role of Shechem in the Conquest of Canaan," in *To Understand the Scriptures: Essays in Honor of William H. Shea*, ed. D. Merling [Berrien Springs: Andrews University Institute of Archaeology, 1997], 245–56; see pp. 247–49 for a review of previous proposals). He proposes that Israel had established a patron-client relationship with the king of Shechem, who allowed them to come into the land under his patronage and protection and expand Shechemite hegemony to the south and the north. There is no scriptural evidence for this, however—indeed, it flies in the face of the consistent indications that Yahweh would give Israel the land and that they were to have no entanglements with the Canaanites. Furthermore, Wood relies too heavily on the discredited equation of the *Habiru/Hapiru* in the Amarna texts with the *Hebrews* in the Bible (see D. M. Howard, Jr., *Introduction to the Old Testament Historical Books* [Chicago: Moody, 1993], 73–74). Alternatively, Keil suggests that the Shechemites, although probably hostile, would not have ventured to challenge Israel in light of its success over Jericho and Ai and in light of the armed forces that Israel possessed (*Book of Joshua*, 90).

[131] Its importance in Canaan as a religious center is confirmed archaeologically. A series of temples, sanctuaries, and ceremonial standing stones from almost every period of its existence has been uncovered in excavations, although archaeologists debate whether specific monuments at the site can be identified with events in Josh 8:30–35 or 24:1–28. See Boling, *Joshua*, 252–53; L. E. Toombs, "Shechem (Place)," *ABD* 5:1174–86; E. F. Campbell, "Shechem," *NEAEHL* 4:1345–54; W. T. Koopmans, *Joshua 24 as Poetic Narrative*, JSOTSup 93 (Sheffield: Academic Press, 84–92, 154–56).

[132] Nelson, *Joshua*, 116. For details of the variant manuscript traditions, see the commentary in chap. 5.

[133] The construction consists of וַיְהִי plus a prepositional phrase indicating a time frame, followed by a *wayyiqtol* verb form. For more on this, see the note at 4:11.

clearly demarcated as a self-contained unit.

Because of these considerations, many scholars have seen this account as a (fictional) "Deuteronomistic" addition, added many years after the writing of the rest of the book.[134] Most such scholars associate the episode with the covenant renewal ceremony described in chap. 24. Indeed, one scholar relocates these verses immediately after the account of that ceremony, after 24:27, even though there is no manuscript tradition supporting this.[135]

Despite the uncertainty concerning the account's location in the text, in its present position it shows the importance of covenant affirmation, sacrifice, and reading of the law at a critical juncture in the nation's history. It had just won two victories over individual cities, but it had suffered a defeat due to its sin. Furthermore, it would soon face challenges of a very different sort: not from individual cities, but from powerful coalitions of cities (9:1–2; 10:1–5). In light of these considerations, the need for the observances here was very great indeed.

The overarching theme in this section is obedience to God through observance of the Mosaic law. Four different times, the text states that an action was taken in accordance with Moses' commands (vv. 31[2x],33,35). Also, the actions themselves were rooted in the instructions in the law. Almost every statement in this passage has roots in the Pentateuch. The most important passages are Deut 27:2–13 and 31:9–12, but many others also figure here.[136] The passage shows the importance to Israel of the Pentateuchal legislation, and it shows Israel's concern to obey.

Furthermore, Joshua's role as a leader also emerges in this account, in that he built the altar (v. 30–31), he copied the law onto stones from a copy he had written (v. 32), and he read the law in the people's hearing (vv. 34–35). He is once again portrayed as a worthy successor to Moses and one who prefigured the kings to come, who were to write in a book a (personal) copy of the law (Deut 17:18–19).

At least five separate activities were involved here: (1) Joshua built an altar (v. 30); (2) the people offered burnt offerings (v. 31); (3) the people sacrificed fellowship offerings (v. 31); (4) Joshua wrote the words of the law on stones (v. 32); and (5) Joshua read the words of the law in public, before all the people (vv. 34–35).

8:30   After the events of 8:1–29, Joshua and the people went to Mount

---

[134] See, e.g., Butler, *Joshua*, 90; Nelson, *Joshua*, 117–19. Boling believes that the episode preserves at least some modicum of a "reliable historical memory" (*Joshua*, 253).

[135] Soggin, *Joshua*, 222, 226.

[136] Nelson (*Joshua*, 118) gives the following correspondences: v. 30: Deut 27:4–5; v. 31: Deut 27:5–7a; v. 32: Deut 27:2–3,4,8 (and 17:18); v. 33: Deut 27:12–13 (and 11:29 and 29:10–11 [Hb. 9–10]); vv. 34–35: Deut 31:11–12 (and 11:26–28). Butler (*Joshua*, 90) gives an even more detailed account, including passages from Exodus, Leviticus, and Numbers, in addition to Deuteronomy.

Ebal, some distance to the north, and there Joshua built an altar to the Lord. Mount Ebal is only mentioned in Deuteronomy (11:29; 27:4,13) and here (vv. 30,33). It—along with Mount Gerizim, directly south of it—was the site to be used in proclaiming blessings and curses when the Israelites came into the land; specifically, it was to be the site of the curses (Deut 11:29; 27:13).[137]

8:31 The altar that Joshua built was done just as Moses had commanded. Deuteronomy 27:5–6 states that Israel was to build such an altar when it entered the land. The stones were uncut fieldstones, just as Moses had instructed, which was in accord with God's earlier instructions about making altars (Exod 20:25).[138]

The ceremony included two different types of sacrifices, offered on the altar that Joshua built: burnt offerings and fellowship offerings. Burnt offerings were sacrifices that entirely consumed the animals, and they were offered as "an aroma pleasing to the LORD" (Exod 29:18; Lev 1:9,13,17) to atone for the sacrificers' sins (Lev 1:4). The fact that these offerings were made indicates that one function of the activities at Mount Ebal was to atone for the nation's sins.

Another function was indicated by the fellowship offerings (sometimes called "peace offerings"; see KJV, NASB, NLT). These were joyful offerings in which portions of the sacrificial animals were to be eaten by the ones presenting them (Lev 3:1–17; 7:11–21), and fellowship with God and others was at their core. The fact that these were offered indicates that another function of the activities was to reestablish a sense of relationship and well-being[139] with God.

8:32 Joshua wrote a copy of the law on stones, which echoes the instructions for a king in Deut 17:18. While Joshua was not a king, several indications in the book show him in a "kingly" light, acting with the authority of a king and in ways in which kings were supposed to act (cp. Josh 1:5–9; Deut 17:14–20).

The stones may have been those of the altar (v. 31) or other stones, such as the two stone tablets given to Moses (Exod 32:15), the twelve stones set up to confirm the Sinai covenant, one for each tribe of Israel (Exod 24:4), or the large stone set up as a witness of the covenant renewal (Josh 24:26–27). The

---

[137] Mounts Ebal and Gerizim are two important peaks in central Palestine, flanking an east-west pass through the north-central hill country; almost the entire promised land is visible from the top of Mount Ebal.

[138] The unfinished stones would have contrasted with the finished stones found in many Canaanite altars, a reminder that, even in such rituals as offering sacrifices (which were shared by the Israelites), the Israelites were to be different. See Boling, *Joshua*, 248.

[139] The NRSV and NJPSV render the term here (שְׁלָמִים) as sacrifices or offerings "of well-being." See E. E. Carpenter, "Sacrifices and Offerings in the OT," *ISBE* 4:268; G. A. Anderson, "Sacrifice and Sacrificial Offerings (OT)," *ABD* 5:877–78, on both of these types of offerings.

most natural reading grammatically would suggest that these stones were the altar stones. However, a careful reading of the instructions in Deuteronomy 27 reveals that there were two sets of stones in view: plaster-covered stones to be set up for writing the words of the law on (vv. 2–4,8), and uncut stones to be set up as an altar for sacrifices (vv. 5–7).[140] Thus, if, as is evident throughout this passage, the instructions in Deuteronomy were being followed closely, we must understand the writing stones to be different from the altar stones, a possibility that is allowed by the grammar.[141]

The last clause in the NIV ("which he had written") suggests that Joshua was copying the law onto the stones from a copy of the law that he himself had written earlier, and this is possible grammatically. On the other hand, the NJPSV understands him to have copied from something Moses had written ("he inscribed a copy of the teaching that Moses had written"), which is also possible grammatically. Deuteronomy 17:18–19 instructs that the king was to write for himself a copy of the law and that it was to stay with him all the days of his life, so the former is certainly possible. However, we cannot be sure from whom (Moses? Joshua?) the copy came that Joshua used. The Old Greek omits the clause altogether; if it was not part of the original Hebrew text, then the question disappears altogether, and presumably the copy Joshua used was one from Moses.

8:33 The list of participants in this verse makes it clear that the entire nation was involved. Both the alien and the native-born citizen were included. The word here for "alien" *(gēr)* refers to those foreigners who lived as permanent residents within Israel. These were different from "foreigners" *(nokrîm)*, who came into incidental contact with Israel, such as travelers or traders, and who had few rights within Israel (e.g., Exod 12:43; Lev 22:25; Deut 14:21; 15:3). Resident aliens, on the other hand, did enjoy certain rights in Israel, even though they were not Israelites by birth. They were allowed to take gleanings from the fields (Lev 19:10; 23:22), and the Israelites were repeatedly instructed to give special care to them, along with the poor, the widow, and the orphan (Exod 22:21; 23:9; Deut 10:17–22; 24:17–18). This special concern for aliens within Israel's borders was rooted in Israel's own alien status in Egypt, which they were to remember in perpetuity (Exod 22:21; 23:9; Deut 10:17–22; 23:7). Most strikingly, the aliens could participate in Israel's festivals, such as the Passover (Exod 12:43–49), the Sabbath (20:10), the Feast of Weeks (Deut 16:10–12) and Tabernacles (16:13–14), and the celebra-

---

[140] See P. C. Craigie, *Deuteronomy*, NICOT (Grand Rapids: Eerdmans, 1976), 328–29.

[141] Writing on plaster (on walls or larger flat surfaces) is known from several ancient Near Eastern sites, including several in Egypt (Craigie, *Deuteronomy*, 328 and n. 3), Tell Deir Alla in the Jordan Valley, and Kuntillet Ajrud in the northern Sinai desert (Boling, *Joshua*, 248). For the Tell Deir Alla texts, see J. A. Hackett, "Deir ʿAlla, Tell: Texts," *ABD* 2:129. For the Kuntillet Ajrud inscriptions, see Z. Meshel, "Kuntillet ʿAjrud," *ABD* 4:107.

tion of the firstfruits (Deut 26:10–11). These celebrations appear to have been open to them so long as they were circumcised (Exod 12:43–49). In this sense, these aliens were true "converts" to faith in Israel's God. Indeed, the Old Greek translates the Hebrew term here with the Greek word *prosēlutos*, which forms the basis of the English word "proselyte" (i.e., one who converts). This shows—as does the story of Rahab—that Israel's faith was not a closed system: it was open to outsiders. In the case of its aliens, Israel was to treat those within its own borders in such a way that they would be desirous of entering fully into a relationship with Israel's God. This is how Christians should relate to those outside the faith as well: Jesus instructed his disciples that they should be a light to the world, conducting themselves in a manner that would point people to their Lord (Matt 5:14–16). Here in Joshua 8, these aliens are participating right along with the rest of the Israelites in the covenant affirmation ceremony.

The people were surrounding the ark on both sides, opposite *(neged)* the Levitical priests[142] carrying it, and divided into two groups. Half of them were in front of *(mûl)* Mount Ebal and half in front of Mount Gerizim, just as Moses had commanded they should do (Deut 27:12–13). A slight change in wording from the instructions in Deuteronomy occurs here. There, the people were to be "on top of" *(ʿal)* the mountains, whereas here they were "in front of" them. Since the people were scrupulously keeping to the instructions that Moses had given, it may be that they were indeed on top of the two mountains and that those on Mount Gerizim were considered those to be "in front of Mount Ebal" and vice versa.

The text does not state that the people did anything except line themselves up in this way. The next verse states that "after this," Joshua read the law, including blessing and curse. In Deut 27:12–13, the people were to participate in reciting the blessing and curse, but if they were so involved here, the text does not state it.

8:34–35 Joshua read the entire book of the law to the people—this is stated explicitly twice in these two verses—but the blessing and the curse are specifically singled out in v. 34. This undoubtedly was to highlight the degree of obedience to the instructions of Deuteronomy 27 that the Israelites were practicing. This was the first public reading of the law mentioned after Moses' death.

Joshua read the law to the entire assembly *(qāhāl)* of Israel, including women, children, and aliens (v. 35). The mention of aliens again reinforces their importance for Israel (see comments on v. 33). The term "assembly" of Israel is often used to denote Israel gathered as a congregation for worship or other religious functions (e.g., Lev 16:17; Deut 31:30; 1 Kgs 8:14; Ezra 10:1; Ps 22:22; etc.), but this is its only use in the Book of Joshua.

---

[142] On these Levitical priests, or "the priests, who were Levites," see the commentary on 3:3.

5. The Gibeonite Treaty (9:1–27)

Chapters 9–11 expand the horizons of the book's action. Whereas previously, Israel's opposition came from individual cities, now it came from coalitions of cities. In this chapter, a coalition of six kings from throughout the land came against the Israelites (9:1–2). In Joshua 10, five southern kings banded together against them and the Gibeonites (10:1–5), and in chap. 11, a coalition of many northern kings did the same (11:1–5). Each group convened as a result of the kings' hearing *(šmᶜ)* about the exploits of Joshua and his people (9:1; 10:1; 11:1).[143]

Israel's reputation had already spread throughout the land: according to 2:9–11 and 5:1 the Canaanites had heard *(šmᶜ)* about Israel and its victories, and their hearts melted. In contrast, now the Canaanites did not appear to fear the Israelites, even after their impressive victories at Jericho and Ai (Joshua 6; 8) because they joined forces to attack Israel. This is a remarkable turnaround in attitude, due, no doubt, to the spectacle of Israel's having been defeated in battle by the men of Ai (chap. 7). The Canaanites' fear of the Israelites was now diminished, and they felt confident in doing battle with them.

This all demonstrates the effects of sin in the nation's life, since, had Achan not sinned, Israel certainly would not have suffered a defeat at Ai. Perhaps it might even have taken the rest of Canaanite territory with a minimum of conflict, on the model of the taking of Jericho. We see here the outworking of the curses recorded in Deuteronomy 28, where the Lord had promised defeat if Israel disobeyed his words: "However, if you do not obey the LORD your God and do not carefully follow all his commands and decrees I am giving you today, all these curses will come upon you and overtake you. ... The LORD will cause you to be defeated before your enemies. You will come at them from one direction but flee from them in seven, and you will become a thing of horror to all the kingdoms on earth" (Deut 28:15,25). The curses in Deuteronomy 28 had the exile as their ultimate fulfillment, but the defeat at Ai and the Canaanites' renewed courage certainly can be seen as early fulfillments of such words. The Book of Haggai records a similar example of cause and effect: "Consider how you have fared. You have sown much, and harvested little; you eat, but you never have enough; you drink, but you never have your fill; you clothe yourselves, but no one is warm; and you that earn wages earn wages to put them into a bag with holes" (Hag 1:5–6, NRSV). Haggai was speaking about the Jews' failure to rebuild the temple, but his point about life's consequences following life's

---

[143] Younger argues that chaps. 9–12 form a unit devoted to several conquest accounts, linked by a "syntagm" (i.e., one of an episode's component parts) oriented to hearing (שָׁמַע). See Younger, *Ancient Conquest Accounts*, 197–237, especially p. 200. Younger in this section provides extensive documentation for extrabiblical parallels to the conquest accounts in these chapters, including much of the stereotypical language.

choices are certainly valid in the case at hand.

Not all Canaanites reacted with paralyzed fear, as the people in Jericho had, or with aggressive attacks, as the coalitions in 9:1–2, 10:1–5, and 11:1–5 did. The Gibeonites heard *(šmᶜ)* about the Israelites' successes, and they devised their own strategy of trickery and accommodation with the Israelites, one that allowed them to survive annihilation, albeit as vassals of Israel. Their strategy is recounted in 9:3–27.

The story in vv. 3–27 breaks down naturally into two sections, which many critical scholars have seen as deriving from two different sources: (1) a story about the Gibeonite treaty with Israel, which was accomplished via trickery (vv. 3–15) and (2) one about the Gibeonite indenture to Israel, which was the consequence of the trickery (vv. 16–27). The issue of hypothetical early sources beyond this is very confused, however, and most scholars do not claim great certainty concerning any of the proposed reconstructions.[144]

The nature of the Gibeonites' treaty with Israel has attracted considerable scholarly attention. Many scholars identify elements of an ancient Near Eastern suzerain-vassal treaty here, in which a relationship between a superior party and an inferior one is established.[145] These elements include (1) the fact that Joshua "made peace" (v. 15) with the Gibeonites (NIV: "Joshua made a treaty of peace with them"); (2) the eating of provisions (v. 14);[146] and (3) the taking of an oath (v. 15). The treaty evidently included provisions for mutual defense as well, because the Israelites came to the Gibeonites' defense when they were attacked (10:1–8). It also appears to have included provisions for punishment of either party if it violated the terms of the treaty, because David delivered seven descendants of Saul over to the Gibeonites for punishment when it was pointed out to him that Saul had earlier tried to annihilate the Gibeonites, thereby breaking the treaty (2 Sam 21:1–8).[147] The

---

[144] E.g., Boling declares that "we lack adequate controls for more detailed source analysis" (*Joshua*, 262), and Nelson states, "Probably a completely satisfying explanation for these irregularities is impossible" (*Joshua*, 123). See the reviews of critical proposals in Soggin, *Joshua*, 110–13; Nelson, *Joshua*, 123–28.

[145] The following are representative studies: F. C. Fensham, "The Treaty between Israel and the Gibeonites," *BA* 27 (1964): 96–100; J. M. Grintz, "The Treaty of Joshua with the Gibeonites," *JAOS* 86 (1966): 113–26; B. Halpern, "Gibeon: Israelite Diplomacy in the Conquest Era," *CBQ* 37 (1975): 303–16. For recent treatments of ancient Near Eastern covenants and treaties, see G. A. Herion and G. E. Mendenhall, "Covenant," *ABD* 1:1179–1202; M. L. Barré, "Treaties in the ANE," *ABD* 6:653–56. On the elements of a treaty here, see Fensham; Soggin, *Joshua*, 114.

[146] Contra scholars such as Fensham and Soggin, however, it is doubtful whether the consumption of the Gibeonites' food in v. 14 was the sharing of a ceremonial meal; more likely it represented the Israelites' testing of the Gibeonites' truthfulness about their food being dry and moldy (v. 12).

[147] For many critical scholars, the account in 2 Samuel 21 is testimony of the historicity of the treaty making in Joshua 9. See, e.g., Soggin, *Joshua*, 113 ("II Samuel 21.1–14 supplies us with an excellent proof of the basic historicity of this story"); Halpern, "Gibeon," 303 ("[The covenant's] existence is attested convincingly in the account of 2 Sam 21:1–14"); Boling, *Joshua*, 262 ("There can be no doubt about the historicity of a treaty with the Gibeonites").

binding nature of this treaty (see v. 18) forms the basis for the actions taken in 10:1–27, where the Gibeonites found themselves threatened by a Canaanite coalition and appealed to the Israelites for help, which they rendered.

(1) Introduction (9:1–2)

¹Now when all the kings west of the Jordan heard about these things—those in the hill country, in the western foothills, and along the entire coast of the Great Sea as far as Lebanon (the kings of the Hittites, Amorites, Canaanites, Perizzites, Hivites and Jebusites)— ²they came together to make war against Joshua and Israel.

This section is set off from what precedes, as we noted earlier (see the introduction to 8:30–35), and it introduces the events of chaps. 9–11 (see the introduction to 9:1–27). However, it also forms the backdrop more specifically to 9:3–27, since the Gibeonites' stance toward the Israelites—the desire to make a treaty—forms a contrast to the belligerent stance taken here by the six kings.

This section also begins almost exactly as 5:1 does:

> And it happened, when all the kings of the Amorites who were beyond the Jordan ... heard. (5:1)

> And it happened, when all the kings who were beyond the Jordan heard. (9:1)

After the nearly identical beginnings, however, the two verses show the contrast between Israel before and after Achan's sin that we have noted, since, in 5:1, the kings were terrified of Israel, whereas here, they gathered to attack Israel.

The region referred to here is, literally, "beyond the Jordan" *(bĕ'ēber hay-yardēn)*, referring to regions west of the Jordan. This phrase is found thirteen times in Joshua, referring both to the region east of the Jordan (what is often called "Transjordan": 1:14–15; 2:10; 7:7; 9:10; 12:1; 13:8; 22:4; 24:8) and the region west of the Jordan (what is sometimes called "Cisjordan": 5:1; 9:1; 12:7; 22:7). Originally, a person's use of the term undoubtedly signaled a reference point where that person stood relative to the Jordan, but in the writing of the book, this was not so clear.[148] Occasionally, the term is clarified by an adverbial prepositional phrase indicating geographical location, such as "toward the sea," that is, to the west (5:1; 12:7) or "toward the sunrise," that is, to the east (1:15; 12:1).

The geographical description laid out shows that the kings opposing Israel came from all parts of the land of Canaan: they were from (1) the hill country, that is, the central highlands, (2) the western foothills, that is, the foothills

---

[148] See also Woudstra, *Joshua*, 153 and n. 1.

between the central highlands and the coastal plain,[149] and (3) the entire coast of the Mediterranean Sea, as far as the "front"[150] of Lebanon.[151] Just as the land that Israel was entering to possess is painted in terms as broad as possible in 1:4, so here, the adversaries Israel was to face are also portrayed as coming from as broad an area as possible.[152] The summary statement in 10:40–42 about Joshua's all-encompassing conquests recalls the territories mentioned here (specifically, the references to the hill country and the western foothills).

The coalition that came up against Israel was led by the kings of six groups of Canaanites, all of whom were listed among the seven groups in 3:10, but in a different order. Of the twenty-one such lists of nations, only the ones in Deut 20:17 and Josh 12:8 match this one exactly.[153] The correspondence with the Deuteronomy list cannot be coincidental, because that list is found in a passage speaking of Israel's going to war (Deut 20:1–20), and it occurs at the precise moment when Moses instructs the Israelites concerning their treatment of the nations indigenous to Canaan: "However, in the cities of the nations the LORD your God is giving you as an inheritance, do not leave alive anything that breathes. Completely destroy them—the Hittites, Amorites, Canaanites, Perizzites, Hivites and Jebusites—as the LORD your God has commanded you. Otherwise, they will teach you to follow all the detestable things they do in worshiping their gods, and you will sin against the LORD your God" (Deut 20:16–18). This is a subtle reminder that Israel was not to make peace with any of these peoples, and it is an ironic introduction to the story that follows, where Israel did precisely that with the Gibeonites.

The coalition came together to fight Joshua *and* Israel (v. 2). Since both Joshua and Israel are prominent in the account of the defeat of Ai, it is not surprising that both are mentioned here. The group came as a unified force: the NIV does not translate the last two words of the verse, which state that the kings came against Israel as "one mouth," that is, unified in purpose against Israel (cf. NASB: "with one accord"). This reinforces the all-encompassing nature of those aligned against Israel that we noted in v. 1. We do not read of any actual fighting between Israel and this coalition, however; the coalition disappears from the scene after v. 2, but it is replaced in chaps. 10 and 11 with different coalitions (although 11:1 reminds us of the coalition here by listing

---

[149] Often called by their Hb. term, the "Shephelah"; see, e.g., NJPSV and NLT text note.

[150] The word is מוּל, "in front of, before," the same word used in 8:33, referring to the placement of half of the people near Mount Ebal.

[151] For geographical details concerning these regions, see Rasmussen, *NIV Atlas of the Bible*, 16–19, 42 (coastal plain and central hill country) and 47–48 (western foothills).

[152] Woudstra, *Joshua*, 154.

[153] See E. C. Hostetter, *Nations Mightier and More Numerous: The Biblical View of Palestine's Pre-Israelite Peoples*, BIBAL Dissertation Series 3 (N. Richland Hills, TX: BIBAL Press, 1995), 34–36, on features of this list.

the same six peoples as part of an even larger coalition). However, the comments in 12:1,7, speaking of kings of the land whom the Israelites defeated, undoubtedly include the kings mentioned here in 9:1–2.[154]

(2) The Gibeonites' Deceit (9:3–15)

³However, when the people of Gibeon heard what Joshua had done to Jericho and Ai, ⁴they resorted to a ruse: They went as a delegation whose donkeys were loaded with worn-out sacks and old wineskins, cracked and mended. ⁵The men put worn and patched sandals on their feet and wore old clothes. All the bread of their food supply was dry and moldy. ⁶Then they went to Joshua in the camp at Gilgal and said to him and the men of Israel, "We have come from a distant country; make a treaty with us."

⁷The men of Israel said to the Hivites, "But perhaps you live near us. How then can we make a treaty with you?"

⁸"We are your servants," they said to Joshua.

But Joshua asked, "Who are you and where do you come from?"

⁹They answered: "Your servants have come from a very distant country because of the fame of the LORD your God. For we have heard reports of him: all that he did in Egypt, ¹⁰and all that he did to the two kings of the Amorites east of the Jordan—Sihon king of Heshbon, and Og king of Bashan, who reigned in Ashtaroth. ¹¹And our elders and all those living in our country said to us, 'Take provisions for your journey; go and meet them and say to them, "We are your servants; make a treaty with us."' ¹²This bread of ours was warm when we packed it at home on the day we left to come to you. But now see how dry and moldy it is. ¹³And these wineskins that we filled were new, but see how cracked they are. And our clothes and sandals are worn out by the very long journey."

¹⁴The men of Israel sampled their provisions but did not inquire of the LORD. ¹⁵Then Joshua made a treaty of peace with them to let them live, and the leaders of the assembly ratified it by oath.

The narrative flow begun by the story of opposition to Israel is arrested by the story of the Gibeonites' treaty with Israel in the rest of this chapter. In the first section (vv. 3–15), the actual process of the making of the treaty is described. The inhabitants of Gibeon also had heard of the Israelite victories, but their response was different from that of the kings mentioned in vv. 1–2. Rather than risk destruction, which they were sure would be their lot, they resorted to a trick to deceive Israel into making a peace treaty with them. They were successful, and they ended up living among the Israelites (v. 27). Their appearance as foreigners who lived among the Israelites has been anticipated by the reference to the "alien" in 8:33.

---

[154] See Younger, *Ancient Conquest Accounts*, 197–98, arguing that these verses represent an "introductory statement and … concluding summaries," part of a unified narrative encompassing chaps. 9–12.

9:3–5   Just as the kings heard *(šmᶜ)* about Joshua's and Israel's victory over Ai (v. 1), so also had the Gibeonites (v. 3; see also v. 24). Gibeon was a city not far from Ai, about five miles northwest of Jerusalem. It is first mentioned here in the Bible. Gibeon would be part of Benjamin's tribal inheritance (Josh 18:25) and also would be apportioned as a Levitical city (21:17). In the Bible, it is known primarily from the story here and the battle that followed (10:1–27).[155]

In response to the threat of the Israelites, the Gibeonites devised a trick by which to deceive Israel into making peace with them.[156] They went to elaborate lengths to make it appear that they had been traveling a long distance and a long time (vv. 4–5). Their bread was dry and crumbly.[157]

9:6   Following up on their actions in vv. 4–5, the Gibeonites claimed that they had come from a faraway country.[158] Israel was allowed to spare and make treaties with cities that were far from them, but they were explicitly directed not to make peace with the cities of the peoples whom the Israelites were dispossessing (see Exod 34:11–12; Deut 20:10–18, esp. vv. 15–18). Thus, if the Gibeonites' claim of v. 6 had been truthful, the treaty that the Israelites made with them would have been permissible; however, the reader knows that this is not true. A hint of this untruth is found in the Gibeonites' own choice of words here (see the note on v. 8). It is obvious that the Gibeonites knew something about Israelite law, since their actions and words corresponded so closely to the Pentateuchal instructions. How they would have known this is unclear, but Israel's reputation had preceded it (Josh 2:9–11; 9:9–10). For a people who took such elaborate steps to spare themselves from any attack by the Israelites, it should not strain credulity to imagine them

---

[155] Scattered biblical references show that it was in existence in exilic and postexilic times (e.g., Jer 28:1; Neh 7:25). Archaeological excavations have identified the site as el-Jib and uncovered an elaborate system of waterworks, but much of the site remains to be excavated. Nevertheless, good evidence is found to show a continuous occupation of the site from the time of Joshua until the destruction of Jerusalem, confirming the affirmations in this chapter that the Gibeonites survived and lived among Israel as permanent residents (see vv. 26–27 and the commentary there). See J. B. Pritchard, *Gibeon: Where the Sun Stood Still* (Princeton: University Press, 1962); id., *NEAEHL* 2:511–14.

[156] Many scholars are skeptical about the trick itself, arguing that it is implausible and contains "confusions" (Soggin, *Joshua,* 111; see also J. Liver, "The Literary History of Joshua IX," *JSS* 8 [1963]: 227–43). However, Younger has shown that such a ruse fits its ancient Near Eastern context remarkably well: several similar examples are known from Assyrian, Hittite, and Egyptian sources (*Ancient Conquest Accounts*, 201–4).

[157] The term translated in NIV as "moldy" (נִקֻּדִּים) occurs only here (vv. 5,12) and in 1 Kgs 14:3, referring to a small cake brought to the prophet Ahijah. Rather than "moldy," it more probably refers to something crumbly, since mold requires moisture for growth, and this bread was dry. For "crumbly," see BDB, 666; *HALOT*, 720; NJPSV.

[158] The syntax, in fronting the prepositional phrase "from a distant country," highlights the place from which they claimed to come.

doing whatever was necessary to find a way to accomplish this (see also on 2:11).

The first reference in the book to a "covenant" *(bĕrît)* other than the one Israel had made with its God is found here.[159] A covenant was a binding agreement between two parties, and in this case the word "treaty" describes the agreement well. We have already discussed the nature and elements of this treaty (see the introduction to this passage).

The geographical setting now shifts to "Gilgal." If this was the place where the Israelites had erected memorial stones and undergone circumcision (see 4:19–20; 5:9–10), then they journeyed twenty-five to thirty miles back to their original starting point in the land, which seems strange. However, it seems more likely that this was a different place with the same name, somewhere in the vicinity of Mounts Ebal and Gerizim, where the covenant renewal ceremony had taken place (8:30–35). There are at least three different places called Gilgal in the Old Testament: (1) the main one, in the Jordan Valley, known from Joshua 4 and 5 and numerous other Scriptures (1 Sam 7:16; 11:14–15; 13:3–4; etc.); (2) a location north of Bethel, in the hill country, where Elijah and Elisha had been staying (2 Kgs 2:1); (3) a town between Jerusalem and Jericho, in the boundary list of Judah's territory (Josh 15:7). It appears that the Gilgal here is a fourth one, the same one that is mentioned in Deut 11:29–30, which was near Mounts Ebal and Gerizim and the oak of Moreh (which, according to Gen 12:6, was near Shechem).[160]

The Israelites in vv. 6–7 are called, literally, "the man of Israel." This term is used frequently as a collective noun referring to the Israelite army (e.g., Judg 7:23; 9:55; 1 Sam 13:6; 17:2; 23:9; cf. 2 Sam 17:24, where *kol,* "all, every," precedes the term), and such is possibly the case here. Some manuscript traditions have a more conventional reading in vv. 6–7: "sons of Israel" or "every man of Israel."[161]

---

[159] The term occurs twenty-two times in Joshua, most often in the phrase "the ark of the covenant" (see, e.g., 3:6,8; 4:9; 6:6). It occurs four times referring to the treaty with the Gibeonites (9:6,7,15,16).

[160] So also Keil, *Book of Joshua,* 92–94; Goslinga, *Joshua, Judges, Ruth,* 91–92; Hess, *Joshua,* 178. Situated as it was in the central highlands of the land, this would have been a much more logical location in which to establish a base camp and from which to divide the land (see 14:6) than the Gilgal east of Jericho, far down in the Jordan Valley at the eastern edge of the land. For more on the manifold identifications of Gilgal, see J. Muilenberg, "The Site of Ancient Gilgal," *BASOR* 140 (1955): 11–27; B. M. Bennett, Jr., "The Search for Israelite Gilgal," *PEQ* 104 (1972): 111–22; A. Zertal, "Israel Enters Canaan: Following the Pottery Trail," *BARev* 17.5 (1991): 28–47, esp. pp. 38,42–43; W. R. Kotter, "Gilgal," *ABD* 2:1022–24.

[161] This expression—אִישׁ יִשְׂרָאֵל—is an important factor in many scholars' critical reconstruction of sources (see the reviews in Butler, *Joshua,* 101–2; Nelson, *Joshua,* 125–26 and n. 1). However, the expression can easily be understood as a collective (so also Butler, *Joshua,* 101; Keil, *Book of Joshua,* 97), or as having undergone textual corruption.

9:7 The Israelites displayed their skepticism concerning the Gibeonites' claim by raising the possibility that the Gibeonites were actually living in their midst and showed their knowledge of the prohibitions in Exod 34:11–12 and Deut 20:15–18 about making treaties with the peoples of the land by asking how they could make such a treaty.

The narrator adds an intriguing signal of his own at this point by calling the Gibeonites "Hivites," although they had not identified themselves as such. Since the Hivites were among the groups to be destroyed (Exod 34:11; Deut 20:17; Josh 3:10) and part of the coalition arrayed against Israel (9:1), the narrator is providing his readers with his own evaluation of the situation: the Gibeonites were "Hivites," enemies of Israel, and no treaty should be made with them.[162]

9:8 The Gibeonites attempted to defuse the situation by depicting themselves as subordinates ("We are your servants"). Joshua, however, maintained a skeptical stance by asking them who they were and whence they had come.

A subtle interplay between Joshua's words in v. 8 and the Gibeonites' in v. 6 reveals their differing perceptions of the situation. The Gibeonites stated in v. 6 that they had "come from a distant country"; the verb form here makes it clear that, in their minds, they had reached their destination, that is, they had "*arrived* from a distant country." By contrast, when Joshua questioned them, the verb form he used made it clear that he believed the Gibeonites were merely passing by. We might paraphrase his words as "from where are you coming as you pass by here?"[163] The Gibeonites' deception was working: their own (secret) destination was the Israelite camp, but Joshua believed that they were on their way to somewhere else.

9:9–13 In response to Joshua's questions, the Gibeonites gave a lengthy explanation and justification of their actions that had brought them to the point of asking for a treaty. They began by reiterating their claim to have come from a distant place (cf. v. 6) and then added that this was occasioned by the name ("fame") of Israel's God (v. 9). This is one of only two direct references in the book to God's name, that is, his reputation.[164]

In vv. 9–10, the Gibeonites uttered words similar to Rahab's (see 2:9–11).

---

[162] There is insufficient extrabiblical evidence for a definitive conclusion concerning the nature of the Gibeonite-Hivite connection in all its details. See J. Blenkinsopp, *Gibeon and Israel: The Role of Gibeon and the Gibeonites in the Political and Religious History of Early Israel* (Cambridge: University Press, 1972), 14–27.

[163] The verb form in v. 6 is a suffixed (perfect) form (בָּאנוּ; cf. also v. 9), which denotes an action that is complete (i.e., the Gibeonites had completed their journey), whereas the verb form in v. 8 is a prefixed (imperfect) form (תָּבֹאוּ), denoting an incomplete action (i.e., Joshua perceived that their journey was still in progress). On the distinction here, see L. McFall, *The Enigma of the Hebrew Verbal System: Solutions from Ewald to the Present* (Sheffield: Almond, 1982), 85.

[164] The other is Josh 7:9. See the commentary on 7:7 and on 7:9 for more on God's name and its significance.

The Israelites' reputation had preceded them, and the Gibeonites had heard about God's mighty acts in Egypt and the Israelites' victories over Sihon and Og. How they had heard is not specified, but v. 24 explicitly says that they had been informed of the details of how God had worked on Israel's behalf. Rahab had only mentioned Sihon and Og, but undoubtedly the events in Egypt were known as well, since they were even more spectacular than the victories in Transjordan. The fact that the Gibeonites mentioned only events outside of Canaan—as opposed to the more recent victories over Jericho and Ai—may have been an intentional part of their plan, suggesting to the Israelites that they were not from nearby (and thus would not know of the most recent events).[165]

In vv. 11–13, the details of the Gibeonites' ruse come out. They claimed to have left so long before that their bread was dry and crumbled and their wineskins were cracked (vv. 12–13). As is often the case with liars, the Gibeonites told partial truths: they had indeed taken provisions,[166] as their elders had instructed (cf. vv. 4–5,11), and they had indeed heard a report (cf. vv. 3,9).[167] However, the whole truth showed them to be liars, and we readers know this because of the information in the text, even if Joshua and the Israelites did not.

9:14 The NIV's "sampled" translates the Hebrew's *wayyiqḥû*, "and they took from." Some scholars maintain that this was part of a covenant-ratifying meal that the Israelites and Gibeonites shared together (see the introduction to chap. 9). However, more probably, this statement merely means that the Israelites took from the Gibeonites' provisions in order to inspect them, to confirm the Gibeonites' words.

The key to understanding Israel's fault in this episode comes in the second half of this verse, which reads (lit.), "But the mouth of the LORD they did not ask [i.e., consult]." This failure was contrary to the explicit instructions the Lord gave to Joshua concerning how to discern his will, that they *should* consult him, by going to Eleazar the priest, who would consult the Lord using the Urim (Num 27:21). The Israelites' confirmation of the Gibeonites' claim was purely in their own strength and on their own initiative. The mistake on Israel's and Joshua's part was not that they were deceived per se, but that they did not ask for the Lord's counsel. This is certainly a warning to all who read this passage: God is there to be consulted, and we ignore him at our peril (cf. 1 Chr 28:9; 2 Chr 15:2; 18:4; 20:4; etc.).

9:15 Apparently, on the basis of sampling the Gibeonites' food, Joshua

---

[165] Nelson, *Joshua*, 133.

[166] The lexeme here—צֵידָה—is the same one used by the Israelite officials when they instructed their people to prepare for the journey to the Jordan River (צֵידָה: 1:11). For more on this term, see footnote at 1:11.

[167] Nelson, *Joshua*, 129.

and the leaders of the Israelite assembly were satisfied with the Gibeonites' story. Joshua and the leaders are distinguished in this verse. Joshua took two actions (merged into one in NIV's translation): (1) they "made peace," and (2) they "made a covenant [or treaty]." These actions spared the Gibeonites' lives, which was their objective from the start. The leaders then swore an oath that ratified the treaty.[168]

A different word for the Israelite assembly is used here (*ʿēdâ*) from the previous chapter (*qāhāl*; see on 8:30). The two terms are essentially synonymous, although, based on its etymology, *ʿēdâ* may indicate a group of Israelites convened for a specific goal,[169] which in this case would have been dealing with the Gibeonites. The specific phrase here—"leaders *[nĕśîʾîm]* of the assembly"—is found eleven times in the Old Testament, including four times in Joshua (9:15,18,19; 22:30) and five times in Numbers (4:34; 16:2; 27:2; 31:13; 32:2). The term *nĕśîʾîm* usually is translated as "leaders," "chiefs," or "princes."

(3) The Gibeonites' Lot (9:16–27)

[16]Three days after they made the treaty with the Gibeonites, the Israelites heard that they were neighbors, living near them. [17]So the Israelites set out and on the third day came to their cities: Gibeon, Kephirah, Beeroth and Kiriath Jearim. [18]But the Israelites did not attack them, because the leaders of the assembly had sworn an oath to them by the LORD, the God of Israel.

The whole assembly grumbled against the leaders, [19]but all the leaders answered, "We have given them our oath by the LORD, the God of Israel, and we cannot touch them now. [20]This is what we will do to them: We will let them live, so that wrath will not fall on us for breaking the oath we swore to them." [21]They continued, "Let them live, but let them be woodcutters and water carriers for the entire community." So the leaders' promise to them was kept.

[22]Then Joshua summoned the Gibeonites and said, "Why did you deceive us by saying, 'We live a long way from you,' while actually you live near us? [23]You are now under a curse: You will never cease to serve as woodcutters and water carriers for the house of my God."

[24]They answered Joshua, "Your servants were clearly told how the LORD your God had commanded his servant Moses to give you the whole land and to wipe out all its inhabitants from before you. So we feared for our lives because of you, and that is why we did this. [25]We are now in your hands. Do to us whatever seems good and right to you."

[26]So Joshua saved them from the Israelites, and they did not kill them. [27]That day he made the Gibeonites woodcutters and water carriers for the community and for the altar of the LORD at the place the LORD would choose. And that is what they are to this day.

---

[168] On the nature of this treaty, see the introduction to chap. 9. On the importance of oaths, see comments below, on 9:18.

[169] E. Carpenter, "עֵדָה," *NIDOTTE* 3:327.

The second major section of the chapter, which explains the Gibeonite indenture to Israel, is marked by the standard syntactical pattern also found in v. 1 (see on 9:1). This section divides naturally into two subsections. The first (vv. 16–21) tells of the Israelites' discovery of the Gibeonites' deceit and the resulting confrontation. Despite the Gibeonite trickery, Israel nevertheless was bound by its oath to keep the treaty. The seriousness of the oath is underscored by the fact that vv. 18–21 are devoted to it. The congregation was angry with its leaders for having done this (v. 18b), but their hands were tied by the oath the leaders had taken. This fact is stated explicitly and in repetitive detail in vv. 19–20. Joshua is not mentioned at all in this section: the fault is laid at the leaders' feet for swearing the oath to the Gibeonites (v. 15b), even though Joshua had made the peace and the actual treaty (v. 15a). Both parties were guilty, but the author downplays Joshua's guilt, perhaps because of his otherwise exemplary leadership role in the book.

The second subsection here (vv. 22–27) tells of Joshua's confrontation with the Gibeonites. This parallels the confrontation between the Israelite leaders and the Gibeonites recounted in vv. 16–21. The leaders and Joshua apparently had acted separately in making peace with the Gibeonites (see especially v. 15), but the results were the same: they both instructed the people to let the Gibeonites live, and the Gibeonites ended up as servants in the Israelite camp (vv. 21,26–27). In the end, the Gibeonites provide another example in Joshua of foreigners assimilated into Israel, although in a different way (see the commentary at 2:11 and 8:33).

9:16 The Gibeonites' trickery is now discovered by the Israelites in an ironic twist: they heard *(šmᶜ)* about the Gibeonites' deceit, just as the Canaanite kings and the Gibeonites earlier had heard *(šmᶜ)* about the Israelites' great successes (vv. 1,3). The Gibeonites were not from a distant land but were from nearby: they actually were living "in their midst" (NIV: "near them").

9:17 We learn that the Gibeonites lived in at least four towns, all of which are mentioned in the Benjaminite tribal allotments (Josh 18:25–26,28). These were all clustered five to ten miles northwest of Jerusalem.[170] Nothing concrete is known of the Gibeonites' political organization, but this reference to "their cities" suggests some type of loose federation (with elders *[zĕqēnîm]* as important leaders in the community: see v. 11). The Philistines had a five-city federation—composed of Gaza, Ashkelon, Ashdod, Ekron, and Gath—ruled by "lords" *(sĕrānîm)*, as indicated by such texts as Josh 13:3; Judg 3:3; 1 Sam 6:16–18; et cetera.

9:18 The Gibeonites were safe from harm at the hands of Israel because of the oath that had been taken (v. 15). Oath taking and swearing are solemn

---

[170] On these towns, see Blenkinsopp, *Gibeon and Israel*, 1–13; Boling, *Joshua*, 266–67 and map, p. 260.

affairs in the Old Testament. To take an oath—the Hebrew words for "swear" and "oath" are from the same root: *šbʿ*—was to give one's sacred and unbreakable word that he would follow through on what was promised. God often swore by himself, his holiness, or his great name to take certain actions (e.g., Gen 22:16–18; Ps 89:35 [Hb. 36]; Jer 44:26). Swearing falsely was a grave sin (Ezek 17:16–21; Zech 5:3–4; Mal 3:5). Because of the sacred, unbreakable nature of an oath, this treaty that the Israelites made with the Gibeonites, even though it was obtained under false pretenses, could not be revoked. A similar situation is visible in Genesis 27, where Jacob tricked Isaac into blessing him, and the rightful recipient of the blessing, Esau, could not then receive it.

The entire assembly grumbled against the leaders. The word used here of grumbling—*lûn*—is found about twenty times in the Old Testament, all but twice (here and Ps 59:15[Hb. 16]) in Exodus and Numbers, referring to the people's grumbling and complaining in the wilderness. It does not appear that the people were simply grumbling because of an ill-advised treaty. Rather, vv. 19–21 imply that the people's desire was to kill the Gibeonites and that their grumbling was because they were now deprived of this opportunity. Verse 26, which states that "Joshua saved [the Gibeonites] from the Israelites," confirms that their intentions were not good.[171]

9:19 The leaders' reply indicates the bind into which they had placed themselves, and its wording gives a slight indication of a defensive, frustrated, or desperate attitude. The emphasis is on themselves as the ones who made the treaty—as opposed to God—and on their inability to retract it. They said, in a wooden translation, "As for us, *we* have sworn to them by the LORD the God of Israel, and now, we are not able to touch them!" Contrary to the human impulse to lie and justify oneself, an impulse indulged far too commonly, the leaders did not deny that they had done this—their words are almost identical to the narrator's report in v. 18—but they were powerless to make any changes. The repeated phrase "by the LORD the God of Israel" in vv. 18–19 emphasizes the solemnity and the binding nature of the oath they had sworn: this was taken in his name and could not be broken.

9:20–21 In v. 20, the leaders acknowledged the obvious necessity incumbent upon them, that they needed to spare the Gibeonites, if only so that they themselves would not suffer wrath because of breaking the oath. Many years later, when Saul killed the Gibeonites in violation of this oath, the Lord brought a famine upon the land (2 Sam 21:1), and this would have been the type of wrath the leaders feared.

The leaders specified that the Gibeonites should be their servants, cutting their wood and carrying their water; thus, in this way, the leaders' word to the

---

[171] I thank Ray Clendenen for this observation (personal communication).

Gibeonites was honored (v. 21). Servitude was the destiny of those cities that made their peace with the Israelites, according to Deut 20:10–11. The specific activities here were mentioned by Moses, in a context that indicates this was already a reality with other aliens: in urging the Israelites to follow the covenant, he included even aliens in his instructions: "Your children and your wives, and *the aliens living in your camps* who chop your wood and carry your water" (Deut 29:11[Hb. 10]).

9:22–23 These verses open the second subsection of 9:16–27 (see comments introducing this section). They are somewhat repetitive of the information in v. 21, but they add several new elements to the story line. Joshua's question about the Gibeonites' deception in v. 22 refers back to his earlier questions of v. 8, the Gibeonites' response in v. 9, and the revelation of their true home in v. 16. The Gibeonites' servant status is now revealed to be a curse (v. 23), in line with the curses to be pronounced on ones who violated God's covenant (see Deuteronomy 27–28). The Gibeonites' service was to be "for the house of our God," which is different from the leaders' more general statement that it was to be "for all the assembly" (v. 21). Verse 27 reveals that their duties included both activities.

The "house of God" in later years signified the temple that Solomon built (see, e.g., 1 Chr 22:2; 23:28; Ps 135:2; Mic 4:2) or the temple rebuilt after the exile (e.g., Ezra 1:4; 3:8). In Joshua's day, however, there was no temple, and the "house of God" may have referred to the tabernacle or to a place such as Shiloh, where there was a house of God in the days before the temple was built (1 Sam 1:7; cf. Josh 18:1).[172]

9:24–25 The Gibeonites now revealed their motives to Joshua, which have been apparent to the reader from the beginning (see vv. 3–4). In doing so, they expressed a knowledge of what God was intending to do for his people, in a way similar to Rahab's confession of her faith in 2:9–11. They placed themselves at Joshua's mercy, stating that they should do to them (lit.), "according to that which is good and right in your eyes." The same expression is found in Jer 26:14, where Jeremiah defended himself before the officials and people of Judah, stating that his mission was from God and that they should do to him "according to that which is good and right in your eyes." If they chose wrongly, however—that is, if they put him to death—then "you will bring the guilt of innocent blood on yourselves and on this city and those who live in it" (v. 15). So too for the Gibeonites: the rightness of their claim of protection was rooted in Israel's law. The expression "to do right in X's eyes" usually refers to doing right in God's eyes. Sometimes it refers to the decision-making process, as here (Josh 9:25; 2 Sam 19:6[Hb. 7]; Jer 26:14; 40:4–5).[173]

---

[172] See further the commentary on 6:19.

[173] For a fuller discussion of "doing right in X's eyes," see D. M. Howard, Jr., "The Case for Kingship in Deuteronomy and the Former Prophets," *WTJ* 52 (1990): 110–11, n. 27.

9:26–27 The wording in v. 26 places Joshua in the role of the Gibeonites' deliverer from the Israelites, who presumably were angry enough to want to abrogate the treaty and kill them (cf. v. 18). As we noted earlier, despite his own role in making the treaty (v. 15), Joshua is in the background in the section where the problem is discussed (vv. 16–21), and his leadership was not questioned as was the Israelite officials' (v. 18).

Verse 27 shows that the Gibeonites' tasks of cutting wood and carrying water were dual in focus, which had already been indicated in vv. 21,23 (see the commentary on v. 23): they were to serve "for the community"[174] (a secular focus) and "for the altar of the LORD" (a religious focus). This was to be done in perpetuity, "to this day," and it was to be done at the place that the Lord would choose.

The reference to the place that the Lord would choose echoes an identical expression that is prominent in Deuteronomy, where it occurs twenty-one times.[175] It indicates that the Gibeonites were to serve only at sanctioned Israelite cultic centers, such as Shiloh (Josh 18:1) or Gibeon itself (1 Chr 16:39), and not Canaanite ones. These sanctioned centers were those where the tabernacle and the ark of the covenant were to be found, because God's presence was there.[176] After the Jerusalem temple was built, it was the place of legitimate worship.

A postscript to the story of the Gibeonites can be seen after the exile, in two lists in the Book of Nehemiah. In both cases, men from Gibeon are listed among the Jews who were repairing the walls or who returned from Babylonian exile (Neh 3:7; 7:25). They appear to have been fully assimilated among the Jews, as much believers in Israel's God as was Rahab and other foreign "converts" and as much the recipients of God's grace (see also the comments on 2:11).

6. The Gibeonite Treaty Tested; Southern Campaign Begun (10:1–27)

Chapters 10–11 tell of Israel's conquest of northern and southern Canaan after it had gained a foothold in central Canaan by defeating Jericho and Ai and making a treaty with Gibeon.

---

[174] The NIV inexplicably renders עֵדָה here and in 9:21 as "community," whereas elsewhere in the chapter it has "assembly" (vv. 15,18[2x]).

[175] See especially in chaps. 12 and 16: 12:5,11,14,18,21,26; 16:2,6,7,11,15,16.

[176] Craigie expresses this point well: "Though there was only one tabernacle, it would be moved from place to place; there would be many places over the course of time, but only one place at a time" (*Deuteronomy*, 217).

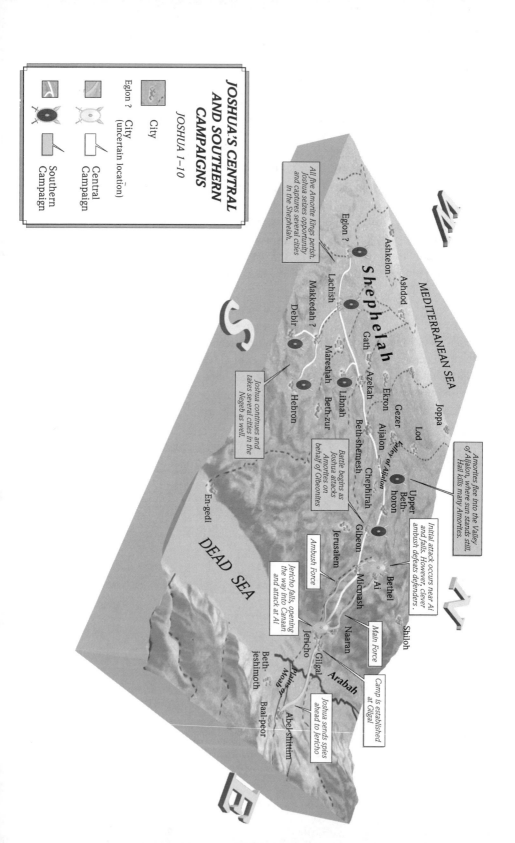

JOSHUA'S CENTRAL AND SOUTHERN CAMPAIGNS

JOSHUA 1–10

City

Eglon? City (uncertain location)

Eglon? Southern Campaign

Central Campaign

MEDITERRANEAN SEA

DEAD SEA

Arabah

S h e p h e l a h

Joppa

Lod

Gezer

Ekron

Ashdod

Ashkelon

Eglon?

Gath

Azekah

Lachish

Makkedah?

Mareshah

Debir

Libnah

Beth-zur

Hebron

Beth-shemesh

Aijalon

Valley of Aijalon

Chephirah

Gibeon

Jerusalem

Michmash

Ai

Bethel

Upper Beth-horon

Shiloh

Naaran

Jericho

Gilgal

Plains of Moab

Beth-jeshimoth

Baal-peor

Abel-shittim

En-gedi

All five Amorite kings perish. Joshua seizes opportunity and captures several cities in the Shephelah.

Joshua continues and takes several cities in the Negeb as well.

Battle begins as Joshua attacks Amorites on behalf of Gibeonites

Amorites flee into the Valley of Aijalon, where sun stands still. Hail kills many Amorites.

Initial attack occurs near Ai and fails. However, clever ambush defeats defenders.

Ambush Force

Jericho falls, opening the way into Canaan and attack at Ai

Main Force

Camp is established at Gilgal

Joshua sends spies ahead to Jericho

Several striking parallels can be seen between the two chapters. Both open with accounts of a coalition of kings who opposed Israel's invasion (10:1–27; 11:1–9). Both mention God's help in repelling the attacks (chap. 10 more than chap. 11, but see 11:6,8). Both open with descriptions of decisive battles (10:1–14; 11:1–9) and are followed by further military activity related to these (10:16–27; 11:10–15). Each account shows one main instigator of the coalition: in chap. 10, it is Adoni-Zedek, king of Jerusalem; in chap. 11, it is Jabin, king of Hazor. Each chapter then ends with an account of the consolidation of power in each area (10:28–43; 11:16–23).[177]

Both chapters are linked with chap. 9 in that in all three chapters, coalitions of Canaanite kings came out against Israel because of what they had heard *(šmᶜ)* of Israel's successes (9:1; 10:1; 11:1).

This section (vv. 1–27) tells of the Israelites' victory over a southern coalition of Canaanite kings who attacked Gibeon as a result of that city's treaty with Israel. Thus, the account here is a test of the validity of the treaty and Israel's commitment to its oath. The question was, Would Israel be true to its word and defend this people with whom it had made a binding treaty? The battle took place near Gibeon (vv. 1–15), but its aftermath unfolded elsewhere, at a cave near Makkedah (vv. 16–27). The battle of Gibeon is the last battle described in any detail in the book (the others are the encounters at Jericho and Ai) since after this the text merely summarizes the campaigns in the south (10:28–43) and in the north (11:1–23).

(1) Southern Coalition Gathered against Gibeon (10:1–5)

[1]Now Adoni-Zedek king of Jerusalem heard that Joshua had taken Ai and totally destroyed it, doing to Ai and its king as he had done to Jericho and its king, and that the people of Gibeon had made a treaty of peace with Israel and were living near them. [2]He and his people were very much alarmed at this, because Gibeon was an important city, like one of the royal cities; it was larger than Ai, and all its men were good fighters. [3]So Adoni-Zedek king of Jerusalem appealed to Hoham king of Hebron, Piram king of Jarmuth, Japhia king of Lachish and Debir king of Eglon. [4]"Come up and help me attack Gibeon," he said, "because it has made peace with Joshua and the Israelites."

[5]Then the five kings of the Amorites—the kings of Jerusalem, Hebron, Jarmuth, Lachish and Eglon—joined forces. They moved up with all their troops and took up positions against Gibeon and attacked it.

This section shows the gathering of the southern coalition of five Canaanite kings and their attack on Gibeon. In vv. 3 and 5, the five kings' cities are identified: Hebron, Jarmuth, Lachish, Eglon, and Jerusalem. These were all cities

---

[177] For some of the syntagmatic patterns within these chapters (i.e., patterns of constituent elements) and in similar ancient Near Eastern texts, see Younger, *Ancient Conquest Accounts*, 204–29.

southwest of Jerusalem. This suggests that the coalitions of 9:1–2 and 10:1–5 were not the same, since the kings in 9:1–2 were from all parts of Canaan, not just the south. Once again, the reputation of Israel's victories had spread among the Canaanites, striking fear into their hearts. In contrast to Rahab, who turned to Israel's God in faith, and to the Gibeonites, who entered into a treaty with the Israelites (by trickery), this coalition decided to resist Israel by force.

10:1 Once again Israel's spreading fame is mentioned, since Adoni-Zedek, king of Jerusalem heard *(šmᶜ)* about Joshua's doings at Ai and Jericho, and about Israel's treaty with Gibeon (cf. the same motif of hearing elsewhere, in 2:9–11; 5:1; 9:1). This verse consists entirely of background information for the action that is to begin in v. 2.[178] Jerusalem is mentioned by this name here for the first time in the Bible, although other names for it are found earlier, at Gen 14:18 ("Salem") and 22:14 ("The LORD Will Provide" and "the mountain of the LORD"). Jerusalem became the most important city in Israel, but this did not happen until many years later, under David (2 Sam 5:6–19).[179]

10:2 By contrast to the Canaanite coalition that gathered to come against Israel in 9:1–2, which seemed to be unafraid of Joshua and Israel, Adoni-Zedek and his people were indeed afraid (v. 2). The crucial difference is that, in the interim, an important Canaanite city—Gibeon—had made peace with the Israelites. Not only was Israel's God helping it, but now one of the Canaanites' very own would be Israel's ally. Their political and military calculations led Adoni-Zedek and the five Canaanite kings to conclude that their only option was to band together and attack Gibeon (see v. 5).

Gibeon appears from v. 2 to have been an important city, militarily and otherwise. It was like a "royal city," that is, one ruled by a king.[180] It was even greater than Ai. From this statement, Ai appears to have been a strong city as well; otherwise, if it had been a small, insignificant city, the point made about Gibeon's strength—that it was even greater than Ai's—would have been a weak one. This contrasts with the indication in 7:3 that Ai *was* an insignificant city, which may reinforce the possibility that Ai was always considered in connection with the larger and stronger Bethel (see commentary on 8:17).

All of Gibeon's men were "good fighters." This expression translates the term *gibbōrîm*, which means "mighty men, heroes." The Israelite force that

---

[178] The syntactical construction is an extended subordinate clause following וַיְהִי, indicating time; the *wayyiqtol* verb form that resumes the main story line is וַיִּֽירְאוּ in v. 2. For more on this syntactical pattern, see the commentary on 3:14–16 and the footnote at 4:11.

[179] For an introduction to the historical and theological significance of Jerusalem, see Howard, *Introduction to the Old Testament Historical Books*, 224–29 and references there.

[180] Thirty-one such cities are listed in western Palestine alone in 12:7–24 (Boling, *Joshua*, 279).

met this coalition's forces (v. 7) was also an elite one: it consisted of the "best fighting men" *(gibbōrê heḥāyil).*[181]

10:3–5 Adoni-Zedek appealed to four other kings to help him, because of the threat that Gibeon posed to them (vv. 3–4). Verse 5 identifies the five as "kings of the Amorites." The term "Amorite" is likely used here in its narrow sense of inhabitants of the central mountain region of Palestine, not its broader sense of any Canaanite (see commentary on 3:10). Only Jerusalem and Hebron were actually in the hill country, but the designation of the entire coalition as an Amorite one may signify the importance of Jerusalem—an "Amorite" city—and its king at the head of the coalition. The four kings joined Adoni-Zedek and attacked Gibeon (v. 5). The four kings were from Hebron, Jarmuth, Lachish, and Eglon,[182] all cities southwest of Jerusalem.[183]

(2) The Battle of Gibeon: Stage One (10:6–11)

⁶The Gibeonites then sent word to Joshua in the camp at Gilgal: "Do not abandon your servants. Come up to us quickly and save us! Help us, because all the Amorite kings from the hill country have joined forces against us."

⁷So Joshua marched up from Gilgal with his entire army, including all the best fighting men. ⁸The LORD said to Joshua, "Do not be afraid of them; I have given them into your hand. Not one of them will be able to withstand you."

⁹After an all-night march from Gilgal, Joshua took them by surprise. ¹⁰The LORD threw them into confusion before Israel, who defeated them in a great victory at Gibeon. Israel pursued them along the road going up to Beth Horon and cut them down all the way to Azekah and Makkedah. ¹¹As they fled before Israel

---

[181] This term is translated in other versions as "mighty men of valor" (KJV, NKJV), "valiant warriors" (NASB), "mighty warriors" (NRSV), "trained warriors" (NJPSV). See the commentary on 1:14 for more on the גִּבּוֹרֵי הֶחָיִל. See on 8:3 on "his entire army" (lit., "all the people of the army").

[182] Debir, king of Eglon, is otherwise known in the Bible as a place name, not a personal name (see Josh 10:38–39; 11:21; 12:13; 13:26; 15:7,15,49; 21:15; Judg 1:11), while Eglon was a Moabite king encountered in Judges 3 (Judg 3:12–14), as well as apparently a place name in Joshua (10:3,5,23,34,36–37; 12:12; 15:39). The Old Greek has "Adullam" for "Eglon" in chap. 10 and other names (not "Eglon") in 12:12 and 15:39. This has led J. Barr to argue that there were actually six cities in this coalition (adding Adullam), or that the place names and personal names were confused at some point ("Mythical Monarch Unmasked? Mysterious Doings of Debir King of Eglon," *JSOT* 48 [1990]: 55–68). The Qumran fragment containing Josh 10:3, however, clearly reads "Eglon" as a place name (see L. Greenspoon, "The Qumran Fragments of Joshua: Which Puzzle Are They Part of and Where Do They Fit?" in G. J. Brooke and B. Lindars, eds., *Septuagint, Scrolls and Cognate Writings*, SBLSCSS 33 [Atlanta: Scholars Press, 1992], 185). For further rebuttal of Barr, see K. L. Younger, Jr., "The 'Conquest' of the South (Jos 10,28–39)," *BZ* 39 (1995): 263–64.

[183] For their locations, see the maps in Rasmussen, *NIV Atlas of the Bible*, 94; T. V. Brisco, *Holman Bible Atlas* (Nashville: Broadman & Holman, 1998), 79. For information on the sites, see Butler, *Joshua*, 114–15; Boling, *Joshua*, 279–80. For conjectures concerning the strategic military significance of these cities, see Hess, *Joshua*, 189–90.

on the road down from Beth Horon to Azekah, the LORD hurled large hailstones down on them from the sky, and more of them died from the hailstones than were killed by the swords of the Israelites.

The account of the battle falls into two sections, each parallel to the other: vv. 6–11 and 12–15. They are not successive stages, but parallel ones: they both describe different facets of the battle of Gibeon.[184] The picture in both sections is of a great and complete victory, with different facets: (1) a successful ambush (vv. 9–10), (2) a deadly hailstorm (v. 11), and (3) a miracle or sign involving the sun and the moon (vv. 12–13). When all was said and done, the wonder of God's listening and responding to a man's appeal stands out (v. 14), showing that God was sensitive to his people.

The first section begins with the Gibeonites appealing to Joshua under terms of the treaty made in chap. 9 and Joshua responding (vv. 6–7). God threw the coalition into a panic, and there was a great slaughter by the Israelites (v. 10). Then, in the retreat, more were killed by a hailstorm than had died in the military encounter (v. 11).

10:6–7 The Gibeonites' words to Joshua were an urgent appeal for protection, because of the impressive forces arrayed against them (v. 6). Because of the treaty they had just concluded with the Israelites, they were able to make such an appeal, and, as such, this episode is a test of Israel's commitment and faithfulness to its word. The number of verbs found in their appeal—all imperatives—add to this sense of urgency: "*Do not let* your hands *drop* from your servants; *get up* to us quickly and *deliver* us and *help* us!" The appeal to "*deliver*" is an emphatic imperative—perhaps best rendered as "*you must deliver us!*"—adding even more to this impression. Joshua did just as the Gibeonites requested (v. 7), coming up from Gilgal with a force of his own against the Amorite coalition (see on v. 2). Despite the trickery by which the treaty had been made, Joshua and his people remained committed and faithful to their word.

10:8–10 God's words of encouragement to Joshua in v. 8 echo closely the words he had spoken to Joshua at the outset of the book.[185] Once again, in case Joshua had forgotten, God reminded him of his presence and empowerment. Joshua came up against the Amorite coalition "suddenly" (NIV: "by surprise"), after having marched all night (v. 9).[186] The word combination here— "came against" *(bw' 'l)*—denotes a hostile military encounter; see the same construction in Gen 32:8 (Hb. 9), where Jacob was worried about

---

[184] See the introduction to vv. 12–15 for a justification of this.

[185] "Do not be afraid [אל־תירא]" echoes 1:9 ("Do not be terrified" [תערץ]); "I have given them into your hand" echoes 1:2 ("I am giving [them] to you"); "Not one of them will be able to withstand [עמד] you" echoes 1:5 ("No one will be able to stand up [יצב] against you").

[186] Depending on the precise location of Gilgal (see on 9:6), the march would have covered twenty to twenty-five miles uphill.

Esau's attacking *(bwᵓ ᵓl)* him.

While Joshua and his force marched all night and took the Amorites by surprise (v. 9), it was Yahweh—and Yahweh alone—who took the decisive actions against the enemies (v. 10). Every verb in this verse is singular, indicating that he alone *confused, struck, pursued,* and *struck* them.[187] It may have been that the fighting force with Joshua (v. 7) was actually involved in this—indeed, this probably was the case, in light of the reference in v. 11 to the Israelites' swords killing people. But, here, the author has chosen to ignore this fact and to focus instead on Yahweh's direct involvement as Israel's warrior. The land and its people were Yahweh's to give, and he did so here.

The geographical clues in this verse show that the pursuit was over a great distance, along the road "going up to Beth Horon" as far as Azekah and Makkedah, a distance of more than twenty miles. This escape route first went northwest, then southwest, down out of the hill country. In v. 11, the road to Beth-Horon is described from a different perspective: "the road down from Beth-Horon."[188]

10:11   Whereas v. 10 summarizes the victory over the Amorites in general terms, with Yahweh receiving the credit, v. 11 gives more details, and Yahweh is again credited with the victory. The verse wraps up the first section describing the battle, and it is set off from its surroundings syntactically. It begins with the common *wayĕhî* plus stage-setting temporal-clause construction (see on 4:11): "And it happened, when they fled ..." In this case, Yahweh is the focus, and we might translate the next clause as follows: "*Yahweh* was the one who hurled great stones upon them." Just as he is in v. 10, God is also given credit here for the victory, but now the means by which he gave the victory is specified: a great deluge of hailstones that killed more people than the Israelite swords did. The verse builds to a climax even in the choice of words for the stones. The first time they are referred to, the expression is general: "great stones from heaven." The second time, however, it is more specific: "hailstones."[189]

---

[187] The NIV's interpretive rendering has *Israel* defeating the Gibeonites and pursuing them. However, the subject of the verb "pursued" is "he," not "Israel." There is some textual evidence for plural verbs in the second half of the verse—the Old Greek, Syr., and a Tg. all have, "And they pursued ... and they struck"—but the consonantal MT is singular. The Vg. (Latin) also has singular verbs here, and "the LORD" is the subject: "And he pursued by the way of the ascent of Beth-horon and he smote as far as Azekah and Makkedah."

[188] For more on the geography here, see D. A. Dorsey, "The Location of Biblical Makkedah," *Tel Aviv* 7 (1980): 185–93; Rasmussen, *NIV Atlas of the Bible*, 94 –95. On the road to Beth-Horon, see Dorsey, *The Roads and Highways of Ancient Israel* (Baltimore: Johns Hopkins University, 1991), 241. An important pass descending to the coastal plain leads along this ascent/descent.

[189] A midsummer hailstorm would have been a rarity, rendering miraculous assistance in this instance. There are only five to eight days of hail per year in the coastal plain, mostly in midwinter. See Boling, *Joshua*, 282. And even then the hail is not usually of deadly force.

The Canaanites' terror is captured in the expression "they fled from the face *(mippĕnê)* of the Israelites." This term—as opposed to the similar *millipnê* ("from before")—suggests more of a sense of urgency, with the idea of causation often attached to it (i.e., the agent of the fear, that which causes it, is often in view).[190] In this case, their immediate fear was Israel, but the agent behind Israel was of course Yahweh. Thus, even this word choice exalts the awesome, fearsome nature of Israel's God. He could be counted on to rout his enemies.

(3) The Battle of Gibeon: Stage Two (10:12–15)

[12]On the day the LORD gave the Amorites over to Israel, Joshua said to the LORD in the presence of Israel:

> "O sun, stand still over Gibeon,
>   O moon, over the Valley of Aijalon."
> [13]So the sun stood still,
>   and the moon stopped,
>   till the nation avenged itself on its enemies,

as it is written in the Book of Jashar.

The sun stopped in the middle of the sky and delayed going down about a full day. [14]There has never been a day like it before or since, a day when the LORD listened to a man. Surely the LORD was fighting for Israel!

[15]Then Joshua returned with all Israel to the camp at Gilgal.

10:12 The second section describing the battle of Gibeon is introduced with the disjunctive adverb *ʾāz*, translated "then" (meaning "at that time"). It introduces important action that took place at the same time as that of vv. 6–11, not something that happened later.[191] This is the function of *ʾāz* when it is followed by a prefixed (imperfect) verb form, as it is here.[192] That is, somehow the hailstorm of v. 11 and the phenomena of vv. 12–13 either were one and the same thing or (more probably) they happened at the same time, as part of the same larger miracle of deliverance for Israel.

---

[190] See BDB, 817–18 for the distinctions between מִפְּנֵי and מִלִּפְנֵי. Other passages in Joshua using this expression (מִפְּנֵי) to show the especially fearsome nature of Israel's God include 2:9–11,24; 3:10; etc.

[191] אָז means "then, at that time," but "not in the sense of 'sequentially, next'" (*DCH* 1:167).

[192] "The action introduced by אָז is to be thought of as having taken place before the completion of the preceding action, and in this sense the nonperfective describes relative action" (*IBHS* § 31.6.3b). See further I. Rabinowitz, "*ʾāz* Followed by Imperfect Verb-Form in Preterite Contexts: A Redactional Device in Biblical Hebrew," *VT* 34 (1984): 53–62. Rabinowitz states that "referring to the foregoing context of narrated past events, *ʾāz* + imperfect indicates this context as approximately the time when, the time or circumstances in the course of which, or the occasion upon which the action … went forward," and he translates it as "this was when …" (p. 54; see p. 60 on Josh 10:12 specifically).

The author's emphasis in the section comes in v. 14. He marvels, not so much at the miracle or sign of v. 13, but rather at the fact that God heard and responded to the voice of a man (v. 14), interceding dramatically for Israel because of Joshua's petition (v. 12)! There had never been such a day, nor would there be ever again. The two previous miracles on Israel's behalf—the stopping of the waters of the Jordan and the victory over Jericho—had been at God's initiative; this time, it was in response to one man's petition. This fact again highlights Joshua's importance in the book, and it also underscores God's faithfulness to his people.

This passage bristles with a host of exegetical and historical questions. Interest in these should not obscure the main thrust of the passage, however, which is that God listened to one man's voice and that he fought for Israel as a result (v. 14). Nevertheless, the exegetical and historical questions deserve to be treated.

One question arises from the reference to an extrabiblical source in v. 13—the *Book of Jashar*—and it concerns the extent of the quotation, if any, from that book. Some scholars appear to assume that the quotation consists of the poetic lines in vv. 12b–13a: Joshua's words to the sun and moon and the confirmation that this happened.[193] Others understand the quotation to be much longer, beginning immediately after the verse's opening words, "Then Joshua spoke to the LORD," and including all of the rest of vv. 12–15.[194] This has the decided advantage of accounting for the insertion of v. 15, which is out of place chronologically and which is repeated again verbatim in v. 43, although there are other, equally credible ways of dealing with this problem (see on v. 15). Still other scholars have proposed that the quotation from the *Book of Jashar* immediately follows—not precedes—the reference to it, in v. 13b.[195]

However, there may be no actual quotation of the *Book of Jashar* at all, only a reference to it. The grammatical pattern introducing this book—"Is it not written upon (=in) the Book of Jashar?"—is the same as that found numerous times in the Books of 1, 2 Kings referring to such sources as "the book of the annals of the kings of Israel" and "the book of the annals of the kings of Judah." There the language is the same—"Are they not written upon (=in) the book of the annals of the kings of Israel/Judah?"—and yet no one

---

[193] The NIV's layout of vv. 12b–13a shows this, and Butler understands it so (*Joshua*, 117). Goslinga understands the quote to begin earlier, and that only the words at the beginning of the verse—"Then Joshua spoke to the LORD"—are not from the *Book of Jashar* (*Joshua, Judges, Ruth*, 100 and n. 80). The reader should note that the NIV's dynamic equivalence rendering places these opening words in the middle of the verse, not at the beginning.

[194] Keil, *Book of Joshua*, 107–8; Woudstra, *Joshua*, 174.

[195] Howard, *Introduction to the Old Testament Historical Books*, 88; J. H. Walton, "Joshua 10:12–15 and Mesopotamian Celestial Omen Texts," in A. R. Millard, J. K. Hoffmeier, D. W. Baker, eds., *Faith, Tradition, and History: Old Testament Historiography in its Near Eastern Context* (Winona Lake: Eisenbrauns, 1994), 187.

supposes that the Books of 1, 2 Kings are in those instances actually quoting selections verbatim from these sources. On the contrary, the references in 1, 2 Kings show that the reader may read further in these sources of the deeds of the various kings and that presumably what is written in 1, 2 Kings can also be found there.[196]

A second question that arises here concerns who is speaking "in the presence of Israel" (v. 12). A literal translation of the beginning of the verse clarifies the issue since the NIV's dynamic equivalent translation rearranges and obscures several words: "At that time, Joshua spoke to the LORD, on the day of the LORD's giving the Amorite [before] the sons of Israel, *and he said* [in] the eyes (=in the presence) of Israel ...." Most interpreters understand the speaker to be Joshua, and, on the face of it, this is the most natural reading of the Hebrew. However, two issues should give us pause in this matter. First, the subject of the verb *wayyōʾmer*, "*and he said*," is not specified, and it is at least possible that God, not Joshua, is the speaker; the grammar would certainly allow for this, even if it is not the first probability.[197] Second, even though the text says that Joshua "spoke *to the LORD*," the words spoken were actually addressed directly to the sun and the moon, not to the Lord. Many commentators have noted this, and some have attributed this to layers of tradition that have been stitched together in this passage,[198] while others have stated that Joshua was addressing the sun and the moon through the power of God, or that he was actually praying to God.[199] However, this tension would be resolved much more easily if it were God speaking rather than Joshua. This suggestion is made more plausible when we remember that God is a far more appropriate subject than Joshua to have addressed the sun and moon directly with a command such as this: he created them, and he was their sovereign (Gen 1:14–17; Isa 40:26; Jer 31:35). If this is the case, then we have in these verses evidence of *God* taking the initiative and demonstrating his great power over these natural phenomena, speaking directly to them, ordering them to obey his command.

In line with this, the end of v. 14 states, "Surely the LORD was fighting for Israel," which can shed some light on a statement in v. 13 (usually read "until the nation avenged itself on its enemies"). If God, in his capacity as their sovereign, commanded the sun and the moon to take their positions, and if, as we have noted in connection with vv. 10–11, God was ultimately solely responsible for doing battle with the Amorites, then here too it should not surprise us

---

[196] On these sources in 1, 2 Kings and 1, 2 Chronicles, see Howard, *Introduction to the Old Testament Historical Books*, 174–75, 238–42.

[197] This suggestion is made by P. D. Miller, Jr., *The Divine Warrior in Early Israel*, 127–28. The Old Greek adds "Joshua" as subject of "he said," and it is followed by the NIV and many versions and commentators, but the Hb. and the Vg. are indefinite.

[198] E.g., Soggin, *Joshua*, 122; Butler, *Joshua*, 116–17; Nelson, *Joshua*, 142.

[199] E.g., Keil, *Book of Joshua*, 108; Goslinga, *Joshua, Judges, Ruth*, 99; Woudstra, *Joshua*, 174.

if God—rather than the Israelites—is described as taking vengeance upon his enemies. This is precisely what the Old Greek states, which reads in v. 13: "until God took vengeance on their enemies." If this is the original reading,[200] then the entire text is consistent: God was the one who sent the hailstorm and struck down the Amorites (v. 11), who commanded the sun and the moon to obey him (v. 12), who avenged himself upon Israel's enemies (v. 13); in short, God fought for Israel (v. 14). Even if the word "God" is not added to the text, we can still see him as the subject of the verb "take vengeance" by postulating that the consonant *m* dropped out of the text just after the verb, which ends with an *m (nqm)*. Then, the Hebrew would read "until he [i.e., God] took vengeance against the nation of his enemies."[201] Thus, in the exposition below, we assume that God was the one who spoke to the sun and the moon, not Joshua (see the translation of vv. 12–14 given near the end of this discussion).

A third question, both exegetically and historically oriented, concerns what actually happened to the sun and moon, and it is the question most often asked of this passage. The answer involves a series of further questions. The discussion below proceeds as follows: (1) a review of the major proposals advanced about this question, (2) an evaluation of some of their strengths and weaknesses, and (3) a conclusion by pointing to what seems to be the most plausible solution.

Proposal 1: The Earth Stopped Rotating.   Traditionally, it has been assumed that a miracle of colossal magnitude took place, that the sun actually stopped in its course across the sky (as well as the moon)—or, in terms of modern science, that the earth's rotation stopped. The apocryphal book called *The Wisdom of Sirach (Ecclesiasticus)* states, "Was it not through [Joshua] that the sun stood still and one day became as long as two?" (*Sir* 46:4, NRSV),[202] and Josephus likewise claimed that this day was longer than the ordinary day (*Ant.* 5.1.17). This interpretation has been supported by a long line of Christian and Jewish interpreters, including Augustine, Jerome, Luther, and Calvin, and various rabbinical commentators.[203]

---

[200] M. J. Gruenthaner argues that it is ("Two Sun Miracles of the Old Testament," *CBQ* 10 [1948]: 271–90 [the relevant pages are 278–79]).

[201] This is the proposal of Miller, and it had been advanced earlier by F. Delitzsch and M. Noth (see Miller, *The Divine Warrior*, 127–28). Miller notes that "with the single exception of this verse, the verb *nāqam* when it takes an object always takes a preposition" (*The Divine Warrior*, 128).

[202] In v. 5, Sirach mentions the hailstorm of Josh 10:11: "He called upon the Most High, the Mighty One, when enemies pressed him on every side, and the great Lord answered him with hailstones of mighty power."

[203] See J. Calvin, *Commentaries on the Book of Joshua* (Grand Rapids: Eerdmans, n.d.), 153–54. For others, see references in Walton, "Joshua 10:12–15," 181–82, 190, and nn. 1,27. In the modern day, Goslinga is one who follows this literal interpretation (*Joshua, Judges, Ruth*, 99–100, 189–93). See also Soggin, *Joshua*, 123: "It seems more prudent to regard the phenomenon as one of the numerous miracles of which the Bible tells us (such as are found elsewhere in the ancient world), remembering that in the biblical message a miracle is always a 'sign' of an extraordinary divine intervention which imparts a grace unmerited by man and inconceivable in any other way." Soggin does not claim to believe this actually happened, but only that this is what the text affirms did happen.

In modern times, some Bible students have claimed to verify this by referring to supposed calculations showing that precisely one day is missing from astronomical history and that this missing day is accounted for by the extra "day" in Joshua 10 and the ten steps (degrees?) that the sun went backwards in Hezekiah's time (2 Kgs 20:9–11). In one such account, it is claimed that a Professor Pickering of the Harvard Observatory traced this missing day back to Joshua's time, and that the ten "degrees" in Hezekiah's time were verified by astronomers from Greenwich and Yale. However, such claims have not been verified; they only exist in popular-level works on the Bible and science.[204]

Another, more recent story makes the same claims—that twenty-three hours and twenty minutes are missing, to be ascribed to Joshua's long day, and the remaining forty minutes are due to the event in Hezekiah's day—but it ascribes this to "our astronauts and space scientists at Green Belt Maryland," who stumbled across the missing day in the course of "checking the position of the sun, moon and planets out in space where they would be one hundred and one thousand years from now." It is claimed that the computer running the measurements came to a halt, until one scientist recalled stories from his Sunday School days that might explain this; following a quick check of the Bible, the calculations verified Joshua's long day and the ten degrees of Hezekiah, and the project was able to proceed.[205] It is difficult to regard such unverified accounts as belonging to anything but a variety of the "urban legend" genre.

Nevertheless, the traditional interpretation cannot be ruled out merely because it involves a phenomenon of colossal magnitude that modern science would dismiss out of hand because it cannot be verified, or because certain attempts to verify it have no credibility.

Proposal 2: The Sun's Light Lingered.   Many scholars have sought explanations in various natural phenomena. It is objected that, while God certainly

---

[204] See B. Ramm, *The Christian View of Science and Scripture* (Grand Rapids: Eerdmans, 1954), 107–10.

[205] One source for this is the *"Evening Star,* a newspaper located in Spencer, IN," according to *The Bone Yard*, a Christian newsletter for the poultry industry circulated from Oakwood, Georgia (*The Bone Yard* 3.4 [1998], 1). I thank my secretary, Carl Kelley, for alerting me to this source. We have since discovered this same story in various permutations on the Internet, some propounding it as fact and others debunking it. L. R. Bush notes the following (personal communication): In the 1970s this story was broadcast on WFAA TV in Dallas by Bob Gooding. When queries were raised, he referred only to an individual who claimed to have lost the documentation giving names and details of the story but who then presented "evidence" showing that NASA had "proved" that the earth did in fact have four corners. Independent research has found no one who claims to have been involved in these "discoveries," and it is difficult to conceive of any computer program that even hypothetically could detect such things. It is surely an embarrassment to Christian people that such claims continue to circulate. There seems to be no actual facts to support them, no one who personally claims to have been there, and no likelihood that such measurements could have been taken in any case.

is capable of performing a miracle on such a grand scale as stopping the earth on its axis, this is out of proportion to his normal ways of working, and so other naturalizing explanations are advanced. Thus, some have proposed a refraction of light that allowed for more light in order that the battle might be completed.[206] Another proposal is that light was diffused due to a rain of meteorites.[207]

Proposal 3: The Sun's Light Was Blocked.   Others argue that there was *less* light, not more, and that a solar eclipse is in view here, basing their argument in part on understanding the verb *dmm* (in vv. 12b and 13a) as "to be dark," rather than its more common translation, "to cease" or "to be quiet." The idea is that the sun ceased from shining, not from moving in its course across the sky.[208] A related proposal states that Joshua's request was for relief from the heat of the sun, in order that the battle might be fought to its conclusion. Thus, the sun "ceased" from shining due to the cloud cover associated with the hailstorm (v. 11), which at the same time killed many of the enemy and gave welcome relief from the sun's heat to the Israelites.[209] However, these views do not explain how the cloud cover would not have refreshed the Amorites as well as the Israelites. Furthermore, they do not adequately account for the parallelism of the verbs in these two verses, *dmm* and *ʿmd* ("stand"; see below).

Proposal 4: A Special Sign Was Involved.   Another set of approaches sees in Joshua's words a request for an omen involving astrological signs. These approaches consider the episode here in the context of ancient Near Eastern culture, where the movements of the sun, moon, stars, and planets were watched carefully as signs of good or ill fortune. In these interpretations, there was no extraordinary interruption of the movement of heavenly bodies, only an alignment that could be taken as a good or evil omen. Thus, one scholar first proposed that Joshua's request was for a favorable sign for Israel, one in which both the sun and moon would be visible at the same time: the sun rising and standing in the sky in the east before the moon had set in the west.[210] The sun would "stop" or "wait" in opposition to the moon, which "stood" or "waited" for the sun. This typically was the fourteenth day of the month in

---

[206] Gruenthaner, "Two Sun Miracles." For citations of older proposals, see Ramm, *The Christian View of Science and Scripture*, 108–9.

[207] W. Pythian-Adams, "A Meteorite of the Fourteenth Century B.C.," *PEQ* 78 (1946): 116–24.

[208] R. D. Wilson, "Understanding 'The Sun Stood Still,'" *PTR* 16 (1918): 46–54 (reprinted in W. C. Kaiser, Jr., ed., *Classical Evangelical Essays in Old Testament Interpretation* [Grand Rapids: Baker, 1972], 61–65). A more recent argument for this is J. Sawyer, "Joshua 10:12–14 and the Solar Eclipse of 30 September 1131 B.C.," *PEQ* 104 (1972): 139–46.

[209] E. W. Maunder, "A Misinterpreted Miracle," *The Expositor* 10 (1910): 359–72; id., "Beth-Horon, The Battle of," *ISBE* 1:469–71; Kaiser, *More Hard Sayings of the Old Testament* (Downers Grove: InterVarsity, 1992), 123–26.

[210] J. S. Holladay, Jr., "The Day(s) the *Moon* Stood Still," *JBL* 87 (1968): 166–78.

ancient Near Eastern omen texts. A slight variation on this argues that, since the Canaanites would likely have seen such an opposition as a sign favorable to them as well (not as an evil omen), Joshua's request was uttered as a polemic in order to demonstrate to the Canaanites that he could control these elements of nature simply by praying to his God.[211] Another variation suggests that Joshua's request was for the sun and moon to stand in opposition, not on the fourteenth day of the month, which the Canaanites would have seen as propitious for them, but rather on the fifteenth, which they would have interpreted as an evil omen for them. Joshua himself need not have believed in such omens, but he asked for this knowing that his enemies would have, thus using their own beliefs against them.[212]

These approaches have the advantage that such omens were clearly part of the cultural and religious environment of the ancient Near East, and it is possible that such a practice was followed here. They have the disadvantage, however, that the text itself gives no indication at all that omens or signs (for good or for evil) were in view here. If what occurred was such a radical event as an omen that the Gibeonites would have interpreted as having been a message to them from Israel's God (whether portending victory for Israel or boding ill for them), then we should expect some sort of indication that they indeed feared the Israelites or their God and that the omen or sign was effective.[213]

Proposal 5: The Passage Is Figurative. Two proposals take into account the nature of poetry, since vv. 12b–13a (and possibly v. 13b, as well) are poetic (see NIV's layout). One such proposal is that the words spoken to the sun and moon in v. 12b originated with the poet who authored the fragment (and perhaps the book), not with Joshua or Yahweh, and they were a command to these heavenly bodies to "be speechless with terror, be stunned into motionless rigidity," that is, that they should have "a stunned reaction in the face of a startling catastrophe or astonishing revelation."[214] This proposal has support in that *dmm*, "to be quiet," does indeed indicate on occasion "silence in the face of an impending catastrophe or one that has already struck, or in preparation for a revelation."[215] It rests on the analogy of such poetic passages as Exod 15:16, where the Moabites, Edomites, and Canaanites are terri-

---

[211] Younger, *Ancient Conquest Accounts*, 212–20, especially p. 215.

[212] Walton, "Joshua 10:12–15."

[213] Among the omen interpretations, Walton's view is the most plausible, since he understands the request to have been for the sun and the moon to align in such a way as to be interpreted as an unfavorable sign to the enemy (not one that the enemy might interpret as favorable). However, Walton's solution involves a number of interpretive assumptions that stretch the limits of normal usage, which makes it less plausible.

[214] Nelson, *Joshua*, 144–45.

[215] A. Baumann, "דָּמָה *dāmāh* II," *TDOT* 3:260–65 (the quote is from p. 261).

fied of Israel: "Terror and dread will fall upon them. // By the power of your arm they *will be as still (dmm)* [i.e., dumbstruck, silent, in awe] as a stone // —until your people pass by, O LORD," or Hab 3:11, which states that "sun and moon *stood still (ʿmd)* [i.e., were dumbstruck, silent, in awe] in the heavens // at the glint of your flying arrows, at the lightning of your flashing spears." This is an attractive option, since it deals with the language of the text on its own terms, but it suffers from the (perhaps fatal) objection that v. 13b makes it clear that the position or movement of the sun and moon were integral parts of the phenomenon; they were not just passive addressees, as this proposal would have it.[216]

Others have argued that the poetic nature of the passage indicates that it was never intended to be taken literally.[217] Rather, it describes the battle in cosmic terms, in the same way that Judg 5:20 mentions that the stars were involved in the Israelites' battle against Sisera and his army: "From the heavens the stars fought, // from their courses they fought against Sisera." We can also cite the aforementioned passage from Habakkuk, where an awe-inspiring appearance of the Lord in a vision is described, and the sun and moon are described in terms similar to what we find here in Joshua 10 (Hab 3:11). No one suggests concerning these two passages that there were any extraordinary astronomical or geophysical phenomena involving the sun, moon, or stars; rather, they are easily recognized as figurative expressions in poetic form, describing the totality of Yahweh's victory over the Canaanites (in the first case) or the awesomeness of Yahweh's appearance (in the second case).

Thus, one scholar asserts that vv. 12b–13b are simply poetic expressions of information contained in corresponding prose assertions. The prose account of the all-night march (v. 9) is described in the poetic text as the moon's standing still (v. 13a), since the moon's light would have facilitated this march; likewise, the prose account of the entire battle, which was a lengthy one and which concluded "at sunset" (v. 27), is described in the poetic text as the sun's stopping in the middle of the sky and delaying setting for a full day (v. 13b).[218] Similar relationships between poetic and prose texts can be found elsewhere, most notably in Exod 15:1–18, which is a poetic description of the events that are told in a prose narrative in Exodus 14, and Judges 5, which is a

---

[216] R. Nelson, who proposes this option, agrees that v. 13b speaks of the movement or position of the sun and moon (*Joshua*, 145), but he argues that the poetic fragment of vv. 12b–13a was supplemented by another author in v. 13b, in "an act of demythologizing, of making orthodox a problematic bit of tradition." According to Nelson, this author was troubled by the direct address to the sun and moon, and so he wrote v. 13b in order to salvage the orthodoxy of the passage, transforming what had been "mythopoetic rhetoric" into an account of a long day. Nelson's approach sees irreconcilable differences between vv. 12b–13a on the one hand and v. 13b on the other.

[217] E.g., R. deVaux, *The Early History of Israel* (Philadelphia: Westminster, 1978), 634–35; J. Sailhamer, *NIV Compact Bible Commentary* (Grand Rapids: Zondervan, 1994), 191.

[218] Sailhamer, *NIV Compact Bible Commentary*, 191.

poetic reflection upon the prose text in Judges 4. Given the fact that poetic texts are indeed frequently figurative in their expression,[219] this possibility has much to commend it.

Evaluation. The extraordinary attention devoted to this passage and the myriad attempts to interpret it should give us pause in declaring with too much certainty what the passage signifies in its every detail.[220] Many plausible elements can be found in almost every solution. Furthermore, almost all of the solutions fall within the parameters of orthodoxy. Most of them are also defended by believing Christians with a very high regard for the Bible's accuracy. Nevertheless, the following points can be made, which may help to narrow the options.

In the first place, the reference to the sun's position over Gibeon and the moon's over the Valley of Aijalon is significant. The town of Aijalon was seven to ten miles west of Gibeon,[221] so the reference points here are to the east and to the west: the sun was to "stand/cease" over Gibeon[222] to the east and the moon over Aijalon to the west. If a naturalistic phenomenon is in view here, then the time of day referred to was the early morning, as the sun was rising in the east and before the moon had set in the west.[223] This would make a request for prolonging the daylight so that the battle could be finished seem rather strange, since the time of day was in the morning. Most interpretations that see the miracle as one of prolonging the daylight—whether by stopping the earth's rotation or by a refraction of light—argue that this request came toward the end of the day, when it would have been obvious that more time was needed to finish the battle. Thus, this observation argues against the traditional interpretations that see a monumental stopping of the

---

[219] See Howard, *Introduction to the Old Testament Historical Books*, 27–28.

[220] The options surveyed above represent the major approaches to this passage, but they by no means exhaust the proposals made. Good surveys of the abundant literature on this topic include the following (although each one emphasizes different aspects of it): Ramm, *Christian View of Science and Scripture*, 107–10, 116–17; Gruenthaner, "Two Sun Miracles"; Goslinga, *Joshua, Judges, Ruth*, 98–101, 189–93; Holladay, "The Day(s) the *Moon* Stood Still," 166; Boling, *Joshua*, 282–85; Nelson, *Joshua*, 141–45.

[221] See Rasmussen, *NIV Atlas of the Bible*, 94.

[222] Even such a seemingly simple matter of translating "over Gibeon" is not without its problems because the preposition here is בְּ, which normally is translated "in, with, by means of." Although prepositions are exceptionally flexible in their meanings, no major lexicon gives a meaning of "over" for בְּ (see BDB, *HALOT, DCH*, s.v.); the normal preposition for this is עַל. If we translate בְּ as "in" here, we must understand it to mean that the sun and moon were to be considered from vantage points in Gibeon and in the Valley of Aijalon. Perhaps בְּ was chosen here, rather than עַל, for poetic reasons (e.g., line length, syllable balancing, or alliteration).

[223] See Keil, *Book of Joshua*, 108–9; B. Margalit, "The Day the Sun Did Not Stand Still: A New Look at Joshua X 8–15," *VT* 42 (1992): 466–91 (observation on pp. 479–80); Walton, "Joshua 10:12–14," 182.

sun (i.e., the earth's rotation) in its tracks.[224]

Second, the proposals that consider the verb *dmm* as meaning "to cease from shining"—and thus speak of the sky darkening, due to a solar eclipse, the hailstorm, or some other means—do not adequately account for the parallel verb *ʿmd*, "to stand," which describes the moon's action in v. 13a and which is used of the sun itself in v. 13b. The poetic parallelism in v. 13a and the narrative fleshing out of the details in v. 13b argue that what is in view here is the movement or positioning of the sun, not a darkening. The postulate of a solar eclipse has the further difficulty that astronomers know exactly when solar eclipses took place in Central Palestine between 1500 and 1000 B.C.: August 19, 1157 (8:35 a.m.), September 30, 1131 (12:53 p.m.), and November 23, 1041 (7:40 a.m.). None of these fits the dates assigned to Joshua, whether one adopts an early or a late date for the exodus.[225]

Third, as we have noted, according to v. 14, there was never a day like this one before or since, not because of some extraordinary astronomical phenomenon, but because the Lord listened to the voice of a man and fought for Israel. The author has chosen to marvel at this fact, and not the supposed marvel of the sun's "stopping." This is either because the sun did not actually stop (and we have misunderstood what did happen) or because, despite whatever ordinary or extraordinary event may or may not have taken place with the sun and the moon, the most important facts for him were these: (1) the interaction between God and his people and (2) the exalting of Joshua, not any cosmic doings for their own sake.

Conclusion. If these points are valid, then the proposal with the least problems would seem to be that the words directed to the sun and moon were figurative, describing the battle in poetic terms but making no comment at all about any extraordinary positioning or movement of the sun and the moon. This approach has the advantage of dealing with a familiar, demonstrable phenomenon found in the texts of the Bible—the often figurative nature of poetry. It has the further advantage of the existence of several other poetic texts that use similar language, which can help in the interpretation here.

Thus, we present a translation of the passage that attempts to clarify the points made above. The indented, italicized lines are poetic. Words in parenthesis are added for clarity in the process of going from one language to

---

[224] If the sun's position at the time these words were spoken can be shown to have been of no consequence, then the likelihood that these verses speak of an actual stoppage of the sun (or the earth's rotation) is increased. Goslinga, who believes that the day was lengthened by the sun stopping still, does understand that "it must have still been morning when Joshua spoke his famous words" (*Joshua, Judges, Ruth*, 100), but he does not explain why Joshua should have made this request at this time of the day.

[225] See B. J. Beitzel, *The Moody Atlas of the Bible* (Chicago: Moody, 1985), 97, on this point.

another. Words in brackets are additions based on textual or grammatical issues discussed above.[226]

[12]At that time, Joshua spoke to (i.e., petitioned) the LORD, on the day of the LORD's giving the Amorites into the power of the sons of Israel. And [the LORD] said in the sight of Israel,

> *"O sun, over Gibeon stop,*
> > *O moon, over the valley of Aijalon (stop)!"*
> [13]*So the sun stopped*
> > *and the moon, it stood still*
> *Until [the LORD] took vengeance [against] the nation of his enemies.*
> Is it not (all) written in the book of Jashar?
> > *And the sun stood still*
> > > *in the midst of the heavens,*
> > *And it did not hurry to go (down)*
> > > *about a complete day.*

[14]And there has not been (a day) like that day before it or after it, when the LORD obeyed the voice of a man, for the LORD fought for Israel.

What, then, do vv. 12–14 tell us? First, Joshua appealed to God for help (v. 12a), but his words are not recorded. Then, in response, God spoke to the sun and moon, ordering them to stop, and they "obeyed." They maintained this obedience until God took his vengeance against his enemies (vv. 12b–13). Then this is all placed into perspective in the amazing fact that the Lord actually listened and responded to the request of one man. (v. 14).

If they are poetic and figurative, the words in vv. 12b–13 do not describe a literal astronomical or geophysical phenomena. They do, however, tie in with the prose account of the day's events by means of a few key-word or associative connections. In the first instance, the words about the sun's stopping, standing still, and not hurrying to go down simply describe the entire day's battle, which ended when the sun did go down (v. 27). The key words here are "sun" *(šemeš)* and "go (down)" *(bôʾ)*, found in both the prose and poetic parts of the passage. Perhaps the day's events simply seemed especially

---

[226] There are nine poetic lines (or half-lines) here (for this terminology and the method of counting stresses here, see Howard, *The Structure of Psalms 93–100* [Winona Lake: Eisenbrauns, 1997], 28–30 and n. 9). They are fairly well balanced in terms of the stresses in the Hb. text: In the first set, we have stress patterns of 3,3,2,2,3, while in the second set, we see 2,2,2,2. We must note that v. 13b (containing the second set of poetic lines) is not generally analyzed as poetry—and this is perhaps the major weakness of this approach, because otherwise it is difficult to deal with the assertions of v. 13b. However, the four lines here are as easily poetic as the three lines in v. 13a (including the presence of a *wayyiqtōl* verbal construction in both sets); virtually no one questions the poetic nature of v. 13a, and, we would argue, v. 13b is no different in kind.

long.[227] The words about the moon's stopping and standing still are linked with the all-night march (v. 9). Here there are no key-word links, but the connections between the moon and such a march are obvious. The second set of poetic lines reiterates what was said in the first set, adding the words about the sun's not hurrying to go down, which reinforces the picture of the sun's "obeying" God's words.

What do the words addressed to the sun and the moon mean, then, if not that the earth stopped rotating or shining (or something similar)? Simply this: that God was directing the sun and the moon to fight for Israel in the same way that the stars fought for Israel in Deborah's day (Judg 5:20), or else that they were to stand amazed as he fought for Israel, just as they did in Hab 3:11. We do not imagine that these statements in Judges and Habakkuk mean anything except that God's victory was total and that his majesty is awe-inspiring. Do we properly read these statements as involving universe-altering astronomical or geophysical phenomena? The issue is the same in Josh 10:12–13. The suggestion offered here is that the language is similar to the psalmist's who urges the rivers to clap their hands and the mountains to sing for joy (Ps 98:8) or the trees of the field to sing for joy (Ps 96:12), or when Isaiah writes that "the mountains and hills will burst into song before you, and all the trees of the field will clap their hands" (Isa 55:12).

The sun and the moon "obeyed" God's commands, and, remarkably, God "obeyed" a man's request (v. 14). The expression in v. 14 is literally, "and the LORD listened [to] the voice of a man." The verbal construction here is one of the most common ways that Hebrew has to express obedience.[228] God was not bound to "obey" Joshua's request, of course. However, the fact that he did is what was so remarkable. Thus, this correspondence between vv. 13 and 14 in terms of obedience highlights the most remarkable feature of the days' events: it was a day on which the Lord himself "obeyed" a mere man and fought for Israel (see also on v. 14). The suggestion of a figurative interpretation is not a denial that God could perform such a miracle, and one does not need to accept the figurative view because of any concern over scientific problems. God rules over all natural laws and can do whatever he chooses to do. The figurative view is suggested because of the literary features mentioned above, not because of any concern over God's sovereignty over nature.

10:13 The *Book of Jashar* was an extrabiblical book from which the author of the Book of Joshua took some or all of the information in this sec-

---

[227] This is suggested by Keil (*Book of Joshua*, 109–12), who understands the day to have been lengthened either in reality *or in the Israelites' perception*. Younger quotes a Confederate soldier's words in a letter about the battle of Antietam to illustrate the latter point; the soldier, commenting on the ferocity of the fighting, wrote, "The sun seemed almost to go backwards, and it appeared as if night would never come!" (Younger, *Ancient Conquest Accounts,* 314, n. 55).

[228] See BDB, 1034, § 1.m.

tion (see discussion above). It is mentioned again in 2 Sam 1:18 and in the Old Greek versions of 1 Kgs 8:13. The reason for its inclusion here probably is not because the author of Joshua was using it as his only source for the information. Rather, he was stating, in effect, "If you don't believe it, go read about it in the *Book of Jashar.* Even that book has a record of this event."

10:14 This is the climax of the section, where the author leaves off describing the events and gives his own evaluation of them. The author of Joshua marvels that the Lord listened to the voice of one man and fought on Israel's behalf as a result. Just as the sun and moon obeyed the Lord's commands, so here the Lord "obeyed" Joshua's request.

In what way was it true that the Lord had never listened to a man before this or since? After all, Moses had spoken with the Lord, and the Lord had listened to him. In the wilderness, for example, the Lord told Moses that he was going to destroy the Israelites and make a great nation out of Moses, but he was dissuaded by Moses' prayerful intervention (Num 14:11–21). Also, Moses himself claimed that the Lord had listened to him (Deut 9:19; 10:10).

The answer lies in the precise wording used here, which is *šāmaʿ bĕqôl*, meaning "to listen to" or "to obey" (lit., "to listen [to] the voice"). This is a much stronger way of expressing obedience than merely to say that someone listened to or heard someone else (i.e., without *qôl*, "voice"). The wording used here is only found three times in the Old Testament with "the LORD" as the subject. In the first instance, the context is similar to that here, but the object is the nation of Israel, not an individual (Num 21:3: "The LORD listened to *[šāmaʿ bĕqôl]* Israel's plea and gave the Canaanites over to them"). The second instance is here in Josh 10:14, the first time this precise wording is found with reference to an individual's voice. In the third instance, the Lord did listen to the voice of a man, as he had to Joshua's, but it was many centuries later, after the writing of the material here in Joshua 10. It involved another great individual, Elijah, when the Lord restored the life of a young boy on the basis of Elijah's plea (1 Kgs 17:22).[229]

This response on the Lord's part was indeed remarkable. He "obeyed" Joshua's request. Not even Moses, the great leader whose shoes Joshua was attempting to fill, had received such an honor. The Lord honored Joshua in many ways throughout his tenure as Israel's leader, but this was one of the most remarkable.

How did the Lord obey Joshua's request? How did he fight for Israel? In the interpretation offered here, it was not by stopping the earth's rotation (although he certainly could have done so had he chosen to), but rather by throwing the enemy into confusion (v. 10), by sending the hailstorm (v. 11),

---

[229] In two other instances, the same wording is found with "God" as subject, not "the LORD": Judg 13:9; Ps 55:19.

and by commanding even the sun and the moon to "fight" for Israel, that is, by declaring total war against the Amorites (vv. 12–13). The author has come at the subject of God's fighting for Israel from several different angles in this passage, and v. 14 shows that he did this at Joshua's request. Because of this, it was a marvelous day like no other before or since! This is an excellent example of the power of one person's influence and of the power of prayer. It also is one more brush stroke in the picture painted in the book concerning Joshua's God-anointed leadership and his position as a worthy successor to Moses.

10:15 Verse 15 is out of place chronologically. It is scarcely possible or logical that Joshua would have interrupted the completion of the battle's business near Gibeon and the other cities (including Makkedah: v. 10) and marched the entire congregation many miles back to their base camp at Gilgal, only to return to Makkedah and conclude the business of dealing with the Amorite coalition (vv. 16–27). The anomaly of v. 15's position is magnified when we realize that the words of this verse are found—intact and verbatim—in v. 43, where they make much more sense.

Four solutions present themselves. First, those who see the *Book of Jashar* quote extending through v. 15 have little problem here, since this verse was thus part of that source, incorporated wholesale into the Book of Joshua. These scholars see v. 15 functioning proleptically, anticipating the end of the matter that comes in v. 43. In the *Book of Jashar,* the account would have omitted the details of the city-by-city conquests of vv. 16–42 and just concluded with the statement of v. 15/v. 43, which occurred just once in that book. Second, both verses could have been included intentionally, each closing off a section of the narrative.[230] Third, other scholars see v. 15 as a scribal duplication (i.e., a transmission error), since the ends of vv. 14 and 42 are similar in Hebrew. Thus, only v. 43 should be seen as original. Fourth, the Old Greek omits both vv. 15 and 43, which may indicate that neither verse was present in the original text. Of these four possibilities, the second or third appears to be the most plausible.

(4) Southern Coalition Kings Defeated (10:16–27)

[16]Now the five kings had fled and hidden in the cave at Makkedah. [17]When Joshua was told that the five kings had been found hiding in the cave at Makkedah, [18]he said, "Roll large rocks up to the mouth of the cave, and post some men there to guard it. [19]But don't stop! Pursue your enemies, attack them from the rear and don't let them reach their cities, for the LORD your God has given them into your hand."

[20]So Joshua and the Israelites destroyed them completely—almost to a man—

---

[230] On this phenomenon, see Davis, *No Falling Words,* 86–87, n. 9.

but the few who were left reached their fortified cities. [21]The whole army then returned safely to Joshua in the camp at Makkedah, and no one uttered a word against the Israelites.

[22]Joshua said, "Open the mouth of the cave and bring those five kings out to me." [23]So they brought the five kings out of the cave—the kings of Jerusalem, Hebron, Jarmuth, Lachish and Eglon. [24]When they had brought these kings to Joshua, he summoned all the men of Israel and said to the army commanders who had come with him, "Come here and put your feet on the necks of these kings." So they came forward and placed their feet on their necks.

[25]Joshua said to them, "Do not be afraid; do not be discouraged. Be strong and courageous. This is what the LORD will do to all the enemies you are going to fight." [26]Then Joshua struck and killed the kings and hung them on five trees, and they were left hanging on the trees until evening.

[27]At sunset Joshua gave the order and they took them down from the trees and threw them into the cave where they had been hiding. At the mouth of the cave they placed large rocks, which are there to this day.

This section completes the story of the battle of Gibeon, begun in vv. 1–5. It tells of the final disposition of the coalition kings, and it also recapitulates some of the previous action (see especially v. 20). After God's decisive interventions (vv. 10–11,12–13), the five Amorite kings fled from the Israelites and hid in a cave at Makkedah, where Joshua sealed them up in order to capture them (vv. 16–19). The Israelites pursued and killed the enemy forces (v. 20), the kings were brought out and executed, and their bodies were hung on five trees until sundown (vv. 22–26), after which they were thrown into the very cave in which they had attempted to hide from Joshua earlier (v. 27). The first time, Joshua had sealed them up in order to capture them, and he now sealed them up permanently.

10:16–18   The five Amorite kings fled the scene and hid in a cave near Makkedah. Joshua's instructions in v. 18 were to seal them up, so that the battle could be pursued to its conclusion, which was to destroy all of the people (vv. 19–20). After this, he would deal with the kings (vv. 22 –27).

10:19–20   Joshua's instructions continue in v. 19, where he shifted the focus to the Israelites and their duty to press the attack on their enemies (cf. v. 11). Addressing the people with an emphatic pronoun, he commanded them *not* to stand or wait (*ʿmd*)—in contrast to the moon, which had earlier done precisely that (*ʿmd;* v. 13); we might paraphrase by saying, "*You*, in contrast to the moon, *you* are not to stand/wait, but rather pursue ..." They were not to allow their enemies to go *(lābôʾ)* into their cities (v. 19). In v. 13b, the sun did not hurry to go down *(lābôʾ)* into its resting place; neither were Israel's enemies to be allowed to go into their places of security. The fortified cities (v. 20) offered sanctuary to their people, which is why the earlier ambush at Ai was designed to draw the people out of their city (8:17).

The assurance that the Lord had already delivered Israel's enemies into their hands once again reminded them of his presence and that God himself was Israel's warrior (see notes on 1:3; 6:2; 10:8). The gifts of the land and the destruction of its people had already been accomplished for Israel.

The slaughter of the Canaanites was great, but some people escaped (v. 20). This explains why there were still people in these towns later (see especially vv. 31–37).

10:21   The battle of Gibeon ended with the people returning safely (literally, "in peace") to the encampment at Makkedah. Things had come to such a peaceful, satisfying conclusion that "no one uttered a word ...." The expression is literally "no one sharpened his tongue," and, in this context, it refers to opposition against Israel.[231] In Exod 11:7, the same expression occurs, when Moses promised a safe night for the Israelites at the same time the Egyptian firstborn were going to be killed, except that it says "no dog will sharpen its tongue against any man or beast" (NIV has "not a dog will bark at any man or animal"). That is, so safe would the Israelites be that not even a dog would bark against them. Dogs were despised, accursed animals in the ancient Near East (in the Bible, see 1 Sam 17:43; 2 Sam 9:8; 2 Kgs 8:13), and the use of almost the exact expression here in Joshua may be the author's way of reminding the Israelites how God miraculously delivered them at an earlier time in Egypt, and subtly equating the accursed Canaanites with dogs (i.e., no Canaanite spoke against the Israelites now, just as no dog had "spoken" against them in Egypt).

There was no opposition now to Israel, and they were able to settle peacefully into this place in the land. In contrast to the result of Israel's disobedience earlier, now things were going well for the nation, illustrating the principle that when the nation obeyed, God blessed.

10:22–23   Joshua instructed that the kings should be brought out from the cave, and the people obeyed. This is a straightforward enough narrative, but it again shows the people's obedience, in contrast to their earlier disobedience at Ai.

10:24–25   Joshua instructed his army commanders to place their feet on their enemies' necks, which they did (v. 24). The word for commander here—*qāṣîn*—is relatively rare and means "ruler, leader, superior" in general, but "commander" in contexts such as this. By etymology, it means "a person who has to decide something."[232] It is different from the term used in 9:15—*nāśîʾ*—which is usually translated as "leader," "chief," or "prince." Here, in a context with more military overtones than the story of the Gibeonite treaty has, its use is appropriate. The term is part of the expression "army command-

---

[231] The NEB has, "No one suffered so much as a scratch on his tongue," and the REB has, "Not one of the Israelites suffered so much as a scratch."

[232] *HALOT*, 1122.

ers" (lit., "commanders of the men of war"); the term "people of war" found in 8:3 is not used here, probably because the focus in this text has more of a military orientation, in contrast to the more community-wide orientation in chap. 8 (see note at 8:3).

When the commanders put their feet on their enemies' necks (v. 24), this was clearly a gesture of victory. In the Bible, we see similar imagery in several texts, including Ps 18:39 (Hb. 40) // 2 Sam 22:40, which says, "You made my adversaries bow under me," and Ps 110:1, where the Lord says to the Messiah, "Sit at my right hand until I make your enemies a footstool for your feet." In the New Testament, this imagery is again applied to Jesus, the Messiah, in 1 Cor 15:25–27, where God places Jesus' enemies "under his feet" (quoting from Ps 8:6).[233]

When Joshua encouraged his commanders in v. 25, he was again demonstrating his leadership qualities. He now had the authority to give the same encouraging exhortation to others with which the Lord had encouraged him: (1) The words "Do not be afraid; do not be discouraged" were spoken to him by God in 8:1, after the defeat at Ai; and (2) "Be strong and courageous" are the same words God spoke to him in his initial charge (1:6–7,9). God had also told him in 10:8, "Do not be afraid of them." God would be with his people, no matter what the circumstance, no matter what the battle.

"This" in v. 25 ("This is what the LORD will do ...") refers back to the subjugation of Israel's enemies described in v. 24. Just as Israel's commanders were physically stepping on these five kings' necks, so the Lord would do to *all* of Israel's enemies, certainly an encouraging thought in light of what lay ahead.

10:26–27 The climactic moment is told tersely: Joshua struck, killed, and hung on trees the five kings (v. 26), doing to them what he had earlier done to the king of Ai (8:29). As he had done before, so now also he took the bodies down before sundown (v. 27), in accordance with the Mosaic legislation against exposure after sundown (see on 8:29). Once again, obedience was now the watchword.

The sun's setting in v. 27 brings to a close the sun's involvement on this momentous day. Regardless of the precise nature of its involvement in vv. 12–14, it now marked the completion of this historic day.

In an ironic twist, the kings' bodies were thrown into the cave where they had been hiding earlier: the place they had thought would be their refuge ended up as their tomb. This cave was sealed with large stones—perma-

---

[233] Cp. also 1 Kgs 5:3; Isa 51:23. Outside the Bible, Tukulti-Ninurta I (ca. 1242–1206 B.C.) described his treatment of Kashtiliah IV, king of Babylon, in similar fashion: "His royal neck I trod with my foot, like a footstool" (quoted in Boling, *Joshua*, 286). Several reliefs from Egypt and Mesopotamia show kings stepping on their enemies, although not their necks specifically. See *ANET,* figs. 308, 393, and R. W. Vunderink, "Foot," *ISBE* 2:332 and figure there.

nently, this time (cf. v. 18): these stones were still there "to this day," that is, at the time of the writing of this account. The section ends almost identically to the way in which the story of the battle of Ai ends: there, too, the king had been hung on a tree, his body taken down before sunset, covered with a pile of large stones, which were still visible "to this day" (8:29; see on 7:22–26). In whatever circumstances—whether facing an enemy in an insignificant town that had defeated them once or a coalition of determined enemies who would initiate the attack—the result was the same: God gave the victory, and the enemies' fate was the same, now that Israel was taking pains to obey its God.

7. Southern Campaign Completed (10:28–43)

Chapter 10 concludes with a quick overview of the rest of the southern campaign, in which seven cities are the focus (vv. 28–39), followed by a summary of the entire area that was subdued, along with a theological evaluation (vv. 40–43).

(1) Seven Cities Destroyed (10:28–39)

[27]At sunset Joshua gave the order and they took them down from the trees and threw them into the cave where they had been hiding. At the mouth of the cave they placed large rocks, which are there to this day.

[28]That day Joshua took Makkedah. He put the city and its king to the sword and totally destroyed everyone in it. He left no survivors. And he did to the king of Makkedah as he had done to the king of Jericho.

[29]Then Joshua and all Israel with him moved on from Makkedah to Libnah and attacked it. [30]The LORD also gave that city and its king into Israel's hand. The city and everyone in it Joshua put to the sword. He left no survivors there. And he did to its king as he had done to the king of Jericho.

[31]Then Joshua and all Israel with him moved on from Libnah to Lachish; he took up positions against it and attacked it. [32]The LORD handed Lachish over to Israel, and Joshua took it on the second day. The city and everyone in it he put to the sword, just as he had done to Libnah. [33]Meanwhile, Horam king of Gezer had come up to help Lachish, but Joshua defeated him and his army—until no survivors were left.

[34]Then Joshua and all Israel with him moved on from Lachish to Eglon; they took up positions against it and attacked it. [35]They captured it that same day and put it to the sword and totally destroyed everyone in it, just as they had done to Lachish.

[36]Then Joshua and all Israel with him went up from Eglon to Hebron and attacked it. [37]They took the city and put it to the sword, together with its king, its villages and everyone in it. They left no survivors. Just as at Eglon, they totally destroyed it and everyone in it.

[38]Then Joshua and all Israel with him turned around and attacked Debir.

³⁹They took the city, its king and its villages, and put them to the sword. Everyone in it they totally destroyed. They left no survivors. They did to Debir and its king as they had done to Libnah and its king and to Hebron.

10:28–39 The battle of Gibeon (vv. 1–27) is the last in the Book of Joshua for which a detailed account is given (the others are Jericho and Ai). Hereafter, only bare-bones summaries are given. The dominant mood now, especially in this section, is that Israel almost effortlessly took every city, king, and people it encountered, by God's power, and that it annihilated every living thing in these cities. The reasons for this annihilation are rooted in the concept of total destruction as a sacral act, the ḥērem, which we have discussed earlier (see the excursus on "Destruction and Devoted Things in Joshua" at the end of chap. 6). Now that Israel had faced its greatest crises—disobedience and defeat at Ai and treaty entanglement with a forbidden people, the Gibeonites—God gave the Canaanites and their cities into the Israelites' hands.

In this section, the kings and people of seven cities are mentioned in a series of formulaic accounts as having engaged Israel in battle and having been completely destroyed. The cities are Makkedah, Libnah, Lachish, Gezer, Eglon, Hebron, and Debir. They were all in the southern portion of the land; the Israelites had entered Canaan in the middle (on a north-south axis), and their campaigns went through the middle first, then turned south (chap. 10), and then north (chap. 11). The fact that there are exactly seven cities here—no more and no less—suggests that this may be a summarizing account, showing the destructions of representative cities and not intended to be comprehensive, detailing every city captured. Furthermore, we read later of four additional cities in the south that Joshua and the Israelites took, which argues in the same direction. The cities were Geder, Hormah, Arad, and Adullam (12:13–15; see further the commentary on 12:7–24).

Certain patterns can be discerned in this account. The overall account is regular, but no one of the seven miniaccounts is exactly the same as the other, which lends a flavor of historical plausibility to the passage.[234] A balanced structure centered around Gezer can easily be seen as follows.[235]

---

[234] Despite Nelson's assertion to the contrary, who prefers the less formulaic stories about some of the cities later in Joshua and in Judges 1 (Nelson, *Joshua*, 147).

[235] This figure is adapted from Boling, *Joshua*, 294. For much more elaborate configurations, see J. K. Hoffmeier, *Israel in Egypt: The Evidence for the Authenticity of the Exodus Tradition* (New York: Oxford University, 1997), 37; Younger, "The 'Conquest' of the South," 259–60.

CITY (OBJECT OF DESTRUCTION)	COMPARISON
A Makkedah (king, city, people)	like Jericho
B Libnah (king, city, people)	like Jericho
C Lachish (city, people)	like Libnah
D Horam, king of Gezer	--------------
C′ Eglon (city, people)	like Lachish
B′ Hebron (king, villages, people)	like Eglon
A′ Debir (king, villages, people)	like Libnah and Hebron

The list is constructed around Gezer, for which there is no record of the Israelites' capture and destruction of its inhabitants, only the defeat of its army (v. 33). This accords with the historical reality recorded in 16:10, which says that the Ephraimites "did not dislodge the Canaanites living in Gezer; to this day the Canaanites live among the people of Ephraim," and in Judg 1:29: "Nor did Ephraim drive out the Canaanites living in Gezer, but the Canaanites continued to live there among them."[236]

Six segments of the list mention "Joshua and all Israel with him" (A, B, C, C′, B′, A′) and the fact that Joshua (A, B, C) or Joshua and all Israel (C′, B′, A′) "put it/them to the sword." Five segments mention that the Israelites "left no survivors" (A, B, D, B′, A′), and one more (C′) states that they "totally destroyed everyone." Six segments conclude by stating that Joshua did to the city in question just as he had done to a previous city or king (A, B, C, C′, B′, A′). For the first two cities, the point of comparison is Jericho; after that, it is the previously mentioned city, until the last one, which in addition refers back to the second one in the list (B and B′).[237] Five segments mention the king of the city; the two that do not are C (Lachish) and C′ (Eglon), both cities whose kings had already been killed (10:3,26). A third city from the coalition earlier in the chapter is also among the seven here: Hebron (B′). Its king *is* mentioned (despite the fact that he had already been killed), probably for reasons of structural balance in the passage.[238]

The list begins with Makkedah (v. 28), where the battle of Gibeon had ended with the Amorite kings' bodies sealed up in a cave. It proceeds in an arc northwest to Libnah (vv. 29–30), southwest to Lachish (vv. 31–32), then it is

---

[236] In addition, Gezer was an important site at a strategic crossroads. For its geographical and archaeological significance, see Younger, "The 'Conquest' of the South," 262, and bibliography there.

[237] Each of these common elements is what Younger calls a "syntagm" (see also n. 1), of which he finds ten in this list. For his complete (and detailed) analysis, see Younger, "The 'Conquest' of the South," 256–60.

[238] Woudstra suggests (*Joshua*, 183) that this king was a new king of Hebron, which would indicate that the process took some time, as 11:18 indicates: "Joshua waged war against all these kings for a long time." This is certainly possible.

interrupted by the encounter with Horam, king of Gezer, who came from some distance away, to the northwest, to the aid of Lachish (v. 33). After this, the list moves southeast to Eglon (vv. 34–35), northeast to Hebron (vv. 36–37), and south to Debir (vv. 38–39). (See map.)[239] The account of Horam, king of Gezer, coming from a distance to help his ally at Lachish and being defeated in the process (v. 33) stands in ironic contrast to the Israelite success in coming to help their new allies, the Gibeonites (vv. 1–14). It was only through the help of their God that Israel was able to succeed.

The nature of the "conquest" of these cities differed from city to city, it would appear. This is because for some, we read later of further efforts to subjugate them (e.g., Hebron: 15:13–14; Judg 1:9–10,20; Debir: Josh 15:15–17; Judg 1:12–13). Also Aijalon, which is mentioned in the battle of Gibeon (10:12), was not conquered until later (Judg 1:35).[240]

(2) Summary of the Campaign (10:40–43)

[40]**So Joshua subdued the whole region, including the hill country, the Negev, the western foothills and the mountain slopes, together with all their kings. He left no survivors. He totally destroyed all who breathed, just as the LORD, the God of Israel, had commanded.** [41]**Joshua subdued them from Kadesh Barnea to Gaza and from the whole region of Goshen to Gibeon.** [42]**All these kings and their lands Joshua conquered in one campaign, because the LORD, the God of Israel, fought for Israel.**

[43]**Then Joshua returned with all Israel to the camp at Gilgal.**

These verses bring to a close the present section, which deals with Israel's campaign in the south (chap. 10). They also hark back to chap. 9, since the first battle in chap. 10, at Gibeon, had its roots in the Gibeonites' treaty with Israel, which they made with Israel as a result of their hearing (*šmᶜ*) about what Joshua had done to Jericho and Ai (9:3). They even hark back to 9:1, where the kings of several regions in Canaan also heard (*šmᶜ*) about these things and gathered to do battle against Israel. Even though these kings are not heard from again after 9:2, the summary here in 10:40 includes two of the regions from which these kings came: the hill country and the western foothills. So, even these kings' lands were now under Israel's sovereignty. The summary is somewhat repetitive, but in v. 40, regions are in view, whereas in v. 41, boundaries or limits are described, and in v. 42, kings are mentioned.

The picture painted in this section is unequivocally one of complete and swift annihilation of people throughout the entire region. This is the implica-

---

[239] For detailed site identifications of these places, see the works in the excursus on "Identifying Geographical Entities" at the end of chap. 12.

[240] For more on the incomplete nature of the conquests, see comments on vv. 40–43.

tion of the statements that Joshua and the Israelites left no survivors in the various cities in vv. 28,30,33,37,39 (cf. also vv. 32,35). This is also the explicit testimony of vv. 40 and 42a, as well (see also the similar summaries in 11:16–23; 21:43–45). The southern campaign is seen as having been accomplished in one fell swoop (v. 42) because God fought for Israel.

However, we should anticipate here that other indications in the Book of Joshua point to a longer-lasting and less all-inclusive campaign. Passages such as Josh 11:22; 13:2–6; 14:12; 15:63; 16:10; 17:12–13; 18:2–3; 19:47; 23:4–5,7,12–13; and Judges 1 show people remaining in areas supposedly conquered and destroyed completely by the Israelites. Also, Josh 11:18 states that "Joshua waged war against all these kings for a long time (lit., 'many days')," which stands somewhat in tension with the statement in v. 42 that "all these kings and their land Joshua conquered in one campaign." Such a long-lasting campaign had been anticipated many years earlier, when the Lord told the Israelites: "I will not drive [the people of the land] out in a single year, because the land would become desolate and the wild animals too numerous for you. Little by little I will drive them out before you, until you have increased enough to take possession of the land" (Exod 23:29–30). Moses also told the people: "The LORD your God will drive out those nations before you, little by little. You will not be allowed to eliminate them all at once, or the wild animals will multiply around you" (Deut 7:22).

Thus, the picture presented in 10:28–43, and especially in vv. 40–42, must be seen as a stylized summary of sorts.[241] From one perspective—a broader, more general perspective—there was indeed a sweeping victory over the Canaanites. No significant opposition remained: the power of the Canaanites was broken and their land effectively belonged now to Israel (or, more accurately, by the end of chap. 11). The author was being hyperbolic here in order to reiterate the theological point made many times in the book that God was indeed giving Israel the entire land. However, the details of the conquest of every last city were not included (see above, on vv. 28–39), and the author acknowledged elsewhere that the conquest was indeed not complete. Thus, from another, more detailed perspective, there was still much work to be done.

The NIV's "subdued" in vv. 40–41 translates nkh, usually rendered "to strike, smite," and "conquered" in v. 42 translates lkd, usually rendered "to capture." These translations are appropriate if we remember that sometimes a "conquest" is not necessarily a complete subjugation. For example, the Germans' "conquest" of France in World War II involved the defeat of the French army and the occupation of most of France, but it did not thereby mean that all French people became German loyalists or that Germany permanently col-

---

[241] Woudstra calls it "a provisional conclusion" (*Joshua*, 184).

onized France or that it killed every French citizen. So too with many of the cities of Canaan, which were "conquered" or "subdued," but only temporarily or only in part.[242]

The dichotomy here is real, but the Book of Joshua acknowledges it. The statements in vv. 40–42 are not an example of a simplistic text uninformed by the historical realities. On the contrary, the book is careful to paint the picture in all its complex texture.[243] Sometimes land remained unconquered due to the Israelites' disobedience or inability (which, in effect, was disobedience, evidencing a lack of faith, since God had promised to be faithful and fight Israel's battles). Examples of this include Judah's failure to dislodge the Jebusites from Jerusalem (15:63), Ephraim's failure to dislodge the inhabitants of Gezer (16:10), Manasseh's failure to occupy several towns (17:12), and several examples in Judges 1.[244] Sometimes it would appear that the conquest simply was not yet complete. The best example of this is in 13:1–6, where the Lord detailed to Joshua the territory remaining to be taken, without censuring him or the people for not having done so.[245]

Thus, the biblical text is abundantly clear that what was a sweeping conquest on one level involved much hard work—and failure—on another level. The concern in 10:40–42, however, is with the broader picture: God gave a sweeping, total, effortless victory to his people in fulfillment of his promises.

10:40 Here is an overview of a region that Joshua subdued in Canaan. It included four areas: (1) the hill country and (2) the western foothills, which had been mentioned earlier (cf. 9:1), but it also encompassed (3) the Negev

---

[242] See Younger, *Ancient Conquest Accounts*, 243–44, for the example from WWII and a helpful discussion of this issue. A useful survey of the different ways in which the Book of Joshua treats those whom the Israelites did not completely destroy is found in G. Mitchell, *Together in the Land: A Reading of the Book of Joshua,* JSOTSup 134 (Sheffield: Sheffield Academic Press, 1993), 152–84.

[243] This is the point of much of L. D. Hawk's usually insightful work (*Every Promise Fulfilled: Contesting Plots in Joshua* [Louisville: Westminster/John Knox, 1991]). He traces the tensions between "conquest and compromise" (pp. 43–55) and "obedience and disobedience" (pp. 56–93), but, unfortunately, he makes little attempt to resolve them. Generally, Hawk makes a valid argument about many of the tensions in the book, but in at least two passages—1:16–18 and chap. 2— he greatly overstates his case (pp. 58–59, 60–71). On chap. 2, see further his "Problem with Pagans," in T. K. Beal and D. M. Gunn, eds., *Reading Bibles, Writing Bodies: Identity and the Book* (London: Routledge, 1997), 153–63. See also my brief critique at 1:17 and 2:12–13.

[244] On the differences between Joshua 10 and Judges 1, see, among many others, G. E. Wright, "The Literary and Historical Problem of Joshua 10 and Judges 1," *JNES* 5 (1946): 105–14; W. R. Roehrs, "The Conquest of Canaan According to Joshua and Judges," *CTM* 31 (1960): 746–60; D. I. Block, *Judges, Ruth,* NAC 6 (Nashville: Broadman & Holman, forthcoming).

[245] Other evangelical treatments of the problem of a complete versus incomplete conquest include Keil, *Book of Joshua*, 125–26 (on 11:16–23) and Hess, *Joshua*, 284–86 (on 21:43–45). See also the work of another evangelical, Younger (*Ancient Conquest Accounts*, 241–47), who shows many parallels to the all-encompassing claims of the Joshua text in the ancient Near East. He rightly labels such claims as hyperbolic.

and (4) the mountain slopes.[246] The hill country was the heart of Canaan, the central highlands that included Ai and Gibeon in the north and Hebron and Debir in the south. The Negev was the wilderness area in the southern part of the land (it is still called this in modern-day Israel). The western foothills is the "Shephelah," the area between the central highlands and the coastal plain.

The mountain slopes are either the western slopes leading down to the lowlands near the Mediterranean Sea or, more probably, the steep slopes going down to the Dead Sea to the east of the central mountainous area (see also 12:8). The reference may be, more precisely, to the stream beds or ravines in one of these areas. The term used here (*ʾăšēdâ*) only occurs six times in the Old Testament, and its meaning is not exactly clear. On the basis of its etymology, which includes the idea of pouring a liquid, as well as the form in Num 21:15 (*ʾešed*), which describes a stream bed in hilly territory (see NASB and NRSV: "the slope of the wadis"), some propose that it refers to waterfalls or "partings of water."[247]

This summary statement covers the central and southern portions of the land of Canaan, but it does not include the coastlands (see 13:2–6, which lists Philistine territory along the coast, along with other lands, as still remaining to be taken).

The destruction of the region's peoples was total, according to this verse. Twice the total annihilation is described: (1) there were no survivors, and (2) Joshua "totally destroyed all who breathed." The first assertion is made five times in the previous battle summary (vv. 28,30,33,37,39); and the second, four times (vv. 28,35,37,39), except that here the statement is more comprehensive: Joshua totally destroyed "*all who breathed.*" This was all done in fulfillment of the Lord's commands (see Deut 20:16–18 and the introduction to chap. 6). Once again the theme of obedience to God's law and his commands is prominent.

10:41 Now the boundaries or limits of the territory that the Israelites subdued are delimited. The southern extreme stretched from Kadesh Barnea in the east to Gaza in the west. Neither town has been mentioned previously in Joshua, and, in the case of Gaza, it was a Philistine city that had not been conquered: it remained unconquered in 13:3 and did not come under Israelite control until the days of David (2 Sam 5:17–25; 1 Kgs 4:24).

The northern extreme stretched from "the whole region of Goshen" as far as Gibeon (see map). Goshen is not the area in the northeastern Nile Delta

---

[246] For geographical details concerning these regions, see Rasmussen, *NIV Atlas of the Bible*, 18–19,42 (hill country), 47–48 (western foothills), 49–51 (Negev). On the "mountain slopes," see next paragraph.

[247] See M. Noth, *Das Buch Josua*, 3d ed., HAT 7 (Tübingen: Mohr [Siebeck], 1971), 60; Soggin, *Joshua*, 121. J. Simons understands these slopes as those sloping eastward down to the Dead Sea (*The Geographical and Topographical Texts of the Old Testament*, §§ 137, n. 24, 509).

where the Israelites had lived in Egypt (Gen 45:10; 46:28; Exod 8:22[Hb. 18]; 9:26). Rather, it is the city in the southern hill country of Canaan mentioned in 15:51 (see also 11:16). Its exact location is unknown.[248]

10:42 The impression given in vv. 28–39, that the Israelites subdued the land effortlessly, is made explicit here: it was "in one campaign," literally, "one time." There is no way of knowing exactly how long this was. The passage in vv. 28–39 mentions several days for the campaign (vv. 28,32,35), and 11:18 states that "many days (NIV: "a long time") Joshua made war ..." However, the point here is that this conquest was part and parcel of one campaign, and the picture painted in vv. 28–39 of a quick, effortless campaign is now reinforced by this reference to a single campaign.[249]

The campaign against many different enemies and over a wide territorial expanse was effortless because Israel's God fought for it. The words here are essentially the same as those found in v. 14. Again and again, the Book of Joshua reminds its readers that God was in control of all the events.

10:43 Finally, after the extensive activities of the chapter, Joshua and the people were able to return to their base camp at Gilgal, from where they had come originally in response to the Gibeonites' appeal for help (v. 7).[250] This verse is identical to v. 15, but it probably is a scribal duplication at that point (see note at v. 15).

8. Northern Campaign Begun (11:1–15)

After the Israelites' success against Adoni-Zedek and the southern coalition that came against them has been told, the text's attention turns in chap. 11 to a northern coalition under another king, Jabin. Israel was able to defeat this northern coalition as well (vv. 1–15). The account of this is followed by a general conclusion to chaps. 10–11 (or 9–11), in vv. 16–23. There are numerous parallels between chaps. 10 and 11 (on which, see the introduction to chap. 10, and further below).

The chapter contains two temporal markers—"at that time"—in vv. 10,21, marking natural breaks there (vv. 1–9,10–20,21–23: see below). The account of the battle against the northern coalition, however, follows the pattern of that of the battle in chap. 10, in which the coalition gathered (10:1–5; 11:1–5), the battle was fought (10:6–15; 11:6–9), and the Israelites followed it up by

---

[248] See Simons, *Geographical and Topographical Texts*, § 285–87, 319 A9; W. A. Ward, "Goshen," *ABD* 2:1076.

[249] J. Niehaus makes the point that the wording here—"one time" or "once"—means that Joshua took the land once but there was "the possibility that later battles were required to take certain locales ("*Pa'am 'Eḥat* and the Israelite Conquest," *VT* 30 [1980]: 236–39); the quote is from p. 238. See also Davis, *No Falling Words*, 88–89.

[250] On Gilgal's location, see commentary on 9:6.

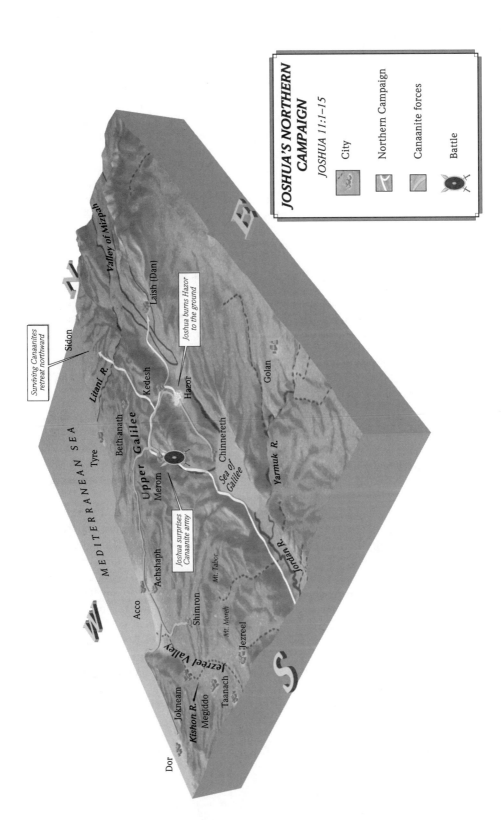

JOSHUA'S NORTHERN CAMPAIGN

JOSHUA 11:1–15

City

Northern Campaign

Canaanite forces

Battle

Surviving Canaanites retreat northward

Joshua burns Hazor to the ground

Joshua surprises Canaanite army

MEDITERRANEAN SEA

Valley of Mizpah

Sidon

Laish (Dan)

Litani R.

Tyre

Kedesh

Beth-anath

Upper Galilee

Hazor

Chinnereth

Sea of Galilee

Golan

Merom

Yarmuk R.

Achshaph

Acco

Mt. Tabor

Jordan R.

Shimron

Mt. Moreh

Jezreel

Jezreel Valley

Jokneam

Taanach

Megiddo

Kishon R.

Dor

N

E

W

S

finishing the task (10:16–27; 11:10–15), so our outline below follows these contours.

The message here is the same as in chap. 10: God was working on his people's behalf to give them the land of Canaan, no matter the odds or the coalition arrayed against them (cf. Deut 20:1). In this case, the coalition is much more impressive, seeming to come from all parts of the north (and even from the south), with a carefully designed strategy against Israel. There is no dramatic miracle of hailstones or a sign involving sun and moon here, but nevertheless it is clear that the battle was the Lord's (see vv. 6,8).

(1) Northern Coalition Gathered against Israel (11:1–5)

[1]When Jabin king of Hazor heard of this, he sent word to Jobab king of Madon, to the kings of Shimron and Acshaph, [2]and to the northern kings who were in the mountains, in the Arabah south of Kinnereth, in the western foothills and in Naphoth Dor on the west; [3]to the Canaanites in the east and west; to the Amorites, Hittites, Perizzites and Jebusites in the hill country; and to the Hivites below Hermon in the region of Mizpah. [4]They came out with all their troops and a large number of horses and chariots—a huge army, as numerous as the sand on the seashore. [5]All these kings joined forces and made camp together at the Waters of Merom, to fight against Israel.

Chapters 10 and 11 begin identically in Hebrew (they are slightly different in the NIV's rendering): "And it happened, when [king's name] heard ..." References to the report of Israel's doings and successes being heard *(šmᶜ)* link chaps. 9–11 (9:1,3; 10:1; 11:1), showing that God was indeed working on Israel's behalf, not only in giving them successes but also in assuring that word of these successes spread throughout the land (see also Rahab's testimony that Israel's reputation was known throughout the land: 2:9–11).

The northern coalition was headed by Jabin, king of the most important city in the north, Hazor. A large army came together: various kings are mentioned in vv. 1–2, and six "nations" are mentioned in v. 3, the same six that are in 9:1. The precise geographical limits of the coalition are difficult to determine with certainty, but Hazor, a far northern city, was clearly the most prominent (see v. 10). The assembled kings and nations were a great and powerful force (v. 4), and they joined together near Hazor, at the "waters of Merom" (v. 5).[251]

The coalition described in vv. 1–3 is not as neat and tidy as the five-king group in chap. 10. It was a broader coalition appears here as a force much more threatening to the Israelites, gathered as it was from such a widely scattered area. Only two kings are named (Jabin and Jobab), but four cities are specified (Hazor, Madon, Shimron, and Acshaph, v. 1), several regions are mentioned

---

[251] For detailed maps of this battle, see Rasmussen, *NIV Atlas of the Bible*, 95; Brisco, *Holman Bible Atlas*, 80.

(the northern mountains, the Arabah south of Kinnereth, the western foothills, Naphoth Dor, v. 2, and the region of Mount Hermon near Mizpah, v. 3), and six peoples are listed (Canaanites, Amorites, Hittites, Perizzites, Jebusites, Hivites, v. 3). The overall effect of the listing of such widely scattered cities, regions, and peoples is to cast a dark cloud of impending doom over the Israelites. This makes the deliverance that is accomplished that much more impressive.

11:1 The coalition was headed by Jabin, king of Hazor (v. 1). In later years, another "Jabin, king of Canaan," who was king in Hazor, opposed the Israelites (Judg 4:2). Many scholars believe that there was only one Jabin and that the Judges 4 account is secondary or else that Joshua 10 and Judges 4 describe one and the same battle.[252] However, "Jabin" appears to have been a dynastic name for kings in Hazor—not a personal name—just as "Pharaoh" was for kings in Egypt and "Ben-Hadad" was in Syria.[253]

Four cities are mentioned in v. 1, of which Hazor was the most important: v. 10 states that it "had been the head of all these kingdoms." It is mentioned several times in the Bible, in different periods (see Judg 4:2,17; 1 Sam 12:9; 1 Kgs 9:15; 2 Kgs 15:29),[254] and its archaeological site is not disputed: its remains can be found on a huge mound, more than two hundred acres in area, about eight miles north of the Sea of Galilee.[255] Biblical and extrabiblical evidence alike point to its having been a large and strategic city.[256]

The other cities appear to have been minor cities. The first, Madon, is known only here and in the list of conquered kings in 12:19.[257] Shimron may

---

[252] See, e.g., Soggin, *Joshua*, 136; J. Gray, *Joshua, Judges, Ruth*, 114; Butler, *Joshua*, 125–26; Y. Aharoni et al., *The MacMillan Bible Atlas*, 3d ed. (New York: MacMillan, 1993), 53–55.

[253] Y. Yadin, *Hazor: With a Chapter on Israelite Megiddo* (London: Oxford University, 1972), 5–6; Boling, *Joshua*, 304; Bimson, *Redating the Exodus and Conquest*, 181.

[254] Several other towns named "Hazor" are also mentioned in the Bible, but almost nothing is known of them and their sites are unknown. See J. M. Hamilton, "Hazor," *ABD* 3:88.

[255] Cp., e.g., the size of Megiddo, another important city in Israel, whose tell occupies only twenty acres.

[256] On the archaeology of Hazor, see Yadin, *Hazor;* A. Ben-Tor and Y. Yadin, "Hazor," *NEAEHL*, 2:594–606; Ben-Tor, "The Hazor Tablet: Foreword," *IEJ* 42 (1992): 17–20; id., "The Yigael Yadin Memorial Excavation at Hazor," *BA* 56 (1993): 131–32. Currently, new excavations at Hazor are being conducted under Ben-Tor, but no publications are yet available. Ben-Tor has reported on the discovery in 1996 of charred remains of a Late Bronze Age palace, which included the deliberate decapitation and mutilation of statues of the Canaanites' gods, in keeping with Moses' injunction in Deut 7:5 that the Israelites should do precisely that. (See Hoffmeier, *Israel in Egypt*, 35, for this datum.)

[257] Its name is not found in Old Greek's Codex Vaticanus, which has "Marron" instead (and also in vv. 5,7: "Waters of Marron" instead of "Waters of Merom"). "Maron" is also known from Egyptian and Assyrian sources. This evidence may suggest that the MT mistakenly has "Madon," while the original may have been "Maron" or "Merom" (see N. Na'aman, *Borders and Districts in Biblical Historiography: Seven Studies in Biblical Geographical Lists*, JBS 4 [Jerusalem: Simor, 1986], 119–43). However, scholarly consensus is not unanimous on this point (see Boling, *Joshua*, 305 and map on p. 112, who sees Madon and Merom as two separate places).

have been somewhat more important, since it is known from several texts outside the Bible. It became part of the territory of Zebulun (19:15), although its
exact location is unknown.[258] Acshaph, whose site is also unknown, appears
only in the Book of Joshua: here, in the list of conquered kings (12:20), and in
the territorial list of the tribe of Asher (19:25).

11:2 After naming two kings and four cities, the text becomes more general, focusing on regions. Four regions are mentioned: the mountains, the
Arabah south of Kinnereth, the western foothills, and Naphoth Dor. Two of
the terms are general and are also found in the summary of the southern conquest (10:40): the hill country (NIV has "hill country" in 10:40 and "mountains" in 11:1 for the same Hb. term: *hār*) and the western foothills (also
known as the Shephelah). These terms are descriptive of terrain and are not
specific place names per se; in this context, they describe regions in the
north.[259] In addition, the term "Negev" is found in both 10:40 and 11:2,
although referring to different areas. In the former instance, it refers to a
region in southern Canaan, while in the latter, it is translated "south."

The "Arabah south of Kinnereth" refers to the Jordan River valley north of
the Dead Sea (see the reference at 12:3, and note on 8:14). "Kinnereth" was
the older name of the Sea of Galilee (see 12:3: "the Sea of Kinnereth" [also in
Num 34:11]). There was also a town called Kinnereth on the northwest side of
this sea (19:35), but here, the text refers undoubtedly to the sea. The meaning
of the name "Naphoth Dor" is uncertain,[260] but the seaport of Dor on the
Mediterranean is mentioned several times in the Bible and is well known
through archaeological excavations.[261]

11:3 The list now turns away from naming kings, cities, or areas and
focuses on six peoples, the same six mentioned in 9:1, although in a different
order. We noted in the comments on 9:1–2 that no conclusion to the attack of
the six kings is given. Although the attack in chap. 11 is clearly broader than
the one in chap. 9, the inclusion of the same six groups as part of the larger
coalition in chap. 11 brings the entire section (chaps. 9–11) to conclusion. On
these peoples, see the commentary on 3:10.

The inclusion of Jebusites, who were the inhabitants of Jebus/Jerusalem, is

---

[258] Scholarly consensus puts it at Khirbet Sammuniyeh, southwest of Hazor, almost due north
of Megiddo, ca. five miles west of Nazareth (see Boling, *Joshua*, 305; P. Benjamin, "Shimron,"
ABD 5:1218–19).

[259] For these regions in general, see on 10:40. The use of "hill country" here is more easily
explained than "western foothills," since the latter term ("Shephelah") usually is more specific to
the southern hills separating Judah from Philistia.

[260] Older interpretations render "Naphoth" as "heights" (BDB, 632), but this is not certain.
More recent proposals for the meaning include "dune" (Boling, *Joshua*, 306) and "yoke" (*HALOT*,
708). There are no hills or heights in the region of Dor (Simons, *Geographical and Topographical
Texts*, § 510.29).

[261] E. Stern, "Dor," *NEAEHL*, 357–68.

striking, since Jerusalem was far to the south, south of Jericho. This may indicate the grave nature of the Israelite threat in the Canaanites' minds, such that help was sought from far and wide.

Mount Hermon was in the far north, the highest point in northern Palestine. "Mizpah" was the name of several cities in Israel's history: there was a city near Lachish (15:38), one in Benjamin in the south (18:26), and another one in Gilead, east of the Jordan River (Judg 10:17). One of these cities (or still another one) was a gathering place for solemn assemblies in later times (Judg 20:1; 1 Sam 7:5–6). The one here is known only in this chapter (vv. 3,8).[262]

11:4–5 The impressive, even overwhelming, nature of the coalition arrayed against Israel—which is hinted at by the wide geographical spread in vv. 1–3—is made explicit now. The language in v. 4 is repetitive, emphasizing the vast numbers of the forces that came against Israel: the term $rāb/rōb$, "many, much," occurs three times in this verse, and the forces are compared with the number of sands on the seashore. The fighting forces were strengthened by their horses and chariotry.[263] Such a vast force surely would have appeared irresistible!

Here again, the enemy brought the attack to Israel. As we have noted earlier, only in the cases of Jericho and Ai did the Israelites initiate the conflicts. The Israelites were not to put their trust in military power: God again is given the credit for Israel's victory (see commentary on 1:7–8; 10:9–11). The reference here to horses is the first time these are mentioned in the book, and it certainly shows a contrast between the Canaanite conduct of war and the model of leadership that Joshua exemplified and that Israel's kings were to exemplify: they were not to multiply horses for themselves (Deut 17:16), that is, not depend on their military might, but rather on God.

The Canaanite coalition encamped together near the "Waters of Merom," whose site is not known with certainty. Since the Middle Ages, it was identified with Lake Huleh, the small lake north of the Sea of Galilee, but most scholars today believe it was somewhere between the Sea of Galilee and the Mediterranean coast.[264]

---

[262] On Mount Hermon, see R. Arav, "Hermon, Mount," *ABD* 3:158–60; for Mizpah, see P. M. Arnold, "Mizpah," *ABD* 4: 879–81.

[263] Horses at this time were for pulling chariots, which were fast, maneuverable, and stable weapons platforms. They did not operate well in hilly areas, however. See Yadin, *The Art of Warfare in Biblical Lands in the Light of Archaeological Study* (New York: McGraw-Hill, 1963), 4–5, 86–90.

[264] Various proposals are advanced. See Simons, *Geographical and Topographical Texts*, § 505; Boling, *Joshua*, 307; Na'aman, *Borders and Districts*, 126; D. C. Liid, "Merom, Waters of," *ABD* 4:705.

(2) The Battle of Merom (11:6–9)

⁶The LORD said to Joshua, "Do not be afraid of them, because by this time tomorrow I will hand all of them over to Israel, slain. You are to hamstring their horses and burn their chariots."

⁷So Joshua and his whole army came against them suddenly at the Waters of Merom and attacked them, ⁸and the LORD gave them into the hand of Israel. They defeated them and pursued them all the way to Greater Sidon, to Misrephoth Maim, and to the Valley of Mizpah on the east, until no survivors were left. ⁹Joshua did to them as the LORD had directed: He hamstrung their horses and burned their chariots.

The battle against the impressive Canaanite coalition was joined by Israel. There was no dramatic, miraculous intervention by God this time, as there had been at the battle of Gibeon (10:6–14), but God did help his people. He promised to hand their enemies over (*ntn:* give), dead, to the Israelites (v. 6). Just as in 10:9–11 the credit extended to Yahweh alone, so here too, he claimed exclusive credit when he declared: "*I* will hand all of them over to Israel" (11:6). And just as Yahweh fought for Israel (10:14), so here too, he "gave *[ntn]* them into the hand of Israel" (11:8).

11:6 God gave Joshua an exhortation and promise, just as he had in the campaign against the southern coalition earlier (see 10:8 and the commentary there). He was not to fear (lit.) "from the face" *(mippĕnê)* of his enemies. The expression here is the same as in 10:11, when Israel's enemies did flee "from the face" *(mippĕnê)* of Israel (on the import of this expression, see 10:11). Israel's enemies did not have Israel's God on their side, so their respective situations contrasted sharply with each other.

God promised to deliver Israel's enemies into its hands by the next day. This was especially significant, in light of the impressive numbers arrayed against Israel in vv. 4–5. Almost exactly the same words were used many years later by Elisha to predict the deliverance of Samaria from a siege imposed by the Syrians (2 Kgs 7:1). In both cases, these words from God were guarantees to his people that indeed came true (cf. also Judg 20:28).

In the perspective presented in v. 6, God would do the killing of the enemies, and all Israel had to do was to hamstring their horses and burn their chariots. According to vv. 7–8, Israel was actively involved in attacking their enemies, but here, once again, the focus is on Israel's God, and the credit and glory are his.

11:7–8 The actual battle is told with almost no details; certainly no extraordinary miracle or sign is reported, as in chap. 10. Here Israel ambushed the enemy, and the Lord gave them into Israel's hands. The emphasis is on God's doings.

More parallels between chaps. 10 and 11 can be seen in v. 7. In both cases, Israel was able to ambush the enemy successfully: the wording is "they came against/upon them suddenly" (10:9; 11:7). Furthermore, the "whole army" came with Joshua; this phrase is literally "all the people of war," an expression found only in Joshua, which apparently emphasizes the unity of the nation (see on 8:3). Significantly, it is used in 10:7 as well: in the accounts of both the southern and northern campaigns, "all the people of war" went out to war against their common enemies.

The victory was clearly from God (v. 8). When Israel attacked its enemies, they repelled and chased them in opposite directions. Sidon was a city to the west, on the Mediterranean coast, and Misrephoth Maim probably was a site along the Litani River, somewhere south of that (its name means "Misrephoth of [the] waters").[265] To the east was the Valley of Mizpah (cf. v. 3). The defeat was a total rout, scattering the enemy in all directions and leaving "no survivors," a statement reminiscent of the oft-repeated assertion in chap. 10 (10:28,30,33,37,39).[266]

11:9 Joshua obeyed the Lord's instructions of v. 6 to the letter; the wording in both verses is identical. Such exact repetition is common in Hebrew narrative and shows the careful execution of commands or fulfillment of promises (see 4:2 for more on this phenomenon). Joshua was being an exemplary leader and an obedient servant. Such behavior ultimately won for him the label of "servant of the LORD" (24:29).[267] Joshua's actions would have prevented any meaningful pursuit by Israel's enemies.

(3) Northern Coalition Defeated (11:10–15)

¹⁰At that time Joshua turned back and captured Hazor and put its king to the sword. (Hazor had been the head of all these kingdoms.) ¹¹Everyone in it they put to the sword. They totally destroyed them, not sparing anything that breathed, and he burned up Hazor itself.

¹²Joshua took all these royal cities and their kings and put them to the sword. He totally destroyed them, as Moses the servant of the LORD had commanded. ¹³Yet Israel did not burn any of the cities built on their mounds—except Hazor, which Joshua burned. ¹⁴The Israelites carried off for themselves all the plunder and livestock of these cities, but all the people they put to the sword until they completely destroyed them, not sparing anyone that breathed. ¹⁵As the LORD commanded his servant Moses, so Moses commanded Joshua, and Joshua did it; he left nothing undone of all that the LORD commanded Moses.

Not only did Israel annihilate the opposing armies, but it also destroyed Hazor, the coalition's leading city, as well as all the people in the cities. They did not destroy the cities themselves, however, except for Hazor, which was

---

[265] See Na'aman, *Borders and Districts*, 48–50.

[266] See the introduction to 10:40–43 for the question of the all-inclusive nature of the conquest.

[267] See 1:1 for more on this "servant of the LORD" motif in the book.

burned (vv. 11,13). This section is a combination of details of the aftermath of the main battle and summarizing statements about the completeness of the victory, taking of spoils, and obedience to Moses' commands.

11:10–11 The Israelites destroyed Hazor, the chief city of the coalition, whose king, Jabin, was its leader. The time frame is somewhat vague—"at that time" does not necessarily specify sequential action—but the verb *wayyāšob,* "and [Joshua] turned back," suggests that this did take place after the events of vv. 6–9.

The prominence of the city and its king explains why its destruction was singled out for special treatment: Hazor had the dubious distinction of being only one of three cities that were actually burned by the Israelites (the others were Jericho and Ai: 6:24; 8:19,28).[268] The rest of the cities were left intact, so that the Israelites would be able to inherit "large, flourishing cities you did not build, houses filled with all kinds of good things you did not provide, wells you did not dig, and vineyards and olive groves you did not plant," just as the Lord through Moses had promised (Deut 6:10–11).

11:12–15 The focus syntactically in vv. 12–14 is on the objects of capture or destruction: first, the royal cities and their kings (v. 12); second, the cities on their mounds and the chief city, Hazor (v. 13); and, third, the plunder from these cities, their livestock, and their people (v. 14).[269] These were what God was giving into the Israelites' hands and what they were to destroy totally or to take for themselves.

The plunder and livestock in this case were allowed to be taken (v. 14), as had been the case with Ai (8:2,27), but in contrast to Jericho, where the Israelites were to destroy everything or bring it to the Lord's treasury (6:17–19). Like both Jericho and Ai, Joshua burned Hazor (v. 13; also v. 11). The treatment for Hazor was the most severe—that is, it was burned, while its fellow cities were not—but the people in all of the cities were accorded the same treatment: they were utterly exterminated, and no one that breathed remained.[270]

The passage also focuses on the succession of commands in vv. 12 and 15. What God spoke to Moses, his servant, Moses had spoken to Joshua. Over and over again we see Joshua faithfully carrying out his orders. The focus here again shows the importance of strict obedience to God's word and the

---

[268] Excavation of Hazor has shown several destructions in the Late Bronze Age, one ca. 1400 B.C. that easily could be attributed to Joshua. On these, see B. K. Waltke, "Palestinian Artifactual Evidence Supporting the Early Date for the Exodus," *BSac* 129 (1972): 33–47, esp. pp. 42–46; Bimson, *Redating the Exodus and Conquest,* 172–87 (with a different dating scheme); on the archaeology of Hazor in general, see notes on 11:1.

[269] In each case, the object of the verb precedes the verb, bringing attention to it.

[270] The endings of v. 11 (describing Hazor) and v. 14 (describing the other cities) are almost identical.

exemplary nature of Joshua as Israel's leader, a worthy successor to Moses.[271] As Butler states: "The conquest narratives from the story of the spies sent to Jericho to the destruction of Hazor and the north stand as a monument to the great faithfulness of Joshua to the Mosaic law. It [his faithfulness] thus stands as a goal for all future leaders of Israel. Rather than being lawmakers, the kings of Israel are law takers and law keepers."[272]

9. Northern Campaign Completed (11:16–23)

Whereas the manner in which the northern and southern campaigns unfolded is described in parallel patterns in chaps. 10 and 11, the concluding summaries are somewhat different. Structurally, 10:28–43 and 11:16–23 parallel each other, in summarizing and painting the conquest with a broad brush, describing a destruction that was comprehensive in scope. But whereas the former summarizes the southern campaign specifically, including seven of the cities conquered, the latter does not end in a parallel manner. It is more of a general summary of the fighting in the whole land, not just the north. Nevertheless, the picture is the same as that found in chap. 10: one of complete annihilation of the people of Canaan.[273]

In this section, Joshua is highlighted as Israel's leader. He alone is identified as the agent in almost all the activities here: he took the entire land (v. 16), captured and killed the kings (v. 17), waged war a long time (v. 18), destroyed the Anakites (v. 21), and took the entire land and distributed it (v. 23). Obviously, the nation was involved in these (v. 19 acknowledges this: "they took them all in battle"), but the emphasis on Joshua is striking. Also, the references to Moses in vv. 15 and 23 show Joshua fulfilling the leadership mandate given to him.

(1) Summary of the Campaigns (11:16–17)

16So Joshua took this entire land: the hill country, all the Negev, the whole region of Goshen, the western foothills, the Arabah and the mountains of Israel with their foothills, 17from Mount Halak, which rises toward Seir, to Baal Gad in the Valley of Lebanon below Mount Hermon. He captured all their kings and struck them down, putting them to death.

---

[271] Woudstra notes the following concerning parallels between Moses and Joshua (*Joshua,* 193, n. 26): (1) God hardened the pharaoh's heart in Moses' day and the Israelites' enemies' hearts in Joshua's (11:20); (2) 12:1–6 gives Moses' victories, and 12:7–24 Joshua's; (3) 13:8–32 gives allotments Moses had given, and chaps. 14–19 Joshua's.

[272] Butler, *Joshua,* 129.

[273] On the incomplete nature of the conquest and the nature of the comments in chaps. 10 and 11 as provisional, see the commentary on 10:40–43.

11:16–17 This summary of territory conquered serves both as a summary of the northern campaign and a general summary to tie off the entire section (chaps. 9–11). The Israelites had now, for all practical purposes, conquered the entire land. Verse 16 mentions the regions that were conquered, and v. 17 gives the northern and southern limits of the territory. The extent of the lands conquered is not as ambitious as the "map" of lands that God was giving to Israel in 1:4, but even this description is programmatic and schematic in light of the lands that still had not been taken (see 13:1–5 and commentary on 10:40–43).

The territories mentioned in v. 16 are almost all southern regions found in 10:40–41: the hill country, the Negev, the region of Goshen, and the western foothills (Shephelah). Only the "mountains of Israel with their foothills" are not mentioned specifically, but this expression is only a summarizing one, encompassing regions already mentioned.[274] In this context, some of these regions most likely refer to the northern extensions as well—for example, the hill country and the western foothills—since these, while usually mentioned with reference to Judah, extended northward throughout the land.

The southern extreme of the land is demarcated by Mount Halak, which is only mentioned here and in 12:7 and whose location is unknown. Mount Halak rose eastward, up toward Seir, which is the name of the country of Edom (Gen 32:3; Deut 2:8), a mountainous land (see Gen 14:6). Seir/Edom was the territory southeast of the Dead Sea, east of the Arabah, although portions of it may have been west of this.[275] In Num 34:4 and Josh 15:3, Mount Halak is mentioned in connection with the ascent of Akrabbim (NIV: "Scorpion Pass"), Zin, and Kadesh Barnea. Kadesh Barnea is mentioned in 10:41, and Mount Halak may have been near it.[276]

The northern extreme of the land reached to Baal Gad in the Valley of Lebanon, near the foot of Mount Hermon. Baal Gad's location is unknown, but its position at the foot of Mount Hermon (see on v. 3) gives a general picture of the extent of the land northward.[277]

(2) Conclusion (11:18–23)

18Joshua waged war against all these kings for a long time. 19Except for the Hivites living in Gibeon, not one city made a treaty of peace with the Israelites, who took them all in battle. 20For it was the LORD himself who hardened their hearts to wage war against Israel, so that he might destroy them totally, extermi-

---

[274] On these regions, see the commentary on 10:40 (and 11:2).

[275] Simons, *Geographical and Topographical Texts*, §§ 434, 435.

[276] See the maps (nos. 4, 17) in Aharoni, *The Land of the Bible*, 71, 234.

[277] On Baal Gad, see Simons, *Geographical and Topographical Texts,* § 509; Aharoni, *Land of the Bible*, 238–39.

nating them without mercy, as the LORD had commanded Moses.

²¹At that time Joshua went and destroyed the Anakites from the hill country: from Hebron, Debir and Anab, from all the hill country of Judah, and from all the hill country of Israel. Joshua totally destroyed them and their towns. ²²No Anakites were left in Israelite territory; only in Gaza, Gath and Ashdod did any survive. ²³So Joshua took the entire land, just as the LORD had directed Moses, and he gave it as an inheritance to Israel according to their tribal divisions.

Then the land had rest from war.

This passage forms the true narrative wrap-up of the first major section of the Book of Joshua (chaps. 1–12), even though an appendix of sorts follows in chap. 12. It looks back to events and ideas presented earlier, and it looks ahead to the distribution of the land in the following chapters. It includes historical and theological reflections on the events of the conquest (vv. 18–20), a final campaign against a significant foe (vv. 21–22), and a final, summarizing statement that encapsulates the most important elements of the book's theology (v. 23).

11:18–20 These verses are reflective, placing the events of the conquest in proper historical and theological perspective. As we have noted earlier, v. 18 helps to correct any misimpressions about the nature of the conquest that may be communicated by the stylized summaries in 10:28–43. The "one campaign" to take the land (10:42) actually took a long time (lit., "many days").[278]

Verses 19–20 show that the events of chaps. 10–11 were orchestrated by God himself. No city made peace with the Israelites as Gibeon had done (chap. 9); rather, Israel took them all in battle. The reason that no city took it upon itself to make peace with Israel was that God hardened their hearts so that he could completely destroy them. They had followed a pattern of opposing God by attacking the Israelites (see 9:1; 10:1–5; 11:1–5; and the comments introducing chap. 9). Thus, the text is stark and harsh: the idea and activity of hardening originated from God himself,[279] and it was for the purpose of destroying the Canaanites through battle. The destructions wrought among the Canaanites had been anticipated and commanded by Moses (see especially Deut 7:1–5; 20:16–18). The people were to make no treaty with the Canaanites and show them no mercy (Deut 7:2). The Canaanites' time for

---

[278] It may have been five (or seven) years for the main phase described in Joshua. This number comes from Caleb's indications in 14:10 that it had been forty-five years since he had spied out the land and received promises about his own inheritance. Subtracting thirty-eight or forty years for the wilderness wanderings, the events in chap. 14 would seem to have come five or seven years after the initial events in the book.

[279] The construction at the beginning of the verse makes this clear: כִּי מֵאֵת יְהוָה ׀ הָיְתָה לְחַזֵּק אֶת־לִבָּם, "for it was of the LORD (or, it was the LORD's doing) to harden their heart"— makes this clear. The preposition מֵאֵת shows that this originated with God himself (see the discussions in BDB, 86; *HALOT*, 101).

punishment had now come (cf. Gen 15:16).

The reference to God's hardening the Canaanites' hearts obviously recalls the same idea in the events of the exodus. There God hardened the pharaoh's heart (Exod 9:12; 10:1,27; 11:10; etc.) and sent the plagues. A careful reading of the Exodus passages shows that God's actions in Egypt were tied to the pharaoh's defiance. He responded to Moses and Aaron's request to be allowed to leave Egypt with a defiant statement: "Who is the LORD, that I should obey him and let Israel go? I do not know the LORD and I will not let Israel go" (5:2). He repeatedly hardened his own heart (7:13–14,22; 8:15[Hb. 11]; etc.). As a result, God sent the plagues, the purpose of which were that the Egyptians would know that "I am the LORD" (7:5,17; 8:10[Hb. 6],22[Hb. 18]; 9:14,16,29; 10:2; 14:4,18). God could have forced Israel's release after just one plague, but his purpose was to display his own power against the Egyptians and against their gods (Exod 12:12 states this clearly: "I will bring judgment on all the gods of Egypt. I am the LORD"). God's hardening of the pharaoh's heart must be seen in the context of the pharaoh's stubbornness and resistance of the Lord.[280]

We must examine the Canaanites' resistance to the Lord in a similar light. We have noted numerous times that the Canaanites heard *(šmᶜ)* about Israel's victories (2:9–11; 5:1; 9:1,3; 10:1; 11:1) and that they reacted differently at different times. Rahab and the Gibeonites were Canaanites who were spared, even if they were for different reasons. Those Canaanites who resisted Israel and its God, however, were shown no mercy and were annihilated. God's hardening of their hearts, then, was due, at least in part, to their own stubbornness and resistance of Israel's God.[281] Had they been willing to react as Rahab (or even the Gibeonites) had done, undoubtedly the results would have been different.[282]

11:21–22 One last military campaign is recorded, against the Anakites. Like the account of the destruction of Hazor, this one is introduced with a vague time reference: "at that time" (see on vv. 10–11).

The Anakites were warriors of great renown, and they had figured prominently at a critical juncture in Israel's history. Their fearsome presence had been the primary cause of the Israelites' rebellion in the wilderness (Num 13:22,28,32–33). The Israelite spies had returned with a report that compared them to the Nephilim, who were descended from the Anakites' ancestor Anak: "we seemed like grasshoppers in our own eyes, and we looked the same to

---

[280] For good discussions of the hardening of the pharaoh's heart, see V. P. Hamilton, *Handbook on the Pentateuch* (Grand Rapids: Baker, 1982), 167–74; Kaiser, *Toward Old Testament Ethics*, 252–56. L. G. Stone makes the same point ("Ethical and Apologetic Tendencies in the Redaction of the Book of Joshua," *CBQ* 53 [1991]: 25–36; the observation is on pp. 33–34).

[281] This is the thrust of Stone's essay cited in the previous note.

[282] See also Kaiser, *Toward Old Testament Ethics*, 268 on this last point.

them" (Num 13:33). As a result the Israelites feared going into the land and rebelled against Moses and Aaron (Numbers 14). Deuteronomy 1:28 states that the Canaanites, including the Anakites, were stronger and taller than the Israelites and that their cities were large, with towering walls. Deuteronomy 9:2 quotes a saying about the Anakites: "Who can stand up against the Anakites?" Thus, Israel had absorbed a consuming fear of these people.

It is fitting, then, that the chronicle of Israel's conquests should end with this account of a triumph over perhaps Canaan's most feared inhabitants. The language used is picturesque: Joshua "cut off [or, "cut out"] the Anakites from the hill country." This expression—"to cut off/out"—is commonly used to describe totally uprooting and exterminating something or someone (twenty-two times; e.g., Lev 20:6 [one who follows mediums or spiritists]; Deut 12:29 [the nations]; Josh 7:9 [the Israelites' name]; etc.). Following this statement, the completeness of the extermination is reinforced in two ways: first, by the naming of the cities and regions from which the Anakites were cut out and second, by the verb *ḥrm*, "to exterminate, destroy completely."

The cities of Hebron and Debir, from which Joshua drove the Anakites, were two of the seven that were exterminated in 10:28–39 (see 10:36–39). The vague time reference in v. 21 may indicate that this campaign against the Anakites actually took place in the context of the southern campaign mentioned in chap. 10. However, the importance of the Anakites as intimidating enemies of Israel may account for the special mention of this campaign here at the end of the listing of the battles in Canaan. Hebron and Debir had to be taken again later by Caleb (Hebron: 14:6–15) and Othniel (Debir: 15:15–17), indicating that the exterminations of 10:36–39 and 11:21–22 were less than complete (see on 10:40–43), or, perhaps more likely in this case, that the area was resettled by Anakites shortly thereafter.

In addition to the cities of Hebron, Debir, and Anab,[283] Joshua cut out the Anakites from all the hill country of Judah and Israel. They only survived in Gaza, Gath, and Ashdod, three cities in Philistine territory, which was in the southwest portion of Canaan, along the Mediterranean coast.

In sum, this short account of the elimination of the Anakites is unusual in its harshness and thoroughness, a factor to be attributed, no doubt, to the Anakites' awesome reputation and their intimidating influence on Israel's attitudes heretofore.

11:23 This verse brings the entire first section of the book to a close. It is remarkable in its simplicity and its comprehensiveness: in its short compass, it captures almost every important element of the book's theology—Joshua's leadership, the taking and giving of the land in fulfillment of God's promises,

---

[283] Anab was ca. fifteen miles southwest of Hebron (Simons, *Geographical and Topographical Texts*, § 507; Boling, *Joshua*, 315; Hess, *Joshua*, 218–19).

and the tribes' peaceful settlement of the land in their allotted territories.

More immediately, this verse ends the section of the Israelites' encounter with the Canaanite peoples (chaps. 9–11). It functions as a "hinge" verse, looking back to summarize the conquests and looking forward to anticipate the inheritance of the land. In both instances, Joshua is highlighted as the agent: he "took the entire land," and he "gave it as an inheritance to Israel according to their tribal divisions." The former statement looks back to the activities detailed in chaps. 10–11, while the latter statement anticipates those in chaps. 13–19. Once again, Joshua's careful observance of the Mosaic commands is noted (see also vv. 15,20).

The statement that "the land had rest from war" clearly shows that the first section of the book is drawing to a close. This is the first mention of rest since Joshua spoke of it to the Transjordan tribes (1:13,15). The idea of rest for the entire nation from their enemies is found in such passages as Deut 12:10 and 25:19, and it is echoed in the summarizing passages in Josh 21:44 and 23:1. In two places, we read that the land itself had rest from war (Josh 11:23; 14:15; cf. Deut 12:9–10; 25:19; 2 Sam 7:1,11; 1 Kgs 8:56). This anticipates the same idea repeated several times in Judges: "So the land had rest X years" (Judg 3:11; 3:30; 5:31; 8:28).

The Book of Hebrews mentions Sabbath rest for God's people as the goal of believers (Hebrews 3–4) and states that Joshua did not give his people rest (4:8). The context previously refers to the rebellious wilderness generation (3:7–19), and this generation and others did not enter into God's rest because of their disobedience (4:6). Certainly the Book of Joshua emphasizes the obedience of Joshua and the people time and again, but the rest spoken of in Joshua was a fragile, tenuous one, as is borne out by the land remaining to be conquered mentioned in numerous references in Joshua 13–19. The rest from war in Joshua was something granted by God (not Joshua), but it was different from the spiritual rest that the writer to the Hebrews was speaking of for God's people, which they were to enter into by their obedience (Heb 4:11).

Despite the differences in outlook from the Book of Hebrews, the land's rest in Joshua is a positive thing, and the intense mood of the confrontations and battles of chaps. 6–11 is dramatically changed with this final statement about rest. A much more peaceful and sedentary mood is found in chaps. 13–24, and this statement sets the stage for those chapters. All the loose ends are being tied up. Joshua is emerging strongly as Israel's leader, the entire land is now pacified, and there is no more war. All that remains before the important and much-anticipated task of the distribution of Israel's inheritance is the list of Canaanite kings who were subjugated (chap. 12).

10. List of Conquered Kings and Lands (12:1–24)[284]

This chapter forms an appendix of sorts to the first major section of the book (chaps. 1–12). A narrative wrap-up is found at 11:16–23, but this chapter recapitulates with a list of kings and territories that the Israelites conquered. It is appropriate to have this list here—even if a sense of closure has already been achieved at the end of chap. 11—because of the great importance placed in the book on Israel's inheritance of the land. Now that the major battles were over and the land subjugated for all practical purposes, the author appends this list, specifying in detail the cities and regions Israel subjugated. After the narrative conclusion in 11:16–23, it is as though the author were saying, "Here is the supporting evidence—the raw data—of what I have written about in the previous chapters." Even though the list is primarily a geographical one, it is couched in terms of the kings of the geographical areas. However, the kings' names are not important, so none are recorded (except for those of Sihon and Og), which contrasts to the practice of listing kings' names elsewhere (esp. 10:1–5; 11:1). The conquest of lands is of paramount importance in the Book of Joshua.

The chapter is divided into two major sections, focusing on Transjordan (vv. 1–6) and Cisjordan (vv. 7–24). Both sections begin similarly (lit.): "And these are the kings of the land which [the Israelites/Joshua] struck/conquered …" Verses 1–6 look back at the lands Israel had conquered east of the Jordan, reaching back into the Book of Numbers to tell of battles and lands won before Joshua was Israel's leader. Verses 7–8 provide an overview of the lands conquered west of the Jordan, and they echo 10:40 and 11:16–17 in most respects. Verse 8 also includes the names of the six nations mentioned in 9:1. Then, vv. 9–24 contain a list of thirty-one kings and their cities that the Israelites conquered in these lands.

The reason for the inclusion of the Transjordan material is that now, truly, Israel was in process of gaining its long-awaited inheritance, and it is fitting to review all of its gains to this point, whether east or west of the Jordan River. It reinforces the theme of national unity mentioned in chap. 1. The chapter also focuses on the leadership of Moses and Joshua (see the introduction to vv. 7–24).

(1) The Kings and Land of Transjordan (12:1–6)

1These are the kings of the land whom the Israelites had defeated and whose territory they took over east of the Jordan, from the Arnon Gorge to Mount Hermon, including all the eastern side of the Arabah:

---

[284] For a note on the process of geographical identifications in this and following chapters, see the excursus at the end of this chapter, "Identifying Geographical Entities."

²**Sihon king of the Amorites, who reigned in Heshbon. He ruled from Aroer on the rim of the Arnon Gorge—from the middle of the gorge—to the Jabbok River, which is the border of the Ammonites. This included half of Gilead. ³He also ruled over the eastern Arabah from the Sea of Kinnereth to the Sea of the Arabah (the Salt Sea), to Beth Jeshimoth, and then southward below the slopes of Pisgah.**

⁴**And the territory of Og king of Bashan, one of the last of the Rephaites, who reigned in Ashtaroth and Edrei. ⁵He ruled over Mount Hermon, Salecah, all of Bashan to the border of the people of Geshur and Maacah, and half of Gilead to the border of Sihon king of Heshbon.**

⁶**Moses, the servant of the LORD, and the Israelites conquered them. And Moses the servant of the LORD gave their land to the Reubenites, the Gadites and the half-tribe of Manasseh to be their possession.**

The down payment on the inheritance of the land had been the Israelites' earlier conquests east of the Jordan, their victories over Sihon, king of Heshbon, and Og, king of Bashan. They were defeated under Moses, and their lands were possessed at that time (v. 6; the fuller story is told in Num 21:21–35 and Deut 2:26–3:11. These lands were the inheritance of the two and one-half tribes that settled there (see commentary on 1:12–15). This list (vv. 2–5) is similar to the one found in 13:9–12.

The details of the geographical descriptions here are usually of little interest to modern-day readers and, in truth, they are not as theologically laden as other portions of the book. However, their importance lies in confirming the veracity of the claims elsewhere that these lands were indeed conquered, in confirming the tribes' claims to the lands mentioned here, and in confirming that God was faithful to his promises to give these lands to his people. He would fulfill his promises, right down to every last village or town and every last border, passing atop this hill over here and descending through that valley over there.

12:1 The list begins by delineating the southern and northern extremes of the land east of the Jordan, the Arnon Gorge and Mount Hermon, respectively, which were both east of the Arabah (see map). The Arnon River flowed through a deep gorge into the Dead Sea from the east about halfway down its length, and Mount Hermon was north of the Sea of Kinnereth (Galilee).

12:2–3 These verses echo almost exactly the geographical description of the same lands that Moses enunciated in his review of what the Lord had done for Israel in Deuteronomy 2–3, especially 2:36–37 and 3:16–17. Nothing new had happened for Israel since that time in Transjordan, so the Book of Joshua simply repeats the information from Deuteronomy.

King Sihon's major city, Heshbon,²⁸⁵ is listed first, and then the southern and northern boundaries, from the city of Aroer, at the edge of the Arnon

---

²⁸⁵ On the site identification, see Hess, *Joshua,* 225–26.

River, including the middle of the river gorge and half of Gilead, north to the Jabbok River (v. 2). The Jabbok River gorge was the next deep gorge to the north, entering the Jordan River valley from the east, near the towns of Adam and Zarethan (mentioned in 3:16). Gilead was a large area east of the Jordan north and south of the Jabbok River;[286] Sihon's sovereignty was over its southern half. His sovereignty also extended along the eastern portion of the Jordan River valley (the Arabah: v. 3), including areas north of the border mentioned in v. 2, the Jabbok River. In this area, it reached all the way north to the Sea of Kinnereth and south to Beth Jeshimoth and even further, to Mount Pisgah, somewhere near the northern end of the Dead Sea.

12:4–5 These verses echo the geographical description that Moses gave in Deut 3:10–11. Og's territory was north of Sihon's, in Bashan. His two capital cities were east of the Sea of Kinnereth, Ashtaroth being north of Edrei. Ashtaroth[287] and Edrei were inherited by members of the half tribe of Manasseh (13:31), and Ashtaroth became a Levitical city (21:27).

The territorial description in v. 5 is not as neat as that in v. 3 (which gives the northern and southern extremes of Sihon's territory). It gives the northwestern and eastern boundaries (Mount Hermon and Salecah), and then mentions the Maacathites and Geshurites, who were people living northeast of the Sea of Kinnereth (see Deut 3:14) and whom the Israelites were not able to expel from their territory (Josh 13:13). The southern border extended to Sihon's territory.

12:6 Moses' role as leader and the one who gave these territories to the two and one-half tribes east of the Jordan is emphasized here. Consistent with the theme of obedience highlighted in chap. 11, Moses is here called "the servant of the LORD." Joshua assumes the same role as Moses in v. 7.

(2) The Kings and Land of Cisjordan (12:7–24)

7These are the kings of the land that Joshua and the Israelites conquered on the west side of the Jordan, from Baal Gad in the Valley of Lebanon to Mount Halak, which rises toward Seir (their lands Joshua gave as an inheritance to the tribes of Israel according to their tribal divisions— **8**the hill country, the western foothills, the Arabah, the mountain slopes, the desert and the Negev—the lands of the Hittites, Amorites, Canaanites, Perizzites, Hivites and Jebusites):

9the king of Jericho one the king of Ai (near Bethel) one **10**the king of Jerusalem one the king of Hebron one **11**the king of Jarmuth one the king of Lachish one **12**the king of Eglon one the king of Gezer one **13**the king of Debir one the king of

---

[286] See W. S. LaSor, "Gilead," *ISBE* 2:468; Y. Aharoni, *The Land of the Bible: A Historical Geography*, rev. ed. (Philadelphia: Westminster, 1979), 38–39; Rasmussen, *NIV Atlas of the Bible*, 52. See further the commentary on 13:11.

[287] See the commentary on 21:27 on its name there.

Geder one [14]the king of Hormah one the king of Arad one [15]the king of Libnah one the king of Adullam one [16]the king of Makkedah one the king of Bethel one [17]the king of Tappuah one the king of Hepher one [18]the king of Aphek one the king of Lasharon one [19]the king of Madon one the king of Hazor one [20]the king of Shimron Meron one the king of Acshaph one [21]the king of Taanach one the king of Megiddo one [22]the king of Kedesh one the king of Jokneam in Carmel one [23]the king of Dor (in Naphoth Dor) one the king of Goyim in Gilgal one [24]the king of Tirzah one thirty-one kings in all.

The recent conquests west of the Jordan (in Cisjordan) are now reviewed. The review begins with a geographical overview in vv. 7–8 that echoes similar overviews in 10:40 and 11:16–17. Then, in vv. 9–24 is a list of thirty-one kings and their cities that the Israelites conquered in these lands.

A certain symmetry exists between the two major sections of the chapter that centers around Moses and Joshua in vv. 6 and 7. With reference to the kings of the land in vv. 1–6 (Transjordan), Moses and the Israelites conquered *(nkh)* them, and Moses gave *(ntn)* their land as an inheritance *(yĕruššâ)* to the two and one-half tribes (v. 6). With reference to the kings of the land in v. 7 (Cisjordan), Joshua and the Israelites conquered *(nkh)* them, and Joshua gave *(ntn)* their land as an inheritance *(yĕruššâ)* to the tribes of Israel (v. 7). The leadership of both Joshua and Moses is highlighted, but the comparison works to Joshua's advantage, since Moses' stature is already assured (he is called "the servant of the LORD" twice in v. 6, whereas nothing comparable is said of Joshua). Once again, Joshua as the worthy successor to Moses is highlighted.

12:7–8   Verse 7 gives the northern and southern limits of the territory that the Israelites had taken, which are the same limits mentioned in 11:17, with the order reversed. The verse looks backwards to the first half of the book when it states that Joshua and the Israelites conquered the kings of the land, it looks forward to the second half in stating that Joshua gave their land as an inheritance to the tribes, in accord with their allotted portions (NIV: "tribal divisions").[288] In this way, it echoes the final verse of the narrative conclusion to the first half (11:23), which also looks back and ahead.

Verse 8 presents an overall, sweeping view of the lands taken, mentioning six areas and six peoples. The six areas have all been mentioned previously in the book, in the summarizing statements of 10:40 and 11:16, or elsewhere in the book: the hill country, western foothills, and the Negev in 10:40 and 11:16, the Arabah in 11:16, the mountain slopes in 10:40, and the desert in 1:4. The six peoples also have been mentioned in 3:10. The references both to territories and to peoples emphasize the completeness of the conquest to this point.

---

[288] For more on the idea of inheritance in the book, see the excursus "Israel's Inheritance of the Land in Joshua" at 13:6–7.

12:9–24 The list mentions thirty-one kings that Joshua and the Israelites conquered and their cities. Of the thirty-one cities listed here, more than half (sixteen) are specifically mentioned in chaps. 6–11 as having been defeated by Israel: Jericho (chap. 6); Ai (chap. 8); Jerusalem, Hebron, Jarmuth, Lachish, Eglon, Gezer, Debir, Libnah, Makkedah (chap. 10); and Madon, Hazor, Shimron (–meron), Acshaph, and Dor (chap. 11). The rest are in the areas already delineated in 10:40–41; 11:16–17; and 12:7–8. The extent of this list—particularly the references to so many cities not mentioned previously—supports the idea that the list of seven conquered cities in chap. 10 may have been merely a schematic list (see the commentary on 10:28–39), indeed, that this may also have been the case in chap. 11. Here, too, the detailed listing of the kings and their cities adds to the impressiveness of Israel's triumph west of the Jordan.

The list begins with the first two cities conquered in Canaan: Jericho and Ai (v. 9). Ai's location near Bethel is mentioned here, perhaps to prepare for the inclusion of Bethel in v. 16 (see also on 8:17).

After this, a general south-to-north orientation is used, vv. 10–16a focusing on kings and cities in the south.[289] The five kings of 10:3 are mentioned first: Jerusalem, Hebron, Jarmuth, Lachish, and Eglon, along with the king of Gezer, who had come up to help Lachish in 10:33 (vv. 10–12). The seven kings of the seven cities in 10:28–39 are scattered throughout vv. 10–16, although in a different order from that in chap. 10: Hebron, Lachish, Eglon, Gezer, Debir, Libnah, and Makkedah.

Cities previously unmentioned in the south include Geder (v. 13), Hormah, Arad (v. 14), and Adullam (v. 15). Geder is mentioned only here in the Bible, although several cities with names similar to it existed (e.g., Beth Gader [1 Chr 2:51]; Gederah [Josh 15:36]; Gedor [Josh 15:58]). This city may have been one of those with a similar name, and its unique spelling possibly was influenced by the spelling of "Gezer" in v. 12.[290] Hormah was a city in the Negev, and it became part of Judah's inheritance (15:30), although by way of Simeon's inheritance, which lay within Judah (19:4). It had been the place toward which the Amorites had pursued the Israelites in their first, misguided attempt to enter the promised land (Num 14:45; Deut 1:44). Arad and Hormah were closely linked geographically and also in a story in Num 21:1–3, where Arad's king attacked the Israelites, who then destroyed him and his allies and renamed the region "Hormah," which means "destruction." Adullam had played no significant role in Israel's history previously (although it was the locale of the events of Genesis 38) and would not until the days of David,

---

[289] Nelson makes this point, noting that, generally, cities in the south are clustered in vv. 10–16a, cities in the center of the land in vv. 16b–18, and cities in the north in vv. 19–24 (*Joshua,* 161).

[290] So Boling, *Joshua,* 326.

when he hid in a cave there on occasion (1 Sam 22:1; 2 Sam 23:13).

Beginning with Bethel, five cities from the central portion of the land are listed in vv. 16b–18: Bethel, Tappuah, Hepher, Aphek, and Lasharon. None of these has been mentioned previously, except for Bethel, which is anticipated in v. 9 and is mentioned in connection with Ai in 7:2; 8:9,12,17 (for more on Bethel, see 8:17). This shows that Jericho and Ai were not the only cities conquered in the central portion of the land.

Tappuah (v. 17) was on the border of Ephraim and Manasseh. The city itself was allotted to Ephraim (16:8; 17:8), but the lands around it were given to Manasseh (17:8). Nothing is known of Hepher (v. 17), although the "land of Hepher" was in one of Solomon's twelve administrative districts (1 Kgs 4:10). Several cities named "Aphek" (v. 18) are known in the Bible, but so little is known of them that even their total number is a matter of dispute (four? five?).[291] Lasharon (v. 18) is mentioned only here in the Bible. Its name could also mean "belonging to Sharon," in which case this would not be a city at all but a phrase modifying "Aphek," to identify which Aphek this was. This is how the Old Greek versions read v. 18 (i.e., "the king of Aphek of Sharon"). However, a difficulty with this understanding is the presence of the word "king" twice, rather than just once, and the total in v. 24 is "thirty-one," which would be incorrect if this city were removed from the list.

The rest of the list (vv. 19–24) deals with cities in the north, with the exception of the last city in the list, Tirzah (v. 24), which was in the north-central hill country. This portion of the list begins with the four cities of the coalition mentioned in 11:1 (although in a slightly different order): Madon, Hazor, Shimron-Meron,[292] and Acshaph (vv. 19–20).

This is the Bible's first mention of Taanach and Megiddo (v. 21), and they are most commonly mentioned together (17:11; Judg 1:27; 5:19; 1 Kgs 4:12). They were strategic cities in the Jezreel Valley, about five miles apart, and they controlled a heavily traveled pass going southwest into the Plain of Sharon.[293] They were both part of Manasseh's inheritance (17:11), and Taanach became a Levitical city (21:25), but the tribe of Manasseh did not drive out the inhabitants of either city (Judg 1:27). Kedesh (v. 22) is likewise previously unmentioned, but it is known elsewhere as "Kedesh in Galilee" (20:7; 21:32); these references reveal that it was assigned as a city of refuge and a Levitical city, respectively. It was assigned to the tribe of Naphtali (19:37),

---

[291] R. Frankel, "Aphek," *ABD* 1:275–77; cf. Simons, *Geographical and Topographical Texts*, 546–47; J. F. Prewitt, "Aphek," *ISBE* 1:150.

[292] In 11:1, the town's name is simply "Shimron." The Old Greek reads "the king of Shimron and the king of Meron" in v. 20, understanding two different cities here (followed by Nelson, *Joshua*, 158). Most probably, however, "Shimron Meron" was the town's full name (so also Boling, *Joshua*, 328; J. Kutsko, "Shimron-Meron," *ABD* 5:1219).

[293] Woudstra, *Joshua*, 206; Boling, *Joshua*, 328–29.

and it was located northwest of Lake Huleh.[294] Jokneam (v. 22) also is not
mentioned previously, but it became part of Zebulun's inheritance (19:11) and
a Levitical city (21:34). The qualifier "of Carmel" may have been added to
distinguish this city from Jokmean, a city in Ephraim (1 Chr 6:68 [Hb.
53]).[295] Dor (v. 23) was already mentioned in 11:2 (see commentary there).

Goyim in Gilgal (v. 23) is a strange name for three reasons. (1) "Goyim" is
the Hebrew word for "nations" or "Gentiles" and is not otherwise known as a
place name. (2) There is no other evidence for a city named "Gilgal" this far
north. (3) The previous two city names are qualified by an area designation
("in Carmel," "in Naphoth Dor"), whereas here, the qualifier would seem to
be a city, not an area ("in Gilgal"). Concerning the first problem, it would
seem that "Goyim" is nevertheless a place name, since the word "king" occurs
twice in v. 23, once for each place named in the verse. Furthermore, if it were
omitted, the total of thirty-one kings in v. 24 would be incorrect. The Old
Greek reads "Goim of Galilee," which would be more consistent with the previous two area designations, and this reading is accepted by most scholars.
Such a reading would connect this site with Isa 9:1 (Hb. 8:23), which mentions "Galilee of the Gentiles."[296] An alternative suggestion sees "Gilgal" and
"Galilee" as variant forms of the same name (both coming from the root *gāl,*
"mound, circle," and both referring to a region in the north).[297] In either case,
however, it is clear that this Goyim is not to be associated with the Gilgal in
earlier chapters of Joshua.

The list ends with Tirzah, to the south of the others in vv. 19–24. It is closer
to the cities in the central highlands of vv. 16b–18. It is known elsewhere only
from references in 1 Kings, where it appears to have served as the first capital
of the Northern Kingdom (1 Kgs 14:17; 15:21,33; 16:6,8–9).

The second major section of Joshua is now complete. As the author of
Joshua presents it, the Israelites have been given the land, with God's help,
and they have completely destroyed their enemies. They have taken possession of most of the lands they were given. Many lands have not been taken, of
course, and much work remains to be done. However, a milestone has been
reached, and the stage has been set for the parceling out of the land and
Israel's settling into it, hundreds of years after it was first promised to Israel's
ancestors.

---

[294] At least three cities are named "Kedesh" in the Bible, and the problems of identifying them
are complex. See R. K. Harrison, *ISBE* 3:5; J. L. Peterson and R. Arav, "Kedesh," *ABD* 4:11–12.

[295] So also Boling, *Joshua,* 329.

[296] E.g., Woudstra, *Joshua,* 206; Soggin, *Joshua,* 139; Nelson, *Joshua,* 158.

[297] See Hess, *Joshua,* 228, n. 1 and the discussion and bibliography there.

EXCURSUS: IDENTIFYING GEOGRAPHICAL ENTITIES

For entities whose location is crucial to the argument at hand, their locations are identified in this commentary, usually with supporting evidence from the Bible and (sometimes) archaeology. Where the information is relevant, further details concerning the history of the locale are also given (e.g., if a locale is the site of previous or subsequent activity relevant to the present account).

In some cases, only a place's locale is identified, sometimes with supporting biblical information and sometimes (if this information is obvious or has been discussed previously) only with reference to an accompanying map. However, a comprehensive attempt to locate precisely each geographical entity mentioned in the text—and to justify each identification—is not made.[298] This detailed pursuit is more properly the province of historical geography. Nevertheless, readers may be well served in some cases to know how geographical identifications are made, so a few comments on this are in order. Such identifications are of several types.

The first type of identification is of geographical entities that have not been verified extrabiblically. Such identifications rely of necessity on the biblical data, which is often less than sufficient to locate a site exactly. Nevertheless, the information provided is usually enough to locate the site in the correct region. One example of this is the location of Mount Pisgah (Josh 12:3), which is not known precisely but which is known from biblical data to have been near the northern end of the Dead Sea. See, for example, Num 21:20, which mentions "the valley in Moab where the top of Pisgah overlooks the wasteland"; Deut 3:17, which mentions that the Reubenites' and Gadites' western border was "the Jordan in the Arabah, from Kinnereth to the Sea of the Arabah (the Salt Sea), below the slopes of Pisgah"; and Deut 34:1, which states that "Moses climbed Mount Nebo from the plains of Moab to the top of Pisgah, across from Jericho." All of these references can help the historical geographer narrow down Pisgah's location to a certain area near the northern end of the Dead Sea with a high degree of certainty, even if the exact mountain peak cannot be identified. Another example of this is Gilgal (Josh 4:19; 5:9–10; 9:6; 10:6; etc.). The best geographical clue to its location comes from Josh 4:19, which places it "on the eastern border of Jericho." However, despite several proposals, its precise location remains unknown.[299]

A second, more precise, type of geographical identification occurs when an entity can be confirmed extrabiblically through the names attached to modern sites. In many cases, names have persisted for thousands of years, and there is no question that the site name today accurately identifies the ancient site of the same name. Obvious examples of this include Jerusalem, Bethlehem, the Jordan River, the Negev, et cetera. Less well-known examples include Aroer (Josh 12:2) and Beth Shemesh (Josh 15:10; 19:22,38), whose modern names have been confirmed archaeologically. Aroer's name survives in a town whose Arabic name is

---

[298] The commentaries by Butler, Hess, and especially Boling provide more of this type of information than most. Nelson (*Joshua*, 285–89) lists the modern site identifications for every place mentioned in the book.

[299] The case of Gilgal is complicated by the fact that more than one place is identified in the Bible by this name, including perhaps two in the Book of Joshua (see the discussion at 9:6).

ʿAraʿir (and there is a large tell there as well). Beth Shemesh is identified with Tell er-Rumeilah, a site near the village of ʿAin Shems, the second element of whose name preserves the biblical "Shemesh."

This type of identification must be made with some caution, however, because in some cases, the modern site name, which is the same as the ancient site's, does not in fact identify the ancient site. One example of this is Eglon (Josh 10:34), which scholarly consensus now places at Tell el-Hesi (or, less probably, Tell ʿAitun), even though a Khirbet ʿAjlan exists nearby ("ʿAjlan" is the Arabic equivalent of "Eglon").[300] Another example is Jericho, which is located on the mound known as "Tell es-Sultan," even though a village named "Er-Riha" is located nearby ("Er-Riha" is the Arabic equivalent of "Jericho").[301] This transfer of names from one site to another one nearby sometimes is known as "site shift."[302]

A third type of geographical identification comes when a site is excavated archaeologically and evidence points to a certain biblical site. Most often, the evidence is only suggestive: the site is in the general area suggested by the biblical evidence, and it was occupied during the period the Bible identifies for the place. Examples of this type are common and include Shechem (Josh 24:1), whose site is Tell el-Balata; Megiddo (Josh 12:1), whose site is Tell el-Mutesellim; and Jokneam (Josh 12:22), located at Tell Qeimun.

Rarely, archaeological excavations uncover written documents identifying the site beyond any doubt. One example of this is Ekron (Josh 15:45–46), where an inscription mentioning the city and several of its kings was found in 1996 at the site (Tell Miqne).[303] Another example is Beth Shan (Josh 17:16), where an inscription was found, dating to the thirteenth century B.C., which mentions "Mekal, the god, lord of Beth-Shan."[304] A third example is Gezer (Josh 12:12), where in 1874 the first of what are now eleven so-called "boundary inscriptions" was found (dating to the intertestamental period), on most of which are written the words "the boundary of Gezer." These were found in an arc to the east and the south of the mound now acknowledged to be Gezer.[305]

Even the presence of written evidence is not foolproof, however. In one well-known case, the site of ancient Lachish (Josh 10:31) was once thought to be Tell el-Hesi, seemingly confirmed by the presence of a letter written in cuneiform on a clay tablet that mentions several kings of Lachish, dating to the period of the Late Bronze Age (ca. 1400–1200 B.C.). However, today the scholarly consensus

---

[300] See C. S. Ehrlich, "Eglon (Place)," *ABD* 2:320–21.

[301] Aharoni, *Land of the Bible*, 124.

[302] For more on this phenomenon, see K. A. Kitchen, *The Bible in Its World* (Downers Grove: InterVarsity, 1977), 13–14; Aharoni, *Land of the Bible*, 123–24; A. F. Rainey, "The Toponymics of Eretz-Israel," *BASOR* 231 (1978): 10.

[303] S. Gitin, T. Dothan, J. Naveh, "A Royal Dedicatory Inscription from Ekron," *IEJ* 47 (1997): 1–16, esp. p. 9.

[304] P. E. McGovern, "Beth Shan," *ABD* 1:694.

[305] See H. D. Lance, "Gezer in the Land and in History," *BA* 30 (1967): 34–47, esp. p. 47; B.-Z. Rosenfeld, "The 'Boundary of Gezer' Inscriptions and the History of Gezer at the End of the Second Temple Period," *IEJ* 38 (1988): 235–45, esp. pp. 234–35. I thank my colleague, R. D. Cole, for alerting me to the examples in this paragraph.

is that stronger evidence exists for the site of Lachish as Tell ed-Duweir, a large and important mound six to seven miles east of Tell el-Hesi.

For readers interested in pursuing geographical and historical information beyond what is provided in this commentary, the following works can be recommended. In the first instance, most Bible encyclopedias provide good geographical, historical, and archaeological information for every biblical locale. Three of the best are M. C. Tenney, ed., *The Zondervan Pictorial Encyclopedia of the Bible*, 5 vols. (Grand Rapids: Zondervan, 1975); G. Bromiley, ed., *The International Standard Bible Encyclopedia*, 4 vols. (Grand Rapids: Eerdmans, 1979–88); and D. N. Freedman, ed., *The Anchor Bible Dictionary*, 6 vols. (New York: Doubleday, 1992).

Bible atlases are also helpful, providing detailed maps and also some other information about geographical locales. The following are among the best atlases: B. J. Beitzel, *The Moody Atlas of the Bible* (Chicago: Moody, 1985); C. G. Rasmussen, *The Zondervan NIV Atlas of the Bible* (Grand Rapids: Zondervan, 1989); Y. Aharoni et al., *The MacMillan Bible Atlas*, 3d ed. (New York: Macmillan, 1993); and T. V. Brisco, *Holman Bible Atlas* (Nashville: Broadman & Holman, 1998).

More in-depth treatments of historical geography may be found in the following classic works: J. Simons, *The Geographical and Topographical Texts of the Old Testament* (Leiden: Brill, 1959); and Y. Aharoni, *The Land of the Bible: A Historical Geography*, rev. ed., trans. and ed. A. Rainey (Philadelphia: Westminster, 1979). Beyond these and similar works, one enters the area of specialized studies. Three such standard, book-length studies are N. Na'aman, *Borders and Districts in Biblical Historiography: Seven Studies in Biblical Geographical Lists*, JBS 4 (Jerusalem: Simor, 1986); Z. Kallai, *Historical Geography of the Bible: The Tribal Territories of Israel* (Leiden: Brill; Jerusalem: Magnes, 1986); J. Svensson, *Towns and Toponyms in the Old Testament with Special Emphasis on Joshua 14–21*, ConB 38 (Stockholm: Almqvist & Wiksell, 1994). An important unpublished work is H. V. D. Parunak, "Geographical Terminology in Joshua 15–19," M.A. thesis, Institute for Holy Land Studies (Jerusalem), 1977.

Simons' is the definitive work devoted to every geographical site mentioned in the Bible, and Kallai's occupies a similar position concerning the tribal territories, with their boundaries and cities, although many scholars will disagree with them on many specific points, and new information renders many of their judgments obsolete. Svensson's recent work is a close literary reading of the lists, not oriented to identifying modern-day sites at all yet very thorough in considering each list in Joshua 14–21, their structures, interplay, and functions in the text.

JOSHUA 6–12: THEOLOGICAL REFLECTIONS

These chapters form the heart of the Book of Joshua. If the book's central message concerns Israel's inheritance of the promised land in fulfillment of God's promises, these chapters show Joshua and the Israelites taking possession of that land. They form a complement to chaps. 13–21, which show

Joshua apportioning the land to all of the tribes. Without the taking of the land recounted in these chapters, there would have been no apportioning of the land.

Israel could not take the land without God's presence among them and going before them. He repeatedly reminded Joshua and the people that he was with them and that they should not fear, for he would fight for them. In every military encounter, God provided the victory for his people. In the major encounters at Jericho, Ai, Gibeon, and the waters of Merom, the text calls attention to the fact that God fought for Israel, that he gave the enemies into Israel's hands. In the minor encounters in chap. 10, the same is stated for most of the cities conquered. Not once did the Israelites win a victory due to their superior military force. In most cases, it was as if the Israelites merely had to stand back and observe God at work on their behalf.

The different manner in which each encounter unfolded shows God at work in different ways. At Jericho, the Israelites merely had to walk into the city to take it after God knocked the walls down (chap. 6). At Ai, they had to set an ambush, but God gave clear instructions for this, and the plan worked to perfection (chap. 8). At Gibeon, the Lord sent a hailstorm that wreaked havoc upon the enemy, and even the sun and the moon fought for Israel (chap. 10). At the waters of Merom, God handed ever the enemy dead to the Israelites (chap. 11). To be sure, each encounter involved the Israelites' participation as combatants, but the text makes it very clear that they were secondary characters in these dramas: God—and God alone—was the victor in these battles against his enemies.

The foundation for Israel's taking the land had been laid many years earlier, when God promised the land to the patriarchs and reiterated his promises to succeeding generations. He also gave detailed instructions through his servant Moses about how Israel was to take the land; and according to these chapters in Joshua Israel carried out those instructions to the letter. Repeatedly we are told about Joshua and the people doing things just as God and/or Moses had commanded. The importance of obedience to God's commands and instructions is very much demonstrated in these chapters.

The battles that were fought, however, were not merely military encounters with the limited goal of ridding the land of its people so that the Israelites could claim their inheritance. They were sacred exercises as well, to remind Israel and the peoples of Canaan of the power and majesty of Israel's God. This is the importance of the detailed preparations of chaps. 1–5. This is the significance of the ceremonial marching around Jericho (chap. 6). This is the importance of the covenant-renewal ceremony at Mount Ebal (chap. 8). In all of these—in the midst of bloody and messy military encounters—Israel was to keep a larger perspective: the land itself was holy (5:15), and it belonged to the Lord, who was in process of giving it to his people.

The land had been defiled by the sins of its inhabitants over the centuries (Gen 15:16), and one of the harsh facts of this section is that God would not tolerate such defilement, such rebellion against him. The Israelites were to exterminate every person in the land in an extreme measure that had as its goal the cleansing of the land and its preparation for God's people to settle there. The Israelites were certainly not inheriting this land because of any merit of their own. Indeed, Deut 9:5 explicitly rejects that reasoning; the Israelites were chief among sinners, as Paul would say about himself many years later (1 Tim 1:15–16) and as the Books of Joshua and especially Judges make abundantly clear.

Yet God had promised this land to the descendants of Abraham, and he intended from the very beginning to make good on his promises (Gen 12:1–3,6–7). This was a critical juncture in his people's history, since they had just escaped four centuries of slavery in a foreign land, and they were now to take up a new existence in a new land. The nation's faith—indeed, its very existence—had not been tested like this before. So the holy God demanded a stiff price at this critical time. The Israelites were to make no accommodation with the peoples of the land that would compromise their standing as his people. If the peoples of the land would adopt Israel's faith, as Rahab did, they might be spared. The Gibeonites found a way to be spared as well; however, it was not through their faith but through trickery. Nevertheless, they too were spared because of the inviolable nature of the treaty the Israelites had made with them. In contrast to Rahab and the Gibeonites, however, most of the peoples of the land took a harsh stance toward the Israelites (chaps. 9–11), and they were dealt with harshly.

Even Israel itself was not exempt from God's requirements of holiness and obedience. When Israel violated his explicit commands about the disposition of the booty at Jericho, Israel itself became like the Canaanites, forfeiting God's protection and becoming subject to defeat (chap. 7). It was only after the sin had been dealt with that the nation regained God's protection.

The question of Israel's leadership continues to be addressed in this section. Now Joshua was firmly established, and he gave Israel its instructions time and time again. His leadership was again confirmed: "So the LORD was with Joshua and his fame spread throughout the land" (6:27). God "obeyed" his voice and fought for Israel (10:14). Yet Joshua's leadership was not exercised in a vacuum. It stood in continuity with Moses', whose instructions he was charged with carrying out. In particular, the covenant renewal ceremony was carried out in accordance with Moses' instructions (chap. 8), as well as the taking of all the land, including the destruction of its inhabitants (chap. 11).

At the end of this section of the book, the picture painted is that the land was pacified and the Israelites had claimed their territories. In reality, much land remained to be taken, and the land was not rid of all the Canaanites. However, the Israelites had obeyed their God in the main, and in the overall picture they succeeded. Plenty of opportunity remained for the biblical writers to remind their readers of the problems that Israel still faced in taking the land completely (in the rest of the Book of Joshua and in the Book of Judges), but here God and his victories and his gift of the land are celebrated.

At the halfway point in the book, Israel stood ready to receive the allotments of the land. Joshua 11:23 summarizes the state of affairs well, looking back and looking ahead and encapsulating the book's major motifs in its short compass: "So Joshua took the entire land, just as the LORD had directed Moses, and he gave it as an inheritance to Israel according to their tribal divisions. Then the land had rest from war." Up to this point, things had gone well for the Israelites. There are discordant notes scattered through chaps. 7–12—Achan's sin, the leaders' failure to consult with the Lord about the Gibeonites, the fact that the wars took a long time (11:18)—and these anticipate further troubles ahead. But, on the whole, Israel had accomplished much, it had been given much, and things were going its way. The concluding listing of the kings and their lands that the Israelites had defeated (chap. 12) is but a further confirmation of that.

III. APPORTIONING THE LAND (13:1–21:45)
    1. The Command to Distribute the Land (13:1–7)
    2. The Transjordan Distribution Recalled (13:8–33)
        (1) General Survey (13:8–13)
        (2) The Levites' Inheritance (13:14)
        (3) Reuben's Inheritance (13:15–23)
        (4) Gad's Inheritance (13:24–28)
        (5) Eastern Manasseh's Inheritance (13:29–31)
        (6) Summary (13:32–33)
    3. The Cisjordan Distribution Introduced (14:1–5)
    4. Judah's Inheritance (14:6–15:63)
        (1) Caleb's Inheritance: Part One (14:6–15)
        (2) Judah's Boundaries (15:1–12)
        (3) Caleb's Inheritance: Part Two (15:13–19)
        (4) Summary (15:20)
        (5) Judah's Cities (15:21–62)
        (6) Judah's Failure Concerning Jebus (15:63)
    5. Joseph's Inheritance (16:1–17:18)
        (1) Joseph's Southern Boundary (16:1–4)
        (2) Ephraim's Boundaries (16:5–19)
        (3) Ephraim's Failure Concerning Gezer (16:10)
        (4) Western Manasseh's Boundaries (17:1–11)
        (5) Western Manasseh's Failure Concerning Its Towns (17:12–13)
        (6) Joseph's Complaint (17:14–18)
    6. The Other Tribes' Inheritance (18:1–19:48)
        (1) Introduction (18:1–10)
        (2) Benjamin's Inheritance (18:11–28)
        (3) Simeon's Inheritance (19:1–9)
        (4) Zebulun's Inheritance (19:10–16)
        (5) Issachar's Inheritance (19:17–23)
        (6) Asher's Inheritance (19:24–31)
        (7) Naphtali's Inheritance (19:32–39)
        (8) Dan's Inheritance (19:40–48)
    7. Joshua's Inheritance (19:49–50)
    8. The Cisjordan Distribution Concluded (19:51)
    9. The Cities of Refuge (20:1–9)
        (1) Introduction: General Instructions (20:1–3)
        (2) Specific Instructions (20:4–6)

III. APPORTIONING THE LAND (13:1–21:45)

The second half of the Book of Joshua is different from the first half in several ways. In terms of subject matter, no more battles are recorded. In terms of literary genre, lists predominate here, whereas earlier, narrative stories are the rule.[1] Furthermore, the sedentary pace, relaxed tone, and relative lack of action contrast dramatically with the first half.

A major emphasis in this section is that God was the great landowner and landgiver. Just as in chaps. 1–12, he is presented as the one who guided and fought for Israel, giving its enemies into its hands, so now he appears as the one who gave Israel the land. The detailed boundary descriptions and lists of cities serve to emphasize the fact that God had been in control of this land all along, and he had the authority to parcel it out as he saw fit.

The two central sections of the book highlight two of the book's key themes: the taking of the land (chaps. 6–12) and the inheritance and distribution of the land (chaps. 13–21). The book is very well balanced in this way. We modern readers, perhaps naturally enough, usually gravitate to the gripping stories in the former section rather than the obscure lists in the latter. And yet, the very inclusion of the great detail in these lists shows the importance of documenting each tribes' inheritance and of demonstrating God's faithfulness to his promises. In the modern day, the heirs at a reading of a deceased person's will are attentive even to the smallest details of that will—even the legal boilerplate that fills much of it—because these details are of vital importance to their future. The provisions of the will perform many functions, including, most obviously, the dividing up of the estate. However, the will also gives

---

[1] For a note on the process of geographical identifications in this and following chapters, see the excursus at the end of chap. 12, "Identifying Geographical Entities."

indications of the deceased person's attitudes and feelings to those left behind, in what is left to whom, how it is distributed, what charities are remembered (if any), and even how the deceased person wants his or her heirs to conduct themselves in the future.

The land distribution lists in Joshua 13–21 functioned in similar ways. They too were of vital importance to Israel's future, and they too gave the Israelites clues about God's attitudes and feelings toward them. His desires for them are seen more fully elsewhere, especially in Joshua's speeches in chaps. 22–24; but it is clear, now that he had fought his people's battles for them, that he certainly was going to follow through and generously give them the lands that were rightfully theirs, based on his earlier promises. The occasion must have been one of great joy. The psalmist reflects something of this when he says in Ps 16:5–6: "LORD, you have assigned [mnh] me my portion [ḥēleq] and my cup; you have made my lot [gôrāl] secure. The boundary lines [ḥebel] have fallen for me in pleasant places; surely I have a delightful inheritance [nāḥălâ]." These two verses are replete with the vocabulary of inheritance found throughout Joshua 13–21 (see the excursus "The Inheritance of the Land in Joshua" after 13:7).

The lists in chaps. 13–21 follow a logical order. After an introductory section (13:1–7), the two and one-half Transjordan tribes' inheritance is detailed, lands that already had been assigned and, essentially, taken (13:8–33). Previews of the Levites' different inheritance are given in vv. 14,33; the cities of their inheritance were scattered throughout the other Israelite lands (see chap. 21).

In chaps. 14–19, the lands west of the Jordan are distributed. Following an introductory section (14:1–5), Caleb's inheritance is described (14:6–15). This singling out of an individual is appropriate, of course, because he and Joshua were the only two surviving adults from the wilderness generation and the two spies who had given a positive report about entering the land many years earlier (Numbers 14).

After the preliminaries in chaps. 13–14, the inheritance of the most important tribe, Judah, is given (chap. 15). Another version of Caleb's inheritance is told (15:13–19), and the boundary descriptions and lists of cities are extensive. Then the inheritance of the tribes of Joseph—those descended from his two sons, Ephraim and Manasseh—is given (chaps. 16–17). Joseph had been Jacob's favorite son (Gen 37:3), and the tribes of Ephraim and Manasseh were the most important in the Northern Kingdom of Israel many years later.

Following the distribution of the lands to the most important tribes, the inheritances belonging to the remaining seven tribes are given in chaps. 17–18. At the end, Joshua is also singled out (as Caleb had been initially), and his inheritance is given in 19:49–50.

The lists conclude with the designation of the cities of refuge (chap. 20) and the cities allotted to the Levites (chap. 21). The concerns here show God's interest in more than just land per se. The land had many sacred functions, of which two were to provide for justice (the cities of refuge) and for God's special ministers (the Levitical cities).

According to one scholar, chaps. 13–21 are organized around the dividing up of Canaan, indicated by the key word *ḥlq,* "to divide."[2] Koorevaar argues that this section is the heart of the book and that, structurally, a concentric or chiastic pattern focuses the attention on the assembly at Shiloh in 18:1–10:

A   13:8–22 Transjordan for two and one-half tribes

  B   14:1–5 The principles of the division

    C   14:6–15 Beginning: Caleb's inheritance

      D   15:1–17:18 The lot for Judah and Joseph

        E   18:1–10 **The Tent of Meeting taken to Shiloh and the apportioning of the land**

      D′ 18:11–19:48 The lot for the seven remaining tribes

    C′ 19:49–51 Ending: Joshua's inheritance

  B′ 20:1–6 God's fourth initiative: designating cities of refuge

A′ 20:7–21:42 Cities of refuge and levitical cities

Many scholars believe that the author of the Book of Joshua was not responsible for producing the lists in chaps. 13–21, and this may very well be true. The lists may have been independent records that the author incorporated into his work, just as the authors of 1–2 Kings, 1–2 Chronicles, and Ezra–Nehemiah used lists and sources in the course of writing their books.[3] These lists undoubtedly came directly from Joshua, Eleazar (see 14:1), or someone else in the nation's leadership (or their scribes). At least some of the lists were produced by the twenty-one surveyors sent out from Shiloh to survey the territories of the seven remaining tribes of chaps. 18 and 19 (see 18:1–10).

Most scholars who have devoted extended attention to the origins and dates of these lists believe they came from sometime during the monarchy, the exile, or after the exile. More to the point, most such scholars do not believe that they accurately reflect any such parceling out of territories during the days of Joshua, but rather that they were retrojections of later political bound-

[2] H. J. Koorevaar, *De Opbouw van het Boek Jozua* (Ph.D. dissertation, University of Brussels, 1990), cited by J. G. McConville, *Grace in the End* (Grand Rapids: Zondervan, 1993), 101–2, and summarized by J. R. Vannoy, "Joshua: Theology of," *NIDOTTE* 4:811–14. Citations here are from Vannoy's summary.

[3] See D. M. Howard, Jr., *An Introduction to the Old Testament Historical Books* (Chicago: Moody, 1993), 173–76, 238–42, 277–80 on the use of sources in these later books.

aries—or idealized boundaries that never existed at any time in history—back
into the time of Joshua. The position taken in this commentary, however, is
that these lists do indeed preserve accurately the distributions that were made
in Joshua's time, regardless of whether or not they were incorporated into the
book at a later time and regardless of whether or not certain tribes ever fully
took possession of their lands.[4]

1. The Command to Distribute the Land (13:1–7)

[1]**When Joshua was old and well advanced in years, the LORD said to him,
"You are very old, and there are still very large areas of land to be taken over.**

[2]**"This is the land that remains: all the regions of the Philistines and Geshurites:** [3]**from the Shihor River on the east of Egypt to the territory of Ekron on the
north, all of it counted as Canaanite (the territory of the five Philistine rulers in
Gaza, Ashdod, Ashkelon, Gath and Ekron—that of the Avvites);** [4]**from the south,
all the land of the Canaanites, from Arah of the Sidonians as far as Aphek, the
region of the Amorites,** [5]**the area of the Gebalites; and all Lebanon to the east,
from Baal Gad below Mount Hermon to Lebo Hamath.**

[6]**"As for all the inhabitants of the mountain regions from Lebanon to Misrephoth Maim, that is, all the Sidonians, I myself will drive them out before the
Israelites. Be sure to allocate this land to Israel for an inheritance, as I have
instructed you,** [7]**and divide it as an inheritance among the nine tribes and half of
the tribe of Manasseh."**

Despite the general picture of complete victory in chaps. 10–11, we are
now reminded that much territory still remained to be taken (vv. 1–6a).[5] This
included territories of the Philistines and their neighbors in the south (vv. 2–

---

[4] A good review of the history of research on these chapters may be found in T. C. Butler,
Joshua, WBC 7 (Waco: Word, 1983), 141–44. See also N. Na'aman, *Borders and Districts in Biblical Historiography: Seven Studies in Biblical Geographical Lists,* JBS 4 (Jerusalem: Simor,
1986); Na'aman devotes five of his seven studies to the lists here in Joshua 13–21. The most important study is Z. Kallai's *Historical Geography of the Bible: The Tribal Territories of the Bible*
(Leiden: Brill; Jerusalem: Magnes, 1986). He reviews the history of study of the lists (pp. 3–15),
and then undertakes the most comprehensive study of the lists to date (the book is 543 pages in
length). He concludes that the lists reflect actual historical realities during the time of the United
Monarchies (see also the comments in the introduction to chap. 21). R. S. Hess's recent study
argues that the lists reflect even earlier realities, from premonarchical, Late Bronze Age traditions
("Asking Historical Questions of Joshua 13–19: Recent Discussion Concerning the Date of the
Boundary Lists," in A. R. Millard, J. K. Hoffmeier, D. W. Baker, eds., *Faith, Tradition, and History: Old Testament Historiography in Its Near Eastern Context* [Winona Lake: Eisenbrauns,
1994], 191–205). Likewise, see D. R. Davis's helpful comments (*No Falling Words: Expositions
of the Book of Joshua* [Grand Rapids: Baker, 1988], 126, n. 9).

[5] On the issue of the complete or incomplete nature of the conquest, see the commentary on
10:40–43.

The Twelve Tribes

Scale of Miles
0 · 10 · 20 · 30

Scale of Kilometers
0 · 10 · 20 · 30 · 40

Sidon
Damascus

Tyre
Mt. Hermon
Laish (*Dan*)

Asher
Naphtali
Kedesh

Merom?
Madon?
Hazor

Acco
Manasseh
Ashtaroth

Acshaph
Kinnereth
Sea of Kinnereth
Golan

Zebulun
Mt. Carmel
Shimron
Yarmuk River
Edrei

Dor
Jokneam
Mt. Tabor
Issachar

Megiddo

Taanach
Ramoth Gilead

Hepher · *Manasseh*
Jordan River

Mt. Ebal ▲
Mt. Gerizim ▲
Tirzah
Shechem
Zarethan
Jabbok River

Aphek
Tappuah
Adam
Gad
Ammon

Mediterranean Sea (Great Sea)

Joppa
Ephraim
Shiloh

Dan
Upper Beth Horon
Bethel
Gilgal
Rabbah of the Ammonites

Gezer
Kephirah
Ai
Gibeon
Jericho
Heshbon
Bezer

Aijalon
Benjamin
Mt. Nebo ▲
Medeba

Kiriath Jearim
Jerusalem
Beth Jeshimoth
Reuben

Ashdod
Jarmuth
Jahaz
Kedemoth

Gath
Azekah
Dead Sea (Salt Sea)

Ashkelon
Libnah
Adullam
Dibon

Gaza
Lachish
Hebron
En Gedi
Aroer

Makkedah
Eglon
Debir
Arnon River

Judah
Arad
Moab

Beersheba
Hormah

Simeon
Wilderness of Judah

Edom

3), the Phoenician coastland to the north (v. 4), and the northern, mountainous territories of Lebanon (vv. 5–6). It was not for Joshua to be involved in the remaining struggle for the land, however: he was too old (v. 1). Besides, God himself would drive out the remaining inhabitants (v. 6a); Joshua merely was to apportion the land to the nine and one-half tribes west of the Jordan, under God's guidance (vv. 6b–7).

Joshua was an old man, ready to move off the scene. In similar circumstances previously, a patriarch or leader had given a farewell speech, blessing those he was leaving behind (see Isaac in Genesis 27, Jacob in Genesis 49, and Moses in Deuteronomy 33).[6] Joshua too gave a farewell speech—two, in fact—but these are not recorded until chaps. 23 and 24. In fact, 23:1 also mentions that Joshua was old, using the exact wording found here (lit.): "Now Joshua was old, moving along in years,"[7] and this is followed by his first farewell speech to the nation. However, at this juncture in 13:1, Joshua still needed to perform the critically important task of distributing the land, and so the narrative flow leading to his farewell is interrupted by the lengthy lists of chaps. 14–21.[8]

As the book had begun with God addressing Joshua, encouraging him and giving him instructions (1:2–9), so now too God spoke to Joshua with instructions for carrying out his tasks (13:1b–7).

13:1 Joshua's advanced age made it necessary that he distribute the land before he gave his farewells to the tribes. Joshua's leadership role is again highlighted, in that he was central to the twin tasks of taking the land and distributing it. There was much land that had not been taken, and vv. 2–5 (or 2–6a) specify them. God's words in this verse begin by highlighting Joshua: the following translation captures the nuances here: "*You*, you are old, moving along in years, but as for the land, very much remains to be possessed." Despite Joshua's advanced age, the land was still important, and it needed to be apportioned, which was Joshua's task.

13:2–5 These verses specify which lands remained to be taken.[9] The description is not neatly symmetrical, but, then, neither was the distribution of the lands that had not yet been taken. The list is built on three geographical

---

[6] See Butler, *Joshua*, 147 on this point.

[7] The wording is וִיהוֹשֻׁעַ זָקֵן בָּא בַּיָּמִים.

[8] Chapters 14–21 are those in which Joshua is portrayed as giving the lands to the tribes. Chapter 13 is a review of distributions Moses had made to the Transjordan tribes, and chap. 22 involves Joshua's farewell to those same tribes.

[9] Good maps of these territories can be found in Y. Aharoni, *The Land of the Bible: A Historical Geography*, rev. ed. (Philadelphia: Westminster, 1979), 234 (and see his discussion on pp. 233–36); and T. V. Brisco, *Holman Bible Atlas* (Nashville: Broadman & Holman, 1998), 82 (although Brisco does not reflect the problems of identifying Geshur and Aphek [see the discussion below]). Extended discussion may be found in J. Simons, *The Geographical and Topographical Texts of the Old Testament* (Leiden: Brill, 1959), § 295; Na'aman, *Borders and Districts*, 39–73.

areas: the south (vv. 2–3), a "Canaanite" region of uncertain parameters (v. 4), and a northern region (v. 5).[10]

The southern region includes the territory of the Philistines and the Geshurites (v. 2), along the coastal plain in the southwestern part of Canaan. The "Geshur" here is almost certainly not the same one mentioned in 12:5; 13:11,13, which was northeast of the Sea of Kinnereth, but rather the Geshur mentioned in 1 Sam 27:8, in southwestern Canaan.[11] The southern region extended from the unknown Shihor River, in the far south,[12] to the area of Ekron (a Philistine city) in the north (v. 3).

The Philistines are mentioned now for the first time in the book. They were a mixed group of peoples who settled in Canaan in large numbers ca. 1200 B.C., but forebears of whom had been in the land since the time of Abraham (see Gen 21:32–24; 26:1; etc.). The reference here is either to these forebears or else the term "Philistine" is used to label the territory that later would become identified by its occupants.[13] The Philistines had five major cities, named here, ruled over by five "lords." The word for "lord" here—*seren*—is the only clearly Philistine word known,[14] and it is used consistently in the Bible to refer to the Philistine rulers of their five-city political organization.

The Avvites are known only here and in Deut 2:23 and 2 Kgs 17:31. They were driven out of their territory by the Caphtorites (who were from Crete), but little is known of them otherwise. They lived near Philistine territory.

The "land of the Canaanites" of v. 4 is unclear because there are several textual difficulties in this verse.[15] The area described by v. 4 was likely between the southern regions mentioned in vv. 2–3 and the far northern regions mentioned in vv. 5–6. The site of "Arah" is unknown. However, many Bible versions render this name as "Mearah," following the spelling in the MT (e.g., NASB, NJPSV, NRSV, NLT), but such a place is also unknown. The parallel with "from the south" at the beginning of the verse suggests that

---

[10] R. D. Nelson, *Joshua: A Commentary*, OTL (Louisville: Westminster John Knox, 1997), 166.

[11] See Simons, *Geographical and Topographical Texts*, § 295 (pp. 110–11). R. G. Boling's reading of "Gezerites," based on the Old Greek, is unconvincing, since the Old Greek spelling for "Gezer" is not what is found here (*Joshua*, Anchor Bible 6 [Garden City: Doubleday, 1982], 333).

[12] Shihor is mentioned in Isa 23:3 and Jer 2:18, referring to the Nile River (or a tributary), but here it appears to be "east" of Egypt, not "in" Egypt. See Butler, *Joshua*, 145–46; A. Betz, "Shihor," *ABD* 5:1212, for fuller discussion.

[13] See Howard, "Philistines," in A. E. Hoerth, G. L. Mattingly, and E. M. Yamauchi, eds., *Peoples of the Old Testament World* (Grand Rapids: Baker, 1994), 231–50, for an introduction to the Philistines, and pp. 234–38 on the issues surrounding their entrance into Canaan.

[14] It may be related to the Greek word τύραννος, "tyrant" (see Howard, "Philistines," 243, n. 42). Recently (in 1996), an important inscription was unearthed at Ekron, a Philistine site, but it was written in Hebrew. See S. Gitin, T. Dothan, J. Naveh, "A Royal Dedicatory Inscription from Ekron," *IEJ* 47 (1997): 1–16.

[15] See Na'aman, *Borders and Districts*, 52–54; Butler, *Joshua*, 146.

"from Arah" should be read here. This town belonged to the region of the Sidonians, which was in the far north along the coast, in the region of the Phoenicians. However, it probably was at the southern extreme of the Sidonian territory, since the construction in the verse is, literally, "from the south ... as far as Aphek as far as the border of the Amorites," which suggests a south-to-north progression. The reference to "Aphek" must be to a northern site, not to the Aphek in the central coastal plain (12:18).[16]

The northern portion of the description of unconquered lands (v. 5) extends to the far northern city of Gebal (also known as Byblos) and, in the east, from Baal Gad to Lebo Hamath. Baal Gad is described here as "below Mount Hermon," whereas in 11:17 and 12:7, it is "in the Valley of Lebanon," which is north and west of Mount Hermon. Baal Gad must have marked the southern point and Lebo Hamath the northern point of the Valley of Lebanon.[17] Lebo Hamath was at the northern end of the Valley of Lebanon and is commonly mentioned in the Bible in boundary descriptions (e.g., Num 13:21; 34:8; Judg 3:3; 1 Kgs 8:65; etc.). Hamath was an important city in biblical times (see 2 Sam 8:9–10; 2 Chr 8:4; etc.), and Lebo Hamath—whose name means "entrance of Hamath"—seems to have been the equivalent of a suburb.

13:6–7   The focus in v. 6a shifts to peoples instead of territories, but v. 6a appears to be the conclusion of the listing of unconquered territories and peoples. It summarizes the third portion of the list (v. 5) by referring to lands in the north. Misrephoth Maim is mentioned again in the Bible only in Josh 11:8 (on its location, see the commentary there).

The emphasis in v. 6a, however, shifts from a simple catalogue of territories (or peoples) to the activity that God promised he would undertake, namely, to drive out these peoples before the Israelites. The objects of God's activity are emphasized syntactically by appearing in the beginning of the verse. Furthermore, God emphasizes his own activity and his own fearsome attributes: "I myself[18] will drive them out before the Israelites." "Before" translates *mippĕnê*, which emphasizes the agent causing the dispossession, that is, God himself (see the commentary on 10:11).

Verses 6b–7 shift the focus away from the unconquered territories and people to Joshua's obligations to divide the land as an inheritance to the tribes west of the Jordan, just as God had commanded him. As such, this passage harks back to v. 1, and it shows vv. 2–5 (or 2–6a) to be a parenthetical aside detailing the lands remaining to be conquered, which are signaled at the end

---

[16] See R. Frankel, "Aphek," *ABD* 1:275–77, and Aharoni's map here (*Land of the Bible*, 234), against Brisco (*Holman Bible Atlas*, 82).

[17] See also Na'aman, *Borders and Districts*, 42–43; Simons, *Geographical and Topographical Texts*, § 509.

[18] The emphasis here on "myself" is to account for the grammatically redundant אָנֹכִי before the verb. Its presence highlights the subject of the verb, in this case, God.

of v. 1. Joshua's obligations are introduced by the restrictive adverb *raq,* "only" (untranslated in NIV).[19] Joshua was not to worry about what was God's to do (dispossessing the peoples, v. 6a), but rather on what he was to do (dividing up the land). He was to focus only on his task, not God's task too. His attention was also arrested by God's use of *wĕʿattâ,* "and now," at the beginning of v. 7 (untranslated in NIV): again, he was instructed to focus on his own task.

EXCURSUS: ISRAEL'S INHERITANCE OF THE LAND IN JOSHUA

The central idea in the Book of Joshua concerns the Israelites' taking possession of the land that God promised to the patriarchs. This is expressed in numerous ways, but key among them is the vocabulary of inheritance and possession of the land, expressed by the constellation of ideas surrounding the Hebrew roots *yrš* (the verb of which is usually translated "to inherit, possess" or "to drive out, dispossess") and *nḥl* (the verb of which is usually rendered "to inherit"). Below we consider these two important lexemes (or roots), as well as several others associated with them.

The overall picture of Israel's inheritance is a richly textured one. The use of so many different words to describe different aspects of it alone demonstrates this. God gave the land to his people as an inheritance, which they were to take possession of. In doing so, they were to dispossess the peoples who were now on this land. This dispossession included the idea of punishment for the displaced peoples. Israel's inheritance also involved their taking legal title of ownership of the land. Then, when the land was taken, it was carefully divided up, each tribe receiving the portion assigned to it by the casting of lots.

"To inherit, possess; drive out, dispossess" (yrš) in Joshua.[20] The root *yrš* is fairly common in the Old Testament, occurring about 230 times as a verb, meaning "to inherit, possess" or "to drive out, dispossess," and twenty-six times in four noun forms, meaning "inheritance, possession." It is found especially often in Deuteronomy and Joshua, which is not surprising, given these books' focus on the issue of God's gift of the land and its inheritance or possession by Israel. It occurs most frequently in Deuteronomy (seventy times) and is found in Joshua thirty times. The analysis below focuses on the two most important verb stems: the basic stem, usually called the *qal,* and the *hiphil* stem, which usually has a causative meaning (although *yrš* in the *hiphil* means "to drive out, dispossess," which is not a causative meaning).

yrš as "to inherit, possess." Throughout the Old Testament, the meaning of the basic stem involves the legal inheritance, or transfer, of family leadership and property (e.g., Gen 15:3–4; Num 27:11) and also the inheritance of territory (e.g.,

---

[19] See the commentary on 1:17 and footnotes there on the functions of רק.

[20] The following are important points of entrée into the discussion of *yrš*: Bird, *YRŠ and the Deuteronomic Theology of the Conquest* (Th.D. Diss., Harvard Divinity School, 1971); N. Lohfink, "ירשׁ *yārāš*," *TDOT* 6:368–96; C. J. H. Wright, "ירשׁ," *NIDOTTE* 2:547–49. I thank Professor Bird for making available to me a copy of her dissertation.

Deut 2:12; Josh 1:15; Judg 11:23–24). The inheritance sometimes is passively received (e.g., Gen 15:3–4; Lev 25:46; 2 Sam 14:7), but most commonly, referring to territory, it is something to be actively taken (e.g., Gen 15:7–8; Deut 11:31). When territory was taken, peoples were dispossessed (e.g., Deut 2:21–22; 12:29), in which case their lands became that which their conquerors inherited (Deut 12:24).

In Joshua all the occurrences of *yrš* in the basic stem refer to Israel's actively taking possession of the Canaanites' land,[21] and the NIV appropriately translates *yrš* as "take possession" or "occupy" in most instances. Two references illustrate the active nature of the verb: (1) "When Joshua was old and well advanced in years, the LORD said to him, 'You are very old, and there are still very large areas of land *to be taken over (yrš)*'" (13:1); (2) "So Joshua said to the Israelites: 'How long will you wait before you begin *to take possession (yrš)* of the land that the LORD, the God of your fathers, has given you?'" (18:3).

yrš as "to drive out, dispossess."   In the *hiphil* verb stem, the meaning of *yrš* primarily involves displacing or ejecting someone from his property or territory in order to be able to possess it for oneself (e.g., Num 32:21; Deut 4:38a; Judg 2:21). In almost every case, God is the subject of the verb, indicating that *he* would do the driving out. Deuteronomy 9:4–5 is a key text showing this: "After the LORD your God has driven them out before you, do not say to yourself, 'The LORD has brought me here *to take possession [yrš, qal]* of this land because of my righteousness.' No, it is on account of the wickedness of these nations that the LORD *is going to drive them out [yrš, hiphil]* before you. It is not because of your righteousness or your integrity that you are going in *to take possession [yrš, qal]* of their land; but on account of the wickedness of these nations, the LORD your God *will drive them out [yrš, hiphil]* before you, to accomplish what he swore to your fathers, to Abraham, Isaac and Jacob."

In Joshua, several references show God working in exactly this way, driving out Israel's enemies (3:10,10; 13:6; 23:5a; 23:9). In other passages, Moses (13:12), Caleb (14:12; 15:14), and the tribes of Ephraim and Manasseh (17:18) drove out peoples and possessed their land, with God's help. Joshua instructed those lying in wait to ambush Ai that they should rise up and take possession of the city (8:7).[22] In a negative sense, several times in Joshua, we read that the Israelites did *not*—or could not—drive out the Canaanites from various parts of the land (13:13; 15:63; 16:10; 17:12,13[2x]), and once, Israel was warned that God would not drive out the nations before them unless they kept themselves pure and did not intermarry with the Canaanites and worship their gods (23:13).

A number of passages in the Old Testament include a wordplay that uses both the major stems of *yrš* (*qal* and *hiphil*). This wordplay illustrates both sides of the idea that God *drove out* the Canaanite peoples *(yrš, hiphil)* so that his own people could *take possession (yrš, qal)* of God's gift of the land.[23] Good examples of

---

[21] Josh 1:11[2x],15[3x]; 12:1; 13:1; 18:3; 19:47; 21:43; 23:5b; 24:4,8.

[22] *yrš* is *hiphil* here; see Bird, *YRŠ*, 267–68 on this anomalous meaning of *yrš, hiphil.*

[23] The list includes Num 21:32; 33:53; Deut 9:4–5; 11:23; Josh 23:5; Judg 11:23–24[2x]. Cf. also Deut 18:12,14 and Ps 44:2–3[Hb. 3–4], where the wordplays are in separate verses.

this are Deut 9:4–5 (quoted above), and Judg 11:23–24: "So then the LORD, the God of Israel, *dispossessed [yrš, hiphil]* the Amorites from before his people Israel; and are you *to take possession [yrš, qal]* of them? Will you not *possess [yrš, qal]* what Chemosh your god *gives you to possess (yrš, hiphil)*? And all that the LORD our God *has dispossessed [yrš, hiphil]* before us, we *will possess [yrš, qal]*" (RSV). In Joshua, this wordplay is found once: "The LORD your God will push them back before you, and *drive them out [yrš, hiphil]* of your sight; and you *shall possess [yrš, qal]* their land, as the LORD your God promised you" (Josh 23:5).[24]

Distribution. The distribution of usage of *yrš* in the Book of Joshua is instructive as well. *yrš* is found primarily in the second half of the book (twenty-four of thirty-three occurrences). This should not be surprising, given that the primary focus in the second half of the book is the land distribution.

Summary. In sum, both the *qal* and *hiphil* forms of *yrš* reinforce the idea that Israel's inheritance was a legal transaction, a transfer of property that was a gift from God: what God gave, Israel inherited as a possession. We have already seen earlier that God was the ultimate source of the gift of the land to Israel, and in several significant passages, the giving and the inheritance are linked.[25] That which God gave, Israel was to receive by taking possession of it. Typical are the following: "Three days from now you will cross the Jordan here to go in and *take possession [yrš]* of the land the LORD your God *is giving [ntn]* you for your own" (Josh 1:11b); "So the LORD gave *(ntn)* Israel all the land he had sworn to their forefathers, and they took possession of it *(yrš)* and settled there" (Josh 21:43).[26]

"To inherit" (nḥl) in Joshua.[27] The root *nḥl* is closely related to *yrš*, and their meanings overlap in large degree. It occurs in Joshua more times than in any other book of the Old Testament, indicating the centrality of this idea in the book.

---

[24] The continuity of meaning between *qal* and *hiphil* is explained well by Bird: "The idea represented by this *hiphil* is simply the corollary or counterpart of that found in the extended use of the *qal* to speak of 'inheriting' by conquest. It is 'inheriting' by dispossessing. The *hiphil* makes essentially the same statement as the *qal*, only it focuses on the former owners rather than their possessions" (Bird, *YRŠ*, 277). The essential idea of the *hiphil*, then, is not "to drive out" per se and certainly not "to destroy"; rather, it is "'dispossess' (with the aim of claiming the property of the dispossessed as an 'inheritance')" (p. 283).

[25] *yrš* and *ntn* are linked in this sense nine times in Joshua (Josh 1:11,15; 8:7; 12:6–7; 18:3; 21:43; 24:4,8). All uses of *yrš* are *qal*, except for 8:7 *(hiphil),* where God gave *(ntn)* Ai for Israel to possess *(yrš, hiphil);* see Bird, *YRŠ*, 267–6,8 on this anomalous meaning of *yrš, hiphil.* In 12:6–7 the defeated kings' lands are given as an inheritance *(yĕruššâ).* The two roots are also linked many times in Deuteronomy and elsewhere. See Bird, *YRŠ,* 338–60, for a broad-ranging discussion of *yrš* and *ntn* in the Deuteronomistic History and her tables on pp. 335–36, listing the collocation of the two roots outside of Joshua.

[26] An influential OT scholar, N. Lohfink, has argued extensively that the *hiphil* of *yrš* means "to destroy, exterminate," not simply "drive out" or "dispossess" *(TDOT* 6:374–75, 382–83 and bibliography there). However, this cannot be supported in light of the root's usage. I have demonstrated this in an essay (March 1998), which I hope to publish in the future.

[27] See the following on *nḥl:* C. J. H. Wright, "נחל," *NIDOTTE* 3:77–81; G. Wanke, "נַחֲלָה Nāḥǎlâ, possession," *TLOT* 2:731–34.

The basic stem of the verb means "to obtain something as a possession," while the noun *nāḥălâ* denotes "essentially inalienable, thus enduring, property, esp. land, which devolves *(npl)* upon individuals or a group as a grant, as an inheritance, or through dispossession of the prior owner. [It] properly implies an enduring claim to possession."[28]

Inheritance (nāḥălâ) as Ownership. In the Old Testament, *nāḥălâ* refers essentially to three ideas, all involving ownership. Ownership is an integral part of the concept of *nāḥălâ*: God owned the land, and he gave it to his people Israel. First, and most commonly, *nāḥălâ* refers to land, whether owned by individuals (e.g., Num 32:18–19; Deut 19:14), by family groups (e.g., Num 33:54a), or by tribes (e.g., Num 33:54b). Since land was given by God, it is not surprising to find it referred to as Yahweh's "inheritance" in several texts (e.g., Exod 15:17; Ps 68:9–10 [Hb. 10–11]; Jer 12:7–9), probably meaning "a special, permanent, and precious possession" (since God did not "inherit" the land from anyone).[29]

Second, the idea of ownership can be seen in the references to Israel as Yahweh's inheritance, in passages such as Deut 4:20; 32:8–9; 1 Sam 26:19. Yahweh did not "inherit" Israel himself, but rather he owned it. Israel belonged to Yahweh, and not any of the other gods (Jer 10:16 // 51:19). In several prayers, the petitioners asked Yahweh to restore his people because they were his inheritance, that is, a permanent, special possession (e.g., Exod 34:9; 1 Kgs 8:52–53; Isa 63:17).[30]

Third, this idea of Israel as Yahweh's inheritance is reversed in some texts, and Yahweh is *Israel's* inheritance or, more specifically, Levi's inheritance. This is expressed in several texts in the Pentateuch (e.g., Num 18:20; Deut 18:2). Along with this, sometimes, the tithes given by the Israelites or the offerings by fire were Levi's inheritance (e.g., Num 18:21; Deut 18:1).

Inheritance (nāḥălâ) in Joshua. In the Book of Joshua, which speaks of this inheritance more than any other book, we find almost all of these ideas expressed. Even more than *yrš*, *nḥl* is found almost exclusively in the second half of the book, where the land is parceled out.[31] Usually the inheritance spoken of is the individual tribes' inheritance of their allotted land portions: the tribes east of the Jordan as a group (13:8,23,28), the tribes west of the Jordan (13:7; 14:2), the tribe of Judah (15:20), the tribes of Ephraim and Manasseh (16:5,8,9; 17:14), and the remaining seven tribes (nineteen times in chaps. 18–19). In a few instances, the entire land of Canaan is mentioned as Israel's inheritance (1:6; 11:23; 13:6). In the case of the tribe of Levi, its inheritance was the offerings by fire (13:14), the Lord himself (13:33), and the priestly service (18:7).

YRŠ **and** *NḤL* **Compared.** The two primary lexemes for inheritance—*yrš* and *nḥl*—have almost identical meanings, as we have seen. Both mean "to inherit." Both are gifts from God. *yrš* focuses a bit more on the taking possession of that which rightfully belongs to the recipient. Both terms refer to the land as that which is inherited, but *nḥl* focuses more exclusively on the land. *yrš (hiphil)*

---

[28] Wanke, *TLOT* 2:731.
[29] Wright, *NIDOTTE* 3:79.
[30] Wright, *NIDOTTE* 3:79–80.
[31] The only exceptions are in 1:6 and 11:23.

focuses on dispossessing the inhabitants of the land, a nuance not found for *nḥl*. *nḥl*, in its association with the division and parceling out of the land (see below, on *ḥlq*), focuses somewhat more on the measuring and demarcating of the boundaries of the inheritance.

yrš and *nḥl* occur in conjunction with each other at least fifteen times in the Old Testament, twice in Joshua.[32] The two instances in Joshua are typical:

> As for all the inhabitants of the mountain regions from Lebanon to Misrephoth Maim, that is, all the Sidonians, I myself *will drive them out [yrš]* before the Israelites. Be sure to allocate this land to Israel for an *inheritance [nāḥălâ]*, as I have instructed you. (Josh 13:6)

> Remember how I have allotted as an *inheritance [nāḥălâ]* your tribes all the land of the nations that remain—the nations I conquered—between the Jordan and the Great Sea in the west. The LORD your God himself will drive them out *[hdp]* of your way. He *will push them out [yrš]* before you, and you *will take possession [yrš]* of their land, as the LORD your God promised you. (Josh 23:4–5)

Other Terms Associated with Inheritance.   While *yrš* and *nḥl* are the two terms most commonly designating inheritance, several other terms are used in conjunction with them, clarifying and expanding their meaning. Sometimes these terms are used instead of *yrš* or *nḥl*. These include *grš*, "to drive out, cast out," *ḥlq* "to divide, apportion" (as a noun: "portion, territory"), *grl*, "lot (noun), to cast a lot (verb)," and *ntn* "to give." We will consider each briefly below (except for *ntn*, "to give," which we have considered at length above [after 1:3]).

"To drive out, cast out" (grš).   This verb occurs forty-seven times in the Old Testament but only twice in Joshua: 24:12,18. Its meaning is close to that of *yrš (hiphil)*, "to dispossess," but there is a slight difference (see next paragraph). *GRŠ* is the term used, for example, when Abraham drove out Hagar from his household (Gen 21:10), when Solomon expelled Abiathar from the priesthood (1 Kgs 2:27), and as a term for a divorced woman, that is, one who is cast out (Lev 21:7,14; 22:13; Num 30:9 [Hb. 10]; Ezek 44:22). It has a special theological nuance when God is the subject of the verb. In almost every case, being cast out *(grš)* involves shame or punishment. For example, God expelled Adam and Eve from the Garden of Eden (Gen 3:24), Cain from his land (Gen 4:14), and he banished Jonah from his sight (Jonah 2:4 [Hb. 5]).

God also expelled *(grš)* the peoples of Canaan from the land so that the Israelites could occupy it.[33] In this respect, *grš* is close to *yrš (hiphil)*, except that *grš*

---

[32] The verb forms occur together five times: Lev 25:46; Deut 19:14; 1 Chr 28:8; Isa 57:13. See also the combination in Ps 69:36 *(yrš)* and thirty-seven *(nḥl)*. The combination of the verb of *yrs*, "to possess," and the noun *nāḥălâ*, "inheritance," appears at least ten times: Num 27:11; 36:8[2x]; Deut 4:38; 15:4; 19:14; 25:19; 26:1; Josh 13:6; Judg 2:6; Ezek 36:12. The combination is also found in Josh 23:4 *(nāḥălâ)* and 5 *(yrš[2x])*.

[33] The instances are as follows: Exod 23:28,29,30; 33:2; 34:11; Deut 33:27; Josh 24:12,18; Judg 6:9; Ezek 31:11 (Egyptians); Ps 78:55. In Exod 23:28 and Josh 24:12, the "hornet" is the subject, but it is either a metaphorical reference to God's activity or a literal swarm sent by God. In Hos 9:15, God warned Israel that he would drive *them* out of the land because of their wickedness.

implies punishment as an integral part of the dispossession. This recalls God's words to Abraham that his descendants would not return to the land of Canaan for four hundred years, "for the sin of the Amorites [i.e., Canaanites] has not yet reached its full measure" (Gen 15:16). The Israelites' entry into the land of Canaan would not only fulfill God's promises to Abraham, but it also would serve as a means of punishment of the wicked Canaanites (see Deut 9:4–5). The term as it is used in Joshua (24:12,18) does not overtly carry this meaning (although it may imply it); rather, it emphasizes God's complete sovereignty and initiative in driving out Israel's enemies.

"To divide, apportion; portion, territory" (ḥlq). The verb of *ḥlq* (meaning "to divide, apportion") and several related nouns (meaning "portion, territory") are closely related to Israel's inheritance of the land. This is because the tribal inheritances were parceled out, or divided, among the tribes. The NIV variously translates the verb in Joshua as "divide," "allot," "or "apportion" and the noun as "division," "allotment," or "portion." That which was apportioned to people or groups was "the portion coming to one by law and custom,"[34] that is, that which belonged to them, whether by legal title, promise, or other factor. The stress is on the allocating or apportioning.[35] The most common use of *ḥlq* is with reference to land, although other uses are found.[36]

In Joshua, the following examples are typical. (1) "And divide *[ḥlq]* it as an inheritance *(nḥl)* among the nine tribes and half of the tribe of Manasseh" (13:7); (2) "These are the territories *[nāḥălâ]* that Eleazar the priest, Joshua son of Nun and the heads of the tribal clans of Israel assigned by lot *[gôrāl]* at Shiloh in the presence of the LORD at the entrance to the Tent of Meeting. And so they finished dividing *[ḥlq]* the land" (19:51); (3) "You are to divide *[ḥlq]* the land into seven parts *[ḥlq]*. Judah is to remain in its territory on the south and the house of Joseph in its territory on the north. After you have written descriptions of the seven parts *[ḥlq]* of the land, bring them here to me and I will cast lots *[gôrāl]* for you in the presence of the LORD our God. The Levites, however, do not get a portion *[ḥlq]* among you because the priestly service of the Lord is their inheritance *[nāḥălâ]*. And Gad, Reuben and the half-tribe of Manasseh have already received their inheritance *[nāḥălâ]* on the east side of the Jordan. Moses the servant of the LORD gave *[ntn]* it to them" (18:5–7).

These representative examples show the close connection between the dividing *(ḥlq)* of the land and the inheritance *(nḥl/nāḥălâ)* of it. They show that God was the giver *(ntn)* of the inheritance. They also show that the apportioning was done by lot *(gôrāl)*, which was controlled by God.

The roots *ḥlq,* "to divide, apportion," and *nāḥălâ,* "inheritance," occur together in five instances in Joshua: 13:7; 18:2,7; 19:9,51.[37] These show that the individual tribes' inheritances were carefully apportioned to them and carefully

---

[34] M. Tsevat, "חָלַק; *chālaq* II," *TDOT* 4:448.

[35] C. Van Dam, "חלק," *NIDOTTE* 2:162.

[36] Ibid.

[37] The other main term for inheritance—*yrš*—does not occur in any immediate proximity to *ḥlq* in Joshua.

accounted for. A good example of this is Josh 19:9: "The inheritance *[nāḥălâ]* of the Simeonites was taken from the share *[ḥbl]* of Judah, because Judah's portion *[ḥlq]* was more than they needed. So the Simeonites received their inheritance *nḥl]* within the territory *[nāḥălâ]* of Judah."

"Lot" (gôrāl). The casting of lots was done in Old Testament times in order to help with decision making. For example, the two goats chosen on the Day of Atonement for sacrificing and for scapegoating were chosen by lot (Lev 16:8–10). The families that were to bring wood for the temple for burning were determined by lot (Neh 10:34[Hb. 35]). In Nehemiah's day, those who were to live in Jerusalem, to repopulate it, were chosen by lot (Neh 11:1).

God was in control of the lot. This is affirmed by 1 Sam 14:41, which states: "Then Saul prayed to the LORD, the God of Israel, 'Give me the right answer.' And Jonathan and Saul were taken by lot *[gôrāl]*, and the men were cleared." This is also affirmed by Prov 16:33, which states that "the lot *[gôrāl]* is cast into the lap, but its every decision is from the LORD."

The Book of Joshua speaks of lot casting more than any other book in the Old Testament, more than a third of the Old Testament occurrences (twenty-six of seventy-seven times), all of them in the land distribution chapters (Joshua 14–21). The distribution of the land was done by casting of the lots, which God controlled. The following passages are representative. (1) "Their inheritances *[nāḥălâ]* were assigned by lot *[gôrāl]* to the nine-and-a-half tribes, as the LORD had commanded through Moses" (14:2). (2) "Joshua then cast lots *[gôrāl]* for them in Shiloh in the presence of the LORD, and there he distributed *[ḥlq]* the land to the Israelites according to their tribal divisions *[ḥlq]*. The lot *[gôrāl]* came up for the tribe of Benjamin, clan by clan. Their allotted *[gôrāl]* territory lay between the tribes of Judah and Joseph" (18:10–11).

These passages show clearly that the casting of lots *(gôrāl)* was bound up with the dividing *(ḥlq)* of the inheritances *(nāḥălâ)* of the tribes of Israel. The inheritance of the land was under God's control, through the casting of lots.

Summary. The portrait of Israel's inheritance of the land of Canaan, the land promised to Abraham, is a richly textured one. First and foremost, it was a gift from Israel's God, Yahweh. It involved a legal transfer to the Israelites of Canaanite lands, which Yahweh owned. Since it was a gift, all that was required of the Israelites was that they take possession of this land, which they did, with Yahweh's help in matters military. As the Israelites took possession, they drove out the Canaanites who lived there in the land, and this was in punishment for their wickedness. The Israelites destroyed the Canaanites on a wide scale, but the idea of Israel's inheriting the land is carefully distinguished from the idea of the destruction of the Canaanites.

Israel's inheritance of the land meant that they owned legal title to it. This was possible because the land was Yahweh's, who gave it to them. Israel itself was Yahweh's inheritance (i.e., he owned it), and Yahweh himself was the Levites' inheritance since they did not inherit their own tribal territory.

The land's importance was such that it was carefully parceled out, with Yahweh guiding the allotments by the lots that were cast. Each tribe's inheritance was a matter of great importance, so much so that the process of the allotments, and their boundaries, are recounted in great deal in the Book of Joshua.

2. The Transjordan Distribution Recalled (13:8–33)

Before Joshua's distribution of the lands west of the Jordan, the previous land distribution is reviewed. It had been done under Moses and was to the tribes of Reuben, Gad, and Eastern Manasseh. This review performs several functions. First, it details the boundaries of the inheritances of the Transjordan tribes, which had not been so detailed before (only general summaries are given in Numbers 32 and Deut 2:26–3:17). Second, it emphasizes the unity of Israel—on both sides of the Jordan—that is important in 1:12–18 and 12:1–6, and that will be seen again in chap. 22. Third, it again emphasizes Joshua's leadership position as Moses' successor: in the same way that Moses had apportioned the Transjordan territories, so now Joshua was to do with the land west of the Jordan. Fourth, it anticipates the "landless" state of the Levites (vv. 14,33) and the Levitical cities to be mentioned later (chap. 21), reminding us of the Levites' importance. Fifth, it serves as a subtle warning that not all is entirely well at this juncture, because some peoples of the land still lived in Israel's territory (see v. 13).

(1) General Survey (13:8–13)

[8]The other half of Manasseh, the Reubenites and the Gadites had received the inheritance that Moses had given them east of the Jordan, as he, the servant of the LORD, had assigned it to them.

[9] It extended from Aroer on the rim of the Arnon Gorge, and from the town in the middle of the gorge, and included the whole plateau of Medeba as far as Dibon, [10]and all the towns of Sihon king of the Amorites, who ruled in Heshbon, out to the border of the Ammonites. [11]It also included Gilead, the territory of the people of Geshur and Maacah, all of Mount Hermon and all Bashan as far as Salecah— [12]that is, the whole kingdom of Og in Bashan, who had reigned in Ashtaroth and Edrei and had survived as one of the last of the Rephaites. Moses had defeated them and taken over their land. [13]But the Israelites did not drive out the people of Geshur and Maacah, so they continue to live among the Israelites to this day.

A general survey of the lands east of the Jordan River now follows (vv. 8–13), before the more detailed listings later in the chapter (vv. 15–31). It is not until chap. 14 that we will read of Joshua beginning to carry out God's instructions of vv. 6b–7. First, Moses, the model leader, is shown having allotted the lands east of the Jordan, and then Joshua will be shown doing the same thing. The lands in this section were those that Moses had allotted to the remaining two and one-half tribes (the nine and one-half tribes west of the

Jordan have just been mentioned at the end of v. 7).[38] The original account is found in Numbers 32.[39] Most of the places mentioned in this short summary are also found in the more detailed listings that follow.[40]

13:8 The section begins awkwardly: "With it, the Reubenites and the Gadites took their inheritance." The pronominal suffix "it" probably refers to the half tribe of Manasseh east of the Jordan River, and most versions supply the fuller reference (so NIV, NASB, NJPSV, NRSV, NLT). The inheritance that Moses had given these tribes is first mentioned in Num 32:33–42 and Deut 3:8–17. Moses' authority as the Lord's servant and as the one eligible to parcel out the land is in view here (see 1:14–15; 22:4), laying the foundation for Joshua to assume that same authority (see 14:1). The taking *(lqḥ)* of the land that the two and one-half tribes did also sets the precedent for the rest of the tribes to do the same thing, although the only other time this verb is used in the book to describe taking of land, it again refers to the two and one-half tribes (18:7). Not once is it said that any of the tribes west of the Jordan took *(lqḥ)* their lands. The focus in the later chapters is on God's and Joshua's *giving* of the land and their *possessing* it—and, sometimes, on the fact that the tribes did *not* dispossess the land's inhabitants.

13:9–12 The description of the territory assigned to the Transjordan tribes moves generally from south to north. The border from Aroer in the Arnon Gorge is already mentioned in 12:2 (and cf. 13:16; 2 Sam 24:5; etc.). It was the Israelites' southern boundary with Moab (see map). The list moves northward to the plains of Medeba and then returns southward to include the town of Dibon (v. 9). The Gadites apparently fortified it (Num 32:24), but it was assigned to Reuben (Josh 13:17).

The description changes from boundary and territorial descriptions in v. 9 to focus on Sihon, the king who ruled in Heshbon (v. 10). Heshbon was at the northeastern edge of Reuben's territory, bordering on the Ammonites' lands (v. 10). Sihon is known from many biblical texts; the principal story of his defeat by the Israelites is told in Num 21:21–31.

The list returns to describing territory in v. 11, describing it in terms similar to those in chap. 12. It included Gilead (cf. 12:2,5), which stretched north-

---

[38] See the maps in B. J. Beitzel, *The Moody Atlas of the Bible* (Chicago: Moody, 1985), 100; C. G. Rasmussen, *Zondervan NIV Atlas of the Bible* (Grand Rapids: Zondervan, 1989), 101; Brisco, *Holman Bible Atlas*, 84. A brief but very useful overview of all the tribal inheritances is in R. S. Hess, "Tribes, territories of the," *ISBE* 4:907–13. Hess's treatment of the Transjordan tribes is on pp. 910–11.

[39] For good treatments of the historical geography of Numbers 32 and other passages, see R. D. Cole, *Numbers*, NAC 4 (Nashville: Broadman & Holman, forthcoming), *ad loc.*

[40] Scholarly conjectures concerning the origins, dates, and provenience of the lists in vv. 8–33 are myriad and complex, but ultimately they add little or nothing to the understanding of them in their present contexts. For reviews of the discussion, see J. A. Soggin, *Joshua: A Commentary*, OTL (Philadelphia: Westminster, 1972), 154–57; Butler, *Joshua*, 158–59.

ward from the Arnon River in the south to Bashan in the north. Gilead was an important area for Israel and is mentioned well over one hundred times in the Old Testament, in most periods of its history. Gilead was a fertile region at high elevation, with abundant forests (Jer 22:6; 50:19) and olives, grains, and vines flourishing on the western slopes. It was especially known for a healing balm used for medicinal purposes (Jer 8:22; 46:11); and spices, balm, and myrrh came from there (Gen 37:25).[41]

The region of the Geshurites and Maacathites is again mentioned (cf. 12:5), along with Mount Hermon in the north (cf. 12:1,5) and the region of Bashan as far east as Salecah (cf. 12:4–5). The region described in v. 11 was essentially the kingdom ruled by the other Transjordanian king defeated by Moses, Og, king in Bashan (v. 12; cf. Num 32:33–35). Og and his kingdom are described here in the same terms as in 12:4.

The concluding comment in this list is that Moses had defeated and dispossessed "them,"[42] that is, everyone in all the territories mentioned in vv. 9–12. This lays the foundation for the contrast in v. 13.

13:13 Immediately following the commendation of Moses for defeating *(nkh)* and dispossessing *(yrš)* the kings and peoples in Transjordan at the end of v. 12, the next words state that the Israelites did not dispossess *(yrš)* the people of Geshur and Maacah, people who are listed as having been defeated *(nkh)* by Moses and the Israelites in 12:5. This shows that the "defeats" mentioned in the Book of Joshua were not always total annihilations. Here, these people's survival is a preview of the motif of incomplete conquest discussed above (see on 10:40–43).[43] Indeed, Geshur figured in events in David's day: Absalom, David's son, was born to a Geshurite princess (2 Sam 3:3), and he took refuge there when he rebelled against his father (2 Sam 13:37–38; 14:23,32; etc.). Maacah too survived to plague David: one thousand men from Maacah were part of an Ammonite coalition that opposed him (2 Sam 10:6,8). These troubles in David's day can be seen as one consequence of the Israelites' failure to follow through on God's instructions in Joshua's day.

(2) The Levites' Inheritance (13:14)

[14]But to the tribe of Levi he gave no inheritance, since the offerings made by fire to the LORD, the God of Israel, are their inheritance, as he promised them.

Instead of a land inheritance, the sacrifices of the Lord himself would be

---

[41] See Simons, *Geographical and Topographical Texts*, § 93; Rasmussen, *NIV Atlas of the Bible*, 52; M. Ottoson, "Gilead," *ABD* 2:1020–22.

[42] The third masculine plural suffix is the object of both verbs here, although it is obscured somewhat in the NIV.

[43] See also the discussion of "Cities and Territories Remaining to Be Conquered" in the excursus "Patterns in the Land Distribution Lists" at the end of this chapter.

the Levites' privileged inheritance. The contrast between the Levites and the other tribes is reinforced by *raq*, "only" at the beginning of the verse (it is untranslated in NIV, but see the comment on v. 6b). The landless state of the tribe of Levi is important in the Book of Joshua, but it had its roots much earlier. It is mentioned here and in v. 33, as well as in 14:3–4 and 18:7. These passages hark back to the Lord's directives to Aaron in Num 18:20–24, where their inheritance was to be the tithes that the Israelites presented to the Lord, and to Moses' words in Deut 18:1–5, where they were to receive the choicest offerings that the people brought to the Lord (cf. also Deut 10:8–9).

These passages show the important nature of the ministry of the Lord's work. While these, his ministers, did not have land, they did have rights to the choicest of the offerings. It was a great privilege to serve the Lord, and he himself would be their inheritance (v. 33). It was to Israel's great shame that, many years later, the Levites and temple singers were having to work in the fields in order to survive because God's people were not bringing their tithes, the portions assigned to the Levites (Neh 13:10–13).

The apostle Paul made a similar point in addressing the church at Corinth when he said, "Don't you know that those who work in the temple get their food from the temple, and those who serve at the altar share in what is offered on the altar?" (1 Cor 9:13). He was speaking of the right that he and fellow servants of the gospel had to be supported by the church (although, for reasons of independence, he did not exercise that right). Thus, the principle of supporting the workers in God's service has its roots in God's earliest instructions for his people and is repeated as binding on the Christian church as well.

Originally, the tribe of Levi had been sentenced to a landless existence for its violent behavior in the matter of the Shechemites (Gen 49:5–7; cf. 34:25–31), but, later, the Levites redeemed themselves (Exod 32:25–28) and were promised a blessing for it (Deut 33:8–11). Their exclusion from inheriting land explains why only twelve tribes are spoken of when, technically, thirteen tribes were now represented: of the original twelve sons of Jacob, Joseph's inheritance was divided into two, for his two sons, Ephraim and Manasseh; so the exclusion of Levi from land inheritance kept the number at twelve. (This is explained in Josh 14:3–4.) However, the Levites did inherit individual cities in the territories of each tribe (chap. 21).

(3) Reuben's Inheritance (13:15–23)

¹⁵This is what Moses had given to the tribe of Reuben, clan by clan:

¹⁶ The territory from Aroer on the rim of the Arnon Gorge, and from the town in the middle of the gorge, and the whole plateau past Medeba ¹⁷to Heshbon and all its towns on the plateau, including Dibon, Bamoth Baal, Beth Baal Meon, ¹⁸Jahaz, Kedemoth, Mephaath, ¹⁹Kiriathaim, Sibmah, Zereth Shahar on the hill in the valley, ²⁰Beth Peor, the slopes of Pisgah, and Beth Jeshimoth ²¹—all the

towns on the plateau and the entire realm of Sihon king of the Amorites, who ruled at Heshbon. Moses had defeated him and the Midianite chiefs, Evi, Rekem, Zur, Hur and Reba—princes allied with Sihon—who lived in that country. [22]In addition to those slain in battle, the Israelites had put to the sword Balaam son of Beor, who practiced divination. [23]The boundary of the Reubenites was the bank of the Jordan. These towns and their villages were the inheritance of the Reubenites, clan by clan.

The Reubenites' inheritance in this section is the first of the twelve apportionments in this and the following chapters. These lists follow certain patterns, which are discussed in the excursus on "Patterns in the Land Distribution Lists" at the end of this chapter.

13:15 The introductory statement emphasizes Moses' part and also the clans (see comments above).

13:16 The list proper begins by demarcating the eastern limits of Reuben's territory, from Aroer in the southeast along the plateau past Medeba to Heshbon in the northeast (v. 17). The description here matches that in v. 9 word for word.

13:17–20 Heshbon in this verse should be considered as the last element of the description that begins in v. 16, where the common pattern "from ... from ... to" is found. After Heshbon, the list focuses on eleven (or twelve?) cities, beginning with Dibon in the south (v. 17), moving to Jahaz, Kedemoth, and Mephaath in the east (v. 18), and ending with several cities in the northwest (vv. 19–20).[44] A brief list of cities that the Reubenites rebuilt is found earlier, in Num 32:37–38, including Heshbon, Elealeh, Kiriathaim, Nebo, Baal Meon, and Sibmah, and all but Elealeh and Nebo are mentioned again here (vv. 17,19). Heshbon later was a Levitical city in the territory of Gad, not Reuben (21:39), which shows the overlapping nature of some of the territorial descriptions (note, e.g., that Heshbon is also mentioned in Gad's territorial allotment [13:26]). Mephaath (v. 18) also became a Levitical city (21:37).

Several of the cities' histories are worth mentioning because of prior connections with Israel. Jahaz (v. 18) became a Levitical city (21:36), and it was the site where Sihon had engaged the Israelites in battle (Num 21:23; Deut 2:32). Kedemoth (v. 18) also became a Levitical city (Josh 21:37), and it was the place where Israel had encamped prior to its encounter with Sihon (Deut 2:26). Beth Peor (v. 20) was the notorious place where the Israelites had succumbed to the Moabite women's seductions and engaged in worshiping their god, the Baal of Peor (Num 25:1–3; 31:16). As it turned out, Balaam the diviner had advised the Moabites to entrap the Israelites in this way (31:16). The inclusion of this city here in Joshua 13 paves the way for the special men-

---

[44] The map in Rasmussen, *NIV Atlas of the Bible*, 101 shows most of these cities clearly. For a detailed discussion, see Simons, *Geographical and Topographical Texts*, § 298.

tion of Balaam in v. 22. The reference to the slopes of Pisgah, northeast of the Dead Sea, is somewhat strange here, since the rest of the locations are cities, and this is a region.[45] It has been mentioned already in 12:3.

13:21–22 The list moves toward its conclusion by stating in a broad sweep that all the towns in the plateau, and, most broadly, all of Sihon's realm, were part of Reuben's inheritance. Moses had defeated Sihon and his five Midianite allies, whose names appear only here and in Num 31:8. The inclusion of the names of defeated kings in this list otherwise concerned only with cities and territories is a small way of celebrating the earlier victories that made this territorial acquisition possible. It also may be a subtle reminder that the current Israelites did not follow through on their obligations and kill all the inhabitants of the land (see v. 13).

The reference to the Midianites is the only one in the Book of Joshua. These were a people well known to the Israelites, beginning with Joseph's being sold to Midianite traders by his brothers (Gen 37:28,36). Moses spent his wilderness years in the land of Midian (Exod 2:15), and he married Zipporah, the daughter of Jethro, a priest of Midian (Exod 2:16–21). Later, the Midianites appeared as enemies of Israel (Numbers 22–24), and the Israelites fought and defeated them in the battle referred to here in Joshua 13 (Numbers 31). The Midianites were enemies of Israel in Gideon's day, as well, and he led Israel when the Lord defeated Midian on Israel's behalf (Judges 6–8).[46]

Balaam is singled out in v. 22 for special mention. He was the Mesopotamian soothsayer hired by Balak, king of Moab, to curse the Israelites in the wilderness (Numbers 22–24). He only spoke what God told him to, yet he later sinned by inciting the Moabite women to seduce the Israelite men (Num 25:1–9; 31:16). This record of Balaam's death echoes the notice found at Num 31:8. The story of God's turning Balaam's desire to curse Israel into a blessing was significant in Israel's history, and it is told several times (see Josh 24:9–10; Deut 23:4–5; Neh 13:2; Mic 6:5).

13:23 Finally, the list ends by giving the western boundary of the Reubenites' territory, the natural one of the Jordan River. The concluding statement—"These towns and their villages were the inheritance of the Reubenites, clan by clan"—is echoed in many of the following lists (see above). The reference to the "towns and their villages" is typical of the lists through chap. 19. The phrase is literally "the cities and their villages," but most of the "cities" here were small enough to justify the NIV's rendering as

---

[45] Boling argues that originally it was the name of a town or village, which would make it fit into the list more easily (Boling, *Joshua*, 324, 343).

[46] The Midianites have been among the more obscure peoples of the Bible extrabiblically, but the light of archaeological and historical inquiry is slowly making them better known. See J. F. A. Sawyer and D. J. A. Clines, eds., *Midian, Moab, and Edom*, JSOTSup 24 (Sheffield: JSOT, 1983); G. E. Mendenhall, "Midian," *ABD* 4:815–18.

"towns." Typically, the largest Canaanite cities were built protected by walls (e.g., Jericho), but many smaller villages sprang up around them. The word for villages here refers to permanent settlements without walls, that is, outlying farming villages.[47] The cities and their villages comprised the small city-states typical of Canaan at this time.[48] On the phrase "clan by clan," see the introduction to this section (13:15–23).

(4) Gad's Inheritance (13:24–28)

[24]This is what Moses had given to the tribe of Gad, clan by clan:

[25]The territory of Jazer, all the towns of Gilead and half the Ammonite country as far as Aroer, near Rabbah; [26]and from Heshbon to Ramath Mizpah and Betonim, and from Mahanaim to the territory of Debir; [27]and in the valley, Beth Haram, Beth Nimrah, Succoth and Zaphon with the rest of the realm of Sihon king of Heshbon (the east side of the Jordan, the territory up to the end of the Sea of Kinnereth). [28]These towns and their villages were the inheritance of the Gadites, clan by clan.

13:24–28 The description of Gad's inheritance is shorter and simpler than that for Reuben.[49] Between the standard introductory and concluding statements (vv. 24,28), there is a general description of areas, with an eastern boundary (v. 25), a list of cities with southern and northern limits given (v. 26), and a concluding list with more cities and the western border (v. 27). The list includes two of the cities that the Gadites had built up, mentioned in Num 32:34–35—Aroer and Jazer—but most of those mentioned in Numbers 32 are not mentioned here.

Jazer (v. 25) was the place to which Moses had sent spies and which the Israelites captured (Num 21:32), and which the Gadites had already taken (Num 32:35). It was both a region (32:1) and a city (32:3). Jazer later became a Levitical city (21:39). The territory of Gilead was a large one, extending far north, but here, the southern portion is in view (cf. 12:2; see also on 13:11). The Aroer mentioned in v. 25 was near *(ʿal-pěnê)* Rabbah, the capital city of the Ammonite kingdom; it was a different Aroer from the one in the south, near the Arnon Gorge (Josh 12:2; 13:9).[50]

---

[47] The word is חָצֵר and more commonly refers to a courtyard or enclosure around a building, but often enough (as here) it refers to a settlement without walls (*HALOT*, 345; *DBH* 3:296–98).

[48] See Z. Herzog, "Social Organization as Reflected by the Bronze and Iron Age Cities of Israel," in *Comparative Studies in the Development of Complex Societies,* ed. T. Champion and M. Rowlands (London: Allen & Unwin, 1986), 2:10; id., "Cities," *ABD* 1:1036–37.

[49] See discussion in Simons, *Geographical and Topographical Texts,* § 300, and the maps in Rasmussen, *NIV Atlas of the Bible*, 101, and Brisco, *Holman Bible Atlas*, 84, on the territory here.

[50] See J. F. Drinkard, Jr., "ʿal pěnê as 'East of,'" *JBL* 98 (1979): 285–86, who shows that this expression means "near, close by, in the vicinity of, in the region of," not "east of." This observation fits the present text very well.

The description in v. 26 outlines the land in a south-to-north orientation. The first part goes from Heshbon in the south to two cities in the middle of Gad's territory (Ramath Mizpah and Betonim), and the second part goes from Mahanaim in the central part northward to the territory of Debir in the far north. Mahanaim later became a Levitical city (21:38).

In v. 27, four cities in the Jordan Valley are mentioned (i.e., on the western border), and then an expansive claim to "the rest of the realm of Sihon" concludes the list, delineating the western border more specifically by mentioning the Jordan River as the western boundary, extending northward all the way to the Sea of Kinnereth.

(5) Eastern Manasseh's Inheritance (13:29–31)

²⁹This is what Moses had given to the half-tribe of Manasseh, that is, to half the family of the descendants of Manasseh, clan by clan:

³⁰The territory extending from Mahanaim and including all of Bashan, the entire realm of Og king of Bashan—all the settlements of Jair in Bashan, sixty towns, ³¹half of Gilead, and Ashtaroth and Edrei (the royal cities of Og in Bashan). This was for the descendants of Makir son of Manasseh—for half of the sons of Makir, clan by clan.

13:29–31 This is the shortest and seemingly the most randomly assembled of the three lists in the chapter.[51] It begins in v. 30 with a line "from Mahanaim" (mentioned in Gad's territory, as well: v. 26) but has no terminus point (no "to" or "as far as"). It includes, in a grand sweep, all the of land of Bashan, all of Og, king of Bashan's realm there. Jair was a descendant of Manasseh, and he had captured a number of settlements in this region (Num 32:41; Deut 3:14), and hence the reference here to "all the settlements of Jair in Bashan." The total number of towns is impressive: sixty.

Bashan was a fertile region on a rugged, high plateau north of Gilead, east and northeast of the Sea of Kinnereth (Galilee). It was surrounded by mountains (Ps 68:15[Hb. 16]), well-forested (Isa 2:13; Ezek 27:6), but its smooth plateau was ideal for the pasturelands that produced fatted cattle (Jer 50:19; Ezek 39:18; Mic 7:14).[52]

The list concludes in v. 31 by mentioning territory assigned to half of the descendants of Makir. First, the northern half of Gilead is mentioned (cf. the mention of the southern half in Gad's territorial list, v. 25), along with the two capital cities of Og, Ashtaroth and Edrei. Both are mentioned together as Og's royal cities in 12:4 and 13:12 (and Ashtaroth also in 9:10). This territory was

---

[51] See Simons, *Geographical and Topographical Texts*, § 302 and the maps noted in <<n. 61>>.
[52] See Rasmussen, *NIV Atlas of the Bible*, 29–30, and J. C. Slayton, "Bashan," *ABD* 1:623–24, for more on this region.

to be "for" (or "belonging to")[53] the descendants of Makir, a son of
Manasseh. The rest of the territory (vv. 29–31) was "for" (or "belonging to")
half of the descendants of Manasseh. The tribe of Manasseh appears here to
be equated with one of its most prominent forebears, the sons of Makir, since
the concluding formula mentions the sons of Makir, not Manasseh.[54] Makir
was a son of Manasseh, grandson of Joseph (Gen 50:23), and his descendants
had earlier captured this region of Gilead (Num 32:39–40; Deut 3:15).

(6) Summary (13:32–33)

**[32]This is the inheritance Moses had given when he was in the plains of Moab
across the Jordan east of Jericho. [33]But to the tribe of Levi, Moses had given no
inheritance; the LORD, the God of Israel, is their inheritance, as he promised
them.**

13:32–33 The concluding summary reiterates Moses' place as the giver
of the land (cf. vv. 8,12,15,24,29) and the Levites' status as a "landless" tribe
(cf. v. 14).

Here, however, we have a slightly different view of what constituted Levi's
inheritance. In v. 14, it was the Lord's sacrifices; here, it is the Lord himself.
These two perspectives show how closely bound up with each other were God
and the sacrifices offered to him. (See further the notes on v. 14.)

EXCURSUS: PATTERNS IN THE LAND DISTRIBUTION LISTS

The Book of Joshua contains the most detailed and extensive lists of cities and
territories in the land settled by Israel in the entire Bible. The reason for this has
to do with the central theme of the book: the inheritance of that land by the Israelites, who had been promised it centuries earlier by their God. The lists are comprehensive, covering the inheritance for every one of the tribes. However, they are
not identical in structure, emphasis, or length. Internally, the lists are composed
of several different elements, the major ones of which we will discuss below.
These include (1) boundary lists and city lists, (2) notices of cities or territories
remaining to be conquered, (3) stories of individuals or groups asking for and
receiving their inheritances, and (4) miscellaneous regularities, mostly involving
stereotypical introductory and concluding statements.

Boundary and City Lists

In the table below, the tribes are listed in the first column, and the passages
where each tribe's inheritance is given are listed in the second. It is clearly visible
that the greatest part of these passages is taken up with the listing of the tribes'

---

[53] The preposition here and in v. 29 is simply -לְ, "to" or "for."

[54] So also Boling, *Joshua*, 333. The problem is complicated by the reference in v. 30 to Jair,
another prominent descendant of Manasseh (see Num 32:41).

boundaries and cities (third and fourth columns).[55] The fourteen tribal lists show these remarkable similarities, but some striking differences as well.[56]

Table 1: The Tribal Inheritance Lists in Joshua

Tribes	Inheritance	Boundary Lists	City Lists
1. Reuben	13:15–23	13:16–21a,23	13:16b–20[a]
2. Gad	13:24–28	13:25–27	-------------
3. E. Manasseh	13:29–31	13:30–31	-------------
4. Judah	14:6–15:63	15:1–12	15:21–62
5. Ephraim	16:5–10	16:5–9	-------------
6. W. Manasseh	17:1–13	17:7–10	-------------
7. Benjamin	18:11–28	18:12–20	18:21–28
8. Simeon	19:1–9	-------------	19:2–8
9. Zebulun	19:10–16	19:10–14	19:15
10. Issachar	19:17–23	19:22	19:18–21
11. Asher	19:24–31	19:26–29	19:25–30[b]
12. Naphtali	19:32–39	19:33–34	19:35–38
13. Dan	19:40–48	-------------	19:41–46
14. Levi	21:1–42	-------------	21:9–42

  a. Reuben's list is not a true city list: it mixes cities and border descriptions through the main portion.
  b. Asher's list mixes cities and border descriptions throughout

---

[55] The distinction between boundary lists and city lists was first proposed by A. Alt in the 1920's and has been accepted by most scholars since. See the brief historical review in Kallai, *Historical Geography*, 3–15, from which the contour of the boundary list here is adapted (p. 113). An accessible and useful study of the nature of the lists is Hess, "A Typology of West Semitic Place Names with Special Reference to Joshua 13–21," *BA* 59 (1996): 160–70.

[56] The arithmetic here differs from the tradition of "twelve" tribes of Israel, descended from the twelve sons of Jacob. We must remember, however, that Joseph's inheritance was split three ways: one for his son Ephraim and two for his son Manasseh (east and west of the Jordan), yielding fourteen lists to be covered in Joshua. The arithmetic is complicated by the fact that Simeon's territory was *within* the territory of Judah (19:1,9) and by the fact that the Danites had difficulty taking their own territory (19:47), and so they migrated north and took territory there (19:47; Judg 18:1).

The most important thing visible here is that each tribe received an inheritance, whether it was described by a boundary list, a city list, or both. God was fulfilling his promises to give Israel the land, even to the most insignificant or the weakest tribe.

Boundary Lists.   For three tribes there is no boundary description. The tribe of Levi received no contiguous territory, only cities, because their inheritance was the Lord himself or the sacrifices of the Lord (see the commentary on 13:14,33; 18:7). Simeon's and Dan's territories are not characterized by any border or territorial descriptions because Simeon was absorbed into Judah (19:1,9) and because the Danites had difficulty taking their own territory (19:47), and so they migrated north and took territory there (19:47; Judg 18:1). Thus, as Kallai notes, their inheritance is downplayed because "the Book of Joshua was written for the purpose of describing the process of the Conquest and Settlement, and these tribes failed to maintain their hold on the allotment assigned to them originally."[57]

The boundary lists have a different feel from the city lists. The city lists are almost exclusively just that: bare-bones lists of city names with almost no further information. The boundary lists, on the other hand, are more "alive," more of a narrative, with complete sentences and verbs leading the reader along while describing the limits of the territories and the directions in which certain boundaries run. The verbs used in the lists vary from list to list and add distinctiveness and "color." They are precisely drawn and pulsate with life; as the reader moves along, he or she can almost watch as the leading edge of the boundary moves down into this valley, around that city, along that slope, up that hill, and ends by extending as far as the sea or the river.[58]

Many different verbs are used to describe the way in which the boundaries operate. H. V. Parunak has highlighted the nine for which the word "boundary" *(gĕbûl)* is the grammatical subject: "to go, walk" *(hlk)*, "to go out along" *(yṣʾ)* (and the cognate noun *tôṣāʾâ*, "outgoing, extremity"), "to go down" *(yrd)*, "to go around" *(sbb/nsb)*, "to pass along" *(ʿbr)*, "to go up" *(ʿlh)*, "to pass by, touch" *(pgʿ)*, "to turn back" *(šwb)*, and "to turn, bend" *(tʾr)*. The verbs link the fixed points, or they give life to a line, such that the reader can enter into the experience of map drawing, so to speak, as did the twenty-one surveyors sent out from Shiloh in 18:4.[59]

Along with directional indicators—prepositions and nouns such as "from," "to," "alongside," "to the north," "to the sea," "to the east"—as well as geographical nouns such as "border," "tongue," "shoulder (slope)," "valley," "hill," "wadi,"

---

[57] Kallai, *Historical Geography*, 331.

[58] The commentary on 15:1–12 highlights in detail each verb used in that boundary description, attempting to give a feeling for the vividness and vitality of the lists in general.

[59] Parunak's is the most thorough study of the boundary list verbs per se (along with many of the nouns, such as "shoulder," "valley," "hill," etc.: "Geographical Terminology in Joshua 15–19," M.A. Thesis, The Institute of Holy Land Studies, 1977). This unpublished work was already cited numerous times by Boling in his commentary, and I thank Dr. Parunak for making available to me a copy.

"sea," et cetera—the verbs combine to generate interesting and precise boundary descriptions. The fact that many of the points described are not known today should not obscure the marvel and precision of the original lists.

City Lists. The city lists for the Transjordan tribes (the first three in the table) are not as important as the boundary lists: Reuben's cities are mixed in with the boundaries, and none are listed for Gad and eastern Manasseh. This is doubtless because the greater focus in the lists—and the Book of Joshua as a whole—is on the settlement west of the Jordan; the land inherited by the Transjordan tribes had already been pacified in Moses' day (Numbers 32). The reason for the exclusion of any true city lists for Ephraim and Western Manasseh, however, is not easily explained.[60] Several cities are mentioned in Ephraim's boundary lists, but only for the purposes of establishing the boundaries. For Manasseh, several cities are mentioned as well (17:11), but they all lay within other tribes' territories, not their own.

In the case of Judah's city list (15:21–62), almost half of the cities are only mentioned in that list, more than half only in Joshua, and more than two-thirds only in lists in Joshua and elsewhere, with nothing more known of them. It appears that the author of the book simply listed many of the city names to create by far the longest and most impressive list for this, the most important tribe. The list itself reflects Judah's prominence.

Cities and Territories Remaining to Be Conquered

Another important type of information in the territorial lists deals with territories and cities that the Israelite tribes failed to conquer. These are described in two sets of passages. The first set described is "the land that remains," and it is found intact in 13:2–6 (see the commentary there). The second set is sometimes called the "conquest lacunae," that is, the cities and territories from which the Israelites were not able to drive out the Canaanite inhabitants. The most organized list of these is found in Judg 1:21,27–35, but previews of much of the same material are found scattered throughout the lists in Joshua. The table below shows these and compares the information on the "conquest lacunae" in Joshua with that in Judges.

Table 2: Cities Not Conquered by the Israelites[a]

Tribes	Joshua[b]	Judges	People	Cities
1. Israelites in general	13:13	---------	---------	(Geshur)[c] (Maacah)
2. Judah	15:63	---------	Jebusites	Jerusalem
3. Benjamin	---------	1:21	Jebusites	Jerusalem

---

[60] Scholarly explanations for this are many and varied, but all are speculative, and none is compelling.

Table 2: Cities Not Conquered by the Israelites[a]

Tribes	Joshua[b]	Judges	People	Cities
4. W. Manasseh	17:11–12	1:27–28	Canaanites	Beth Shan, Taanach, Dor, Ibleam, Megiddo, Endor,* Naphoth*
5. Ephraim	16:10	1:29	Canaanites	Gezer
6. Zebulun	---------	1:30	Canaanites	Kitron, Nahalol
7. Asher	---------	1:31–32	Canaanites	Acco, Sidon, Ahlab, Aczib, Helbah, Aphek, Rehob
8. Naphtali	---------	1:33	Canaanites	Beth Shemesh, Beth Anath
9. Dan	19:47	1:34–35	Amorites	Leshem*

a. This is a list of the so-called "Conquest Lacunae," consisting primarily of *cities* the Israelites did not conquer (see Kallai, *Historical Geography*, 102–11). It differs from the list of "Remaining Lands," which are listed together in Josh 13:2–6 and consist of *territories* the Israelites did not conquer (in addition to Kallai, see Na'aman, *Borders and Districts*, 39–73).

b. The list in Judges 1 is the most unified and complete. Asterisked entries indicate additional information gathered from Joshua. In those cases where the information is found in both Joshua and Judges and there is no asterisk, then the information given is the same in both books.

c. Geshur and Maacah were regions, not cities.

The information here is exceedingly important, because it gives a counterbalancing view (1) to the seemingly all-encompassing boundary and city lists and (2) most certainly to the all-encompassing summary statements of 10:40–42; 11:16–23; and 21:43–45. There were vast and important territories left yet to conquer (13:2–6), as well as many cities and regions that the Israelites did not take. This is a very realistic picture of the state of affairs in Joshua's day, and it lays the foundation for understanding the many troubles the Israelites were to encounter in the period of the Judges and beyond.[61]

Land Grant Narratives

Scattered throughout the lists of territories and cities are five stories in which characters ask for and receive their inheritance. Each case has its own unique features, but there are similar patterns running throughout all of them as well. These have been identified and labeled as "land grant narratives" by Nelson, who identifies four main elements in the pattern.[62] First, there is a confrontation that estab-

---

[61] See the discussion at 10:40–43 on the issue of a complete or an incomplete conquest.

[62] Nelson, *Joshua*, 177–78. Like any form-critical structure that scholars have identified, this is not a fixed, rigid pattern whose elements are found in all cases, but it does manifest itself in a remarkably consistent way in these five instances.

lishes the setting and the characters. Second, the would-be grantees present their case and make a request for land. Third, the land is granted. Fourth and finally, a summary of the episode's resolution is given. The five stories are as follows: Caleb (14:6–15); Caleb's daughter, Acsah (15:18–19); the daughters of Zelophehad (17:3–6); Joseph (17:14–18); and the Levites (21:1–3).

Miscellaneous Patterns

The remaining patterns in the lists are to be found in the introductory and concluding statements that bracket the details of each list. The most regular lists are the first three (the Transjordan tribes—Reuben, Gad, and eastern Manasseh: chap. 13) and the last seven (Benjamin, Simeon, Zebulun, Issachar, Asher, Naphtali, and Dan: chaps. 18–19). The most irregular lists belong to the most important tribes: Judah (chap. 15) and the Joseph tribes, Ephraim and western Manasseh (chaps. 16–17). The Levites, of course, receive their own special treatment (13:14,33; 18:7; chap. 21).

Among the regular elements in the apportionment passages, most are fairly stereotypical, but in at least one case—the phrase "clan by clan"—there is some theological significance as well (see below). Indeed, the very regularity of all these lists attests to the importance of the land distribution and the fulfillment of God's promises in the Pentateuch.

Following are some of the regular elements in these passages. The introductory statements in chap. 13 emphasize Moses' part: "This is what Moses had given to the tribe of *X,* clan by clan" (13:15,24,29). In later chapters, Joshua and Eleazar the high priest allotted the lands (14:1), but in the first set of introductory statements their names are missing, and the statements are similar to Judah's (15:1): "The allotment for the tribe of Judah" (see 16:5 [Ephraim]; 17:1 [Manasseh]). In the remaining seven tribes' allotments, their portions are introduced by references to the lots themselves, and they are numbered (e.g., "the *second lot* came out for the tribe of Simeon": 19:1).

One element found in each introductory statement—without exception—is the phrase "clan by clan" (with a slight variation for Manasseh in 17:1–2).[63] This phrase is also found in most of the concluding summary statements.[64] The careful attention to this detail is undoubtedly to show that yet another provision of the law of Moses was being kept. In Leviticus 25, the law of the year of Jubilee and redemption of the land is given, and it is clear that land was to remain in the clan and that clan members were obligated to redeem the land for their constituent families (see vv. 23–28 and esp. vv. 41,49).[65] The ordering of society progressed from tribes to clans to families, as we saw in Josh 7:14. In Num 36:6–12, the point is also made forcefully that land was to remain within the tribes and clans:

---

[63] See 13:15,24,29; 15:1; 16:5; 18:11; 19:1,10,17,24,32,40. The NIV's "clan by clan" renders one Hb. word, מִשְׁפְּחוֹת, "clans."

[64] See 13:23,28,31; 16:8; 19:8,16,23,31,39,48. This phrase occurs in the middle of the passage dealing with Judah's inheritance (15:20; cf. also 15:12), and it occurs with variations for western Manasseh (17:2) and Benjamin (18:28)

[65] See Nelson, *Joshua,* 173, and bibliography there for this trenchant observation.

the daughters of Zelophehad (a man who had no sons: Num 26:33) married their cousins in order for their father's land to remain within the clan.

Most of the lists are composed of names of towns and villages allotted to the respective tribes, and the first two and the last six of them end with the same summary statement: "These towns and their villages were the inheritance of the tribe of *[X]*, clan by clan" (see 13:23,28; 19:16,23,31,39,48). The others are not so regular.

Concluding Remarks

What is the importance of the mind-numbing detail of these lists? Why is it significant that there are certain patterns to them? There are several answers to these questions. First and foremost, as we have indicated, these lists are the heart of the book, in that they "prove" to the Israelites and to the book's readers that God was being true to his promises. On one level, it was not enough simply to assert that God gave Israel the land, to state that he fulfilled his promises, and to ask the reader to take the author's word for it.[66] For such promises as these, given so many centuries earlier, such simple assertions would have been profoundly anticlimactic. A deep sense of satisfaction would come if the reader could actually trace the fulfillment of these promises city by city, hill by hill, wadi by wadi, border by border. It is akin to a good book that a person becomes engrossed in, which he or she is reluctant to have come to an end. The reader wants every word and detail to count. So too here.

The most important commercial transaction that ordinary American citizens make is the purchase of a house. There can be several ways of identifying that house's location. For some people, it may simply be known as "the McGillicuddy place." For others, it is the big white frame house on the corner with three stories and the big porch. For others, it is the place with the bird feeders in the yard. For others, it is "the place where all those nice children are." For others, it is known by its postal address, "3 West Maple Avenue."

However, in the eyes of the law, the description of the house and the property on which it sits is much more complicated and precise. It will contain terminology such as "Lot 56 in Block 212 in Uptown unit no. 23, being a subdivision of the southeast quarter of the southwest quarter of Section 18, Township 34 north, Range 8, east of the sixth principal meridian, according to the plat thereof, recorded on [DATE] as document no. 987654, in Book 42 of plats, page 29 in Lincoln County." This language is virtually unintelligible to most normal adults, but, when the time comes to buy a home, it is of crucial importance, and the buyers are glad that someone—their lawyer and their survey company, at least—understands it and has looked it over carefully. Accurate, precise language such as this is critical to the successful completion of a sale.

So too are the lists of the lands that Israel inherited. Israel's God not only had promised this land to them, but he had carefully prepared it and parceled it out.

---

[66] On the level of ontological or ultimate reality, it would of course have been enough for this to have been asserted, since the God-inspired author's word on this issue should indeed have been enough.

He gave precise descriptions, sometimes by describing borders that ran up this hill, turned back at that town, went down into this ravine, ran along that brook, and sometimes by naming the cities that belonged to the tribes in question.

The details of the lists are significant also on a military level, not only on the level of inheritance and real estate legalities. The Israelites had waged several difficult campaigns against the Canaanites over the lands mentioned here. Even though the Book of Joshua emphasizes God's part in waging war and in giving the land and its people into the hands of the Israelites, and their part is downplayed, it is clear that they did have to move across the terrain and actually kill many hundreds or thousands of people. They already had had intimate connections with the land of Canaan, experiences that would have been indelibly imprinted in their memories. As one person notes: "To a soldier who has fought for every hill and town, maybe street [to street and] house to house fighting and who has shed some blood on those hills and in those towns and maybe lost a friend or a loved one in the battles ... you bet the details are important and to be celebrated. ... [It is] a celebration of victory hard fought and dearly paid for."[67]

The regularities in the lists' patterns that we have noted are important, just as regularity in modern real estate surveys is important. Unintelligible as the language of the imaginary real-estate survey we have just written is to the normal person, to those familiar with it and responsible for overseeing real estate transactions, the very regularity of the language makes it intelligible and precise. So too for the Joshua lists. The very fact that each tribe's inheritance is described in language that is almost identical to the others' in its general contours guaranteed that each tribe would be able to take its inheritance confidently, knowing that it was of a piece with that of its fellow tribes.

And yet, the differences are important too. We can assume, for example, that a sprawling country estate of hundreds of acres spanning several townships will have a far more complicated survey description than a simple bungalow on San Martín Boulevard or an obscure street. Certainly the numbers and the names in each survey will be different. So too here in the Joshua lists. Each one follows general patterns, but each one is unique as well. Oftentimes it is the irregularities that are the most significant. As we have noted, the differences in the descriptions for Judah, the Joseph tribes, Simeon, Dan, and Levi all are important theologically. The stories of the claims of individuals show God's fulfillment of his promises even down to individual people's claims. Tribes, clans, families, and even individuals mattered in God's scheme of things. And his provision for the Levites, his priests and special servants, demonstrates other important things about his character and about the religious priorities to be followed in Israelite society.

Thus, despite their seeming impenetrability, the lists in Joshua will richly repay any time invested in understanding them. They are indeed the core of the Book of Joshua. They are the "legal data" supporting the tribes' claims to their territories and validating their God's faithfulness to them. They give a deep sense of rootedness to the people. This principle of land ownership—or, for some cul-

---

[67] Stephen G. Howard, personal communication, August 1998. I thank my brother, a retired naval officer, for these observations.

tures, the idea of rootedness in the land, without specific ownership of specific territories—is one of the most fundamental principles of human societies. In this most geographically rooted of all biblical books, these truths shine forth very clearly. As K. A. Mathews notes: "Theologically, we should remember that the land is God's who has given it to the Israelites as new tenants. Hence, the land became the concrete evidence of each family's claim on the covenant promises. A psyche of land possession = identity became entrenched in the Hebrew mind" (personal communication).

3. The Cisjordan Distribution Introduced (14:1–5)

[1]Now these are the areas the Israelites received as an inheritance in the land of Canaan, which Eleazar the priest, Joshua son of Nun and the heads of the tribal clans of Israel allotted to them. [2]Their inheritances were assigned by lot to the nine-and-a-half tribes, as the LORD had commanded through Moses. [3]Moses had granted the two-and-a-half tribes their inheritance east of the Jordan but had not granted the Levites an inheritance among the rest, [4]for the sons of Joseph had become two tribes—Manasseh and Ephraim. The Levites received no share of the land but only towns to live in, with pasturelands for their flocks and herds. [5]So the Israelites divided the land, just as the LORD had commanded Moses.

This passage functions as an introduction to the entire land distribution in chaps. 14–19. The distributions to the tribes east of the Jordan River described in chap. 13 actually had been accomplished earlier, under Moses (see esp. Numbers 32). Therefore, the land distributions west of the Jordan now described are what is new.

The distributions in chaps. 14–19 follow a pattern of sorts. The most important tribes are dealt with first: Judah (chap. 15), the tribes of Joseph (Ephraim and western Manasseh: chaps. 16–17). Then lands belonging to the remaining seven tribes are listed (chaps. 18–19). The entire listing is introduced by a lengthy account of Caleb receiving his inheritance (chap. 14) and concluded by a short account of Joshua receiving his inheritance (19:49–50).[68]

The geographical setting of the distributions is not specified directly, but there are some clues indicating that they took place in at least two different locations, places of religious significance in the life of the nation. In 14:6, the men of Judah came to Joshua at Gilgal, presumably the site near Jericho that had served as the first religious center in the land (see 4:19–20; 5:9–10).[69] It would appear that the first set of allotments, belonging to Judah and the Joseph tribes, was given out from here. In 18:1, the entire congregation gath-

---

[68] For more on the patterns in these chapters, see the excursus "Patterns in the Land Distribution Lists" at the end of chap. 13.

[69] A different Gilgal appears to be in view in chaps. 9 and 10; see the commentary on 9:6.

ered at another religious center, at Shiloh, and it served as the primary religious center until the end of Joshua's life (see 18:1,8–10; 19:51; 22:2,9,12). It
presumably was here where Joshua delivered his first great farewell speech
(chap. 23). In chap. 24, the scene shifts again, to Shechem (24:1), the city
where Joseph's bones were buried (24:32); it was near Mount Ebal, where the
covenant had been renewed earlier (8:30).

The passage here (14:1–5) can be said to pick up where chap. 11 leaves
off, since the idea of the inheritance *(nāḥal / nāḥălâ)*, as well as that of
Joshua giving *(ntn)* or parceling out *(nḥl)* the land, is found both in 11:23 and
14:1. On the other hand, chaps. 12 and 13 have specific functions in the text,
and so the material here must be seen in its present context.

This is an overall introduction to the land distribution, but it emphasizes
the Levites (vv. 3–4), who have just been mentioned in the previous passage
(13:14,33). It also emphasizes God as the one who gives the land to Israel. It
does this by mentioning his commands to Moses (vv. 2,5) and by mentioning
Eleazar the priest's assistance in the land distribution. This shows that the
inheritance of the land was a religious matter, and not merely a real estate
transaction (v. 1), since Eleazar was a priest, son of Aaron the high priest; and
he had been designated earlier to help Joshua with the distribution, along with
representatives from the twelve tribes (Num 32:28; 34:18–29).

14:1   This verse is yet another introduction to the land distributions. It
contains the first reference in the book to "the land of Canaan," and it introduces the main characters in the land distributions, Joshua and Eleazar, and
the heads of the clans. Joshua is identified as the "son of Nun" at important
junctures in the book.[70] The land distribution lists are bracketed by this name
(14:1; 19:49,51).

Eleazar was the high priest, Aaron's son and successor (Exod 6:25; Num
20:26–28), and he had exercised important duties earlier in the wilderness
(Num 3:4,32; 4:16; 16:37,39; etc.). Significantly, he had been involved in the
commissioning service for Joshua as Moses' successor (Num 27:18–23).
Now he was involved with Joshua in one of the most important and sacred
tasks of their day: distributing the land to the tribes that had been promised to
them for centuries.

According to God's instructions in Num 34:16–29, Joshua, Eleazar, and
one leader per tribe were to distribute the land. The inclusion here of "the
heads of the tribal clans" (lit., "the heads of the fathers of the tribes") once
again shows Israel obeying God's commands.[71]

---

[70] 1:1; 2:1,23; 6:6; 14:1; 17:4; 19:49,51; 21:1; 24:29.

[71] The word used of the tribal leaders here is not נָשִׂיא, the one found in Numbers 34, causing
Boling to understand that many more leaders were involved here (*Joshua*, 354). It is puzzling why
נָשִׂיא is not used in a passage that echoes the earlier one so closely, but it nevertheless seems best
to understand the leaders here as the twelve tribal leaders called for earlier.

14:2 The inheritances were parceled out by lot to the nine and one-half tribes west of the Jordan, according to the Lord's commands through Moses. The casting of lots to determine Israel's inheritance had been commanded by God (Num 26:52–56; 33:54); thus, far from being a matter of chance, God himself was in control of the lot (cf. 18:6,8,10; Prov 16:33). This is the first reference in the book to the lot, but it is mentioned again in 15:1; 16:1; 17:1; 18:6,8,10.[72]

14:3–4 Another notice about the Levites' inheritance is inserted here, lest they be forgotten, it would seem. We learn that the Levites did not receive territories per se but that they did receive towns (cities) and surrounding pasturelands (v. 4). These cities are delineated in chap. 21.[73] Also, the arithmetic of the number of tribes is explained: Jacob had twelve sons, but the descendants of one of these (Joseph) became two tribes (Ephraim and Manasseh), both receiving inheritances. The Levites' "landless" condition kept the number of tribal territories fixed at twelve.[74]

14:5 Along with v. 2, this verse provides an anticipatory summary of the activities to come. The second half of each verse is almost identical, in speaking of the allotments being made in fulfillment of the Lord's commands to Moses. There is a subtle distinction between the expressions, however. Here the wording is "just as the LORD had commanded Moses," whereas in v. 2 it is "just as the LORD had commanded through [lit., "by the hand (of)"] Moses." The expression, "by the hand of Moses," is found thirty-two times in the Old Testament, always referring to Moses as God's obedient instrument, in most cases as his instrument for commanding the people to obey: the expression usually is "just as the LORD spoke/commanded by the hand of Moses." In a few instances, God accomplished certain things "by the hand of Moses."[75] A reference to the hand of someone often signifies their power (e.g., Deut 32:36; Dan 12:7). However, in the passages in question here, the

---

[72] See the excursus after 13:7 on "Israel's Inheritance of the Land in Joshua" for more on the lot.

[73] See the commentary on 13:14 for more on the Levites' landless condition.

[74] The number "twelve" was somewhat fluid since Manasseh essentially was two tribes (eastern and western Manasseh), each with its own territory, whereas Simeon only received its portion *within* that of Judah (see 19:1,9). Nevertheless, "twelve" was the operative number, and it fit the situation by more than one method of counting. See also n. 55 in chap. 13.

[75] In twenty-five cases, God spoke or commanded something "by the hand of Moses" (including here), and in the other cases, he accomplished something. The twenty-five instances of God's speaking are divided as follows: (1) with the verb "to speak" (דבר), eight times (Exod 9:35; Lev 10:11; Num 16:40[Hb. 17:5]; 27:23; Josh 20:2; 1 Kgs 8:53,56; 35:6); (2) with the verb "to command" (צוה), eleven times (Exod 35:29; Lev 8:36; Num 15:23; 36:13; Josh 14:2; 21:2,8; Judg 3:4; 2 Chr 33:8; Neh 8:14; 9:14); (3) with the expression "according to the mouth (of)" (עַל פִּי), six times (Num 4:37,45,49; 9:23;10:13; Josh 22:9). In five instances, God accomplished something "by the hand of Moses" (Lev 26:46; Num 33:1; Neh 10:29 [Hb. 30]; 2 Chr 34:14; Ps 77:20 [Hb. 21]). In two instances, the reference is literally to Moses' hand (Exod 17:12; 34:29).

reference would seem to be more to Moses' function as God's scribe: the commandments, statutes, and ordinances that God spoke "by the hand of Moses" were written down because of their importance. In Josh 14:2 the use of this expression would refer back to the lists and accounts that Moses had written.

4. Judah's Inheritance (14:6–15:63)

Judah, as the most important tribe in Israel's history and the recipient of a special blessing from Jacob many years earlier (Gen 49:8–12), received the most land west of the Jordan, and the attention devoted to its lands is the most detailed and extensive of all the tribes. For more detailed introductions to Judah's tribal inheritance, see the introductions to chap. 15 and to 15:21–62.[76]

(1) Caleb's Inheritance: Part One (14:6–15)

⁶**Now the men of Judah approached Joshua at Gilgal, and Caleb son of Jephunneh the Kenizzite said to him, "You know what the LORD said to Moses the man of God at Kadesh Barnea about you and me. ⁷I was forty years old when Moses the servant of the LORD sent me from Kadesh Barnea to explore the land. And I brought him back a report according to my convictions, ⁸but my brothers who went up with me made the hearts of the people melt with fear. I, however, followed the LORD my God wholeheartedly. ⁹So on that day Moses swore to me, 'The land on which your feet have walked will be your inheritance and that of your children forever, because you have followed the LORD my God wholeheartedly.'**

¹⁰**"Now then, just as the LORD promised, he has kept me alive for forty-five years since the time he said this to Moses, while Israel moved about in the desert. So here I am today, eighty-five years old! ¹¹I am still as strong today as the day Moses sent me out; I'm just as vigorous to go out to battle now as I was then. ¹²Now give me this hill country that the LORD promised me that day. You yourself heard then that the Anakites were there and their cities were large and fortified, but, the LORD helping me, I will drive them out just as he said."**

¹³**Then Joshua blessed Caleb son of Jephunneh and gave him Hebron as his inheritance. ¹⁴So Hebron has belonged to Caleb son of Jephunneh the Kenizzite ever since, because he followed the LORD, the God of Israel, wholeheartedly. ¹⁵(Hebron used to be called Kiriath Arba after Arba, who was the greatest man among the Anakites.)**

Then the land had rest from war.

Before the narrative in chap. 14 details Judah's inheritance, Caleb, a prominent figure in an earlier story, is given his inheritance. Caleb was from the

---

[76] A brief but useful overview of all the tribal inheritances is Hess, "Tribes, Territories of the," *ISBE* 4:907–13. Hess's treatment of Judah's territories is on p. 909.

tribe of Judah (Num 13:6), and he had been one of the twelve spies sent into Canaan from the wilderness. He and Joshua alone had given a favorable report (Num 14:6–9), resulting in their being the only ones from their generation allowed to enter Canaan (14:30). We are told three times of his taking his inheritance, although with different emphases each time (Josh 14:6–15; 15:13–19; Judg 1:12–15). The fact that three episodes tell of his inheritance highlights his prominent status in Israel.

Caleb reviewed his actions and obedience for Joshua before asking him for land in the hill country of Judah; he would drive out the remaining Anakites from that land (vv. 6–12). Joshua granted his wish, giving him Hebron, a prominent city that previously had been captured (10:3,36–37; 12:10), but which may have been taken again by the Anakites who were not destroyed by the Israelites (cf. 11:22).

The story of Caleb's inheritance is one of five stories in chaps. 14–21 in which characters ask for and receive their inheritance: Caleb (14:6–15); Acsah (15:18–19); the daughters of Zelophehad (17:3–6); Joseph (17:14–18); and the Levites (21:1–3). These have been identified and labeled as "land grant narratives" by Nelson, and they follow a similar pattern in most cases.[77] First, there is a confrontation that establishes the setting and the characters. Then the would-be grantees present their case and make a request for land. Following this, the land is granted, and, finally, a summary of the resolution is given.

14:6 We hear nothing after this of the men of Judah who came to Joshua, but Caleb, a Judahite (Num 13:6), was with them, and this is his story. Joshua was at Gilgal, which presumably is the Gilgal near Jericho (see the commentary on 9:6 on another possible Gilgal). The next geographical indicator about where Joshua was comes in 18:1, where the entire nation assembled at Shiloh, another significant religious site for Israel.

Though Caleb is called a "Kenizzite" (14:6,14; cf. Num 32:12), he was also from the tribe of Judah (Num 13:6; 1 Chr 2:9; 4:15). Since we know that a non-Israelite group called Kenizzites lived in Canaan like the Kenites, Kadmonites, Hittites, Perizzites, et cetera (Gen 15:19), scholars have puzzled over Caleb's exact lineage. The simplest solution is to remember that the term "Kenizzite" means "son of Kenaz." Caleb's brother Othniel is called "son of Kenaz" in Josh 15:17, so Caleb may have been a "Kenizzite" by virtue of being associated with a relative or ancestor named Kenaz. Thus the Kenizzites of Caleb's line were one of the family groups within the tribe of Judah and were not related at all to the non-Israelite Kenizzites of Gen 15:19. This is

---

[77] Nelson, *Joshua*, 177–78. Like any form-critical structure that scholars have identified, this is not a fixed, rigid pattern whose elements are found in all cases, but it does manifest itself remarkably in these five cases.

made more plausible by the fact that Caleb himself had a descendant named Kenaz (1 Chr 4:15).[78]

Caleb's words to Joshua recall their experience together forty years earlier as the two spies who gave a favorable report to Moses. His words in this verse emphasize Joshua's role and can be paraphrased as "You (of all people),[79] you know the word that the LORD spoke to Moses, the man of God, concerning me and concerning you, at Kadesh Barnea." The reference here is to God's promises to Joshua and Caleb to bring them into the land of Canaan and give them inheritances there (Num 14:24,30).[80]

14:7–9 These verses review the events of Numbers 13 and 14. While Caleb's (and Joshua's) report was positive, the other spies' report had the effect of making the Israelites' hearts melt because of the fearsome nature of the land's inhabitants (vv. 7–8). Ironically, this was precisely the reaction of Canaan's inhabitants earlier, when they had heard of Israel's exploits (Josh 2:9,11,24; 5:1).

Caleb emphasized his own faithfulness in contrast to his fellow spies' faithlessness, stating that he had "fully" followed the Lord.[81] Caleb's passion is revealed by the manner in which he spoke. We have already noted his special emphasis on Joshua in v. 6. Here, in v. 8, he displayed a similar passion when he stated, "As for me, I have fully followed the LORD."[82] He was confident of his faithfulness to the Lord and now, forty-five years later (see v. 10), he wanted to claim that which had been promised to him.

Moses' promise to Caleb (v. 9) is recorded in Num 14:24 and especially Deut 1:36, where the wording is similar to that here. We learn here that Moses had actually sworn (*šbᶜ*) to Caleb, a fact not recorded in the earlier passages. (See also the commentary on 19:49–50.) Caleb was not being self-serving by claiming that he had fully followed the Lord; he was simply stating a fact that Moses also had recognized (see the words at the end of v. 9, which are found in the Lord's mouth almost verbatim in Num 14:24 and in Moses' mouth in Deut 1:36).

14:10–12 In vv. 10–11, Caleb's focus shifts from the past to the present, specifically, on his own condition and readiness to claim his inheritance. Despite the fact that he was now eighty-five years old (adding the forty years

---

[78] For surveys of the entire complex question, see C. F. Keil, *The Book of Joshua* (Grand Rapids: Eerdmans, 1975 reprint), 148; G. F. Hasel, "Caleb," *ISBE* 1:573–74; M. H. Woudstra, *The Book of Joshua*, NICOT (Grand Rapids: Eerdmans, 1981), 227 and n. 1.

[79] This accounts for the pleonastic (i.e., redundant) pronoun אַתָּה, "you," whose discourse function is to highlight Joshua.

[80] Caleb is even called a servant of the Lord in Num 14:24.

[81] The NIV's "wholeheartedly" translates the verb מָלֵא, which means "to be full"; Caleb was claiming to have fully and completely followed after the Lord.

[82] Again, a pleonastic pronoun—this time אָנֹכִי, "I"—is used, performing the same discourse function found in v. 6 (see n. 79).

of v. 7 to the forty-five years of v. 10), he still claimed physical vigor and a readiness and willingness to do battle. His words were insistent and animated, revealing the vigor and eagerness of a man far younger. For example, he used the expression "and now" *(wĕ῾attâ)* three times (vv. 10[2x],12), which shows him carefully, but insistently, building a logical case for himself; it can be translated as "now then," as the NIV does at the beginning of v. 10.[83] The reference to God's promise is to Num 14:24.

The time periods referred to in vv. 7 and 10 give us an insight into the period of time covered by most of the Book of Joshua. Israel was sentenced to forty years of wandering in the wilderness after the spies came back with their report (Num 14:33–34). Verse 10 shows that forty-five years had elapsed since the time of this sentence, so the conquest to date had occupied some five years (or perhaps seven, if the two years Israel had already been in the wilderness— Num 10:11—are counted in the forty years). Joshua's farewell addresses may have come many years later, however (see the commentary on 23:1).

On the basis of the promises of God and Moses to him, and his own physical vigor (and, presumably, because at his advanced age he would not have had many more years left to him), Caleb presented his request to be given his inheritance (v. 12). His passion is revealed again in his words at the outset of v. 12 (lit.): "Now then *[wĕ῾attâ]*, give to me this hill country." He again appealed to Joshua as one who was present forty-five years earlier, who would know of the fearsome nature of the land's inhabitants and their cities. But he hoped for the Lord's help, since God had promised that Caleb would indeed inherit the land (Num 14:24). Caleb's faith is also revealed in his confession that it was Yahweh himself who had kept him alive these forty-five years, so that he could inherit his land (v. 10).

The Israelites' destruction of the Anakites is recounted in 11:21–22.[84] However, some were able to survive outside of Israelite territory, in the cities of Gaza, Gath, and Ashdod. The reference to them here (and in 15:14) would seem to indicate that Anakites had returned to at least some of their former places.[85]

14:13 Verses 13–15 show the "resolution" (v. 13) and the "results" (vv. 14–15) of the entire episode.[86] No words of Joshua's are recorded in response to Caleb's extended and impassioned speech (vv. 6–12). This fact may signal that Caleb's words were singularly effective and that no verbal response was

---

[83] This expression may also have an emphatic function, in which case Caleb's passion shows that much more clearly. See *IBHS* § 39.3.4f.

[84] On these people, see the commentary on 11:21–22.

[85] See also C. J. Goslinga, *Joshua, Judges, Ruth*, BSC (Grand Rapids: Zondervan, 1986), 193; Woudstra, *Joshua*, 229–30.

[86] The terms here come from Nelson's form-critical study (*Joshua*, 179, and the section "Land Grant Narratives" in our excursus "Patterns in the Land Distribution Lists" [chap. 13]).

necessary, only action. Joshua blessed Caleb and gave him the city of Hebron as his inheritance.

This verse records only the second instance in the book of a blessing *(brk)*.[87] The concept of a blessing is a rich one in biblical thought. God's blessing upon his people bestowed abundant and effective life upon them (e.g., Gen 27:27–29; 49:1–28). It involved bestowing material abundance upon them, such as children (e.g., Gen 1:28; 28:3), land (Gen 26:3; 28:4), or wealth (Gen 28:12–14), as well as upon others (Gen 12:3; 22:18). When people blessed God, they were worshiping him, ascribing worth to him and his great name (e.g., Ps 103:1–2; 104:1). When people blessed each other, it conveyed a desire for God's best to befall them (e.g., Gen 47:10; Judg 5:24; Neh 11:2; Prov 30:11). Blessing someone was more than wishful thinking, however, since blessing in the name of the Lord tapped into the power and resources of God himself.

In the Book of Joshua blessings are bestowed by both God and men. God's blessings through the reading of the blessings in the law were given to the people at Mount Ebal (Josh 8:33–34). Joshua blessed Caleb (14:13) and the Transjordan tribes (22:6–7), and Caleb's daughter Achsah asked her father for a blessing of a land grant (15:19). And the Israelites blessed God (i.e., they praised him: see NIV) when the misunderstanding about the Transjordan tribes' building of an altar was resolved (22:33).

14:14–15 The episode resulted in the city of Hebron becoming Caleb's inheritance ever since (lit., "until this day"). Caleb's whole-hearted devotion to God had never been in question, even in the wilderness (this is affirmed in Num 14:24; Deut 1:36; Josh 14:14). As a result, he received as a reward the land that he requested. His faithfulness to God over a period of forty-five years of waiting for God's promises to be fulfilled was certainly remarkable and worthy of emulating today.

The episode ends with an explanation of the city's name and a concluding comment about rest for the land, just as the account of the southern and northern campaigns had ended (11:23).

The former name of the city of Hebron had been Kiriath Arba. It was where Sarah had died many years earlier (Gen 23:2). Its former name meant "city of Arba" (i.e., "Arbatown"). Arba was the most prominent man of the Anakites, although he is not known except for references here and in 15:13 and 21:11, where he is said to have been the founding ancestor of the Anakite people. This passage explaining why this place received a new name is sometimes labeled by scholars as an etiology (see following excursus).

---

[87] The verb "to bless" is found eight times in the book: 8:33; 14:13; 17:14; 22:6,7,33; 24:10[2x]. The noun "blessing" is found in 8:34 and 15:19.

EXCURSUS: ETIOLOGY IN JOSHUA

On several occasions in Joshua, the name of a place is explained in terms of events that took place there, or the reason for a certain state of affairs is given. The story of Caleb's inheritance of Hebron is a good example (14:6–15). The city of Hebron originally was named "Kiriath Arba," that is, "city of Arba" (Gen 23:2; Josh 14:15) because it was inhabited by the Anakites (11:22; 14:12), whose most prominent leader was Arba. However, it was given to Caleb as his inheritance, and it remained his "until this day" (*ʿad hayyôm hazzeh*) (14:14). Another example is Gilgal, whose name is explained in chap. 5. The place where the Israelites were circumcised was originally called Gibeath-haaraloth, which means "Hill of Foreskins" (5:3). It was now called "Gilgal," however, "until this day" (5:9), in a wordplay on the reproach of Egypt's being rolled away (since Hb. *gālal* means "to roll"). The story of Rahab and the spies in chap. 2 explains why descendants of Rahab lived among the Israelites "until this day" (6:25).

Such explanations of place names or the current state of affairs belong to a class of stories called "etiologies." This term is derived from the Greek word *aitiologia* (consisting of *aitia*, "cause," + *logia*, "description"), and it means "the assignment of a cause, origin, or reason for something." It is used in biblical studies to describe those stories that explain how an existing name, custom, or institution came into being. The pages of Joshua contain several such examples. In addition to the three mentioned above, see the stories explaining the heap of stones near the Jordan (chap. 4); the name of the Valley of Achor (7:26); the status of the Gibeonites as Israel's servants (chap. 9); the presence of Geshurites and Maacathites among the Israelites (13:13), Jebusites in Jerusalem (15:63), and Canaanites in Gezer (16:10).[88] In all of these cases, the phrase *ʿad hayyôm hazzeh*, "until this day," occurs, and usually this refers to the time of the writing of the book.[89] However, not all occurrences of this phrase are in etiological contexts. In all of the examples in chaps. 22 and 23 (22:3,17; 23:8–9), the use of "until this day" refers to the very day on which Joshua was addressing the people, not sometime many years later, and it is not used to explain any existing name or custom.

Many scholars have seen any sign of an etiology in the Bible as a signal that this explanation is fanciful, that the need to explain a place name gave rise in the popular culture to various stories that would do this and that these stories, of necessity, arose many years after anything they attempted to explain. The assumption is that the explanations given are historically false but that they reveal the folk traditions that gave rise to them.

This scepticism about the historicity behind etiologies has drawn much criticism, however, and recent work is much more conservative in understanding

---

[88] Some scholars would point to the name of Ai as a further example (supposing its name to mean "the Ruin": see 8:28). However, this meaning for "Ai" cannot be sustained (see the excursus "The Archaeology of Jericho and Ai" at the end of chap. 6 and the footnote there).

[89] This occurs a total of eighty-seven times in the OT, seventeen times in Joshua, more than in any other book: 4:9; 5:9; 6:25; 7:26[2x]; 8:28,29; 9:27; 10:27; 13:13; 14:14; 15:63; 16:10; 22:3,17; 23:8,9.

them. There is no inherent reason why such stories could not, in fact, be true. Thus, many scholars—evenagelical and nonevangelical alike—recognize that these stories were not invented to give an etiological explanation for a later phenomenon, and it is even conceded by some that the biblical text may indeed preserve the actual reasons for certain names or customs. This is certainly a reasonable and defensible conclusion, and it is the position taken here.

An early critique of the etiological notion advanced by many scholars[90] was by J. Bright.[91] B. S. Childs showed that the formula "until this day" was used as a commentary of sorts to confirm the veracity of an account, and he argued that etiologies were not *by definition* false.[92] B. O. Long's was the most extensive study of the etiologies, and he showed that seldom if ever was an etiological story the driving force behind the construction of a narrative.[93] In recent years, when greater attention has been focused on the literary qualities of narratives, the older emphasis on diachronic study of etiologies is further criticized, even to the point of questioning whether many narratives labeled as etiologies indeed have such a labeling function as their primary point. Rather, the narrative functions of heightening interest is emphasized in many so-called etiologies.[94]

(2) Judah's Boundaries (15:1–12)[95]

[1]The allotment for the tribe of Judah, clan by clan, extended down to the territory of Edom, to the Desert of Zin in the extreme south.

[2]Their southern boundary started from the bay at the southern end of the Salt Sea, [3]crossed south of Scorpion Pass, continued on to Zin and went over to the south of Kadesh Barnea. Then it ran past Hezron up to Addar and curved around to Karka. [4]It then passed along to Azmon and joined the Wadi of Egypt, ending at the sea. This is their southern boundary.

---

[90] H. Gunkel, H. Gressmann, A. Alt, and M. Noth being foremost among them.

[91] J. Bright, *Ancient Israel in Recent History Writing* (London: SCM, 1956), 91–110.

[92] B. S. Childs, "A Study of the Formula 'Until This Day,'" *JBL* 82 (1963): 279–92; id., "The Etiological Tale Re-examined," *VT* 24 (1974): 385–97.

[93] B. O. Long, (*The Problem of Etiological Narrative in the Old Testament*, BZAW 108 (Berlin: A. Töpelmann, 1968).

[94] See especially P. J. van Dyk, "The Function of So-Called Etiological Elements in Narratives," *ZAW* 102 (1990): 19–33, and H. C. Brichto, *Toward a Grammar of Poetics: Tales of the Prophets* (Oxford: Oxford University Press, 1992), 28–30. For further, accessible introductions to the entire question, see J. F. Priest, "Etiology," IDBSup, 293–95; Butler, *Joshua*, xxx–xxxiii; R. S. Hess, *Joshua: An Introduction and Commentary*, TOTC (Downers Grove: InterVarsity, 1996), 110–11.

[95] For in-depth introductions to the Judahite listings (including boundary and city lists), see Simons, *Geographical and Topographical Texts*, §§ 310–1,5 and map 2b; Kallai, *Historical Geography*, 115–24, 372–97, and map 4 (after p. 516); Svensson, *Towns and Toponymns*, 30–51. See also the maps in Beitzel, *Moody Atlas of the Bible*, 100; Rasmussen, *NIV Atlas of the Bible*, 97; Aharoni et al., *MacMillan Bible Atlas*, 105–6; Brisco, *Holman Bible Atlas*, 84. A brief but useful overview of all the tribal inheritances is Hess, "Tribes, Territories of the," *ISBE* 4:907–13. Hess's treatment of Judah's territories is on p. 909.

⁵The eastern boundary is the Salt Sea as far as the mouth of the Jordan.

The northern boundary started from the bay of the sea at the mouth of the Jordan, ⁶went up to Beth Hoglah and continued north of Beth Arabah to the Stone of Bohan son of Reuben. ⁷The boundary then went up to Debir from the Valley of Achor and turned north to Gilgal, which faces the Pass of Adummim south of the gorge. It continued along to the waters of En Shemesh and came out at En Rogel. ⁸Then it ran up the Valley of Ben Hinnom along the southern slope of the Jebusite city (that is, Jerusalem). From there it climbed to the top of the hill west of the Hinnom Valley at the northern end of the Valley of Rephaim. ⁹From the hilltop the boundary headed toward the spring of the waters of Nephtoah, came out at the towns of Mount Ephron and went down toward Baalah (that is, Kiriath Jearim). ¹⁰Then it curved westward from Baalah to Mount Seir, ran along the northern slope of Mount Jearim (that is, Kesalon), continued down to Beth Shemesh and crossed to Timnah. ¹¹It went to the northern slope of Ekron, turned toward Shikkeron, passed along to Mount Baalah and reached Jabneel. The boundary ended at the sea.

¹²The western boundary is the coastline of the Great Sea. These are the boundaries around the people of Judah by their clans.

The boundaries of Judah, in the southern portion of Canaan, are now described (vv. 1–12). This boundary list is one of the clearest and most detailed of the tribes, which should not be surprising, given Judah's prominence. Judah was the most important tribe in later Israelite history, since King David and his descendants were from this tribe (and, ultimately, Jesus: Matt 1:1). But its importance is signaled as early as the time of Jacob, who gave a blessing to Judah that included the promise of kingly authority (Gen 49:8–12).

Judah's boundary list is painstaking and true to life in its presentation, describing, it seems, every twist and turn, every dip and rise, every right angle of the lines that marked off this tribe. It is a dynamic, vibrant boundary (not static), almost lifelike in its movement. In this section, we will focus on the verbs used to describe the unfolding of the boundary, to give the reader a flavor for the dynamics of the lists.[96] In vv. 2–11, nine different verbs are used a total of thirty-five times to describe the movements of the southern and northern boundary lines, as they move from east to west.[97] Along with directional indicators—prepositions and nouns such as "from," "to," "alongside," "to the north, to the sea, to the east"—as well as geographical nouns such as "border," "tongue," "shoulder (slope)," "valley," "hill," "wadi," "sea," et cetera, the verbs combine to generate interesting and precise boundary descriptions. The fact that many of the points described are not known today should not obscure

---

[96] However, we will not do this for the rest of the lists.

[97] There are actually eight verbs—היה, יצא, עבר, עלה, סבב, פנה, תאר, and ירד—and one noun related to the verb יצא: תּוֹצְאוֹת. These words are translated and discussed briefly in the paragraphs below.

the marvel, detail, and precision of the original lists.

Furthermore, the word "boundary" *(gĕbûl)* occurs an astonishing twenty-one times in these twelve verses, a remarkable proportion, since the word occurs a total of eighty-four times in the book. Thus, the Judahite boundary list accounts for fully 25 percent of the occurrences of this word. This confirms the importance of Judah and its tribal boundaries. Such repetition of the word *gĕbûl* adds to the feeling of vitality in this list in particular. The combination of so many verbs linked to so many occurrences of *gĕbûl* places one in the ancient equivalent of what is today called "virtual reality": watching a borderline being drawn in "real time" with a computer-generated line, moving up and down, in and out, twisting and turning. The reader is drawn into the actual creation of the line, it seems, and given a "bumps-and-all" tour of the land.

15:1 Judah's allotment was in the south, extending down to the territory of Edom (south and east of the Dead Sea), and as far south as the Wilderness of Zin (whose exact location is not known with certainty). Readers should remember here and elsewhere that the English word "allotment" is related to the word "lot," both of which translate the Hebrew *gôrāl*. As we have noted in the excursus on "Israel's Inheritance of the Land in Joshua," God controlled even the casting of lots so that each tribe would receive its intended inheritance, that is, its allotment.

15:2–4 The southern boundary is first. It pulsates with life, as it wends its way westward from the southern end of the Dead Sea to the Mediterranean Sea. Attention to the verbs here highlights this, describing the "movement" of the boundary as it travels east to west. In v. 2, the eastern edge of the southern boundary was *(hyh)* opposite the edge of the Dead Sea, from the bay (lit., the "tongue") at the southern end. In v. 3, the boundary started west: it went out along a valley or streambed *(yṣ²)*[98] to the south of the Scorpion Pass and passed along or around *(ᶜbr)*[99] to Zin and went up *(ᶜlh)* from the south to Kadesh Barnea, and it passed along *(ᶜbr)* by Hezron and went up *(ᶜlh)* to Addar, and turned the corner *(sbb)*[100] to Karka. In v. 4, the boundary passed along *(ᶜbr)* over to Azmon, and then it went out along *(yṣ²)* the Wadi of Egypt, which carried the boundary out toward *(tōṣĕ²ôt)*[101] the sea.

---

[98] This verb means "went out." Parunak suggests that in the boundary descriptions, it has a more specialized meaning, used to designate "a boundary that follows a lowland route, and whenever possible, a wadi-bottom" ("Geographical Terminology," 60). (A wadi is a river or streambed that is dry during part of the year.)

[99] The verb אבר in lists such as this emphasizes that there is intervening territory and that the movement from Point A to Point B is not a straight line, but rather a circuitous one, describing perhaps a "bulge" in that portion of the boundary or a detour (ibid., 83–84).

[100] For this translation, see Parunak, "Geographical Terminology," 76–77.

[101] This word is a noun, not a verb, but it is related to the verb "to go out" (יצא) and is commonly used in the boundary lists (nineteen of twenty-three times; ibid., 54–55).

Most of the sites mentioned in vv. 2–4 are not known with certainty, but the general picture is clear, and the boundary is sure when it reaches the Wadi of Egypt.[102]

15:5a Judah's eastern boundary was simple enough: the western shores of the Dead Sea.

15:5b–11 The northern boundary is described in the most detail. This boundary corresponds closely to the southern boundary of Judah's neighbor, Benjamin, which is described in 18:15–19. This was a boundary with which people would have been very familiar, since people from Judah and Benjamin lived and traveled along it and across it, and they knew the cities and geographical markers listed for it. This undoubtedly explains the great detail here, especially when the boundary reaches Jerusalem, where the greatest detail is given (vv. 7b–8).

In v. 5, the northern boundary started at the bay (lit., "tongue") at the north end of the Dead Sea, at the mouth of the Jordan. In v. 6, it *went up (ʿlh)* past Beth Hoglah, traveling in a northerly direction initially. It then *passed along* or *around (ʿbr)* to the north of Beth Arabah and *went up (ʿlh)* to the Stone of Bohan, son of Reuben. No son of Reuben named "Bohan" is otherwise known, and the site of the "Stone of Bohan" is unknown. Yet, the very mention of a topographical feature such as this suggests that people of the day would have known it as a familiar landmark.[103]

In v. 7, the boundary went up *(ʿlh)* to Debir from the Valley of Achor and turned *(pnh)* north to Gilgal (the Gilgal near Jericho: 4:19;5:10). The boundary then passed along or around *(ʿbr)* to the Waters of En Shemesh, which was near Jerusalem.[104] Finally, the boundary line arrived at *(tōšĕʾôt)*,[105] the first site in the Jerusalem area itself, En Rogel, the spring just south of what later came to be known as the City of David, in the Kidron Valley.

In Jerusalem (v. 8), the boundary *went up (ʿlh)* the Hinnom Valley, which entailed moving west and north along the southern shoulder (NIV: "southern slope") of Jerusalem. The city is actually called by the name it bore in that day—"Jebus" (or, lit., here, "the Jebusite"), after its inhabitants—but the reader is also informed parenthetically that this city was the one better known as "Jerusalem." This parenthetical aside serves to link this alien city with the familiar place that was so prominent and important in Israel's later history. The border then *went up (ʿlh)* again to the top of the hill west of the Hinnom

---

[102] See Kallai, *Historical Geography*, 116–18, and map 4.

[103] For discussion of the various issues involved here, see Kallai, *Historical Geography*, 119; D. W. Baker, "Bohan, Stone of," *ABD* 1:772.

[104] See Kallai, *Historical Geography*, 120–21 and n. 48.

[105] On this nuance of תֹּצְאֹות see Parunak, "Geographical Terminology," 54. It is used with אֶל, "to, unto," when a city or a geographical feature—in this case, the En Rogel spring—is the destination.

Valley, at the north end of the Valley of Rephaim.

Leaving Jerusalem, the boundary in v. 9 turned the corner *(tʾr)*[106] from the hilltop to the spring at Nephtoah, and it went out along *(yṣʾ)* the course of the wadi bed[107] to the cities of Mount Ephron. It then turned the corner *(tʾr)* again to Baalath (i.e., Kiriath Jearim).

In v. 10, the boundary turned the corner *(nsb)* once again, this time westward to Mount Seir, and it passed along *(ʿbr)* the shoulder of Mount Jearim to the north, and it went down *(yrd)* to Beth Shemesh[108] and passed along or around *(ʿbr)* to Timnah.

In v. 11, the boundary *went out along (yṣʾ)* to the shoulder of Ekron to the north, and it *turned the corner (tʾr)* toward Shikkeron, and *passed by (ʿbr)* Mount Baalah and *went out along (yṣʾ)* to Jabneel. Here the boundary reached *out toward (tōṣĕʾôt)* the sea.

15:12   The verse begins by giving the last border—the western one—at the Mediterranean Sea. This and the eastern border are simple enough, and they are simply given, with no drawn-out descriptions (cf. v. 5a).[109]

The summary statement in the second half of the verse echoes the introductory statement in v. 1 by emphasizing the clans of the tribe of Judah.[110] An interesting feature here is the picture painted in the verse of the borders "surrounding" *(sābîb)* the clans of the tribe of Judah. In this concluding statement, a sense of security is conveyed, in that the tribe had well-defined borders that surrounded them, protecting them, in a sense, from that which was outside the borders.

(3) Caleb's Inheritance: Part Two (15:13–19)

¹³In accordance with the LORD's command to him, Joshua gave to Caleb son of Jephunneh a portion in Judah—Kiriath Arba, that is, Hebron. (Arba was the forefather of Anak.) ¹⁴From Hebron Caleb drove out the three Anakites— Sheshai, Ahiman and Talmai—descendants of Anak. ¹⁵From there he marched against the people living in Debir (formerly called Kiriath Sepher). ¹⁶And Caleb said, "I will give my daughter Acsah in marriage to the man who attacks and captures Kiriath Sepher." ¹⁷Othniel son of Kenaz, Caleb's brother, took it; so Caleb gave his daughter Acsah to him in marriage.

---

[106] See Parunak, "Geographical Terminology," 79–80 for this definition.

[107] See Kallai, *Historical Geography*, 122, and n. 98 above.

[108] This city should not be confused with the Beth Shemesh of Issachar (19:22) or of Naphtali (19:38).

[109] The western border included Philistine territories, which, according to 13:2–3, remained unconquered. However, certainly by the time of David and Solomon, this land was in Judah's hands (see Kallai, *Historical Geography*, 303–6).

[110] See the excursus on "Patterns in the Land Distribution Lists," Section 4, for more on the appearance of the clans in the introductory and concluding sections of the lists.

¹⁸**One day when she came to Othniel, she urged him to ask her father for a field. When she got off her donkey, Caleb asked her, "What can I do for you?"**

¹⁹**She replied, "Do me a special favor. Since you have given me land in the Negev, give me also springs of water." So Caleb gave her the upper and lower springs.**

The second passage about Caleb's inheritance (see 14:6–15 for the first such passage) explains his further acquisition of Debir, another city that originally had been taken by Joshua (10:38–39). Here, again, the assumption must be that it had fallen back into foreign hands (see on 14:12). This section closely parallels Judg 1:12–15. Either the present passage is an anticipation of what would happen later, inserted here for the sake of completeness, or the Judges passage is a "flashback." This story is bounded on either side by a summarizing statement about Judah's inheritance (vv. 12b and 20).

15:13–14 These verses are closely related to 14:13,15. However, some new details emerge. First, Joshua gave Caleb his inheritance at the Lord's command. Strictly speaking, the Bible does not mention this command earlier, but the Lord's words to Moses about Caleb's inheritance do mention it, and we may presume that the Lord's words to Moses were passed on to Joshua as well (13:6; cf. Num 14:24,30). This same chain-of-command pattern is visible earlier in the book (see esp. 4:8–10), where a previous command is assumed and expanded upon in a later portion of the text.

Second, we learn from v. 14 that Caleb actually had to drive out the Anakites in order to take possession of his land, specifically their three leaders, Sheshai, Ahiman, and Talmai. These three are mentioned in Num 13:22 as having been at Hebron when Caleb and the other spies went into the land the first time, forty-five years earlier. So there is a certain poetic justice in Caleb's now driving them out of the land that he had urged the Israelites to take a generation earlier.

15:15–19 A third thing we learn concerns Debir, a city near Hebron (10:38–39; 11:21). Caleb went up against this city (v. 15), but, as it turned out, Othniel actually captured the city. Caleb offered his daughter Acsah in marriage to whomever would do this, and Othniel did (vv. 16–17). Othniel was part of the Kenizzite clan, being Caleb's nephew (v. 17), so the land remained in the family. Othniel later was one of the twelve judges whom God used in delivering the Israelites from foreign oppressions during the turbulent period described in the Book of Judges (3:9–11).

In vv. 18–19, we have the second account of an individual or group asking for their inheritance (see Section 3 of the excursus "Patterns in the Land Distribution Lists" at the end of chap. 13). These two verses are set off syntactically from the rest of the section, forming a discrete account. Several items make the text somewhat awkward. First, Acsah "urged" Othniel (?) to ask her father for a field. The word translated "urged" is almost always used negatively to mean "incite, allure, instigate,"[111] which raises a question about the appropriateness of this request (although the question is not answered). Second, whom she addressed is not specified, but we may presume that it was her husband, Othniel. Third, strangely enough, Othniel does not figure again in the text, but Acsah went ahead and spoke with her father about her wishes.[112] Fourth, Acsah first mentioned a field (v. 18), but, when her father spoke with her, she asked for springs of water (v. 19). It may be that the "land in the Negev" to which she referred was the fulfillment of her first request for a field and that v. 19 refers to a second request, for springs of water on that land.

Acsah asked her father, Caleb, for a blessing (NIV: "special favor") when he asked what he could do for her. The blessing consisted of springs of water that would complement Debir and the land in the Negev[113] that he had given her (where there is little water), and her father complied with her request.

(4) Summary (15:20)

20This is the inheritance of the tribe of Judah, clan by clan:

An earlier summary statement at the end of Judah's boundary list is found at v. 12. The summary statement here does not correspond merely to the story of Caleb's land in vv. 13–19, however, but to all of 14:6–15:19. Against NIV's paragraph division and punctuation, this verse does not introduce what follows but rather summarizes what precedes. The exact wording here—"This is the inheritance of X, clan by clan"—is found twelve times in Joshua, always and only as a summarizing statement: Josh 13:23,28; 15:20; 16:8; 18:20,28; 19:8,16,23,31, 39,48.[114] A third summary statement for Judah is found at 15:63.

(5) Judah's Cities (15:21–62)

21The southernmost towns of the tribe of Judah in the Negev toward the boundary of Edom were:

Kabzeel, Eder, Jagur, 22Kinah, Dimonah, Adadah, 23Kedesh, Hazor, Ithnan, 24Ziph, Telem, Bealoth, 25Hazor Hadattah, Kerioth Hezron (that is, Hazor),

---

[111] The verb is the *hiphil* form of סות. See BDB, 694; *HALOT*, 749.

[112] Probably reflecting this tension, the Old Greek and Vg. in the parallel text at Judg 1:14 read that *Othniel* nagged at *Acsah* to make the request (followed by REB). However, reading with the MT, we may suppose that when Acsah spoke further with her father, she was doing so in agreement with her husband (see Butler, *Joshua*, 180).

[113] Boling notes that this likely does not refer to the Negev desert in the south (the Hb. word *negeb* means "south, southland"), but to *Hebron's* "southland," i.e., to the "hills falling away to the desert fringe" to the south of Hebron (Boling, *Joshua*, 375).

[114] The Hb. here is לְמִשְׁפְּחֹתָם ... זֹאת נַחֲלַת, "this is the inheritance [of X], according to their clans"; the "X" is either "tribe [of TRIBAL NAME]" or "sons [of TRIBAL NAME]."

^{26}Amam, Shema, Moladah, ^{27}Hazar Gaddah, Heshmon, Beth Pelet, ^{28}Hazar
Shual, Beersheba, Biziothiah, ^{29}Baalah, Iim, Ezem, ^{30}Eltolad, Kesil, Hormah,
^{31}Ziklag, Madmannah, Sansannah, ^{32}Lebaoth, Shilhim, Ain and Rimmon—a
total of twenty-nine towns and their villages.

^{33}In the western foothills:
Eshtaol, Zorah, Ashnah, ^{34}Zanoah, En Gannim, Tappuah, Enam, ^{35}Jarmuth,
Adullam, Socoh, Azekah, ^{36}Shaaraim, Adithaim and Gederah (or Gederoth-
aim)—fourteen towns and their villages.
^{37}Zenan, Hadashah, Migdal Gad, ^{38}Dilean, Mizpah, Joktheel, ^{39}Lachish, Boz-
kath, Eglon, ^{40}Cabbon, Lahmas, Kitlish, ^{41}Gederoth, Beth Dagon, Naamah and
Makkedah—sixteen towns and their villages.
^{42}Libnah, Ether, Ashan, ^{43}Iphtah, Ashnah, Nezib, ^{44}Keilah, Aczib and Mareshah—nine towns and their villages.
^{45}Ekron, with its surrounding settlements and villages; ^{46}west of Ekron, all
that were in the vicinity of Ashdod, together with their villages; ^{47}Ashdod, its surrounding settlements and villages; and Gaza, its settlements and villages, as far as
the Wadi of Egypt and the coastline of the Great Sea.

^{48}In the hill country:
Shamir, Jattir, Socoh, ^{49}Dannah, Kiriath Sannah (that is, Debir), ^{50}Anab, Esh-
temoh, Anim, ^{51}Goshen, Holon and Giloh—eleven towns and their villages.
^{52}Arab, Dumah, Eshan, ^{53}Janim, Beth Tappuah, Aphekah, ^{54}Humtah, Kiriath
Arba (that is, Hebron) and Zior—nine towns and their villages.
^{55}Maon, Carmel, Ziph, Juttah, ^{56}Jezreel, Jokdeam, Zanoah, ^{57}Kain, Gibeah
and Timnah—ten towns and their villages.
^{58}Halhul, Beth Zur, Gedor, ^{59}Maarath, Beth Anoth and Eltekon—six towns
and their villages.
^{60}Kiriath Baal (that is, Kiriath Jearim) and Rabbah—two towns and their vil-
lages.

^{61}In the desert:
Beth Arabah, Middin, Secacah, ^{62}Nibshan, the City of Salt and En Gedi—six
towns and their villages.

15:21–62   The cities that Judah inherited are now listed.[115] Only their
names are given, except for three cities in Philistine territory (vv. 45–47). The
cities are organized into eleven groups in the MT (twelve in the Old Greek
versions), which are arranged in five larger units. The larger units are (1) the
southland (*negeb*), composed of one group (vv. 21–32), (2) the western foothills (*šĕpēlâ*), with three groups (vv. 33–44), (3) three Philistine cities, listed
in one group (vv. 45–47), (4) the hill country (*har*), with five or six groups

---

[115] The most detailed map of this section is to be found in Kallai, *Historical Geography*, Map 2
(after p. 516); see pp. 372–97 for a discussion of the entire Judahite city list. See also Simons, *Geographical and Topographical Texts*, § 316–20, and the map in Rasmussen, *NIV Atlas of the Bible*,
97.

(vv. 48–60), and (5) the desert *(midbār)*, with one group (vv. 61–62).

If one counts the number of cities in the MT, the total is 122, but the running totals given at vv. 32,36,41,44,51,54,57,59,62 yield 115 (see below, on vv. 21–32). If the eleven extra cities in the Old Greek versions in v. 59 are added, then the totals are 133 and 126. If one subtracts the three Philistine cities, the numbers drop accordingly. Almost half of all the cities in the MT of this chapter are never mentioned anywhere else in the Bible—a total of fifty-eight. In addition, more than half are never mentioned outside of the Book of Joshua—a total of sixty-nine. Beyond this, fourteen additional cities are only mentioned in lists, primarily in 1 Chronicles and Nehemiah. Thus, fully two-thirds of the cities mentioned in this chapter (83 out of 122) are found only in contexts such as this, and nothing further is known about them. In addition, many of their locations are uncertain.

These uncertainties should not obscure the larger and obvious point, that the very magnitude of the list—the largest of any of the tribal lists—is intended to reflect Judah's prominence as a tribe. It is not surprising that we know nothing further about so many of these cities. The author of the book included them here to make a theological point, and the fact that they were of no historical significance to any other biblical writer merely reinforces the use to which the author of Joshua put them: to highlight Judah's importance. Further evidence of the continuing importance of this list (and this tribe) comes in the numerous places where a later name is given alongside an earlier one (represented in NIV by parenthetical statements), in vv. 8–10,13,15,25,49, 54,60. This helped readers in a later time identify these locales.[116]

One of these cities— Kiriath Arba (i.e., Hebron), mentioned in v. 54—was Judah's representative among the six cities of refuge (20:7–8). All nine of the Levitical cities mentioned in 21:13–16 as having come from the tribes of Judah and Simeon are mentioned in this chapter, one in Judah's boundary description—Beth Shemesh (v. 10)—and eight in this city list: Ain (v. 32), Libnah (v. 42), Jattir (v. 48), Debir (v. 49), Eshtemoh (v. 50),[117] Holon (v. 51), Hebron (v. 54), and Juttah (v. 55).

Nine of Judah's cities are also listed among the eighteen cities of Simeon in 19:2–9. This is in accordance with the information in 19:1,9, that Simeon in fact received its entire inheritance within Judah's borders. (See further the commentary at 19:1–9.)

A number of cities in Judah's list are found in the city or boundary lists of the other tribes as well. The following cities were later assigned to Dan: Eshtaol and Zorah (v. 33; cf. 19:41), Ekron and Timnah (vv. 45,47; cf. 19:43).

---

[116] We cannot know who added these names, nor when. However, the presence of these "updatings" shows the importance of making the list understandable to later generations.

[117] "Eshtemoh" is more commonly spelled "Eshtemoa": Josh 21:14; 1 Sam 30:28; 1 Chr 6:57.

However, Dan never took possession of these (19:47), and even Judah did not gain complete control over these cities in or near Philistine territory until the time of David. Beth Arabah (v. 61) was on the border between Judah and Benjamin; it appears in both Benjamin's boundary and city lists (18:18,22).[118]

15:21–32: UNIT ONE: THE SOUTHLAND (*negeb*). The cities here are at the southernmost extreme of Judah's territory,[119] and they occupy the single largest area of the groupings in this chapter. Thirty-six cities are listed, although the running total given in v. 32 is only "twenty-nine."[120] Possibly some locales listed were not considered to be substantial enough settlements to have merited inclusion in the running total,[121] or an early copying error may account for the discrepancy.[122] After this, all city listings and running totals in the chapter agree with each other. As we have noted above, several cities in this section of Judah's list are also found in Simeon's list in 19:1–9. We should also note that the three cities named "Hazor" in vv. 23,25 are to be distinguished from the northern Hazor mentioned in chap. 11.

15:33–44: UNIT TWO: THE WESTERN FOOTHILLS (*šĕpēlâ*). This unit is composed of three groups of cities, located at least twenty-five miles southwest of Jerusalem. The first is the northernmost of the three (vv. 33–36), with fourteen cities; the second is to the southwest (vv. 37–41), with sixteen cities, and the third is to the southeast (vv. 42–44), with nine cities.[123] The total number of cities listed is thirty-nine, which accords with the running totals in vv. 36,41,44.

The first two names in this list—Eshtaol and Zorah (v. 33)—were later allotted to Dan (19:41) and, when Judah's boundary lines are considered, they were slightly outside of the boundaries. They were near the area where Samson had some of his confrontations with the Philistines (see Judg 13:25; 16:31).

Several cities in this section have identical names to other cities elsewhere in the lands the Israelites inherited. Kedesh (v. 23) is not to be confused with the important northern city in Naphtali's territory (19:37) that also was a city of refuge and a Levitical city (20:7; 21:32). Its name is a variant form of

---

[118] See commentary on 18:22 for a brief discussion of the possibility of shifts in the allotments.

[119] The Hb. term used is מִקְצֵה, "edge, end, extreme."

[120] Some scholars, by reconstructing the list or combining names, arrive at different totals: Boling finds thirty-three city names here (*Joshua*, 384), as does Nelson (*Joshua*, 182, 184); Kallai finds at least thirty-four, but he also suggests that a total of twenty-one could be arrived at by removing every locale with the element חָצֵר "Hazar" in its name (since "Hazar" means "settlement") (*Historical Geography*, 379). The Old Greek lists thirty cities (although its running total is twenty-nine, like the MT's). NIV, NASB, NJPSV, and NRSV all give thirty-six city names.

[121] Kallai, *Historical Geography*, 379.

[122] So Keil, *Book of Joshua*, 163.

[123] See Kallai, *Historical Geography*, 379–84, for a justification of the geographical locations of the three groupings, which runs slightly counter to the scholarly consensus (which groups them in the north, south, and middle, respectively).

"Kadesh Barnea" (see 10:41; 14:6–7; 15:3). Tappuah (v. 34) is not to be con-
fused with a northern city mentioned several times in connection with
Ephraim and Manasseh (16:8; 17:7–8), which was defeated earlier by Joshua
and the people (12:17), nor is En Gannim (v. 34) to be confused with the city
in Issachar's city list (19:21), which became a Levitical city (21:29). Beth
Dagon (v. 41) should not be confused with another city of the same name in
Issachar's boundary list (19:27); its name means "house (or temple) of
Dagon," and it should be no surprise to find more than one city in Canaan
named after a Canaanite god. Neither is Iphtah (v. 43) to be confused with the
Valley of Iphtah El in Asher's boundary list (19:27), or Aczib (v. 44) with the
Aczib in that same list (19:29)

15:45–47: UNIT THREE: PHILISTINE CITIES.   The three cities in this
section—Ekron, Ashdod, Gaza—all were Philistine cities found earlier in the
listing of lands remaining to be conquered by the Israelites in 13:2–6 (specifically, 13:3). The format of this short list is distinctly different from the rest of
the city list: it is much fuller, with directional markers and mention of surrounding villages, and it has no running total at the end, as do all the other city
groups in the chapter. Ekron, the northernmost of the three cities, was later
assigned to the tribe of Dan (19:43). The irregularities in this section are no
doubt because the entire area covered by these cities remained unconquered
by Judah. Yet this section is included because, according to the boundary listings, Judah's territory included even these cities (see 15:4,11–12).

15:48–60: UNIT FOUR: THE HILL COUNTRY *(har)*.   This unit is composed of five or six groups, running in a general south-to-north listing. The
first group is the southernmost (vv. 48–51), just to the north of the first large
unit of vv. 21–32. It has eleven cities. The second and third groups are just to
the north, the second to the west of the first. The second group has nine cities
(vv. 52–54), and the third ten (vv. 55–57). The fourth group is north of the
second group and consists of six cities (vv. 58–59).

The city of Jezreel in v. 56 is not the same as the northern Jezreel in Issachar's territory (19:18). The Gibeah of v. 57 is not the one in Benjamin's territory (18:28), nor the one in Ephraimite territory, where Eleazar the priest was
buried (24:33). Kiriath Baal (i.e., Kiriath Jearim) in v. 60 is specifically mentioned as being a town of Judah at the southwestern corner of Benjamin's
boundary description (18:14–15).

The Old Greek versions preserve a fifth group in v. 59 that is not found in
the MT. It consists of eleven additional cities and reads: "Tekoa, Ephrathah,
that is, Bethlehem, Peor, Etam, Culon, Tatam, Sores, Carem, Gallim, Baither,
and Manach: eleven towns in all with their hamlets" (REB).[124] This group is

---

[124] See also NJPSV's text note. REB's "hamlets" is "villages" in most versions. The spellings
of these city names is not certain in every case, due to the vagaries of reconstructing a Hb. form
from a sometimes imprecise Gk. text. Cf. the slightly variant lists in Kallai, *Historical Geography*,
392; Nelson, *Joshua*, 183.

north of the fourth, centering around Bethlehem, south of Jerusalem. It is plausible that this group dropped out early in the copying process because the word wĕḥaṣrêhen, "and their villages," occurs at the end of the fourth group and at the end of this one; and a scribe's eye easily could have jumped from the one to the other, causing him to omit an entire section.[125]

The sixth group (the fifth in the MT) is small, consisting merely of two cities: Kiriath Baal/Jearim and Rabbah (v. 60).[126] It was north of the previous group, some twenty miles west of Jerusalem. Kiriath Jearim is mentioned in the boundary list at v. 9. Rabbah was not the Ammonite city in Transjordan, which was not part of the Israelites' territory (cf. 13:25).

15:61–62: UNIT FIVE: THE DESERT (midbār).   The final major unit is somewhat narrowly, and yet vaguely, described, with only one group, composed of six cities. They were all located in the desert along the northwestern half of the Dead Sea, but the geographical limits of the unit may have extended south to the end of the Dead Sea.[127] The major city in the list is En Gedi, an oasis halfway down the Dead Sea.

(6) Judah's Failure concerning Jebus (15:63)

[63]Judah could not dislodge the Jebusites, who were living in Jerusalem; to this day the Jebusites live there with the people of Judah.

15:63   In the first "Conquest Lacuna" specifying an individual tribe's failure to drive out certain inhabitants of Canaan, the tribe of Judah was not able to drive out the Jebusites, who remained with them "to this day." Since David was able to capture the city from the Jebusites (ca. 1003 B.C.), we can presume that this reference predates that time. On the "Conquest Lacunae," see the excursus "Patterns in the Land Distribution Lists," Section 2, at the end of chap. 13.

The references to the Jebusites and Jerusalem are somewhat complicated when considered in conjunction with later information about these. Judges 1:21 is an almost verbatim repetition of this verse, except stating that Benjamin (not Judah) did not drive out the Jebusites. The reason for this dual assignment of the city undoubtedly is that Jerusalem sat astride the boundary between Benjamin and Judah, and it was not strongly identified with either tribe. On the one hand, Jerusalem was a Benjaminite city: in the Benjaminite tribal allotment, the boundary line runs "down the Hinnom Valley along the

---

[125] See the discussions of this grouping in Keil, Book of Joshua, 172–73; Kallai, Historical Geography, 393–93.

[126] Rabbah's site is unknown; some suggest that it is to be identified with a city known from Egyptian sources as R-b-t and from the Amarna Letters as Rubute (e.g., Kallai, Historical Geography, 394), but this identification is not certain (see W. R. Kotter, "Rabbah," ABD 5:600).

[127] See Kallai's discussion (Historical Geography, 395–96) and Map 2 (after p. 516).

southern slope of the Jebusite city and so to En Rogel" (Josh 18:16), and "the Jebusite city (that is, Jerusalem)" appears in the Benjaminite city list (18:28). On the other hand, Jerusalem also appears in the Judahite boundary list: the description in 15:8 uses almost the same language as is found in the Benjaminite list: "Then it ran up the Valley of Ben Hinnom along the southern slope of the Jebusite city (that is, Jerusalem)."

Further complicating the matter is that the tribe of Judah did capture Jerusalem later (Judg 1:8), but then we are told that Benjamin did not drive out the Jebusites in their portion (Judg 1:21). The solution to this difference in perspective lies in understanding that Judah's success may have been limited and temporary, while Benjamin's failure was total.[128] In either case, Jebusites and Israelites lived intermingled, according to Josh 15:63 and Judg 1:21, and the city was not taken decisively by Israelites until the time of David, ca. 1003 B.C. (2 Sam 5:5–10). Indeed, in the period of the judges, Jebus was considered to be a non-Israelite city since it was called an "alien city" by the Levite from the hill country of Ephraim who was passing by with his concubine and his servant (Judg 19:11–12).

5. Joseph's Inheritance (16:1–17:18)

The descendants of Joseph—Ephraim and Manasseh—received two large portions west of the Jordan, in the center of the land, plus a portion in Transjordan for half of the tribe of Manasseh. This reflects the favor that was to be shown Joseph, mentioned years earlier in Jacob's blessing on his sons (Gen 49:22–26). However, the author of the book clearly considers the tribes of Joseph to be one with each other, giving us several lines of evidence that point to this. First, they received one lot (16:1). Second, the southern boundary of Ephraim, the southernmost tribe of the two, is in some sense considered the southern extremity for both tribes. It is given in detail in 16:1–3, then 16:5 gives Ephraim's southern border in an abbreviated form.[129] Third, the story about the tribes' demanding two portions underscores this even further (17:14–18).

After a general summary of the two tribes' southern boundary (16:1–4), Ephraim's land is marked out (16:5–10), followed by Manasseh's (17:1–13). The two tribes are listed in reverse order of their ancestors' birth; this perhaps reflects the favor that was to be shown the younger son, Ephraim (see Genesis 48). As we have noted, these two tribes were only apportioned land by one

---

[128] Some have suggested that the Judahite victory may have been against the undefended western hill, while the Benjaminites' failure was against the impregnable fortress on the southeastern hill. However, no settlement from this time period is attested archaeologically; the city was only settled on the walled southeastern hill (see Kallai, *Historical Geography*, 136–37).

[129] Manasseh's southern boundary proper is described in 17:7–9, but the point in 16:1–4 is that Ephraim and Manasseh were closely bound together.

lot—the word *gôrāl*, "lot, allotment," is singular in 16:1—which caused them to complain to Joshua (17:14–18). They are the only tribes settling west of the Jordan for which no city lists per se are preserved. Two cities in its boundary descriptions, however, were among those that became Levitical cities: Gezer (vv. 3,10; see 21:21) and Beth Horon (vv. 3,5; see 21:22).

The two chapters are full of interpretive difficulties, some of them because the Hebrew is unclear, some of them because of textual difficulties, and some of them because the locations mentioned are not known.[130]

(1) Joseph's Southern Boundary (16:1–4)

[1]The allotment for Joseph began at the Jordan of Jericho, east of the waters of Jericho, and went up from there through the desert into the hill country of Bethel. [2]It went on from Bethel (that is, Luz), crossed over to the territory of the Arkites in Ataroth, [3]descended westward to the territory of the Japhletites as far as the region of Lower Beth Horon and on to Gezer, ending at the sea. [4]So Manasseh and Ephraim, the descendants of Joseph, received their inheritance.

The southern boundary of the Joseph tribes—Ephraim and Manasseh—is given in some detail in vv. 1–3,[131] moving from the Dead Sea in the east to the Mediterranean Sea in the west. It corresponds to the northern boundary of Benjamin (18:12–13), although there are elements in each description not found in the other. The common elements in both lists, however, show that the line was drawn and understood fairly precisely. However, since there are no city lists preserved for either Joseph tribe, this may account for some of the interpretive difficulties mentioned above.[132]

16:1 The boundary line for the sons of Joseph began in the east near Jericho, which was north of Judah's boundary. Judah's boundary began at the northern "bay" of the Dead Sea (15:5), leaving a short stretch of Benjaminite territory between the two (see 18:19–20).

The text actually states that the lot (not the boundary) "went out," but the idea is that the lot was cast and the boundary line started out as a result.[133] It

---

[130] See the following works on parts or all of these two chapters: Simons, *Geographical and Topographical Texts*, §§ 323–24; Kallai, *Historical Geography*, 138–78; Na'aman, *Borders and Districts*, 145–66 (on the boundary between Ephraim and Manasseh); Svensson, *Towns and Toponymns*, 63–65. The textual variants and other difficulties are discussed in these and the standard commentaries. The treatment here generally follows the NIV's interpretive rendering in most places. Good, general maps may be found in Boling, *Joshua*, 398; Rasmussen, *NIV Atlas of the Bible*, 98; Brisco, *Holman Bible Atlas*, 84.

[131] A reason for this is suggested at 16:4.

[132] See Woudstra, *Joshua*, 257.

[133] The opening words of Simeon's inheritance in 19:1 also are "and the lot went out," but the syntactical pattern after that is different from the pattern in 16:1: the words in 19:1 are part of the introductory framework, and the boundary description does not begin until 19:2. See also the commentary on 19:1.

ran to the "waters of Jericho"[134] east of Jericho. Like Jerusalem (see on 15:63), Jericho appears in the inheritance lists of two different tribes (it also appears as part of Benjamin's boundary line in 18:12). It went up from the desert (or wilderness) near Jericho, at its location far below sea level in the Jordan River valley, rising sharply as it ran northwest up into the hill country near Bethel.

16:2 Bethel and Luz are distinguished here (lit., "from Bethel to Luz"), but because of their close association elsewhere (18:13; Gen 28:19; Judg 1:23), the NIV's rendering of the phrase as "from Bethel (that is, Luz)" is certainly defensible.[135] At Bethel, the boundary, which had been moving northwest, turned to go southwest. The Arkites were a people listed among the Canaanite peoples in Gen 10:17; one of David's close advisors, Hushai, was an Arkite (2 Sam 15:32; 16:16; etc.). Ataroth was not the same one that was on Ephraim's northern border (Josh 16:7), but it is mentioned again in 16:5 and 18:13, as part of Benjamin's boundary. It was near Bethel, southwest of it.

16:3 The boundary line went westward (or "toward the sea"; Hb. *yāmmâ* can be translated either way),[136] through the Japhletites' territory. The Japhletites are otherwise unknown, except as descendants of Asher (1 Chr 7:30–33). Two fixed points—Lower Beth Horon[137] and Gezer—are mentioned, but these are not anywhere near the sea. The boundary description ends by stating that "(the boundary) was outgoing *[tōṣĕ'ôt]* to the sea," but the fifteen miles (roughly) from Gezer to the sea are not detailed at all. The boundary would appear to move now to the sea in a sharply northwestern direction, on the basis of the Danite city list in 19:40–48, particularly the cities of Joppa, on the coast, and Gath Rimmon, near the Mediterranean and just south of the Yarkon River.[138]

16:4 The unified treatment of the two Joseph tribes now ends, completing the common southern boundary that separated them from the southern

---

[134] This undoubtedly refers to the perennial spring east of the city, ʿAin es-Sultan (see T. A. Holland and E. Netzer, "Jericho," *ABD* 3:724).

[135] For various other proposals, see Woudstra, *Joshua*, 258; Boling, *Joshua*, 396; Kallai, *Historical Geography*, 129–31,143; Nelson, *Joshua*, 196.

[136] The directional reference points in the Hb. mental map were oriented with one facing east with the Mediterranean Sea at one's back. East was a reference point in front or toward the rising of the sun, west behind, toward the sea, or toward the setting of the sun, south was toward the right hand, and north was toward the left hand. See Y. Aharoni et al., *The Macmillan Bible Atlas,* 3d ed. (New York: Macmillan, 1993), 11; J. F. Drinkard, Jr., "Direction and Orientation," *ABD* 2:204; P. S. Alexander, "Geography and the Bible," *ABD* 2:979. For more detail, see the articles on the compass points (east, west, north, south) in any Bible dictionary or encyclopedia.

[137] Beth Horon was one of the locations where the Israelites chased the Amorite coalition during the battle of Gibeon (10:10–11).

[138] See the commentary on 19:40–48 and the maps in Beitzel, *Moody Atlas of the Bible*, 100; Rasmussen, *NIV Atlas of the Bible*, 102; Brisco, *Holman Bible Atlas*, 84.

tribes of Benjamin and Judah. From this point on, the boundaries are given for each tribe individually. The importance of this southern border may reflect real geographical, cultural, and political divisions between north and south, even at an early stage in the nation's history. Such divisions are hinted at during the united monarchy under David, where "Judah" is distinguished from "Israel" even before there had been a split (e.g., 2 Sam 2:9–10; 3:10,19,37; 4:1).

(2) Ephraim's Boundaries (16:5–9)

⁵This was the territory of Ephraim, clan by clan:
The boundary of their inheritance went from Ataroth Addar in the east to Upper Beth Horon ⁶and continued to the sea. From Micmethath on the north it curved eastward to Taanath Shiloh, passing by it to Janoah on the east. ⁷Then it went down from Janoah to Ataroth and Naarah, touched Jericho and came out at the Jordan. ⁸From Tappuah the border went west to the Kanah Ravine and ended at the sea. This was the inheritance of the tribe of the Ephraimites, clan by clan. ⁹It also included all the towns and their villages that were set aside for the Ephraimites within the inheritance of the Manassites.

16:5 Ephraim's inheritance *(nāḥălâ)*[139] in the central portion of the land is now detailed. In vv. 5–6a, the southern boundary detailed in vv. 1–3 is briefly reviewed, again dispensing with any detail quite a distance from the sea (see comments on v. 3). Both fixed points here are mentioned in the more detailed listing in vv. 2–3: Ataroth (Addar) and (Upper) Beth Horon. The focus is now on Ephraim as a tribe by itself rather than on both Ephraim and Manasseh as the Joseph tribes. However, since the southern boundary was the same from both perspectives, its description is abbreviated here.

16:6–7 The eastern portion of the northern boundary is now given. It began with Micmethath (mentioned again only in Manasseh's list: 17:7),[140] from where it curved eastward and then southeastward, passing Jericho until it reached the Jordan, ending where the southern boundary had started (cf. v. 1). The specific points between Micmethath and Jericho are not easily identified from the biblical data, although the general direction of the boundary is clear enough. Two of the places—Taanath Shiloh and Naarah—are mentioned only here, and a third—Janoah—occurs only here (vv. 6–7) and in 2 Kgs 15:29, where it is listed with several cities captured by the Assyrian king Tiglath-Pileser.

---

[139] See also v. 9; contrast the characterization of Manasseh's portion in 17:1: the allotment (גּוֹרָל).

[140] Kallai believes that it may have been a geographical reference point, such as a mountain or a valley, not a city, since it is written with the definite article -הַ, i.e., "the Micmethath" (Kallai, *Historical Geography*, 150–51).

16:8a   The western portion of the northern boundary is now given, completing the picture begun in v. 6, except for a short gap that is left between Micmethath (v. 6) and Tappuah (v. 8).[141] The boundary went westward from Tappuah (which was southwest of Micmethath), along the Kanah Ravine all the way to the sea. The last phrase here—*wĕhayû tōṣĕʾōtāyw hayyāmmâ*, "and it was outward to the sea"—is the same as in v. 3 (see also 17:9, describing the same border).[142] In contrast to the vagueness in v. 3, however, the northern boundary would seem to be more precise than the southern one at its western extremity because it ran along an identifiable geographical feature, the Kanah Ravine. If this is the Wadi Qanah, as is generally supposed,[143] then this wadi can easily be traced even today.

16:8b–9   Just as in v. 5, Ephraim's land is called its "inheritance" in the concluding statement in v. 8b (on this as a concluding statement, see comments on 15:20). According to v. 9 some of Ephraim's cities were actually part of Manasseh's inheritance. The reason for this is not clear, but it may have its basis in the greater blessing extended to Ephraim by Jacob (Genesis 48). Manasseh also inherited cities from other tribes' territory: from Issachar and Asher (17:11) and even from Ephraim (17:9).

(3) Ephraim's Failure Concerning Gezer (16:10)

10They did not dislodge the Canaanites living in Gezer; to this day the Canaanites live among the people of Ephraim but are required to do forced labor.

16:10   At the conclusion of the short treatment of the Ephraimites' boundaries, we are told that they too, like the Judahites, failed to drive out certain Canaanites from their territories (on Judah, see 15:63 and the commentary there), in this case, the inhabitants of Gezer (see also Judg 1:29).[144] Joshua had earlier conquered Gezer to some degree (Josh 10:33), but evidently it was not a complete conquest, or else it had been repopulated in the interim. Gezer remained outside of Israelite control until the time of Solomon, when the Egyptian pharaoh captured it and gave it as a dowry for his daughter, Solomon's bride (1 Kgs 9:16).

In contrast to the statement about Judah and the Jebusites in 15:63, the Ephraimites did place the inhabitants of Gezer under their control, as forced laborers. The term used here, *lĕmas ʿōbēd*, can be rendered "and it [i.e., Gezer] was working at forced labor." The idea of forced labor or compulsory service *(mas)* was something the Israelites were subjected to under the Egyp-

---

[141] This boundary line is complemented by the Manassite boundary description in 17:7–9.

[142] With the exception of the definite article on "sea," which is absent in v. 3.

[143] Kallai, *Historical Geography*, 153; H. O. Thompson, "Kanah," *ABD* 4:5. See the map in Rasmussen, *NIV Atlas of the Bible*, 98.

[144] Essentially the same statement is found in Judg 1:29 as well.

tians (Exod 1:11) but to which they were to subject any faraway peoples who accepted an offer of peace with them (Deut 20:11), as the Gibeonites did (see Josh 9:27).[145] The tribe of Manasseh subjected to forced labor the Canaanites living in the towns they were to capture (17:12–13; Judg 1:28), as did the tribes of Zebulun and Naphtali with residents of cities within their territorial inheritances (Judg 1:30,33; cf. also v. 35).

In these contexts the subjugation of the Canaanites was not a positive accomplishment for the Israelites, however, because they did this without making any peace with them. According to Deut 20:16–18, they should have completely annihilated the peoples, not spared them and subjected them to forced labor. Thus, the Ephraimites and the rest failed in their duties, even though the lasting result was their subjugation of native peoples. The status of the inhabitants of Gezer with respect to the Ephraimites was somewhat similar to that of the Gibeonites (see 9:27), except that there was no treaty involved here, so the status of these Canaanites was somewhat lower than that of the Gibeonites.

(4) Western Manasseh's Boundaries (17:1–11)

¹This was the allotment for the tribe of Manasseh as Joseph's firstborn, that is, for Makir, Manasseh's firstborn. Makir was the ancestor of the Gileadites, who had received Gilead and Bashan because the Makirites were great soldiers. ²So this allotment was for the rest of the people of Manasseh—the clans of Abiezer, Helek, Asriel, Shechem, Hepher and Shemida. These are the other male descendants of Manasseh son of Joseph by their clans.

³Now Zelophehad son of Hepher, the son of Gilead, the son of Makir, the son of Manasseh, had no sons but only daughters, whose names were Mahlah, Noah, Hoglah, Milcah and Tirzah. ⁴They went to Eleazar the priest, Joshua son of Nun, and the leaders and said, "The LORD commanded Moses to give us an inheritance among our brothers." So Joshua gave them an inheritance along with the brothers of their father, according to the LORD's command. ⁵Manasseh's share consisted of ten tracts of land besides Gilead and Bashan east of the Jordan, ⁶because the daughters of the tribe of Manasseh received an inheritance among the sons. The land of Gilead belonged to the rest of the descendants of Manasseh.

⁷The territory of Manasseh extended from Asher to Micmethath east of Shechem. The boundary ran southward from there to include the people living at En Tappuah. ⁸(Manasseh had the land of Tappuah, but Tappuah itself, on the boundary of Manasseh, belonged to the Ephraimites.) ⁹Then the boundary continued south to the Kanah Ravine. There were towns belonging to Ephraim lying among the towns of Manasseh, but the boundary of Manasseh was the northern side of the ravine and ended at the sea. ¹⁰On the south the land belonged to

---

[145] General discussions of the forced labor represented by מַס can be found in R. North, "מַס mas," *TDOT* 8:427–30; G. A. Klingbeil, "מַס," *NIDOTTE* 2:992–95.

Ephraim, on the north to Manasseh. The territory of Manasseh reached the sea and bordered Asher on the north and Issachar on the east.

[11]**Within Issachar and Asher, Manasseh also had Beth Shan, Ibleam and the people of Dor, Endor, Taanach and Megiddo, together with their surrounding settlements (the third in the list is Naphoth).**

Manasseh's allotment is given here as a continuing part of the larger treatment of the Joseph tribes' inheritance in chaps. 16–17. This section is longer than the one for Ephraim, partly because of the episode in vv. 3–6 and the details of vv. 1–2. Manasseh, Joseph's firstborn, nevertheless is treated in second position, probably because of the favor that was to be shown to Ephraim mentioned in Genesis 48.

17:1–2 Makir, Manasseh's firstborn, was his only son (Gen 50:23; Num 26:29). His descendants represented the half-tribe of Manasseh that had already received a separate portion east of the Jordan, in Gilead and Bashan (13:29–31). The rest of Manasseh's portion was west of the Jordan (17:2,7–11).

Verse 1 reads, literally, "And the allotment was for Manasseh, for (Hb. *kî*) he was Joseph's firstborn." This would seem to imply a causal relationship between the first and second clauses here, that is, that somehow his firstborn status was the cause of the allotment here. However, *kî* can also be read emphatically, as "indeed, in fact," and that is how it should be read here.[146] The NIV's rendering rightly avoids making the causal connection here.

The focus in the second part of v. 1 is on Makir's inheritance of Gilead and Bashan. In a wooden translation, it reads (somewhat awkwardly), "To Makir, Manasseh's firstborn, the father of the [region of] Gilead[147]—because he, he was a man of war—so it was that to him belonged Gilead and Bashan." Makir is thus highlighted in the verse. The reference to the "man of war" also highlights Makir; it is in line with the fighting ascribed to Makir's descendants in Gilead many years earlier (Num 32:39).

Verse 1 thus explains why a portion of Manasseh's descendants inherited the lands east of the Jordan, and it forms the backdrop for understanding why the rest of Manasseh's descendants received their inheritance west of the Jordan (v. 2).

Now in v. 2 the true focus of the passage comes into view: the allotment to

---

[146] *GBH* § 164b; *IBHS* § 39.3.4e; see also Nelson, *Joshua*, 199. Woudstra's difficulties with the construction would be solved had he read כִּי emphatically (*Joshua*, 263).

[147] "Gilead" here is actually "the Gilead" (הַגִּלְעָד), referring to the region, not the person. Keil's suggestion—"*lord* (possessor) *of Gilead*"—captures the nuance well. He points out that the person is consistently referred to without the definite article, whereas the region just as consistently takes the article (*Book of Joshua*, 179). Nevertheless, Num 26:29 makes it clear that Makir was the father of Gilead the man as well. The region would appear to have received its name from the descendants of Gilead who settled there.

Manasseh's other descendants west of the Jordan. Six of them are named, all of them descendants of Gilead, according to Num 26:30–32. These six sons are specifically said to be the male descendants *(zĕkārîm)* of Manasseh at the end of v. 2, which lays the foundation for the discussion in vv. 3–6 of five *daughters* descended from one of these sons.

17:3–6   One of the six sons of Gilead named in v. 2, Hepher, had a son Zelophehad who had five daughters, but no sons. Because the inheritance of land normally passed through the male descendants, Zelophehad's family was at risk of losing its inheritance, and his daughters knew this. They had approached Moses about the problem many years earlier, and he had inquired of the Lord about it. The Lord's answer was that these women's claim was legitimate and that they should receive their father's portion. He went further and made it a general principle that the inheritance of a man dying without sons was to go to his daughters, or, lacking daughters, to his brothers, or, lacking brothers, to his uncles, or, lacking uncles, to his next nearest relatives. This story is told in some detail in Num 27:1–11.[148] In the account in Joshua, Zelophehad's daughters reminded Eleazar and Joshua of the Lord's ruling and command, and Joshua gave them their rightful inheritance.[149]

Several features of this account bear mentioning. First, the daughters' names and Zelophehad's genealogy are carefully recorded in v. 3. This is to show the legal legitimacy of their claim, to prevent any misunderstandings or misinterpretations arising from confused identities. The case is introduced clearly, and the precedent in Numbers 27 can be easily checked. The care with which the tribes' boundaries and cities are recorded extends down to the inheritance for individuals, even these daughters. Second, "Eleazar the priest" and "Joshua son of Nun" were the officials to whom the daughters presented their case. This too shows that everything was being done carefully and in order. Eleazar's role in the land distribution lists is always linked with Joshua's as one who gave the tribes their rightful inheritance. In each case he is identified as "Eleazar the priest," and Joshua is called by his full name, "Joshua son of Nun" (14:1; 17:4; 19:51; 21:1). Third, the account (esp. v. 4b) shows once again Joshua's concern to obey the word of the Lord down to the very letter. Fourth, it reinforces the principle enunciated in Numbers 27 that daughters could indeed—and did indeed—inherit land, under the conditions mentioned there. Indeed, they received a total of five portions, not one to divide between all five. The entire account makes this point, but v. 6 explic-

---

[148] See the discussion of this passage in G. J. Wenham, *Numbers: An Introduction and Commentary,* TOTC 4 (Downers Grove: InterVarsity, 1981), 191–94; P. J. Budd, *Numbers,* WBC (Waco: Word, 1984), 299–303; Cole, *Numbers, ad loc.* On the issue of the daughters' inheritance, see Z. Ben-Barak, "Inheritance by Daughters in the Ancient Near East," *JSS* 25 (1980): 22–33.

[149] This is the third of the "land grant narratives" identified by Nelson. See the excursus "Patterns in the Land Distribution Lists," Section 3, at the end of chap. 13.

itly states, lest the point be missed, that "the daughters of Manasseh received an inheritance among the sons." Fifth, this story accounts for the number of land tracts inherited by the tribe of Manasseh (see v. 5). East of the Jordan, the descendants of Gilead had received two tracts: Gilead and Manasseh. West of the Jordan, the total was ten. This was accounted for as follows: five tracts for the descendants of the five sons in v. 2—Abiezer, Helek, Asriel, Shechem, and Shemida. The lineage of Hepher, the sixth son, went through Zelophehad to his five daughters, and they each received one portion. In this way, Hepher's inheritance was multiplied fivefold. Thus, the grand total of portions in Manasseh's inheritance was twelve, two east of the Jordan and ten to the west.

17:7–10 Manasseh's actual inheritance is outlined now, primarily in the form of a boundary list, although it is abbreviated and contains some significant gaps. A few cities are mentioned in vv. 7–10 (the boundary list proper), and several more are given in v. 11, which delineates Manassite sovereignty within other tribes' territories, but there is no city list proper.[150] Two cities in its boundary description became Levitical cities: Shechem (vv. 2,7; see 21:21) and Taanach (v. 11; see 21:25).

In v. 7a the northern and southern extremes of Manasseh's territory are given: its "boundary" was from the tribe of Asher in the north to Michmethath (also in 16:6) in the south.[151]

In vv. 7b–10a the southern boundary is described. This boundary has already been described in Ephraim's border description in 16:6–8a (i.e., Ephraim's northern boundary was Manasseh's southern boundary), and the two descriptions correspond in several places. From Michmethath, the boundary ran southward to include the inhabitants of En Tappuah (i.e., the spring of Tappuah), but not Tappuah itself (v. 7b).[152] As v. 8 states, the territory near Tappuah belonged to Manasseh, but Tappuah itself belonged to

---

[150] Detailed discussions of Manasseh's boundaries can be found in Simons, *Geographical and Topographical Texts*, §§ 323–24; Na'aman, *Borders and Districts*, 148–51; Kallai, *Historical Geography*, 167–78; Svensson, *Towns and Toponymns*, 65–68. See also the maps in Beitzel, *Moody Atlas of the Bible*, 100; Rasmussen, *NIV Atlas of the Bible*, 98; Brisco, *Holman Bible Atlas*, 84.

[151] One problem with this understanding is that there is no preposition or other marker (e.g., עַד, "as far as," or directional ה, "to") attached to "Michmethath"; the text reads simply "from Asher Michmethath, which was opposite Shechem." Nevertheless, a directional preposition would seem to be implied here: "from Asher *to* [or *as far as*] Michmethath." Kallai (in discussing another list) agrees that direction can be implied "without recourse to an unequivocal grammatical expression thereof," and he gives several examples of this (*Historical Geography*, 131).

[152] The Old Greek reads a place name here—Iasib—for יֹשְׁבֵי, "inhabitants." It can easily be postulated that "Iasib" became "Yashub" (יָשׁוּב), which would be "Yāsūf" in Arabic, the name of a village in the vicinity today (see Kallai, *Historical Geography*, 151–53). However, the presence of יֹשְׁבֵי, "inhabitants," four times in v. 11, in identical constructions as here (i.e., "the inhabitants of *X*"), argues against accepting the Old Greek reading here.

Ephraim (this is also indicated in 16:8).

In v. 9 the boundary went southward to the Kanah Ravine. This ravine is also mentioned in Ephraim's northern border description in 16:8; and, in both places, it is the last geographical marker before the border extended quickly out to the sea (*wĕhayû* [or *wayĕhî*] *tōṣĕʾōtāyw hayyāmmâ*, "and it was outward to the sea"). In v. 9 we also are told that some Ephraimite towns lay among the towns of Manasseh, although their names are not given.[153] This echoes the statement in 16:9, in the account of Ephraim's inheritance, and it anticipates the statement in v. 11 that several of Manasseh's cities lay within the territories of Issachar and Asher.

The end of v. 9 and the beginning of v. 10 show that the Kanah Ravine formed the boundary between the tribes of Ephraim and Manasseh. Verse 10 concludes by mentioning, very briefly, that Manasseh's northern boundary was with Asher (cf. v. 7a) and its eastern boundary with Issachar. The greatest part of Manasseh's eastern boundary was formed by the Jordan River, although this is not stated here.

17:11 Several of Manasseh's towns lay within the territories of Issachar and Asher. Two towns are mentioned alone, with their surrounding villages: Beth Shan and Ibleam. The others are mentioned in connection with their inhabitants: Dor, Endor, Taanach, and Megiddo. That is, the text literally states, "The inhabitants of Dor and its daughters [i.e., its surrounding villages], and the inhabitants of Endor and its daughters," et cetera. The distinction between the cities and their inhabitants is clear grammatically, although its import is difficult to discern because sovereignty over a city's inhabitants would certainly imply sovereignty over the city itself as well.[154]

The phenomenon of cities belonging to one tribe lying within the area assigned to another tribe is not limited to this one instance. It also occurs with four of Judah's cities, Eshtaol and Zorah (15:33), Ekron and Timnah (15:45,57). The same is true of several of Ephraim's cities (16:9; 17:8–9), as well as cities lying along the boundaries between two tribes, such as Jerusalem (see commentary on 15:63), Beth Arabah (15:61; 18:18,22), and Jericho (16:1; 18:12).

The last two words in the verse in Hebrew—rendered by the NIV as "(the third in the list is Naphoth)"—have occasioned much discussion. The NIV's rendering is easily defensible: it refers to the third city in the list in v. 11, which is "Dor," and informs the reader that an alternate name for it was "Naphoth." Because other Scriptures refer to Naphoth Dor (Josh 11:2; 12:23;

---

[153] The Hb. here is awkward, but the essential thrust is clear.

[154] This construction is also found in v. 7: "the inhabitants of En Tappuah." See the discussion there.

1 Kgs 4:11), this possibility makes good sense.[155] An alternative rendering of the phrase, however, is "the three-heights country," referring to the geography of the last three cities in v. 11.[156]

(5) Western Manasseh's Failure Concerning Its Towns (17:12–13)

[12]Yet the Manassites were not able to occupy these towns, for the Canaanites were determined to live in that region. [13]However, when the Israelites grew stronger, they subjected the Canaanites to forced labor but did not drive them out completely.

For the third time in as many chapters, we again read of a tribe's failure to drive out the inhabitants of part of its territory. The first two were Judah (the Jebusites from Jebus: 15:63) and Ephraim (the Canaanites from Gezer: 16:10). Here the Manassites were unable to dislodge the Canaanites from "these cities," presumably those just listed in v. 11. The reason was that the Canaanites "stubbornly" (NJPSV) stayed on as inhabitants of this region.[157]

The notice here is somewhat different from those in 15:63 and 16:10 in that it emphasizes the Canaanites' stubborn determination in v. 12, whereas no such statement is made in the earlier notices. This is reinforced by v. 13, which states that when the Israelites were able to grow strong enough, they did put the Canaanites to forced labor. Nevertheless, the result was the same as earlier: they were not able to drive out the inhabitants of these cities completely (see further the commentary on 15:63; 16:10). Ironically, the three most important tribes, highlighted by their place and prominence in the lists, all were not able to drive out the Canaanites from portions of their lands. As E. R. Clendenen notes, they had the power to remove the Canaanites from the land and so to be God's instruments of judgment to remove wickedness, but they chose to tolerate wickedness and to use for their own purposes that which God had devoted to destruction. And so they sowed the seeds of their own destruction. Just like Achan. Peace with wickedness is preferred to war for righteousness (personal communication).

---

[155] This is not the normal way in Hebrew of indicating an alternate name for a city name, which follows the pattern "Kiriath Arba (that is, Hebron)" (15:13,54), but it would seem to be the best explanation for a difficult phrase. For further discussion, see G. Dahl, "The 'Three Heights' of Joshua 17 11," *JBL* 53 (1934), 381–83; Nelson, *Joshua*, 199–200. The NLT's rendering essentially follows the NIV's. Boling's rendering—"(*Re*: the third [Dor]. Is it Napheth?)"—accounts for the ה on נֶפֶת (understanding it as an interrogative ה) and it is in line with the NIV's rendering in seeing a connection between Dor and Napeth/Naphoth (Boling, *Joshua*, 407).

[156] This is the interpretation of Keil, *Book of Joshua*, 182; Woudstra, *Joshua*, 266.

[157] The Hb. word is יָאַל, "to be keen, pleased, determined" (see BDB, 383–84; *HALOT*, 381). Most translations do not capture this nuance of the Canaanites' stubborn determination to stay put.

(6) Joseph's Complaint (17:14–18)

¹⁴The people of Joseph said to Joshua, "Why have you given us only one allotment and one portion for an inheritance? We are a numerous people and the LORD has blessed us abundantly."

¹⁵"If you are so numerous," Joshua answered, "and if the hill country of Ephraim is too small for you, go up into the forest and clear land for yourselves there in the land of the Perizzites and Rephaites."

¹⁶The people of Joseph replied, "The hill country is not enough for us, and all the Canaanites who live in the plain have iron chariots, both those in Beth Shan and its settlements and those in the Valley of Jezreel."

¹⁷But Joshua said to the house of Joseph—to Ephraim and Manasseh—"You are numerous and very powerful. You will have not only one allotment ¹⁸but the forested hill country as well. Clear it, and its farthest limits will be yours; though the Canaanites have iron chariots and though they are strong, you can drive them out."

The two-chapter account of the Joseph tribes' inheritance comes to an end as it began, with the tribes of Ephraim and Manasseh being considered together, as one unit (cf. 16:1–4). They are called "the sons of Joseph" in both 16:4 and 17:14, and they speak as one, using first-person singular address— "me" and "I"—and Joshua addresses them in the second-person singular ("you" [singular]). These two tribes are depicted as being dissatisfied with their allotted territory, challenging Joshua, and being challenged by him in return. Among other things, the episode serves as another reminder that much land remained to be possessed (see 13:1). The episode unfolds through two verbal exchanges between Joshua and the tribes: vv. 14–15 and vv. 16–18. This is the fourth of the "land grant narratives" in the lists.[158] However, it has a decidedly more negative tone than the others.

17:14–15 In the first exchange, the people from the Joseph tribes presented Joshua with a complaint: they felt that they had been shortchanged in the allotments and presented their great numbers and the Lord's blessing as evidence that something should change. In the end of v. 14, the Hebrew is difficult. However, by following the Old Greek and Syriac traditions, which lack one word in the Hebrew text (ʿad, "as far as, until"; Hb. reads lit. "but I am a numerous people *until* which [until now] Yahweh blessed me"), the sentence can be translated, "But I am a numerous people whom Yahweh has blessed until now," an understanding followed by NASB, NJPSV, NRSV, and, it would appear, NIV.

The Joseph tribes exhibited a degree of arrogance and greed in their confrontation with Joshua. The tone here sharply contrasts with the far more

---

¹⁵⁸ These are identified as such by Nelson. See the excursus "Patterns in the Land Distribution Lists," Section 3, at the end of chap. 13 for a fuller explanation.

humble requests presented by Caleb (14:6–12) and the daughters of Zelophe-had (17:4), both of whom appealed to the Lord's promises as the basis for their requests. Here these tribes cited no such precedent, only their subjective evaluation that their great numbers justified the request. Furthermore, they challenged the outcome of the lot *(gôrāl)*, which was controlled by God. Thus, in their request they were challenging the very workings of God himself.

Joshua responded with a challenge of his own (v. 15). If they were too con-stricted[159] in "Mount Ephraim," then they should clear out[160] land from the forests where the Perizzites and Rephaites lived. Joshua's reference to "Mount Ephraim" is rendered in the NIV and other versions as "the hill coun-try of Ephraim," which is acceptable grammatically, although it is not the only possible rendering. The argument in the section proceeds from the narrower to the broader: in v. 16, instead of *har-ʾeprāyim,* "Mount Ephraim," the Joseph tribes use the broader term *hāhār,* "the hill country." The occurrence of *har-ʾeprāyim* in 1 Kgs 4:8, in a list clearly dealing with individual places, not vast areas, supports the notion that Joshua was referring to a specific hill or moun-tain, not the entire hill country.[161]

An alternate proposal is that the hill country of Ephraim referred to here was east of the Jordan and that Joshua was telling the Ephraimites to expand in that direction. Support for this is adduced from a reference to "the forest of Ephraim" in 2 Sam 18:6, which was east of the Jordan, as well as from the reference to the Rephaites, a people who appear almost exclusively east of the Jordan (Deut 2:11,20; 3:11,13; Josh 12:4; 13:12).[162]

Both proposals have the difficulty that the Perizzites and Rephaites are never otherwise mentioned together, and they appear most often on opposite sides of the Jordan. However, a "Valley of Rephaim" (i.e., Rephaites) is found southwest of Jerusalem (15:8; 18:16), and it thus is possible that the Rephai-tes were to be found west of the Jordan as well. This would argue in favor of the first proposal.

The Rephaites were associated primarily with Bashan, east of the Jordan (Deut 3:11,13; Josh 12:4; 13:12), and they were considered to be fearsome giants (see Deut 2:10–11; 3:11). The Perizzites are mentioned several times earlier in the book, all west of the Jordan (3:10; 9:1; 11:3; 12:8), but little else is known of them.

---

[159] The word here is אוץ "to be pressed, confined, narrow" (BDB, 21). The NIV's "too small" is adequate, but it misses something of the nuance here.

[160] The verb here is ברא III: "to cut, clear" (see *HALOT,* 154; *DCH* 2:259); it is unrelated to ברא I, "to create," as BDB (135) supposes.

[161] See Nelson, *Joshua,* 204, for this observation. Woudstra also speaks of "the mountain of Ephraim," but he does not elaborate further *(Joshua,* 268).

[162] See Woudstra, *Joshua,* 268, who mentions this view but who does not adopt it.

17:16–18 A further aspect of the Joseph tribes' greed is visible in the second exchange. Whereas Joshua had challenged them to clear the forests of "Mount Ephraim," they retorted that the (entire) hill country was not enough for them (v. 16). They also revealed a fear of the Canaanites living in the plain, who had iron chariots. These were not effective in the hills, especially in forested areas.[163] However, the Joseph tribes felt hemmed in by the Canaanites' dominance in and around Beth Shan and the Jezreel Valley, which were in the northern portions of Manasseh's territory.[164] Their complaints here about the Canaanites is reminiscent of similar complaints by the ten spies who came back from the land in Moses' day (Num 13:26–33); they too were cowed by the Canaanites' seeming superiority.

Joshua once again turned the Joseph tribes' challenge back on them in vv. 17–18: because they were numerous and powerful, they would not be limited to only one allotment (v. 17). They would take the forested hill country out to its extreme edges and, by extension, project their power into the plains, driving out the Canaanites in their iron chariots (v. 18).

This extra allotment is never referred to again, and it is not taken into account in counting the tribes (i.e., the two Joseph tribes are not counted as three or four as a result). Perhaps this is not surprising, given the confrontational attitude displayed by these tribes and given the fact that God did not sanction their request. Joshua's granting of the extra portion was dependent on the two tribes' own numbers and power. In effect, he told them, "If you can do the job in your own strength, then the land is yours. But, the LORD does not commit himself to fight for you, as he has done previously for his people."

6. The Other Tribes' Inheritance (18:1–19:48)

After the most important tribes have been dealt with in previous chapters, the land distribution is rapidly concluded now in two chapters that detail the remaining seven allotments. The allotment descriptions for each tribe are much shorter and much more uniform than those of Judah and the two Joseph tribes. The unity of the two chapters is indicated by the regularly patterned allotments for all the remaining tribes, by the accounting for every tribe—including those mentioned previously, and Levi, to be mentioned later—and even by the opening and closing verses (18:1; 19:51), which both mention Shiloh and the tent of meeting. The literary unity reflects the historical unity that was to be the standard for the entire nation (see 1:12–18; cf. chap. 22).

---

[163] For more on chariots, see the commentary on 11:4.

[164] Beth Shan is mentioned in v. 11, and the Jezreel Valley was the large valley running roughly northwest to southeast at the northern edge of Manasseh's territory. In it were several cities mentioned in v. 11: Megiddo, Taanach, and Ibleam. On this valley see Rasmussen, *NIV Atlas of the Bible*, 36.

Until now, Israel's central encampment in the land appears to have been at
Gilgal, but now the entire congregation moved to Shiloh (18:1), and the tent
of meeting was set up there. At this assembly at Shiloh Joshua charged Israel
with the task of mapping out and possessing the land for the remaining seven
tribes (18:2–10). After the surveying was done, lots were cast, and the land
was apportioned out accordingly. The seven tribes were Benjamin, Simeon,
Zebulun, Issachar, Asher, Naphtali, and Dan. The lists for each of these are
similar and straightforward, for the most part, listing boundaries and/or cities
belonging to each tribe. Simeon inherited land within Judah's allotment
(19:1,9), and Dan would later lose its territory and migrate northward (19:47;
cf. Judg 1:34–35; 18:27–31). The other tribes are not forgotten, however.
Joshua carefully mentioned each one: the two and one-half Transjordan tribes,
Judah, the two Joseph tribes (Ephraim and Manasseh), and Levi (vv. 5–7).
The detail and inclusiveness here shows the importance of (1) the land in
God's plans for Israel and (2) the unity of the nation.

The format of the distribution lists changes in these two chapters from the
previous chapters. It is uniform and regular for all seven tribes dealt with, as
we have noted. The lot *(gôrāl)* was involved in each one, but the territories
were surveyed before the lots were cast. Previously, the distribution for the
two and one-half Transjordan tribes involved no lot, since the account in chap.
13 is essentially a review of what had already happened under Moses. In the
distributions to the important tribes of Judah and Joseph (chaps. 15–17), the
lot is mentioned, but no surveying was done and the *gôrāl* was more of a
static nature ("allotment") rather than the active nature seen in chaps. 18–19,
where the lot appears actually to have been cast.[165]

God's presence throughout these two chapters, but especially in 18:1–10,
is indicated in at least three ways: (1) the presence of the tent of meeting
(18:1; 19:51); (2) the presence of the Lord (18:6,8,10; 19:51); and (3) the
actual casting of the lots, since God controlled even the lot (18:6,10–11;
19:1,10,17,24,32,40,51).

(1) Introduction (18:1–10)

**[1]The whole assembly of the Israelites gathered at Shiloh and set up the Tent of
Meeting there. The country was brought under their control, [2]but there were still
seven Israelite tribes who had not yet received their inheritance.**

**[3]So Joshua said to the Israelites: "How long will you wait before you begin to
take possession of the land that the LORD, the God of your fathers, has given you?
[4]Appoint three men from each tribe. I will send them out to make a survey of the
land and to write a description of it, according to the inheritance of each. Then
they will return to me. [5]You are to divide the land into seven parts. Judah is to**

---

[165] See Nelson, *Joshua,* 206–7, on this point.

remain in its territory on the south and the house of Joseph in its territory on the north. **⁶After you have written descriptions of the seven parts of the land, bring them here to me and I will cast lots for you in the presence of the LORD our God. ⁷The Levites, however, do not get a portion among you, because the priestly service of the LORD is their inheritance. And Gad, Reuben and the half-tribe of Manasseh have already received their inheritance on the east side of the Jordan. Moses the servant of the LORD gave it to them."**

⁸As the men started on their way to map out the land, Joshua instructed them, "Go and make a survey of the land and write a description of it. Then return to me, and I will cast lots for you here at Shiloh in the presence of the LORD." ⁹So the men left and went through the land. They wrote its description on a scroll, town by town, in seven parts, and returned to Joshua in the camp at Shiloh. ¹⁰Joshua then cast lots for them in Shiloh in the presence of the LORD, and there he distributed the land to the Israelites according to their tribal divisions.

This section represents an important turning point in the land distribution lists and is arguably the focal point of all of chaps. 13–21 (see the introduction to these chapters). A new location—Shiloh—is the setting, and the tent of meeting is mentioned for the first time in the book. God's presence is emphasized as the passage opens and closes, through the references to the tent of meeting in v. 1 and "the presence of the LORD" in v. 10.

Koorevaar sees the emphasis on God's presence here as the fulfillment of the Lord's last promise in the list of blessings in Leviticus 26: "I will put my dwelling place among you, and I will not abhor you. I will walk among you and be your God, and you will be my people" (Lev 26:11–12).[166] Joshua 18:1–10 also is the fulfillment of God's promises in Deuteronomy 12 about placing his name in the place he would choose.[167]

18:1–2 Up to this point, Israel's central encampment in the land appears to have been at Gilgal, near Jericho, where the nation had observed several religious ceremonies (4:19–20; 5:2–12). This was where Caleb had approached Joshua to ask for his inheritance (14:6).[168] Now the entire congregation moved to Shiloh (18:1), about fifteen miles northwest of Jericho, and the tent of meeting was set up there. Shiloh was in the territory of Ephraim (see 16:6), and it would remain an important Israelite religious center for several hundred years, until the taking of Jerusalem in David's day (see 19:51; 21:2; Judg 18:31; 21:12; 1 Sam 1:9). The ark was kept there (1 Sam 3:3), and it was brought into battle against the Philistines, who captured it in Samuel's day (1 Samuel 4). Soon after that event, Shiloh was

---

[166] Koorevaar, *De Opbouw van het Boek Jozua*, 290, cited by Vannoy, "Joshua: Theology of," *NIDOTTE* 4:814.

[167] McConville, *Grace in the End*, 102, n. 90.

[168] Gilgal is mentioned in chaps. 9–10 as well, but it may have been another place with the same name. See the commentary on 9:6.

destroyed (Ps 78:60; Jer 7:14).[169]

The only other reference to the tent of meeting (i.e., the tabernacle) in Joshua is at the end of the two-chapter section, in 19:51. The tabernacle was a large portable tent that served as God's "home" when the Israelites were in the wilderness. In it were the ark of the covenant and other holy items. It was made of fine boards covered with layers of rich fabrics (Exodus 26). There was also a different tent called the "tent of meeting," which Moses used to pitch outside of the camp, where he and the people could also meet God (Exod 33:7). It was a temporary tent during the Israelites' days in the wilderness, and it is not referred to later in the Old Testament.[170]

These two verses introduce the situation that needed to be remedied, and they set the stage geographically and spiritually in the process by mentioning Shiloh and the tent of meeting. The situation was that though the land was essentially subdued, seven tribes still had not received their allotted territories.

18:3–7 Joshua's question in v. 3 sounds on the face of it like an accusation, and it very well may have been. However, no specific command to take the land had been given as yet, and Joshua's words may have been merely rhetorical, as a preface to his detailed instructions in vv. 4–7. The already-accomplished aspect of God's gift of the land that is first introduced in 1:3 is again emphasized here (see the commentary on 1:3 and the excursus there on "The Giving of the Land in Joshua"). Joshua reminded the people that it was the God of their fathers who had given them the land. "Your fathers" refers to the patriarchs Abraham, Isaac, and Jacob; and the expression "the God of your fathers" was an important one: God used it with Moses at the burning bush (Exod 3:13,15–16), and Moses used it several times in Deuteronomy as he exhorted the people (1:11,21; 4:1; 6:3; 21:1: 27:3). This is its first use in Joshua, and it is a subtle reminder of the promises God had made to the patriarchs about the land (e.g., Gen 12:7; 15:18–21 [Abraham]; 26:3–4 [Isaac]; 28:4,13; 35:12 [Jacob]).

In order to accomplish the equitable dividing, taking, and settlement of the remaining lands, Joshua instructed that three men from each of the seven remaining tribes be appointed as surveyors who would travel throughout the land and record its description (v. 4).[171] The seriousness of the task is empha-

---

[169] Most scholars date the destruction of Shiloh to ca. 1050 B.C. and David's taking of Jerusalem to ca. 1003 B.C. (or, less probably, 993 B.C.).

[170] The view just enunciated here is not generally accepted in critical scholarship. However, it is based on a plain reading of the text of Exodus 33 and other Scriptures, not hypothetical reconstructions of supposedly earlier and later sources. See also S. Westerholm, "Tabernacle," *ISBE* 4:703; W. C. Kaiser, Jr., "Exodus," EBC 2:483.

[171] It is grammatically possible that thirty-six men were intended, i.e., one from each of the twelve tribes (not just the seven who had not yet received their inheritances). However, the impression and the focus here favor seeing twenty-one rather than thirty-six.

sized by the repeated references to writing in this passage. Three times the text specifies that the men were to write down what they found (vv. 4,6,8). Then, in v. 9, the execution of the command to do this is mentioned: they carefully wrote down on a scroll the land's contours by its cities and by its seven divisions. These things show the importance of the task as well as the fact that later generations were to know of it because it was to be written down.

In vv. 5–7, the unity of the nation and the equitable distribution of the land are the primary focus. All fourteen land distribution units are accounted for here: the tribes of Judah, Ephraim, and Manasseh (v. 5), the seven remaining tribes (v. 6), the Levites (v. 7a), and the three tribal units east of the Jordan (v. 7b).[172] Before the nation hurried ahead to complete its remaining land distributions, Joshua made sure that they remembered the previous distributions.

Three items bear mentioning here. First, Joshua's leadership is visible because he was actively involved in parceling out the lands. The twenty-one surveyors were to bring their findings to him, and he would cast lots before the Lord (v. 6). Second, the Lord's presence was with the people, and he oversaw the lots (v. 6). Third, the Levites' special inheritance is again singled out for attention and augmented. Previously, their inheritance had been identified as "the offerings made by fire to the LORD" (13:14) and "the LORD, the God of Israel" (13:33). Now, a third way of looking at their inheritance is introduced: it was "the priestly service of the LORD" (v. 7).

18:8–10   Verse 8 is somewhat repetitive of information already recorded in vv. 4 and 6. The repetition of Joshua's words shows the importance and solemnity of the occasion. Verse 9 records the execution of the commands Joshua gave in vv. 4–6. Then v. 10 states that Joshua did what he said he would do. There is little new here that is not already anticipated in vv. 4–6, but the report of the execution of the commands is consistent with the same pattern throughout the book. Joshua and the people took extreme care to do things as they should.

The description of the land that was written down on the scroll (v. 9) was presumably that which is now found in the following portions of the Book of Joshua: 18:11–19:48.[173]

This key passage ends, then, with the assurance that each tribe did indeed receive its allotted territory. The previous allotments were a matter of record, the Levites' inheritance was the Lord's service, and the remaining tribes did receive their lands equitably and in order. The unity of the nation was still

---

[172] See the excursus "Patterns in the Land Distribution Lists" at the end of chap. 13, n. 56, on the arithmetic problem of the twelve-tribe unit and also the commentary on 14:3–4.

[173] It is difficult to deny that this portion of the book, at least, comes directly from the time of the events recorded. Even scholars of the source-critical or tradition-historical persuasion mostly admit that these chapters preserve very early materials. See, e.g., Butler, *Joshua*, 201–2; Nelson, *Joshua*, 208 (who presents a positive view of the provenience and present function of 18:1–10).

holding firm. The rest of chaps. 18–19 are devoted to detailing the allotments, but by 18:10 the allotments were complete, an accomplished fact.

(2) Benjamin's Inheritance (18:11–28)

[11]The lot came up for the tribe of Benjamin, clan by clan. Their allotted territory lay between the tribes of Judah and Joseph:

[12]On the north side their boundary began at the Jordan, passed the northern slope of Jericho and headed west into the hill country, coming out at the desert of Beth Aven. [13]From there it crossed to the south slope of Luz (that is, Bethel) and went down to Ataroth Addar on the hill south of Lower Beth Horon.

[14]From the hill facing Beth Horon on the south the boundary turned south along the western side and came out at Kiriath Baal (that is, Kiriath Jearim), a town of the people of Judah. This was the western side.

[15]The southern side began at the outskirts of Kiriath Jearim on the west, and the boundary came out at the spring of the waters of Nephtoah. [16]The boundary went down to the foot of the hill facing the Valley of Ben Hinnom, north of the Valley of Rephaim. It continued down the Hinnom Valley along the southern slope of the Jebusite city and so to En Rogel. [17]It then curved north, went to En Shemesh, continued to Geliloth, which faces the Pass of Adummim, and ran down to the Stone of Bohan son of Reuben. [18]It continued to the northern slope of Beth Arabah and on down into the Arabah. [19]It then went to the northern slope of Beth Hoglah and came out at the northern bay of the Salt Sea, at the mouth of the Jordan in the south. This was the southern boundary.

[20]The Jordan formed the boundary on the eastern side. These were the boundaries that marked out the inheritance of the clans of Benjamin on all sides.

[21]The tribe of Benjamin, clan by clan, had the following cities:

Jericho, Beth Hoglah, Emek Keziz, [22]Beth Arabah, Zemaraim, Bethel, [23]Avvim, Parah, Ophrah, [24]Kephar Ammoni, Ophni and Geba—twelve towns and their villages.

[25]Gibeon, Ramah, Beeroth, [26]Mizpah, Kephirah, Mozah, [27]Rekem, Irpeel, Taralah, [28]Zelah, Haeleph, the Jebusite city (that is, Jerusalem), Gibeah and Kiriath—fourteen towns and their villages. This was the inheritance of Benjamin for its clans.

Of the seven remaining tribes, Benjamin was the most prominent, and its allotment is given in the most detail (eighteen verses). For the rest, an average of eight verses suffices. This is most likely due to Benjamin's geographical location between Judah on the south and "Joseph" (i.e., Ephraim) on the north (see v. 11). It shared some reflected glory because of the prominence of these other tribes.[174] The detail here also reinforces some of the boundary points in

---

[174]Benjamin's prominence may also be due in some measure to the fact that he—along with Joseph—was the son of his father's favorite wife, Rachel (Gen 35:24). Of the thirteen tribal units, the five most important ones were descended from Jacob's two wives, Leah and Rachel (see Gen 35:23–26): Judah and Levi from Leah, and Ephraim and Manasseh (Joseph) and Benjamin from Rachel. And, we should note, with the exception of Levi, their territories were the largest, and all together in the south and central part of the land, nearest Jerusalem.

Judah's list in 15:1–12 and Joseph's and Ephraim's lists in 16:1–5.[175] After the introductory verse, the description proceeds in a counterclockwise direction, beginning with the northern boundary.

18:11 The introduction to Benjamin's boundary description begins a pattern that is followed in each of the next six allotments as well (in chap. 19). The boundary lists in this chapter coordinate well with the parallel boundary lists for the neighboring tribes, especially Judah to the south and Ephraim to the north.[176]

18:12–13 Benjamin's northern boundary was the same as the Joseph tribes' southern boundary, described in 16:1–4, or Ephraim's, described briefly in 16:5. Every place mentioned here is found already in 16:1–5, except for the desert of Beth Aven. Beth Aven was between Jericho and Bethel, but its exact site is disputed.[177] The "desert" of Beth Aven is not known, but it obviously refers to a region associated with the town.[178]

18:14 Benjamin's western boundary was short; the tribal territory was wide in an east-to-west direction, but very short north to south. From the northern boundary, the western one "turned the corner" *(p̄'r)* and "went along" *(nsb)* southward along the western side, from the hill opposite Beth Horon down to Kiriath Baal (i.e., Kiriath Jearim). The sudden southward move here left room to the west for the territory of Dan.[179] The only two fixed points here are found where they would be expected in other lists: the northern point, Beth Horon, is mentioned twice in the Joseph tribes' southern boundary (16:3,5); and the southern point, Kiriath Baal/Jearim, is listed among Judah's cities (15:60). It also is included in Judah's northern boundary description (15:9), as "Baalah (that is, Kiriath Jearim)."

18:15–19 Benjamin's southern boundary is given in the most detail; that may be because it was the border with Judah, the most important tribe. As with its northern boundary, this one corresponds closely with the corresponding boundary description elsewhere, in this case, Judah's in 15:5–11. Indeed,

---

[175] Detailed discussions of Benjamin's boundary and city lists are found in Simons, *Geographical and Topographical Texts*, §§ 326–27; Kallai, *Historical Geography*, 125–37, 398–404; Svensson, *Towns and Toponymns*, 54–59. See also the maps in Beitzel, *Moody Atlas of the Bible*, 100; Rasmussen, *NIV Atlas of the Bible*, 98; Brisco, *Holman Bible Atlas*, 84.

[176] Kallai, *Historical Geography*, 125.

[177] P. M. Arnold, "Beth Aven," *ABD* 1:682. Its location is bound up with the problem of the identification of Ai and Bethel (see the excursus at the end of chap. 6, "The Archaeology of Jericho and Ai"). B. G. Wood suggests ("Notes on the Locations of Ai and Beth Aven," unpublished notes, 1998) that the modern site of Beitin could be ancient Beth Aven (and not Bethel, as most scholars suppose).

[178] The NIV's rendering of מִדְבָּר as "desert" is misleading because the area from Jericho up to Bethel is more properly a desolate wilderness. NASB, NJPSV, NRSV, and NLT all have "wilderness" here, a more accurate translation of מִדְבָּר in this context.

[179] See the maps in Beitzel, *Moody Atlas of Bible Lands*, 100; Brisco, *Holman Bible Atlas*, 84.

the degree of correspondence is remarkable: every place named here is found in its corresponding place in chap. 15. The directions for the two are opposite, however: Benjamin's southern boundary description runs from west to east whereas Judah's runs east to west.

The boundary description begins in v. 15 at Kiriath Jearim by "going out" *(yṣʾ)* to the west *(yammâ)* and then "going out" *(yṣʾ)* to the waters of Nephtoah (which was eastward). The NIV's rendering here makes it sound as though Kiriath Jearim were "on" the west, but *yammâ* is a directional word, "to the west" (or, "toward the sea"). It seems as though the boundary line here was moving first in one direction, and then the opposite direction, from the same starting point. That is, the boundary went westward to some undefined point from Kiriath Jearim (presumably not too far away because Benjamin's western border was not at the sea, according to v. 14), and it went eastward to the waters of Nephtoah.[180] This portion of the description is a mirror image of Judah's in 15:9, except that in 18:15 the towns of Mount Ephron are not mentioned.

The precincts of Jerusalem are described in v. 16, again carefully mirroring the description in 15:8. In vv. 17–18, the eastern portion of the southern boundary is given, ending at the northern bay of the Dead Sea, once again almost exactly duplicating the description in 15:6–7, although in reverse order. The one major difference from the Judahite list is that Gilgal there is replaced with "Geliloth" here. "Geliloth" is the word for "districts" or "territories" (see, e.g., 13:2; Joel 3:4[Hb. 4:4]), and it is related etymologically to "Gilgal," so the references would appear to be to the same place (i.e., "Gelioth" was "Gilgal"). The Targum, in fact, reads "Gilgal" here. Either "Geliloth" refers to the "districts" facing the Pass of Adummim or else it was an alternate name for Gilgal.[181]

18:20 Benjamin's eastern boundary was easily identified: it was the Jordan River.

18:21–28 Benjamin's territorial description ends with a list of its cities, which is divided into two sections: (1) twelve cities in the eastern portion (vv. 21–24) and (2) fourteen cities in the western portion (vv. 25–28). The city names as given in the NIV add up to the totals given in vv. 24,28.[182] Benjamin's is the third-longest city list of all the tribes, after those belonging to the tribes of Judah and Levi.

---

[180] See Kallai, *Historical Geography*, 133–34.

[181] So also Boling, *Joshua*, 367,430; Nelson, *Joshua*, 213–14; Kallai, *Historical Geography*, 120. Simons sees it as a small district in the vicinity (*Geographical and Topographical Texts*, § 326).

[182] See Kallai, *Historical Geography*, 403–4, who arrives at different totals by considering Zelah Haeleph in v. 28 to be one city, not two; likewise in v. 28, he considers Gibeath-Kiriath [Jearim] to be one name, not two. NASB, NJPSV, REB, NRSV, NLT all agree with the NIV.

Cities mentioned previously in boundary descriptions include the following: Jericho (v. 21), on the Ephraimite border (16:1,7; 18:12); Beth Hoglah (v. 21), on the Judahite border (15:6; 18:19); Bethel (v. 22), on the Ephraimite border (16:1–2; 18:13); and Jerusalem (v. 28), also on the Judahite border (15:63).[183] Cities that became Levitical cities include Geba (v. 24) and Gibeon (v. 25; see 21:17). Beth Horon (from the boundary list in vv. 13–14) also was a Levitical city.

Beth Arabah was now assigned to Benjamin (v. 22). Earlier, it had been part of Judah's boundary list (15:6) and its city list (15:61). Its presence in both lists—not just in the boundary lists, but also the city lists—suggests that it was on the boundary, perhaps to be shared by the two tribes, or else that the allotments in chaps. 18–19, coming as they did at a time later than those in the earlier chapters, were adjusted slightly and some cities reassigned.[184]

Several cities have the same name as others in other lists but should not be confused with each other. Ophrah (v. 23) is not to be confused with the city in Manasseh's territory (Judg 6:24; 8:27). Ramah (v. 25) is not to be confused with cities bearing the same name along Asher's northern border (Josh 19:29), in Naphtali's territory (19:36), or in Simeon's territory (19:8). Its name means "height," so it is not surprising that several places should be so named. Mizpah (v. 26) was not the same as the Mizpah in Judah's list (15:38). Gibeah (v. 27) was not the Gibeah in Judah (15:57) nor the Ephraimite city where Eleazar was buried (24:33). Kiriath (v. 28) appears to have been different from the Kiriath-Jearim belonging to Judah (15:60; 18:14–15).

Ten of the cities here never occur elsewhere in the Bible: Emek Keziz, Avvim, Parah, Kephar Ammoni, Ophni, Mozah, Irpeel, Taralah, Zelah, and Haeleph.

(3) Simeon's Inheritance (19:1–9)

[1]The second lot came out for the tribe of Simeon, clan by clan. Their inheritance lay within the territory of Judah. [2]It included:

Beersheba (or Sheba), Moladah, [3]Hazar Shual, Balah, Ezem, [4]Eltolad, Bethul, Hormah, [5]Ziklag, Beth Marcaboth, Hazar Susah, [6]Beth Lebaoth and Sharuhen—thirteen towns and their villages;

[7]Ain, Rimmon, Ether and Ashan—four towns and their villages— [8]and all the villages around these towns as far as Baalath Beer (Ramah in the Negev). This was the inheritance of the tribe of the Simeonites, clan by clan. [9]The inheritance of the Simeonites was taken from the share of Judah, because Judah's portion was more than they needed. So the Simeonites received their inheritance within the territory of Judah.

---

[183] For more on Jerusalem's status, see the commentary on 15:63.

[184] So also Keil, *Book of Joshua*, 152; Woudstra, *Joshua*, 236.

Simeon was not given an independent allotment, but rather, it inherited scattered cities (and their surrounding villages) within Judah's allotment.[185] The stated reason for this was that "Judah's portion was more than they needed" (v. 9). As we noted in the discussion of Judah's cities, nine of them appear here in Simeon's city list, confirming this unique arrangement.[186] Judah and Simeon worked together in concert in Judges 1, when they fought the Canaanites side by side (Judg 1:3). First Chronicles 4:27 shows Simeon to have been a small tribe relative to Judah, stating that "[Simeon's] entire clan did not become as numerous as the people of Judah." No boundary description is given for Simeon, for obvious reasons.

Another perspective on why Simeon did not inherit land independently is provided by Jacob's prophecy in Genesis 49:5–7:

> Simeon and Levi are brothers—
> > their swords are weapons of violence.
> Let me not enter their council,
> > let me not join their assembly,
> for they have killed men in their anger
> > and hamstrung oxen as they pleased.
> Cursed be their anger, so fierce,
> > and their fury, so cruel!
> I will scatter them in Jacob
> > and disperse them in Israel.

Thus, from many centuries earlier, Simeon and Levi already had been condemned to be scattered among their fellow tribes. The land inheritance lists show the fulfillment of this because neither Simeon nor Levi received independent territory; both tribes received cities scattered throughout the others' lands.

What was behind Jacob's harsh prophecy concerning these two tribes? The text does not specifically give a reason, but Jacob's words about his two sons' violence hark back to the violence they had perpetrated against the inhabitants of Shechem, when they annihilated every man in the city while these men were recuperating from having been circumcised (Gen 34:24–30). In v. 30, Jacob had foreshadowed his later prophecy by rebuking his sons for their violence. Thus, Simeon's and Levi's "landless" status was a punishment for their taking violent, personal vengeance.

---

[185] In this chapter, no attempt is made to refer the reader to individual sections of the historical-geographical works relied on heretofore for each of the six tribes dealt with, except when they are specifically cited. The primary works used are Simons, *Geographical and Topographical Texts;* Kallai, *Historical Geography;* Svensson, *Towns and Toponymns;* Beitzel, *Moody Atlas of the Bible;* Rasmussen, *NIV Atlas of the Bible;* Brisco, *Holman Bible Atlas.* Readers who need to consult these will easily be able to find their way to the information sought.

[186] These nine cities represent half of Simeon's total of eighteen. The shared cities are Moladah, Hazar Shual, Ezem, Eltolad, Hormah, Ziklag, Ain, Ether, and Ashan.

The tribe of Levi, however, was greatly favored by the Lord, and they received a special inheritance far greater than Simeon's. Forty-eight cities throughout the land (see chap. 21), the Lord himself, the offerings by fire, and the priestly service (13:14,33; 18:7) were all components of their inheritance. What accounts for the difference in treatment between Simeon and Levi? Again, the text gives no specific answers. Moses and Aaron were from the tribe of Levi, and God singled them out to be the special instruments of accomplishing his will for reasons known only to him (Exod 6:13–27).

However, the Levites as a tribe did vindicate themselves in the episode involving the golden calf, and this no doubt is the main reason for their different treatment from Simeon's. When Moses discovered the Israelites' sin in worshiping the golden calf, he directed that "whoever is for the LORD, come to me," and only the Levites responded (Exod 32:26). Moses then directed them to kill the offenders among them, which they did, killing about three thousand people. For their faithfulness Moses blessed the Levites and declared them to be set apart to the Lord (Exod 32:27–29). The difference between the slaughter here and in Genesis 34 is that here it was sanctioned by the Lord, who reserves all vengeance to himself (Deut 32:35). And so the Levites were not engaged in personal, private vengeance, as their ancestor had been in the matter at Shechem.

19:1 Simeon's was the second lot cast among the seven remaining tribes. The backdrop to this is found in 18:1–10, where the lands for the remaining tribes were surveyed and allotted. As we noted earlier, the word *gôrāl* ("lot, allotment") appears now in an active sense, wherein the lots actually were cast for these tribes, as opposed to previously, when the allotments already seem to have been set. The reference to the "second lot" is repeated with the appropriate number in each of the following lists: vv. 10,17,24,32,40 (cf. 18:11).

19:2–8 Simeon's eighteen cities are now listed in two groups: (1) thirteen cities in the southern portion, the Negev (vv. 2–6), and (2) four cities, two in the Negev and two in the western foothills, the Shephelah (v. 7). One additional city in the far south is mentioned (v. 8), for a total of eighteen. The cities are, for the most part, obscure. The cities of Balah, Bethul, Hazar Susah, Beth Lebaoth, Sharuhen, and Baalath Beer are known only from this list. Most of the rest are known only from other lists, with the exception of Hormah, Ziklag, and Rimmon.

Six of the thirteen cities in the first group are mentioned in Unit One of Judah's city list, in the Negev (15:21–32): Moladah, Hazar Shual, Ezem, Eltolad, Hormah, and Ziklag. All four in the second group also appear in Judah's city list: Ain and Rimmon were also in Unit One, in the Negev (15:32),[187] and Ether and

---

[187] The MT and most manuscript traditions clearly distinguish between Ain and Rimmon, both here and in 15:32 (as well as in parallel list in 1 Chr 4:32), in two ways: (1) in grammatical structuring (-ו "and," separates them) and (2) in running totals (they are counted as two). The NIV and most other major Bible versions follow the MT here. A place called En Rimmon appears in Neh 11:29, leading some scholars to judge that Ain and Rimmon here are not two cities but one (e.g., RSV; Boling, *Joshua*, 435; Nelson, *Joshua*, 215 [the names "Ain" and "En" have the same consonants in Hb.: עין]). However, the running totals favor the MT rendering, and ample precedent exists in the lists in Joshua and elsewhere for more than one place having similar or identical names. Therefore we judge that Ain and Rimmon were two different places (also Kallai, *Historical Geography*, 357).

Ashan were in Unit Two, in the western foothills (15:42). The list begins and ends with cities in the far south: Beersheba (v. 2) and Baalath Beer (i.e., "Ramah in the Negev") (v. 8).[188] The reference to the last city functions to define the extent of the Simeonite cities to the south, since it is not part of the two lists preceding it.

19:9 This concluding statement echoes v. 1, and it also gives a rationale about why Simeon's inheritance was within Judah: Judah's portion was "more than it needed" (or, "too much for them": *rab mēhem*). For an additional reason see the introduction to this passage.

(4) Zebulun's Inheritance (19:10–16)

[10]The third lot came up for Zebulun, clan by clan:

The boundary of their inheritance went as far as Sarid. [11]Going west it ran to Maralah, touched Dabbesheth, and extended to the ravine near Jokneam. [12]It turned east from Sarid toward the sunrise to the territory of Kisloth Tabor and went on to Daberath and up to Japhia. [13]Then it continued eastward to Gath Hepher and Eth Kazin; it came out at Rimmon and turned toward Neah. [14]There the boundary went around on the north to Hannathon and ended at the Valley of Iphtah El. [15]Included were Kattath, Nahalal, Shimron, Idalah and Bethlehem. There were twelve towns and their villages. [16]These towns and their villages were the inheritance of Zebulun, clan by clan.

Zebulun's was the third lot cast, and it was the first of five small tribes in the north whose territories are now listed. Very little except for standard boundary and city lists is given for each of these five tribes. After Zebulun, the city lists are an important component in any attempt to reconstruct the boundaries of the tribes because the information in the boundary descriptions is so sparse.[189] Among the descriptions for these tribes, there is "a terseness that increases from tribe to tribe ... [Zebulun's] description is the most complete amongst them."[190] The final tribe, Dan, was also a small tribe; it was allotted territory in the south, but it had trouble taking its lands and migrated north as a result (19:47). Zebulun was a small tribe nestled between Issachar, western Manasseh, Asher, and Naphtali, although its boundary description is suffi-

---

[188] Identification of this site is uncertain, including its exact name. The position adopted here is reflected in the NIV, that "Ramah in the Negev" was another name for Baalath Beer. It seems likely that this is the same site as Bealoth in 15:24. See also Woudstra, *Joshua,* 281; D. W. Baker, "Bealoth," *ABD* 1:628–29; P. M. Arnold, "Ramah," *ABD* 5:614.

[189] Kallai, *Historical Geography,* 193–94.

[190] Ibid., 179.

ciently vague that it cannot easily be correlated with the others.[191]

19:10–14 Zebulun's boundary description is given in vv. 10–14, and a short city list in v. 15 (five cities). The boundary description is different from the preceding ones in that it appears to consist primarily of border cities near which the boundaries ran rather than fixed boundary points through which the boundary went. The total of twelve cities given in v. 15 does not correspond to the numbers of cities listed in v. 15 (which is five) nor the number of cities in the boundary description (which is thirteen). Possibly some cities dropped out, as appears to have been the case at 15:59 (see the commentary there), or else this number in our current manuscripts is simply incorrect, having been miscopied at some early point. Many of the sites named in Zebulun's boundary list are not known, so absolute precision in delineating its borders is not possible.

The southern boundary is described first (vv. 10–11). Sarid serves as a fixed point for two sections of the boundary.[192] First, it went from there to the west, extending as far as the ravine near Jokneam.[193] Then the western portion of the southern boundary is described (v. 12). The border "returned" *(šwb)*, which means that it began again at Sarid, moving eastward this time as far as Japhia, whose site is uncertain.[194] From there, the boundary ran north, forming Zebulun's eastern border (v. 13). The text states that it "passed along eastward to the east" (v. 13), but Kallai points out that this should be understood as "the direction which the border faces" (i.e., eastward) rather than the direction that the border runs (i.e., northward).[195] The main site in v. 13 is Rimmon.[196] The boundary then went around *(nsb)* on the north side past Hannathon (whose location is unknown) to the Valley of Iphtah El (v. 14). Zebulun's western boundary is very loosely defined, if at all.[197]

19:15–16 Zebulun's city list proper is truncated, consisting of only five cities (v. 15). Two of these are never mentioned anywhere else in the Bible—

---

[191] Like Judah, Benjamin, Ephraim, and western Manasseh before it, Zebulun also was unable to drive out the Canaanites from some of its territories, the cities of Kitron and Nahalol, according to Judg 1:30. Kitron is otherwise unknown, but "Nahalol" of Judges 1 is undoubtedly the "Nahalal" of Josh 19:15.

[192] Sarid is usually identified with Tel Shadud, which corresponds with the Old Greek, Vg, and Syr. readings. The ר (r) and ד (d) were easily confused in most Hb. scripts. See Aharoni, *Land of the Bible,* 117; Kallai, *Historical Geography,* 179–80.

[193] Its site is identified with Tell Qeimun (Tel Yoqneam) in the Jezreel Valley (see A. Ben-Tor, "Jokneam," *ABD* 3:933).

[194] See Parunak, "Geographical Terminology," 69; Kallai, *Historical Geography,* 183.

[195] Kallai, *Historical Geography,* 186.

[196] Arnold, "Rimmon," *ABD* 5:773; Kallai, *Historical Geography,* 187. On the difficulties with וּמְתֹאָר הַנֵּעָה, see Kallai, *Historical Geography,* 187–88; Nelson, *Joshua,* 218.

[197] Kallai believes that the reference to the "goings out" at the Valley of Iphtah El refers to a brook that defines the western boundary, but others disagree. See Kallai, *Historical Geography,* 189.

Kattah and Idalah— and one—Nahalal—only occurs again in the list of Levitical cities (21:35).[198] Shimron was one of the cities of the northern Canaanite coalition that attacked the Israelites (11:1). The city named "Bethlehem" is not the one in Judah known as the birthplace of the Messiah (Judg 17:7; Ruth 1:1; 1 Sam 16:1; Mic 5:2; Matt 2:1; etc.). Rather, it was in Zebulun, the site where Ibzan, the judge, was buried (Judg 12:8–10). Three cities from Zebulun's boundary description later became Levitical cities: Jokneam (v. 11; see 21:34), Nahalal (v. 15; see 21:35), and Daberath (v. 12; see 21:28). Daberath is credited in chap. 21 to Issachar, however, indicating its fluid position on the border between these two tribes.

(5) Issachar's Inheritance (19:17–23)

[17]The fourth lot came out for Issachar, clan by clan. [18]Their territory included:

Jezreel, Kesulloth, Shunem, [19]Hapharaim, Shion, Anaharath, [20]Rabbith, Kishion, Ebez, [21]Remeth, En Gannim, En Haddah and Beth Pazzez. [22]The boundary touched Tabor, Shahazumah and Beth Shemesh, and ended at the Jordan. There were sixteen towns and their villages. [23]These towns and their villages were the inheritance of the tribe of Issachar, clan by clan.

Issachar, whose lot was the fourth cast, was the second small tribe in the north, in the region of Galilee. Its boundary description consists of only three cities (v. 22), and its city list contains thirteen cities. The running total given of sixteen incorporates the cities in both lists (three + thirteen). Issachar's general location is clear: it was north of western Manasseh, east and south of Zebulun, west of the Jordan, and south of Naphtali. However, the details of its boundaries are not so clear.

19:18–21 Of the thirteen cities mentioned in the city list in vv. 18–21, well over half (nine) are only mentioned here in the Bible, although some are known elsewhere by different names or spellings: Kesulloth,[199] Hapharaim, Shion, Anaharath, Rabbith,[200] Ebez, Remeth,[201] En Haddah, and Beth Pazzez. In addition, Kishion and En Gannim only occur again as Levitical cities (21:28–29),[202] and one of the three boundary cities—Shahazumah (v. 22)—never is mentioned elsewhere. Thus, fully three quarters of the cities mentioned in connection with Issachar's list are known only from this or

---

[198] Although the "Nahalol" of Judg 1:30 is undoubtedly the same city.

[199] This town is known as Kisloth Tabor in Zebulun's boundary list (v. 12). It was ca. three miles west of Mount Tabor. See R. Frankel, "Chisloth-Tabor," *ABD* 1:910–11.

[200] Some scholars identify Rabbith (v. 20) with Daberath (19:12; 21:28), but this identification is not without problems. See D. W. Baker, "Rabbith," *ABD* 5:604–5.

[201] This town is mentioned in the Levitical list in 21:29 as "Jarmuth" (see n. 11 in chap. 21).

[202] A different En Gannim occurs in Judah's city list (15:34).

other lists (twelve of sixteen).[203]

The thirteen cities appear to be arranged in four groups, based on the Masoretic accents (i.e., verse divisions).[204] The first group—Jezreel, Kesulloth, Shunem (v. 18)—were on a north-south line in the western portion of Issachar. The second group—Hapharaim, Shion, Anaharath (v. 19)—also represents a north-south line, just east of the first group. The Old Greek text adds a fourth city to this group: "Reeroth."[205] The third group—Rabbith, Kishion, Ebez (v. 20)—appears to have been concentrated in the north, near Mount Tabor. The fourth group—Remeth, En Gannim, En Haddah, Beth Pazzez (v. 21)—was in the eastern portion of the tribal lands.

19:22–23 The sparse boundary description in v. 22 lists only three cities: Tabor,[206] Shahazumah, and Beth Shemesh. Scholars differ on their precise locations, but the general contour is clear: this boundary description delineates Issachar's northern border, which was also part of the southern borders of Zebulun and Naphtali. It begins in the northwest at Mount Tabor and ends in the east at the Jordan River.

Issachar's eastern boundary was naturally the Jordan River. Its southern boundary was also the eastern portion of western Manasseh's northern boundary (cf. 17:10), although details are sparse. Its western boundary is not specified at all and can only be reconstructed from the corresponding descriptions of Zebulun's and western Manasseh's boundaries. Issachar's territory included the fertile Jezreel Valley, in which the city of Jezreel lay.[207]

(6) Asher's Inheritance (19:24–31)

24The fifth lot came out for the tribe of Asher, clan by clan. **25**Their territory included:

Helkath, Hali, Beten, Acshaph, 26Allammelech, Amad and Mishal. On the west the boundary touched Carmel and Shihor Libnath. 27It then turned east toward Beth Dagon, touched Zebulun and the Valley of Iphtah El, and went north to Beth Emek and Neiel, passing Cabul on the left. 28It went to Abdon, Rehob, Hammon and Kanah, as far as Greater Sidon. 29The boundary then turned back toward Ramah and went to the fortified city of Tyre, turned toward Hosah and came out

---

[203] Scholars have proposed site identifications for most of these, and many are reasonable. See the relevant discussions in the works in n. 1 and in such works as *ISBE* and *ABD*.

[204] See the discussion on this in Kallai, *Historical Geography*, 421–26, and his map 3 (after p. 516). See also the good map in Rasmussen, *NIV Atlas of the Bible*, 99.

[205] This may be another form of "Beeroth," which should not be confused with the Beeroth in Benjamin's territory. See Kallai, *Historical Geography*, 424; Butler, *Joshua*, 199.

[206] "Tabor" may have been a city associated with Mount Tabor, or the reference may be to the actual mountain. The total in v. 22 of "sixteen towns and villages" treats Tabor as a city. Alternatively, if the Old Greek's extra city—Reeroth/Beeroth (v. 20)—is added, then "Tabor" would more likely refer to the mountain.

[207] M. Hunt, "Jezreel (Place)," *ABD* 3:850.

at the sea in the region of Aczib, ³⁰Ummah, Aphek and Rehob. There were twenty-two towns and their villages. ³¹These towns and their villages were the inheritance of the tribe of Asher, clan by clan.

19:24   Asher's was the fifth lot cast, and its territory lay in a long, narrow strip in the far northwest of the tribal inheritances, with the Mediterranean Sea as its western boundary and the tribes of Zebulun and western Manasseh at its eastern edge. Its territorial description is not neatly separated into boundary and city lists, as are the others. Rather, small groups of cities are included at different points along the boundary descriptions. No compelling reason for this difference has been advanced, although Nelson well notes that this "kaleidoscopic totality," this "indiscriminate mingling of two sorts of materials" shows that "[f]rom the standpoint of the national claim on territory, both boundary cities and interior cities serve the same basic function."[208] That is, whether one is considering a boundary line that runs this way or turns that way or a city list consisting of those certain cities, in both cases, the Bible is asserting Israel's rightful claims to the territories so described or encompassed.

The total number of cities listed is twenty-three, whereas "twenty two" is the total given in v. 30. However, no definitive conclusion can be drawn from this discrepancy because we are unable to determine exactly how the count was made. At least three cities known to have been part of Asher's territory—Acco, Ahlab, and Helbah (Judg 1:31)—are not included in the list here.[209] Furthermore, not all readings of the names of towns are certain. For example, the NIV translates *mēḥebel ʾakzîbâ* in v. 29 as "in the region of Achzib" (so also the NASB), whereas the NLT understands these two words to refer to two cities: "Mahalab, Achzib" (so also NJPSV, REB, NRSV).[210] Seven cities are not mentioned elsewhere in the Bible: Hali, Beten, Allamelech, Amad, Beth Emek, Neiel, and Ummah, nor is Shihor Libnath, which is probably a geographical feature (a river? a swamp?). All four of the Levitical cities listed in 21:30–31 as coming from Asher are found in this section: Helkath (v. 25), Mishal (v. 26), Abdon (v. 28), and Rehob (v. 28).

19:25–26   Although many sites named in this list are unknown or their locations disputed, the broad plan of the boundary/city list can be followed. The first portion is the southern boundary, with a starting point at Helkath. It

---

[208] Nelson, *Joshua,* 223–24.

[209] The readings of "Ahlab" and "Helbah" have difficulties of their own, which need not detain us here. See M. J. Fretz, "Ahlab," *ABD* 1:123; Hunt, "Helbah," *ABD* 3:117.

[210] So also Nelson, *Joshua,* 216, 218. A third alternative is Boling's proposal that מֵחֶבֶל should be read as "from Achlab," referring to Achlab's presence in Judg 1:31 (*Joshua,* 453). Despite the uncertainties, the NIV's rendering—based on the use of the term חֶבֶל elsewhere to refer to territories (e.g., Josh 17:14; 19:9)—appears to be the most likely. On this point, see Parunak, "Geographical Terminology," 12.

ran first to the west, where it reached (or extended toward) Mount Carmel and Shihor Libnath, which probably was a river, perhaps the outlet of the Kishon River at the sea (vv. 25–26).[211] Interrupting the boundary description is a list of seven cities, most of whose identities are uncertain.[212] Then the point of reference returned *(šwb)* to Helkath to begin the eastern portion of the southern boundary, moving eastward toward Beth Dagon (v. 27).[213]

19:27 The boundary then proceeded northward, touching Zebulun and the Valley of Iphtah El on the east—Iphtah El is described earlier at the western end of Zebulun's northern border (v. 14)—and passing Cabul "on the left" (v. 27).[214] Cabul is known otherwise only from an episode in 1 Kgs 9:11–13, where King Solomon gave twenty cities in the Galilee region to Hiram, king of Tyre, in return for building supplies for the temple in Jerusalem. However, Hiram was displeased with this gift, and he gave it a disparaging name, "the Land of Cabul" (1 Kgs 9:13).[215] The city of Cabul was presumably part of the district of twenty cities that Solomon gave to Hiram, and it gave its name to the entire region.[216]

19:28 From Cabul the boundary extended north and west to "Greater Sidon" (v. 28). Sidon was an important coastal city, and Asher's territory appears to have included it (and not just moved in its direction); this is because Judg 1:31 includes the inhabitants of Sidon among those whom Asher was unable to displace.[217] The boundary description is interrupted by a short list of cities in the "expansive northern area of the allotment which was defined only in the north":[218] Abdon,[219] Rehob, Hammon, and Kanah (v. 28).

---

[211] See Kallai, *Historical Geography*, 208–9; Frankel, "Shihor-Libnath," *ABD* 5:1212–13. REB has "the swamp of Libnath."

[212] See Kallai, *Historical Geography*, 430–31.

[213] See Parunak, "Geographical Terminology," 68–70 on this use of שׁוּב, including a discussion of 19:27.

[214] The word here, מִשְּׂמֹאל is literally "from [the] left," but it can also be translated "from [the] north" because north was to the left in the biblical system of orientation (see the commentary on 16:3 and note there). Thus, many scholars understand the expression here to be referring to the northerly direction in which the boundary was proceeding at this point. See, e.g., NASB ("on north to Cabul"), NJPSV ("to Cabul on the north"), NRSV ("in the north to Cabul"), NLT ("north to Cabul"); Nelson (Joshua, 216: "to Cabul on the north"). Kallai understands the expression as follows: "to Cabul on the left hand" (*Historical Geography*, 210).

[215] The exact meaning of the name is uncertain. The word sounds like כְּבָל, which means "like nothing," i.e., "good-for-nothing." See NIV text note at 1 Kgs 9:13; *HALOT*, 458.

[216] The identification of Cabul is relatively certain: a modern village of Kabul sits ca. ten miles east-northeast of Mount Carmel, ca. nine miles southeast of Acco. It is mentioned by Josephus and in Talmudic literature as well. See Kallai, *Historical Geography*, 210; R. J. Hughes, "Cabul," *ISBE* 1:567; Frankel, "Cabul," *ABD* 1:797.

[217] See the more extended discussion in Kallai, *Historical Geography*, 212–14.

[218] Ibid., 432.

[219] The Hb. here has "Ebron," a place otherwise unknown. The NIV's "Abdon" comes from the Levitical city in Asher in 21:30 (see also 1 Chr 6:74 [Hb. 59]). The Tg. also has "Abdon."

19:29   The boundary now turned southward along the coastline and included the cities of Ramah, Tyre (the fortified city), Hosah, and Achzib along the coast. The language in the verse uses the unusual combination of *šwb* ("returned") twice. As Parunak has pointed out, this verb indicates a 180-degree reversal in direction. Sometimes, as in vv. 27,34, what this means is that the boundary description moves out from a fixed point in one direction and then returns to that same point to go out in the other direction (see comment on v. 27). However, here in v. 29a *šwb* appears to indicate that the boundary line reversed itself from its previously northward direction culminating in Greater Sidon (v. 28) and came south to Ramah and the other cities. Then, to include the fortress of Tyre, the line would have had to go out to the island city, then reverse itself *(šwb)* to come back to Hosah (v. 29b). The border then went out toward *(tōṣēʾōt)* the sea, in the territory of Achzib.[220] The boundary actually reached the sea at both Sidon and Tyre, but it is mentioned for the first time only with Achzib. Ramah in this verse should not be confused with another Ramah in Naphtali (19:36).

19:30   The list ends in the southwest portion of Asher's territory, near Acco, on the coast, by listing three cities in the region: Ummah (or Acco?),[221] Aphek, and Rehob (v. 30). The Rehob here probably is different from the one mentioned in v. 28, although many scholars identify the two.[222] Also, at least five different cities named Aphek are known; this is the only one in Asher.[223] As we noted, the total of twenty-two does not fit the number of towns listed.[224]

(7) Naphtali's Inheritance (19:32–39)

32The sixth lot came out for Naphtali, clan by clan:
33Their boundary went from Heleph and the large tree in Zaanannim, passing

---

[220] The understanding here is indebted to Parunak ("Geographical Terminology," 68–76, esp. 70–76). The issues involved with the "fortress of Tyre" and Hosah are complex. Kallai argues that the "fortress of Tyre" is not the large and well-known island city but an outpost some distance inland from it. Furthermore, he argues that "Hosah" is an alternate name for the "fortress of Tyre" (Kallai, *Historical Geography*, 215–20). However, Parunak's arguments are more compelling: he convincingly challenges Kallai's separation of the "fortress of Tyre" from Tyre itself ("Geographical Terminology," 74–76), and his analysis pays much more careful attention to the meanings of the verb שׁוּב and the noun תֹּצָאוֹת than does Kallai's.

[221] Many scholars propose that "Ummah," which is otherwise unknown, represents a scribal error in copying "Acco." Supporting this is one manuscript of the Old Greek, which reads "and Acco." In Judg 1:31, Acco is listed as one of the cities that Asher did not subdue, which also supports this suggestion.

[222] Absolute certainty is not possible here. On the issues involved, see W. S. LaSor, "Rehob," *ISBE* 4:71–72; J. L. Peterson, "Rehob (Place)," *ABD* 5:660–61.

[223] See Frankel, "Aphek," *ABD* 1:275–77.

[224] According to Judg 1:31–32, Asher did not drive out the Canaanites from several of its cities: Acco, Sidon, Ahlab, Aczib, Helbah, Aphek, or Rehob. Of these, Acco (v. 30; perhaps Ummah: see above), Aczib (v. 29), Aphek (v. 30), and Rehob (v. 30) are all mentioned in this chapter.

Adami Nekeb and Jabneel to Lakkum and ending at the Jordan. ³⁴The boundary ran west through Aznoth Tabor and came out at Hukkok. It touched Zebulun on the south, Asher on the west and the Jordan on the east. ³⁵The fortified cities were Ziddim, Zer, Hammath, Rakkath, Kinnereth, ³⁶Adamah, Ramah, Hazor, ³⁷Kedesh, Edrei, En Hazor, ³⁸Iron, Migdal El, Horem, Beth Anath and Beth Shemesh. There were nineteen towns and their villages. ³⁹These towns and their villages were the inheritance of the tribe of Naphtali, clan by clan.

Naphtali's was the sixth lot cast, and it received the rich, forested land in the heart of the Galilee region. Asher was to the west, Zebulun and Asher to the south, and the Jordan River and eastern Manasseh to the east. Its territory is described by means of a sketchy boundary description (vv. 33–34) and a separate city list (vv. 35–38). Several cities in Naphtali's listing have the same name as cities elsewhere (cf. Jabneel [v. 33] in Judah [15:11]; Ramah [v. 36] in Asher [v. 29]; Edrei [v. 37] in Transjordan, one of Og's royal cities [13:12]; Kedesh [v. 37] in Judah [15:23]; Beth Shemesh [v. 38] in Judah [15:10] and in Issachar [19:22]).

19:33–34 Only Naphtali's southern boundary is given in any detail (vv. 33–34a). It began at Heleph and ran eastward to the Jordan River. Then it returned *(šwb)* to its starting point and ran westward to Hukkok. Hukkok was presumably at the western edge, near the eastern boundary of Asher. Of the seven cities marking this southern border, only Zaanannim is mentioned again—in Judg 4:11, where it is near Kedesh—which makes it difficult to correlate Naphtali's southern boundary with the northern boundaries of Zebulun and Issachar.

Verse 34 ends by giving a general overview of three of Naphtali's four borders, mentioning the natural abutments of each: Zebulun on the south (although Issachar also bordered it on the south), Asher on the west, and the Jordan River on the east (north of the Sea of Galilee). The NIV smooths over a difficulty in the Hebrew here, which does not read simply "the Jordan," but "Judah of the Jordan" (see NASB: "to Judah at the Jordan"). This is either an unknown town in the far north or it represents a textual corruption. The NIV opts for the latter solution, following the Old Greek, which omits "Judah."

19:35–38 Naphtali's city list begins like that of no other tribe: it states that the cities in the list were "fortified cities." The word "fortified" *(mibṣār)* occurs only three times in Joshua (here, in v. 29 ["fortified city of Tyre"], and in 10:20). Presumably the cities in Naphtali's territory were not the only ones in Canaan that were fortified—see especially 10:20, where the kings of the southern coalition retreated to fortified cities in the south, and Num 13:28, where the Israelite spies reported on the fortified cities (*bāṣûr*, a word related to *mibṣār*) of Canaan that they saw—but it is only in this list that the author bothers to give us this information.

Sixteen cities are listed here, which does not correlate with the total of nineteen mentioned in v. 38. This is similar to the problem with the totals in Asher's list (see above). As there, at least one city known to have been in Naphtali's territory is not mentioned here: Kartan (see 21:32). Thus, we cannot draw any definitive conclusions about the totals.[225]

Of the sixteen cities in Naphtali's city list, all whose locations can be verified are in the southern portions of Naphtali's territory, leaving an unexplained gap in cities of the north.[226] Nine are not mentioned elsewhere in the Bible: Ziddim, Zer,[227] Hammath, Rakkath, Adamah, En Hazor, Iron, Migdal El, and Horem.[228]

(8) Dan's Inheritance (19:40–48)

[40]The seventh lot came out for the tribe of Dan, clan by clan. [41]The territory of their inheritance included:

Zorah, Eshtaol, Ir Shemesh, [42]Shaalabbin, Aijalon, Ithlah, [43]Elon, Timnah, Ekron, [44]Eltekeh, Gibbethon, Baalath, [45]Jehud, Bene Berak, Gath Rimmon, [46]Me Jarkon and Rakkon, with the area facing Joppa.

[47](But the Danites had difficulty taking possession of their territory, so they went up and attacked Leshem, took it, put it to the sword and occupied it. They settled in Leshem and named it Dan after their forefather.) [48]These towns and their villages were the inheritance of the tribe of Dan, clan by clan.

The final tribe, the seventh in the lot casting, was the tribe of Dan. The Danites' territorial interests were overshadowed by their inability to take their own land and their subsequent migration to a region far to the north, which was where they settled. Thus, the detailed description found in vv. 41–46 is primarily for historical interest because the Danites settled in the north, at Leshem, which they renamed "Dan" (v. 47). Their territorial allotment was in the south, abutting Judah and other tribes. However, they are listed here with the northern tribes in Galilee undoubtedly because that is where they eventually settled.

19:41–46   There is no boundary description for Dan, only a city list consisting of eighteen cities. This should not be surprising, given that they never appear to have settled permanently in the region described for them here. Although no borders are given, the known cities in their list, coupled with adjoining boundary descriptions, allow us to know where their territory was:

---

[225] The total is missing entirely from the Old Greek at this point.

[226] See Kallai, *Historical Geography,* 437.

[227] Alternate proposals have been advanced to account for Ziddim and Zer, involving textual corruption. However, nothing certain can be concluded. See the discussions in Kallai, *Historical Geography,* 434–35; Boling, *Joshua,* 457; Nelson, *Joshua,* 218.

[228] Like several other tribes, Naphtali failed to drive out the Canaanites from portions of its territory: Beth Shemesh and Beth Anath, according to Judg 1:33. Both cities are mentioned in Josh 19:38.

it was bounded on the west by the Mediterranean Sea (Joppa in v. 46 was an important seaport), on the south by Judah, on the east by Benjamin, and on the east and north by Ephraim and Manasseh.

Seven of Dan's cities are not mentioned elsewhere in the Bible, at least as they appear here: Shaalabbin,[229] Ithlah, Elon,[230] Jehud, Bene Berak, Me Jarkon,[231] and Rakkon. Several of Dan's cities are also mentioned in connection with Judah's inheritance: Zorah and Eshtaol (v. 41; 15:33), Ir Shemesh (v. 41; 15:10: as "Beth Shemesh"), Timnah (v. 43; 15:57), Ekron (v. 43; 15:11,45–46). Baalath (v. 44) should not be confused with Baalath Beer in Simeon's possession (19:8). All four of the Levitical cities listed in 21:23–24 as coming from Dan are found here: Aijalon (v. 42) Eltekeh and Gibbethon (v. 44), and Gath Rimmon (v. 45).

19:47 The defining characteristic for Dan was not just that they were unable to drive out the Canaanites from their territories.[232] After all, several other tribes had the same problem. However, the Danites were unique in that they abandoned their allotted territory and migrated elsewhere. They traveled to the far north of Canaan and took a city called Leshem, renaming it Dan.[233] This became an important city as a marker of the northern extreme of the land, included in the phrase "from Dan to Beersheba" (e.g., Judg 20:1; 1 Sam 3:20; 1 Kgs 4:25). It was one of the cities where Jeroboam I erected a golden calf (1 Kgs 12:29–30).

The Book of Judges gives us further perspectives on Dan's migration. Judges 1:34 states that the tribe migrated because of pressure from the Canaanites, who confined them in the hill country. Judges 18 tells the entire story about their migration, the details of which are mostly sordid, showing the Danites' apostasy (see esp. 18:27–31).[234]

7. Joshua's Inheritance (19:49–50)

⁴⁹When they had finished dividing the land into its allotted portions, the Israelites gave Joshua son of Nun an inheritance among them, ⁵⁰as the LORD had commanded. They gave him the town he asked for—Timnath Serah in the hill country of Ephraim. And he built up the town and settled there.

---

[229] This probably is the same city as the Shaalbim of Judg 1:35 and 1 Kgs 4:9.

[230] This probably is the same city as Elon Bethhanan in 1 Kgs 4:9.

[231] This actually may be "the waters of Jarkon" (מֵי is the word for "waters") or "on the west, Jarkon" (following the Old Greek).

[232] Literally, the text states "and the territory went out from them," which may mean, to use a modern expression, that it slipped through their fingers, i.e., that their enemies took it from them.

[233] Leshem is unknown except for here. In Judg 18, it is called "Laish" (vv. 7,14,27,29).

[234] The Old Greek gives a longer text in vv. 47–48 that differs in several ways from the MT. There is little that is not found in Josh 19:47 and Judg 1:34–35, however, and it must be judged to have been a secondary addition. See also Nelson, *Joshua,* 225–26.

19:49   The land distributions west of the Jordan begin with Caleb's family inheritance (14:6–15), and they end, fittingly enough, with Joshua's. Joshua, who was usually the agent distributing the land, now received it from the Israelites (v. 49). He could not give himself his own portion.[235]

The specific command of God mentioned here that granted Joshua this inheritance is not recorded anywhere in Scripture, but God's words to the rebellious Israelites in Num 14:30 were a general promise to Caleb and Joshua, the two faithful spies: "Not one of you will enter the land I swore with uplifted hand to make your home, except Caleb son of Jephunneh and Joshua son of Nun." Both spies not only entered the land, but they both also received special portions in it.

Joshua's territory was the city of Timnath Serah, in the hill country of Ephraim. Joshua himself was from this tribe (Num 13:8), and he was buried in the city given to him (Josh 24:30). The two references to this city in Joshua are the only two in the Bible. A city named Timnath Heres is mentioned in Judg 2:9, also in the hill country of Ephraim, and most scholars believe the two are one and the same.[236] It would seem that Timnath Serah was Joshua's own personal possession because it does not appear in Ephraim's tribal list (nor in any other list, for that matter). No other Israelite received any inheritance in this manner, that is, as a personal possession; even Caleb's city, Hebron, belonged to the tribe of Judah (15:13,54), and it was both a city of refuge (20:7) and a Levitical city (21:11,13). This certainly contributes to the picture of Joshua as an extraordinary individual, one who demonstrated extraordinary faithfulness to God and who was the leader par excellence.

8. The Cisjordan Distribution Concluded (19:51)

[51]These are the territories that Eleazar the priest, Joshua son of Nun and the heads of the tribal clans of Israel assigned by lot at Shiloh in the presence of the LORD at the entrance to the Tent of Meeting. And so they finished dividing the land.

19:51   The summary statement here is a conclusion to the immediate section (chaps. 18–19), given the references to Shiloh and the tent of meeting (see 18:1). However, the statement also serves as a fitting conclusion to the entire section of chaps. 14–19, in which the land distributions west of the Jordan were accomplished. The major characters involved in the distributions are mentioned, identified by their full names: Eleazar the priest, Joshua son of

---

[235] On the significance of the agents of giving, see the excursus "The Giving of the Land in Joshua" at 1:3.

[236] This is because the second elements of both names have the same consonants, only reversed: סרח, "-Serah," and חרס, "-Heres." See A. Van Selms, "Timnath Serah," *ISBE* 4:856; H. R. Weeks, "Timnath Heres," *ABD* 6:557–58.

Nun, and the heads of the tribal clans. The same cast of characters opens the section in 14:1. This concluding reference to them brings the entire arduous, and at times tedious, process full circle, assuring us that throughout the entire proceedings, these God-appointed representatives were involved.

The key passage in 18:1–10 is echoed here as well. The gathering at Shiloh is mentioned (cf. 18:1), as is the assignment of everything by lots (cf. 18:6,8,10), the Lord's presence with his people (cf. 18:6,8,10), and the tent of meeting (cf. 18:1). The division of the land into portions *(ḥlq)* is also mentioned here, as it is in 18:2,5[2x],6,7,9,10. The importance of 18:1–10 that has been noted on other grounds (see the introduction to chap. 13) is echoed by the repetitions here.

Now all the tribes except for Levi had received their inheritances. All that remained was to delineate the Levites' inheritance and to designate the special cities of refuge. The greatest portion of the task, however, was completed.[237]

9. The Cities of Refuge (20:1–9)

Finally, the task of apportioning the lands east and west of the Jordan to the twelve tribes was complete. Two final items remained to be taken care of: (1) the designation of the cities of refuge (chap. 20) and (2) the Levitical cities (chap. 21). The instructions here rely heavily on Mosaic legislation that first mentions both of these two types of cities. The two groups of cities were related to each other, since the cities of refuge were a subset of the Levitical cities: there were forty-eight Levitical cities, out of which the six cities of refuge were designated.

In the Pentateuch, the Israelites were first instructed that six cities of refuge should be designated as safe havens where a man could flee if he accidentally killed someone. In Exod 21:12–14, the provision for this is placed at the beginning of the laws dealing with capital offenses: premeditated murder was to be punished by death (vv. 12,14), but accidental killing was not (v. 13). In Num 35:9–29, provisions for this are spelled out in much more detail, including the Lord's instructions that the Israelites should select six cities, three on each side of the Jordan (Num 35:9–15). Deuteronomy 4:41–43 reports that Moses did precisely that for the tribes east of the Jordan (three cities). In Deut 19:1–10, Moses gave instructions that the same should be done with three cities west of the Jordan. And we are told in Num 35:6 that these six cities were to be designated from among the cities to be allotted to the Levites.

The legislation concerning the cities of refuge shows, on the one hand, God's mercy, in that those who killed accidentally could find a place of refuge. And

---

[237] The final summary statement is found in 21:43–45, which is more sweeping, more overarching, and more theological than this statement.

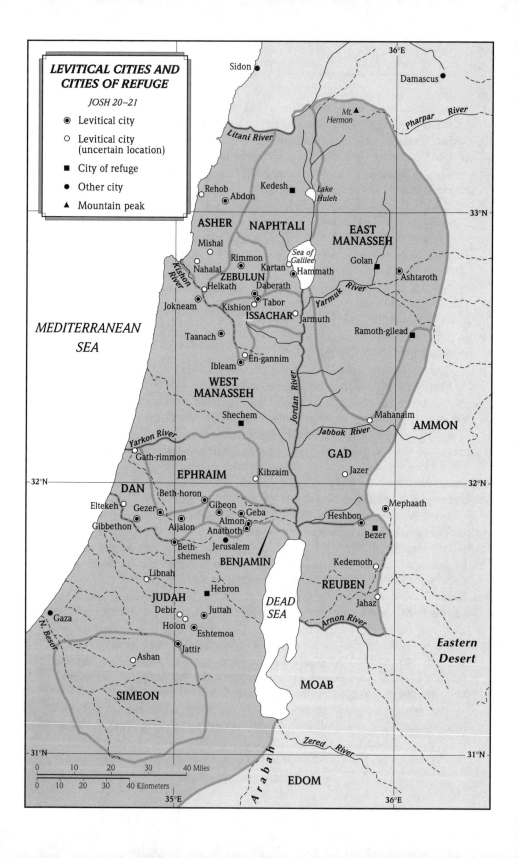

LEVITICAL CITIES AND
CITIES OF REFUGE

JOSH 20–21

◉ Levitical city
○ Levitical city
(uncertain location)
■ City of refuge
● Other city
▲ Mountain peak

36°E

Sidon

Damascus

Mt. Hermon

Pharpar River

Litani River

33°N

Rehob
Abdon
Kedesh
Lake Huleh

ASHER   NAPHTALI   EAST MANASSEH

Mishal
Rimmon
Sea of Galilee
Golan
Ashtaroth

Nahalal
Kartan
Hammath
ZEBULUN
Helkath
Daberath
Jokneam
Kishion
Tabor
ISSACHAR
Jarmuth

Yarmuk River

Taanach

Ramoth-gilead

Ibleam
En-gannim

WEST
MANASSEH

Jordan River

Shechem

Mahanaim
Jabbok River
AMMON

Yarkon River

GAD

Gath-rimmon

Kibzaim
Jazer

EPHRAIM

32°N   32°N

DAN

Beth-horon
Gibeon
Geba
Heshbon
Mephaath

Eltekeh
Gezer
Almon
Gibbethon
Aijalon
Anathoth
Bezer

Beth-shemesh
Jerusalem
Kedemoth

BENJAMIN

Libnah

Hebron
REUBEN

JUDAH
Debir
Juttah
Jahaz

Holon
Eshtemoa
DEAD SEA

Gaza
Jattir

Arnon River

Ashan

Eastern
Desert

SIMEON

MOAB

MEDITERRANEAN
SEA

Zered River

31°N   31°N

0   10   20   30   40 Miles
0   10   20   30   40 Kilometers

35°E   EDOM   36°E

yet, on the other hand, it also affirms the sanctity of human life, in that even an accidental death caused blood guilt that could be avenged if the killer did not go to a city of refuge. Furthermore, the killer who escaped to such a city was not free to return home until another death had taken place, that of the high priest (Num 35:25,28).

It appears that the altar in the tabernacle and the temple functioned as a place of temporary refuge, but these cities were to provide long-term refuge. For example, in Exod 21:14 God said: "If a man schemes and kills another man deliberately, take him away from *my altar* and put him to death" (author italics). The implication here is that the murderer was taking refuge at the altar. This is illustrated by two episodes in 1 Kings, where Adonijah and Joab sought temporary refuge by clinging to the altar (1 Kgs 1:50–53; 2:28). The cities of refuge were to provide a long-term place of refuge for those guilty of accidental killing.

Almost everything in this chapter comes from the Pentateuchal passages noted above; there is little that is new. However, what *is* new is the combination of elements here—the instructions for designating the cities, the rationale for this, the six cities so designated (including the names of the three cities west of the Jordan, which had not been named previously), and the setting in which this was finally accomplished. This was done in the context of the distribution of the rest of the promised land, which had just now been completed at the end of chap. 19. Thus, the rich theology of protection of accidental killers by setting up safe havens for them has now come to fruition: the earlier instructions and rationale are repeated (vv. 1–6), and now, finally, the execution of the commands to do this is accomplished. That which had earlier merely been anticipated was now a reality (vv. 7–9).

(1) Introduction: General Instructions (20:1–3)

¹Then the LORD said to Joshua: ²"Tell the Israelites to designate the cities of refuge, as I instructed you through Moses, ³so that anyone who kills a person accidentally and unintentionally may flee there and find protection from the avenger of blood.

20:2 God gave Joshua the instructions for designating the cities of refuge, just as he had instructed "by the hand of Moses."[238] The instructions referred to here are found in Exod 21:12–14; Num 35:9–29; and Deut 19:10 (see above). God told the Israelites, literally, to "give to yourselves" the cities of refuge (v. 2), that is, they were a gift to themselves from cities they already possessed. They would be a gift because any innocent person could avail him-

---

[238] See the commentary on 14:5 on this expression, which shows Moses as God's agent of accomplishing his will.

self of the protection offered there.

The purpose of these cities was so that the one who killed without murderous intention could flee there and receive protection. The word for "killer" here is *rôṣēaḥ*, which can refer to one who premeditates a murder (e.g., Num 35:16,21; Deut 22:26) or to someone who killed accidentally, as here (e.g., Num 35:6,11; Deut 4:42; 19:3,4,6). The word is related to the verb found in the Ten Commandments—"You shall not murder *[rṣḥ]*"—and denotes illegal and inappropriate killing.[239] Even though there is an exception to the laws of capital punishment here, the deed itself is not condoned: the guilty one simply was to be spared death at the hands of an "avenger of blood." He was still guilty, but the law treated him more leniently. This shows that the biblical legislation did make distinctions in degrees of guilt and that God's law was sensitive to motives and intent of the heart, in providing more lenient treatment for what modern criminal codes call "manslaughter" (as opposed to premeditated murder).

20:3 The law's sensitivity to motives and intent becomes clear in v. 3 when we consider the words in question here. The NIV speaks of killing someone "accidentally and unintentionally." In the first instance, "accidentally" translates *šĕgāgâ,* which refers to inadvertent wrongdoing.[240] Such inadvertent sins were due to one of two things: (1) negligence, that is, although the sinner knew that an action was wrong, he was negligent, accidentally committing the sin, such as an accidental homicide (Num 35:22–24; Deut 19:4–5); or (2) ignorance, that is, the sinner was aware of his actions but remained unaware that they were sinful (e.g., 1 Sam 26:21; Ps 19:12[Hb. 13; "hidden faults"]; Prov 5:23 ["great folly"]; Ezek 45:20). In both cases, the sinner was guilty: in the former instance, negligence resulting in accidents was to be accounted for, and, in the latter case, ignorance of the law was no excuse (just as today).

In the second instance in Josh 20:3, the NIV's "unintentionally" is literally "he did not know," the meaning of which is clear; it is essentially synonymous with the second meaning of *šĕgāgâ.* Here, too, ignorance when the law was broken did not excuse the sinner.

However, God's law was not rigidly blind. It did indeed take into account intentionality when considering sins, and it imposed lesser punishments and allowed for atonement. This is clear from our passage here in Joshua 20 (and its predecessors). It is clear from Leviticus 4, which is devoted in its entirety to instructions related to atoning for sins committed unintentionally or inadvertently—the term *šĕgāgâ* (or the related verb *šgh*) occurs four times in this

---

[239] See *HALOT*, 1283; W. R. Domeris, "רצח," *NIDOTTE* 3:1188–89.

[240] The seminal study on שְׁגָגָה is J. Milgrom, "The Cultic שְׁגָגָה and Its Influence in Psalms and Job," *JQR* 58 (1967): 115–25. See also A. E. Hill, "שׁגג," *NIDOTTE* 4:42–43.

chapter: vv. 2,13,22,27—by means of the purification offering (sometimes known as the "sin offering").[241] It is also clear from Lev 5:1–13, which deals with sins that are "hidden" (ʿlm) from the sinner and that he then becomes aware of (see esp. vv. 2–4). Finally, it is clear from Lev 5:14–6:7[Hb. 5:14–26], where sinning unintentionally (šĕgāgâ in v. 14; "not knowing" in v. 17) and "acting unfaithfully" (mʿl in 6:2[Hb. 5:21]) are all to be atoned for by the reparation offering (or "guilt offering").[242] In all of these cases, the unwitting or accidental sins are atoned for and not punished as severely as intentional sins.

This raises a related point not directly addressed in this passage but important nevertheless: Did the Old Testament allow for the atonement of intentional sins—sins committed consciously and deliberately—in addition to inadvertent sins? Some have argued that in the sacrificial system explicated in Leviticus 1–7, there is no sacrifice for deliberate sin. Indeed, Num 15:30–31 would seem to indicate that there is no forgiveness in the Old Testament for deliberate sin: "But anyone who sins defiantly, whether native-born or alien, blasphemes the LORD, and that person must be cut off from his people. Because he has despised the LORD's word and broken his commands, that person must surely be cut off; his guilt remains on him." The NIV's "defiantly" in v. 30 is literally "with a high [or raised] hand," and the idea is that of a fist raised skyward in rebellion against God. Because of arguments such as this, some Christians have further argued that Christ's sacrifice was superior to the Old Testament sacrifices because his sacrifice covered *all* sins, not just inadvertent ones.

By way of answering the question, we must first affirm that Christ's sacrifice was indeed infinitely superior to the Old Testament sacrifices. The Book of Hebrews makes this abundantly clear (see Heb 7:27; 10:2–14). However, concerning the more limited question of whether deliberate sins could be atoned for in the Old Testament, the answer certainly is yes. Otherwise, no Old Testament believer could ever have been forgiven.[243] We can make at least two points in support of this.

First, the burnt offering (Leviticus 1) was "clearly propitiatory and expiatory (for 'wrath,' 'guilt,' 'offense,' 'sin'),"[244] at least in part. This fact is

---

[241] "Purification offering" is the better term: see J. Milgrom, *Leviticus 1–16*, AB 3 (New York: Doubleday, 1991), 253–54; J. E. Hartley, *Leviticus*, WBC 4 (Dallas: Word, 1992), 55.

[242] On this terminology, see Milgrom, *Leviticus*, 339–45; Hartley, *Leviticus*, 76–80.

[243] If it is countered that OT believers were atoned for by Christ's sacrifice, not by their own sacrifices, the answer is "of course." However, to argue in this fashion would obviate the need for sacrifices even for inadvertent sins. The question then would be, Why should there be sacrifices for one type of sin in the OT and not another, if Christ's atoned for both in any case? Better not to have any sacrifices at all, then, and await Christ's perfect sacrifice. The question being probed here is whether the OT only knows of sacrifices for inadvertent sins, not whether Christ's sacrifice covers one or another type of sin, or all types.

[244] Milgrom, *Leviticus*, 175.

attested by the very words for the offering itself, in Lev 1:4: "It will be accepted on his behalf to make atonement for him." Leviticus 14:19–20 speaks of the priest offering a burnt offering on the altar, along with the grain offering, to "make atonement for him, and he will be clean," and Lev 16:24 is similar.[245] Thus, the burnt offering is proof positive that there was atonement for deliberate sins in the Old Testament.

Second, Num 5:6–8 shows that a person who "is unfaithful *[mᶜl]* to the LORD" must confess his or her sin and also make restitution, and then the sins can be forgiven. The verb "to be unfaithful" here *(mᶜl)* is the same one found in Lev 6:2[Hb. 5:21] (see above) and is perhaps better translated "to commit a sacrilege."[246] It is also used with reference to Achan's sin in Josh 7:1. The key here is the confession of sin. It would appear, then, that the sin committed "with a high hand" in Num 15:30–31 was a deliberate rebellion against God in which there was no confession; rather, the sinner was standing defiantly before God, with an upraised fist, not humbly, with a broken spirit and a broken and contrite heart (see Ps 51:17[Hb. 19]). This would be the Old Testament equivalent of the blasphemy against the Holy Spirit of which Jesus spoke (see Matt 12:31; Mark 3:29; Luke 12:10).

If someone had indeed killed inadvertently, he could flee to a city of refuge to escape the "avenger of blood" *(gōʾēl haddām)*. This person is mentioned in only four contexts in the Old Testament, three of them legal or semilegal and one a narrative, all of them dealing with the same principle.[247] A more general term (the *gōʾēl*) is mentioned close to fifty times and is usually translated as "close relative," "kinsman redeemer," or something similar. The *gōʾēl* seems to have been one who had certain obligations to fulfill, whether they were recovering people or property that had been lost through indenture, or they were paying a fee (usually by a relative or an owner), or they were meting out punishment for killing someone. The law of the *gōʾēl* is given in Leviticus 25, where provisions for redeeming family property (vv. 25–28), dwellings (vv. 29–34), and needy relatives (vv. 47–49) are made. The best-known example of this being played out in practice is from the Book of Ruth, where Boaz and an unnamed relative (a "kinsman redeemer") were involved in a legal situation over their obligations to the widowed Ruth (Ruth 4).[248]

---

[245] Outside of the legal corpus, several narrative examples show that burnt offerings were to turn away God's wrath and atone for sin. See, e.g., Gen 8:20–21; Num 15:24; 2 Sam 24:25; Job 1:5; 42:8; and cf. 2 Chr 29:7–8. See the discussion in G. J. Wenham, *The Book of Leviticus*, NICOT (Grand Rapids: Eerdmans, 1979), 57–58, on this issue.

[246] See Milgrom, *Leviticus*, 345–56.

[247] Num 35:19,21,24,25,27[2x]; Deut 19:6,12; Josh 20:3,5,9; 2 Sam 14:11.

[248] On the "kinsman redeemer" (גֹּאֵל) in general, see H. Ringgren, "גָּאַל *gāʾal*," *TDOT* 2:350–55; R. L. Hubbard, Jr., "The *Goʾel* in Ancient Israel: Theological Reflections on an Israelite Institution," *BBR* 1 (1991): 3–19; id., "גָּאַל," *NIDOTTE* 1:789–94.

The idea of blood vengeance behind our passage here in Joshua 20 (and the related passages in Numbers 35 and Deuteronomy 19) is more limited than the broader idea of the "kinsman redeemer." The "avenger of blood" was not free to take private vengeance: the Bible clearly reserves vengeance to God alone (Deut 32:35; Isa 34:8; Rom 12:19). Numbers 35 states clearly that the avenger of blood was only free to kill someone who had killed another if (1) that person ventured forth from a city of refuge (Num 35:26–28) or (2) that person was guilty of murder, and not manslaughter (Num 35:16–21). The avenger of blood had a legal status in society to carry out society's (i.e., God's) judgments and was by no means one who was to exact private vengeance.[249]

(2) Specific Instructions (20:4–6)

[4]"When he flees to one of these cities, he is to stand in the entrance of the city gate and state his case before the elders of that city. Then they are to admit him into their city and give him a place to live with them. [5]If the avenger of blood pursues him, they must not surrender the one accused, because he killed his neighbor unintentionally and without malice aforethought. [6]He is to stay in that city until he has stood trial before the assembly and until the death of the high priest who is serving at that time. Then he may go back to his own home in the town from which he fled."

20:4–6 The circumstances of what was to happen to the manslayer are now given. The details in v. 4 are not found in the earlier passages in Numbers and Deuteronomy. The one who fled was to state his case before the elders of the city who, according to Deut 19:12, had the power to return him to his original city and into the hands of the blood avenger. However, here the presumption is that he was innocent, and he was to be given a place to live.

The elders were to protect the one who fled from the blood avenger (v. 5), and he was to remain there until two things happened (v. 6): (1) until he had had a chance to make his case and defend his innocence[250] and (2) until the high priest died. Then he was free to return home with no fear of reprisal.

It is not specifically stated what removed the manslayer's guilt. He was sentenced to a period of exile in the city of refuge, away from his home, and he could not return home until the high priest died. Many have argued that the high priest's death marked a period of amnesty ushering in a new era. How-

---

[249] A. Philips has proposed that the גֹּאֵל may have been an official of the state, but his view has not attained very wide currency; see *Ancient Israel's Criminal Law* (Oxford: Basil Blackwell, 1970), 99–109, and the comments by P. Craigie (*Deuteronomy*, NICOT [Grand Rapids: Eerdmans, 1976], 266 and n. 9) and Butler, *Joshua*, 216–17.

[250] In Num 35:24–25 it appears that he was to stand trial back in his home city and to be returned to the city of refuge if he were found innocent.

ever, a more probable explanation is that since the high priest represented the sacrificial system, his death atoned for the sins of the manslayer.[251] No ransom was to be accepted for a murderer or for a manslayer (Num 35:30–31). Only on the occasion of a death—the high priest's—was the manslayer free to leave. As Greenberg states, "The sole personage whose religious-cultic importance might endow his death with expiatory value for the people at large is the high priest."[252] In Numbers 35, the high priest is mentioned as having been anointed with "holy oil" (v. 25), which would tend to support his position as the acceptable "sacrifice." For Christians, the typological associations with the death of Jesus Christ—the great High Priest whose death atones for their sins—are certainly visible here.

(3) The Cities of Refuge Set Apart (20:7–8)

7So they set apart Kedesh in Galilee in the hill country of Naphtali, Shechem in the hill country of Ephraim, and Kiriath Arba (that is, Hebron) in the hill country of Judah. 8On the east side of the Jordan of Jericho they designated Bezer in the desert on the plateau in the tribe of Reuben, Ramoth in Gilead in the tribe of Gad, and Golan in Bashan in the tribe of Manasseh.

20:7–8 The six cities of refuge are now listed, the three west of the Jordan first (v. 7) and the three on the east side second (v. 8).[253] To the west of the Jordan, "Kedesh in Galilee," in the north, was mentioned already in 12:22 and 19:37. It was part of Naphtali's territory. Shechem was in the central highlands, in the territory of Ephraim, listed as marking the border of western Manasseh in 17:2,7. The third city, Kiriath Arba (Hebron), was in the south, in Judah's territory (11:21; 14:13–15; 15:13–14; etc.).

East of the Jordan (v. 8), the three cities are mentioned almost word for word as they were specified by Moses in Deut 4:41–43. However, the only other times they appear in Joshua are in the list of Levitical cities (21:27,36,38). The list here is south to north: (1) Bezer was on the desert plateau east of the Dead Sea, in Reubenite territory; (2) Ramoth in Gilead, east of the Jordan, in Gad's territory; and (3) Golan in Bashan, east of the Sea of Kinnereth (Galilee), in eastern Manasseh's territory.

No place in the land was more than a day's journey from one of these cities. All six of these cities are mentioned again in the next chapter, since they

---

[251] See the discussions in Woudstra, *Joshua*, 301; G. J. Wenham, *Numbers: An Introduction and Commentary*, TOTC (Downers Grove: InterVarsity, 1981), 238; R. B. Allen, "Numbers," *Expositor's Bible Commentary* (Grand Rapids: Zondervan, 1990), 1004; and esp. M. Greenberg, "The Biblical Conception of Asylum," *JBL* 78 (1959): 125–32.

[252] Greenberg, "The Biblical Conception of Asylum," 130.

[253] See the maps in Rasmussen, *NIV Atlas of the Bible*, 102; Brisco, *Holman Bible Atlas*, 86.

also were Levitical cities. Despite their importance here and in the Pentateuch, however, they do not appear again in the Old Testament.

(4) Summary (20:9)

⁹Any of the Israelites or any alien living among them who killed someone accidentally could flee to these designated cities and not be killed by the avenger of blood prior to standing trial before the assembly.

This verse summarizes the law of the cities of refuge well, adding the intriguing information that any alien *(gēr)* living among the Israelites was to be afforded the same protections. This adds to the inclusive vision found in the Pentateuch and the Book of Joshua that we have noted earlier (see the commentary at 2:11,21; 8:33).

10. The Levitical Cities (21:1–42)

Forty-eight cities were designated at Shiloh as ones in which the Levites could live and graze their cattle nearby, but they were to have no other land portion (see 13:14,33; 14:3; 18:7). The Levites were to be "salt and light" among their fellow Israelites, scattered as they were throughout the tribes. One important function of the Levites was that they were to be teachers of the law (Deut 33:10; cf. 2 Chr 17:7–9; 35:3; Mal 2:6–9), and they could more easily do this if they lived scattered throughout the land.[254] Levi's status as a landless tribe originated in a curse Jacob pronounced on Simeon and Levi (Gen 49:5–7), but the Levites did vindicate themselves during the time of Moses (see the commentary on 19:1–9 for a full discussion).

The Levitical cities were apportioned by lot, as the tribal territories had been, to the descendants of Levi's three sons: Kohath, Gershon, and Merari (Gen 46:11). As was the case with the cities of refuge, this too was in fulfillment of Mosaic legislation, which stated that the cities were to come from the territories of the other tribes (Num 35:1–8). The care for the Levites evidenced by this allotment reinforces the special stature assigned to this tribe that we noted at 13:33 (see also 14:4). We do not read of any campaigns to take most of these cities (and, indeed, a number of them may have remained unoccupied by the Levites for some time). Rather, the emphasis here is on the allotment of these cities to the Levites as their inheritance from the Lord.

This list of cities is preserved almost intact in 1 Chr 6:54–81[Hb. 39–66], but it is better organized than the one in Chronicles (e.g., the totals do not add up correctly in the Chronicles list, due to several omissions of city names, and

---

[254] See D. Garrett, *Rethinking Genesis: The Sources and Authorship of the First Book of the Pentateuch* (Grand Rapids: Baker, 1991), 199–232, on the teaching function of the Levites.

there is no overall summary in Chronicles as there is in Joshua). The preservation of this list so many centuries later shows the importance the Levites and their city allotments had in Israel.

The list has been studied extensively by critical scholars, and it is almost universally rejected as an unhistorical, utopian fantasy from a much later time.[255] Nelson's comments are typical. He marvels that the elaborate rhetorical strategy in the chapter "has induced many scholars to accept the historical existence of this artificial system" and states that "it is best to see the catalogue as a largely artificial construction."[256] However, one important scholar, Kallai, argues that the list is indeed historical, reflecting the historical realities of the end of the Davidic monarchy and Solomon's reign.[257]

We should note that many attempts to verify (or disprove) the historical moorings of this list ignore the fact that the chapter does not claim that these forty-eight cities actually were captured in Joshua's day (or in the period of the judges), nor that the Levites actually settled in all of them. Rather, as we have noted, the chapter emphasizes the allotment of the cities—the word *gôrāl,* "lot," is used eight times in the chapter (vv. 4[2x],5,6,8,10,20,40).[258] Just as we saw at the end of chap. 20 that the cities of refuge are not mentioned again in the Old Testament—which neither proves nor disproves their original designation and existence—so too here, the fact that some of the cities cannot be proven to have been settled by the Levites does not prove or disprove their original designation as Levitical cities. Indeed, there is evidence for occupation in many of the Levitical cities during the Iron II Age (ca.

---

[255] The literature is extensive. Four representative studies are (1) W. F. Albright, "The List of Levitical Cities," in *Louis Ginzberg Jubilee Volume* (New York: American Academy for Jewish Research, 1945), 49–73 (who postulates one, relatively early list that both Joshua and Chronicles drew upon); (2) Na'aman, *Borders and Districts,* 203–36 (who argues that the list originally only contained thirteen cities from Judah and that it dates to the late seventh century B.C.); (3) A. G. Auld, "The 'Levitical Cities': Texts and History," *ZAW* 91 (1979): 194–206 (who argues that the Joshua list is late, composed on the basis of the 1 Chr 6 list); (4) E. Ben-Zvi, "The List of the Levitical Cities," *JSOT* 54 (1992): 77–106 (who also argues that the list is late exilic or postexilic). For further discussion and bibliography, see Soggin, *Joshua,* 202–6; Butler, *Joshua,* 225–26; Nelson, *Joshua,* 236–40; Kallai, *Historical Geography,* 447–76; Svensson, *Towns and Toponymns,* 83–89. The greatest amount of scholarly discussion is devoted to determining the date of the original list, from which the Joshua and 1 Chronicles lists supposedly came, or determining the relationship between the two lists. Dates ranging from the United Monarchy to the postexilic period are proposed. Good maps of the cities of refuge and the Levitical cities may be found in Beitzel, *Moody Atlas of the Bible,* 101; Rasmussen, *NIV Atlas of the Bible,* 102.

[256] Nelson, *Joshua,* 237, 239. By his comment concerning the "historical existence" of the system of cities laid out in this chapter, he refers to scholars who at least believe that such a system existed at some point in Israel's history, although certainly not in Joshua's day and not the forty-eight-city system so neatly laid out in Joshua 20.

[257] Kallai, *Historical Geography,* 445–76, esp. pp. 447–58.

[258] See Woudstra, *Joshua,* 304–5, and nn. 1–2 on this point.

1200–1000 B.C.), according to at least one scholar.[259]

We will make some observations here about the patterns in the actual listing of the cities (vv. 9–42), including dealing with the major exceptions to the patterns. Our actual discussion of the list will be brief, since most of the cities have been mentioned previously and since, once the patterns are visible, very little remains to be stated.

The list of forty-eight cities is well organized and remarkably consistent structurally. The tribes averaged four cities apiece as their contributions to the Levites. The true number was four for every tribe except for Naphtali, which contributed only three cities (v. 32), but this was offset by Judah's and Simeon's combined contribution of nine cities (instead of the "expected" eight) (vv. 13–16). Western and eastern Manasseh functioned as one tribe for purposes of contributing to the Levites, contrary to their more usual functioning as two separate tribes: each contributed two cities, totaling four from the tribe as a whole. All the cities are named, the totals for each tribe are given, and, in every case, the numbers of cities listed and the running totals agree with each other.

The distributions were made to the divisions within the tribe of Levi that corresponded to his three sons, Kohath, Gershon, and Merari. Furthermore, the Kohathite branch was divided according to those who were descended from Aaron and those who were not (see comments on vv. 4–8).

The list names all forty-eight Levitical cities, as we have seen. A remarkable internal unity can be seen between this list and the previous territorial listings. In most cases, the cities here are found in the listings of their corresponding tribes, and the assignments to the tribes match in both passages. This shows again the care with which this and the other lists were compiled. It also can be related to the book's concern to show that promises were fulfilled and commands executed: here, information from the previous listings is carefully collated into the list.

Despite the remarkable correspondences between this and the earlier lists, however, some cities in this list cannot be correlated with ones in chaps. 13–19, or there appear to be conflicts between the information given here and in the earlier lists. For example, five cities are known only from this list, although in some cases, this may be due to textual corruption (i.e., copyists' errors): Kibzaim (from the tribe of Ephraim: v. 22), Be Eshtarah (from eastern Manasseh: v. 27),[260] Hammoth Dor and Kartan (from Naphtali: v. 32), and

---

[259] J. Peterson, *A Topographical Surface Survey of the Levitical "Cities" of Joshua and 1 Chronicles 6*, Ph.D. dissertation, Chicago Institute of Advanced Theological Studies (Evanston: Seabury-Western, 1977), cited in Hess, *Joshua*, 281, n. 2. See also Kallai's work (*Historical Geography*, 445–76).

[260] This city, however, is probably "Ashtaroth," a city in eastern Manasseh's territory (13:31). The parallel reading in 1 Chr 6:71[Hb. 56] has "Ashtaroth," as does the Syriac version.

Dimnah (from Zebulun: v. 35).[261] Four of the six cities of refuge are only mentioned again in the book in chap. 20, not in the land distribution lists of chaps. 13–19. These include all three cities of refuge east of the Jordan—Golan in Bashan (v. 27), Bezer (v. 36), and Ramoth in Gilead (v. 38)—which occur again in 20:7–8, and Kedesh in Galilee (v. 32), west of the Jordan (20:7). Anathoth and Almon (v. 18) are not mentioned again in Joshua, although they are found elsewhere.

In several cases, cities are listed here as being contributed by one tribe whereas they appear in another tribe's inheritance list earlier. This raises questions about the consistency and accuracy of the lists. However, simple solutions are available for each case. (1) Shechem is listed from Ephraim (v. 21), but it also appears in Manasseh's southern boundary description (17:2,7). This causes no problem, however, because Manasseh's southern boundary was Ephraim's northern one. (2) Gath Rimmon is listed from Dan (v. 24) and from western Manasseh (v. 25); it appears in Dan's city list (19:45). Here, the problem is a textual one. The Old Greek reads "Ibleam" in v. 25, as does the parallel list in 1 Chr 6:70[Hb. 55],[262] and it would appear that a scribe miscopied "Gath Rimmon" (instead of "Ibleam") because of its presence already in v. 24. If the Gath Rimmon in v. 25 is indeed Ibleam, then the problem disappears because Ibleam is attributed to western Manasseh in 17:11. (3) Daberath is listed from Issachar (v. 28), but it appears in Zebulun's boundary list (19:12). Because these two tribes adjoined each other, there is no problem here. (4) Jarmuth is listed from Issachar (v. 29), but a city of the same name appears in Judah's city list (15:35). The solution here is that these were two different cities, as we have seen is the case repeatedly earlier in the lists.[263] Jarmuth is called "Remeth" in Issachar's city list (19:21).[264] (5) En Gannim is listed from Issachar (v. 29), and it does indeed appear in Issachar's city list (19:21), but it also appears in Judah's city list (15:34). Here too the issue is two cities with the same name.[265]

All six of the cities of refuge in chap. 20 were also Levitical cities, and five out of the six are identified as such in chap. 21: Hebron (v. 13), Shechem

---

[261] Here too a textual corruption may be present. The Old Greek has "Rimmon" here, and the parallel reading in 1 Chr 6:77[Hb. 62] is "Rimmono." The ר (r) and ד (d) were easily confused in Hebrew, and "Rimmon" is a likely reading here. Rimmon appears in Zebulun's boundary list (19:13), and this fits with the claim here that "Dimnah" was from Zebulun.

[262] The MT in 1 Chr 6:70[Hb. 55] has "Bileam," but substantial manuscript evidence supports a reading of "Ibleam."

[263] See P. de Miroschedji, "Jarmuth," *ABD* 3:644–46.

[264] The Old Greek has "Remmath" here, confirming this reading. The difference in the Hb. consonantal text is only one consonant plus a vowel letter: ירמות, "Jarmuth," vs. רמת, "Remeth." The parallel passage in 1 Chr 6:73[Hb. 58] has ראמות, "Ramoth," which is also related to the other two.

[265] So also Boling, *Joshua*, 450.

(v. 21), Golan in Bashan (v. 27), Kedesh in Galilee (v. 32), and Ramoth in Gilead (v. 38). The exception is Bezer, which is listed but not mentioned as having been a city of refuge (v. 36).

We should note that some of the cities were not actually in Israel's possession at this time (e.g., Gezer: v. 21), and some appear never to have been for any significant length of time (e.g., the Philistine cities of Elteke and Gibbethon: v. 23). This does not necessarily indicate that these lists must have come from later periods, when Israel did possess most or all of them, or that they were late, idealized projections of what should have been. They just as easily could be reflecting the actual allotments in Joshua's day (although not necessarily the actual possession of lands). This reflects the view so often found in these land distribution chapters, that much land did remain to be possessed, even after it was allotted (13:1; 15:63; 16:10; 17:12–13).

Several overall observations should be taken from this chapter. (1) The nation obeyed the Lord. This is visible in several ways. Verse 3 states that the Israelites obeyed the Lord's command to give cities to the Levites, and the detailed descriptions that follow bear this out. Even the organization of the chapter bears this out. The chapter is extraordinarily precise and well organized, the second lengthiest city list in chaps. 13–21 (the longest being Judah's in chap. 15), and it is precisely drawn and recorded. The nation took great care in making sure the Lord's commands were carried out to the letter. (2) The nation looked after God's servants. The repeated litany that tribe X or Y or Z contributed the next four cities draws all Israel into the support and care for the Levites that was the ideal. The Levites could not live and do their work as God intended unless the tribes supported and provided for them. (3) The nation functioned as a unity. Every tribe contributed something, in almost equal proportions.

(1) Introduction (21:1–3)

¹Now the family heads of the Levites approached Eleazar the priest, Joshua son of Nun, and the heads of the other tribal families of Israel ²at Shiloh in Canaan and said to them, "The LORD commanded through Moses that you give us towns to live in, with pasturelands for our livestock." ³So, as the LORD had commanded, the Israelites gave the Levites the following towns and pasturelands out of their own inheritance:

21:1 Previously, the "heads of the fathers of the tribes" were involved in distributing the land. They are mentioned along with Eleazar the priest and Joshua, son of Nun, as overseeing the allotments (see 14:1 and the commentary there). At the end of the process, they are mentioned again along with Eleazar and Joshua (19:51).

In this passage, they were again involved, this time as those to whom the Levitical leaders came to present their claim to their lands (v. 1). The Levitical leaders were themselves "the heads of the fathers of the Levites," which indicates that the system of organization at the national level (twelve such leaders: see on 14:1) was mirrored at the tribal level as well.

This episode is the last of the five in which individuals or groups came to Joshua to claim their lands.[266] God himself had promised cities to the Levites throughout the territories (Num 35:1–8), and now that all the other tribes had received their allotments, the Levites asked for theirs. As they had been previously, Eleazar and Joshua were prominent in the distribution (see also 14:1; 17:4; 19:51).

21:2 The setting was at Shiloh, the place where the Israelites had gathered previously and from where they had sent out twenty-one surveyors to aid in the remaining land distributions (18:1–10). This was a significant religious center in Joshua's day and remained so for many years (see the commentary on 18:1).

Shiloh is specifically said to be "in the land of Canaan" (NIV has "in Canaan" here), which was certainly an unnecessary bit of information from one perspective, since any reader would have known this. However, the only previous occurrence of this phrase is in 14:1, at the beginning of the land apportionments, and the reference here ties the Levites' inheritance to that of the rest of the tribes. Even though their inheritance was different, in that they only received scattered cities, they still were given an inheritance by God on a par with that of the other tribes (*naḥălâ*: v. 3); they were *all* "in the land of Canaan," just as God had promised to Abraham. This reinforces the notion of the unity of the nation.

The Levites reminded Eleazar, Joshua, and the tribal leaders of God's promise "by the hand of Moses,"[267] which was given in Num 35:1–8. They had been promised forty-eight towns, along with their pasturelands (Num 35:7), and that was what they asked for here. The word for pasturelands *(migrāš)* refers to the grazing lands around the cities. It occurs about 110 times in the Old Testament, almost always in connection with the Levites' inheritance (it occurs ninety-eight times in Joshua 21 and its parallel passage in 1 Chronicles 6).

21:3 In keeping with the themes of harmony, unity, and obedience found in the book, now the Israelites obeyed "the mouth of the LORD" and gave the Levites what God had promised them.

(2) General Overview (21:4–8)

⁴The first lot came out for the Kohathites, clan by clan. The Levites who were descendants of Aaron the priest were allotted thirteen towns from the tribes of

---

[266] The others were Caleb (14:6–15); Acsah (15:18–19); the daughters of Zelophehad (17:3–6); and Joseph (17:14–18). See the excursus "Patterns in the Land Distribution Lists," Section 3, at the end of chap. 13.

[267] On this phrase, see the commentary on 14:5.

Judah, Simeon and Benjamin. ⁵The rest of Kohath's descendants were allotted ten towns from the clans of the tribes of Ephraim, Dan and half of Manasseh.

⁶The descendants of Gershon were allotted thirteen towns from the clans of the tribes of Issachar, Asher, Naphtali and the half-tribe of Manasseh in Bashan.

⁷The descendants of Merari, clan by clan, received twelve towns from the tribes of Reuben, Gad and Zebulun.

⁸So the Israelites allotted to the Levites these towns and their pasturelands, as the LORD had commanded through Moses.

21:4–8 This general overview is followed by a detailed listing of cities in vv. 9–40. In this overview, however, the general contours of the list are set out. We are told, for example, that the distribution was divided among the descendants of the three sons of Levi: Kohath (vv. 4–5), Gershon (v. 6), and Merari (v. 7) (cf. Gen 46:11; Exod 6:16). The Kohathite descendants of Aaron had an allotment (v. 4), while the rest of the Kohathites received a separate allotment (v. 5). Aaron—who was the first high priest and Moses' brother—was descended from Kohath (Exod 6:16–20), and undoubtedly Aaron's special status accounted for this special distribution to his descendants. We also learn that the cities were chosen by the lot. The word "lot" *(gôrāl)* occurs five times in these five verses (vv. 4[2x],5,6,8), showing the importance of this God-directed method of choosing the cities. God was in control of every aspect of the process. The allotments came from all twelve tribes of Israel, indeed, thirteen if the dual apportionments from the tribe of Manasseh are counted twice (vv. 5–6).²⁶⁸ Thirteen of the cities were for the Aaronic Kohathites (v. 4), ten for the other Kohathites (v. 5), thirteen for the Gershonites (v. 6), and twelve for the Merarites (v. 7), for a total of forty-eight cities, which accords with the number promised by God in Num 35:7. Finally, v. 8 echoes v. 3, that the Israelites obeyed, doing just as the Lord had commanded "by the hand of Moses."

(3) The Priestly Kohathites' Inheritance (21:9–19)

⁹From the tribes of Judah and Simeon they allotted the following towns by name ¹⁰(these towns were assigned to the descendants of Aaron who were from the Kohathite clans of the Levites, because the first lot fell to them):

¹¹They gave them Kiriath Arba (that is, Hebron), with its surrounding pastureland, in the hill country of Judah. (Arba was the forefather of Anak.) ¹²But the fields and villages around the city they had given to Caleb son of Jephunneh as his possession.

¹³So to the descendants of Aaron the priest they gave Hebron (a city of refuge for one accused of murder), Libnah, ¹⁴Jattir, Eshtemoa, ¹⁵Holon, Debir, ¹⁶Ain, Juttah and Beth Shemesh, together with their pasturelands—nine towns from

---

²⁶⁸ On the arithmetic problem of counting the number of tribes, see the commentary on 14:3–4.

these two tribes.

[17]**And from the tribe of Benjamin they gave them Gibeon, Geba,** [18]**Anathoth and Almon, together with their pasturelands—four towns.** [19]**All the towns for the priests, the descendants of Aaron, were thirteen, together with their pasturelands.**

21:9–19 The first set of Levitical cities is now listed by name. The priestly branch of the Kohathites, descended through Aaron, received thirteen cities, from Judah, Simeon, and Benjamin (vv. 4,9–19), which left thirty-five cities for the nonpriestly Kohathites and the rest of the Levites. Their inheritance included one city of refuge: Hebron (v. 13).

The Kohathites had the most important duties among the tribe of Levi. They had responsibility for the sanctuary (Num 3:28), specifically, "for the care of the ark, the table, the lampstand, the altars, the articles of the sanctuary used in ministering, the curtain, and everything related to their use" (Num 3:31).

The Kohathites' allotment within Judah is significant since the tribe of Judah was the only one to survive in the centuries ahead, and Jerusalem (with its temple) was in Judah's territory. The Aaronic priests were thus strategically located to serve in the temple, beginning in the days of Solomon and continuing until the fall of Jerusalem, and in territory that remained in the hands of descendants of Judah through the years before and following the Babylonian exile.

(4) The Nonpriestly Kohathites' Inheritance (21:20–26)

[20]**The rest of the Kohathite clans of the Levites were allotted towns from the tribe of Ephraim:**

[21]**In the hill country of Ephraim they were given Shechem (a city of refuge for one accused of murder) and Gezer,** [22]**Kibzaim and Beth Horon, together with their pasturelands—four towns.**

[23]**Also from the tribe of Dan they received Eltekeh, Gibbethon,** [24]**Aijalon and Gath Rimmon, together with their pasturelands—four towns.**

[25]**From half the tribe of Manasseh they received Taanach and Gath Rimmon, together with their pasturelands—two towns.** [26]**All these ten towns and their pasturelands were given to the rest of the Kohathite clans.**

21:20–26 The nonpriestly Levites received thirty-five cities among them. The rest of the Kohathites (i.e., those who were not descended from Aaron) received ten cities, from Ephraim, Dan, and Manasseh (west of the Jordan) (vv. 5,20–26). This included one city of refuge: Shechem (v. 21).

(5) The Gershonites' Inheritance (21:27–33)

[27]**The Levite clans of the Gershonites were given:**
from the half-tribe of Manasseh, Golan in Bashan (a city of refuge for one

accused of murder) and Be Eshtarah, together with their pasturelands—two
towns; [28]from the tribe of Issachar, Kishion, Daberath, [29]Jarmuth and En Gannim, together with their pasturelands—four towns; [30]from the tribe of Asher,
Mishal, Abdon, [31]Helkath and Rehob, together with their pasturelands—four
towns; [32]from the tribe of Naphtali, Kedesh in Galilee (a city of refuge for one
accused of murder), Hammoth Dor and Kartan, together with their pasturelands—three towns. [33]All the towns of the Gershonite clans were thirteen,
together with their pasturelands.

21:27–33 The Gershonites received thirteen cities, from Issachar, Asher,
Naphtali, and Manasseh (east of the Jordan) (vv. 6,27–33). This included two
cities of refuge: Golan in Bashan (v. 27) and Kedesh in Galilee (v. 32).

(6) The Merarites' Inheritance (21:34–40)

[34]The Merarite clans (the rest of the Levites) were given:
from the tribe of Zebulun, Jokneam, Kartah, [35]Dimnah and Nahalal, together
with their pasturelands—four towns; [36]from the tribe of Reuben, Bezer, Jahaz,
[37]Kedemoth and Mephaath, together with their pasturelands—four towns;
[38]from the tribe of Gad, Ramoth in Gilead (a city of refuge for one accused of
murder), Mahanaim, [39]Heshbon and Jazer, together with their pasturelands—
four towns in all. [40]All the towns allotted to the Merarite clans, who were the rest
of the Levites, were twelve.

21:34–40 The Merarites received twelve cities, from Reuben and Gad
(east of the Jordan) and Zebulun (vv. 7,34–40). Their inheritance included two
cities of refuge: Bezer (v. 36; cf. 20:8) and Ramoth in Gilead (v. 38).

(7) Summary (21:41–42)

[41]The towns of the Levites in the territory held by the Israelites were forty-
eight in all, together with their pasturelands. [42]Each of these towns had pasturelands surrounding it; this was true for all these towns.

21:41–42 The Levitical distribution is summarized in the last two verses of
this section (vv. 41–42). The emphasis here is on the exactness of the distributions and the fact that they were scattered throughout Israel. Verse 41 specifies
the forty-eight cities, including the surrounding pasturelands, and it mentions
that the Levitical cities were to be found throughout Israel's territorial holdings
($\bar{?}\check{a}huzzat$). Verse 42 is somewhat obscure,[269] but it focuses on the fact that each
city was properly allotted. Nothing was left out, and nothing was left to chance.
    At the end of v. 42, a substantial addition in the Old Greek text is found.
The first part of it parallels 19:49–50 fairly closely. The table below sets out

---

[269] It reads, lit., "These cities will be—each one and its pasturelands surrounding it—thus for
all of these cities."

the parallel Hebrew and Old Greek texts in such a way as to show the parallels
between the two (author's translation).

Joshua 19:49–50 (Hebrew)	Joshua 19:49–50 (Greek)	Joshua 21:42 (Greek addition)
And they completed dividing the land	And they went over to take possession of the land	And Joshua completed dividing the land
according to its boundaries,	according to their boundary,	into their boundaries,
and the sons of Israel gave an inheritance to Joshua son of Nun in their midst	and the sons of Israel gave an allotment [Gk. *klēros*] to Joshua son of Nun among them,	and the sons of Israel gave a portion [Gk. *merida*] to Joshua,
according to the commandment [lit., "mouth"] of the LORD,	because of *[dià]* the commandment of God.	according to *[katà]* the commandment of the Lord.
they gave to him the city which he requested,	And they gave to him the city which he requested,	They gave to him the city which he requested.
Timnath Serah, in the hill country of Ephraim,	Timnath Serah,[a] which is in Mount Ephraim [or, "the hill country of Ephraim"].	Timnath Serah they gave to him in Mount Ephraim [or, "the hill country of Ephraim"].
and he built the city and he dwelt in it.	And he built the city and he dwelt in it.	And Joshua built the city, and he dwelt in it. And Joshua took the knives of stone with which he circumcised the sons of Israel who were born on the way in the desert, and he put them in Timnath Serah.

a. Greek θαμνασαραχ (*thamnasarach*).

The Greek of 19:49–50 follows the Hebrew there faithfully, but the addition in
21:42 has no parallel in any extant Hebrew manuscript.

Furthermore, the Greek addition in 21:42 tells us that Joshua stored the
flint knives in his hometown, the ones with which he had circumcised the Israelites earlier (see 5:2–3). This too is unknown from elsewhere, but it anticipates another addition in the Old Greek text at 24:30, which states that Joshua
was buried with these flint knives (see the commentary on 24:30). It is difficult to imagine the Greek translators creating this addition on their own
authority, so the Hebrew manuscript tradition with which they were working

probably had this addition in it. Whether this accurately reflects the *original* text of Joshua, however, is difficult to know. The duplication of most of 19:49–50 in 21:42 makes it more likely that this addition was not original, despite the independent material about the knives at the end. It seems likely that the entire section was added at once because the material about the knives is linked with the material about Joshua's allotment. By itself, the material about the knives is very unlikely to have been added directly to 21:42 of the Hebrew text. Thus, we conclude that the entire addition in Greek was secondary, not original, despite its fascinating contents.

11. The Land Distributions Concluded (21:43–45)

[43]So the LORD gave Israel all the land he had sworn to give their forefathers, and they took possession of it and settled there. [44]The LORD gave them rest on every side, just as he had sworn to their forefathers. Not one of their enemies withstood them; the LORD handed all their enemies over to them. [45]Not one of all the LORD's good promises to the house of Israel failed; every one was fulfilled.

A glorious spiritual summary concludes the entire section devoted to the land distributions (chaps. 13–21). Davis calls it "the theological heart of the Book of Joshua."[270] Several significant themes from earlier in the book are reiterated here (esp. from chap. 1). It is a fittingly triumphant ending to the third major section of the book, the heart of the book in terms of the real-world lands, borders, allotments, cities, et cetera, that the Israelites inherited. Everything God had promised his people for centuries had now been meticulously delineated and allotted, with scrupulous attention to detail and fairness.

Structurally, it has been noted that this short passage summarizes everything that precedes. Verse 43 (which speaks of the land in which Israel settled) summarizes chaps. 13–21. Verse 44 (which speaks of the conflicts with Israel's enemies) summarizes chaps. 1–12. Verse 45 summarizes everything that precedes.[271] In terms of its content, Davis has well noted that this short section consists of *praise* to God. It is not just dispassionate reporting; rather, it praises him for his complete fidelity to his promises. Our awesome and reliable God is described in these verses.[272]

These verses emphasize the totality of Israel's success, the overarching picture of complete victory, and the all-encompassing nature of God's faithfulness to his promises and his people. It is of a piece with similar passages, such as 10:40–42; 11:16–23; and 23:1. It does not echo the passages that

---

[270] Davis, *No Falling Words,* 157.

[271] So K. Gutbrod, *Das Buch vom Landes Gottes,* Die Botschaft des Alten Testament, 3d ed. (Stuttgart: Calwer, 1965), 137, cited by Davis, *No Falling Words,* 157.

[272] Davis, *No Falling Words,* 158–60.

stand in tension with it, which speaks of unfinished business, of lands that remained to be captured. Yet on its own terms, it does present an accurate picture of the prevailing situation at the time.[273]

21:43 The Lord's *gift* of the land is stressed here, as it had been from the beginning (1:3). His *promises* are also stressed (cf. 1:6), as is the people's *inheritance* (see on 1:11). In a new emphasis, their settlement in the land is also highlighted.

21:44 *Rest* for the land is highlighted again (see also 11:23). The enemies' inability to withstand Israel echoes God's promise in 1:5. The Lord's handing over of all the Israelites' enemies echoes God's promise of his presence wherever Joshua went (1:5,9), as well as repeated statements about God fighting for Israel throughout the second major section of the book (see 6:2; 8:1,7; 10:10–11,14,19,42; 11:8; etc.).

21:45 The final, sweeping affirmation is that everything that God had promised Israel came to pass; none of his promises failed. This is certainly a fitting note on which to end this extraordinary section of the book.

JOSHUA 13–21: THEOLOGICAL REFLECTIONS

Chapters 13–21 stand as a very real counterpart to chaps. 6–12, and together these two sections form the heart of the Book of Joshua. Whereas chaps. 6–12 tell of the taking of the land, chaps. 13–21 tell of the distributing of that land. Once the land had been taken and its peoples defeated, then it remained to clarify which groups in Israel would receive which territories. These chapters are lengthy and detailed, and, considered as a whole, they form a massive center of gravity for the book.

The very massiveness of this material indicates its importance. God's promise of the land to Abraham was an important part of the covenant with

---

[273] See further the commentary on 10:40–43 for an extended discussion of this tension. R. Polzin paints a much different picture here. He sees an irreconcilable tension between the overarching, generalizing summary that emphasizes God's good graces in giving his people the land (21:43–45) and the more "realistic" picture in which much land remained to be taken (13:1). He states that "there is absolutely no way that the reader can extricate himself from the overwhelmingly negative reaction produced by the reading of 21:43–45; everything that the narrator has previously placed before his eyes causes him to recoil from the ideological position underlying the phraseology of these concluding verses of the second section of Joshua. ... We have no clearer example in Joshua of the explicit formulation of an ideological point of view which must be immediately and categorically denied by the reader if he chooses to continue to read and accept the basic ideological position of the text before him. ... [I]f one is to understand and accept the ideology that controls all of 13:1–21:40, the ideology that supports the phraseology of 21:43–45 must be categorically rejected" (*Moses and the Deuteronomist: A Literary Study of the Deuteronomistic History*, Part One: *Deuteronomy, Joshua, Judges* [Bloomington: Indiana University Press, 1980], 132). His judgment is overly and unnecessarily harsh, however. See Nelson, *Joshua*, 242–43, for a much more moderate assessment; see also the discussion at 10:40–43.

him and his descendants, and so much of the Pentateuch consistently points toward Israel's inheritance of the land and gives instructions for how to live in it. It therefore should not surprise us that when the time finally arrives that Israel entered into possession of the land, the Book of Joshua lingers over and savors this wonderful fulfillment. Israel's possession of the land is looked at from several perspectives in the Book of Joshua, including the military encounters that made it possible in the first place (chaps. 6–12), as well as the detailed "legal" descriptions of the borders and cities in the land (chaps. 13–21).

These chapters show us that Yahweh was a promise-keeping God. In general, the detailed listings fulfill his land promises to give the land that he had repeated so many times previously. More specifically, chap. 13 reviews the lands that the Transjordan tribes inherited. They had already been given to these tribes (Numbers 32), but chap. 13 shows that what God had promised, he would deliver. Also, the setting aside of the cities of refuge and the Levitical cities fulfilled God's instructions in the Pentateuch concerning these (Exod 21:12–14; Numbers 35). Furthermore, the individual inheritances of Caleb (14:6–15; 15:13–19) and the daughters of Zelophehad (17:3–6) fulfilled specific promises to each of them (Num 14:24 and Deut 1:36 for Caleb; Num 27:1–11 for the daughters of Zelophehad). In addition, the statements about the people and the land having rest (14:15; 21:44) fulfilled promises about this also (see Deut 12:10; 25:19). Likewise, none of Israel's enemies was able to withstand them (Josh 21:44), just as God had promised (1:5). In sum, "Not one of all the LORD's good promises to the house of Israel failed; every one was fulfilled" (21:45).

The lists in these chapters also emphasize the unity of the nation. Every tribe, no matter how large or small, received its duly-appointed portion, and each portion is described in some detail. Every tribe was considered part of the nation, even Levi, so no tribe could claim to have been left out. Indeed, in the case of Levi, the fact that each tribe contributed roughly four cities apiece shows the nation coming together in a gesture of national unity as well.

The careful tracing of almost every boundary line and the detailed listings of city after city in the various tribal territories show the importance of land inheritance and ownership. The way in which the boundary lines "move" from one geographic feature to another shows an intimate knowledge of the land and a love for it. Further evidence of this care is that several joint boundaries (such as Judah's and Benjamin's, or Benjamin's and Ephraim's) are described in two places and that the descriptions match so closely.

The detail and care employed in these chapters shows that all of the tribes—indeed, even individuals—were important in God's estimation. None was too small or insignificant to be included. The attention to the individual inheritances of Caleb, the daughters of Zelophehad, and Joshua also shows this. At the same time, the lists realistically show which were the most important tribes. Judah, the most important, is devoted the most space, and its boundary descriptions and city lists are the most detailed (chaps. 14–15). Ephraim and Manasseh, the most important tribes of the later Northern Kingdom, also receive a significant amount of space (chaps. 16–17). And Levi, the tribe of the priests and their helpers, also figures prominently (chap. 21).

Concern for justice is a hallmark of these chapters. This can be seen in the simple fact that every tribe received its due inheritance. It can also be seen in the distributions to individuals. The story of the daughters of Zelophehad's inheritance shows this particularly well (17:3–6). Justice is the major backdrop for the designation of cities of refuge, where those who unintentionally had killed could flee (chap. 20). It even is visible in the assignment of the Levitical cities (chap. 21) because this tribe was landless otherwise.

The fact that God was the giver of the land is certainly a part of these chapters. He is specifically stated to have given Israel the land in 18:3 and 21:43. In addition, he controlled the lots that were cast (see especially 14:2; 18:6,8,10; 19:51). Furthermore, Joshua and Eleazar acted on his behalf in distributing the lands (14:1; 19:51).

Religious concerns play a significant part in these chapters. Not only is Joshua, the nation's leader, involved in the land distributions, but so too is Eleazar, the high priest. His presence shows that there was a religious component to what was being done. Furthermore, the assembly in 18:1–10 at Shiloh, where the Tent of Meeting was, also shows that this was a religious exercise. The lots were cast there in God's presence (18:6,8,10). And the setting aside of Levitical cities (chap. 21) shows the importance of God's special servants in charge of religious matters as well as the special notices about the meaning of the Levites' inheritance (13:14,33; 18:7).

Alongside the major themes of harmony, obedience, and completeness of the distributions, a minor note of discord is sounded, however, in two ways. First, despite the thoroughness of the previous victories, much land remained to be taken (13:2–6). Second, several tribes failed to drive out the Canaanite inhabitants of lands or cities that they were assigned. These included Judah (15:63), Ephraim (16:10), western Manasseh (17:11–12), and Dan (19:47). Thus, the seed was planted for much trouble in the years following. (For more on this see the "Theological Reflections" on chaps. 22–24.)

IV. FAREWELLS (22:1–24:33)
1. Joshua's Farewell to the Transjordan Tribes (22:1–8)
    (1) Joshua's Exhortation (22:1–5)
    (2) Joshua's Blessing (22:6–8)
2. A Crisis of Loyalties (22:9–34)
    (1) The Crisis Develops (22:9–12)
    (2) The Accusation (22:13–20)
    (3) The Defense (22:21–29)
    (4) The Crisis Resolved (22:30–34)
3. Joshua's First Farewell to All Israel (23:1–16)
    (1) Introduction (23:1–2)
    (2) Exhortations and Admonitions: Part One (23:3–8)
    (3) Exhortations and Admonitions: Part Two (23:9–13)
    (4) Admonitions (23:14–16)
4. Joshua's Second Farewell to All Israel (24:1–28)
    (1) Introduction and Review of the Past (24:1–13)
    (2) Covenant Affirmations (24:14–24)
    (3) Sealing the Covenant (24:25–28)
5. Conclusion: Burial Notices (24:29–33)
    (1) Joshua's Burial (24:29–31)
    (2) Joseph's Burial (24:32)
    (3) Eleazar's Burial (24:33)

IV. FAREWELLS (22:1–24:33)

The final three chapters all deal with farewells of sorts: (1) Joshua bade farewell to the Transjordan tribes, dismissing them to their inheritances east of the Jordan (chap. 22); (2) he bade farewell to the entire nation in a speech urging them to follow the Lord (chap. 23); and (3) he again bade farewell to the nation and led them in a covenant renewal ceremony, at a different place and with different emphases (chap. 24). Even the final section of the book, where three short burial notices are found, is, in effect, the author's farewell to his readers, assuring them that everything had been completed faithfully and in order (24:29–33).

Joshua's leadership role in the final three events is clear: in three separate addresses, he blessed the people, urged them to follow the Lord, warned of the consequences of disobedience, reviewed the Lord's faithfulness to them, and challenged them to follow him in reaffirming their covenant with their God. As a result, when Joshua is mentioned for the last time in the book, the author bestows on him the coveted title, heretofore held only by Moses, of "the servant of the LORD." The question raised at the beginning of the book (see commentary on 1:1) about Joshua's fitness to be Moses' successor is answered in a definitive way: he was worthy of the same title that attached to Moses, that is, both were servants of the Lord.

All three chapters look toward the future as well as the past. After Joshua praised the Transjordan tribes for their faithfulness, a misunderstanding arose concerning the tribes' relationship with each other, one that was important to resolve in order for future relationships to be clear. The focus of chap. 22 deals in large measure with the issue of the tribes' loyalties to each other and, more importantly, to the Lord. This harks back not only to the loyalties that Joshua urged at the beginning of the book (1:12–15), but it also anticipates the importance of loyalty in the years to come (22:21–29). Chapter 23 looks ahead to Israel's life in the land, stressing not only how God had fought for the nation and given it the land, but how it was now to live in the land. Chapter 24 focuses on the past to a much greater degree than chap. 23, but it also stresses Israel's obligations to its God and the covenant that bound it to him.

We do not find any new initiatives on God's part in these chapters, undoubtedly because his promises were now all fulfilled (see 21:43–45).[1] The focus now is on the people's loyalty, obedience, and service to him.

1. Joshua's Farewell to the Transjordan Tribes (22:1–8)

After all that had transpired and all that the nation had gone through together, the time had now come for the tribes to return to their inheritances and begin their settled lives in the land. The tribes whose inheritances were east of the Jordan had been faithful in their commitment to God and to their word, in that they had helped their brothers take their lands, even while their own lands had been, in effect, waiting for them. The episode here echoes and fulfills Joshua's earlier exhortation to these tribes to be faithful to God and to their fellow Israelites (see 1:12–15 and the commentary there). It also echoes these tribes' response to Joshua's exhortation (1:16–18).

---

[1] H. J. Koorevaar has analyzed the book's overall structure in terms of God's initiatives: (1) that the Israelites should cross the Jordan (1:1–9); (2) that they should take Jericho and the land (5:13–6:5); (3) that they should divide Canaan (13:1–7); and (4) that they should designate cities of refuge (20:1–6). The last section of the book is dominated by three initiatives of Joshua (22:1; 23:1–2; 24:1), not God, because God's promises had now been fulfilled. See the summary of Koorevaar's analysis in J. R. Vannoy, "Joshua: Theology of," *NIDOTTE* 4:811–14; the original work is H. J. Koorevaar, *De Opbouw van het Boek Jozua* (Ph.D. dissertation, University of Brussels, 1990).

(1) Joshua's Exhortation (22:1–5)

¹**Then Joshua summoned the Reubenites, the Gadites and the half-tribe of Manasseh ²and said to them, "You have done all that Moses the servant of the LORD commanded, and you have obeyed me in everything I commanded. ³For a long time now—to this very day—you have not deserted your brothers but have carried out the mission the LORD your God gave you. ⁴Now that the LORD your God has given your brothers rest as he promised, return to your homes in the land that Moses the servant of the LORD gave you on the other side of the Jordan. ⁵But be very careful to keep the commandment and the law that Moses the servant of the LORD gave you: to love the LORD your God, to walk in all his ways, to obey his commands, to hold fast to him and to serve him with all your heart and all your soul."**

22:1 The time frame for the action now is not specified. The NIV's "Then" is *ʾāz,* which means "at that time," but it does not give any specific indication about the time relationship between events in chap. 22 and those in the preceding chapters.[2] The reference in this verse to the two and one-half Transjordan tribes follows up on the references to them in chap. 13, where their land inheritance is mentioned.

22:2–3 Joshua commended these tribes for their faithfulness to what Moses, Joshua, and God himself had commanded them: they were not to settle into their lands until the entire land of Canaan had been taken (see commentary on 1:12–15 for the background to this passage). The tribes' obedience is stressed here: they did everything that Moses had commanded, they obeyed what Joshua had commanded, and they kept the charge[3] that God had given them.

The length of time that the Transjordan tribes had deferred their own settling down was "a long time now" (v. 3).[4] No specific indication of the length of time is given, but this reference combines with the similar reference in 11:18—"Joshua waged war against these kings for a long time"—to indicate that the taking of the land was not done in a single, short campaign, contrary to the impression sometimes given by the battle summaries in chaps. 10–11.

22:4–5 God too had been faithful to his promises: he had given rest to the tribes west of the Jordan (v. 4).[5] Joshua instructed the Transjordan tribes to return home and settle there (v. 4) and also that they should take special care to remain obedient to the Lord (v. 5).

Joshua's words in v. 5 are passionate, and they capture the heart of the chap-

---

[2] On this function of אָז see the commentary on 10:12 and the footnote there.

[3] The NIV has "carried out the mission" for this expression.

[4] The NIV's "now" translates זֶה, which usually means "this, that." However, here it functions as a demonstrative adverb, meaning "now." See *GBH* § 143a.

[5] On the concept of "rest," see the Introduction, and the commentary at 11:23 and 21:44.

ter's message about faithfulness and loyalty. The words echo similar exhortations in Deuteronomy (Deut 4:29; 6:5–6; 10:12,13; 11:13) and in Joshua (1:7–8; see commentary there) that the Israelites should be faithful to God. What God had urged Joshua himself to do in chap. 1, Joshua now urged the people to do. This exhortation is the essence of the "first and greatest commandment," to love God passionately, with every fiber of one's being (Deut 6:5; Matt 22:37–38). The verbs in v. 5 give a comprehensive picture of what a proper relationship to God was to include: to love God, to walk in all his ways, to obey his commands, to hold fast (or cling) to him, and to serve him. These were to be done not as a matter of external conformity but "with all your heart and all your soul."

(2) Joshua's Blessing (22:6–8)

⁶Then Joshua blessed them and sent them away, and they went to their homes. ⁷(To the half-tribe of Manasseh Moses had given land in Bashan, and to the other half of the tribe Joshua gave land on the west side of the Jordan with their brothers.) When Joshua sent them home, he blessed them, ⁸saying, "Return to your homes with your great wealth—with large herds of livestock, with silver, gold, bronze and iron, and a great quantity of clothing—and divide with your brothers the plunder from your enemies."

22:6–8 Joshua's blessing was of the nature of a parting farewell, as is seen in several other places in the Old Testament: see Gen 31:55[Hb. 32:1]; 47:10; 2 Sam 13:25; 19:39[Hb. 40].[6]

The farewell blessing is interrupted in v. 7 by the author's parenthetical explanation of the unique situation of the tribe of Manasseh, which had two land portions, one on each side of the Jordan (cf. 13:29–31; 17:1–13). Both Moses and Joshua are acknowledged as distributors of the land here. The insertion undoubtedly was for the purpose of stressing the unity of this tribe, which symbolized within its own tribal context the larger unity that was to characterize the entire nation. This unity was strained by the events narrated in the following verses, but ultimately the unity was preserved, and the Transjordan tribes' loyalty to their brethren and their God was established beyond any doubt.

In v. 8, the great wealth[7] that the Israelites had gathered from the Canaanites is elaborated, with the livestock, precious metals, and clothing that they had taken. The Transjordan tribes were to divide up the spoils with their brethren in

---

[6] See T. C. Butler, *Joshua,* WBC 7 (Waco: Word, 1983), 245.

[7] The word for "wealth," נְכָסִים, is relatively rare, occurring only here and in 2 Chr 1:11–12; Eccl 5:19[Hb. 18]; 6:2. It is only plural and means "riches, treasures, wealth" (BDB, 647; *HALOT,* 699 [*HALOT* mistakenly has "Isa 22:8" for "Jos 22:8"]).

another display of unity and loyalty.[8] An earlier such dividing up of the spoils was when Moses instructed the Israelites to do so after their battle with the Midianites: "Divide the spoils between the soldiers who took part in the battle and the rest of the community" (Num 31:27; cf. also 1 Sam 30:21–25, where David gave similar instructions to his own fighting men).

2. A Crisis of Loyalties (22:9–34)

The Israelites' unity as a nation was immediately threatened when the Transjordan tribes left to return to their homes east of the Jordan. Ironically, it was a gesture on their part—which they intended as a symbol of unity—that precipitated the crisis that almost tore the nation apart. However, when their true intentions were revealed to have been honorable, and not rebellious, the crisis was resolved, and the Israelites on both sides of the river settled in their own lands.

(1) The Crisis Develops (22:9–12)

[9]So the Reubenites, the Gadites and the half-tribe of Manasseh left the Israelites at Shiloh in Canaan to return to Gilead, their own land, which they had acquired in accordance with the command of the LORD through Moses.

[10]When they came to Geliloth near the Jordan in the land of Canaan, the Reubenites, the Gadites and the half-tribe of Manasseh built an imposing altar there by the Jordan. [11]And when the Israelites heard that they had built the altar on the border of Canaan at Geliloth near the Jordan on the Israelite side, [12]the whole assembly of Israel gathered at Shiloh to go to war against them.

This section sets the stage for the crisis in bare outline. Several critical details that explain the crisis do not emerge until later. We do not know, for example, the reason that the Transjordan tribes built their altar (v. 11). We are not told what was wrong with this and why the rest of the Israelites gathered for war against them (v. 12). However, something clearly was wrong.

22:9–10 The Transjordan tribes left their fellow Israelites at Shiloh, where the climactic gathering had been held and the final land distributions had been made (see 18:1), to return to their own lands. The references in v. 9 to "Shiloh in Canaan" and "Gilead, their own land" emphasize the fact that the two portions of Israel were going to different places, one portion remaining in Canaan proper and the other leaving, to go to a land (Gilead) that was not, strictly speaking, in Canaan. This anticipates the problem of a divided nation

---

[8] The NIV's "Return to your homes ... and divide with your brothers" should not be taken to mean that the dividing was to be done after the Transjordan tribes had returned home. These were two parallel instructions, indicated by the lack of any conjunction joining the two imperatival clauses (i.e., NIV has added "and" where there is no such word in Hebrew).

that is addressed in the remainder of this chapter.

The tribes arrived at Geliloth, near the Jordan, which appears to have been the site of Gilgal, the place where they had first entered the land and set up a pillar of memorial stones and circumcised the nation (4:19–20; 5:9–10).[9] At this place significant in the nation's history, the Transjordan tribes built a large altar.[10] Its imposing size, visible from afar, explains the significance of this altar west of the Jordan. In the first place, its erection west of the Jordan by the tribes living east of the Jordan emphasized something the Transjordan tribes wanted to affirm: the nation's unity and their own loyalty to the God who gave Canaan to his people. However, for a people living east of the Jordan, its position across the river could potentially have caused it to have been forgotten. Thus, its imposing size would have allowed it to be seen from vantage points across the river and thus remembered.

22:11–12 Verse 11 is somewhat awkward syntactically, but it reports in direct speech the Israelite tribes' surprised reaction to the altar's presence (lit.): "And the Israelites heard, saying, 'Look! [The Transjordan tribes] have built the altar opposite (or, at the border of)[11] the land of Canaan! At Geliloth of the Jordan! At the side of the sons of Israel!' "[12] Three times the location of the altar is mentioned. Clearly the altar was west of the Jordan, which was not in territory allotted to the Transjordan tribes. That is, they had built a large altar in land belonging to Judah or Benjamin (15:7; 18:17), not their own land east of the Jordan.

The tribes west of the Jordan (the Cisjordan tribes) reacted strongly to this altar by assembling to go to war (v. 12). As we have noted, the reason for their reaction is not revealed until later (vv. 16–20), as is the motivation for the Transjordan tribes' having built the altar in the first place (vv. 21–29). The basis for the Cisjordan tribes' reaction is found in the law against offering a burnt offering or sacrifice at any location other than the tabernacle (Lev 17:8–9) and in the more general law in Deut 13:12–15 against worshiping other gods. In both instances, the Israelites were authorized to kill the offenders, and this was why they now prepared to go to war against their fellow Israelites.

It is striking to notice one of the terms used for the Cisjordan tribes here. Even though they were only nine and one-half tribes, they are called by an

---

[9] The word "Geliloth" means "districts," and the NASB, NJPSV, NRSV all render it here as "region" rather than a proper name. See the discussion at 18:17.

[10] The Hebrew here has "large altar for/of appearance." The NIV has "imposing altar"; the NASB, "a large altar in appearance"; and NJPSV, "a great conspicuous altar."

[11] The word here is מוּל, which means "front," or "opposite," particularly when preceded by אֶל, as here. Cf. the commentary on 9:1. The Old Greek has "border" here, which would reflect Hebrew גְּבוּל.

[12] The NIV's rendering loses the tone of surprise and urgency conveyed by the direct speech and by the awkward syntax.

inclusive term in v. 12: "the whole assembly of Israel" (see also v. 16, and "the whole community of Israel" vv. 18,20). The two and one-half Transjordan tribes are clearly not included in this designation, that is, they were not considered to be part of the Israelite assembly, at least at this point. A survey of the rest of the chapter reveals that the narrator and the speakers consistently maintain such a distinction until the misunderstanding about the altar has been explained in a satisfactory manner (by v. 30). Beginning with v. 30, there is no reference again to such all-inclusive terms as "all Israel"[13] or "the whole community," only to the more general terms, "the Israelites" or "the community."

The significance of these careful distinctions is that the story is being presented in order to highlight two facts about the altar: (1) the grave danger posed by its existence and (2) its potential for irreparably dividing the nation. The Cisjordan tribes had already inherited their lands in Canaan proper, which was where Abraham had been promised his lands (Gen 17:8). The Transjordan tribes' inheritance lay outside of Canaan, so if they were to be considered truly a continuing part of Israel, they needed to demonstrate this clearly. Their building of an altar—which the Cisjordan tribes interpreted as being a rival altar to the one at the tabernacle, one devoted to sacrifices to false gods—threatened their place as true Israelites. The author, by carefully labeling the tribes in this chapter, preserves a distinction between the tribes until the altar's true nature and intent has been made clear: the Cisjordan tribes were "true" Israelites, living in the land promised to Abraham, whereas the Transjordan tribes, living outside the land, were not yet to be included with "all Israel" until the nature of their commitment to the Lord was clarified. After the clarification, however (i.e., after v. 29), all twelve tribes are treated as part of the one nation, Israel. Thus, the issues of the unity of the nation and the tribes' loyalties are reflected even in the way in which the narrator labels the tribes.[14]

(2) The Accusation (22:13–20)

[13]So the Israelites sent Phinehas son of Eleazar, the priest, to the land of Gilead—to Reuben, Gad and the half-tribe of Manasseh. [14]With him they sent ten of the chief men, one for each of the tribes of Israel, each the head of a family division among the Israelite clans.

[15]When they went to Gilead—to Reuben, Gad and the half-tribe of Manasseh—they said to them: [16]"The whole assembly of the LORD says: 'How could you break faith with the God of Israel like this? How could you turn away from the LORD and build yourselves an altar in rebellion against him now? [17]Was not the sin of Peor enough for us? Up to this very day we have not cleansed ourselves from that sin, even though a plague fell on the community of the LORD!

---

[13] The NIV renders כֹּל, "all," as "whole."

[14] These insights are noted in a trenchant discussion by R. Polzin, *Moses and the Deuteronomist* (Bloomington: Indiana University Press, 1980), 135–37.

[18]And are you now turning away from the LORD?

"'If you rebel against the LORD today, tomorrow he will be angry with the whole community of Israel. [19]If the land you possess is defiled, come over to the LORD's land, where the LORD's tabernacle stands, and share the land with us. But do not rebel against the LORD or against us by building an altar for yourselves, other than the altar of the LORD our God. [20]When Achan son of Zerah acted unfaithfully regarding the devoted things, did not wrath come upon the whole community of Israel? He was not the only one who died for his sin.'"

The Cisjordan tribes confronted their fellow Israelites across the Jordan, raising the specter of terrible punishment on the entire nation resulting from what they regarded as their fellows' sin. They pointed to two cases: the Israelites' sin at Peor in the wilderness (Numbers 25) and, more immediately, Achan's sin at Jericho (Joshua 7). As we have noted, the backdrop for their reaction is found in the laws against offering a burnt offering or sacrifice at any location other than the tabernacle (Lev 17:8–9) and against worshiping other gods (Deut 13:12–15).

22:13–14 These verses reflect the emphasis on unity from another vantage point: they show ten carefully chosen representatives, leaders of the nine and one half (i.e., ten) tribes west of the Jordan. The representatives were each heads of family divisions—literally, "head of the house of their fathers" *(rôʾš bêt ʾăbôtām)*—within the Israelite clans *(ʾălāpîm)*, each representing a tribe *(maṭṭēh)*.[15]

The presence of Phinehas, the priest, shows the emphasis on true (i.e., correct) ritual. It especially recalls his own actions in the incident at Peor, when he had taken drastic measures to stop a plague that had broken out because of Israel's disobedience (Numbers 25, esp. vv. 7–13). That incident is specifically recalled in v. 17. Thus, the seriousness of the potential problem is underscored by Phinehas's role and by the reference to the Peor incident. Joshua is not mentioned in this chapter after v. 7. Rather, Phinehas and the Cisjordan tribes are the characters who raised their concerns about all Israelites remaining loyal to God. Perhaps Phinehas's priestly role is emphasized because the laws forming the backdrop to the incident here are given in the Pentateuchal legislation falling under the priest's concerns (Lev 17:8–9; Deut 13:12–15) and because of Phinehas's earlier role at Peor.

22:15–20 Phinehas and the ten representatives crossed the Jordan themselves into Gilead in order to confront their fellow Israelites with what they saw as a great offense (v. 15). These representatives are called "the whole assembly of the LORD," that is, they stood as representatives of the entire godly portion of the nation. At this juncture, the faithfulness of the Transjordan tribes is still

---

[15] These represented the three basic social units within Israelite society. Similar societal divisions are noted in 7:14–18, although the terms there are slightly different. See the commentary on 7:14 and footnote there, as well as Butler, *Joshua,* 246.

in doubt. (On the significance of such labels, see the comments on vv. 11–12.)

The seriousness with which the Cisjordanian delegation regarded the Transjordan tribes' action in building the altar is seen in the term they used for it *(mᶜl)*, found twice here in v. 16 (as a verb, "break faith," and as a noun, "rebellion"). It is the same term used of Achan's sin in v. 20 ("acted unfaithfully") and in 7:1 (see the commentary on 7:1 for further discussion of *mᶜl*). They understood the altar to have been a major breach in relationship with the Lord. They equated the offense of this altar not only with Achan's sin, but also with the sin committed at Peor.[16] The sin at Peor had occurred many years earlier in the wilderness. It had involved the Israelites' prostituting themselves by bowing to the Moabite gods—specifically, the Baal of Peor—seduced by the women of Moab to do so. A plague had broken out in the Israelite camp as an expression of the Lord's displeasure, and twenty-four thousand people had died before Phinehas had intervened and caused the Lord's anger to abate (Num 25:6–9).

The Cisjordan tribes' fear was that such a horror could happen again. Indeed, they claimed that the stain of this sin remained with them "up to this very day," that the plague was still (lit.) "in" (*b-*) the congregation (v. 17).[17] The plague itself was not still raging because Num 25:8 states that it had stopped.[18] Nevertheless, its effects were still being felt in a very real way. The implication is that Israel had never truly rid itself of this sin, that it always flirted with—if not participated in—idolatry and the allure of pagan religious systems. Achan's case was proof positive of this, and the Cisjordan tribes feared that this altar represented another such case.

The Cisjordan representatives did not ask a question (as the NIV suggests in v. 18), but rather they pointed an accusing finger (verbally) at their fellow tribes and accused them of having turned back from following after the Lord.[19] They also stated their belief in a domino effect of sorts: their rebellion would result in the Lord's anger against the rest of the nation (just as had happened with the case of Achan: see v. 20).[20] The stain of sin was infectious, and its effects were catching.

---

[16] The place is called "Baal Peor" in Deut 4:3 and Hos 9:10.

[17] The NIV's "even though a plague fell on the community of the LORD" is unnecessarily interpretive here and implies a contrast that is not truly present in Hebrew. The Hebrew simply states "And the plague was in the congregation of the LORD." If anything, the conjunction *wāw* here should be read as "because," not "even though." That is, the effects were still being felt many years later because the plague was within the congregation.

[18] Also, if such a plague that killed twenty-four thousand in the wilderness were literally still raging, certainly intervening texts in Numbers, Deuteronomy, and/or Joshua would have mentioned it.

[19] The pleonastic (i.e., redundant) אַתֶּם, "you (plural)," adds to the accusatory tone.

[20] The NIV's condition expressed here—"If you rebel"—is justified grammatically despite the absence of a conditional word (אִם); see BDB, 225: "The arrangement is peculiar, and the condit. is expressed without אִם."

Following their accusations, the Cisjordan representatives urged their Transjordanian brothers to take drastic action (v. 19), to abandon their inheritance east of the Jordan and settle west of the river if the land of their possession was unclean (NIV: "defiled"). The tabernacle resided there, symbolizing God's presence and standing as the fulfillment of God's instructions about setting his name in the place where he would choose (see Deuteronomy 12 and the commentary introducing 18:1–10). From their perspective, it was better that the Transjordan tribes abandon their possession and pursue true worship than to keep their land and engage in apostasy. The "land of *your* possession" east of the Jordan is contrasted with "the land of *the LORD's* possession" west of the Jordan in this verse. Implied is the idea that perhaps the land east of the Jordan was not actually to be considered the Lord's possession, certainly not so if its Israelite inhabitants were to succumb to pagan worship. In the same sense in which Achan "made himself a Canaanite" by his actions (see the comments introducing 7:1–26), so also here the question arises: Were the Transjordan tribes truly Israelites, or were they becoming Canaanites? The crucial difference from Achan, however (as we learn in the next section), was that the Transjordan tribes were not guilty at all of what they were accused of.

A certain self-interest reveals itself in the Cisjordan tribes' comments in that they feared for their own lives (v. 20). They feared that their fellow Israelites' "sin" would result in the entire nation's being punished, just as it had in Achan's case.

(3) The Defense (22:21–29)

[21] Then Reuben, Gad and the half-tribe of Manasseh replied to the heads of the clans of Israel: [22]"The Mighty One, God, the LORD! The Mighty One, God, the LORD! He knows! And let Israel know! If this has been in rebellion or disobedience to the LORD, do not spare us this day. [23]If we have built our own altar to turn away from the LORD and to offer burnt offerings and grain offerings, or to sacrifice fellowship offerings on it, may the LORD himself call us to account.

[24]"No! We did it for fear that some day your descendants might say to ours, 'What do you have to do with the LORD, the God of Israel? [25]The LORD has made the Jordan a boundary between us and you—you Reubenites and Gadites! You have no share in the LORD.' So your descendants might cause ours to stop fearing the LORD.

[26]"That is why we said, 'Let us get ready and build an altar—but not for burnt offerings or sacrifices.' [27]On the contrary, it is to be a witness between us and you and the generations that follow, that we will worship the LORD at his sanctuary with our burnt offerings, sacrifices and fellowship offerings. Then in the future your descendants will not be able to say to ours, 'You have no share in the LORD.'

[28]"And we said, 'If they ever say this to us, or to our descendants, we will answer: Look at the replica of the LORD's altar, which our fathers built, not for burnt offerings and sacrifices, but as a witness between us and you.'

[29]"Far be it from us to rebel against the LORD and turn away from him today by building an altar for burnt offerings, grain offerings and sacrifices, other than the altar of the LORD our God that stands before his tabernacle."

The Transjordan tribes responded passionately that they were innocent of any rebellion or breach of faith. The entire paragraph shows them to have been innocent of anything malicious: they never intended to use this altar for sacrifices to God himself, let alone to other gods. Rather, they intended it only as a memorial or witness for their children (vv. 26–27). Their concern was the same as that of the tribes west of the Jordan: that the unity of Israel be maintained and that their loyalty be to the Lord alone (vv. 25,27). This echoes their response, along with that of the other tribes, in 1:16–18.

The defense is the climax of the passage in terms of the plot's unfolding because the Transjordan tribes' motivations in building the altar are not revealed until now (vv. 27–28). We learn that their intentions, previously suspected to be sinful, were entirely honorable. The defense is passionate, and this is reflected in the syntax. It is choppy in places, and much repetition is found in these verses. It reflects the agitated state of mind in which the Transjordan tribes found themselves, and we can easily imagine them stumbling breathlessly (and perhaps even indignantly) over their words in order to clarify the matter and justify themselves. Structurally as well, this section represents the heart of the passage, as D. Jobling has pointed out.[21]

(a) Transjordanians build an altar (v. 10)
  (b) Cisjordanians threaten war (v. 12)
    (c) Cisjordanians send an embassy (vv. 13–15a)
      (d) Accusatory speech by the embassy (vv. 15b–20)
        (e) Transjordanians' reply (vv. 21–29)
      (d′) Accepting speech by the embassy (vv. 30–31)
    (c′) Return of the embassy to Cisjordan (v. 32)
  (b′) Withdrawal of the Cisjordan threat of war (v. 33)
(a) Transjordanians name the altar (v. 34)

22:21–23 The Transjordan tribes began their defense in v. 22 by calling God as their witness in the strongest possible terms: three terms for God are used, each set repeated twice. The NIV and most Bible versions have three terms, each one independent of each other: ʾēl, "God" or "the Mighty One," ʾĕlōhîm, "God" (which can also be "gods"); and yhwh, "the LORD" or "Yahweh." The Hebrew may be rendered in other ways as well. For example, NRSV has "The LORD, God of gods," the REB has "The LORD the God of gods," and

---

[21] D. Jobling, "The Jordan a Boundary: Transjordan in Israel's Ideological Geography," in *The Sense of Biblical Narrative: Structural Analyses in the Hebrew Bible II*, JSOTSup 39 (Sheffield: JSOT, 1986), 88–134, especially pp. 98–99.

Nelson has "Yahweh is God of gods."[22] The exact wording here is found again only in Ps 50:1, where the same range of meanings is possible. In Gen 33:20, we find *ʾēl ʾělōhê yiśrāʾēl*, which the NIV text note indicates could be "God, the God of Israel" or "mighty is the God of Israel."

The piling up of the terms for God here, and their repetition, is unique in the Old Testament, and it indicates the agitated state of mind of the Transjordan tribes and their eagerness to have their position vindicated. They affirmed as forcefully as possible their loyalty to this God. After the string of terms for God is ended, we find an interesting sequence in which the idea of knowing is important: the tribes affirmed that, as for God, "He knows!" Then, they stated that, as for Israel, "it *will* know!" (or, following the NIV, "*let* Israel know!"). In affirming God as they did, these tribes were also appealing to him as their witness to vindicate them. Then their Israelite brethren would know the truth.

Following their opening exclamations, the Transjordan tribes cast themselves on the mercy of their fellow tribes (v. 22b) and on God himself (v. 23). They were willing to suffer whatever consequences would be meted out, if indeed they were guilty of what they were being accused of. They used words that their accusers had used: *mrd*, "rebellion" (cf. vv. 16,18,19[2x]), *mʿl*, "to act unfaithfully" (cf. vv. 16,20),[23] and *šwb*, "to turn away" (cf. vv. 16,18). They were willing for God himself to "seek" *(bqš)* them (NIV has "call us into account"). They had nothing to hide, and they were anxious to prove it. Their attitude demonstrated a refreshing transparency, which came from their certainty of their innocence.

The Cisjordan tribes had not mentioned sacrifices or offerings of any kind, but the Transjordan tribes did in their response, five times: vv. 23,26,27,28,29. They were well aware of the prohibitions against false worship and sacrifice, and they took care to show that this was not their intent.

22:24–25 Turning the argument away from asserting their innocence, the Transjordan tribes now gave the reason for what they did: it was rooted in their fear of being cut off from their fellow Israelites sometime in the future. The Jordan River formed a natural boundary between them and their brethren, and they feared that their descendants might be rejected by their brothers' descendants. Worse than that, however, they feared that the Cisjordanian's descendants might cause the Transjordanian's descendants to cease their worship of God (v. 25). They would do this by referring to the obvious boundary between them—the Jordan River—and then claiming, by extension, that only those living west of the Jordan, in "the LORD's land," had a legitimate portion in the Lord (cf. v. 19). In this way, their descendants might be completely cut off from

---

[22] R. D. Nelson, *Joshua: A Commentary*, OTL (Louisville: Westminster John Knox, 1997), 244. M. H. Woudstra lists other possible renderings: "God, God the Lord; God of gods, the Lord; El, God, the Lord" (*The Book of Joshua*, NICOT [Grand Rapids: Eerdmans, 1981], 327, n. 1).

[23] The NIV has "disobedience" here, which is surely inadequate to capture the sense of מַעַל.

the blessings promised to all Israel.

The Transjordan tribes' urgency and sincerity is indicated in many ways, including the content of their words, their insistence in uttering them, and even in the way in which they vowed their innocence. Following the insistent appeal to God in v. 22, their words at the beginning of v. 24 take on the nature of an oath and can be translated as "Now *surely*, on account of anxiety did we do this!"[24]

In v. 25, only the Reubenites and the Gadites are mentioned as targets of the Transjordan tribes' rejection (i.e., eastern Manasseh was not included with them). This was because eastern Manasseh would have still been considered to have had roots west of the Jordan, by virtue of the Manassites who settled there. Note that ten representatives from Transjordan had been sent (v. 14); these represented all ten of the landed tribes there, including western Manasseh (but excluding the Levites). This highlights the question in the chapter in another way: whether the tribes *east* of the Jordan, outside of Canaan, could legitimately be considered part of Israel. In vv. 32–34, only the Reubenites and Gadites are mentioned again, but by this time, their status had been settled: they were truly a part of a unified Israel.

22:26–29   The climax of the passage is now reached. After heightening the suspense yet again, restating what the altar was not intended for, the author reveals the Transjordan tribes' motivation for building the altar. The altar was to be a witness (*ʿēd*) between the two parts of Israel. It would represent the unity of eastern and western tribes in the proper worship of the Lord at his true sanctuary. They would offer the sacrifices and offerings there, not at the altar they had built. The use of the term "witness" for the first time in the book reveals the legal status of the altar in the minds of the Transjordan tribes. As a noun, *ʿēd (or ʿēdâ)* frequently functions as "a legal witness to the truth of a matter."[25] Such a witness was usually a person or group (e.g., Ruth 4:9–11; Isa 8:2; Jer 32:10,12,25). In some cases, inanimate objects were called to witness, as we see here and in Josh 24:27, where Joshua erected a great stone to be a witness to the people's renewal of their covenant with God. God himself called the heavens and the earth to be witnesses of whether or not his people would choose to obey him (Deut 30:19).

The altar that the Transjordan tribes had built is revealed in v. 28 not to have been a true altar at all, but only a replica *(tabnît)*[26] of the true altar. True wor-

---

[24] "Now surely" translates וְאִם־לֹא. This expression is commonly used in oaths to underscore the certainty of what is being sworn; BDB states that the expression אִם־לֹא becomes an emphatic affirmative after an oath (expressed or implied) (BDB, 50; see also *DCH* 1:304). The NIV has "No!" for אִם־לֹא, which does not exactly capture the nuance here.

[25] R. B. Chisholm, "עוּד," *NIDOTTE* 3:337.

[26] This word refers elsewhere to the "pattern" for the tabernacle given to Moses in Exod 25:9,40, as well as to that of the temple (1 Chr 28:11,12,18,19).

ship was in no jeopardy; this imitation altar was merely to serve as a reminder to the Transjordan tribes of the true altar at which they would offer their true worship of God and as a reminder and a witness to *all* the tribes of the unity between them.

The altar's location should have been a clue from the beginning as to its purpose. Significantly, the Transjordan tribes did not build it on their side of the Jordan, but across the river from where they would live. It served little useful purpose to them there; for it to have been used regularly to offer sacrifices, it would need to have been east of the river. Here, its imposing size comes into play (cf. v. 10). There it would stand, west of the Jordan, out of practical reach for regular offerings, yet functioning as a silent reminder of the true altar at the Lord's sanctuary. It beckoned the Transjordan tribes to cross the Jordan to offer their sacrifices at the altar of which it was only a copy. And when these tribes reached the climactic point in their defense where they revealed the altar's nature as a copy, they told their brethren to "look" at it (v. 28). The word for "look" here *(rʾh)* and the word for "appearance" in v. 10 *(marʾeh)*[27] come from the same root, and so the Cisjordan tribes are invited to look at it and its imposing appearance to see what the Transjordan tribes would see in years to come. The reason for its imposing size is thus revealed.

The Transjordan tribes' final words are another emphatic denial that they would ever contemplate offering sacrifices of any type except at the true altar at the tabernacle (v. 29). They again used the vocabulary that had been used against them: they would not *rebel* against the Lord nor *turn away* from him (see the comments above on vv. 22–23). Thus, their denial of any wrongdoing comes to a close. Their innocence and proper intentions could not be doubted.

(4) The Crisis Resolved (22:30–34)

[30]**When Phinehas the priest and the leaders of the community—the heads of the clans of the Israelites—heard what Reuben, Gad and Manasseh had to say, they were pleased.** [31]**And Phinehas son of Eleazar, the priest, said to Reuben, Gad and Manasseh, "Today we know that the LORD is with us, because you have not acted unfaithfully toward the LORD in this matter. Now you have rescued the Israelites from the LORD's hand."**

[32]**Then Phinehas son of Eleazar, the priest, and the leaders returned to Canaan from their meeting with the Reubenites and Gadites in Gilead and reported to the Israelites.** [33]**They were glad to hear the report and praised God. And they talked no more about going to war against them to devastate the country where the Reubenites and the Gadites lived.**

[34]**And the Reubenites and the Gadites gave the altar this name: A Witness Between Us that the LORD is God.**

---

[27] See note above on this translation.

The Transjordan tribes' impassioned defense quickly defused the crisis, satisfying the people's representatives. The response of Phinehas and the leaders occupies only one verse (v. 30), an abrupt ending to a crisis that has been described in twenty verses (vv. 10–29). The passage concludes with assurances and peace on all sides and a formalizing of the altar's purpose with a name for it (vv. 31–34). The unity of the nation is preserved, the place of the Transjordan tribes assured, and a civil war and the Lord's punishment is avoided.

22:31 The threat of the Lord's wrath being poured out on the entire nation, which was a very real fear (vv. 18,20), was now averted. The Cisjordan tribes were now assured that their eastern brothers had not been acting faithlessly *(m⁽l)*. In a very real sense, then, they had "rescued" the nation from catastrophe.

22:32–33 The conclusion of the episode is signaled by the leaders' return home in v. 32. The formal identification of Phinehas—"Phinehas son of Eleazar, the priest"—helps to bring matters to a close, as well, echoing the way in which he is introduced in the account (v. 13). Things came to a happy conclusion, with the western tribes rejoicing and praising God when they heard the news (v. 33). The war thus avoided would have been a fearsome thing: the word used here—"devastate" *(šḥt)*—denotes complete destruction and ruination; this is the only occurrence in Joshua of this otherwise common word. Given that this term indicates destruction and despoiling of cities and property as well as people, the potential war would have been far more destructive than most of the encounters with the Canaanites, where the term is not used and where only people were killed, for the most part.[28]

Only two of the Transjordan tribes are referred to now in vv. 32–34: Reuben and Gad. Eastern Manasseh, which was clearly also allied with them (see vv. 1,7,10,13, etc.), is not mentioned, for reasons noted above (see v. 25).

22:34 The climax of the chapter reveals the full meaning of the altar: it was to testify to God himself. Previously, the account had revealed that it was to be a witness (vv. 27,28), but the earlier verses do not reveal the precise nature or function of the "witness." Now we see that it was to affirm that Yahweh was God. It was a symbol of Israel's national unity, and this symbol was to testify to Israel's God. In a similar vein, Jesus told his disciples that people would know they were his disciples by seeing their love for each other, that is, their love would point people to Christ (John 13:35).

The general thrust of the verse is clear, communicating what we have just noted. However, the specifics are more difficult. The most intelligible reading restores the word *ʿēd*, "witness," after the word "altar,"[29] yielding the follow-

---

[28] See BDB, 1007–8; D. Vetter, "שחת *šḥt* pi./hi. to ruin," *TLOT,* 1317–20.

[29] This is based on some meager manuscript evidence from the Tgs. and on the Syr. version, which has *ʿēd* here. See the discussions in Butler, *Joshua,* 241; Nelson, *Joshua,* 246.

ing reading: "and the Reubenites and the Gadites called the altar 'Witness,' for it is a witness between us that the LORD is God." This reading is followed by most modern Bible versions (NASB, REB, NRSV, NLT). The NIV understands the verse slightly differently, with a lengthy name as the title of the altar.

3. Joshua's First Farewell to All Israel (23:1–16)

The final two chapters of the book contain Joshua's two farewell speeches to the entire nation, delivered at the end of his life. Both were given in the pastoral, hortatory style found in Moses' speeches in Deuteronomy, also delivered at the end of his life. The fact that Joshua gave such speeches to the nation places him on a level with Moses as God's anointed leader over the nation, and it reinforces again the picture presented many times in the book: Joshua was the worthy successor to Moses.

Because of the similarities between these two speeches, some scholars argue that these chapters represent two versions of only one event or speech, one or both of which are Deuteronomistic compositions dating many centuries later.[30] However, significant differences exist between the two that must be taken into account. (1) The first speech is very pastoral, urging Israel to keep the law and to follow the Lord and warning it against turning away from him; as such, it is oriented to the future in significant ways. The second speech, while doing much of the same thing, reviews the past record of God's faithfulness to Israel in a much more systematic way. (2) The first speech was apparently delivered to the leaders of Israel (see v. 2), while the second appears to have been to all the nation (24:1–2).[31] (3) The first speech apparently was delivered at Shiloh, which had been the Israelites' religious center for some time (see 18:1,8–10; 19:51; 21:1), while the next was delivered at Shechem (24:1). (4) The first is less formal than the second, since it consists entirely of Joshua's words of exhortation and admonition to his audience, while the second is followed by the people's response and by a covenant renewal ceremony.[32]

Joshua's speech in chap. 23 is reminiscent of the last speeches of Jacob

---

[30] See, e.g., J. A. Soggin, *Joshua*, OTL (Philadelphia: Westminster, 1972), 218; J. Gray, *Joshua, Judges, Ruth*, NCBC, 3d ed. (Grand Rapids: Eerdmans, 1986), 173, 176.

[31] In truth, both chapters contain sections referring to the past, but in chap. 23 these are more limited, concerning the land allotments in Joshua's day, whereas in chap. 24 they are much broader, concerning the ways in which Yahweh interceded for his people, beginning with Abraham and ending with the people in Joshua's own day.

[32] Butler mentions this last difference as the major one and adds four others: (1) the setting is established temporally in chap. 23 (Joshua's old age) but geographically in chap. 24 (at Shechem); (2) focus on the land allotments in chap. 23 but on Yahweh's victories in chap. 24; (3) obedience to the law is stressed in chap. 23 but serving the Lord in chap. 24; (4) marriage entanglements are warned against in chap. 23 but worshiping foreign gods in chap. 24 (*Joshua*, 265–66).

(Genesis 49), Moses (Deuteronomy 32–33), and David (2 Sam 23:1–7). In it, Joshua summed up most of the important motifs introduced throughout the book, passionately urging Israel to be steadfast in loving God, in obeying his law, and in keeping themselves uncontaminated by the religious practices of their neighbors. Joshua promised that God would be with Israel in the as-yet-unfinished task of driving out their enemies, just as he had been in the past (vv. 3–5, 9–10). The promises of God and their fulfillment are emphasized again here (vv. 10, 14–15; cf. 21:45).

This chapter, while warm in its exhortations to Israel, also contains sobering warnings. If Israel would not love and obey God and keep themselves pure, then he would not drive out the nations, and they would remain as torments (v. 13). Furthermore—and more seriously—Israel stood to lose the land itself, this very land that was so central to the nation's endeavors up to this point (vv. 15–16). Just as good things would happen if they obeyed, so also bad things would happen if they disobeyed. This follows the pattern of much of the theology in Deuteronomy (see esp. Deuteronomy 27–30).

A striking feature of the speech is its realistic assessment of the situation heretofore. While on the one hand, Joshua affirmed in v. 9 that no one remained who had opposed the Israelites, in several other places he spoke of the "nations" remaining among the Israelites, and he warned the Israelites against them (vv. 3,4,7,9,12,13).

With these emphases on the peoples remaining among them, on the warnings, and on the potential problems that lay before the nation, the speech is of a piece with those passages in Joshua that tell of the peoples whom the Israelites did not drive out and of land that yet remained to be conquered (see 13:2–6,13; 15:63; 16:10; 17:11–12; 19:47). Such texts lay the foundation for the Book of Judges. The Israelites did *not* fulfill their mandate in its entirety, so the seeds of their corruption were in place from the beginning in the form of peoples and nations who remained living among them.

God's ownership of the land is emphasized in this speech. Ultimately, the land belonged to God, not Israel. These warnings saw their most dramatic fulfillment when Judah was carried into Babylonian captivity because of its repeated transgression of the covenant (2 Kings 25). But they also were relevant almost immediately, during the period of the judges, when Israel began to do precisely what was warned against here (see esp. Judg 2:16–23, 3:1–6).[33]

Most of Joshua's words here echo words found earlier in the book, as well as in Deuteronomy.[34] This is fitting, given that his speech was a farewell in

---

[33] On this point, see also Butler, *Joshua*, 253.

[34] For example, M. Weinfeld has shown that clauses or sentences from every verse of Joshua's speech (vv. 3–16) can be found in Deuteronomy (*Deuteronomy and the Deuteronomic School* [Winona Lake: Eisenbrauns, 1992 reprint], 320–57 [*passim*]). (Weinfeld neglects to treat v. 10, but the reference to God's fighting for Israel is found in Deut 1:30 and elsewhere.)

which he urged the people to remain faithful to God, to his law, and to all of the instructions they had received heretofore.

The chapter consists of repetitions of ideas and piling up of thoughts,[35] which does not lend itself to a clear pattern or structure emerging. Neither does the syntax of the passage offer any clear pattern.[36] For our purposes, we can identify three major sections of Joshua's speech: vv. 3–8,9–13,14–16.[37] In each section, Joshua looked back at what the Lord had done for Israel (vv. 3–5,9–10,14).[38] Then, Joshua instructed the people as to what they needed to do to obey and to avoid the Lord's judgment (vv. 6–8,11–13,15–16). Whereas the first set of these instructions contains no added warnings (vv. 6–8), the second begins with instructions (v. 11) but quickly turns to dire warnings of punishment if Israel should reject the Lord (vv. 12–13). The third set consists entirely of dire warnings (vv. 15–16). Thus, as Nelson notes, "there is a clear escalation in the severity of the rhetoric," and "the perspective moves from a focus on the positive potentials in Israel's present and future (vv. 5,8,9–10) to the real possibility of disobedience and destruction (vv. 13,15–16)."[39]

Israel certainly was to obey the Lord because of what he had done for them in the past (vv. 3–4,9–10,14) and out of a motivation of love for him (v. 11). However, if such positive motivations did not work, the negative motivation of the threat of punishment also figured in Joshua's speech, becoming more prominent as his speech progressed (vv. 12–13,15–16). Sometimes, both then and now, people are not motivated to act purely out of positive motivations (the "carrot")—which are clearly the best motivations for any action—but require

---

[35] The most detailed analysis of the passage from a literary standpoint, with a sensitivity to such repetitions, is W. T. Koopmans, "The Poetic Prose of Joshua 23," in W. van der Meer and J. C. de Moor, eds., *The Structural Analysis of Biblical and Canaanite Poetry,* JSOTSup 74 (Sheffield: Sheffield Academic Press, 1988), 83–118. Koopmans understands the literary genre of the passage to be "poetic prose" or "poetic narrative," which he places midway on the continuum between prose and poetry. As such, its repetitions are not on the level of internal parallelism (as with classic poetic texts), but rather on the higher levels of external parallelism (p. 116).

[36] Illustrating this point are the following paragraph divisions from several Bible versions: NJPSV, REB: vv. 1–5, 6–8, 9–13, 14–16; NASB, NRSV: vv. 1–13, 14–16; NIV, NLT: vv. 1–5, 6–8, 9–11, 12–13, 14–16. Following are several scholars' analyses: vv. 1–2, 3–13, 14–16 (C. F. Keil, *The Book of Joshua* [Grand Rapids: Eerdmans, 1975 reprint], 223–26); vv. 1–8, 9–13, 14–16 (Woudstra, *Joshua,* 331–39); vv. 1–2, 3–10, 11–16 (R. G. Boling, *Joshua,* AB 5 [Garden City: Doubleday, 1982], 519–20); vv. 1–2, 3–5, 6–8, 9–10, 11, 12–13, 14, 15–16 (Butler, *Joshua,* 253); vv. 1–5, 6–10, 11–13, 14–16 (Koopmans, "Joshua 23," 90–92); vv. 1–5, 6–11, 12–16 (R. S. Hess, *Joshua: An Introduction and Commentary,* TOTC (Downers Grove: InterVarsity, 1996); vv. 1–2, 3–8, 9–13, 14–16 (Nelson, *Joshua,* 253–55).

[37] These divisions are also proposed by Woudstra and Nelson (see previous note).

[38] In v. 5 the focus is on what the Lord would do in the future.

[39] Nelson, *Joshua,* 256. E. R. Clendenen (personal communication) suggests the following structure: (1) setting, vv. 1–2a, (2) situation, vv. 2b–3, (3) exhortation, vv. 4–7, (4) motivation, vv. 8–16 (positive—vv. 8–11, negative—vv. 12–16).

motivations formulated negatively (the "stick") in order to compel certain behaviors. In Israel's case, tragically, even such negative formulations were not enough to deter it from lapsing into disobedience many times, beginning with the period of the judges and continuing down to the time of the exile and even afterwards.

(1) Introduction (23:1–2)

¹After a long time had passed and the LORD had given Israel rest from all their enemies around them, Joshua, by then old and well advanced in years, ²summoned all Israel—their elders, leaders, judges and officials—and said to them: "I am old and well advanced in years.

23:1 This entire verse sets the stage for the activity of the chapter. Syntactically, it is all prefatory to the main action, which begins in v. 2.[40] Every statement in this verse echoes earlier ones. The "long time" harks back to 22:3; the idea of "rest" echoes earlier statements in 11:23; 14:15; 21:44; and the statement on Joshua's advanced age repeats a similar statement in 13:1. All three statements refer to the passage of time in one way or another. Because of this passage of time, because the land now had rest, and because Joshua was old and his end was near, it was now appropriate for him to look back to remind the people of God's faithfulness and to look ahead, exhorting and warning them about the future.

The exact time intended here is impossible to know with certainty, but it appears to refer to a time many years after the events in chaps. 13–21, and even chap. 22. The verse clearly echoes 13:1 in stating that Joshua was "old and well advanced in years," and it also echoes 21:44—both verses state that the Lord had given the people rest. Some scholars believe that the "long time" here is calculated from the *beginning* of the book (i.e., when God began to give rest to the land).[41] However, it is also possible—and, in actuality, more probable— that the "long time" should be calculated from the *completion* of the process (i.e., that the speeches in chaps. 23 and 24 came "a long time" after the land distribution was completed, when God had finally given true rest to the land).[42] In support of this, we may note that the farewell speeches, as they are presented in chaps. 23 and 24, appear to have come at the end of Joshua's life. Indeed, in 23:14, Joshua stated that he was about to go "the way of all the earth today," indicating that his death was fairly close at hand. He was 110 years old when

---

[40] The *wayĕhî* + prepositional phrase construction, indicating a time reference, is not resolved until the *wayyiqtōl* verb form at the beginning of v. 2, indicating that everything in v. 1 sets the stage for what follows. For more on this construction, see note at 4:11.

[41] E.g., Woudstra, *Joshua*, 332.

[42] Keil (*Book of Joshua*, 223) and C. J. Goslinga (*Joshua, Judges, Ruth*, BSC [Grand Rapids: Zondervan, 1986], 164) both appear to take this position.

he died (24:29), and, if he was anywhere near Caleb's age of eighty-five when the land was distributed (see 14:10), then his farewell speeches would have come about twenty-five years after the main events in the book. (See also the note on 14:10.)

23:2   This was an all-inclusive speech in the sense that it was delivered to a wide range of the nation's leaders, who represented the entire nation. By way of contrast, in 24:2 we are told that Joshua spoke directly to "all the people" in addition to the leaders of the nation.

(2) Exhortations and Admonitions: Part One (23:3–8)

³You yourselves have seen everything the LORD your God has done to all these nations for your sake; it was the LORD your God who fought for you. ⁴Remember how I have allotted as an inheritance for your tribes all the land of the nations that remain—the nations I conquered—between the Jordan and the Great Sea in the west. ⁵The LORD your God himself will drive them out of your way. He will push them out before you, and you will take possession of their land, as the LORD your God promised you.

⁶"Be very strong; be careful to obey all that is written in the Book of the Law of Moses, without turning aside to the right or to the left. ⁷Do not associate with these nations that remain among you; do not invoke the names of their gods or swear by them. You must not serve them or bow down to them. ⁸But you are to hold fast to the LORD your God, as you have until now.

23:3–4   Joshua's speech more properly begins at the end of v. 2, where he acknowledged what the narrator had stated in v. 1, that he was "old and well advanced in years." He referred to himself—"*As for me*, I am old"—in order to contrast himself with his addressees, to whom his first words were "*As for you*, you have seen."[43]

In vv. 3–4, Joshua took his first look back at what God had done for the nation. In v. 3, he reminded the nation that the Lord had fought for them, and that they themselves had been witnesses of this ("you have seen"). The reference to God's fighting for Israel repeats the idea that the land was God's and that he would give it to them, even to the extent of fighting on their behalf (see also Deut 7:1; 11:23–25; Josh 1:5,9; 8:7; 10:14,19,42; etc.).

In v. 4, Joshua shifted the focus to his own role as distributor of the tribes' inheritances. That Joshua had been a primary figure in the land distributions was well established (see 11:23; 12:7; 14:12,13; 15:13; 17:4,14; 21:2; 22:7). What had not been emphasized previously was Joshua's claim to individual conquest, which the NIV's rendering indicates: "the nations I conquered"

---

[43] In each case, a pleonastic (i.e., redundant) pronoun is found before the verb, indicating this emphasis on the two contrasting subjects.

(lit., "all the nations that I cut off" [krt]).[44] It was Yahweh who had fought Israel's battles, not any individual. Nevertheless, a precedent for this unusual claim is found in 11:21, which states that "Joshua went and destroyed (lit., "cut off" [krt]) the Anakites from the hill country: from Hebron, Debir, and Anab, from all the hill country of Judah, and from all the hill country of Israel. Joshua totally destroyed them and their towns." Later in the same passage we are told that "Joshua took the entire land, just as the LORD had directed Moses, and he gave it as an inheritance to Israel according to their tribal divisions" (11:23). Both in chap. 11 and here Joshua's individual conquests are linked to his giving of lands as the Israelites' proper inheritance. Even though he is said to have given the tribes their inheritances, we know that ultimately it was God who did this (i.e., Joshua acted as his agent). These references to Joshua's fighting and conquering peoples must be understood in the same way: God fought for Israel, and Joshua was his agent in several cases.

Joshua's speech emphasizes the foreign nations that remained among the Israelites in a way that no other speech heretofore has done (see esp. vv. 3,4 [2x],7,9,12,13). The term for "nations" (gôyîm) is found seven times in this chapter, as opposed to only six times previously.[45] This term normally refers to foreign, pagan nations, and here the danger from these godless nations is emphasized. The lands belonging to the nations in Canaan had been allotted as the Israelites' inheritance in the earlier transactions of allotting the territories (on the allotment, see the commentary on 14:2).

23:5 After looking back at what God had done for Israel in vv. 3–4, Joshua now looked forward to what he would do. He would drive out Israel's enemies so that Israel could possess the land, in fulfillment of his promises (cf. Deut 9:3–5; Josh 3:10; 13:6).

23:6–8 Then, after focusing on what God had done and would do for his people, Joshua exhorted them in terms similar to what God had said to Moses and to him on earlier occasions. The Israelites' success was dependent on their obedience and on the centrality of the law in their lives (v. 6). Joshua here charged the Israelites in terms almost identical to God's charge to him (see 1:7–8) and, to a lesser extent, with which he had exhorted the Transjordan tribes (22:5).

The Israelites were to keep themselves uncontaminated by the nations who remained among them and by the gods they worshiped (v. 7). The problem of mixing with the peoples of the land and adopting their worship loyalties was the most severe problem throughout Israel's history in the land, affecting it in

---

[44] This verse in fact is the subject of some discussion on a textual level because the syntax is somewhat awkward. However, the major versions follow the MT, and it is intelligible—if not completely smooth—as it stands. See the discussions in Boling, *Joshua,* 521; Butler, *Joshua,* 252.

[45] See 3:17; 4:1; 5:6,8; 10:13; 12:23.

almost every era. It quickly became the dominant problem in the period of the judges (Judg 2:10–19). It was the cause of Solomon's downfall and the split in the kingdom (1 Kings 11). It was the cause of the fall of the Northern Kingdom of Israel (2 Kgs 17:7–23), as well as of the Southern Kingdom of Judah (2 Kgs 21; 24:3–4). It was a problem even in the postexilic period, when the people should have learned their lesson (Ezra 9:1–2; Neh 13:23–27). Thus, while Joshua's speech was warm-hearted and hortatory in tone, it nevertheless contained ample warnings and signs of the troubles that were to come, troubles that would be caused by Israel's associations with the nations that remained among them (Josh 23:4,7,12–13).

Instead of following the Canaanites' gods, the Israelites were to cling to their own God (v. 8). The word translated "hold fast" (*dbq:* also used in v. 12 and in 22:5) means "to cling tightly." The root refers to the soldering process in Isa 41:7 (i.e., a process in which things are joined together inseparably).[46] This word has a rich theological content, showing the extreme closeness that people were to have with their God. For example, Hezekiah, a good king par excellence in Judah, is commended in terms of his trusting and "holding fast" (*dbq*) to God (2 Kgs 18:5–6).

(3) Exhortations and Admonitions: Part Two (23:9–13)

[9]"The LORD has driven out before you great and powerful nations; to this day no one has been able to withstand you. [10]One of you routs a thousand, because the LORD your God fights for you, just as he promised. [11]So be very careful to love the LORD your God.

[12]"But if you turn away and ally yourselves with the survivors of these nations that remain among you and if you intermarry with them and associate with them, [13]then you may be sure that the LORD your God will no longer drive out these nations before you. Instead, they will become snares and traps for you, whips on your backs and thorns in your eyes, until you perish from this good land, which the LORD your God has given you.

23:9–10 Once again Joshua looked back at what God had done for Israel (cf. vv. 3–4). An important emphasis here again is God's faithfulness to his

---

[46] The root here—דבק—is the basis for Modern Hebrew's word for "glue" (דֶּבֶק), illustrating the point further. The word is used in the OT in a literal sense of a hand clinging to a sword (2 Sam 23:10), sections of armor (1 Kgs 22:34) or the scales of a crocodile (Job 41:17,23[Hb. 9,15]) forming a joint, metal being joined by a blacksmith (Isa 41:7), a belt clinging to a man's waist (Jer 13:11), the tongue sticking to the roof of one's mouth (Ezek 3:26; Ps 22:15[Hb. 16]; 137:6; Job 29:10; Lam 4:4); skin clinging to bones (Ps 102:5[Hb. 6]; Job 19:20); or of dirt hardened by lack of rain (Job 38:38). In personal relations it describes "a state of loyalty, affection, or close proximity" (G. J. Brooke, "דבק," *NIDOTTE* 1:911). It is used of loyalty to Yahweh in Deut 4:4; 10:20; 11:22; 13:4,20; Josh 22:5; 2 Sam 18:6; Ps 63:8. The LXX usually translates it with κολλάω (or προσκολλάω), "to glue, cement, join," which is found twelve times in the NT including Matt 19:5 (quoting Gen 2:24).

promises. He had indeed driven out the nations before the Israelites, in fulfillment of his promises (see comments on v. 5), such that no one had been able to
withstand them (v. 9b); the language here is similar to God's words to Joshua
in 1:5.[47]

God had also promised to fight for Israel, and he had fulfilled this too (see
on v. 3). He had done so to such an extent that one Israelite would be able to
rout a thousand of its enemies (v. 10). These words about the Israelites' prowess echo the words in Moses' song in Deut 32:30:

> How could one man chase a thousand,
>   or two put ten thousand to flight,
> unless their Rock had sold them,
>   unless the LORD had given them up?

They are also similar to God's promises in Lev 26:7–8: "You will pursue your
enemies, and they will fall by the sword before you. Five of you will chase a
hundred, and a hundred of you will chase ten thousand, and your enemies will
fall by the sword before you." When God fought for his people, the odds
increased by factors of hundreds, even thousands, in their favor.

23:11   At the heart of his speech (almost exactly midway through it),
Joshua challenged the people to love the Lord their God, which was the heart
of their duties as his people. Everything else—including the important exhortations to obey everything in the law (v. 6) and to avoid pagan entanglements—
was a means to an end, which was that Israel should have a close and loving
relationship with its God. This exhortation is rooted in Moses' words in Deut
6:5: "Love the LORD your God with all your heart and with all your soul and
with all your strength." It is the substance of what Jesus called the first and
greatest commandment (Matt 22:37 and parallels). The constant exhortations
to Israel to be faithful to God were not given in a sterile or harshly demanding
environment. Rather, they were issued in service of the larger principle that
God wanted a loving relationship with his people: he promised to be with them
(Josh 1:9), and in return he desired their loyalty and their love.

23:12–13   After the brief but important instruction of v. 11, Joshua turned
to an extended and serious admonition or warning in vv. 12–13. If Israel chose
to reject the Lord and cling instead to the nations remaining among them, then
what God had already done and what he promised to continue to do for the
Israelites—to drive out the nations before them (cf. vv. 5,9)—he would no
longer do (v. 13). Instead, the nations would become obstacles of the worst
kind for the Israelites: they would be snares and traps to them (for earlier passages stating the same idea, see Exod 23:33; Deut 7:16; and especially Num
33:55). This prediction came true with a vengeance during the period of the

---

[47] The NIV's "withstand" in 1:5 and 23:9 translates two different Hebrew terms—יצב and
עמד, respectively—but their meanings in these contexts are similar.

judges (see Judg 2:14–15,21–23; 3:1–6). The nations would become such obstacles to the Israelites that they would even cause them to lose the land itself, a land that was good, a land that had been God's gift to his people. Rejecting God was such a serious offense that it would yield even such a drastic result. God's standards would not be relaxed even for his own people.

A wordplay in vv. 8 and 12 involves a contrast. In v. 8, Israel was to cling (*dbq*) to the Lord himself, and in v. 12, if Israel clung (*dbq;* NIV has "ally" here) instead to the nations, God would bring punishment.

The dangers of intermarriage with unbelieving foreigners was such that this was strictly forbidden to the Israelites (Exod 34:11–16; Deut 7:1–4). A dramatic example of how faith was polluted by intermarriage can be seen in Solomon's case (1 Kgs 3:1; 11:1–8). In a later time, when the Israelites discovered that many among them had indeed intermarried, the drastic step of a mass divorce was taken (Ezra 9–10; cf. also Neh 13:23–27).[48] The same prohibition was given by the apostle Paul: "Do not be yoked together with unbelievers. For what do righteousness and wickedness have in common? Or what fellowship can light have with darkness?" (2 Cor 6:14).

(4) Admonitions (23:14–16)

[14]"Now I am about to go the way of all the earth. You know with all your heart and soul that not one of all the good promises the LORD your God gave you has failed. Every promise has been fulfilled; not one has failed. [15]But just as every good promise of the LORD your God has come true, so the LORD will bring on you all the evil he has threatened, until he has destroyed you from this good land he has given you. [16]If you violate the covenant of the LORD your God, which he commanded you, and go and serve other gods and bow down to them, the LORD's anger will burn against you, and you will quickly perish from the good land he has given you."

Joshua concluded his speech with a third set of admonitions and warnings. This time there were no further reviews of the past, except for an assertion that every one of the Lord's promises had been fulfilled (v. 14). Beyond this, Joshua laid forth what the Lord would do if Israel violated the covenant (vv. 15–16).

23:14 Joshua indicated that he was about to die soon (lit., "today"). His words—"I am about to go the way of all the earth"—were also spoken by David to his son Solomon when he was about to die (1 Kgs 2:2).[49] The pas-

---

[48] Concerning the difficult ethical question of such a mass divorce in Ezra, see, briefly, D. M. Howard, Jr., *An Introduction to the Old Testament Historical Books* (Chicago: Moody, 1993), 295–96.

[49] The only other time the expression "the way of all the earth" occurs in the OT is in Gen 19:31, where Lot's daughters lamented that there was no man to lie with them in "the way of all the earth," i.e., in the custom or manner practiced everywhere, which is a different usage of the expression.

sion with which they were to regard the Lord is indicated by the phrase "with all your heart and soul," an expression used in Deut 6:5 to indicate the passion with which the Israelites were to love him (cf. the link to Deut 6:5 in v. 11). Not only were they to love him in this manner, they were also to know with the same degree of certainty that his promises did come to pass. The repeated affirmations that God's promises were fulfilled highlights an important motif in the book, and they pick up most specifically on the similar statement in 21:45 (cf. also 22:4).

23:15–16 Joshua's logic as he concluded his speech was that, just as surely as the Lord's promises had come true for Israel's good, so also his swift and devastating punishment would come upon the Israelites if they violated the covenant. God's anger would burn *(ḥrh)* against his people, and, indeed, this did happen many times in Israel's history. Whenever the Lord's anger burned against his people, they suffered, usually at the hands of a foreign enemy. The following passages are typical: (1) "The anger of the LORD burned *[ḥrh]* against Israel so that he sold them into the hands of Cushan-Rishathaim king of Aram Naharaim, to whom the Israelites were subject for eight years" (Judg 3:8); (2) "He became angry with them [lit., "the anger of the LORD burned *(ḥrh)* against them"]. He sold them into the hands of the Philistines and the Ammonites" (Judg 10:7); (3) "So the LORD's anger burned *[ḥrh]* against Israel, and for a long time he kept them under the power of Hazael king of Aram and Ben-Hadad his son" (2 Kgs 13:3). In Joshua, this had already happened once previously (7:1: "So the LORD's anger burned *[ḥrh]* against Israel"), and the results had been devastating.

This time, however, the results would be even more devastating. Joshua promised Israel that they would perish from the good land in which they lived if they forsook the Lord (cf. also v. 13). The land belonged to God, and it was his to give and his to take away. This promise saw its dramatic fulfillment when Judah was carried into Babylonian captivity because of its repeated transgression of the covenant (2 Kings 25). In this way, too, God's promises came to pass: if his people obeyed him, they enjoyed great blessing; but if they disobeyed him, they would suffer great calamity. God displayed remarkable patience, suffering through centuries of his people's covenant violations and disobedience. He repeatedly sent foreign oppressors to punish and prophets to warn, until the time came when his patience reached an end, and he sent them into exile.

4. Joshua's Second Farewell to All Israel (24:1–28)

Joshua's second farewell to Israel took place at Shechem, site of the earlier covenant renewal ceremony (8:30–35). Although this address reflected the one in chap. 23 in several ways, there are also significant differences.[50] The most significant difference between chaps. 23 and 24 is that the latter contains a covenant renewal ceremony, in which the people actually committed themselves to serving the Lord.

Although the contents of the chapter are straightforward and clear enough, the chapter nevertheless has been the subject of extensive study from many different perspectives.[51] One of the most productive approaches has focused on the covenant entered into in this chapter, and comparisons have been drawn with ancient Near Eastern treaties, especially the Hittite treaties of the second millennium B.C. A standard outline was followed in such treaties, which governed relations between kings who considered themselves equals to each other (parity treaties) or cases in which one was the overlord and the other was the vassal (suzerainty treaties).

G. E. Mendenhall was the first to identify such a treaty structure in Joshua 24, correlating it with parallels in the ancient Near East.[52] On the basis especially of Hittite treaties of the second millennium B.C., scholars prior to Mendenhall had highlighted the following elements of international treaties:

1. *Preamble:* identifies the author of the covenant
2. *Historical Prologue:* describes the previous relationship between the two parties
3. *Stipulations:* the vassal's obligations to the overlord
4. A. *Deposit in the Temple*
   B. *Periodic Public Reading*
5. *Witnesses:* the gods are called to witness the covenant
6. *Curses and blessings:* the gods will punish or bless, depending on whether the covenant is kept

Mendenhall's particular contribution was to note the parallels between such treaty forms and various covenants in the Bible. The overlord (or "suzerain") in these covenants was God, and his vassal was Israel. In Joshua 24, Mendenhall identified the following elements of the standard second-millennium treaty form:[53]

---

[50] See the introduction to chap. 23 for a discussion of the differences.

[51] See the summaries of research in Butler, *Joshua*, 257–61, 266–69, and Nelson, *Joshua*, 265–67. The most extensive study of the chapter is that of W. T. Koopmans, *Joshua 24 as Poetic Narrative*, JSOTSup 93 (Sheffield: Sheffield Academic Press, 1990); see pp. 1–163 for his survey and evaluation of previous scholarship.

[52] G. E. Mendenhall, "Covenant Forms in Israelite Tradition," *BA* 17 (1954): 50–76. A useful catalog and brief discussion of the fifty-seven ANE treaties extant through the 1980's may be found in J. H. Walton, *Ancient Israelite Literature in Its Cultural Context* (Grand Rapids: Zondervan, 1989), 95–107.

[53] Mendenhall, "Covenant Forms," 67. He holds to the same basic structure in his most recent survey of the subject: G. E. Mendenhall and G. A. Herion, "Covenant," *ABD* 1:1179–1202.

1. *Preamble*: "the LORD, the God of Israel" (v. 2a)
2. *Historical Prologue:* history of God's relationship with Israel from Terah and Abraham until the present (vv. 2b–13)
3. *Stipulations:* — — —[54]
4. A. *Deposit in the Temple:* — — —
   B. *Periodic Public Reading:* — — —
5. *Witnesses:* the people (v. 22) and the great stone (v. 27)
6. *Curses and blessings:* — — —

K. A. Kitchen has identified more details that fit into the pattern:[55]

1. *Preamble* (vv. 1–2)
2. *Historical Prologue* (vv. 2–13)
3. *Stipulations* (vv. 14–15 [and vv. 16–25])
4. A. *Deposit* (v. 26: the Writing in the book of the law)
   B. *Periodic Public Reading* — — —
5. *Witnesses* (vv. 22,27)
6. *Curses and blessings* (implicit in vv. 19–20)

K. Baltzer, in an extensive study of ancient Near Eastern and Biblical treaties and covenants, added an element to the list used by Mendenhall, which he called the "Statement of Substance Concerning the Future Relationship of the Partners to the Treaty" and which took the place of the deposit and public reading in previous outlines of ancient Near Eastern treaties.[56] He saw the following structure in Joshua 24:[57]

Part One: Conditions of the Covenant (vv. 2–14)
1. Preamble (v. 2)
2. Antecedent History (vv. 2–13)
3. Statement of Substance (v. 14)
Part Two: Confirmation of the Covenant by Oath (vv. 15–27)
1. Transition: Joshua Speaks for the People (v. 15)
2. Antecedent History Referred To (vv. 17–18a)
3. Statement of Substance Echoed (vv. 16,18b)
4. Witnesses (and Curses and Blessings) (vv. 19–24)
5. Written Documentation (vv. 25–27)

---

[54] Mendenhall notes that the people's words forswearing the worship of other gods (v. 16) reports on what would have been the foundational stipulation ("Covenant Forms," 67).

[55] K. A. Kitchen, *Ancient Orient and Old Testament* (Chicago: InterVarsity, 1966), 96–97; id., *The Bible in Its World* (Downers Grove: InterVarsity, 1977), 82–84. See also his recent article comparing ANE treaty forms with each other and with biblical materials: "The Patriarchal Age: Myth or History?" *BARev* 21.2 (1995): 48–57, 88–95; on p. 56 (footnote) he gives a slightly modified version of the above outline for Joshua 24.

[56] K. Baltzer, *The Covenant Formulary in Old Testament, Jewish, and Early Christian Writings* (Philadelphia: Fortress, 1971) [trans. D. E. Green from the 1964 ed.], 9–18.

[57] Ibid., 19–27.

Baltzer was forced to stretch the ideas of God as a witness and of blessings and curses in vv. 19–24, however, in order to accommodate the scheme.

The outlines drawn up by Mendenhall, Kitchen, Baltzer, and other scholars have been criticized as being overly rigid, forcing elements of Joshua 24 into the scheme in an artificial way. It has been noted that Joshua 24 does not claim to be the *text* of a treaty or covenant but rather a *report* of a covenant-renewal ceremony. This distinction is a helpful one, and it accounts for the variations from the standard treaty outline. Joshua 24 is best understood against the general backdrop of the covenant treaty forms but with an eye to the differences as well as the similarities.[58]

This chapter constitutes an appropriate capstone to the book's message and to Joshua's life. Joshua did in a short address much the same as Moses had done in several longer addresses at the end of his life (see Deuteronomy 1–11)—looking back over what the Lord had done for him and the people and urging them to serve the Lord and to avoid apostasy. Joshua was functioning as a true spiritual leader and as Moses' worthy successor in doing so.

As a report of a covenant renewal ceremony, the chapter reminds us that, first and foremost, a covenant established (or ratified) a relationship between two parties. This is certainly an important part of the biblical covenants. For example, in the Abrahamic Covenant, God committed himself to doing many good things for Abraham (Gen 12:1–3,7; 15:4–5,7, 18–21; 17:2,6–8; etc.). At the establishment of the Mosaic Covenant, God first emphasized the relationship with his people Israel that he had established—and how he intended to strengthen it—*before* he placed any demands on his people (Exod 19:4–6; 20:2; Deuteronomy 1–11). The same is true in Joshua 24: the first major portion of the chapter is devoted to a review of what God had done for his people (vv. 2–13) before any requirements or warnings are uttered.[59]

(1) Introduction and Review of the Past (24:1–13)

¹Then Joshua assembled all the tribes of Israel at Shechem. He summoned the elders, leaders, judges and officials of Israel, and they presented themselves before God.

²Joshua said to all the people, "This is what the LORD, the God of Israel, says: 'Long ago your forefathers, including Terah the father of Abraham and Nahor,

---

[58] See Koopmans, *Joshua 24 as Poetic Narrative*, 146–54, especially 152–54.

[59] The issue of covenant is a vast and multi-faceted subject that cannot be adequately entered into here. For introductions to the concept and the literature, see J. B. Payne, "Covenant (in the Old Testament)," *ZPEB*, 1:1000–1010; J. A. Thompson, "Covenant (OT)," *ISBE* 1:790–93; M. Weinfeld, "בְּרִית *běrîth*," *TDOT* 2:253–79; Mendenhall and Herion, "Covenant," *ABD* 1:1179–1202; G. J. McConville, "בְּרִית," *NIDOTTE* 1:747–55. See also the works listed in D. M. Howard, "The Case for Kingship in Deuteronomy and the Former Prophets," *WTJ* 52 (1990): 114, n. 39; Koopmans, *Joshua 24 as Poetic Narrative*, 49–83.

lived beyond the River and worshiped other gods. ³But I took your father Abraham from the land beyond the River and led him throughout Canaan and gave him many descendants. I gave him Isaac, ⁴and to Isaac I gave Jacob and Esau. I assigned the hill country of Seir to Esau, but Jacob and his sons went down to Egypt.

⁵"'Then I sent Moses and Aaron, and I afflicted the Egyptians by what I did there, and I brought you out. ⁶When I brought your fathers out of Egypt, you came to the sea, and the Egyptians pursued them with chariots and horsemen as far as the Red Sea. ⁷But they cried to the LORD for help, and he put darkness between you and the Egyptians; he brought the sea over them and covered them. You saw with your own eyes what I did to the Egyptians. Then you lived in the desert for a long time.

⁸"'I brought you to the land of the Amorites who lived east of the Jordan. They fought against you, but I gave them into your hands. I destroyed them from before you, and you took possession of their land. ⁹When Balak son of Zippor, the king of Moab, prepared to fight against Israel, he sent for Balaam son of Beor to put a curse on you. ¹⁰But I would not listen to Balaam, so he blessed you again and again, and I delivered you out of his hand.

¹¹"'Then you crossed the Jordan and came to Jericho. The citizens of Jericho fought against you, as did also the Amorites, Perizzites, Canaanites, Hittites, Girgashites, Hivites and Jebusites, but I gave them into your hands. ¹²I sent the hornet ahead of you, which drove them out before you—also the two Amorite kings. You did not do it with your own sword and bow. ¹³So I gave you a land on which you did not toil and cities you did not build; and you live in them and eat from vineyards and olive groves that you did not plant.'

This section introduces the passage and reviews the past in terms of God's gracious provisions for his people. The review of God's gracious actions on Israel's behalf goes back to Terah, Abraham's father, and continues up to the taking of the land. It begins with a reminder that Israel's ancestors had served other gods (v. 2), and it is followed by an exhortation not to serve these or any gods (vv. 14–15). It ends with yet another reminder that the land was God's gift to Israel (vv. 12–13; cf. Deut 6:10–11). Verses 1 and 2 present evidence suggesting the more formal nature of this chapter because the Israelite leaders "presented themselves before God" (v. 1) and because the historical review is introduced with the traditional prophetic speech formula, "Thus says the LORD God of Israel" (v. 2).

24:1 Joshua gathered the Israelites at Shechem,[60] which represented a new location for their national gatherings (most recently the setting appears to have been at Shiloh: see 18:1). This is the first time this important city is mentioned in Joshua (except in the land distribution lists), although the covenant renewal ceremony in 8:30–35 took place at Mount Ebal, near Shechem. It was

---

[60] Here and in v. 25, the Old Greek traditions read "Shiloh" instead of "Shechem," undoubtedly to correlate with the previous gathering site (18:1; 22:12). The reading "Shechem" is followed here.

at Shechem that God first promised to give Abraham the land (Gen 12:6–7), and now, centuries later, God's promises finally had come true, and the covenant was renewed in the very place where he had made them.[61]

The officials at this gathering were the same as in chap. 23—the elders, leaders, judges, and officials (cf. 23:2)—but this time the entire nation is also mentioned as being present (cf. also v. 2: "all the people"). They all presented themselves "before God," which was undoubtedly before the ark.[62]

24:2–4 Joshua's review of God's gracious acts for his people began with a reference to their ancestors as far back as Terah, who lived in Mesopotamia[63] and who worshiped other gods (v. 2). Illustrative evidence of some of their ancestors' worship of many gods can be found in the account of Laban, Jacob, and Rachel, where Rachel stole the household gods in Laban's house (Gen 31:19,34–35). This is also illustrated by the account in Gen 35:2–4, where Jacob urged his household to divest themselves of the foreign gods they had kept among them, which they did.

Terah had three sons—Abraham, Nahor, and Haran (Gen 11:27), of whom Nahor and Abraham are mentioned here. God chose only Abraham, however, to bless and to use as a means of blessing to others, and thus the text here states that God took him from his homeland.[64]

God led Abraham through "all the land of Canaan" (NIV: "throughout Canaan"), just as the Book of Genesis affirms (Gen 12:6–9; 13:17–18). He also gave him many descendants, beginning with his son Isaac and his grandsons Jacob and Esau (vv. 3–4). Of these two, the blessing passed through Jacob, who went down to Egypt (v. 4; cf. Gen 15:13; 28:10–15; 35:9–13; 46:5–7). Esau, meanwhile, was granted land east of the Jordan (cf. Gen 32:3; 36:8). A contrast is drawn between Esau and Jacob in the syntax here: "But as for Jacob and his sons, they went down to Egypt." Even though Jacob was the one through whom the promise to Abraham would be mediated, he and his descendants spent a long "exile" in Egypt before finally returning to the promised land. God's plans for the Canaanites had not come to fruition until now (Gen 15:16).

24:5–7 The second phase of God's gracious acts for his people involved what he had done for them in Egypt. He sent leaders for his people—Moses and Aaron. Furthermore, he afflicted the Egyptians through the plagues (cf.

---

[61] For more on the significance of Shechem, see introduction to 8:30–35 and footnote there.

[62] Examples in Joshua where the expression "before the LORD" signifies "before the ark" include 4:13; 6:8 (and possibly 7:23). The expression "before God" does not occur elsewhere in Joshua, but it signifies "before the ark" in 1 Chr 13:8 and 16:1.

[63] "The River" here (and in vv. 3,14–15) refers to the Euphrates River in Mesopotamia, as it does in Gen 31:21; Exod 23:31; Num 22:5; etc.

[64] The text of Gen 11:31 states that *Terah* took Abram from their home in Ur of the Chaldeans, but ultimately it was God's doing.

Exodus 7–12) and brought the Israelites out of Egypt (v. 5; cf. Exod 12:31–39). Then he dramatically delivered the Israelites and destroyed the Egyptians at the Red Sea (Exodus 14–15). Following that was a long sojourn in the desert. The text here does not mention that this sojourn was due to the previous generation's rebellion against the Lord (see Numbers 14). Rather, because the present generation was a new one, which was not guilty of this rebellion, the desert sojourn is simply mentioned in passing.

A dramatic shift in perspective occurs in these verses. Whereas previously God had spoken of the people's ancestors in the distant past and in third-person address ("he," "they"), in v. 5 "you" occurs for the first time, and "you" alternates with "they" through v. 7. After that, "you" is used exclusively. This puts the focus on the present generation in a dramatic way. The alternation also shows the unity of this generation with the fathers. A great number of people in this generation had actually witnessed and experienced many of the mighty deeds God had done for his people. They would have been the people who were under the age of twenty when the nation had left Egypt (see Num 14:29–33). Indeed, the major part of the review of the past in vv. 2–13 focuses on what God had done for those now alive and present with Joshua at Shechem. This shows that God did not just make himself known in ages past; he also worked mightily and graciously for the people being addressed. The impact of God's words was greater because of this focus on them. Christians today are still part of that great spiritual heritage (see, e.g., Rom 11:11–24; Hebrews 11).

24:8–10 The third phase of God's gracious acts for his people involved his work on their behalf before they crossed the Jordan River, and it is divided here into two parts: (1) the victories against Sihon and Og (v. 8; cf. Num 21:21–35) and (2) the thwarting of Balak's evil intentions (vv. 9–10; cf. Numbers 22–24). Sihon and Og are not mentioned here by name, but v. 8 clearly refers to them.

When God said that he was not willing to listen to Balaam (v. 10), he was referring to Balaam's implicit request that God should put a curse on Israel, which he refused to do (Num 22:10–12).[65] The NIV's "he blessed you again and again" here is somewhat misleading. The construction is more properly translated "he indeed blessed you" and expresses the surprise inherent in Balaam's blessing Israel, since his original intention was *not* to do so (see the similar construction in Num 23:11; 24:10).[66]

24:11–13 The fourth and final phase of God's gracious acts concerned his interventions and his blessings in the land of Canaan, that is, the activities

---

[65] Strictly speaking, Balaam was only passing on Balak's request of him, but the context suggests fairly strongly that Balaam's inclinations were in accord with Balak's desires.

[66] The clause here is וַיְבָרֶךְ בָּרוֹךְ אֶתְכֶם, with a (rare) postpositive infinitive absolute. On this construction, see *GBH* § 123l; GKC § 113r; *IBHS* §§ 35.3.1–2.

covered in the Book of Joshua. The people's first great encounter at Jericho is mentioned specifically, but the other battles are only generically referred to by means of the references to the seven peoples of the land and to the hornet (vv. 11–12). God's gift of the land is emphasized in v. 13.

The seven peoples listed here are the same as those listed in 3:10, only in a different order. In 3:10 Joshua had promised the Israelites that God would drive out these peoples from before them. The book comes full circle now in affirming that God had done what he promised: he had delivered the Canaanites into the Israelites' hands (v. 11), and he had driven them out (v. 12).[67]

In v. 12 a reference to "the hornet" that drove the peoples out has occasioned much discussion. The affirmation that God had sent the hornet to do this echoes God's the promise in Exod 23:28 that he would "send the hornet ahead of you to drive the Hivites, Canaanites and Hittites out of your way." In the next verses God had stated that the process would take a long time: "But I will not drive them out in a single year, because the land would become desolate and the wild animals too numerous for you. Little by little I will drive them out before you, until you have increased enough to take possession of the land" (Exod 23:29–30). This is confirmed by statements in the Book of Joshua (see esp. 11:18; 22:3; 23:1, and the commentary on 23:1).

Three suggestions usually are advanced about the identity of the "hornet." (1) It is usually understood as a metaphor representing the terror or panic that an encounter with Israel's God would engender. Passages such as 2:9–11,24; 5:1; 6:27; Exod 15:14–16; 23:27 all show this terror, speaking of it using different terminology (cf. also Gen 35:5).[68] (2) Some have identified the hornet as the power of the pharaoh of Egypt, whose symbols were a bee or hornet.[69] However, the text does not mention Egypt or even hint that Egypt is in view here; furthermore, nowhere in the Bible is such an identification made. (3) Others suggest taking the word literally, arguing that such insects have been used at different points in history in warfare.[70] Even though this practice is known in history in certain places at certain times, however, it is not known from anywhere in the ancient Near East, and such an argument depends on many inferences and assumptions that, in the end, appear to be unlikely.[71]

---

[67] For brief treatments of the seven peoples listed here, see the commentary on 3:10.

[68] See *HALOT* 1056–57 (point b). So also Keil, *Book of Joshua*, 230; Goslinga, *Joshua, Judges, Ruth*, 174–75; Hess, *Joshua*, 304; Butler, *Joshua*, 264.

[69] See J. Garstang, *Joshua and Judges* (London: Constable: 1931), 258–61; O. Borowski, "The Identity of the Biblical ṣirʿâ," in E. L. Meyers and M. O'Connor, eds., *The Word of the Lord Shall Go Forth: Essays in Honor of David Noel Freedman in Celebration of His Sixtieth Birthday* (Winona Lake: Eisenbrauns, 1983), 315–19.

[70] E. Neufeld, "Insects as Warfare Agents in the Ancient Near East (Exod 23:28; Deut 7:20; Josh 24:12; Isa 7:18–20)," *Or* 49 (1980): 30–57.

[71] Neufeld states that "there is a total lack of information from Egypt and from cuneiform sources of Mesopotamia about such military operations" (ibid., 39).

Hornets are not mentioned in the actual battle descriptions in chaps. 6–12, and, in any case, the reference is to "*the hornet*," not "*hornets*." Thus, the first possibility appears to be the most likely (i.e., that we are dealing with a metaphor here). We should remember, however, that the larger point is that God fought for Israel, regardless of how we interpret the reference to "the hornet."

On the face of it, the two kings in v. 12 were Sihon and Og, whom Israel had defeated in the wilderness (Num 21:21–35) and now are called "the kings of the Amorites" (Deut 3:8; 31:4). However, the Israelites' triumph over the Amorites east of the Jordan is told in v. 8; the verses here refer to actions west of the Jordan. It is possible that Adonizedek and Jabin, the heads of the northern and southern coalitions that opposed Israel in chaps. 10–11, are in view here. In chap. 10 the coalition is characterized as "Amorite" (10:6). The Old Greek traditions have "twelve kings" instead of "two kings," but this number—although it is a common one and is also found in Assyrian royal inscriptions referring to the number of enemy kings killed[72]—does not correlate with any groupings of kings in Joshua. Syntactically, the phrase "the two Amorite kings" is not connected to anything else in the verse, and perhaps the simplest solution to this difficulty is to understand that the author is here inserting a brief flashback to victories east of the Jordan to go along with those west of the Jordan.

As this first section comes to an end in vv. 12b and 13, God once again reminded the people that their present position in the land was entirely his doing. Not only did he send "the hornet" to drive out the Canaanites, but this was accomplished even without their own weapons as the instruments. The victories were God's, not dependent upon military power (cf. Ps 44:2–3[Hb. 3–4]). Obviously, the Israelites did wield their weapons on occasion. For example, at Jericho we are told that they "destroyed with the sword every living thing in it" (6:21), or at Ai the enemy "had been put to the sword" (8:24), or in the battle of Gibeon many "were killed by the swords of the Israelites" (10:11). Therefore, God's statement that it was *not* "with your sword or your bow" must be understood as saying that it was not by their own power, by the might or ferocity of their own weapons, that they had success. Only by God's power did they accomplish what they did, something the book affirms over and over again.

The hyperbole here places the emphasis squarely where it belongs, on God's initiatives and provisions for his people. Jesus used similar hyperbolic language when he said, "If anyone comes to me and does not hate his father and mother, his wife and children, his brothers and sisters—yes, even his own life—he cannot be my disciple" (Luke 14:26), even though he had stressed elsewhere that people were to love their neighbors as themselves (Matt 22:39; Mark 12:31,33;

---

[72] See *ANET*, 279–81, 291, 294.

Luke 10:27). His point was that, compared to their love for their neighbors or family, their love for God should cause that human love to appear like hate. So too here: in the overall scheme of things, the Israelites' swords had nothing to do with their inheriting and taking the land. It was all God's doing.

That this was God's work is emphasized in the final statements of the historical review portion of Joshua's address. Essentially everything they now possessed had been given to them by God. They had not worked the land, built the cities, or planted the vineyards and olive groves that they now were enjoying. This fulfilled the promise God had made earlier, in Deut 6:10–11, where he told the Israelites that the land they were coming into was "a land with large, flourishing cities you did not build, houses filled with all kinds of good things you did not provide, wells you did not dig, and vineyards and olive groves you did not plant." Once again God was faithful to his promises. The land was nothing but God's gracious gift to his people.

(2) Covenant Affirmations (24:14–24)

[14]"Now fear the LORD and serve him with all faithfulness. Throw away the gods your forefathers worshiped beyond the River and in Egypt, and serve the LORD. [15]But if serving the LORD seems undesirable to you, then choose for yourselves this day whom you will serve, whether the gods your forefathers served beyond the River, or the gods of the Amorites, in whose land you are living. But as for me and my household, we will serve the LORD."

[16]Then the people answered, "Far be it from us to forsake the LORD to serve other gods! [17]It was the LORD our God himself who brought us and our fathers up out of Egypt, from that land of slavery, and performed those great signs before our eyes. He protected us on our entire journey and among all the nations through which we traveled. [18]And the LORD drove out before us all the nations, including the Amorites, who lived in the land. We too will serve the LORD, because he is our God."

[19]Joshua said to the people, "You are not able to serve the LORD. He is a holy God; he is a jealous God. He will not forgive your rebellion and your sins. [20]If you forsake the LORD and serve foreign gods, he will turn and bring disaster on you and make an end of you, after he has been good to you."

[21]But the people said to Joshua, "No! We will serve the LORD."

[22]Then Joshua said, "You are witnesses against yourselves that you have chosen to serve the LORD."

"Yes, we are witnesses," they replied.

[23]"Now then," said Joshua, "throw away the foreign gods that are among you and yield your hearts to the LORD, the God of Israel."

[24]And the people said to Joshua, "We will serve the LORD our God and obey him."

The proper response to God's gracious dealings was for Israel to forsake other gods and follow him, the one true God. Joshua himself would lead the way by example (vv. 14–15). The people's response was one of commitment (vv. 16–18), after which Joshua warned them about the consequences of this commitment, which the people were willing to accept (vv. 19–21). A formal covenant renewal or covenant ratification ceremony seems to be in view in vv. 22–24, with the people testifying as witnesses to their own actions, although these verses only report on such a ceremony (i.e., they may not contain the entirety of what was said and done).[73]

24:14–15 Now God left off speaking directly, and Joshua addressed the people, charging them to be faithful in serving the God who had been so faithful in helping them. He again mentioned the gods of their ancestors (cf. v. 2) and urged the people to remove them ("throw away") from their midst. In v. 14 the NIV's "serve him with all faithfulness" is literally "serve him with integrity *(tāmîm)* and truth *(ʾĕmet)*." The NASB renders the phrase here as "sincerity and truth," the NRSV as "sincerity and … faithfulness," the REB as "loyalty and truth," the NLT as "wholeheartedly." The word *tāmîm* connotes the idea of wholeness, blamelessness, integrity, even "perfection," and thus Joshua's exhortation is a passionate one that the people should be totally devoted—blameless—in their worship of their God. The first part of v. 14 contains a concentration of theologically freighted words: the Israelites should fear *(yrʾ)* the Lord, and they should serve *(ʿbd)* him with integrity *(tāmîm)* and truth *(ʾĕmet)*. Joshua was urgently impressing on the people what they should do.

The phrase "in Egypt" in v. 14 adds something new here. In v. 2 we have learned that Israel's ancestors had worshiped other gods early on, when they were still in Mesopotamia (see comments on v. 2). However, Joshua now stated that this also had been true in Egypt. There is no direct reference to such false worship from the narrative texts in Exodus about Israel's time in Egypt. However, twice reference is made in the Pentateuch to the gods the Israelites had worshiped there: (1) Lev 17:7 mentions goat idols that the Israelites had sacrificed to, and (2) in Deut 32:16–17 they are charged with worshiping "demons," which were foreign gods, idols, which had not been worshiped in Israel until recent times (i.e., in Egypt, or the wilderness).[74] In v. 15 Joshua added a third set of gods, "the gods of the Amorites, in whose land you are living." Thus, false worship had been a hallmark not only of Israel's distant ancestors or of their more immediate ancestors in Egypt, but even of themselves, here in the land of Canaan. Joshua's implication was that the nation had never truly rid itself of false worship, and he was urging the people in the strongest terms possible to do so now.

---

[73] On elements of the covenant form and questions of the relationship of the material in this chapter to that form, see the introduction to the chapter.

[74] Further references to idol worship in Egypt are found in Ezek 20:7–8; 23:3,8.

In v. 15 Joshua laid out two choices for the people, made the more urgent by his insistence that the choice be made "today" ("this day").[75] If they found serving the Lord to be "evil in your eyes" (NIV: "undesirable to you"), then they should choose between the gods of Mesopotamia whom their distant ancestors had served or the more immediate gods of the Amorites (i.e., Canaanites), among whom they were living. In his famous words at the end of the verse, Joshua took his stand clearly and unambiguously on the Lord's side. Joshua stands as a good example of a leader willing to move ahead of his people and commit himself, regardless of the people's inclinations. His bold example undoubtedly encouraged many to follow what he pledged to do, in their affirmations of vv. 16–18.

The choice laid out here for Israel was a breathtaking one. The language about choice is not found elsewhere in the Old Testament.[76] Normally, God was the one who did the choosing, having chosen Israel from among the nations to be his people (see, e.g., Deut 4:37; 7:6–7; 10:15; 14:2). But now, *Israel* was being asked to choose *its* loyalties, something the pagan nations did not have to do because they could embrace all the gods. The Israelites were being asked to do what Rahab had done, namely, to embrace this *one* God and, by doing so, to reject all others (see on 2:9–11). Joshua laid out for Israel the choice, but he did not threaten them or try to coerce them. The choice was simple, and he set an example by his own choice.[77]

24:16–18 The people rose to Joshua's challenge and promised to serve the Lord, not other gods (vv. 16,18). They echoed the spirit of God's words in vv. 2–13, acknowledging that it was indeed he who had delivered them at each step of the way, but they focused on different aspects of his deliverance. They also added to God's words (e.g., mentioning "that land of slavery," v. 17), showing that they were well aware of their history and God's part in it. The Israelites saw *(rʾh)* in these signs the hand of God, just as God had said that they had seen *(rʾh, v. 7)*. Joshua had suggested that perhaps it was evil in their eyes to follow the Lord (v. 15), but they insisted that they did see things aright now, and they would serve him. This is an incisive reminder for the present day as well, since often, when God does cause events to work out for his people, they do not see his hand in it, but rather attribute it merely to chance or coincidence.

---

[75] The urgency is highlighted even further by the paragogic *nun* in תַעֲבֹדוּן. As we noted at 3:7, this morpheme involves a contrast of some type, which, in this case, is the contrast between Yahweh and the foreign gods. The choice for the people was between these two, which explains the contrast inherent in the paragogic *nun*. See on 3:7 and the note there for more on the paragogic *nun*.

[76] In Deut 30:19, Israel is urged to "choose life," which obviously is a similar situation. However, there blessings and curses are attached, whereas here the choice is simply laid out with no accompanying threats or consequences.

[77] See Butler, *Joshua*, 273–74 for the basic insight here concerning Israel's choice.

24:19–20   Joshua's statement that Israel was not capable of serving the Lord introduces a "deep paradox" here,[78] one that Butler calls "perhaps the most shocking statement in the OT."[79] Joshua had just urged Israel in vv. 14–15 to serve the Lord with all faithfulness, and he had done so in passionate terms. He also laid out what appeared to be a true choice for the people. And yet now, when the people responded that they would do so, he turned the tables on them and stated that they were *not* capable of doing so. Furthermore, he stated that God himself would not forgive their rebellion and sin. These were harsh words indeed.

The key to understanding these statements comes in two other statements that Joshua made, which affirmed two of God's defining characteristics: he is a holy God and also a jealous God (v. 19). Both of these characteristics are part of God's very nature and set him apart from all other gods and from his people.[80] In Lev 19:2 the Israelites are urged to be holy because of God's own holy nature: "Be holy because I, the LORD your God, am holy." God's holiness pervades the instructions in the Pentateuch about the building of the tabernacle, the offering of the sacrifices, and the celebrating of the festivals. Wherever God was, that place was holy, whether it was a piece of ground (Exod 3:5; Josh 5:15), a physical structure such as the tabernacle (Exod 26:33–34; 28:35–36; etc.) or the altar (Exod 29:37; 30:10), or even a day dedicated to him (i.e., the Sabbath: Gen 2:3; Exod 20:8,11; Deut 5:12).

God's jealous nature also set him apart from other gods. They were jealous among themselves, displaying endless petty rivalries. However, God's jealousy played itself out with the consequences being visited on his own people when they were unfaithful. This was (and is) part of God's very nature: he would not brook any competition for his people's loyalties.[81] This is clear in the Second Commandment in Exod 20:4–6: "You shall not make for yourself an idol in the form of anything in heaven above or on the earth beneath or in the waters below. You shall not bow down to them or worship them; for I, the LORD your God, am a jealous God, punishing the children for the sin of the fathers to the third and fourth generation of those who hate me, but showing love to a thousand generations of those who love me and keep my commandments." Butler well notes that "[God] loves [his people] so much that he wants their undivided love in return. He will not share them with any other god."[82]

---

[78] Nelson, *Joshua*, 276.

[79] Butler, *Joshua*, 274.

[80] Butler notes that both ideas are found in the Canaanite traditions of their gods, but that in their biblical expression they are unique (*Joshua*, 275).

[81] W. Eichrodt calls it "the basic element in the whole OT idea of God" (*Theology of the Old Testament* [Philadelphia: Westminster, 1961], 210, n. 1). See Eichrodt's broader discussion of this aspect of God's nature on p. 210.

[82] Ibid.

Joshua's response to the people that they were unable to serve the Lord properly communicates the absolute and awesome nature of God's holiness and his jealousy. He would not forgive them if they persisted in sin. However, Exod 20:6 shows that even this jealous God would show his love in a most bountiful way if his people loved him and kept his commandments.[83] Joshua himself assumed that the Israelites would make a choice (Josh 24:14–15). His dramatic words here emphasize the solemnity of the requirements, to purge from the Israelites any false notions of "cheap grace." Theirs was not to be a nominal, superficial faith. As J. H. Michaelis noted, Israel could not serve the Lord "by your own resolution only, and without the assistance of divine grace, without solid and serious conversion from all idols, and without true repentance and faith."[84]

Verse 20 makes it clear that what Joshua stated in v. 19 about God's not forgiving his people was not an absolute, timeless statement, but that his forgiveness depended on whether or not his people forsook him in favor of "foreign gods." As Calvin stated, "when it is said that he will not spare their wickedness, no general rule is laid down, but the discourse is directed, as often elsewhere, against their disobedient temper. It does not refer to faults in general, or to special faults, but is confined to gross denial of God, as the next verse demonstrates."[85] After all the good that he had done for them, God would reward any rejection of him by his people with harsh judgment. This is not, however, the action of a capricious God. He had graciously taken the initiative again and again with his people and provided for them over and over again, as vv. 2–13 affirm. Yet if his people persisted in rebellion in spite of such loving and sustained overtures, he would not tolerate this forever.

24:21–24   The second section of the chapter ends with a set of exchanges between Joshua and the people about their resolve to serve the Lord. First, the people protested that Joshua was mistaken when he said they were not capable of serving him (v. 21). No doubt they were sincere, and no doubt they obeyed for a time. However, as the Book of Judges makes clear, they soon demonstrated that theirs was indeed a shallow, superficial faith.

In response to their protest of loyalty to the Lord, Joshua held the people responsible to be witnesses against themselves—that they had indeed chosen to serve the Lord—and they readily agreed (v. 22). As we noted in the introduction to the chapter, calling the gods as witnesses between two parties was a standard part of ancient Near Eastern treaties. However, since here Yahweh was God alone and the entire point was that there were no other gods, such gods could not be invoked. Rather, Joshua held the people to be their own

---

[83] Note that God promised to visit the people's sins down to the *third* and *fourth* generations but to show love to a *thousand* generations (Exod 20:5–6).

[84] J. H. Michaelis, quoted in Keil, *Book of Joshua*, 231.

[85] J. Calvin, *Commentary on Joshua* (Grand Rapids: Eerdmans, n.d.), 278.

witnesses. Later he erected a large stone that would serve the same purpose (v. 27).

The expression in v. 23, "incline your heart to the LORD" ("yield your hearts ..."), indicates an attitude of commitment to him, rejecting others. In 1 Kgs 11:2,4,9 we are told that Solomon's heart inclined after foreign gods because of his foreign wives, which was precisely the type of behavior Joshua was warning against.

This section ends in v. 24 as it began in v. 21: with the Israelites vowing to serve the Lord (and to obey him).

(3) Sealing the Covenant (24:25–28)

[25]On that day Joshua made a covenant for the people, and there at Shechem he drew up for them decrees and laws. [26]And Joshua recorded these things in the Book of the Law of God. Then he took a large stone and set it up there under the oak near the holy place of the LORD.

[27]"See!" he said to all the people. "This stone will be a witness against us. It has heard all the words the LORD has said to us. It will be a witness against you if you are untrue to your God."

[28]Then Joshua sent the people away, each to his own inheritance.

In the structure of the covenant treaty form discussed at the beginning of this chapter, some of the information here would correspond to the deposit in the sanctuary, public reading (v. 26), and witnesses (v. 27) (so Kitchen), or a written documentation (so Baltzer). However, as we have noted, it is not clear that this chapter is intending to reproduce faithfully every element of such a treaty, so certainty is impossible. For the first (and only) time in the chapter, the word "covenant" is mentioned. This has occasioned much scholarly discussion about the precise nature of the covenant because God's involvement is limited to the recital of his past deeds; he does not appear as an active party at the end of the proceedings. What is clear is that the people were binding themselves to serve and obey him. The writing down of the decrees and laws and the calling of the great stone as a witness against them both served to seal their solemn commitment to this.[86]

24:25 Joshua made a covenant "for" or "on behalf of" the people (the Hb. preposition can mean either). Once again he functioned as the nation's leader. This covenant bound the people in a strong commitment to serve and obey only Yahweh their God, as over against the gods of the Canaanites or any other foreign gods. He established ("drew up") the terms "for it" (i.e., for the covenant; NIV has "for them"): the decrees and laws. The terms here *(hōq ûmišpāṭ)* are actually singular, "a statute and an ordinance" (NASB). They are

---

[86] The extensive discussion about the precise nature of the covenant here may be entered via the discussions and bibliographies in Butler, *Joshua*, 276; Nelson, *Joshua*, 276–77.

used forty-one times together, five times in the singular: Exod 15:25; Josh 24:25; 1 Sam 30:25; Ezra 7:10; Ps 81:4[Hb. 5].[87] In Exod 15:25 and 1 Sam 30:25, what is in view is a specific ordinance for the specific context. In Ezra 7:10 the larger context of the law is in view, as it is many times when the two terms are plural. In Ps 81:4 [Hb. 5] the decree and the law are for the establishment of festival observances. Here in Joshua 24 the "decree and law" that Joshua established centered around a specific ordinance, which was the primary concern and focus of the chapter, namely, that Israel would be committed to Yahweh alone. By extension, of course, such a commitment would entail Israel's keeping the entirety of the law, but the immediate focus is more intensely concentrated on this single-minded and whole-hearted commitment to God.

24:26 The covenant was sealed by (1) the recording of the words in a book and (2) the setting up of a stone as a "witness" to it. "These words" (or, with NIV, "these things") refers to either the words spoken by God, Joshua, and the people in this chapter or else, more broadly, to an account of everything that had transpired, including the words and the events of that day. The book in which this was recorded is called "the Book of the Law of God." This term is used again only in Neh 8:8,18, where it refers to "the Book of the Law of Moses," that is, the entire corpus of the law (see Neh 8:1). Here the nature of this book is not so clear. The words of the covenant ceremony in Joshua 24 are not found in the Pentateuch in this form. Thus, by writing *these words in the Book of the Law of God,"* Joshua was not contributing to the writing of the Pentateuch itself. He may have recorded the words of the ceremony in a copy of the law that was in his possession, or, more probably, he may have recorded these words in another book, which was called "the Book of the Law of God" by virtue of its contents. The essence of its contents is known to us via the present canonical Book of Joshua.

The covenant was also sealed by the erecting of a large stone under an oak tree. This oak tree was near the Lord's "holy place," which probably was not a formal building or temple but a reference to the "holy place" created at Shechem by the bringing of the tabernacle there, where it would have stayed, at least for a time. The reference in v. 1 to the people's presenting themselves "before God" suggests that the tabernacle was now here, housing the ark.[88] The stone under the oak tree functioned as a legal reminder or guarantor (a "witness") of the covenant just entered into (v. 27). Now the stone and the people were both witnesses to this covenant (v. 22). This also echoes the function of the altar built by the Transjordan tribes, which also was a "witness" (22:34).

---

[87] The first lexeme is represented by חֹק (twenty-seven times) or חֻקָּה (fourteen times).

[88] See the commentary on v. 1. On the tabernacle, see the commentary on 18:1–2.

We have good evidence of the significance of large trees at Shechem and elsewhere. In the Bible they appear primarily as landmarks or gathering places. For example, a great tree "of Moreh" was a distinguishing marker of Shechem as far back as Abraham's day (Gen 12:6), and "great trees of Moreh" are mentioned in Deut 11:30. Jacob buried items of foreign worship under an oak tree at Shechem (Gen 35:4; perhaps the same one that Abraham saw?). In Judg 9:6 "all the citizens of Shechem and Beth Millo gathered beside the great tree at the pillar in Shechem to crown Abimelech king"; no doubt this passage refers to the same tree and stone mentioned in Joshua 24. Other prominent trees include "the great trees of Mamre at Hebron" in Abraham's day (Gen 13:18; 14:13; 18:1); "the Palm of Deborah between Ramah and Bethel in the hill country of Ephraim," where Deborah rendered legal decisions (Judg 4:5); "the great tree in Zaanannim near Kedesh," where Heber pitched his tent (Judg 4:11); "the oak in Ophrah," where the angel of the Lord met Gideon (Judg 6:11,19); and "the great tree of Tabor," where Saul was to meet three men (1 Sam 10:3).

We also have evidence elsewhere of the significance of large standing stones such as the one here. They were used primarily as markers to memorialize significant events or people. Jacob set up the stone he had used for a pillow as a pillar to mark the place where God had met him and where he had made a vow (Gen 28:18,22; 31:13; cf. also 35:14). He also set up a stone, as well as a pile of stones next to it, to mark (as "witnesses") the agreement he made with Laban about their future interactions (Gen 31:44–52). He also set up a stone to mark his wife Rachel's tomb (Gen 35:20). Moses built an altar and twelve stone pillars at the foot of Mount Sinai to mark the giving of the covenant there (Exod 24:4). Absalom erected a pillar as well, but it was a monument to himself, not to the Lord (2 Sam 18:18).[89]

24:27 The stone itself was now a witness of the covenant (as were the people in v. 22). It had "heard" everything that the Lord had said to Israel. The text only claims that the stone had heard what God had said (i.e., vv. 2–13), not the rest of the ceremony (vv. 14–24). So its presence would serve as a testimony to God's faithfulness to his people, just as the twelve stones that Joshua erected on the bank of the Jordan were to serve as testimonies to what he had done at the Jordan (4:9,20–24). Such a reference to the stone's "hearing" is obviously a literary metaphor, in the same way that references to rivers

---

[89] A large standing stone, dating to the Late Bronze Age (i.e., roughly the time represented in this story), has been found at Shechem, which some scholars have associated with the stone mentioned here. However, other scholars dispute this. Indeed, attempts have been made to correlate several archaeological finds at Shechem (including a large temple area) with Joshua 24, but certainty is not possible. See Hess, *Joshua*, 174; Koopmans, *Joshua 24 as Poetic Narrative*, 84–92, 154–56. Concerning the general significances that standing stones had, see C. F. Graesser, "Standing Stones in Ancient Palestine," *Biblical Archaeologist Reader* 4 (Garden City: Doubleday, 1983), 293–321.

clapping their hands and mountains singing for joy (Ps 98:8) or to the trees of the field singing for joy (Ps 96:12) are metaphors.

24:28   With a short, laconic statement, the main story line of the book of Joshua is concluded. There were no more lands to be taken, no more territorial distributions to be made, no more speeches to be given, no more covenants to be entered into. Everyone was able to return to his inheritance, which was the goal from the beginning of the book.

5. Conclusion: Burial Notices (24:29–33)

The Book of Joshua ends on a satisfying, peaceful note, giving the accounts of Joshua's death and burial (vv. 29–31) and of the burial of Joseph (v. 32) and of Eleazar the priest (v. 33). Fittingly, the motif of land inheritance is the common thread in the three burial notices: the bodies of all three men were buried in land that belonged to the inheritance of their families. The burials of these three men signified the ends of eras: Joshua the leader and Eleazar the priest were the last recent links with Egypt, whereas Joseph represented a more distant link with Egypt and with the promises to the patriarchs. God's promises to give his people the land were now indeed fulfilled: every tribe had received its inheritance, and Israel's leaders died peaceful deaths and were buried in land that was finally their own. This peaceful ending to the book gives little hint of the troubles in that land that were to come shortly, in the Book of Judges. However, the Book of Joshua has already given hints of these troubles (see the commentary on 10:40–43). The point here is that Joshua's and the people's obedience was rewarded and especially that Yahweh is a God who keeps his promises.

(1) Joshua's Burial (24:29–31)

[29]**After these things, Joshua son of Nun, the servant of the LORD, died at the age of a hundred and ten.** [30]**And they buried him in the land of his inheritance, at Timnath Serah in the hill country of Ephraim, north of Mount Gaash.**

[31]**Israel served the LORD throughout the lifetime of Joshua and of the elders who outlived him and who had experienced everything the LORD had done for Israel.**

The account of Joshua's death and burial is longer than the others, and it serves as a brief epitaph for this leader (although it is shorter and less glowing than Moses' epitaph in Deut 34:10–12). Joshua died at a ripe old age, was buried on his own land, and Israel served the Lord all his days and the days of his successors. This account is introduced by the same episode-initial syntactical construction found at 1:1 and elsewhere.[90]

---

[90]I.e., וַיְהִי plus a time margin (prepositional phrase) plus a *wāw*-consecutive. See the commentary on 1:1 and 4:11 for more on this construction.

Joshua 24:28–31 is repeated in Judg 2:6–9, with a few differences. The main difference is that the content of v. 31 is placed between that of vv. 28 and 29. The author in Judges reveals his own particular purposes in his rearranging of the material and in his addition of v. 10, which states that "after that whole generation had been gathered to their fathers, another generation grew up, who knew neither the LORD nor what he had done for Israel." That is, here in Joshua the passage ends on a positive note, with the people serving the Lord all the days of Joshua and the elders who outlived him (lit.), "who had known *[ydᶜ]* all the work that the LORD had done for Israel" (24:31). However, this verse is moved earlier in the section in the Judges passage, and v. 10, a new and much more somber one, ends the passage. Judges 2:10 tells us that the new generation did *not* know *(ydᶜ)* the Lord or the work he had done.[91]

The Old Greek traditions have a lengthy addition at the end of v. 30. It reads: "There they placed with him in the tomb, into which they buried him, the stone knives with which he circumcised the sons of Israel in Gilgal, when he brought them out of Egypt, just as the Lord had commanded them, and they are there to this day." This picks up on the previous addition in the Old Greek versions that we noted at the end of 21:42. As we noted, that addition closely parallels 19:49–50, and then it adds the information that Joshua took the flint knives and deposited them in Timnath-Serah. The addition here, then, completes the story of the flint knives. The addition has the ring of authenticity to it, although it is impossible to know for certain if it was on the original.

24:29 Joshua's full name is given for a final time, and now, for the first time, he is called "the servant of the LORD." The book carefully avoids calling him by this label until now—as opposed to Moses, who is called this fourteen

---

[91] A problem of chronology arises here because Joshua's death is mentioned already in Joshua 24, as well as twice in Judges 1–2: in 1:1 and in 2:8. Many scholars see this duplication as due to the convergence of independent traditions (e.g., Boling, *Judges,* 36,72; Soggin, *Judges,* 20,40–42). At least one scholar treats Judg 1:1a—"After the death of Joshua"—as a title to the entire book and sees the events in chap. 1 as all taking place *before* Joshua died. Thus, in this understanding, the account of his death in 2:6–10 is correctly placed chronologically (A. E. Cundall, *Judges: An Introduction and Commentary,* TOTC [Downers Grove: InterVarsity, 1968], 19, 51). This suggestion is attractive since it resolves the problem of Judg 1:11–15, which essentially duplicates Josh 15:15–19. However, the grammatical construction in v. 1 is a common one, demanding that the reference to Joshua's death be read in conjunction with the words immediately following, not detached from them. Thus the judgment here is that Judg 1:1 is correctly placed: most of the events in Judges 1 followed Joshua's death. In this way, then, the reference in 2:6–10 about Joshua's death is out of place chronologically. It is a "flashback" inserted at the beginning of the second section of the book (2:6–3:6). As we have noted, it duplicates Josh 24:28–31 almost word for word, and its purpose is to tie the material that follows closely to the Book of Joshua. Indeed, P. Cassell has shown the function of Judg 2:6–10 by aptly titling the passage "an extract from the Book of Joshua showing when and through what occasion the religious apostasy of Israel began" ("The Book of Judges," in *A Commentary on the Holy Scriptures,* ed. J. P. Lange, ed. [New York: Scribners, 1871], 54).

times in the book (and only four more times in the entire Old Testament). Yet by now, Joshua had clearly "grown into the job" that Moses had vacated. God had exalted him (3:7; 4:14), Joshua had acted as God's spokesman throughout the book, and he had acted authoritatively in leading the nation into battle (chaps. 6–11), in distributing the lands to them (chaps. 13–21), and in exhorting the nation to serve the Lord and renew the covenant (chaps. 22–24). The use of this epithet here brings the book around full circle, recalling the references in 1:1 to Moses as the servant of the Lord and to Joshua as merely Moses' assistant.[92]

24:30 Joshua was buried on his own land, in the city he had asked for and built, Timnath-Serah (see 19:50). The exact location of Mount Gaash is unknown. One manuscript of the Old Greek has "Gilead" for "Gaash," but this cannot be correct since Gilead was east of the Jordan. The same manuscript reads "Gaash" correctly in Judg 2:9.

24:31 This verse forms a fitting epitaph for Joshua: the people under his leadership served the Lord for many years during his lifetime and after his death. They evidently followed his example when he challenged them to choose whom they would serve and when he asserted that he and his household would serve the Lord (vv. 14–15).

(2) Joseph's Burial (24:32)

[32]And Joseph's bones, which the Israelites had brought up from Egypt, were buried at Shechem in the tract of land that Jacob bought for a hundred pieces of silver from the sons of Hamor, the father of Shechem. This became the inheritance of Joseph's descendants.

The brief account of the transfer of Joseph's body to Canaan from Egypt serves as another case of motifs from the Pentateuch being fulfilled in Joshua. Israel kept the promise that Joseph's brothers made hundreds of years earlier, recorded in Gen 50:25–26: "And Joseph made the sons of Israel swear an oath and said, 'God will surely come to your aid, and then you must carry my bones up from this place.' So Joseph died at the age of a hundred and ten. And after they embalmed him, he was placed in a coffin in Egypt." Joseph had died at the same age that Joshua did: 110 years old. He was buried at Shechem, the site of the covenant renewal ceremony in this chapter, on land that had been purchased in a legal transaction. This transaction is recorded earlier—"For a hundred pieces of silver, [Jacob] bought from the sons of Hamor, the father of Shechem, the plot of ground where he pitched his tent" (Gen 33:19)—and the account here wraps up one more final detail from an earlier time.

---

[92] See the commentary on 1:1 and n. 4 there for a fuller discussion of Moses and Joshua as servants of the Lord. See also J. A. Vadnais, "The Characterization of Joshua: From Minister of Moses to Servant of the Lord," Ph.D. diss., New Orleans Baptist Theological Seminary (in progress).

(3) Eleazar's Burial (24:33)

³³**And Eleazar son of Aaron died and was buried at Gibeah, which had been allotted to his son Phinehas in the hill country of Ephraim.**

Eleazar the high priest had figured significantly in the land distribution (see 14:1; 17:4; 19:51, and the commentary on 14:1–5), and now he too received a decent burial on his own land.

JOSHUA 22–24: THEOLOGICAL REFLECTIONS

The Book of Joshua ends with a series of reflections on what has transpired up to this point. More than most Old Testament books, it ends on a settled, peaceful, and harmonious note. Almost every loose end has been tied up, and things have come to a satisfactory conclusion.

The issue of the nation's unity was resolved by the confrontation and resolution surrounding the altar that the Transjordan tribes built (chap. 22). The issue of the land inheritances was finally settled when these tribes returned to their places east of the Jordan (chap. 22), when Joshua dismissed the entire nation to return to their inheritances (24:28), and when Joshua, Joseph, and Eleazar were buried in lands belonging to their own tribal inheritances (24:29–33). The land goal toward which the entire Pentateuch (and most of the Book of Joshua) had moved was now achieved.

An uncommon unity of purpose and outlook among the tribes marks these chapters. The crisis in chap. 22 was precipitated precisely because the Transjordan tribes did not want their descendants to be disenfranchised by their brethren west of the Jordan. Prior to the crisis, these tribes had demonstrated their loyalty to their brethren by fighting alongside them, even though their own lands had been taken; and Joshua commended them for this loyalty and faithfulness (22:1–9). In chap. 24, the tribes passionately committed themselves with one voice to following and serving the Lord. To a tribe and to a man, they bound themselves to these things.

God's faithfulness to his people shines brightly in these chapters, primarily chaps. 23 and 24. Significant portions of Joshua's first speech to the entire nation are devoted to looking back at what God had done for his people (23:3–5,9–10,14). In 23:14 he asserted definitively that none of God's good promises had failed; they had all come to pass. Joshua's final speech reported God's words directly, in which he rehearsed the history of his gifts to his people and his help for them (24:2–13). Even in the peaceful burial notices, where God is not mentioned at all as an actor in the events there, his presence is still felt because everything was ending in an ordered manner. God's promises about the land had finally come true, such that Israel's most significant leaders could be buried there.

The dangers and pitfalls of false worship pervade these chapters as well. The crisis in chap. 22 centered around the Cisjordan tribes' fear that the altar their Transjordan brethren had built was designed for false worship. In chap. 23, Joshua repeatedly warned Israel against entanglements with the Canaanites and their gods. And in the interchange between Joshua and the people in 24:14–24, the gods of the nations form the backdrop to Joshua's warnings and challenges and the people's affirmations: they would not serve these gods but only Yahweh. They were not to serve these gods but to throw them away (24:14,23).

On the positive side, loyalty to the true God is also stressed in these chapters. The Transjordan tribes erected their altar as a reminder and a witness that they should worship the Lord at his sanctuary (22:27). Joshua urged the people to obey him (23:6), to cling to him (23:8), to love him (23:11), to serve him (24:14), and to incline their hearts to him (24:23).

These chapters are remarkable for their sense of serenity and the peaceable ending they portray. And yet, the very insistent warnings that Joshua sounded in his last two speeches—from the warnings in chap. 23 against associating with the Canaanites to his startling words in 24:19 that the Israelites would not be able to serve the Lord and that he would not forgive them—hint that all was not well. Things were certainly much better than they had been in the wilderness and certainly much better than they would become in the period of the judges. Yet the seeds of the religious and political chaos of that period had already been sown in the time of Joshua, when the tribes had not driven out every Canaanite from his land (see 13:2–6,13; 15:63; 16:10; 17:11–12; 19:47).

The book ends in a very satisfying way, with the nation at peace with itself, occupying the land it had looked forward to for centuries in covenant relationship with its God and with its leaders buried properly on lands that were their own. A period of harmony, stability, and peace followed for a number of years (24:31). Yet, it was only a temporary state of affairs, the calm before a great storm. That storm is recounted in the next book.

Selected Bibliography

Albright, W. F. "Archaeology and the Date of the Hebrew Conquest of Palestine." *BA-SOR* 58 (1935): 10–18.

———. "The Israelite Conquest of Canaan in the Light of Archaeology." *BASOR* 74 (1939): 11–23.

———. "The Amarna Letters from Palestine." *CAH* 2.2:98–116.

———. *Yahweh and the Gods of Canaan.* Garden City: Doubleday/Anchor, 1968.

Allis, O. T. *The Five Books of Moses.* Nutley, N.J.: Presbyterian and Reformed, 1949.

Alt, A. "The Settlement of the Israelites in Palestine." In his collected *Essays on Old Testament History and Religion.* Translated by R. A. Wilson. Garden City, NY: Doubleday [Anchor], 1968.

Barthélemy, D. et al., eds. *Preliminary and Interim Report on the Hebrew Old Testament Text Project.* Vol. 2: *Historical Books.* New York: UBS, 1979. [Joshua: pp. 1–67]

Bartlett, J. R. *Cities of the Ancient World: Jericho.* Grand Rapids: Eerdmans, 1982.

Beitzel, B. J. "Review of Norman Gottwald, *The Tribes of Yahweh.*" *TrinJ* 1 (1980): 237–43.

Benjamin, P. "The Theology of Land Presented in the Book of Joshua." Th.D. dissertation, Lutheran School of Theology, Chicago, 1986, 1987.

Bennett, W. H. *Joshua: A New English Translation.* Polychrome Bible.

Bienkowski, P. *Jericho in the Late Bronze Age.* Warminster: Aris and Phillips, 1986.

Bimson, J. J. and D. Livingston. "Saving the Biblical Chronology." *BAR* 13.5 (1987): 40–53, 66–68.

Bimson, J. J. *Redating the Exodus and Conquest.* 2d ed. JSOTSup 5. Sheffield: Almond, 1981.

———. "The Origins of Israel in Canaan: An Examination of Recent Theories." *Themelios* 15.1 (1989): 4–15.

Boling, R. G. *Joshua.* AB 6. Garden City: Doubleday, 1982.

Bright, J. *Ancient Israel in Recent History Writing.* London: SCM, 1956.

———. *A History of Israel.* 3d ed. Philadelphia: Westminster, 1981.

Brueggemann, W. *The Land: Place as Gift, Promise, and Challenge in Biblical Faith.* Philadelphia: Fortress, 1977.

Butler, T. C. *Joshua.* WBC 7. Waco: Word, 1983.

Callaway, J. A. "Ai (et-Tell): Problem Site for Biblical Archaeologists." In *Archaeological and Biblical Interpretation.* Edited by L. G. Perdue, L. E. Toombs, G. L. Johnson. Atlanta: John Knox, 1987.

Campbell, E. F., Jr., "The Amarna Letters and the Amarna Period." *BAR* 3 (1970): 54–75.

Cazelles, H. "The Hebrews." In *Peoples of Old Testament Times.* Edited by D. J. Wiseman. Oxford: Oxford University Press, 1973, 1–28.

Chaney, M. "Ancient Palestinian Peasant Movements and the Formation of Premonarchic Israel." *Palestine in Transition.* Edited by D. N. Freedman and D. F. Graf. Sheffield: Almond/ASOR, 1983, 39–90.

Childs, B. S. *Introduction to the Old Testament as Scripture.* Philadelphia: Fortress,

1979.

———. "The Etiological Tale Reexamined." *VT* 24 (1974): 385–97.

———. "A Study of the Formula, 'Until This Day.'" *JBL* 82 (1963): 279–92.

Clines, D. J. A. *The Theme of the Pentateuch.* JSOTSup 29.

Coote, R. B. and K. W. Whitelam. *The Emergence of Early Israel in Historical Perspective.* Sheffield: Almond, 1987.

Dever, W. G. *Recent Archaeological Discoveries and Biblical Research.* Seattle: University of Washington Press, 1990.

Drower, M. S. "The Amarna Age." *CAH* 2.1:483–93.

———. "Ugarit." *CAH* 2.2:130–60.

Edelman, D., ed., "Toward a Consensus on the Emergence of Israel in Canaan." *JSOT* 2 (1991): 1–116.

Eissfeldt, O. *The Old Testament: An Introduction.* Oxford: Basil Blackwell, 1965.

Finkelstein, I. *The Archaeology of the Israelite Settlement.* Jerusalem: Israel Exploration Society, 1988.

Freedman D. N. and E. F. Campbell. "Chronology of Israel and the Ancient Near East." In *The Bible and the Ancient Near East.* Winona Lake: Eisenbrauns, 1979, 203–28.

Frick, F. S. *The Formation of the State of Ancient Israel.* Sheffield: Almond, 1985.

Fritz, V. "Conquest or Settlement?" *BA* 50 (1987): 84–100.

Garstang, J. and J. B. E. Garstang. *The Story of Jericho.* 2d ed. London: Marshall, Morgan, and Scott, 1948.

Goetze, A. "The Struggle for the Domination of Syria (1400–1300 B.C.)." *CAH* 2.2:1–20.

Goslinga, C. J. *Joshua, Judges, Ruth.* Translated by R. Togtman. Bible Student's Commentary. Grand Rapids: Zondervan, 1986.

Gottwald, N. K. *The Tribes of Yahweh.* Maryknoll, N.Y.: Orbis, 1979.

Gray, J. *The Canaanites.* New York: Praeger, 1964.

———. *The Legacy of Canaan.* 2d ed. VTSup 5 (1965).

Greenberg, M. "Hab/piru and Hebrews." In *World History of the Jewish People: Patriarchs*, 2. Edited by B. Mazar. Rutgers: Rutgers University, 1970, 188–200.

———. *The Hab/piru.* American Oriental Series 39. New Haven: AOS, 1955.

Green, W. B. "The Ethics of the Old Testament." *PTR* 28 (1929): 313–66. Reprinted in W. C. Kaiser, Jr., ed. *Classical Evangelical Essays in Old Testament Interpretation.* Grand Rapids: Baker, 1972, 206–35.

Grintz, J. M. "Ai Which Is Beside Beth-Aven." *Bib* 42 (1961): 201–16.

Harrison, R. K. *Introduction to the Old Testament.* Grand Rapids: Eerdmans, 1969.

Hayes, W. C. "Egypt: Internal Affairs from Thutmosis I to the Death of Amenophis III." *CAH* 2.1:338–46.

———. "Egypt: From the Death of Ammenemes III to Seqenenre II." *CAH* 2.1:42–76.

Holladay, J. S., Jr. "The Day(s) the *Moon* Stood Still." *JBL* 87 (1968): 166–78.

Hopkins, D. *The Highlands of Canaan.* Sheffield: Almond, 1985.

Howard, D. M., Jr. "All Israel's Response to Joshua: A Note on the Narrative Framework in Joshua 1." In the David Noel Freedman Festschrift. Edited by A. Bartels et al. Winona Lake: Eisenbrauns, forthcoming.

———. "The Case for Kingship in Deuteronomy and the Former Prophets." *WTJ* 52 (1990): 101–15.

———. "The Philistines." In *Peoples of the Old Testament World.* Edited by A. Hoerth, G. Mattingly, and E. Yamauchi. Grand Rapids: Baker, 1993.

Kaiser, W. C., Jr. *Toward Old Testament Ethics.* Grand Rapids: Zondervan, 1983.

————, ed. *Classical Evangelical Essays in Old Testament Interpretation.* Grand Rapids: Baker, 1972.

Kallai, Z. *Historical Geography of the Bible: The Tribal Territories of Israel.* Leiden: Brill; Jerusalem: Magnes Press, 1986.

Kenyon, K. M. "Palestine in the Time of the Eighteenth Dynasty." *CAH* 2.1:526–56.

————. "Jericho." In *Archaeology and Old Testament Study.* Edited by D. W. Thomas. London: Oxford University, 1967.

————. *Digging Up Jericho: The Results of the Jericho Excavations 1952–1956.* New York: Praeger, 1957.

————. *Archaeology in the Holy Land.* 4th ed. London: 1979.

Keil, C. F. *The Book of Joshua.* Grand Rapids: Eerdmans, 1975 reprint.

Kitchen, K. A. *Ancient Orient and Old Testament.* Chicago: InterVarsity, 1966.

————. *The Bible in Its World.* Downers Grove: InterVarsity, 1977.

————. "The Basics of Egyptian Chronology in Relation to the Bronze Age. " In *High, Middle or Low?* Edited by P. Åström. Part I. Gothenburg: Paul Åströms, 1987, 37–55; Part III, 1989, 152–59.

Lapp, P. W. "The Conquest of Palestine in the Light of Archaeology." *CTM* 38 (1967): 283–300.

Livingstone, D. "Location of Biblical Bethel and Ai Reconsidered." *WTJ* 33 (1970): 20–44.

————. "Traditional Site of Bethel Questioned." *WTJ* 34 (1971): 39–50.

Long, B. O. *The Problem of Etiological Narrative in the Old Testament.* BZAW 108. Berlin: Alfred Töpelmann, 1968.

Malamat, A. "Israelite Conduct of War in the Conquest of Canaan." In *Symposia.* Edited by F. M. Cross. Cambridge, Mass.: ASOR, 1979, 35–55.

Maunder, E. W. "A Misinterpreted Miracle." *The Expositor* 10 (1910): 359–72.

Mendenhall, G. E. "The Hebrew Conquest of Palestine." In *BAR* 3 (1970), 100–20.

————. "Ancient Israel's Hyphenated History." In *Palestine in Transition*, 91–103. Edited by D. N. Freedman and D. F. Graf. Sheffield: Almond/ASOR, 1983.

————. *The Tenth Generation.* Baltimore: Johns Hopkins University, 1973.

Merling, D. "The Book of Joshua: Its Structure and Meaning." In *To Understand the Scriptures: Essays in Honor of William H. Shea.* Berrien Springs: Andrews University Institute of Archaeology, 1997, 7–27.

Merrill, E. H. *Kingdom of Priests: A History of Old Testament Israel.* Grand Rapids: Baker, 1987.

————. "Palestinian Archaeology and the Date of the Conquest: Do Tells Tell Tales?" *GTJ* 3 (1982): 107–21.

Miller, J. M. "The Israelite Occupation of Canaan." In *Israelite and Judaean History* Edited by J. H. Hayes and J. M. Miller. Philadelphia: Westminster, 1977, 213–84.

————. "Is It Possible to Write a History of Israel without Relying on the Hebrew Bible?" In *The Fabric of History.* Edited by D. V. Edelman. Sheffield: JSOT, 1991, 93–102.

Miller, P. D., Jr. "The Gift of God: The Deuteronomic Theology of the Land." *Int* 23 (1969): 451–65.

Niehaus, J. J. "Joshua and Ancient Near Eastern Warfare." *JETS* 31 (1988): 37–50.

Noth, M. *The History of Israel.* 2d ed. Translated by P. R. Ackroyd. New York: Harper and Row, 1960.

————. *The Deuteronomistic History.* JSOTSup 15. 2d ed. Sheffield: JSOT, 1991.

Polzin, R. *Moses and the Deuteronomist.* New York: Seabury, 1980.

Rad, G. von. "The Promised Land and Yahweh's Land in the Hexateuch." Originally appeared in 1943 in *The Problem of the Hexateuch and Other Essays.* Translated by E. W. T. Dicken. New York: McGraw Hill, 1966, 79–93.

————. "There Remains Still a Rest for the People of God: An Investigation of a Biblical Conception." Originally appeared in 1933 in *The Problem of the Hexateuch and Other Essays,* 79–93.

Rainey, A. F. "Bethel Is Still *Beitîn.*" *WTJ* 33 (1971): 175–88.

Ramsey, G. W. *The Quest for the Historical Israel.* Atlanta: John Knox, 1981.

Rendsburg, G. "The Date of the Exodus and the Conquest/Settlement: The Case for the 1100s." *VT* 42 (1992): 510–27.

————. Two Book Reviews. *JAOS* 107 (1987): 554–57.

Ringgren, H. *Religions of the Ancient Near East.* Philadelphia: Westminster, 1973.

Rowley, H. H. *From Joseph to Joshua: Biblical Traditions in the Light of Archaeology.* London: Oxford University, 1950.

Thiele, E. R. *The Mysterious Numbers of the Hebrew Kings.* 3d ed. Grand Rapids: Zondervan, 1983.

Thompson, J. A. *The Bible and Archaeology.* 3d ed. Grand Rapids: Eerdmans, 1982.

Thompson, T. L. *Early History of the Israelite People.* Leiden: Brill, 1992.

Waltke, B. K. "Palestinian Artifactual Evidence Supporting the Early Date for the Exodus." *BSac* 129 (1972): 33–47.

————. "The Date of the Conquest." *WTJ* 52 (1990): 181–200.

Weippert, M. *The Settlement of the Israelite Tribes in Palestine.* London: SCM, 1971.

————. "The Israelite 'Conquest' and the Evidence from Transjordan." *Symposia.* Edited by F. M. Cross. Cambridge, Mass.: ASOR, 1979, 15–34.

Wenham, G. "The Date of Deuteronomy: Linch-pin of Old Testament Criticism. Part One." *Themelios* 10.3 (1985): 15–20.

————. "The Date of Deuteronomy: Linch-pin of Old Testament Criticism. Part Two". *Themelios* 11.1 (1985): 15–18.

Wilson, R. D. "Understanding 'The Sun Stood Still.'" *PTR* 16 (1918): 46–54. Reprinted in W. C. Kaiser, Jr., ed. *Classical Evangelical Essays in Old Testament Interpretation.* Grand Rapids: Baker, 1972, 61–65.

Winther-Nielsen, N., and E. Talstra. *A Computational Display of Joshua: A Computer-Assisted Analysis and Textual Interpretation.* Amsterdam: VU University Press, 1995.

Wood, B. G. "Did the Israelites Conquer Jericho? A New Look at the Archaeological Evidence." *BARev* 16.2 (1990): 44–58.

Wood, L. *A Survey of Israel's History.* Rev. ed. Grand Rapids: Zondervan, 1986.

Woudstra, M. H. *The Book of Joshua.* NICOT. Grand Rapids: Eerdmans, 1981.

Wright, G. E. *Biblical Archaeology.* Rev. ed. Philadelphia: Westminster, 1962.

Yadin, Y. *The Art of Warfare in Biblical Lands.* 2 Vols. New York: McGraw-Hill, 1963.

Selected Subject Index

Person Index

Selected Scripture Index

460